T0260459

LARGE SCALE NETWORK-CENTRIC DISTRIBUTED SYSTEMS

LARGE SCALE NETWORK-CENTRIC DISTRIBUTED SYSTEMS

Edited by

Hamid Sarbazi-Azad

Sharif University of Technology and
Institute for Research in Fundamental Sciences (IPM)
Tehran, Iran

Albert Y. Zomaya

School of Information Technologies
The University of Sydney
Sydney, Australia

Library of Congress Cataloging-in-Publication Data:
Large scale network-centric distributed systems / edited by Hamid Sarbazi-Azad, Albert Y. Zomaya.
    pages cm
    ISBN 978-0-470-93688-7 (pbk.)
  1. Electronic data processing–Distributed processing. I. Sarbazi-Azad, Hamid. II. Zomaya, Albert Y.
    QA76.9.D5L373 2013
    004'.36–dc23

                           2012047719

CONTENTS

5 DATA DISTRIBUTION MANAGEMENT   **103**

Azzedine Boukerche and Yunfeng Gu

8   MOBILITY EFFECTS IN WIRELESS MOBILE NETWORKS   167
Abbas Nayebi and Hamid Sarbazi-Azad

**9   ANALYTICAL MODEL OF TIME-CRITICAL WIRELESS SENSOR
    NETWORK: THEORY AND EVALUATION   183**
Kambiz Mizanian and Amir Hossein Jahangir

10 MULTICAST TRANSPORT PROTOCOLS FOR LARGE-SCALE DISTRIBUTED COLLABORATIVE ENVIRONMENTS 203

Haifa Raja Maamar and Azzedine Boukerche

PART 4 GRID AND CLOUD COMPUTING

**18 GAME-BASED MODELS OF GRID USER'S DECISIONS IN
     SECURITY-AWARE SCHEDULING   431**
     Joanna Kolodziej, Samee U. Khan, Lizhe Wang, and Dan Chen

**19 ADDRESSING OPEN ISSUES ON PERFORMANCE
     EVALUATION IN CLOUD COMPUTING   463**

*Beniamino Di Martino, Massimo Ficco, Massimiliano Rak,
and Salvatore Venticinque*

22 VIRTUALIZED ENVIRONMENT ISSUES IN THE CONTEXT OF A SCIENTIFIC PRIVATE CLOUD

Bruno Schulze, Henrique de Medeiros Klôh, Matheus Bousquet Bandini, Antonio Roberto Mury, Daniel Massami Muniz Yokoyama, Victor Dias de Oliveira, Fábio André Machado Porto, and Giacomo Victor McEvoy Valenzano

PREFACE

On one hand, the cost of computing resources has decreased rapidly, and on the other hand, the availability of them has increased swiftly in recent years. In the meanwhile, a great amount of intensive applications with greater performance and fault tolerance requirements has emerged. These trends collectively have made centralized designs of the information systems less desirable and distributed systems more widespread in several domains, despite them having more technical difficulties. Obviously, it is the network that sticks the components of such systems together, and it has become apparent that the effectiveness of the operation of the network together with the way it is exploited, primarily determines the quality of the cooperation of those components. Today, network centric computing systems is a subject of interest in the whole extent to which distributed systems operate, from those which are composed of multiple cores on a single chip to those which take advantage of a great number of computers connected together in order to create grids, clouds, and other network-based distributed systems.

In this book, a range of relevant topics in the scope of *Large Scale Network-Centric Distributed Systems* is presented, which covers a selection of its many aspects. It is composed of five parts, each of which includes different chapters authored by the researchers in the field and selected based on a peer-review. A brief summary of the chapters is provided below to give an initiatory sight of the scope of the book.

Part 1 is dedicated to network-based systems-on-chip (SoC) comprising multiple cores. The number of cores on a chip has been growing in recent years and according to ITRS projection, chips with several hundred to thousand cores are on their way. These cores are usually interconnected via a network for data interchange between the different tasks, programs, and threads running on different cores. Studying different issues related to multicore SoCs, from hardware and architectural techniques to software solutions, is of utmost importance. This part includes three chapters.

Chapter 1 introduces a reconfigurable network-on-chip (NoC) which can adapt network topology to the communication requirements of the applications running on different cores. Network topology is the most critical part of an NoC and mainly determines its performance. Having a network with a dynamic topology to adapt the communication requirements of the applications can effectively improve performance and reduce energy consumption. Design issues and experimental evaluation of the proposed reconfigurable architecture is detailed in this chapter.

Chapter 2 briefly reviews different programming models for current multicore systems (espcially GPUs (Graphics Processing Units) which have gained great importance for building large supercomputers) and the state of the art on compilers and support tools helping programmers both in developing and porting codes for multicore systems with an emphasis on automatic parallelization compilers, techniques and tools that do source-to-source transformation of sequential code into parallel. This chapter introduces a tool developed by the authors, to do static analysis on source code in order to represent it along with knowledge extracted from it. The tool integrates an algorithmic recognizer to find instances of known algorithms, and a transformer to automatically transform sequential code into a parallel version by using libraries, so that it could be used in GPUs.

In Chapter 3, authors propose a multi-threaded branch-and-bound (B&B) approach to solve the flow-shop scheduling problem on a multi-core system. Several exact resolution methods used in combinatorial optimization are B&B like algorithms. The proposed approach is implemented using the POSIX Threads programming model. The experiments demonstrate that the use of the total available power in a multi-core CPU does not mean that the maximum speedup is achieved. These experiments show that a multi-threaded B&B approach must take into account the characteristics of its hardware and software environment, such as the size of the random-access memory.

Ubiquitous computing (UC) or pervasive computing is a paradigm where machines fit the human environment instead of forcing humans to enter theirs. Contemporary human-computer interaction models, whether command-line, menu-driven, or GUI (Graphical User Interface)-based, are inappropriate and inadequate to the ubiquitous case. This suggests that the natural interaction paradigm appropriate for a fully robust UC has yet to emerge, although there is also recognition in the field that in many ways we are already living in an ubicomp world. Contemporary devices that lend some support to this latter idea include mobile phones, digital audio players, radio-frequency identification tags, GPS, and interactive whiteboards. Peer-to-peer (P2P) computing or networking is a distributed application architecture that partitions tasks or workloads between peers. Peers are equally privileged, equipotent participants in the application. They are said to form a P2P network of nodes. Peers make a portion of their resources, such as processing power, disk storage or network bandwidth, directly available to other network participants, without the need for central coordination by servers or stable hosts. Peers are both suppliers and consumers of resources, in contrast to the traditional client–server model where the consumption and supply of resources is always divided. Part 2 deals with some important problems in pervasive/ubiquitous computing and peer-to-peer systems. It comprises of three chapters.

In Chapter 4, a new P2P approach is introduced which can handle a huge amount of computational resources in a fully distributed way; that is without the need of any centralized coordinator. The state-of-the-art large scale approach for solving NP-hard permutation-based problems using parallel B&B techniques is based on a Master-Slave model which is known to be limited in terms of scalability. Authors present simple and efficient fully distributed algorithms dealing with major parallel B&B issues such as work sharing, dynamic load balancing and termination detection. The proposed P2P approach has a scalability which is exponentially better in theory compared to the Master-Slave technique, while having a negligible communication overhead in a worst case-scenario, namely poly-logarithmic.

In addition, a more detailed analysis of performance of the proposed approach is realized through studying its different execution phases and its behavior when solving some instances of the Flow-Shop Scheduling Problem from scratch, a well-known permutation-based problem in the field of Combinatorial Optimization.

In Chapter 5, Data Distribution Management (DDM) is addressed in two different network environments: P2P overlay networks and cluster-based networks. Although DDM provides the same data indexing service in both distributed network environments, it serves upper layer applications for very different purposes, and is supported by underlying networks with distinctive infrastructures. In P2P overlay networks, peers share part of their resources.

They might have different capacities to share the load, some might join or leave the system, or even fail, and the connectivity between them is unstable. DDM in P2P overlay networks is more feasible for massive data sharing systems or massively parallel computing. On the other hand, all peers in a cluster network are dedicated resources of the distributed environment. The cluster network might have very limited size, but the status of a peer is highly reliable, and the connectivity is always stable. DDM in such network environments has been commonly used to support more intensive interactive simulations. Because of the fundamental differences at both the application layer and the underlying network layer, the study of DDM has to follow very different methodologies, which in turn divert our interests and objectives in each area significantly.

Chapter 6 introduces some background concepts on ubiquitous computing (UC) and then presents the state-of-the-art in the field of middleware for UC. It then addresses the requirement of the integration of UC middleware and describes an existent solution that addresses this requirement, the Open COntext Platform Integration (OpenCOPI). OpenCOPI provides: (i) an automatic service composition; (ii) a standardized context and communication model; and (iii) a fault tolerance mechanism that handles service failures. Another important feature of OpenCOPI is the use of semantic workflows. The composition model adopted by OpenCOPI is based on both services functionalities and services metadata, enabling a better choice between available services with similar functionalities.

Wireless networks are the communication backbone of mobile networks surrounding us. Mobility is an important characteristic of most of personal electronic/computing devices and plays a crucial role both in a positive way (e.g., in delay-tolerant networks) and in a negative way (e.g., creating problems for topology control). Wireless networking is also a key component of today's sensor systems with a wide range of applications. Part 3 is dedicated to some important issues in mobile and wireless networks. It includes five chapters.

Chapter 7 focuses on the challenges faced in the design of new techniques for enabling new decentralized solutions to large scale wireless sensor networks (WSNs) in the Structural Health Monitoring (SHM) domain. First, the definition of SHM along with the concept of WSNs is given. Authors cite several challenges and solutions found in the literature which are considered to be of utmost importance for understanding the context of this domain of WSN applications, guiding further studies in it. This chapter can be a useful reference for everyone who wishes to research in this domain of WSN applications.

Chapter 8 deals with the mobility issue of wireless networks. Mobility is an important factor that affects performance of wireless networks including wireless sensor networks, mobile ad hoc networks, and wireless mesh networks. In fact, the topology of a mobile wireless network is prone to continuous changes, which considerably affect the performance of routing protocols. In order to ease the analysis of mobility effects on the performance of wireless networks, the concept of intermediate performance modeling (IPM) is introduced in this chapter. IPM can divide the analysis into two steps: analysis of the effects of mobility on some intermediate performance measures (e.g., link life-time), and analysis of the effects of the intermediate performance measures on some final performance measures (e.g., packet loss ratio). Thus, using IPM, one may reuse results of the first step for several evaluations. Moreover, given the results of the first step for several mobility conditions, a particular protocol can be evaluated for all of them.

Chapter 9 considers time-critical WSNs. The WSN should be capable of fulfilling its mission, in a timely manner and without loss of important information. In this chapter, a new analytical model for calculating Real-Time (RT) degree and Reliable Real-Time (RRT) degree in multi-hop WSNs is introduced. Packet loss probability is modeled as a function of the probability of link failure when the buffer is full, and the probability of node failure when the node's energy is depleted. Most network properties are considered as random variables and a queuing theory-based model is derived. In this model, the effect of network load on the packets' delay, RT degree, RRT degree, and node's energy depletion rate are considered.

Chapter 10 gives an overview of the multicast transport protocols. Collaborative Virtual Environments (CVEs) require that geographically distributed users collaborate in closely coupled and highly synchronized tasks to manipulate shared objects. In order to keep the users updated with the changes, and to maintain the synchronization between them, an efficient transport protocol to deliver data is needed. The traditional unicast model that Transport Control Protocol (TCP) offers is inefficient for such applications. In fact, it is not useful to transmit the same data to each receiver across the network. CVE applications use large scale distributed simulations where hundreds or even thousands of distributed users intercommunicate in real time. For this reason, it is necessary to use the multicast approach to deliver data.

As the size of WSNs grows, their complexity increases substantially, rendering traditional centralized control methods unsuitable. Considering the characteristics of WSNs, distributed methods are adopted to solve problems during the process of their design. Most complex problems currently tackled in WSNs share properties with similar scenarios and functions found in nature such as adaptation, self-organization, optimization, topology control, aggregation and communication. These functions are simultaneously handled by biological organisms at different scales and levels to make living creatures more efficient in dealing with different situations. Efficient techniques developed in nature have attracted the attention of computer scientists and engineers for many years and the techniques have been explored and applied to a wide range of problems. Chapter 11 presents a thorough literature survey, introduces the most popular nature-inspired algorithms and shows how these algorithms are applied to a wide range of problems in WSNs.

The grid and cloud computing paradigm has been an incredible success in the last decade. It is based on the idea of delegating every kind of resource to the provider, and letting the users access them in a self-service fashion. The Cloud paradigm has largely been adopted in several different contexts and applied to an incredibly large set of technologies. It is an opportunity for IT users to reduce costs and increase efficiency, providing an alternative way of using IT services. It represents both a technology for using computing infrastructures in a more efficient way and a business model for selling computing resources. It gives small and medium enterprises the possibility of using services and technologies that were the prerogative of large ones, by paying only for the resources needed and avoiding upfront investment. Part 4 is dedicated to different issues of the grid and cloud computing areas and includes eleven chapters.

Chapter 12 discusses Remote Procedure Call (RPC) based computing on grids and clouds. The RPC paradigm is widely used in distributed computing. It provides a straight-forward procedure for executing parts of an application on a remote computer. GridRPC is a standard promoted by the Open Grid Forum, which extends the traditional RPC. GridRPC differs from the traditional RPC in that the programmer does not need to spec-ify the server to execute the task. When the programmer does not specify the server, the middleware system is responsible for finding the remote executing server. When the program runs, each GridRPC call results in the middleware mapping the call to a remote server and then the middleware is responsible for the execution of that task on the mapped server. A number of Grid middleware systems have recently become GridRPC compliant including GridSolve, Nint-G and DIET.

Chapter 13 studies resource allocation in clouds. Pervasive use of cloud computing and the resulting rise in the number of hosting datacenters (which provide platform or software services to clients who do not have the means to set up and operate their own facilities) have brought forth many challenges including energy cost, peak power dissipa-tion, cooling, carbon emission, etc. With power consumption becoming an increasingly important issue for the operation and maintenance of the hosting datacenters, corporate and business owners are becoming increasingly concerned. Furthermore, provisioning resources in a cost-optimal manner so as to meet different criteria such as response time, throughput, network bandwidth, etc. has become a critical challenge. The goal of this chapter is to provide a review of resource provisioning and power management strate-gies that optimize server-related energy costs in a datacenter while meeting the stipulated service level agreements in terms of throughput and response time.

A strong thrust on the use of virtualization technology to realize Infrastructure-as-a-Service (IaaS) has led enterprises to leverage subscription-oriented computing capa-bilities of public clouds for hosting their application services. In parallel, research in academia has been investigating transversal aspects such as security, software frame-works, quality of service, and standardization. In Chapter 14, the current status of cloud computing is assessed by providing a reference model, discussing the challenges that researchers and IT practitioners are facing and will encounter in the near future, and presenting the approach for solving them from the perspective of the Cloudbus toolkit, which comprises a set of technologies geared towards the realization of Market Oriented Cloud Computing vision.

Chapter 15 presents a cloud broker architecture for deploying virtual infrastructures across multiple clouds. The main challenges of the brokering problem in multi-cloud environments are analyzed, and different scheduling policies that can guide the brokering decisions, based on cost criteria, performance criteria, resource consumption, etc., are proposed. Some preliminary results are reported in this chapter to prove the benefits of using the proposed broker architecture in a single cloud, using different pricing schemes, and in multi-cloud environments.

Chapter 16 studies energy-efficient resource utilization methods in clouds. In cloud computing systems, the energy consumed by the underutilized resources accounts for a substantial amount of the actual energy consumption. Recent studies reported that energy consumption (in servers) scales linearly with (processor) resource utilization. In this chapter, two existing energy-conscious heuristics for task consolidation are analyzed. Both heuristics aim to maximize resource utilization, with the main difference being whether the energy consumption to execute the given task is implicitly or explicitly considered. To improve the energy efficiency of task consolidation, an algorithm that combines the two heuristics is proposed, in order to take advantage of both. According to the experimental results, the proposed algorithm increases the energy efficiency of the task consolidation problem without performance degradation.

Grid is expected to evolve from a computing and data management facility to a pervasive, world-wide resource-sharing infrastructure. To fully utilize the wide range of grid resources, effective resource discovery mechanisms are required. However, resource discovery in a large-scale grid is challenging due to the considerable diversity, large number, dynamic behavior, and geographical distribution of the resources. Existing resource discovery approaches have difficulties in achieving both rich searchability and good scalability. Chapter 17 investigates the resource discovery problem for open-networked large-scale grids.

Chapter 18 summarizes authors' recent research on game theoretical models of grid user behavior in security-aware scheduling. The main scheduling attributes, generic model of security-aware management in local grid clusters, and several scenarios of users' games are presented. Four GA (Genetic Algorithm)-based hybrid schedulers have been implemented for the approximation of the equilibrium states of the exemplary simple symmetric game of the grid end users. The proposed hybrid resolution methods are empirically evaluated through the grid simulator under the heterogeneity, security, large-scale and dynamic conditions.

The possibility of dynamically acquiring and using resources and services on the basis of a pay-per-use model in clouds, implies incredible flexibility in terms of management, which is otherwise often hard to address. On the other hand, because of this flexibility new problems emerge, which involve the evaluation and monitoring of the quality of the acquired resources and services as well as threats that can compromise performance and availability of services provided to final users. Chapter 19 describes some open challenges to performance evaluation and provisioning in cloud, and presents a survey on the solutions and technologies proposed by researchers and open community to face such issues.

Many data-intensive applications from several fields, including data mining and computational biology, have been modeled as Bag-of-Tasks (BoT) applications. BoT applications are parallel applications whose tasks are independent of each other. In a BoT application, the tasks do not communicate with each other during the execution.

Based on the results obtained from the execution of some of the tasks, other tasks may be canceled or modified. Hence cloud computing is an attractive platform for running such BoT applications.

With a plethora of Cloud Service Providers (CSPs) offering various kinds of services, it is quite difficult for a new user to choose an appropriate CSP or a set of CSPs for doing a particular job. Chapter 20 introduces a broker-mediated Cloud Aggregation mechanism for BoT applications wherein the users can submit their applications along with the task execution requirements to the broker, and the broker distributes the tasks to various CSPs based on these requirements.

In Chapter 21, a budget aware scheduler for handling large-scale workflow applications in clouds is proposed. A cloud environment is suitable for a large scale many-task workflow (MTW) to be executed in a scalable manner (e.g., scale up, scale out, and scale down). This chapter proposes a budget-conscious scheduling algorithm for scheduling MTWs on Clouds, referred to as ScaleStar. ScaleStar is able to adapt a selected task to a virtual machine which has a higher comparative advantage so as to effectively balance the execution time and monetary cost. We evaluate the performance of our strategies on six different MTWs from real world applications using three major important metrics.

Chapter 22 focuses on aspects related to performance in private Clouds. Several works have been identified concerning the performance analysis, with focus only on the performance of the virtual environment, not addressing the aspects concerning the operating system, the processor architecture and their impact on performance. In this chapter, an approach is proposed differing from others in the literature, using the virtualization advancements developed so far and the knowledge obtained by tests results to verify the use of hybrid virtual environments. These hybrid models are created based on the characteristics of the running applications, combining the use of different types of hypervisors, and at the same time, using the best features of each, in order to improve the execution performance. The study and evaluation of the use of these hybrid models and their analysis were motivated by a real demand, to provide access to a cloud appliance with a GUI for distributed image processing applications. The basic idea is to offer users remote access to virtualized platforms dedicated to their needs and hosted in a cloud environment.

Part 5 is dedicated to some other important and daily topics in network-based computing. It consists of four chapters.

Chapter 23 considers bandwidth scheduling in e-science networks. Many large-scale scientific and commercial applications produce large amounts of data, of the order of terabytes to petabytes, which must be transferred across wide-area networks. When data providers and consumers are geographically distributed, dedicated bandwidth channels are critical to offer (i) large capacity for massive data transfer operations, and (ii) dynamically stable bandwidth for monitoring and steering operations. Bandwidth reservation systems operate in one of two modes: (a) in on-demand scheduling, bandwidth is reserved for a time period that begins at the current time; (b) in in-advance scheduling, bandwidth is reserved for a time period that begins at some future time. In this chapter, a set of in-advance scheduling problems are defined and corresponding algorithms are proposed and evaluated. Moreover, a multiple path scheduling problem, Earliest Finish

Time File Transfer Problem (EFTFTP), is proposed and solved by both optimal solutions and heuristics.

Chapter 24 studies routing and wavelength assignment problems in optical networks. Many high speed networks that provide dedicated connections are based on optical interconnects and optical switches. For these networks, the bandwidth along a given link can be decomposed into multiple wavelengths. The bandwidth scheduling and path computation problem in the context of optical networks is usually called Routing and Wavelength Assignment (RWA). In this chapter, the Extended Bellman-Ford (EBF) algorithm is extended to incorporate the wavelength sharing and wavelength continuity constraints. Moreover, a deferred wavelength assignment strategy is presented. This strategy only counts the number of wavelengths that are used on a link. The actual assignment of the wavelength is done when the request is actually fulfilled. A new network model is proposed which can emulate the existing full-conversion algorithms when only a subset of nodes has a wavelength converter. The algorithms are evaluated on three performance metrics: blocking probability, average start time and scheduling overhead.

Handling the constant stream of data from health care, security, business, and social network applications requires new algorithms and data structures. A new approach for parallel massive analysis of streaming, temporal, graph-structured data is proposed in Chapter 25. This chapter proposes an extensible and flexible data structure for massive graphs called Spatio-Temporal Interaction Networks and Graphs Extensible Representation (STINGER). For the large scale-free graphs, the proposed method uses novel batching techniques that exploit the scale-free nature of the data and run over three times faster than prior methods. This is a new framework which is the first to handle real-world data rates, opening the door to higher-level analytics such as community and anomaly detection.

Chapter 26 presents an ontology-based framework to reflect various aspects of the semantic relationships among the components in the intelligent Water Distribution Network (WDN), and illustrate the powerful automatic reasoning capabilities of the ontology. A complete test case scenario is provided to demonstrate the efficacy of the ontology-based service to assist automatic decision-making in cyber infrastructure when failure occurs in physical infrastructure. By utilizing the ontology to capture the information flow in a complex system, one can have more profound and multi-perspective understanding towards the semantic relationships existing among the interacting components. This is the first time that an ontology-based approach is adopted to assist automatic decision-making based on the raw data collected by sensors, particularly in the domain of WDN. Due to the automatic-reasoning capability of ontology, the ontology-based framework can also be expanded for transportation system and power grid.

ACKNOWLEDGMENTS

We should first thank the chapter authors and acknowledge their contributions to the book, as well as their support and patience. We would also like to thank the reviewers for their useful comments and suggestions that helped in improving the earlier outline of the book and presentation of the material. We should extend our deepest thanks to Simone Taylor, Melissa Yanuzzi, and Diana Gialo from Wiley (USA) for their collaboration, guidance, and most importantly, patience in finalizing this volume. Last but not the least, we are very grateful to the lovely team from Wiley's production department for their extensive efforts during the many phases of this project and the timely fashion in which the book was produced.

Hamid Sarbazi-Azad

Sharif University of Technology & IPM

Albert Y. Zomaya

The University of Sydney

LIST OF FIGURES

LIST OF TABLES

LIST OF CONTRIBUTORS

David A. Bader, School of Computational Science and Engineering, Atlanta, GA, USA

Matheus Bousquet Bandini, Laboratório Nacional de Computação Científica, Petrópolis, Brazil

Thais Batista, Departamento de Informática e Matemática Aplicada, Centro de Ciências Exatas e da Natureza, Universidade Federal do Rio Grande do Norte, Lagoa Nova, Brazil

Azzedine Boukerche, SITE, University of Ottawa, Ottawa, Ontario, Canada

Pascal Bouvry, Faculty of Science, Technology and Communications, University of Luxembourg, Luxembourg

Thomas Brady, UCD, Dublin, Ireland

Rajkumar Buyya, Cloud Computing and Distributed Systems (CLOUDS) Lab, Department of Computing and Information Systems, The University of Melbourne, Melbourne, Australia

Pasquale Cantiello, Dipartimento di Ingegneria Industriale e dell'Informazione, Second University of Naples, Naples, Italy

Dan Chen, School of Computer Science, China University of Geosciences, Wuhan, China

Claudio M. de Farias, Núcleo de Computação Eletrônica, Universidade Federal do Rio de Janeiro, Brazil

Flávia C. Delicato, Departamento de Ciência da Computação, Instituto de Matemática, Universidade Federal de Rio de Janeiro, Brazil

Henrique de Medeiros Klôh, Laboratório Nacional de Computação Científica, Petrópolis, Brazil

Victor Dias de Oliveira, Laboratório Nacional de Computação Científica, Petrópolis, Brazil

Bilel Derbel, INRIA Lille-Nord Europe, France

Beniamino Di Martino, Department of Ingegneria Industriale e dell'Informazione, Second University of Naples (SUN), Naples, Italy

Mathieu Djamaï, INRIA Lille-Nord Europe, France

Igor L. dos Santos, Núcleo de Computação Eletrônica, Universidade Federal de Rio de Janeiro, Brazil

David Ediger, School of Computational Science and Engineering, Atlanta, GA, USA

Massimo Ficco, Department of Ingegneria Industriale e dell'Informazione, Second University of Naples (SUN), Naples, Italy

Oleg Girko, UCD, Dublin, Ireland

Nasir Ghani, ECE Department, University of New Mexico, Albuquerque, NM, USA

Hadi Goudarzi, Department of Electrical Engineering Systems, University of Southern California, Los Angeles, CA, USA

Yunfeng Gu, SITE, University of Ottawa, Ottawa, Ontario, Canada

Ali Hurson, Missouri University of Science and Technology, Rolla, MO, USA

Amir Hossein Jahangir, Department of Computer Engineering, Sharif University of Technology, Tehran, Iran

Eunsung Jung, Samsung, Seohyun-dong, Kyunggi-do, South Korea

Samee U. Khan, Electrical and Computer Engineering Department, North Dakota State University, Fargo, ND, USA

Joanna Kolodziej, Institute of Computer Science, Cracow University of Technology, Cracow, Poland

Bjorn Landfeldt, Department of Electrical and Information Technology, Lund University, Lund, Sweden

Alexey Lastovetsky, UCD, Dublin, Ireland

Juan Li, Electrical and Computer Engineering Department, North Dakota State University, Fargo, ND, USA

Wei Li, School of Information Technologies, The University of Sydney, Sydney, Australia

Xiaorong Li, Institute of High Performance Computing, A*STAR, Singapore

Yan Li, Google, Cupertino, CA, USA

Jing Lin, Missouri University of Science and Technology, Rolla, MO, USA

Ignacio M. Llorente, Facultad de Informatica, Universidad Complutense de Madrid, Madrid, Spain

Frederico Lopes, Escola de Ciências e Tecnologia, Universidade Federal do Rio Grande do Norte, Lagoa Nova, Brazil

José Luis Lucas-Simarro, Facultad de Informatica, Universidad Complutense de Madrid, Madrid, Spain

Haifa Raja Maamar, SITE, University of Ottawa, Ottawa, Ontario, Canada

Fábio André Machado Porto, Laboratório Nacional de Computação Científica, Petrópolis, Brazil

Giacomo Victor McEvoy Valenzano, Laboratório Nacional de Computação Científica, Petrópolis, Brazil

Daniel Massami Muniz Yokoyama, Laboratório Nacional de Computação Científica, Petrópolis, Brazil

Nouredine Melab, LIFL, Université de Lille 1, France

Henning Meyerhenke, Institute of Theoretical Informatics, Karlsruhe Institute of Technology (KIT), Karlsruhe, Germany

Mohand Mezmaz, MathRO, University of Mons, Belgium

Kambiz Mizanian, Department of Computer Engineering, Sharif University of Technology, Tehran, Iran

Mehdi Modarressi, Electrical and Computer Engineering, College of Engineering, University of Tehran, Tehran, Iran

Rubcn S. Montero, Facultad de Informatica, Universidad Complutense de Madrid, Madrid, Spain

Rafael Moreno-Vozmediano, Facultad de Informatica, Universidad Complutense de Madrid, Madrid, Spain

Francesco Moscato, Dipartimento di Ingegneria Industriale e dell'Informazione, Second University of Naples, Naples, Italy

Antonio Roberto Mury, Laboratório Nacional de Computação Científica, Petrópolis, Brazil

Abbas Nayebi, Google, Mountain View, CA, USA

Ganesh Neelakanta Iyer, Department of Electrical and Computer Engineering, National University of Singapore (NUS), Singapore

Suraj Pandey, Cloud Computing and Distributed Systems (CLOUDS) Lab, Department of Computing and Information Systems, The University of Melbourne, Melbourne, Australia

Massoud Pedram, Department of Electrical Engineering Systems, University of Southern California, Los Angeles, CA, USA

Paulo F. Pires, Departamento de Ciência da Computação, Instituto de Matemática, Universidade Federal de Rio de Janeiro, Brazil

Luci Pirmez, Núcleo de Computação Eletrônica, Universidade Federal do Rio de Janeiro, Brazil

Massimiliano Rak, Department of Ingegneria Industriale e dell'Informazione, Second University of Naples (SUN), Naples, Italy

Sanjay Ranka, CISE Department, University of Florida, Gainesville, FL, USA

Nageswara S. Rao, Oak Ridge National Laboratory, Oak Ridge, TN, USA

Jason Riedy, School of Computational Science and Engineering, Atlanta, GA, USA

Sartaj Sahni, CISE Department, University of Florida, Gainesville, FL, USA

Iñigo San Aniceto, Facultad de Informatica, Universidad Complutense de Madrid, Madrid, Spain

Hamid Sarbazi-Azad, Department of Computer Engineering, Sharif University of Technology and School of Computer Science, Institute for Research in Fundamental Sciences (IPM), Tehran, Iran

Sahra Sedigh, Missouri University of Science and Technology, Rolla, MO, USA

Franciszek Seredynski, Department of Mathematics and Natural Sciences, Cardinal Stefan Wyszynski University in Warsaw, Warsaw, Poland

Bruno Schulze, Laboratório Nacional de Computação Científica, Petrópolis, Brazil

Javid Taheri, School of Information Technologies, The University of Sydney, Sydney, Australia

Daniel Tuyttens, MathRO, University of Mons, Belgium

Giorgio L. Valentini, Faculty of Science, Technology and Communications, University of Luxembourg, Luxembourg

Christian Vecchiola, Cloud Computing and Distributed Systems (CLOUDS) Lab, Department of Computing and Information Systems, The University of Melbourne, Melbourne, Australia

Bharadwaj Veeravalli, Department of Electrical and Computer Engineering, National University of Singapore (NUS), Singapore

Salvatore Venticinque, Department of Ingegneria Industriale e dell'Informazione, Second University of Naples (SUN), Naples, Italy

Lizhe Wang, Center for Earth Observation and Digital Earth, Chinese Academy of Sciences, Beijing, China

Lingfang Zeng, Department of Electrical and Computer Engineering, National University of Singapore (NUS), Singapore

Albert Y. Zomaya, School of Information Technologies, The University of Sydney, Sydney, Australia

Part **1**

MULTICORE AND MANY-CORE (MC) SYSTEMS-ON-CHIP

1

A RECONFIGURABLE ON-CHIP INTERCONNECTION NETWORK FOR LARGE MULTICORE SYSTEMS

Mehdi Modarressi and Hamid Sarbazi Azad

CONTENTS

Large Scale Network-Centric Distributed Systems, First Edition. Edited by Hamid Sarbazi-Azad and Albert Y. Zomaya.
© 2014 John Wiley & Sons, Inc. Published 2014 by John Wiley & Sons, Inc.

1.1 INTRODUCTION

1.1.1 Multicore and Many-Core Era

With the recent scaling of semiconductor technology, coupled with the ever-increasing demand for high-performance computing in embedded, desktop, and server computer systems, the current general-purpose microprocessors have been moving from single-core to multicore and eventually to many-core processor architectures containing tens to hundreds of identical cores [1]. Major manufacturers already ship 10-core [2], 16-core [3, 4], and 48-core [5] chip multiprocessors, while some special-purpose processors have pushed the limit further to 188 [6], 200 [7], and 336 [8] cores.

Following the same trend, current multicore system-on-chips (SoC) have grown in size and complexity and consist of tens to hundreds of logic blocks of different types communicating with each other at very-high-speed rates.

1.1.2 On-Chip Communication

As the core count scales up, the rate and complexity of intercore communications increase dramatically. Consequently, the efficiency of on-chip communication mechanisms has emerged as a critical determinant of the overall performance in complex multicore system-on-chips (SoCs) and chip multiprocessors (CMPs). In addition to the performance considerations, on-chip interconnects of a conventional SoC and CMP account for a considerable fraction of the consumed power, and this fraction is expected to grow with every new technology point. The advent of deep submicron and nanotechnologies and supply voltage scaling also brings about several signal integrity and reliability issues [9]. As a result, interconnect design poses a whole new set of challenges for SoC and CMP designers.

1.1.3 Conventional Communication Mechanisms

Conventional small-scale SoCs and CMPs use the legacy bus and ad hoc dedicated links to manage on-chip traffic. With dedicated point-to-point links, the intercore data travel on dedicated wires directly connecting two end-point cores. Thus, they can potentially yield the ideal performance and power results when connecting a few cores. However, when the number of on-chip components increases, this scheme requires a huge amount of wiring to directly connect every component, with less than 10% average wire usage in time [10]. Consequently, the poor scalability due to considerable area overhead is a prohibitive drawback of dedicated links. In addition, the dedicated wires in submicron and nanotechnologies need special attention to manage hard-to-predict power, signal integrity, and performance issues. Furthermore, due to their ad hoc nature, dedicated links are not reusable. These issues bring the design effort to the forefront as the second drawback of the dedicated wires.

Bus architectures are the most common and cost-effective on-chip communication solution for traditional multicore SoCs and CMPs with a modest number of processors. However, bus-based communication schemes, even those utilizing hierarchies of buses, can support a few concurrent communications. Connecting more components to a shared bus would also lead to large bus lengths that in turn result in considerable energy overhead and unmanageable clock skew. Therefore, when the number of devices that need to communicate is high, bus-based systems show poor power and performance scalability [9]. Such scalability problems continue to increase, as technology advances allow more cores to be integrated on a single chip. The scalability and bandwidth challenges of the bus have led to a shift in the board-level interchip communication paradigm and the widely used PCI bus is replaced by the switch-based PCI Express network-on-board.

The on-chip communication has traveled the same path in the past decades: the problems of the bus and dedicated links and the efficiency of packet-based interconnection networks in parallel machines motivated researchers to propose switch-based network-on-chips (NoCs) to connect the cores in a high-performance, flexible, scalable, and reusable manner [10–12].

1.1.4 Network-on-Chip

Networks on chip have now expanded from an interesting area of research to a viable industrial solution for multicore processors ranging from high-end server processors [5] to embedded SoCs [13]. The building blocks of on-chip networks are the routers at every node that are interconnected by short local on-chip wires. Routers multiplex multiple communication flows (in the form of data packets) over the links and manage the traffic in a distributed fashion. Relying on a modular and scalable infrastructure, NoCs can potentially deliver high-bandwidth, low-latency, and low-power communication. From the communication perspective, this allows integration of many components on a single chip.

The benefits of NoCs in providing scalable and high-bandwidth communication are substantial. However, the need for complex and multistage pipelined routers presents several challenges in reaching the potential latency and throughput of NoCs, due to their tight area and power budgets. Authors in [1] show that the bandwidth demands of future server and embedded applications is expected to grow greatly and project that in future CMPs and multicore SoCs, the power consumption of the NoCs implemented by the current methodologies will be about 10 times greater than the power budget that can be devoted to them. Therefore, much research has focused on improving NoC efficiency to bridge the existing gap between the current and the ideal NoC power/performance metrics.

Application-specific optimization is one of the most effective methods to increase the efficiency of the NoC [1]. This class of optimization methods tries to customize the architecture and characteristics of an NoC for a target application. These methods can work at either design time, if the application and its traffic characteristics are known in advance (which is the case for most embedded applications running on multicore SoCs), or at run time for the NoCs used in general-purpose CMPs.

There has been substantial research on application-specific optimization of NoCs, varying from simple methods that update routing tables for each application to sophisticated methods of router microarchitecture and topology reconfiguration [14].

1.1.5 NoC Topology Customization

The performance of a NoC is extremely sensitive to its topology, which determines the placement and connectivity of the network nodes. Proper topology, consequently, is an important target for many NoC customization methods. An equally important problem in specialized multicore SoCs is core (or processing node) to NoC node mapping, which determines on which NoC node each processing core should be physically placed. Mapping algorithms generally try to place the processing cores communicating more frequently near each other; note that when the number of intermediate routers between two communicating cores is reduced, the power consumption and latency of the communication between them decreases proportionally.

Topology and mapping deal with the physical placement of network nodes and links. As a result, the mapping and topology cannot be modified once the chip is fabricated and will remain unchanged during system lifetime. Due to this physical constraint, most current design flows for application-specific multicore SoCs are only effective in providing design time mapping and topology optimization for a single application [15–18]. In other words, they generate and synthesize an optimized topology and mapping based on the traffic pattern of a single application.

This makes problems for today's multicore SoCs that run several different applications (often unknown at design time). Since the intercore communication characteristics can be very different across different applications, a topology that is designed based on the traffic pattern of one application does not necessarily meet the design constraints of other applications. Even the traffic generated by a single application may vary significantly in different phases of its operation. For example, the IEEE 802.11n standard (WiFi) supports 144 communications modes, each with different communication demands among cores [19]. In [20], more than 1500 different NoC configurations (topology, buffer size, and so on) are investigated and it has been shown that no single NoC can be found to provide optimal performance across a range of applications.

1.1.6 NoCs and Topology Reconfigurations

In this chapter, we introduce a NoC with reconfigurable topology, which can dynamically match the communication pattern of the currently running application.

The reconfiguration of the proposed architecture is achieved by inserting several simple switches in the network, allowing the network to dynamically change the internode connections and implement the topology that best matches the communication pattern of the running application. In other words, we try to reduce the hop count (or number of routers) between the source and destination nodes of high-volume (or heavy) communication flows by bypassing the intermediate routers. This can lead to considerable performance improvement since the latency (power) of the router pipeline stages makes a significant contribution to the total NoC latency (power). For example, in Intel's 80-core TeraFlops, more than 80% of the on-chip communication power is consumed by routers [4].

We then explore different reconfigurable NoC architectures by altering the placement of routers and switches. The most interesting structure is achieved by grouping the processors into some mesh clusters and using the reconfigurable switches to connect the clusters in a hierarchical fashion. This hierarchy consists of several clusters with fixed topology at the first level and a reconfigurable topology at the second level.

The topologies proposed for on-chip networks vary from regular tiled-based [21–23] to fully customized [15, 16] structures. Because fully customized NoCs are designed and optimized for some specific applications, they give the best performance and power results for those applications. However, distorting the regular structure of standard topologies leads to a nonreusable ad hoc topology with several implementation issues such as uneven wire lengths and routers with varying number of ports. On the other hand, regular NoC architectures provide standard structured interconnects that ensure well-controlled electrical parameters. In these topologies, designers can solve usual physical design issues like crosstalk tolerance, timing closure, and wire routing for a specific regular topology and reuse it in several designs. This reusability effectively reduces the design time.

Our reconfigurable NoC stands between these two extreme points of NoC design schemes and benefits from both worlds. While this NoC architecture is designed and optimized like a regular NoC, it can be dynamically reconfigured to a topology that best matches the traffic pattern of the currently running application. In other words, this architecture realizes application-specific topologies over structured and regular components.

1.1.7 Reconfigurations Policy

The NoC architecture introduced in this chapter and its design flow can be employed in both homogenous CMPs and heterogeneous multicore SoCs. Here, we focus on multicore SoCs, where the set of target applications is often known a priori. Each application is described as a set of concurrent tasks that have been already assigned and scheduled onto a set of selected IP cores. In such systems, mapping involves physical placement of the cores into the network nodes at design time. The design flow associated with this reconfigurable architecture can then find a customized topology for each application (based on the NoC mapping and application traffic demand) and load it onto the network when the application starts execution. The dynamic run-time reconfiguration policy for supporting homogenous CMPs with unpredictable traffic can be found elsewhere [24].

The reconfigurable topology of this chapter can be coupled with some CMP management schemes to boost their performance. The key to most of these techniques is to allocate data accessed by threads to cache banks or memories closer to the processing core that is executing the thread. For example, R-NUCA, a state-of-the-art block placement and cache-management policy for CMPs, suggests decomposition of a large-scale CMP into virtual clusters [25], each with its own subset of the cache shared by the cores within the cluster. Since most data transfers occur among the cores within a cluster, the proposed reconfigurable topology, in particular in the extended hierarchical form, can be customized to support power- and performance-efficient communication among cluster cores.

Similarly, the specialization methods that trade the silicon real estate for energy efficiency and performance can benefit from the reconfigurable topology. Recent works [26, 27] have shown that, as transistor counts grow with each process generation, increasing core counts would not lead to performance improvements, because chips are physically constrained in power and off-chip bandwidth. Therefore, a fraction of on-chip transistors, referred to as *dark silicon*, must be power-off or underutilized to stay within power and bandwidth budgets. Specialization is the most promising solution to the dark silicon problem [26, 28]. In this approach, the unused dark silicon is exploited to implement a large number of specialized accelerator cores and power up only the subset of these cores that most closely match the requirements of the executing workload at a given time. Specialized cores are designed by characterizing the target workloads and identifying the functional units that execute different parts of the codes in a performance- and power-efficient manner. The specialized cores include ASIC accelerators, GPUs, DSPs, and FPGAs. The reconfigurable topology introduced in this section is one of the best options for implementing the network-on-chip in such manycore CMPs. It can dynamically set up a customized topology among the active cores at any time to efficiently manage the intercore traffic of the current workload.

1.2 TOPOLOGY AND RECONFIGURATION

A large body of research has focused on different optimization methods for on-chip networks to reduce the power consumption and message latency. Some of these methods aim to reduce the power consumption and latency within a network hop by optimizing the microarchitecture of the router and switching mechanism [29–31]. To reduce the message latency, most of these (often general-purpose) optimization methods try to cut down the router critical path delay by parallelizing multiple pipeline stages [29, 32, 33]. Similarly, the power reduction is mostly achieved by reducing the router activity and the total capacitance switched per cycle [34, 35]. These methods are all orthogonal to our reconfigurable topology, which aims to reduce the hop count rather than per hop energy and latency. Mapping, routing, and topology selection mechanisms, on the other hand, try to decrease the length of the path taken by the packets.

A popular choice for modern NoCs is regular topologies such as mesh, which is laid out on a two-dimensional plane [22, 23, 36]. Despite the advantages of meshes for on-chip implementation, some packets may suffer from long latencies due to lack of short paths between remotely located nodes. Owing to the fact that the communication traffic characteristics of multicore SoCs used in embedded systems are nonuniform and can usually be obtained statically, an application-specific NoC with a custom topology that satisfies the design objectives and constraints of the target application is more appropriate [15–17, 37]. The problems of topology selection and core-to-NoC mapping have been explored in the past [17, 38, 39], but almost all of them are only effective in optimizing the topology based on a set of communication constraints obtained from a single application. Some solutions, however, have considered customizing NoC topology for multiple applications by using reconfigurability [20, 40–44].

In [41], topology reconfiguration is achieved by wrapping the NoC routers by some logic called *topology switch*. In this architecture, topology can be dynamically reconfigured by bypassing some routers through such switches. The authors report 56% reduction in power consumption and 10% area overhead for a multimedia application [41]. Authors in [20] introduce a polymorphic NoC with a configurable set of buffers, crossbars, and links on which an arbitrary network can be constructed. The network can be configured to offer the same performance as a fixed function network while incurring 40% area overhead, on average. However, authors have not analyzed the power consumption of their NoC architecture. In [44], a NoC is designed based on the worst-case delay and throughput constraints of a set of input applications. By applying DVS and DFS at run time, the power consumption of the NoC is optimized while the performance constraints of the currently running application are met.

Virtual point-to-point connections (VIPs) [45], express virtual channels (EVCs) [31], and shortcut paths (SCPs) [46] try to reduce the average packet hop count over a regular mesh topology by virtually bypassing some intermediate nodes along packet paths. A semiregular topology is presented in [18] by inserting some physical long links between distant nodes in a mesh, based on the traffic pattern of the target application. Long-range links target the nodes with high traffic volumes and are constructed statically at design time. The authors reported significant improvements over a conventional mesh. In addition to lack of support for multiple applications, this NoC cannot fully exploit the reusability and predictability of regular topologies; physical design and optimization procedures must be repeated for each NoC as the long links are specific to that specific NoC.

1.3 THE PROPOSED NOC ARCHITECTURE

1.3.1 Baseline Reconfigurable NoC

The proposed reconfiguration mechanism relies on an array of simple switches to dynamically change the internode connections. Figure 1.1 shows how the proposed reconfiguration is added to a conventional 2D mesh network. In this architecture, the network nodes, which are composed of a processing element and a router (represented by squares in Fig. 1.1) are not connected directly to each other, but through simple switch boxes, called *configuration switches* (represented by circles in Fig. 1.1). This structure is inspired by the reconfigurable processor arrays in [47].

Figure 1.1 also shows the internal structure of a configuration switch. It consists of some simple switching fabric that can establish connections between incoming and

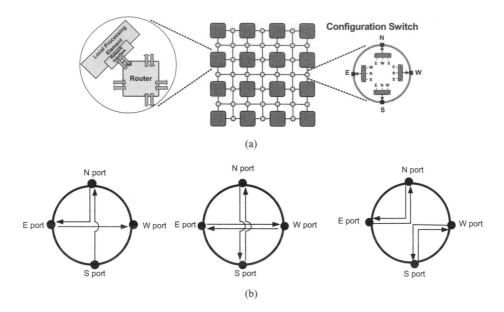

Figure 1.1 The reconfigurable NoC architecture (a) and three possible switch configurations (b).

outgoing links. Actually, the internal connections can be implemented by either a crossbar or four multiplexers, each at an output port of the switch. Figure 1.1 displays three possible switch configurations.

Compared to a router, switches have no buffers, no arbitration and routing logic, and smaller switching fabric (4×4 crossbars with negligible activity on the *select line* of cross-points, compared to a 5×5 crossbar of mesh routers). Furthermore, since a connection coming through an input port does not loop back, a smaller number of cross-points can be used. Some details about optimizing the switch structure and several implementation issues can be found in [48].

An important consideration in the proposed topology is that long links that may be generated by merging a number of channel segments by chaining the configuration switches. Such long links may decrease the NoC clock frequency, if the link delay exceeds one clock period. This problem can be solved by segmenting the long links into fixed-length links connected by a 1-flit register buffer and sending flits over them in a pipelined fashion. Since the connection between two adjacent nodes (on which flits travel in a single NoC cycle) consists of two channel segments, the registers should be placed in some configuration switches in such a way that each flit is buffered after passing through two channel segments. Figure 1.2 shows the switches in which the flits are latched. For example, the bold wire segments in the figure form a long link between nodes X and Y. Here, each flit passes over this link in five cycles, in a pipelined manner.

This NoC can be configured to implement arbitrary topologies, including some standard topologies, if the configuration switches are set properly. For example, Fig. 1.3.a

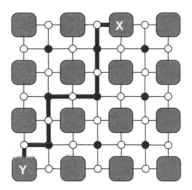

Figure 1.2   Flits traverse the connection between nodes X and Y (the black solid line) in five cycles in a pipelined fashion. Flits are buffered at the black switches.

displays an 8 × 8 network configured as a 2D mesh. Figure 1.3.b shows the case where a workload is running on a selected set of specialized cores (with black color) and the other cores are left dark (inactive). In this figure, the active nodes are connected by a mesh topology implemented on the reconfigurable NoC.

Although we used the mesh topology as the base of our reconfigurable NoC architecture, the proposed reconfiguration mechanism can be applied to other well-known topologies, such as torus, hypercube, and the general k-ary n-cube. It can also be used in some modern topologies, such as concentrated mesh (or X-mesh) networks, to further improve their performance when dealing with multiple applications.

The proposed NoC is not restricted to specific switching and routing schemes. The NoC routers in this study adopt a wormhole switching mechanism; note that wormhole

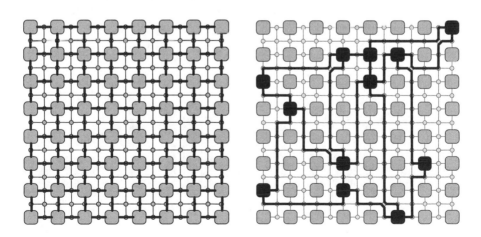

Figure 1.3   The implementation of a mesh on the reconfigurable topology among all network nodes (a) and a selected set of cores, where the black nodes are active and the gray cores are inactive (dark) (b).

switching best suits the limited buffering resources and low-latency communication requirements of on-chip networks. Like most application-specific optimized NoCs, this NoC applies a table-based routing scheme. This allows the NoC to support any static routing algorithm and is a suitable choice due to the irregular nature of application-specific topologies. It also allows the designer to exploit our understanding of the application traffic characteristics and avoid network congestion and load unbalance by appropriately allocating paths to traffic flows.

The NoC reconfiguration process can be initiated by a configuration manager, whenever a switching takes place between two applications. Switching between network configurations is done in parallel with application switching. In most SoC designs, the application switching time is of the order of few milliseconds, which is the time needed to load the data and code of a new application into the SoC, sending control signals to different parts of the SoC and shutting down the old application [44]. Because the configuration data of the proposed NoC architecture are small and can be stored in configuration switches and routers, the NoC configuration switching time is far smaller than the time needed to switch between applications and does not impose any additional delay to the application switching procedure. It has been shown in [44] that, even if the configuration data are stored in an off-chip memory, it can be loaded and distributed around the NoC in few microseconds, which is still shorter than the application switching time. The energy dissipated for configuration switching can also be ignored due to infrequent switching and the small amount of data transition during each switching event.

In general, dynamic hardware reconfiguration can only be implemented on reconfigurable devices; hence, most of the reconfigurable architectures are implemented using FPGAs. However, since the reconfigurable part of the proposed NoC is limited to some simple configuration switches, this NoC can be implemented on both FPGA and ASIC platforms.

The proposed reconfigurable network pays for the flexibility with additional area overhead. Figure 1.4 shows the effects of different architectural parameters, including buffer depth, network size, and link width, on the area overhead of the proposed

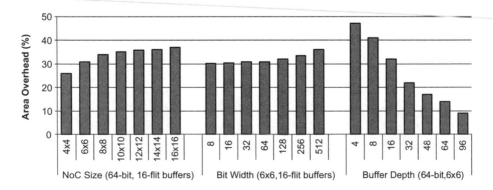

Figure 1.4 The area overhead of the reconfigurable NoC for different buffer depths (flits), network sizes (number of nodes), and link widths (bits).

reconfigurable NoC over a conventional NoC. The results are obtained by a detailed area model for NoC components [48]. The figure reports 10–45% area overhead over a conventional NoC for some common NoC configurations. Please note that Fig. 1.4 reports the area overhead over a conventional network, not the entire chip (cores+network).

1.3.2 Generalized Reconfigurable NoC

We can explore different reconfigurable structures by altering the placement of routers and switches. Figure 1.5 shows two interesting reconfigurable structures. The structure in Fig. 1.5.a is achieved by increasing the number of configuration switches between two adjacent routers, or NoC *corridor width*, to two switches. Reconfigurable NoCs with wider corridor widths best match the applications with a large number of intercore communication flows.

The other alternative placement is depicted in Fig. 1.5.b. In this structure, the nodes are grouped into four-node clusters. The connection among the nodes within a cluster is fixed, but the clusters are interconnected via configuration switches. The idea behind this structure is to benefit from the interesting characteristics of the mesh topology while avoiding its drawbacks. From the traffic management perspective, a mesh NoC is efficient in handling local traffic patterns where each node communicates with its adjacent nodes, but it suffers from the lack of short paths between remotely located nodes.

The proposed architecture can efficiently support local traffic by mapping the tasks generating high intertask traffic flows into the same cluster. Unlike the baseline reconfigurable NoC in Fig. 1.1, in this new architecture, the local traffic does not pass through configuration switches, hence the power consumed in theses switches during data communication between adjacent nodes is saved. The problem associated with

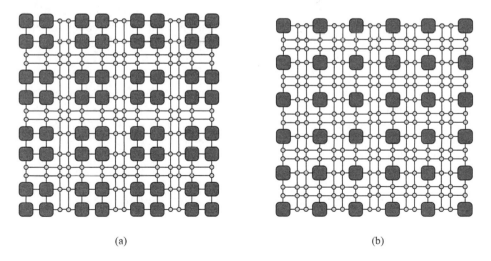

(a)   (b)

Figure 1.5   Reconfigurable NoC with the corridor width of 2 (a) and a cluster-based reconfigurable NoC with cluster size of 4 (b).

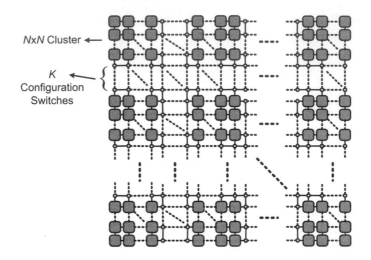

NxN Cluster ←

K ← ⎰
Configuration ⎱
Switches

Figure 1.6 The generalized cluster-based reconfigurable structure.

communication between far nodes can be also mitigated by configuring the intercluster connections in order to make a direct connection, to reduce the hop count, between the endpoint nodes of long traffic flows.

These reconfigurable structures can be extended to a more generalized reconfigurable NoC structure depicted in Fig. 1.6. This architecture offers a hierarchical clustered communication infrastructure with two parameters: cluster size and corridor width. This structure can be considered as a hierarchical topology in which several mesh subnetworks, which provide the first-level local communication structure, are connected via a higher-level global network implemented by reconfigurable switches. Like other hierarchical NoCs [49–51], this two-tier topology facilitates local and global communication between cores. Consequently, this structure is an ideal candidate for the next generation many-core CMPs and MPSoCs where hundreds and thousands of cores are integrated into a single chip.

As mentioned before, the reconfigurability is the advantage of our architecture over the existing hierarchical NoC architectures. The intracluster topology is not limited to mesh, and any topology can be used for this purpose. In particular, when the cluster size is small (Fig. 1.5), using a bus or crossbar may be a more practical choice to support the local communication.

1.4   ENERGY AND PERFORMANCE-AWARE MAPPING

1.4.1   The Design Procedure for the Baseline Reconfigurable NoC

In this section, we address the mapping and routing problems in the baseline reconfigurable NoC. It is assumed that each input application is spatially partitioned into several tasks, each of which is nonmigratory and assigned to a processing core. The intercore communication pattern remains relatively static as each core performs a fixed task. Each input application is described as a Communication Task Graph (CTG). The CTG is a directed graph $G(V, E)$, where each $v_i \in V$ represents a task, and a directed edge $e_{i,j} \in E$ represents the communication flow from v_i to v_j. The communication volume (bits per second) corresponding to each edge $e_{i,j}$ is also provided and is denoted by $t(e_{i,j})$.

Simply stated, for a given set of input applications whose tasks are assigned to a specific set of processing cores, our objective is to (1) map the cores into different nodes of a reconfigurable NoC, (2) find a customized topology for each application based on the mapping in previous step and the application traffic characteristics, and (3) find a route for the traffic flows of each application based on the topology found for the application.

We develop a two-step algorithm for this problem, where core-to-network mapping is done at the first step and then topology and route generation are done concurrently at the second step. The idea behind splitting the procedure into two steps is that, in our proposal, the reconfigurability only changes the connectivity among the cores and not the physical placement of them; so, our system is comprised of some nodes with fixed placement and a reconfigurable set of links. Consequently, mapping and topology selection should be done per MPSoC and per application, respectively. This suggests that our procedure must be carried out in two subsequent steps: the first step handles physical placement of cores by considering all applications and the second step works on each individual application and forms a proper topology for it.

1.4.1.1 *Core-to-Network Mapping*

In the first step, our objective is to figure out how to physically map the cores required by input applications onto different tiles of a mesh network such that the distances between the communicating cores are minimized. We assign a weight to each task graph based on its criticality, for example, the percentage of time that the corresponding application is run on the NoC. Assigning weights enables the designer to bias the mapping for major or critical applications.

This step is performed by constructing a synthetic average task graph (the average task graph) from the task graphs of the given set of input applications. This average task graph includes all the nodes of all task graphs of the input applications. For the edge between every pair of nodes, the average weight of the volumes relating to the corresponding edges across all task graphs are calculated and used in the average task graph. If an edge does not exist in a task graph, its volume is considered to be zero. More formally, the weight (communication volume) of each edge is calculated as

$$t_{avr}(e_{x,y}) = \left(\sum_{\forall applications} t_i(e_{x,y}) \times W_i \right) / n$$

where W_i represents the weight of the ith task graph and $t_i(e_{x,y})$ and $t_{avr}(e_{x,y})$ denote the volume of $e_{x,y}$ (which defines the edge between nodes v_x and v_y) in the ith task graph and the average task graph, respectively, and n is the number of input task graphs.

The mapping problem can be formulated as follows. Given a synthetic average CTG constructed from the task graphs of the input applications and a reconfigurable NoC (satisfying $size(CTG) < size(NoC)$), find a mapping M from CTG to the NoC nodes as $Min \left\{ \sum_{\forall e_{i,j}} t(e_{i,j}) \times dist(M(v_i), M(v_j)) \right\}$ such that for every node $v_i \neq v_j$ of the CTG, we have $M(v_i) \neq M(v_j)$. The constraint states that each core should be mapped to exactly one NoC node, and no node can host more than one core. $dist(a, b)$ shows the Manhattan distance between nodes a and b in the network, and $M(v_i)$ is the network node to which CTG node v_i is mapped. $size(CTG)$ and $size(NoC)$ denote the number of CTG and NoC nodes, respectively. Again, $t(e_{i,j})$ denotes the volume of $e_{i,j}$, which represents the edge between vertex v_i and vertex v_j.

Central to network mapping is an NP-hard problem [52], therefore rather than searching for an optimal solution, it has been solved heuristically in prior works [22, 37, 53]. As the focus of this chapter is the topology reconfiguration, we perform mapping for the average graph using NMAP, a well-known and popular heuristic method presented in [22]. NMAP uses a heuristic algorithm for power-aware mapping of task graph nodes on a mesh-based network and selects a route for each task graph edge. We only use the mapping algorithm of NMAP and then, in the next step, propose a topology and route selection algorithm based on the reconfigurable network links.

In NMAP, all cores are initially unmapped. Then, the core mapping is accomplished as follows:

Step 1. Map the core with the maximum communication demand onto one of the mesh nodes with maximum number of neighbors.

Step 2. Select the core that communicates the most with already mapped cores and examine all unallocated mesh nodes for placement. Select the node that minimizes the communication cost between the current core and already mapped cores. The communication cost of mapping vertex v_i of the CTG into node x of the NoC is given by $\sum_{\forall j | e_{i,j} \in CTG} (t(e_{i,j}) \times dist(x, M(v_j)))$, where $dist(x, M(v_j))$ is the Manhattan distance between x and the node to which CTG vertex v_j is mapped.

The process is repeated until all cores are mapped. We refer interested readers to [22] for more details on the NMAP.

1.4.1.2 Topology and Route Generation.

Once the mapping is obtained from the average task graph, a suitable topology is constructed for each individual application, aiming to reduce the NoC average power consumption and message latency when the application is being processed. To achieve this goal, we implement a topology for each application where the number of hops between the source and destination nodes of heavy communication flows is as small as possible. The main idea is to choose the heaviest communication flow that is not yet assigned a route and find a path with minimum possible hop counts for it. Finding this route may involve configuring the switches that are not yet configured in order to skip over some intermediate routers and make a shorter connection between the end nodes. As a result, route selection and topology construction are done in parallel, within the same procedure. The algorithm can configure the unconfigured internal connections of the configuration switches but not the connections that have been configured at previous iterations of the algorithm for the edges with higher volumes.

Initially, in the topology selection algorithm, all edges of an application task graph are stored in a decreasing order (based on their communication volumes) and the internal connections of all configuration switches are unconfigured. Then, for each edge in the order, a branch-and-bound algorithm chooses the path with lowest cost between its source and destination nodes. We calculate the cost of a path based on the routers and configuration switches it includes. We assign a cost of 1 to a link ending to a configuration switch and a cost of 4 to a link ending to a router. This cost assignment scheme reflects the power/latency ratio of the switches and routers and encourages the algorithm to find a path through the configuration switches, hence creating a long, pipelined link between the flow endpoint nodes. The algorithm searches for the optimal path by alternating the following branch and bound steps:

Branch: Starting from the source router of the selected edge, the algorithm makes a new branch by adding a router/configuration switch adjacent to the current node of the partial path. Current node is defined as the last node added to a partial path through which the path is extended. The added node must be located within the shortest path area, that is, between the source and destination nodes of the edge. The shortest path area is defined by the nodes and configuration switches located along one of the shortest paths between the source and destination nodes, as well as their adjacent configuration switches. If the current node is a router, the path is extended by including its neighboring configuration switches along the shortest path toward the destination node. If the current node is a configuration switch, the path is extended by adding the neighboring routers or configuration switches along the shortest path. However, if a switch is already configured in previous steps of the algorithm for the flows with higher traffic rates (e.g., by connecting its E input port to S output port), the algorithm cannot consider some other paths that involve establishing conflicting turns on the switch (e.g., connecting E input port to W input port).

Bound: A partial path is bounded (discarded) in some conditions. First, it is bounded if, by adding the new node, the predefined bandwidth constraints of the newly added link are violated. More formally, the bandwidth constraint of each NoC link l_k must be satisfied as

$$\forall l_k, BW(l_k) \geq \sum_{\forall e_{i,j} \in E} X^k(i, j)$$

where $BW(lk)$ is the bandwidth of link l_k and $X^K(i, j)$ is obtained by

$$X^k(i, j) = \begin{cases} t(e_{i,j}) & , \; if \; l_k \in path(e_{i,j}) \\ 0 & , \; otherwise \end{cases}$$

where $path(e_{i,j})$ represents the set of links on which task graph edge $e_{i,j}$ (with volume $t(e_{i,j})$) is mapped.

In addition, if the cost of a partial path reaching a node is larger than the minimum cost of the partial paths already reaching that node, the path is discarded. The minimum cost of the already-found paths is also kept by the algorithm and a partial path is bounded when its new cost exceeds this value. Finally, we perform a connectivity check to verify that there is at least one path between the source and destination nodes of all edges that are not mapped yet. If the current partial path configures the switches in such a way that all possible paths between the source and destination nodes of at least one unmapped edge are blocked, the partial path is removed.

After the path with the minimum cost is found, it is established in the NoC by configuring all corresponding configuration switches within the path. Then, the algorithm continues with the next edge. The algorithm is repeated for all the edges of the application CTG. Once all task graph edges are mapped to a path in the NoC, the paths are analyzed for detecting potential deadlocks. To this end, all cyclic dependencies among paths are broken by adding a virtual channel in one of the nodes of the cycle.

In this procedure, we assume that the applications are run on the NoC one at a time. Nonetheless, simultaneous execution of multiple applications is a likely scenario in MPSoCs. We can easily support simultaneous execution of multiple applications by the same procedure. To this end, we combine the CTGs of the applications that may run simultaneously, or within overlapping time intervals, into a single CTG and perform the topology generation and route selection steps for the new task graph. The selected configuration will then be loaded into the network when the applications are run simultaneously.

1.4.2 Mapping and Topology Generation for Cluster-Based NoC

The algorithm developed for the baseline-reconfigurable NoC is extended to a four-step algorithm to support the generalized cluster-based version of the reconfigurable NoCs. Here, applications with v vertices and a reconfigurable NoC with n nodes arranged as n/k clusters of size k are the inputs of the algorithm. For the sake of simplicity, we assume that $v = n$. We outline the steps of this algorithm below. The details of each step can be found in [54].

CTG partitioning: Partition the input CTG into n/k partitions of size k such that the partitions are disjoint and have equal size, and the sum of the weights of the edges with endpoints in different partitions is minimized. We then allocate each NoC cluster to a partition. This graph partitioning approach aims to group the frequently communicating CTG nodes in the same partition and eventually place them in the same cluster in order to reduce the intercluster connections by localizing the traffic. Graph partitioning is a well-known problem in graph theory, and a large number of algorithms have been proposed to solve it. Here, we use the Kernighan-Lin algorithm, one of the most efficient heuristic multilevel algorithms presented in [55].

Partition-to-cluster mapping: This step deals with allocating the NoC clusters to the CTG partitions. The graph partitioning algorithm of Step 1 guarantees that the endpoint nodes of heaviest communication flows are mapped into the same cluster, but there are still communication demands between nodes located at different partitions. The aim of this step is to reduce the intercluster communication by mapping partitions with high interpartition traffic loads into nearby clusters. We perform the mapping using NMAP. By considering the partitions of a partitioned graph as a super-node and grouping all edges between any two given partitions as a super-edge, we get a new CTG. This new CTG is then fed to NMAP to allocate the NoC clusters to the CTG partitions.

Partition-node to cluster-core mapping: Once the partitions are mapped, this step aims to reduce the traffic inside each cluster and figures out how to map different nodes of each partition into the nodes of the target cluster. We again use NMAP for this step.

Intercluster topology implementation: Once all nodes are mapped, the configuration switches should be configured to establish connections among the clusters, based on the current intercluster communication pattern. This step applies a modified version of the branch and bound algorithm of the previous section to find a path with minimum weight for intercluster edges.

1.5   EXPERIMENTAL RESULTS

To evaluate the performance of the proposed NoC architecture and its design procedure, we use some existing SoC designs that have been widely used in the literature, including Multi-Window Display (MWD) [56], Video Object Plane Decoder (VOPD) [22], GSM [57], and Multi Media System (MMS) [23]. The MMS benchmark contains H.263 decoder, H.263 encoder, MP3 encoder, and MP3 decoder applications. GSM also contains the GSM decoder and encoder applications. However, for the first two SoCs that have a single application task graph, we synthesize additional task graphs, called X-50% and X-25%, where X is the name of the application. The X-25% and X-50% task graphs are generated by replacing the source and destination nodes of the edges of task graph X with other randomly chosen nodes (i.e., moving the position of the task graph edges) with a probability of 25% and 50%, respectively. We assign a weight of 0.5 to the base task graph X, a weight of 0.25 to X-25% and X-50% task graphs, and then integrate the task graphs into a single NoC, according to the design flow described in the previous section.

The conventional NoC used for the sake of comparison applies the same mapping as its reconfigurable counterpart, but its topology is fixed during execution of the applications. The communication flows of the conventional NoC are directed by the conventional dimension-order deterministic routing algorithm.

Simulation experiments are performed using Xmulator NoC simulator [58] for a 64-bit-wide system with speculative four-stage pipelined wormhole routers [59] with 16-flit buffers. The power results are reported by Orion power library [60] in 65-nm technology. In simulation experiments, packets are generated with exponential distribution, and the communication rates between any two nodes are set to be proportional to the communication volume between them in the task graph.

The task graphs of different MMS applications are depicted in Fig. 1.7, where the edge tags represent the communication volume between the source and destination nodes of the edge in kilobits per second. The applications use the same set of processing cores,

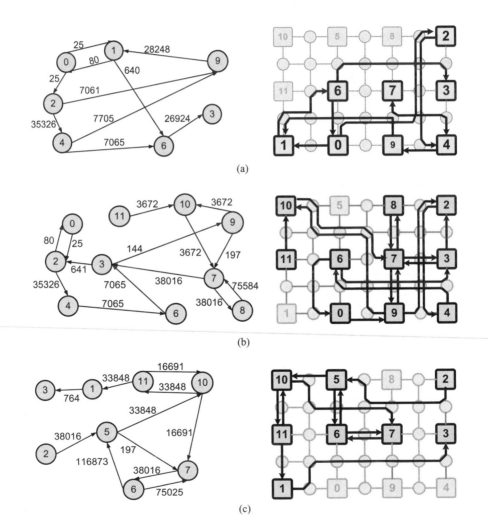

(a)

(b)

(c)

Figure 1.7 The communication task graph and corresponding topology for MP3 (encoder+decoder) (a), H263 decoder (b), H63 encoder (c).

but the traffic pattern among the cores is different for each application. In Fig. 1.7, the edges belonging to each individual application are bolded in the task graph corresponding to their applications. Different tasks of this application suite are mapped on 12 cores. The physical mapping is accomplished based on the average graph of the four input task graphs. The algorithm then finds a suitable topology for each application, which is illustrated next to the corresponding task graph in Fig. 1.7.

1.5.1 Baseline Reconfigurable NoC

Figure 1.8 displays the average packet latency and power consumption of the reconfigurable NoC and its equivalent conventional NoC for the mentioned multicore SoC benchmarks. The results show considerable power and performance improvements over a conventional NoC using NMAP. As the figure indicates, reconfiguration can effectively adapt the topology to different applications and reduce the power consumption and average packet latency of the NoC by up to 28% (16% on average) and 26% (10% on average), respectively.

As the results for MMS applications show, the power and performance gain obtained by the proposed architecture for MP3 encoder/decoder are higher than H.263 encoder/decoder. The reason is that the volume of the communication flows of H.263 applications, which are larger than the communication volumes of MP3 applications, biases the mapping for H.263 encoder and decoder. As a result, the source and destination nodes of H.263 applications are mapped near each other, while the nodes required by MP3 applications are placed at greater distances. However, we can configure the NoC to establish a direct connection between almost all communicating nodes of MP3 encoder and decoder. This leads to power and performance values close to the case when the communicating cores are mapped into nearby nodes.

Similarly, for the MWD and VOPD benchmarks, the weight of the original application is increased over the two synthetic applications which that make the mapping biased for the original application. As a result, reconfiguration provides more power and performance gains for the synthetic applications (X-25% and X-50%).

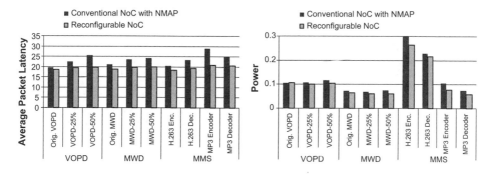

Figure 1.8 Power consumption (Watts) and packet latency (cycles for 8-flit packets) in a conventional and a reconfigurable NoC. The conventional NoC uses NMAP.

The reported power includes both dynamic and static parts. In this work, a dynamic power management scheme is used to deactivate unused router and switch ports in order to decrease the static power consumption of the reconfigurable NoC. The idle routers and links of the conventional NoC are also deactivated. The VOPD benchmarks, however, require more connections compared with other benchmarks, and thus involve more active switches, routers, and links. Consequently, the static power consumption of the reconfigurable NoC, when running the VOPD applications, is higher than the static power of a conventional NoC. This higher static power consumption may not be compensated by the obtained dynamic power saving, as reported for the VOPD original application in Fig. 1.8. Nonetheless, the proposed reconfigurable NoC enhances the NoC dynamic power consumption by 21%, on average.

1.5.2 Performance Evaluation with Cost Constraints

In this section, we compare the proposed NoC with a conventional NoC under cost constraints to investigate what improvements would be obtained if the extra logic used in our reconfigurable NoC is invested to increase the NoC bit width or buffer depth.

First, we use the extra logic to make NoCs with additional buffering capacity. Our area model reveals that a conventional NoC with two virtual channels and 8-flit buffers (Conv. 2VC, 8-flit buffers, 128-bit), a conventional NoC with one virtual channel and 16-flit buffers (Conv. 1VC, 16-flit buffers, 128-bit), and a reconfigurable NoC with corridor width of one, one virtual channel, and 8-flit buffers (Reconfig-C1, 1VC, 8-flit buffers, 128-bit) all have approximately the same area.

The extra area overhead can also be invested to increase the NoC bit width. By increasing the NoC bit width, the area of the NoC data-path components (buffers, links, and crossbars) is increased. According to our area model, the area of a 128-bit reconfigurable NoC (Reconfig-C1, 1VC, 8-flit buffers, in Fig. 1.9) is almost the same as the area of a conventional NoC with bit width of 158 (Conv. 1VC, 8-flit buffers, 158-bit, in Fig. 1.9).

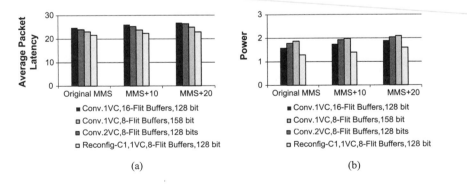

Figure 1.9   The average message latency (cycles for 8-flit packets) (a) and power (Watts) (b) of the three NoC configurations with the same area under the MMS traffic and its variants.

Figure 1.9 compares the power and latency results for these NoC configurations. The figure shows that our reconfigurable NoC efficiently exploits the area overhead to provide smaller latency and power consumption than the three equivalent conventional configurations. In this experiment, MMS benchmark of the previous section is used. In order to evaluate the impact of increasing on-chip traffic on performance improvement of the considered architectures, we generate two other task graphs, MMS+10% and MMS+20%, by randomly adding new edges to the MMS task graph in such a way that the volume of the MMS intercore traffic is increased by 10% and 20%, respectively.

Another possible way to invest the area overhead of the reconfigurable NoC is to use larger, more powerful processing cores. Our area model reveals that the reconfigurable NoC imposes less than 3% overhead to the entire area used by the MMS cores. This result is obtained by considering the reconfigurable NoC of Fig. 1.9 (Reconfig-C1, 1VC, 8-flit buffers) and an average size of 1 mm × 1 mm for each core. According to Pollack's rule [61], the increase in processor performance is roughly proportional to the square root of the increase in its area. Consequently, investing the area overhead to increase the area of the cores in the SoC with a conventional NoC leads to about a 1% increase in the performance of each core. As a result, investing this area overhead to increase the network performance would be a better choice, especially in the case that the network is in the critical path of the system.

1.5.3 Comparison Cluster-Based NoC

To compare the cluster-based and baseline reconfigurable NoCs, we again use the *GSM, MMS*, and *VOPD* applications. We adopt a cluster-based NoC with four clusters of size 2 × 2 for VOPD (with 16 cores), 9 clusters (arranged as a 3 × 3 mesh) of size 2 × 2 for *H263 + MP3* (with 36 cores), and 12 clusters (arranged as a 3 × 4 mesh) of size 2 × 2 for *GSM* (with 48 cores). The MMS application is the same as the application used in the previous section, but by using a different task-to-core assignment scheme its size is increased to 36 cores.

We perform the entire design flow (graph partitioning, mapping, and topology generation steps) for one primary application of each set (*GSM encoder, H.263 + MP3encoder, and VPOD*). Next, to evaluate the adaption capability of the proposed architecture, we assume that a new application of each set (*GSM decoder H.263 + MP3 decoder, and VPOD-50%*) is added to the system after chip fabrication. Again, note that as the NoC is already synthesized, the design steps related to physical core-to-network mapping (graph partitioning, partition to cluster mapping, and partition-node to cluster-core mapping) cannot be done for the new application, and, hence, we directly head to the topology generation step.

Figure 1.10 shows the power and latency results offered by the three networks. The improvement over the baseline reconfigurable NoC comes from the better mapping algorithm (by applying a graph partitioning algorithm together with the NMAP algorithm), as well as the more efficient switch placement of the cluster-based NoC.

For the primary applications, for which the physical mapping is done, we again observe that the improvement is not considerable. The reason is that the source and destination nodes of *GSM encoder* are mapped near each other and this leaves little room

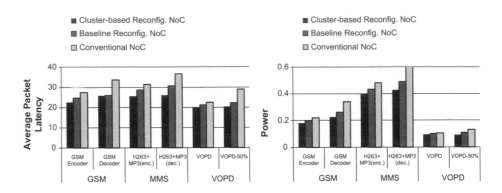

Figure 1.10 The average message latency (cycles for 8-flit packets) (a) and power (Watts) (b) of the three NoC configurations.

(the gap between the conventional and reconfigurable NoC results) for improvement. However, when a new application is run, such as *GSM decoder*, the nodes required by this application are potentially placed at farther distances (since the mapping is performed for some application with a different traffic pattern), so they can enjoy more from the reconfigurable long links.

We have also compared our proposed architecture with a state-of-the-art topology: the *Concentrated Mesh* (CMesh) topology proposed in [36]. In this topology, each router is connected to four processors. Although this topology takes full advantage of the locality of the intercore communication, it increases the switch size and introduces an additional router stage for switch preparation [36]. The simulation parameters and architectural properties of the cluster-based NoC are the same as the previous experiment. For the CMesh topology, we use our partitioning algorithm to create four-task partitions and apply NMAP to map the partitions onto the routers. Figure 1.11 shows the energy and latency results of the proposed NoC architecture and CMesh. As the figure

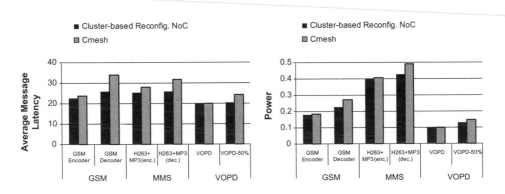

Figure 1.11 Comparing the average message latency (cycles for 8-flit packets) (a) and power (Watts) (b) with the CMesh topology.

indicates, our proposed architecture exhibits better average energy and latency results when compared with CMesh. Note that, again, the reconfigurability of our proposed NoC leads to more improvement over CMesh (with fixed connections) for the applications that are introduced after the NoC synthesis (i.e., GSM decoder, H.263+MP3 decoder, and VOPD50%).

1.6 CONCLUSION

We proposed a reconfigurable architecture for networks-on-chip (NoCs) on which arbitrary application-specific topologies can be implemented. Since entirely different applications may be executed on a SoC at different times, the on-chip traffic characteristics can vary significantly across different applications. However, almost all existing NoC design flows and the corresponding application-specific optimization methods customize NoCs based on the traffic characteristics of a single application. The reconfigurability of the proposed NoC architecture allows it to dynamically tailor its topology to the traffic pattern of different applications.

In this chapter, we first introduced the baseline reconfigurable NoC architecture. We next addressed the two problems of core to network mapping and topology exploration in which the cores of a given set of input applications are physically mapped to the network and then a suitable topology is found for each individual application. Experimental results, using some multicore SoC workloads, showed that this architecture effectively improves the performance of NoCs by 29% and reduces the power consumption by 9% over one of the most efficient and popular mapping algorithms proposed for conventional NoCs.

We then extended the baseline reconfigurable NoC to a generalized reconfigurable NoC architecture. This new cluster-based structure consists of several mesh clusters alongside a reconfigurable connection fabric that handles the intercluster communication. It can support both local and global traffic patterns in an efficient manner. Our evaluation results showed the effectiveness of the proposed architecture in reducing the latency and energy of on-chip communication.

In all, compared with previous reconfigurable proposals and regarding the imposed area overhead and power/performance gains, the proposed NoC introduces a more appropriate trade-off between the cost and flexibility.

REFERENCES

[1] J. Owens, W.J. Dally, R. Ho, D.N. Jayasimha, S.W. Keckler, and L.S. Peh, "Research challenges for on-chip interconnection networks," *IEEE Micro*, Vol. 27, No. 5, pp. 96–108, 2007.

[2] Intel Xeon Processor E7 Family, http://www.intel.com/content/www/us/en/processors/xeon/xeon-processor-e7-family.html, Apr. 2012.

[3] P. Conway, et al., "Cache hierarchy and memory subsystem of the AMD Opteron processor," *IEEE Micro*, Vol. 30, No. 2, pp. 16–29, Mar.–Apr. 2010.

[4] SPARC T3 Data Sheet, http://www.oracle.com/products, Apr. 2012.

[5] J. Howard, et al., "A 48-Core IA-32 message-passing processor with DVFS in 45nm CMOS," in *Proceedings of International Solid State Circuits Conference*, pp. 108–110, 2010.

[6] Vega Processor, http://www.azulsystems.com/products/vega/processor, May 2012.

[7] PC202 processor, http://www.picochip.com/page/75/, Apr. 2012.

[8] Am2045: Ambric's new parallel processor, www.ambric.info/pdf/MPR_Ambric_Article_10-06_204101.pdf, May 2012.

[9] V. Raghunathan, M.B. Srivastava, and R.K. Gupta, "A survey of techniques for energy efficient on-chip communication," in *Proceedings of the Design Automation Conference*, 2003.

[10] W.J. Dally and B. Towles, "Route packets, not wires: on-chip interconnection networks," in *Proceedings of the Design Automation Conference*, pp. 681–689, 2001.

[11] L. Benini and G. De Micheli, "Networks on chip: A new paradigm for systems on chip design," *IEEE Computer*, Vol. 35, No. 1, pp. 70–78, 2001.

[12] A. Jantsch and H. Tenhunen, *Networks on Chip*, Kluwer Academic Publishers, 2003.

[13] Arteris NoC Customers, http://www.arteris.com/customers, Apr. 2012

[14] T. Bjerregaard and S. Mahadevan, "A survey of research and practices of network-on-chip," *ACM Computing Surveys*, Vol. 38, No. 1, pp. 1–51, 2006.

[15] J. Cong, Y. Huang, and B. Yuan, "A tree-based topology synthesis for on-chip network," in *Proceedings of International Conference on Computer-Aided Design*, pp. 651–658, 2011.

[16] J. Chan and S. Parameswaran, "NoCOUT: NoC topology generation with mixed packet-switched and point-to-point networks," in *Proceedings of the Asia and South Pacific Design Automation Conference*, pp. 256–270, 2008.

[17] S. Murali and G. De Micheli, "SUNMAP: A tool for automatic topology selection and generation for NoCs," in *Proceedings of Design Automation Conference*, pp. 914–919, 2004.

[18] U. Ogras and R. Marculescu, "Application-specific network-on-chip architecture customization via long-range link insertion," in *Proceedings of Design Automation Conference*, 2005.

[19] A. Jerraya, "System compilation for MPSoC based on NoC," in *the 8th International Forum on Application-Specific Multi-Processor SoCs*, Netherlands, 2008.

[20] M. Kim, J. Davis, M. Oskin, and T. Austin, "Polymorphic on-chip networks," in *Proceedings of International Symposium of Computer Architecture*, pp. 101–112, 2008.

[21] Y. Hoskote, S. Vangal, A. Singh, N. Bokar, and S. Bokar, "A 5-GHz mesh interconnect for a Teraflops processor," *IEEE Micro*, Vol. 27, No. 5, pp. 51–61, 2007.

[22] S. Murali and G. De Micheli, "Bandwidth-constrained mapping of cores onto NoC architectures," in *Proceedings of Design Automation and Test in Europe*, pp. 896–901, 2004.

[23] J. Hu, and R. Marculescu, "Energy- and performance-aware mapping for regular NoC architectures," *IEEE Transactions on Computer-Aided Design of Integrated Circuits and Systems*, Vol. 24, No. 1, pp. 551–562, 2005.

[24] M. Modarressi, H. Sarbazi-Azad, and A. Tavakkol, "An efficient dynamically reconfigurable on-chip network architecture," in *Proceedings of Design Automation Conference*, pp. 310–313, 2010.

[25] N. Hardavellas, M. Ferdman, B. Falsafi, and A. Ailamaki, "Reactive NUCA: Near-optimal block placement and replication in distributed caches," in *Proceedings of International Symposium of Computer Architecture*, pp. 184–195, 2009.

[26] N. Hardavellas, M. Ferdman, B. Falsafi, and A. Ailamaki, "Toward dark silicon in servers," *IEEE Micro*, Vol. 31, No. 4, pp. 6–15, July–Aug. 2011.

[27] H. Esmaeilzadeh, E. Blem, R. St. Amant, K. Sankaralingam, and D. Burger, "Dark silicon and the end of multicore scaling," in *Proceedings of International Symposium of Computer Architecture*, pp. 365–376, 2011.

[28] N. Goulding-Hotta, et al., "The GreenDroid mobile application processor: an architecture for silicon's dark future," *IEEE Micro*, Vol. 31, No. 2, pp. 86–95, Mar.–Apr. 2011.

[29] R. Mullins and S. Moore, "Low-latency virtual-channel routers for on-chip networks," in *Proceedings of International Symposium of Computer Architecture*, pp. 188–197, 2004.

[30] P. Abad, V. Puente, J. Gregorio, and P. Prieto, "Rotary router: An efficient architecture for CMP interconnection networks," in *Proceedings of International Symposium of Computer Architecture*, pp. 116–125, 2007.

[31] A. Kumar, L.S. Peh, P. Kundu, and N.K. Jha, "Express virtual channels: towards the ideal interconnection fabric," in *Proceedings of International Symposium of Computer Architecture*, pp. 150–161, 2007.

[32] L.S. Peh and W.J. Dally, "A delay model for router microarchitectures," *IEEE Micro*, Vol. 2, No. 1, pp. 26–34, 2001.

[33] K. Kim, S. Lee, K. Lee, and H.J. Yoo, "An arbitration look-ahead scheme for reducing end to-end latency in networks-on chip," in *Proceedings of International Symposium on Circuits and Systems (ISCAS)*, pp. 2357–2360, 2005.

[34] J. Kim, C. Nicopoulos, D. Park, V. Narayanan, M. Yousif, C. Das, "A gracefully degrading and energy-efficient modular router architecture for on-chip networks," in *Proceedings of International Symposium of Computer Architecture*, pp. 4–15, 2006.

[35] P. Meloni, S. Murali, S. Carta, M. Camplani, L. Raffo, and G. De Micheli, "Routing aware switch hardware customization for networks on chips," in *Proceedings of NanoNet*, 2006.

[36] J. Balfour and W.J. Dally, "Design tradeoffs for tiled CMP on-chip networks," in *Proceedings of the International Conference of Supercomputing*, pp. 178–189, 2006.

[37] A. Weichslgartner, S. Wildermann, and J. Teich, "Dynamic decentralized mapping of tree-structured applications on NoC architectures," in *Proceedings of the International Symposium on Networks-on-Chip*, pp. 201–208, 2011.

[38] J. Hu and R. Marculescu, "Energy-aware mapping for tile-based NoC architectures under performance constraints," in *Proceedings of Asia and South Pacific Design Automation Conference*, pp. 233–239, 2003.

[39] D. Bertozzi, A. Jalabert, S. Murali, R. Tamahankar, S. Stergiou, L. Benini, and G. De Micheli, "NoC synthesis flow for customized domain specific multiprocessor systems-on-chip," *IEEE Transactions on Parallel and Distributed Systems*, Vol. 16, No. 2, pp. 113–129, 2005.

[40] B. Zafar, J. Draper, and T.M. Pinkston, "Cubic ring networks: a polymorphic topology for network-on-chip," in *Proceedings of International Conference on Parallel Processing*, pp. 443–452, 2010.

[41] M. Stensgaard and J. Sparsø, "ReNoC: A network-on-chip architecture with reconfigurable topology," in *Proceedings of International Symposium on Networks-on-Chip*, pp. 55–64, 2008.

[42] S. Vassiliadis and I. Sourdis, "Flux networks: Interconnects on demand," in *Proceedings of International Conference on Embedded Computer Systems: Architectures, Modeling and Simulation*, pp. 160–167, 2006.

[43] M. Modarressi and H. Sarbazi-Azad, "Power-aware mapping for reconfigurable NoC architectures," in *Proceedings of the International Conference on Computer Design*, pp. 417–422, 2007.

[44] S. Murali, M. Coenen, R. Radulescu, K. Goossens, and G. De Micheli, "A methodology for mapping multiple use-cases onto networks on chips," in *Proceedings of Design Automation and Test in Europe*, pp. 118–123, 2006.

[45] M. Modarressi, A. Tavakkol, and H. Sarbazi-Azad, "Virtual point-to-point connections in NoCs," in *IEEE Transactions on Computer Aided Design for Integrated Circuits and Systems*, Vol. 29, No. 6, pp. 855–868, June 2010.

[46] N. Teimouri, M. Modarressi, A. Tavakkol, and H. Sarbazi-Azad, "Energy-optimized on-chip networks using reconfigurable shortcut paths," in *Proceedings of the Conference of Architectures for Computing Systems*, pp. 231–242, 2011.

[47] K. Hwang and F.A. Briggs, *Computer Architecture and Parallel Processing*, McGraw-Hill Pubs., New York, 1984.

[48] M. Modarressi, A. Tavakkol, and H. Sarbazi-Azad, "Application-aware topology reconfiguration for on-chip networks," in *IEEE Transactions on Very Large-Scale Integrated Circuits and Systems*, Vol. 19, No. 11, pp. 2010–2022, Nov. 2011.

[49] K. Lee, et al., "Low-power network-on-chip for high-performance SoC design," *IEEE Transactions on Very Large-Scale Integrated Circuits and Systems*, Vol. 14, No. 2, 2006.

[50] S. Bourduas and Z. Zilic, "A hybrid ring/mesh interconnect for network-on-chip using hierarchical rings for global routing," in *Proceedings of the International Symposium on Networks-on-Chip*, pp. 195–204, 2007.

[51] R. Das, S. Eachempati, A.K. Mishra, N. Vijaykrishnan, and C.R. Das, "Design and evaluation of a hierarchical on-chip interconnect for next-generation CMPs," in *Proceedings of International Symposium on High Performance Computer Architecture*, pp. 175–186, 2009.

[52] G. Ascia, M. Catania, and M. Palesi, "An evolutionary approach to network-on-chip mapping problem," in *Proceedings of the IEEE Congress on Evolutionary Computation*, pp. 112–119, 2005.

[53] K. Srinvasan, K. Chatha, and G. Konjevod, "Linear programming-based techniques for synthesis of network-on-chip architectures," in *IEEE Transaction on Very Large-Scale Integrated Circuits and Systems*, Vol. 14, No. 4, pp. 407–420, 2006.

[54] M. Modarressi and H. Sarbazi-Azad, "Reconfigurable cluster-based networks-on-chip for application-specific MPSoCs," in *Proceedings of the International Conference of Application-Specific systems, Architectures, and Processors*, 2012.

[55] G. Karypis and V. Kumar, "A fast and high quality multilevel scheme for partitioning irregular graphs," *SIAM Journal of Sci. Computing*, Vol. 1, No. 20, pp. 359–392, Dec. 1998.

[56] K. Srinvasan and K. Chatha, "A low complexity heuristic for design of custom network-on-chip architectures," in *Proceedings of Design Automation and Test in Europe*, pp. 130–135, 2006.

[57] M. Schmitz, Energy minimization techniques for distributed embedded systems, Ph.D. thesis, University of Southampton, 2003.

[58] Xmulator NoC Simulator, 2008, http://www.xmulator.org, May 2012.

[59] W.J. Dally and B. Towles, *Principles and Practices of Interconnection Networks*, Morgan-Kaufmann Publishers, 2004.

[60] A. Kahng, B. Lin, L. Peh, and K. Samadi, "ORION 2.0: A fast and accurate NoC power and area model for early-stage design space exploration," in *Proceedings of Design Automation and Test in Europe*, 2009.

[61] S. Borkar, "Thousand core chips: a technology perspective," in *Proceedings of the Design Automation Conference*, pp. 746–749, 2007.

2

COMPILERS, TECHNIQUES, AND TOOLS FOR SUPPORTING PROGRAMMING HETEROGENEOUS MANY/MULTICORE SYSTEMS

Pasquale Cantiello, Beniamino Di Martino, and
Francesco Moscato

CONTENTS

Large Scale Network-Centric Distributed Systems, First Edition. Edited by Hamid Sarbazi-Azad and Albert Y. Zomaya.
© 2014 John Wiley & Sons, Inc. Published 2014 by John Wiley & Sons, Inc.

2.1 INTRODUCTION

In the last few years, the continuous growth of processors' clock speed has stopped and processor improvements follow a different path by multiplying the number of processing units on a chip. Not only systems for scientific commodity applications but also personal computers include multiple multicore CPUs and GPUs. It is hard to write parallel code or to port existing sequential code to new architectures. It is a costly process requiring skilled developers. This chapter presents, after a brief introduction of different programming models for current many/multicore and GPUs systems, a review of the state of the art of compilers and support tools tailored to help programmers both in developing and porting code for many/multicore CPUs and GPUs. The emphasis will be on automatic parallelization compilers, techniques, and tools that do source-to-source transformation of code to convert sequential code into parallel. The chapter includes a presentation of a tool developed by the authors, to do static analysis on source code, to represent it in a language-neutral way along with knowledge extracted from it. The tool integrates an algorithmic recognizer to find instances of known algorithms and a transformer to automatically transform sequential code to a parallel version using libraries to be used on GPUs.

2.2 PROGRAMMING MODELS AND TOOLS FOR MANY/MULTICORE

In recent years, multicore devices have quickly evolved in both architecture and core count. This has motivated software developers to define programming models that are able to decouple code from hardware because new applications must automatically scale as new architectures and processors are introduced. In addition, adequate programming models can also enhance performance if proper optimization methodologies are enacted.

All major CPU vendors now exploit explicit parallelism in their processors, both to improve power efficiency and to increase performance, but only parallelized applications provide real improvements.

With these new architectures, dealing with data parallelism is appealing because multiple cores can reduce latency when dealing with data accesses, or can execute the same program on distributed data with a SPMD (Single Program, Multiple Data) model.

Unfortunately, multicore hardware is evolving faster than software technologies and new software multicore standards are rising in order to cope with the complexity of embedded multicore systems

The single-thread computational approach is no longer useful for scaling performance on new architectures [14, 20]. The main reason is that recent multicore and manycore systems do not use only the symmetric multiprocessing (SMP) model but are heterogeneous both in architecture and features. Programmers must acknowledge heterogeneity of hardware and software in order to produce optimized applications.

The main problem in multicore is that, even with the opportunity to increase performance, software usually needs to explicitly exploit multicore features in order to fulfil the potential. Traditional approaches like multithreading force programmers to define proper thread management in order to design parallel algorithms.

The use of SPMD models in parallel programming has been proposed as a programming model of Graphics Processing Units (GPUs) for general-purpose processing. It arises from the demonstration [29] that OpenGL [33] architecture can be abstracted as a Single Instruction Multiple Data (SIMD) processor. Usually, SIMD processing involves significant memory use. In order to reduce bandwidth waste, graphics hardware now executes small threads loading and storing data to local temporary registers and cache memories, trying to exploit computational and data locality through the use of streams (a collection of records requiring similar computation) and kernels (functions that can be executed on local streams).

Identifying kernels to execute in parallel on local data is crucial to improving performance. In recent years, several programming models, techniques, and tools have been proposed for general purpose programming of GPUs.

In the following, some models, languages, and tools for programming many/multicore are described. They usually face the problem of heterogeneity of hardware resources by using a high-level language to describe computation in order to simplify the development of parallel applications and to decouple programming models from hardware. Proper middleware is used then to optimize, compile, and execute programs on the best available target architecture.

2.2.1 OpenMP

A shared memory programming model is useful when developing software for embedded multicores following a SPMD model. Adequate optimization techniques can be used to enhance performance on different architectures. The OpenMP [6, 9] standard works well in decoupling code from hardware. It is based on a set of directives libraries and callable runtime libraries, leaving the base language (C, C++, and FORTRAN) unspecified. The execution model of OpenMP is based on the *fork/join model* [9]. An OpenMP program begins execution as a single process (called a master thread) and then defines parallel regions (by means of a *parallel* directive) that are executed by multiple threads, as shown in the following.

Algorithm 2.1

```
Master Thread ...
#pragma omp parallel
{
    func();
}
Master Thread continues ...
```

Threads are synchronized at the end of a region, where the master thread continues execution. This model allows for the execution of *parallel* regions following a pure SPMD model. *func()* is assigned for execution to each thread in the pool of OpenMP pool and executed once for each thread.

More complex options allow for dividing loop iterations among threads, for defining shared and local variables in parallel regions, and for defining reduction variables.

Parallel regions are optimized by OpenMP compilers in a transparent way, as in shared memory management.

2.2.2 Brook for GPUs

Brook for GPUs [4] is a framework for general purpose computation on GPUs that exploits a streaming programming model. Brook manages memory via streams, and data-parallel operations on GPUs are specified as calls to kernels. Many-to-one reductions can be implemented on stream elements.

Primitives of Brook programming language are not embedded in a general-purpose programming language (like C or Fortran). Brook uses its own language (similar to C) to write Brook programs, which are then translated in C and compiled with a native C compiler.

Main Brook primitives are used to manage streams and to define kernels. Streams are declared with angle-bracket syntax, similar to array (i.e., **double v<5,9>** declares a two-dimensional stream of **doubles**). Kernels are associated with special functions, specified by the **kernel** keyword.

Algorithm 2.2

```
kernel void sum(float4 a<>, float4 b<>, out float4 c<>) {
    c=a+b;
}
void main() {
    float vA[100], vB[100], vC[100];
    float a<100>, b<100>, c<100>;
```

```
      initialize vA and vB
      streamRead(a,vA);
      streamRead(b,vB);
      sum(a,b,c);
      streamWrite(c,vC);
}
reduce void sum2 (float v<>, reduce float red<>) {
red +=v;
}
```

The code above is an example of streams and kernel definitions. For kernels, input and output streams must be declared explicitly. Brook forces programmers to distinguish between data streamed as input and other arrays because Brook divides kernel invocation among available GPU processors, making different stream parts available to kernel instances running on different processors. **streamRead** and **streamWrite** functions are used to copy data from memory to streams and vice versa. The kernel is executed on GPU processors simply by invoking the kernel function.

Kernels are used to apply a function to a set of data that is automatically managed by Brooks. In addition, this provides a data-parallel reduction method for evaluating a single data from a set of records. Reductions are usually used in arithmetic sums or matrices products. Reductions accept a single-input stream and produce a smaller output stream. The function **sum2** is defined as a **reduce** function, and it produces from the stream *v* the element *red* that contains the sum of all the elements in *v*.

Brook also provides a collection of stream operators that can be used to manage, manipulate, and organize streams (i.e., grouping elements into new streams, extracting substreams, etc.).

One of the strengths of Brooks is the way it manages kernels. As shown in the code above, kernels and streams are associated with processors on GPUs transparently. Users do not necessarily have to explicitly split data streams on processors in the code.

2.2.3 Sh

Sh is an open-source metaprogramming language for General Purpose Graphic Processing Units (GPGPUs). The Sh language is built on the top of C++, thus having a similar syntax. Sh code is embedded inside C++, hence no extra compile tools are necessary. In order to generate executables, Sh uses a staged compiler. Parts of code are generated when C++ code is compiled and the rest is compiled at runtime.

The following code shows an example of a Sh program:

Algorithm 2.3

```
ShPoint3f point1(0,0,0);
ShMatrix4f Matr;
ShProgram progr = SH_BEGIN_PROGRAM("gpu:stream") {
```

```
      ShInputAttrib1f a;
      ShInputPoint3f point2;
      ShOutputPoint3f pointOut = Matr | (point1+a*normalize(point2));
} SH_END;
ShChannel <ShPoint3f> channel1;
ShChannel <ShAttrib3f> channel2;
ShStream datastream = channel1 & channel2;
channel1 = progr << datastream; //executes prog.
```

Proper directives allow for variable definition. In Sh, all operations are strongly type checked. Because Sh is a metaprogramming language, all legal C++ constructs are legal. In particular, stream operators are used to assign a stream to a programming function and to run it. As in Brook, allocation and optimization of functions is managed by a Sh framework in a transparent way. Streams are composed by channels that are concatenated to build streams.

Sh was defined in order to be a shared language and it remains highly coupled with pixel shader functions.

2.2.4 CUDA

CUDA (*Compute Unified Device Architecture*) is a scalable programming model and a software environment for parallel computing for NVIDIA GPUs [28]. It exposes an *SPMD* programming model where the kernel is run by a large number of threads grouped into blocks.

The specific GPU hardware is abstracted by *CUDA PTX*, a virtual machine for parallel thread execution. This provides a low-level interface separated from the target device. All the threads within a block form a *Cooperative Thread Array* (CTA) in the PTX domain. The threads in a CTA run concurrently, communicating through shared memory, while multiple CTAs can only communicate through global memory. The PTX indexing schema assigns a position to each CTA within the grid and a position to each thread within a CTA, as shown in Fig. 2.1. Each thread can thus determine what data to work on based on the block and thread ID.

The language supported by CUDA is an extension to C, with some features from C++ as templates and static classes. A *kernel* is a function compiled into a PTX program that can be executed by all threads in a CTA and that can access GPU memory and shared memory. A kernel is executed in a CUDA context, and one or more contexts can be bound to a single GPU. While it is possible to assign multiple contexts among multiple GPUs, there are no spanning mechanisms or load-balancing techniques to distribute a single context over multiple devices. This must be managed by the host program. Kernel executions and CPU-GPU memory transfers can run asynchronously.

2.2.4.1 Memory Management. Memory allocation on a GPU device can be done by calling the `cudaMalloc()` function, while memory transfer from host to devices is enacted by the `cudaMemcpy()` function.

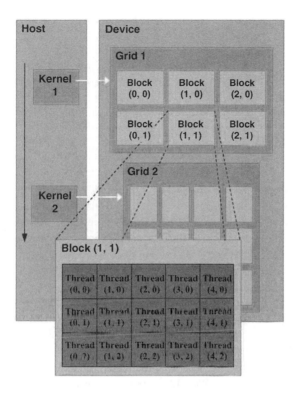

Figure 2.1 CUDA grid and block addressing (courtesy of nVIDIA).

Similarly, to free memory no longer needed, a call must be done to the `cudaFree()` function.

2.2.4.2 Kernel Creation and Invocation. In CUDA, a kernel function specifies the code to be executed by all threads by following the SPMD model.

A kernel function must be called with an execution configuration. The execution contest of a kernel is given by a *Grid* of parallel threads, as shown in Fig. 2.1. Each grid contains a certain number of *Blocks*, addressed with a unique two-dimensional coordinate. In each block, a three-dimensional coordinate system addresses the threads.

Just before invoking the kernel, the *execution configuration parameters*, in terms of grid and blocks, must be created. The special <<< and >>> symbol sequences are CUDA extensions to specify the execution configuration parameters.

The parameters to the kernel function are passed with the normal C syntax. Obviously, pointers passed as parameters must only point to device memory space. An example of kernel invocation follows.

Algorithm 2.4

```
__global__ void KernelFunc(...);
dim3 DimGrid(100, 50); // 5000 thread blocks
dim3 DimBlock(4, 8, 8); // 256 thread per block
size_t SharedMemBytes = 64; // Shared memory
KernelFunc <<< DimGrid, DimBlock, SharedMemBytes >>>(...);
```

2.2.4.3 Synchronization. Threads in a block can coordinate their execution using a barrier synchronization function `__syncthreads()`. When a thread calls this function, it will be held until all the other threads in the block reach the same location. This can be done to ensure that all threads have completed a phase before beginning the next one.

2.2.5 HMPP

HMPP [13] is a Heterogeneous Multicore Parallel Programming environment that was designed to allow for the integration of hardware accelerators. HMPP aims at simplifying the use of accelerators while maintaining code portability. It is based on a set of compiler directives (like in OpenMP [9]), tools, and software runtimes that decouples application code and hardware accelerator.

Basic HMPP directives are used to define functions, named *codelets*. Codelets are pure functions that are suitable for hardware acceleration. Codelets in HMPP are managed by a middleware that choses the best runtime implementation for hardware accelerators (if available). The HMPP runtime is not designed for a specific architecture and HMPP applications can be compiled with off-the-shelf compilers. Dynamic linking mechanisms are employed to use new or improved codelets without having to compile the whole application source.

To define codelets, HMPP directives address data exchange among host and devices. In addition, HMPP is able to handle different accelerator targets in the same application and to execute code running on CPUs and other devices simultaneously, if proper compiled codelets exist for target architectures.

HMPP provides a programming interface that is based on directives used to annotate original code with instructions that will be used to produce proper compiled codelets on a hardware accelerator. Applications are first preprocessed and then linked to a HMPP runtime. Codelets for different devices are compiled with third-party tools. An example of codelet definition in HMPP follows.

Algorithm 2.5

```
#pragma hmpp func codelet, output=outv
void func(int n, float *inv, unsigned int N1[1],
float *outv, unsigned int N3[1]) {
        int i;
```

```
          out
          for (i = 0 ; i < n-1 ; i++) {
              outv[i] = inv[i] + inv[i+1];
          }
}
#pragma hmpp func callsite
          func(n, inc, N1, outv, N1);
```

HMPP codelet is identified by a *pragma* directive that declares *func* as a codelet function. Notice that this function is realized with the *pure function* abstraction. The standard requires that, in codelet definitions, each array-based parameter is followed by a parameter (an array itself) containing the dimension of the previous one (e.g., the declaration of *inv* and *outv* are, respectively, followed by the declaration of *N1* and *N3*). Several other directives can be used to exploit loop unroll, tiling, and other optimizations.

Codelets can be executed synchronously or asynchronously with the application running on the main CPU. HMPP runtime must be invoked for this purpose by defining proper execution directives (*callsite*). Hardware accelerators on which codelets must be run can be chosen explicitly or assigned by the HMPP runtime.

Different data-transfer and synchronization directives can be used in HMPP to implement synchronization patterns and to optimize data transfer from CPU host to device. OpenMP and MPI code are also supported and HMPP is compatible with several GPU devices.

Recent analyses [15] prove that HMPP-based programs have good performance and speed-up.

In summary, OpenHMPP is a high-level programming paradigm that allows for transparent execution of functions (codelets) on several target architectures. Generation of executable code for codelets can be enacted by using third-party tools, compilers, and libraries. HMPP also supports shared memory systems, automatically exploiting symmetric multi-processor systems (SMP), and it is also able to generate communication through MPI interfaces if needed.

2.2.6 OpenCL

OpenCL [32] is an open industry standard that provides a common language, programming interfaces, and hardware abstraction for developing task-parallel and data-parallel applications in heterogeneous environments. The environment consists of a host CPU and any attached OpenCl-compliant device. OpenCL offers classic compilation and linking features, and it also supports runtime compilation that allows the execution of accelerated kernels on devices unavailable when applications were developed. Runtime compilation in OpenCL allows a developed application to be independent from instruction sets of devices. If device vendors change or upgrade instruction sets of their devices (e.g., when new devices are marketed), old applications can be recompiled and optimized at runtime, exploiting new devices' potentialities.

The OpenCL programming model abstracts CPUs, GPUs, and other accelerators like SIMD processing elements (PEs). As with CUDA, computation kernels are associated with PEs with a *thread-safe* semantics, allowing access to shared memory only for one thread at once. OpenCL also abstracts memory, defining four types of memory: *global*, *constant*, *local*, and *private*.

In order to compile, to allocate device memory, and to launch kernels, *contexts* must be created and associated with a device. Memory allocation is associated within a context and not to devices. Resources (memory, number of PEs, etc.) can be reserved to contexts. OpenCL controls whether any device exists with resources required by contexts. Devices with inadequate resources will be excluded from context allocation.

An example of OpenCL code is shown below (the full code is available at [3]).

Algorithm 2.6

```
    // create a compute context with GPU device
    context = clCreateContextFromType(NULL, CL_DEVICE_TYPE_GPU,
NULL, NULL, NULL);
    // create a command queue
    ...
    queue = clCreateCommandQueue(context, device_id, 0, NULL);
    ...
    // create the compute program
    program = clCreateProgramWithSource(context, 1,
&fft1D_1024_kernel_src, NULL, NULL);
    // create the compute kernel
    kernel = clCreateKernel(program, "fft1D_1024", NULL);
    // set the args values
    clSetKernelArg(kernel, 0, sizeof(cl_mem), (void *)
&memobjs[0]);
    ...
    __kernel void fft1D_1024 (__global float2 *in, __global float2
*out,
    __local float *sMemx, __local float *sMemy) {
    ...
    }
```

In OpenCL, kernels and memory are associated with contexts that in turn are associated with one or more devices. When creating contexts, OpenCL verifies whether adequate devices exist to allocate resources associated with context. Once contexts are allocated, OpenCL programs are compiled at runtime and optimized for target devices. Operations within kernels are managed using command queues associated with target devices.

The *clCreateContextFromType* routine is used to create a new context (it is also possible to specify the type of the device to use). Kernels, buffers, and queues are then associated with the context.

2.2.7 OpenAcc

The OpenACC [2] approach is represented by a set of compiler directives designed to specify loops and regions of code in standard C, C++, and Fortran that can be offloaded from a host CPU to an attached accelerator.

OpenACC is a nonprofit corporation founded by four companies: CAPS Enterprise, CRAY Inc., the Portland Group Inc. (PGI), and NVIDIA. Their mission was to create a cross-platform API that would easily allow acceleration of applications on many-core and multicore processors using directives. This allows portability across operating systems, host CPUs, and accelerators.

The directives and programming model allow programmers to create high-level host+accelerator programs without all the concerns about the initialization of the accelerator, or data and program transfer between the host and the accelerator.

OpenACC API-enabled compilers and runtimes hide these concerns inside the programming model. This allows the programmer to provide additional information to the compilers, including locality of data to an accelerator and mapping of loops onto an accelerator.

The API is composed of a collection of compiler directives for C, C++, and Fortran languages. They apply to the immediately following structured block or loop, as a single statement or a compound statement for C and C++, or a single-entry/single exit sequence of statements for Fortran.

For C language, the standard form of a declaration is as follows:

Algorithm 2.7

```
#pragma acc directive-name [clause [[,] clause]...] new-line
```

directive-name is the name of the action that must be applied on the following structured block, and *clause* are optional parameters characterizing the action. Directives fall into the main categories briefly described above.

- *Accelerator Compute Constructs*: These specify the start of parallel executions on the acceleration device. As an example of the `parallel` construct, the compiler creates gangs of workers to execute the accelerator parallel region. One worker in each gang begins executing the code in the structured block of the construct. Optional clauses in this construct can control the number of gangs, or workers, the asynchrony of the execution, or the specification of copy-in and copy-out data between host and accelerator.
- *Data constructs*: The data construct defines data regions (scalars, arrays, or subarrays) to be allocated in the device memory for the duration of the region and the eventual copy-in and copy-out between host and device memories.
- *Loop constructs*: The loop directive applies to the loop immediately following it. It can describe what type of parallelism to use to execute the loop and declare loop-private data (variables and arrays) and reduction operations if required.

- *Cache directives*: The cache directive may appear at the top of (inside of) a loop to specify elements of the array or subarrays to be fetched into the highest level of the cache for the body of the loop.
- *Declare directive*: This can be used in the declaration section of a Fortran block, or following a variable declaration in C/C++ to specify that a variable or array is to be allocated in the device memory for the duration of the block of execution, and to specify whether the data values are to be transferred.
- *Executable directives*: The update directive is used to force the update of data in accelerator memory to the values present in host memory or vice versa. The wait directive causes the program to wait for completion of an asynchronous activity.

In addition to the directive, a runtime library with a set of functions is defined in OpenACC. They can be used, for example, to query the system at runtime to discover the number and typologies of device present, the available amount of memory, to control the synchronization of execution, or the allocate and free memory chunks.

An example of OpenACC code is reported where the operation $Y = aX + Y$ is performed.

Algorithm 2.8

```
void saxpy_parallel(int n, float a, float *x, float *restrict y)
{
#pragma acc kernels
for (int i = 0; i < n; ++i)
y[i] = a*x[i] + y[i];
}
```

The code is a standard sequential loop, but the directive will cause the compiler to generate the kernel allocation on processors.

2.3 COMPILERS AND SUPPORT TOOLS

2.3.1 RapidMind Multicore Development Platform

The RapidMind multicore development platform [26, 27] was born as a framework for expressing data-parallel computations from within C++ code to be executed on a multi-core processor. The platform was bought by Intel Corporation and has been embedded in its framework for parallel development. The platform is based on a programming API and in middleware for optimization and analysis of code. RapidMind supports several compilation back-ends and optimization: it is possible to compile programs running on NVIDIA and ATI GPUs, Intel and AMD CPUs, Cell BE Blade, and Cell Accelerator.

When programs are compiled, RapidMind runtime chooses the best available hardware and optimizes the application using the proper back-end.

RapidMind programs are based on three basic types: values, programs, and arrays. *Values* and *Arrays* are used to define variables and arrays, respectively. They are identified by proper data types in order to discriminate data that will be used in code parts to execute in a parallel environment. *Programs* are used to identify codes to optimize for parallel execution. A program is identified by proper macros, as shown in the following:

Algorithm 2.9

```
Program myprogram = RM_BEGIN {
  In<Value1f> v1;
  Out<Value1f> v2;
  Value1ui i;
  RM_FOR (i = 0, i < 5, i++) {
    v2[i]=v1[i]+1;
  } RM_ENDFOR;
} RM_END;
```

Programs are contained between *RM_BEGIN* and *RM_END* keywords; *v1* and *v2* are, respectively, input and output array for the program; *i* is a variable used as index. The program produces as output *v2* by executing a *for* statement that is optimized in the RapidMind Program.

2.3.2 OpenMPC

OpenMPC [22] is a framework that proposes a programming interface able to merge OpenMP directives and API with the set of CUDA-related directives in order to extend OpenMP features for CUDA in a heterogeneous multicore/GPU environment.

OpenMPC provides programmers with abstraction of the (more complex) CUDA programming model. It consists of a toolchain where (1) OpenMPC code is parsed by Cetus [23]; (2) OpenMP code is analyzed to identify possible CUDA kernels; (3) possible kernels are annotated with CUDA directives; and (4) OpenMP kernels are translated into optimized CUDA kernels following a code transformation approach.

To fulfil optimization, a Tuning Engine is used. It performs various compilation, execution, and measurements of produced code in order to collect information to enhance performances.

2.3.3 Source-to-Source Transformers

Under the heading of source-to-source (S2S) transformers fall tools able to convert a software program written in a given source language to a new version in the same language or in a different one, always in source code. Thus, their output is a code still readable and modifiable by a programmer and that must be compiled for the target architecture.

A type of S2S transformer was used in the past as the *cross-compiler* built to provide a new language on an architecture for which a base language compiler (typically assembly) is already present.

Today, they are conceived mainly with one or more of the following objectives:

- Transform a sequential version of code into a parallel version for a target architecture.
- Transform an already parallel source code written with a particular paradigm (e.g., OpenMP) to a different paradigm/language (e.g., OpenCL).
- Apply source code optimization on regions of code (e.g., loop-nests) in order to take advantage of hardware features or to improve data locality.

The process of transformation of code generally is not a priori fixed, but it can be driven in several ways:

- By users who can annotate code regions they want to transform, with directives (pragmas) that instruct the transformer regarding what and how to modify the code.
- Automatically by the code itself, for example, by analyzing dependences on data inside loop nests.
- By the size of the data involved, as in a distributed memory architecture in which execution and communication times must be taken into account when deciding what must be computed on remote nodes. There are systems that produce multiple versions of the translated code regions with software probes that can select among them only upon runtime, depending on the size of the data and the configuration of the architecture. These are known as *auto-tuning* systems.

More powerful S2S systems are programmable in a high-level language, allowing users to develop custom analyzers and transforms. Some of them are mentioned above.

2.3.3.1 CHiLL. CHiLL [7] is a source-to-source compiler transformation and code generation framework that can transform sequential loop nests. It provides a scripting language to describe composable compiler transformation recipes [18] such as tiling, striping, and unrolling. CHiLL has served as a base for CUDA-CHiLL [31], which extends the scripting language with commands to drive the data moving between compute devices or to extract execution kernels and produce a CUDA syntax. Still based on CHiLL is the auto-tuner compiler described in [8], which combines performance analysis with transformations.

2.3.3.2 Cetus. Cetus [23] is compiler infrastructure for source-to-source transformation. It provides a front-end to parse programs written in C90 language (and C99 with some limitations), model the parsed code in an object-oriented hierarchy representation, and expose a set of Java APIs to access and manipulate it. The user can easily write analysis, transformation, and optimization passes, letting the framework do the parsing and unparsing operations. It does not provide prebuilt transformation routines. The original code structure and statements are preserved. On top of Cetus, tools such as OpenMP-to-GPU [24] have been built to automatically translate standard OpenMP source code into CUDA-based GPU applications.

2.3.3.3 ROSE Compiler. ROSE Compiler [30] is an open source infrastructure for building source-to-source program transformation and analysis tools for C/C++ and Fortran programs. It is based on the EDG front-end [16] to parse C and C++ and on Open Fortran Parser [17] for Fortran 90. By using these parsers, ROSE presents a common object-oriented, open source intermediate representation (IR) for the three supported languages. This IR includes an abstract syntax tree, symbol tables, and control flow graph. The class hierarchy of ROSE provides query, visit, and transformation functions to be used by a program written by the user in C++. The IR preserves original source syntax with comments and directives. Automatic parallelization using ROSE is described in [25].

2.3.3.4 LLVM. LLVM (Low Level Virtual Machine) [21] is a compiler framework designed to support program analysis and transformation for arbitrary programs by providing high level information to compiler transformations at compile-time, link-time, run-time, and in idle time between runs. By defining low-level code representation in static single assignment (SSA) form, it can provide a language-independent representation. The main drawback that derives with this abstraction is the loss of the original control structures (e.g., for() loops are replaced by if() and gotos instructions) after code unparsing.

2.4　CALUMET: A TOOL FOR SUPPORTING SOFTWARE PARALLELIZATION

This section presents CALuMET (Code Analyser and knowLedge ModEller for Transformation), a prototype tool implementing a component-based architecture designed to assist the user in the process of software migration by showing extracted knowledge from code and by driving automatic transformation of parallelizable regions of code. It is designed to parse source code files in C/C++, Java, and Fortran languages and to perform several analyses on them using component-based approach. Graph structures with dependence informations are also built and modeled within the representation.

Results are presented to the user within a GUI, but also emitted in a machine-readable format to enable interoperability. This can be used in a tool chain to do further investigation or to do code transformation driven by the extracted knowledge.

2.4.1　Component-Based Source Code Analysis Architecture

The architecture of the CALuMET Tool is shown in Fig. 2.2 as a block diagram.

The Graphical User Interface (GUI) is the presentation module. It has been designed to be user friendly to minimize learning time for the user and provide a clear view of the

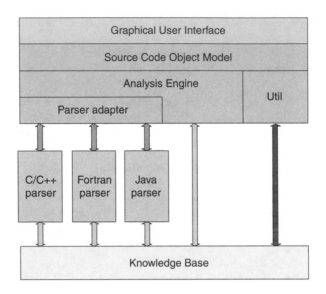

Figure 2.2 Tool architecture.

results. In our case, it has been designed as a multipanel view to permit at any moment a side-by-side comparison between the object of the view (graph, concepts, etc.) and the source code it was built from. Point and click interface with highlighting of related objects between views can be useful to the user.

The *SCOM* component implements the *Language Neutral* representation of code. The GUI interacts with this module to invoke specific analysis, to extract graphs, and to persist data in the Knowledge Base. Additional modules that can be added to the system can use this component to interface with the representation.

The *Analysis Engine* implements the core of the analysis functions and acts as a bridge between the SCOM and the parsers. Requests for analysis from the GUI through the class methods of the SCOM are performed by this module.

In detail, the analysis engine, upon a request of the GUI to parse a file, invokes the corresponding parser through the appropriate adapter, passing to it the environment and the path of the file, and receives the results.

It has also the duty of building standard analysis graphs. It can serialize and deserialize the results of the analysis in a common format. Additional external analyzers can be added as components interfaced with the *SCOM*.

Parser construction is different among target languages and cannot be done in the same environment as the core components. They are built as external executable programs and installed as plug-in modules into the environment. A complete analysis for a given language can be done in several steps with a tool chain of different programs.

Each parser is invoked as an external process by passing it the pathname of the source file to be analyzed, a set of options related to the analysis to perform, the format of the output files, and their location. Thus, the adapter, along with the parser, act as an *interface* between the analysis engine and the source code under analysis.

The *Util* component contains a set of packages that provide common functionalities to the other components of the architecture. It contains, among the others, classes to do:

- Graph management: A package exposes base classes for *Directed Graphs* with methods to do typical operations on nodes and edges (add(), remove(), find(), visit(),...).
- Serialization and deserialization: All the functionalities to persist graphs to and from disks as XML files are present.
- Graph visualization: Another package exposes classes for graph and multigraph visualization along with legends. These classes can be inherited and customized for the particular domain and their visualization can appear inside a panel view.
- Attribute extraction: Due to the design allowing expansions of the model, a subclassed entity can add additional attributes that cannot be ignored by all the other components. To do this, methods are provided to discover and extract them at runtime using reflection.

A *parser* is a module that directly processes the source code files and performs basic analysis on it. Its output populates the Knowledge Base. For each file the parser builds the *Abstract Syntax Tree* as an intermediate representation of code in memory.

By traversing the so-built AST, it identifies the nodes that are relevant to the construction of the analysis graphs for each function, procedure, or method found in the AST. From each procedure, a multigraph is built with these nodes as starting points. Each node has a reference to the node of the AST from which it originates.

Parser construction requires different approaches for each language. At present, there are no *Swiss knife* tools that can be used for all languages, so different external components have been integrated in the prototype.

One of the objectives that led to the design of the architecture was to allow analysis results to be exchanged not only among the core components but also to and from other external components. As an example, a source-to-source transforming processor that modifies sequential code, in order to execute it on a parallel machine, can have in input the results of the analysis already done. Knowing that a certain portion of code implements a known algorithm and the given host architecture can help the transformer to pick a well-suited implementation of the algorithm for the target platform and to transform the code accordingly.

Analysis can be a time-consuming process, so it is wise to do it off-line and only once for each file. Its results can be reused later whenever a new platform must be used or a new implementation of the algorithm is written. Therefore, one of the requirements of the design of the architecture was to permit easy interchange of analysis data and all of the results are produced in GXL format [19].

2.4.2 Algorithmic Recognizer Add-on

The modularity and the expandability of the architecture has been proven with the integration of an add-on module to perform algorithmic recognition and enrich the knowledge base. This module, previously designed and developed by one of the authors [10], implements a technique for automated algorithmic concepts recognition in source code [12].

Algorithmic concepts recognition is a program comprehension technique to recognize in source code the instances of known algorithms. The recognition strategy is based on a hierarchical parsing of algorithmic concepts. Starting from an intermediate representation of code, *Basic Concepts* are recognized first. Subsequently, they become components of *Structured Concepts* in a hierarchical and/or recursive way. This abstraction process can be modeled as a hierarchical parsing by using *Concept Recognition Rules* that act on a description of concept instances found in the code [11, 12].

2.4.3   Source Code Transformer for GPUs

A further extension to the architecture has been the integration of a source-to-source transformer that, starting from the results of the algorithmic concept recognizer, does the transformation of the code region implementing a known algorithm into a new version that takes gain of an accelerator device (a GPU in our case) [5].

The component interfaces not only with the GUI, to let the user express preferences, but mainly with the *SCOM*, from which it can derive recognized algorithm instances and the references to the related code. The repository must contain, for each recognizable algorithm and for each supported target architecture, one or more possible alternative implementations, stored in parametric format. The parameters should be mapped to input and output data involved in the algorithm. The user can drive the selection of the code within the repository by setting preferences on alternative implementations. At present, rules have been implemented mapping basic linear algebra algorithms to CUBLAS calls [1].

The transformer directly manipulates the intermediate representation of the analyzed source program. By using the references stored in *SCOM* entities, the abstract syntax tree is modified with the following steps:

- The sub-tree corresponding to the code region is pruned from the AST and, if desired, a comment block with the original code is inserted.
- A new sub-tree is generated with transformed code. If needed (as in GPUs), it also contains memory allocation on device, memory transfer from CPU to device, library invocation, memory transfer from the device back to the CPU, and memory deallocation.
- This tree is appended in the AST at the removal point, just after the comment block.

After all the transformations done on the AST, an *un-parsing* operation permits generation of the code ready to be compiled on the target platform.

A transformation of this code so it is legal can only be done after verifying dependence information on eventual extra statements not being part of the concepts that are mixed with the code.

By using in input the same source code of a sequential C implementation of a matrix-matrix multiplication seen before, in the following the produced source code with the calls to CUBLAS library is shown, assuming the user has chosen that implementation. Commented code blocks have been omitted.

Algorithm 2.10

```
// .... omitted commented code ...
// -> Added by Transformer - - -
void* _dptr_x;
void* _dptr_y;
void* _dptr_z;
// Memory allocation
cudaMalloc ((void **)&_dptr_x, 10*10*sizeof(double));
cudaMalloc ((void **)&_dptr_y, 10*10*sizeof(double));
cudaMalloc ((void **)&_dptr_z, 10*10*sizeof(double));
cublasCreate(&handle );
// Data transfer CPU >GPU
cublasSetMatrix (10, 10, sizeof(double), x, 10, _dptr_x, 10);
cublasSetMatrix (10, 10, sizeof(double), y, 10, _dptr_y, 10);
// Matrix x Matrix Multiplication
cublasDgemm (handle, CUBLAS_OP_N, CUBLAS_OP_N, 10, 10, 10,
0.0, _dptr_x, 10, _dptr_y, 10, 0.0, _dptr_z, 10);
// Data transfer GPU->CPU
cublasGetMatrix (10, 10, sizeof(double), _dptr_z, 10, z, 10);
// Memory deallocation
cublasDestroy (handle);
cublasFree (_dptr_x);
cublasFree (_dptr_x);
cublasFree (_dptr_x);
```

2.5 CONCLUSION

In this chapter a review has been presented of the main programming models, tools, and techniques to develop and port code for many/multicore CPUs and GPUs. Compilers, techniques, and source-to-source transformer frameworks to program or to convert sequential code into parallel are also summarized.

The chapter also presents a tool developed by the authors to do static analysis on source code, to represent it in a language neutral way. It integrates an algorithmic recognizer to find instances of known algorithms in the code, model the extracted knowledge, and drive a source-to-source transformer to convert sequential code to a parallel version by using libraries for GPUs.

REFERENCES

[1] CUDA CUBLAS library. http://developer.nvidia.com/cuBLAS (Aug. 2010).

[2] OpenACC corporation. http://www.openacc.org/ (Aug. 2012).

[3] Opencl fft example. http://developer.apple.com/library/mac/#samplecode/OpenCL_FFT/Introduction/Intro.html (Aug. 2012).

[4] I. Buck, T. Foley, D. Horn, J. Sugerman, K. Fatahalian, M. Houston, and P. Hanrahan. "Brook for GPUs: Stream computing on graphics hardware." In *ACM Transactions on Graphics (TOG)*, Vol. 23, p. 777–786. ACM, 2004.

[5] P. Cantiello and B. Di Martino. "Automatic source code transformation for GPUs based on program comprehension." In *Euro-Par 2011: Parallel Processing Workshops*, Vol. 7156 of *Lecture Notes in Computer Science*, p. 188–197. Springer, Berlin/Heidelberg, 2012.

[6] B. Chapman, G. Jost, and R. Van Der Pas. *Using OpenMP: Portable Shared Memory Parallel Programming*, Vol. 10. The MIT Press, Cambridge, MA, 2007.

[7] C. Chen, J. Chame, and M. Hall. A Framework for Composing High-Level Loop Transformations. Technical Report 08-897, University of Southern California, 2008.

[8] C. Chun, J. Chame, M. Hall, and J.K. Hollingsworth. "A scalable auto-tuning framework for compiler optimization." In *IEEE International Symposium on Parallel & Distributed Processing*, IPDPS. IEEE, 2009.

[9] L. Dagum and R. Menon. "Openmp: An industry standard api for shared-memory programming." *Computational Science & Engineering, IEEE*, 5(1):46–55, 1998.

[10] B. Di Martino. "ALCOR—An algorithmic concept recognition tool to support high level parallel program development. In *Applied Parallel Computing*, Vol. 2367 of *Lecture Notes in Computer Science*, p. 755–755. Springer, Berlin/Heidelberg, 2002.

[11] B. Di Martino. "Algorithmic concept recognition to support high performance code reengineering." *Special Issue on Hardware/Software Support for High Performance Scientific and Engineering Computing of IEICE Transaction on Information and Systems*, E87-D:1743–1750, Jul 2004.

[12] B. Di Martino and H.P. Zima. "Support of automatic parallelization with concept comprehension." *Journal of Systems Architecture*, 45(6-7):427–439, 1999.

[13] R. Dolbeau, S. Bihan, and F. Bodin. "Hmpp: A hybrid multi-core parallel programming environment." In *Workshop on General Purpose Processing on Graphics Processing Units (GPGPU 2007)*, 2007.

[14] M. Domeika. "Software development for embedded multi-core systems: A practical guide using embedded intel architecture." In *Newnes*, 2008.

[15] S. Grauer-Gray, L. Xu, R. Searles, S. Ayalasomayajula, and J. Cavazos. Auto-tuning a high-level language targeted to GPU codes. Innovative Parallel Computing (InPar), 2012, IEEE, 978-1-4673-2632-2.

[16] The Edison Design Group. The Edison Design Group C/C++ front-end. http://www.edg.com/ (last accessed 17 Jun 2013).

[17] The Open Fortran Group. The Open Fortran Project. http://fortran-parser.sourceforge.net/ (last accessed 17 Jun 2013).

[18] M. Hall, J. Chame, C. Chen, J. Shin, G. Rudy, and M. Khan. "Loop transformation recipes for code generation and auto-tuning." In *Languages and Compilers for Parallel Computing*,

Vol. 5898 of *Lecture Notes in Computer Science*, p. 50–64. Springer, Berlin/Heidelberg, 2010.

[19] R.C. Holt, A. Schürr, S. Elliott Sim, and A. Winter. "GXL: A graph-based standard exchange format for reengineering." *Science of Computer Programming*, 60(2):149–170, 2006.

[20] W.-M. Hwu, K. Keutzer, and T.G. Mattson. "The concurrency challenge." In *IEEE Design and Test*, Vol. 25, p. 312–320. IEEE, 2008.

[21] C. Lattner. "LLVM: a compilation framework for lifelong program analysis and transformation." In *IEEE International Symposium on Code Generation and Optimization*, CGO, p. 75–86. IEEE, 2004.

[22] S. Lee and R. Eigenmann. "Openmpc: Extended openmp programming and tuning for GPUs." In *Proceedings of the 2010 ACM/IEEE International Conference for High Performance Computing, Networking, Storage and Analysis*, p. 1–11. IEEE Computer Society, 2010.

[23] S.-I. Lee, T. Johnson, and R. Eigenmann. "Cetus—An extensible compiler infrastructure for source-to-source transformation." In: L. Rauchwerger, ed., *Languages and Compilers for Parallel Computing*, Vol. 2958 of *Lecture Notes in Computer Science*, p. 539–553. Springer, Berlin/Heidelberg, 2004.

[24] S. Lee, S.-J. Min, and R. Eigenmann. "OpenMP to GPGPU: A compiler framework for automatic translation and optimization. *SIGPLAN Not.*, 44:101–110, Feb. 2009.

[25] C. Liao, D. Quinlan, J. Willcock, and T. Panas. "Extending automatic parallelization to optimize high-level abstractions for multicore." In: M. Muller, B. de Supinski, and B. Chapman, eds., *Evolving OpenMP in an Age of Extreme Parallelism*, Vol. 5568 of *Lecture Notes in Computer Science*, p. 28–41. Springer, Berlin/Heidelberg, 2009.

[26] M.D. McCool and B. D'Amora. "Programming using rapidmind on the Cell BE." In *Proceedings of the 2006 ACM/IEEE Conference on Supercomputing*, p. 222. ACM, 2006.

[27] M.D. McCool, K. Wadleigh, B. Henderson, and H.Y. Lin. "Performance evaluation of GPUs using the rapidmind development platform." In *Proceedings of the 2006 ACM/IEEE Conference on Supercomputing*, p. 181. ACM, 2006.

[28] NVIDIA. CUDA: Compute Unified Device Architecture. http://www.nvidia.com/cuda/ (last accessed 17 Jun 2013).

[29] M.S. Peercy, M. Olano, J. Airey, and P.J. Ungar. "Interactive multi-pass programmable shading." In *Proceedings of the 27th Annual Conference on Computer Graphics and Interactive Techniques*, p. 425–432. ACM Press/Addison-Wesley Publishing Co., 2000.

[30] D. Quinlan. ROSE Compiler project. http://www.rosecompiler.org/ (last accessed 17 Jun 2013).

[31] G. Rudy, M. Khan, M. Hall, C. Chen, and J. Chame. "A programming language interface to describe transformations and code generation." In: K. Cooper, J. Mellor-Crummey, and V. Sarkar, eds., *Languages and Compilers for Parallel Computing*, Vol. 6548 of *Lecture Notes in Computer Science*, p. 136–150. Springer, Berlin/Heidelberg, 2011.

[32] R. Tsuchiyama, T. Nakamura, T. Iizuka, A. Asahara, and S. Miki. *The OpenCL Programming Book*. Fixstars Corporation, 2009.

[33] M. Woo, J. Neider, T. Davis, and D. Shreiner. *OpenGL Programming Guide: The Official Guide to Learning OpenGL, Version 1.2*. Addison-Wesley Longman Publishing Co., 1999.

3

A MULTITHREADED BRANCH-AND-BOUND ALGORITHM FOR SOLVING THE FLOW-SHOP PROBLEM ON A MULTICORE ENVIRONMENT

Mohand Mezmaz, Nouredine Melab, and Daniel Tuyttens

CONTENTS

Large Scale Network-Centric Distributed Systems, First Edition. Edited by Hamid Sarbazi-Azad and Albert Y. Zomaya.
© 2014 John Wiley & Sons, Inc. Published 2014 by John Wiley & Sons, Inc.

3.1 INTRODUCTION

Many real-world problems encountered in different industrial and economic fields, such as task allocation, job scheduling, network routing, cutting, and packing, are of a combinatorial nature. Such combinatorial optimization problems are known to be large in size and NP-hard to solve. One of the most popular exact methods for solving to optimality a combinatorial optimization problem, is the branch-and-bound (B&B) algorithm.

This algorithm is based on an implicit enumeration of all the feasible solutions of the problem to be tackled. The space of potential solutions, called the search space, is explored by dynamically building a tree for which the root node designates the initial problem. The internal or intermediate nodes represent subproblems obtained by the decomposition of upper subproblems. The leaf nodes designate potential solutions or subproblems that can not be decomposed. Building the B&B tree and its exploration are performed using four operators: branching, bounding, selection, and pruning.

The execution time of a B&B often increases significantly with the instance size, and often only small or moderately sized instances can be practically solved. For this reason, over the last decades, parallel computing has been revealed as an attractive way to deal with larger instances of combinatorial optimization problems. A taxonomy of the various models used to parallelize the B&B algorithm is presented in [11]. Four models are identified: the multiparametric parallel model, the parallel tree exploration model, the parallel evaluation of bounds model, and the parallel evaluation of a bound model.

Recently, multicore processors have been used for the parallelization of several algorithms. A multicore processor is a computer unit containing two or more cores. Before the advent of multicore processors, semiconductor chip makers, like Intel and AMD, increased the power of their products by raising the frequency of their single-core processors. But this method has finally reached its limits. Indeed, the increase in frequency of a processor requires an increase in the electrical power supplied. In addition, the thermal energy generated, which should be dispelled, increases.

Unlike distributed computing systems, one of the advantages of multicore systems is the possibility to parallelize a B&B algorithm using threads instead of processes. Unlike processes, which have their own virtual memory, the threads of a process share the same virtual memory. Therefore, communications between these threads are faster than between processes. Many programming models based on the use of threads have been developed. Some of these models can be considered as low-level models, such as POSIX Threads [14], and others as high-level models, such as OpenMP [3].

Optimization methods based on multithreaded B&B algorithms are proposed in many research works, such as [1, 2, 5, 15, 16]. These multithreaded B&B methods can be classified into two categories: low-level multithreaded B&B and high-level multithreaded B&B. In low-level multithreaded B&B, a low-level thread model is used, and in high-level multithreaded B&B, a high-level thread model is used.

The approach we propose for solving the flow-shop scheduling problem on a multicore system belongs to the low-level multithreaded B&B category and uses POSIX Threads. The obtained results show that our approach uses almost all the computing power available in the used multicore CPU. However, the use of the total available power in a multicore CPU does not mean that the maximum speed-up is achieved. Indeed, this work shows the importance of taking into account some issues related to the hardware and software environment, such as the size of the random-access memory (RAM).

The chapter is organized in five main sections. Section 3.2 briefly describes the flow-shop scheduling problem. Section 3.3 explains the different models used to parallelize B&B algorithms. Section 3.4 describes some research works done in the literature to parallelize a B&B algorithm using threads. Section 3.5 presents our multithreaded B&B approach. In Section 3.6, we report the obtained experimental results. The chapter ends with conclusions drawn from this work and its perspectives.

3.2 FLOW-SHOP SCHEDULING PROBLEM

The flow-shop belongs to the category of scheduling problems. A scheduling problem is defined by a set of jobs and resources. The flow-shop is a multioperation problem, where each operation is the execution of a job by a machine. In this problem, the resources are machines in a production workshop. The machines process jobs according to the production chain principle. The machines are arranged in a certain order. Thus, a machine can not start processing a job if all the machines, which are located upstream, have not finished their treatment. A duration is associated with each operation. This duration is the time required for the machine to finish its treatment. An operation cannot be interrupted, and the machines are critical resources because a machine processes one job at a time. The *makespan* of a solution corresponds to the time when the last job ends on the last machine. The objective is to find a solution that minimizes the *makespan*. In [6], it is shown that the minimization of *makespan* is NP-hard from three machines upwards.

The performance of a B&B algorithm depends mainly on the relevance of the used bounding operator. The lower bound proposed by Lageweg et al. [10] is used in our bounding operator. This bound is known for its good results and has complexity with $O(M^2 Nlog(N))$, where N is the number of jobs and M the number of machines. This lower bound is mainly based on Johnson's theorem [8], which provides a procedure for finding an optimal solution for a flow-shop scheduling problem with two machines. The

Johnson algorithm assumes assigning jobs at the beginning and at the end of a partial schedule associated with a subproblem.

3.3 PARALLEL BRANCH-AND-BOUND ALGORITHMS

Several exact resolution methods used in combinatorial optimization are B&B-like algorithms. These algorithms are based on an implicit enumeration of all the solutions of the problem being solved. The space of potential solutions (search space) is explored by dynamically building a tree where

- The **root node** represents the initial problem.
- The **leaf nodes** are the possible solutions.
- And the **internal nodes** are subspaces of the total search space.

B&B algorithms can significantly reduce the computing power needed to explore all solution space. However, such power may be still huge, especially when solving large instances. Using many processors in parallel is an effective means for reducing the exploration time. Many approaches to parallelize B&B algorithms are proposed in the literature. This section gives a brief classification of these methods.

A taxonomy of the various models used to parallelize the B&B algorithm is presented in [11]. Four models are identified: the multiparametric parallel model, the parallel tree exploration model, the parallel evaluation of bounds model, and the parallel evaluation of a bound model. The next four subsections present these models.

3.3.1 Multiparametric Parallel Model

The multiparametric parallel model, relatively little studied in the literature, is based on the use of several B&B algorithms run in parallel. This is a coarse-grained model. Several variants of this model may be considered according to the choice of one or more parameter(s) of the B&B algorithm. The parallel B&B algorithms differ only by the branching operator in [13]. These parallel algorithms are different only by the selection operator in [7], where a variant of the depth-first exploration strategy is used. Each algorithm randomly selects the next subproblem to be addressed among the last generated subproblems. In [9], each algorithm uses a different upper bound in their tests. The idea is that one algorithm uses the best upper bound found while the others use this bound reduced by an ϵ value (ϵ-optimal, where $\epsilon > 0$). Another variant of this parallel model consists of decomposing the interval defined by the lower and upper bounds of the subproblem to solve into subintervals. Each subinterval is assigned to one of these algorithms.

The main advantage of the multiparametric parallel model is its genericity, allowing its use in a transparent manner to the end-user. Its disadvantage is the overhead in computing it generates, since some subproblems in the tree are explored in a redundant manner.

However, this extra computing cost has less consequence when the model is deployed on a high-performance computing system since it has many computing resources.

3.3.2 Parallel Tree Exploration Model

The parallel tree exploration model consists of simultaneously exploring several sub-problems that define different research subspaces of the initial problem. This means that selection, branching, bounding, and pruning operators are executed in parallel synchronously or asynchronously by different processes exploring these subspaces. In synchronous mode, a B&B algorithm has different phases. During each phase, the B&B processes of the algorithm do their exploration independently. Between the phases, the B&B processes are synchronized to exchange information, such as the best solution found. In asynchronous mode, the B&B processes communicate in an unpredictable manner.

Compared with other models, the parallel tree exploration model is more frequently used and is the subject of much research for two main reasons. On the one hand, the degree of parallelism of this model may be important in large instances, justifying the use of multicore computing or a high-performance computing system. On the other hand, the implementation of the model raises several issues that constitute interesting research challenges in the field of parallel algorithms. Among these issues, we can include the placement and management of the list of subproblems to solve, the distribution and sharing of the load (generated subproblems), the communication of the best solution found, detecting the termination of the algorithm, and fault tolerance.

3.3.3 Parallel Evaluation of Bounds

The parallel evaluation of bounds model allows the parallelization of the bounding of subproblems generated by the branching operator. This model is used in the case where the bounding operator is performed several times after the branching operator. The model does not change the order and the number of explored subproblems in the parallel B&B algorithm compared to the sequential B&B. Besides the fact that the bounding phase is faster in the parallel evaluation of bounds B&B than the sequential B&B, the main advantage of this model is its genericity. However, this model can be inefficient in some parallel computing environments for the following reasons:

- The model is synchronous and therefore unsuitable for heterogeneous and volatile contexts.
- Its granularity (the cost of the bounding operator) can be fine and therefore unsuitable for high-performance computing systems. For example, in the case of the flow-shop problem, the cost of the bounding operator is not big enough to justify the use of a distributed computing system.
- The degree of parallelism of this model depends on the problem addressed. In the flow-shop problem, the more a problem is deep in the tree, the more the number of its subproblems decreases, so the less this model is suitable.

The combination of this model with the parallel tree exploration model can generate a higher degree of parallelism than using this model alone.

3.3.4   Parallel Evaluation of a Bound Model

This model does not change the design of the algorithm because it is similar to the sequential version except that the bounding operator is faster. The efficiency of this centralized and synchronous model depends on the addressed problem. Because of its scalability, the efficiency of this model depends on its combination with another model.

The parallel evaluation of a bound model is mainly interesting when computing the bound of the initial root problem. Indeed, the cost of the bounding operator when used for the initial problem is often much more costly than for the other subproblems. This happens especially when solving mixed integer linear programming problems. In such problems, computing the bound of a subproblem is based on the bound of its father subproblem. In this algorithm, the branching operator adds one new constraint for a problem to define its subproblems. Therefore, the calculation of the bound is often done relatively quickly. But the calculation of the bound of the initial problem usually starts with no constraints. PICO [4] is one of the B&B parallel platforms based on the parallel evaluation of a bound model. In PICO approach, this model is recommended for computing the bound of the initial root problem. Once the bound of the initial problem is computed, PICO can continue the resolution according to parallel tree exploration model.

3.4   A MULTITHREADED BRANCH-AND-BOUND

An implementation of a multithreaded B&B is proposed in many research works. These multithreaded B&B algorithms can be classified into two categories: low-level multithreaded B&B and high-level multithreaded B&B. In low-level multithreaded B&B, a low-level thread model, such as POSIX Threads, is used, and in high-level multithreaded B&B, a high-level thread model, such as OpenMP, is used.

3.4.1   Low-Level Multithreaded B&B

BNB-Solver (branch-and-bound solver) [5] is a software platform allowing the use of sequential, shared memory and distributed memory B&B algorithms. MPI is used for the implementation of the distributed memory B&B, while POSIX Threads is used for the implementation of the shared memory B&B. The shared memory architecture of BNB-Solver is composed of a number of threads. Each thread has a local pool of subproblems, and all threads share a common pool.

As mentioned previously, a B&B algorithm proceeds in several iterations. In BNB-Solver, each thread is set by a fixed number N of iterations. During the N iterations, the generated new subproblems are stored in the local pool. At the end of these N iterations, the thread transfers a part of its subproblems from the local pool to the global pool.

At each iteration, the thread tries to select from its local pool the next subproblem to be processed. If the local pool is empty, the thread selects a subproblem from the global pool. If the global pool is empty, the thread blocks itself until a thread puts at least one subproblem in the global pool. Once the global pool is not empty, blocked threads are released and take subproblems from the global pool. As the global pool is used by all threads, it is necessary to protect it with a semaphore. BNB-Solver ends when the global pool is empty and all threads are blocked.

PAMIGO [2] (parallel advanced multidimensional interval analysis global optimization) is a parallel B&B algorithm on shared memory multicore architecture based on the use of POSIX Threads. Two versions of this algorithm, called Global-PAMIGO and Local-PAMIGO, are developed. In Global-PAMIGO, threads share the same pool of subproblems. In Local-PAMIGO, each thread has its own pool of subproblems. A synchronization mechanism between threads, using semaphores, is necessary in Global-PAMIGO. In Local-PAMIGO, a dynamic load-balancing mechanism among threads and termination detection mechanisms are implemented. One of the major issues addressed by the authors of PAMIGO is the number of threads. In Global-PAMIGO, the number of threads is always equal to the number of cores, and the number of threads in Local-PAMIGO must be equal to or less than the number of cores.

In Local-PAMIGO, a thread stops when its local pool of subproblems is empty. At each iteration, a thread checks the number of threads that are running. A thread creates a new thread if two conditions are checked. The first is that the number of threads is less than the total number of computing cores, and the second is that the current thread contains at least two subproblems in its local pool. The new thread is initialized by one of the subproblems of the current thread. Local-PAMIGO ends when there are no threads that are running, and Global-PAMIGO ends when the global pool is empty.

As already indicated, PAMIGO is set by the maximum number of threads, which is equal to the number of cores. According to the number of available computing cores, [16] provides three decision models to fix the number of threads in Local-PAMIGO. In each of these three models and at each iteration, a thread requests permission to create a new thread. In the first model, a new thread is created if the work done per thread and per second has not decreased since the last iteration. The second model is based on the different execution states of threads since the last iteration. A new thread is created if no thread was in the asleep state since the last iteration. In Linux, for example, one can check the file */proc/[process_id]/tasks/[thread_id]* to know the state of the thread *thread_id* belonging to the process *process_id*. The third decision model is more complex to implement than the first two models but gives better results. The third model assumes a compilation of the operating system providing thread management. In Linux-like operating systems, it is therefore necessary to recompile the kernel. Linux runs the so-called idle thread in each processor when this processor becomes idle. The idea is to change this idle thread to test all files */proc/[process_id]/tasks/[thread_id]*. The idle thread has to create a new thread if there is no thread in the asleep state.

3.4.2 High-Level Multithreaded B&B

OpenMP has been used in [15] to implement a parallel B&B algorithm with a combination of Lipschitz bounds for multi-core computers. The authors of [15] use a breadth-first strategy to explore the B&B tree. Only the bounding operator is parallelized in this approach. The number of threads, used to bound each subproblem, is indicated by the OpenMP directive *omp_set_num_threads*. The OpenMP directive *#pragma omp for schedule(dynamic,1)* indicates that the B&B loop iterations are executed in parallel and dynamically assigned. The directive *#pragma omp critical* allows threads to access some shared variables, such as the best solution found, in an exclusive way.

In [1], the authors compare the serial, OpenMP (shared memory parallel model) and MPI (distributed memory parallel model) B&B approaches. These algorithms are used to solve a mixed integer programming problem. A common approach to solve this problem, using a B&B, is to convert subproblems of the mixed integer problem to linear programming problems, thereby eliminating some of the integer constraints, and then trying to solve these subproblems using an existing linear program approach. In the OpenMP approach of [1], threads share the same pool of subproblems. The obtained speed-ups were better in the MPI approach than the OpenMP approach. It seems that the main reason for the poor speed-up of the OpenMP approach is that the used LP solver GNU/GLPK was not "thread safe," which made it impossible to run a shared memory model approach without the use of some explicit mechanisms of control in the implementation. This work demonstrates the interest in avoiding misuse of the control and synchronization mechanisms in order to not drastically decrease the performance of an OpenMP B&B.

3.5 THE PROPOSED MULTITHREADED B&B

Algorithms 3.1 and 3.2 describe our approach. Algorithm 3.1 is the main program and Algorithm 3.2 is a B&B thread. Algorithm 3.1 declares some global variables used by all threads of Algorithm 3.2. These variables are:

- *NUMBER_OF_THREADS* gives the number of threads. In our approach, *NUMBER_OF_THREADS* is equal to the number of computing cores.
- *pool* contains the list of active subproblems that are not yet branched or solved.
- *best* saves the best found makespan.
- *mutex_pool* provides exclusive access to the variable *pool*.
- *mutex_best* provides exclusive access to the variable *best*.
- *sem_pool* is a queue used to control the number of threads trying to take a subproblem from the list *pool*. The idea is that the number of threads allowed to take a subproblem from the list *pool* should not exceed the number of subproblems of this list.

Algorithm 3.1 starts by creating and putting the initial problem *root* in *pool*. As shown on the line 13, Algorithm 3.1 then launches *NUMBER_OF_THREADS* threads. Each of these threads is an execution of Algorithm 3.2, and each thread runs a B&B using the same list of subproblems *pool*.

All B&B threads of Algorithm 3.2 have access to global variables *pool* and *best*. Therefore, and as indicated by the lines 6, 18, and 46, the access to the variable *pool* is protected by *mutex_pool*, and, as indicated by the lines 32 and 37, the access to the

---

Algorithm 3.1 Our multithreaded B&B

`branch_and_bound_thread()`

```
 1: int NUMBER_OF_THREADS
 2:
 3: subproblems pool
 4: pthread_mutex_t mutex_pool
 5: sem_t sem_pool
 6:
 7: int best
 8: pthread_mutex_t mutex_best
 9:
10: subproblem root
11: insert(pool,root)
12: sem_post(&sem_pool)
13: for i = 1 → NUMBER_OF_THREADS do
14:    pthread_create(NULL,NULL,branch_and_bound_thread,NULL)
15: end for
```

---

variable *best* is protected by *mutex_best*. This protection is accomplished by surrounding the instructions reading these variables by *pthread_mutex_lock* and *pthread_mutex_unlock* functions.

The B&B algorithm implemented in Algorithm 3.2 proceeds in several iterations. At the beginning of each iteration, the algorithm checks whether the resolution is finished. B&B threads terminate if and only if two conditions are checked. The first is that there are no subproblems in *pool*. The second condition is that all threads except the current thread are in the asleep state. In other words, they are blocked at the semaphore *sem_pool* waiting for a subproblem. Line 3 allows one to read the number of threads blocked on the semaphore *sem_pool*, line 6 allows one to know the number of subproblems in the list *pool*, and lines 9 and 10 determine whether the resolution has to stop. When the termination condition is satisfied, the role of lines 12 and 13 is to wake up all threads in order to stop their execution.

Line 16 controls the number of threads trying to take subproblems from *pool*. The purpose of this instruction is that this number should not exceed the number of subproblems in *pool*. To do this, the value of the semaphore *sem_pool* must always be equal to the number of subproblems in *pool*. When a subproblem is added to the *pool*, *sem_pool* is incremented by the function *sem_post* (see line 12 of Algorithm 3.1 and line 48 of Algorithm 3.2). When a subproblem is removed from the pool, *sem_pool* is decremented by the function *sem_wait* (see line 16 of Algorithm 3.2).

A thread reaches the instruction of line 17 for two reasons. The first is that it is authorized to take a subproblem to branch or to solve. In this case, *pool* is not empty and a subproblem will be taken from *pool*. The second reason is that the resolution is complete. In this case, *pool* is empty and no subproblem will be taken from *pool*. As shown in line 21, the B&B thread stops when *pool* is empty.

Otherwise, the subproblem is either an internal subproblem or a leaf subproblem. A leaf subproblem is simple and admits only one solution. An internal subproblem is more complex and has several solutions.

Algorithm 3.2   A B&B thread

```
void * branch_and_bound_thread(void *)
 1: while true do
 2:     int blocked_threads
 3:     sem_getvalue(&sem_pool,&blocked_threads)
 4:     int active_subproblems
 5:     pthread_mutex_lock(&mutex_pool)
 6:     active_subproblems←size(pool)
 7:     pthread_mutex_unlock(&mutex_pool)
 8:     bool terminaison
 9:     terminaison←(blocked_threads=(NUMBER_OF_THREADS-1))
10:     terminaison←terminaison and (active_subproblems=0)
11:     if terminaison then
12:        for i = 1 → NUMBER_OF_THREADS do
13:           sem_post(&sem_pool)
14:        end for
15:     end if
16:     sem_wait(&sem_pool)
17:     pthread_mutex_lock(&mutex_pool)
18:     subproblems p←take(pool)
19:     pthread_mutex_unlock(&mutex_pool)
20:     if p=NULL then
21:        stop while
22:     end if
23:     int cost
24:     if leaf(p) then
25:        cost←evaluate(n)
26:     else
27:        cost←bound(n)
28:     end if
29:     if leaf(p) then
30:        pthread_mutex_lock(&mutex_best)
31:        if best>cost then
32:           best←cost
33:        end if
34:        pthread_mutex_unlock(&mutex_best)
35:     else
36:        pthread_mutex_lock(&mutex_best)
37:        bool bound←(best>cost)
38:        pthread_mutex_unlock(&mutex_best)
39:        if bound then
40:           continue
41:        end if
42:        subproblems ps←decompose(p)
43:        foreach p in ps
44:        for all p ∈ NUMBER_OF_THREADS do
45:           pthread_mutex_lock(&mutex_pool)
46:           insert(pool,p)
47:           pthread_mutex_unlock(&mutex_pool)
48:           sem_post(&sem_pool)
49:        end for
50:     end if
51: end while
52: pthread_exit(NULL)
```

If the subproblem is a leaf,

1. Line 25 calculates the cost of its single solution.
2. Line 31 tests whether this cost improves the minimum cost stored in *best*.
3. If this cost is actually improved, line 32 updates the value of *best*.

In the case where the subproblem is an internal node of the tree,

1. Line 27 computes a lower bound for the solutions of this subproblem.
2. Line 37 compares the obtained bound to the minimum cost stored in *best*.
3. If the obtained bound is greater than *best*, line 40 stops the current iteration and forces the thread to move to the next subproblem.
4. If the obtained bound is lower than *best*, line 42 branches the subproblem, and the loop of line 46 inserts the obtained subproblems in *pool*.

After the execution of line 21, the thread exits the loop and executes the function *pthread_exit* of line 52. This function stops the thread and releases its memory resources.

3.6 EXPERIMENTS AND RESULTS

In this section, we present an experimental study to evaluate the performance of our multithreaded B&B approach on a multicore system.

3.6.1 Flow-Shop Instances

In our experiments, we used the flow-shop instances defined by Taillard [17]. These standard instances are often used in the literature to evaluate the performance of methods that minimize the makespan. Optimal solutions of some of these instances are still not known. These instances are divided into groups of 10 instances. In each group, the 10 instances are defined by the same number of jobs and the same number of machines. The groups of 10 instances have different numbers of jobs, namely 20, 50, 100, 200, and 500, and different numbers of machines, namely 5, 10, and 20. For example, there are 10 instances with 20 jobs and 20 machines belonging to the same group of instances.

In our experiments, we used only the 10 instances where the number of machines and the number of jobs are equal to 20. Instances where the number of machines is equal to 5 or 10 are easy to solve. For these instances, the used bounding operator gives such good lower bounds that it is possible to solve them in few seconds using a sequential B&B. Therefore, these instances do not require the use of a multithreaded B&B algorithm. Instances where the number of jobs is equal to 50, 100, 200, or 500, and the number of machines is equal to 20 are very hard to solve. To solve these instances, one needs to use high-performance computing systems like cloud computing.

3.6.2 Hardware and Software Testbed

The experiments were done on a computer with Intel 12 cores 3.20GHz processor and 4Go RAM. Our multithreaded B&B algorithm is executed using the Linux command *time*; *time* runs a program and determines which information to display about the resources used by this program according to the options specified. Options to *time* must appear on the command line before the program to execute and the arguments of this program. In our experiments, and for each B&B process, we collected the following information:

- **Wall clock time**: Elapsed real time used by the process, in seconds.
- **Percentage of CPU usage**: Percentage of the CPU that the process got. This is just user and system times divided by the total running time.
- **Total RAM usage**: Maximum resident set size of the process during its lifetime, in kilobytes. The resident set size is the portion of a process's memory that is held in RAM. The rest of the memory exists in swap or the filesystem (never loaded or previously unloaded parts of the executable).
- **Number of page faults**: Number of minor, or recoverable, page faults. These are pages that are not valid (so they fault) but which have not yet been claimed by other virtual pages. Thus the data in the page is still valid but the system tables must be updated.
- **Number of voluntary context switches**: Number of times that the program was context switched voluntarily, for instance, while waiting for an input or output operation to complete.
- **Number of involuntarily context switches**: Number of times the process was context switched involuntarily (because the time slice expired).

3.6.3 Experimental Protocol

To evaluate our approach, our ideal experimental protocol is to solve the 10 instances with 20 jobs and 20 machines by varying the number of threads from 1 to 12. However, there are two problems.

The first problem is that when an instance is solved twice using a multithreaded B&B, the number of explored subproblems is often different between the two resolutions. To compare the resolution times obtained with different numbers of threads, the number of explored subproblems should be exactly the same between the different tests. Therefore, we chose to always initialize our B&B by the optimal solution of the instance to solve. With this initialization, we are sure that the number of explored subproblems is the same regardless of the resolution even when the number of threads changes.

The second problem is that all the instances used in our experiments are extremely hard to solve. Indeed, the resolution of some of these instances requires several days of computation on one CPU core. Optimal solutions for some of these instances are obtained using high-performance computing systems. Using the approach defined in [12], it is possible to obtain a random list L of subproblems, such as the resolution of

L lasts T seconds with a one-threaded B&B. So, by initializing the pool of our one-threaded B&B with the subproblems of this list L, we are sure that the resolution of the one-threaded B&B will last T' seconds, such as T' will be approximately equal to T. Therefore, it will be possible to initialize the pool of our multithreaded B&B with the same list L of subproblems. With this experimental protocol, the subproblems explored by the 1-threaded, 2-threaded, and so on to 12-threaded B&B will be exactly the same.

Therefore, evaluating our approach, for an instance, we:

1. compute, using the approach defined in [12], a list L of subproblems, such as the resolution of L lasts 600 seconds with a one-threaded B&B;
2. initialize the pool of a one-threaded B&B with the subproblems of this list L;
3. solve the subproblems of this pool with our one-threaded B&B and using the *time* command;
4. get the number of explored subproblems, the wall clock time, the percentage of CPU usage, total RAM usage, the number of page faults, and the number of voluntary and involuntarily context switches;
5. repeat the steps 2, 3, and 4 using a 1-threaded, 3-threaded, and so on to 12-threaded B&B resolutions;
6. check that the number of explored subproblems is the same in these 12 resolutions;
7. and, finally, repeat steps 2, 3, 4, and 5 for all the remaining instances.

3.6.4 Performance Analysis

As indicated in Table 3.2, the obtained results show that the the average resolution wall clock time decreases each time a computing core is added. Furthermore, these results show that our approach uses almost all the computing power available in the multicore CPU. Experiments with 12 threads use on average 1194% of the available multicore computing power (the total available power is equal to 1200%). We note that there is a slight loss of the percentage of CPU usage each time a new core is added. For example, our approach uses 996% (instead of 1000%) of the available computing power when using 10 cores, and uses 1095% (instead of 1100%) of our multicore CPU with 11 cores. However, this loss is very small and experimentation shows that the approach continues to use almost all the available power each time a new thread (i.e., a new computing core) is added.

T A B L E 3.1 Number of Explored Subproblems for Each Instance

Inst.	21	22	23	24	25	26	27	28	29	30
N. Nod.	299412	302958	340373	369861	284662	335749	358652	309405	306701	382456

The first line gives the number of an instance and the second line the number of explored subproblems for this instance. As explained in subsection 3.6.3, this number is always the same whatever the number of used threads.

T A B L E 3.2 Results Obtained for Each Instance

No. Thr.	21	22	23	24	25	26	27	28	29	30	Avg.	CPU Usa. (%)
1	582	563	586	575	588	590	578	564	590	589	580	99
2	357	350	374	367	355	372	370	348	370	377	364	199
3	271	269	292	287	267	289	292	267	286	296	282	299
4	220	220	242	239	214	238	245	218	235	246	232	399
5	190	192	214	211	184	210	218	190	206	218	203	499
6	173	176	197	194	166	192	200	173	191	201	186	598
7	161	164	185	180	155	181	185	162	176	185	173	698
8	152	155	173	170	147	169	176	152	166	175	163	797
9	144	147	164	162	139	160	165	145	157	167	155	997
10	138	140	157	155	133	153	159	138	151	158	148	996
11	132	135	150	147	128	147	152	133	145	153	142	1095
12	127	129	144	141	123	141	146	128	139	146	136	1194

The first column gives the number of used threads. The number of threads varies from 1 to 12 threads. Each of these 12 columns concerns the results obtained for an instance. For example, the intersection of column 2 and line 3 means that the resolution wall clock time of the instance 21 using 2 threads is equal to 357 seconds. The second-to-last column gives the average resolution wall clock time of the 10 instances. For example, the intersection of the second-to-last column and line 3 means that the average resolution wall clock time of the 10 instances using 3 threads is equal to 364 seconds. The last column gives the average percentage of CPU usage during the resolution of the 10 instances. For example, the intersection of the last column and line 3 means that the average percentage of CPU usage of the 10 instances using 3 threads is equal to 199%.

However, using almost all the available computing power in the CPU does not mean getting an almost maximum speed-up. Figure 3.1 shows the gap between the obtained and ideal curves. According to these curves, the larger the number of threads, the bigger the gap between these two curves. It seems that an additional computation is performed every time a thread is added. Indeed, the use of an additional core provides some additional computing power but also involves some extra computing cost. When the number of threads increases, the operating system handles additional page faults and context switches.

3.6.5 Page Faults

When a page fault occurs, the operating system takes control of the computer. The system has to find a free space in the main memory to allocate it to the process responsible for this page fault. But maybe there is no free space in the main memory. In this case, the pagination algorithm has to select a page in the main memory. This page is either immediately reassigned to the requesting process or is first saved to the hard disk drive, and the entry of the page table, that references it, is updated.

The page faults can significantly reduce the performance of a B&B. Therefore, a B&B algorithm must take into account this issue. Threads must collaborate to ensure that the size of the pool of subproblems remains reasonable and reduce the risk of a page fault. Figures 3.2 and 3.3 show that the higher the number of threads, the larger the pool

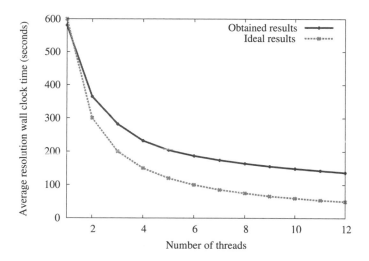

Figure 3.1 Average resolution wall clock times of the 10 instances using different numbers of threads. The abscissa gives the number of used threads and the ordinate the average resolution wall clock time. Each point of the obtained result curve gives the average resolution wall clock time using different numbers of threads. This curve corresponds to the times in the second-to-last column of Table 3.2. And each point of the ideal result curve gives the ideal resolution wall clock time that should be obtained using different numbers of threads. The ideal resolution wall clock time is the time that should be obtained if the speed-up of a parallel application is perfect.

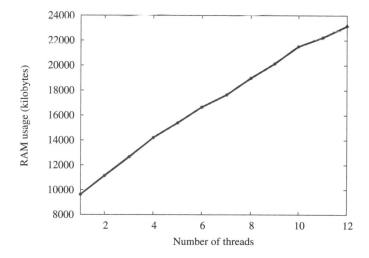

Figure 3.2 Evolution of the average size of the total RAM usage when solving the 10 instances according to the number of threads.

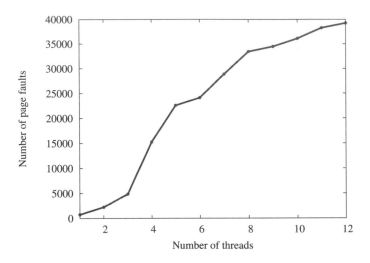

Figure 3.3 Evolution of the average number of page faults when solving the 10 instances according to the number of threads.

size, the total RAM usage, the number of page faults, and the time used in loading pages will be.

3.6.6 Context Switches

A context switch, in a multitasking operating system, consists of saving the state of a process to restore in its place the state of another process. This operation can be more or less time consuming according to the hardware architecture used, the operating system, and the type of the process. Indeed, in the case of a heavyweight process, it always requires a change of the address space, while the threads of the same process share the same address space, and then the address space does not need to be loaded. The saved context must include at least a significant portion of the processor state (general registers, status registers, etc.) and the necessary data to the operating system to manage this process. The context switch may be voluntary, at the end of a time slice, or involuntary, in the middle of a time slice. Figure 3.4 shows that the higher the number of threads, the bigger the number of context switched involuntarily or voluntarily, and therefore the used time in context switches will be.

3.7 CONCLUSION

In this chapter, we proposed a multithreaded B&B algorithm for solving the flow-shop scheduling problem on a multicore system. In addition to presenting the flow-shop problem and multicore systems, the chapter explains, in general, the different models used for parallelization of a B&B, and, in particular, their parallelization using threads. We

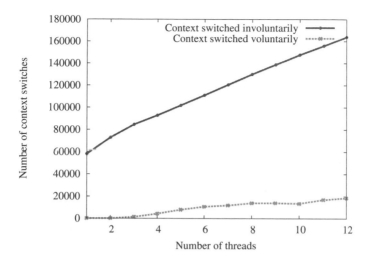

Figure 3.4 Evolution of the average number of context switches (involuntarily or voluntarily) when solving the 10 instances according to the number of threads

identify two main classes of a multithreaded B&B: low-level multithreaded B&B and high-level multithreaded B&B. The approach we proposed for solving the flow-shop problem on a multicore system is a low-level multithreaded B&B approach that is based on POSIX Threads.

The obtained results using our parallel algorithm show that our B&B approach uses almost all the computing power available in the multicore CPU. Indeed, experiments with 12 threads use on average 1194% of the available multicore computing power, which is in total equal to 1200%. However, using almost all the available computing power in the CPU does not mean getting an almost maximum speed-up. Moreover, our experiments demonstrate the importance of taking into account some issues when designing a multithreaded B&B algorithm.

Indeed, the algorithm must take into account its hardware and software environment. The complete use of the available computing power is not enough to have an optimal speed-up. One must also take into account the characteristics of the memory, mainly its size. When the size of the memory is not sufficient, the algorithm must control the size of the pool of subproblems in order to reduce the total RAM usage and thus avoid many page faults. The policy used by the operating system to schedule threads is another element that may influence the obtained performance.

In a future version, we plan to improve our algorithm to better take into account hardware and software features of the multicore CPU used. We also plan to estimate the time cost of page faults and context switches. One way to get these values is to modify the Linux kernel and recompile it. In addition, our goal is to estimate the other parameters that are important in multithreading computing, like the latency and bandwidth of the main memory.

REFERENCES

[1] L. Barreto and M. Bauer. Parallel branch and bound algorithm-a comparison between serial, openmp and mpi implementations. In *Journal of Physics: Conference Series*, Vol. 256,
p. 012018. IOP Publishing, 2010.

[2] L.G. Casado, J.A. Martinez, I. Garcia, and E.M.T Hendrix. Branch-and-bound interval
global optimization on shared memory multiprocessors. *Optimization Methods & Software*,
23(5):689–701, 2008.

[3] B. Chapman, G. Jost, and R. Van Der Pas. *Using OpenMP: Portable Shared Memory Parallel
Programming*, Vol. 10. Cambridge: The MIT Press, 2007.

[4] J. Eckstein, C.A. Phillips, and W.E. Hart. PICO: An object-oriented framework for parallel
branch-and-bound. Research Report 40–2000, RUTCOR, 2000.

[5] Y. Evtushenko, M. Posypkin, and I. Sigal. A framework for parallel large-scale global optimization. *Computer Science-Research and Development*, 23(3):211–215, 2009.

[6] M.R. Garey, D.S. Johnson, and R. Sethi. The complexity of flow-shop and job-shop scheduling. *Mathematics of Operations Research*, 1:117–129, 1976.

[7] V.K. Janakiram, D.P. Agrawal, and R. Mehrotra. A randomized parallel branch-and-bound
algorithm. In *Proc. of Int. Conf. on Parallel Processing*, p. 69–75, Aug. 1988.

[8] S.M. Johnson. Optimal two and three-stage production schedules with setup times included.
Naval Research Logistis Quarterly, 1:61–68, 1954.

[9] V. Kumar and L. Kanal. Parallel branch-and-bound formulations for and/or tree search. *IEEE
Trans. Pattern. Anal. and Machine Intell.*, PAMI-6:768–778, 1984.

[10] J.K. Lenstra, B.J. Lageweg, and A.H.G. Rinnooy Kan. A general bounding scheme for the
permutation flow-shop problem. *Operations Research*, 26(1):53–67, 1978.

[11] N. Melab. Contributions à la résolution de problèmes d'optimisation combinatoire sur grilles
de calcul. LIFL, USTL, Nov. 2005. Thèse HDR.

[12] M. Mezmaz, N. Melab, and E-G. Talbi. A grid-enabled branch and bound algorithm for
solving challenging combinatorial optimization problems. In *Proc. of 21th IEEE Intl. Parallel
and Distributed Processing Symp. (IPDPS)*. Long Beach, CA, March 2007.

[13] D.L. Miller and J.F. Pekny. The role of performance metrics for parallel mathematical programming algorithms. *ORSA J. Computing*, 5(1):26–28, 1993.

[14] B. Nichols, D. Buttlar, and J.P. Farrell. *Pthreads Programming*. O'Reilly Media, 1996.

[15] R. Paulavičius and J. Žilinskas. Parallel branch and bound algorithm with combination of
lipschitz bounds over multidimensional simplices for multicore computers. *Parallel Scientific
Computing and Optimization*, p. 93–102, 2009.

[16] J.F. Sanjuan-Estrada, L.G. Casado, and I. García. Adaptive parallel interval branch and bound
algorithms based on their performance for multicore architectures. *The Journal of Supercomputing*, p. 1–9, 2011.

[17] E. Taillard. Benchmarks for basic scheduling problems. *Journal of Operational Research*,
64:278–285, 1993.

Part **2**

PERVASIVE/UBIQUITOUS COMPUTING AND PEER-TO-PEER SYSTEMS

4

LARGE-SCALE P2P-INSPIRED PROBLEM-SOLVING: A FORMAL AND EXPERIMENTAL STUDY

Mathieu Djamaï, Bilel Derbel, and Nouredine Melab

CONTENTS

Large Scale Network-Centric Distributed Systems, First Edition. Edited by Hamid Sarbazi-Azad and Albert Y. Zomaya.
© 2014 John Wiley & Sons, Inc. Published 2014 by John Wiley & Sons, Inc.

4.1 INTRODUCTION

4.1.1 Motivations

Today, more and more computational resources are needed to tackle real-life combinatorial optimization problems, for example, in physics, bioinformatics, and graphical simulation. Indeed, these kinds of problems require a huge amount of computational resources to be solved in an optimal way. However, even having huge computational power at hand, it is not straightforward to design efficient large-scale software platforms and algorithms that allow us to fully take advantage of these resources available from both large-scale computational grids and personal computers connected through Internet. It is a challenge to design a highly scalable platform for solving large NP-hard combinatorial problem instances. To achieve this goal, we propose a peer-to-peer (P2P) approach that allows us to gain in scalability while efficiently managing challenging issues related to the local nature of fully distributed environments. From a pure optimization point of view, we are interested in solving optimally permutation-based problems (e.g., flow-shop, etc.). More specifically, we focus on parallel/distributed branch-and-bound (B&B) techniques for solving very large instances requiring the use of a huge amount of computational resources.

Much work has been done [4, 8, 11, 14] to take benefit from the relatively weak dependencies between the tasks generated by B&B techniques when exploring the search space. However, most of existing parallel/distributed approaches are based on the master-slave paradigm. In other words, the parallel exploration of the search space depends strongly on a central entity that guides the B&B by distributing tasks and controlling information sharing among computational resources. The master-slave paradigm is indeed a relatively simple technique that is well suited to the parallel execution of many independent tasks in a distributed environment. However, using a central coordinator is an obstacle to scalability. In fact, it generally induces costly synchronization operations, high communication delays, and more importantly, it creates a communication bottleneck around the master.

Getting rid of such a central coordinator turns out to be a challenging issue from many perspectives. In fact, having no central coordinator, able to communicate directly with other resources, means that no global view of the system is available at any computational node. In particular, for the case of an exact optimization algorithm such as B&B, coordinating the search process in a local manner so that the computed global solution can be guaranteed to be optimal is critical. One could argue that classical distributed algorithms may enable emulation of the master-slave paradigm in a fully decentralized environment, using, for instance, election and flooding based techniques [16]. However, keeping the communications low between computational nodes and avoiding network congestion is difficult to achieve. Moreover, while one can intuitively think that a fully distributed architecture (i.e., a pure peer-to-peer approach) would straightforwardly lead to manage an increasing number of computational resources, it is not clear that the parallel efficiency[1] can be improved. In fact, because computational nodes need to communicate distributively to self-coordinate the B&B search process, distributed communication and synchronization issues may slow down the overall process and lead to poor performance compared to a master-slave framework using fewer computational resources.

4.1.2 Contribution and Results

We tackle the above-mentioned issues and propose a new P2P fully distributed B&B approach, allowing us to design efficient and scalable algorithms for solving large permutation-based problem instances. Compared to the most related distributed B&B frameworks [11, 14, 15], the scalability of our approach is shown to be highly better. Our approach can manage (theoretically) exponentially more computational nodes while having a negligible communication overhead in a worst-case scenario, namely poly-logarithmic. These results are obtained as a byproduct of several techniques that can be summarized as follows:

- Efficient distributed algorithms managing work sharing in a local manner and ensuring a good load balancing.
- Efficient termination detection distributed algorithms.
- A structured peer-to-peer architecture based on a small-degree, small-diameter network overlay, namely a pastry-like overlay.[2]

Whereas these issues are handled in a simple way in a master-slave approach (due to the central entity having a global view on the network), they require more sophisticated solutions to be solved in a fully distributed environment. The algorithmic solutions

---

[1] The ratio of the time spent to explore the search space out of the overall execution time.

[2] We note, however, our approach is to be overlay independent.

we propose in this chapter are the core elements of the our peer-to-peer approach. To validate the P2P approach from a more practical perspective, we implemented the above-mentioned techniques and made extensive real experiments on top of the Grid'5000 nationwide French grid [12]. The targeted application is the flow-shop scheduling problem [28]. Compared to the state-of-the-art master-slave B&B approach [20], our experiments show that within the same fixed execution time:

- The parallel efficiency of our approach stays relatively constant as the number of computational resources increases, namely above 90%, whereas the performance of the master-slave approach goes down to 15%.
- The P2P approach is up to 625% more efficient than the master-slave approach in terms of number of solutions explored during the B&B search process.
- The communication overhead is kept relatively low, computational nodes exchange about 11 times more messages while exploring more solutions (pruning more branches).
- The intrinsic performances study (more precisely, the different execution phases when solving completely small instances of the flow-shop problem) show that our approach is well suited for extreme scale computing.

Finally, the P2P solution-space search process is optimal since a region of the solution space is never explored twice by computational nodes. This is not guaranteed by the state-of-the-art master-slave approach, which leads to redundancy in the search process and thus to loss of efficiency.

4.1.3 Related Works

One can find many studies in the literature demonstrating the importance of parallel B&B algorithms for solving hard optimization problems on grids and large-scale computational platforms. In [1, 2], a master/slave-based parallel B&B algorithm is proposed and deployed on a grid. The latter approach shows a limited scalability as it creates a bottleneck on the master process. This issue is studied in [8], however, a hierarchical master/slave model is used therein. In [20], an efficient encoding representation of the search space is proposed to reduce message size. The overall parallel efficiency is then improved compared to previous solutions. The approach of [20] can be considered as the best parallel B&B approach that can be applied in a large-scale computational environment such as grids. In particular, it was successfully applied to find the optimal solution of an unsolved flow-shop hard instance, namely the Ta056 instance [19, 28]. The latter approach is also based on the Master-slave model. In [4], the authors show that by allowing slaves to directly communicate together after receiving a task from the master, the redundancy induced by [20]'s approach when exploring the search space can be significantly reduced. In [8], a middleware called "*Grid'BnB*" is described. It enables emulation of master-slave-based parallel B&B techniques on P2P networks or platforms. The main difference with a classical master-slave model is that messages are relayed through peers towards the master. The main goal of [8] is, in fact, to design a middleware that hides the network architecture/topology for computational applications. Bendjoudi et al. [5] have proposed a fault-tolerant hierarchical B&B, named FTH-B&B, in order to deal with the fault tolerance and scalability issues in large-scale unreliable environments. Their algorithm is composed of several fault-tolerant M/W-based B&Bs, organized hierarchically. Some other works, for example, Cabani et al.'s PHAC ([7]), Saffre et al.'s Hypergrid [26], aim to dynamically redesign the topology in order to confront communication bottleneck issues.

4.1.4 Outline

The rest of the chapter is organized as follows. In Section 4.2, we give some background concerning the parallelization of the B&B algorithm. In Section 4.3, we describe the peer-to-peer approach and detail the main distributed challenges. In Section 4.4, we provide an analysis of our P2P approach from scalability and congestion perspectives. In Section 4.5, we provide experimental results on an instance of the flow-shop problem (Ta057), comparing our approach with the state-of-the-art one. We also provide a detailed analysis of the intrinsic performances of our approach through the study of the different execution phases. In Section 4.6, we draw the conclusions and list some open questions raised by our P2P approach

4.2 BACKGROUND

Roughly speaking, for a permutation-based problem, a basic B&B strategy can be represented by a tree where the root designates the problem to be solved, a leaf represents a solution (a permutation), and a node inside the tree represents a partial solution (equivalently, a subproblem) where only some variables in the permutation are fixed. From a parallel/distributed point of view, the most efficient B&B algorithms are based on depth-first strategy when exploring the search space [17, 24, 29]. A sequential depth-first strategy explores the tree in a depth-first manner branching and bounding according to some branching and bounding policies. A parallel version of this strategy is to run several depth-first explorations in parallel on different parts of the search tree. As soon as a new lower bound for the problem is found, it is communicated to other processes, which allows them to update their own local lower bound and thus to speed up the overall search process.

One major difficulty when setting up this general idea in a distributed environment is to carefully encode the nodes of the B&B tree in order to reduce the cost of exchanging messages between computational nodes and decide which part of the tree should be explored by which computational node. A trivial approach would be to encode a subproblem of the B&B tree in a fully comprehensive way by providing all necessary information. In [13], a tree node (a subproblem) is encoded as a path from the root to the node itself, which is still expensive. In [19, 20], an extremely simple and efficient encoding is proposed. Roughly speaking, the tree is labeled in such that a way a subset of nodes (corresponding to a subproblem) can be encoded by an interval, that is, two

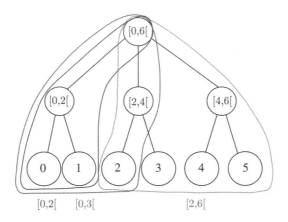

Figure 4.1   Example with a three-variable permutation.

integers. A centralized model is then adopted to distribute intervals among computational nodes. More specifically, the approach described in [19, 20] consists in defining a central computational entity (the master), which is in charge of controlling assignment of intervals (work units) to other computational nodes (the slaves).

In this chapter, we will adopt the interval-based encoding of [20] while removing the need of a central coordinator. To make the chapter self-contained, we briefly give an example to illustrate the tree encoding. For the sake of clarity and to make our results more comprehensive, we also recall the basic ideas of the master-slave approach and the main challenges we are addressing. Figure 4.1 gives a simple example with a p-variable permutation problem (with $p = 3$), and the optimal solution of our problem is one of the $3! = 6$ possible ordering of our variables. More precisely, a label (integer) is assigned to each leaf of the tree, corresponding to a specific permutation. Then, an interval $[x, y[\subseteq [0, p![$ refers to a subtree of the whole search tree. For instance, one can see in Fig. 4.1 the subtrees corresponding to intervals $[0, 3[, [0, 2[$, and $[2, 6[$. Having this labeling, two operators, defined in [20], allow us to switch from the tree representation to the interval-based representation and conversely. Notice that exploring intervals $[0, 3[$ and $[2, 6[$ in parallel implies exploring the same region of the search space (permutation 3) twice, while exploring only interval $[0, 2[$ and $[2, 6[$ may fail to produce the optimal solution since permutation 2 is not explored.

In [19], this tree encoding is coupled with a master-slave model. More precisely, the master owns initially the whole interval to be explored (i.e., the whole tree). Then, slaves ask the master for a subinterval (a piece of the tree) to explore. The master continuously removes from the list the subintervals that are already explored and distributes those not yet explored. However, since many slaves having different computational power can ask for some work at the same time, some slaves may end up exploring the same part of the search tree, inducing a so-called "*redundancy*." Redundancy issue is highlighted in [19] and further work dealing with this issue can be found in [15]. We also remark that each time a slave finds a new and better solution (i.e., an ordering of variables), it directly informs the master, which broadcasts this information to other slaves. Hence,

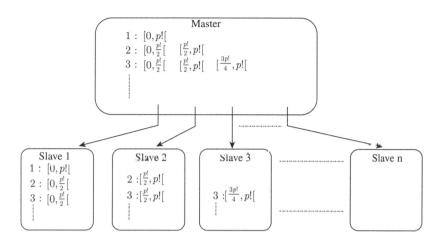

Figure 4.2 Operation of a master-slave based architecture.

sharing the best known solution is straightforward and does not induce any technical difficulty from a pure distributed/parallel point of view. In addition, termination of the whole distributed search process can be easily detected by the master, that is, when the list of remaining subintervals maintained by the master becomes empty. Load balancing is also quite simple since the master can control slaves' progress and reassign work units directly to under-used slaves.

A concrete scenario is proposed in Fig. 4.2. Assume that we have initially n slaves. Assume that a first slave wants to start participating in the exploration process. Then, it sends a work request to the master. When receiving that request, the master answers with the whole problem to process (since until now the master has not received any request). In the second step, suppose that the master receives a work request from a second Slave. To balance the load, the master splits the original interval into two parts and shares it equally between both slaves. Now, suppose that in the third step, a new request coming from slave 3 reaches the master. The master shall choose one of the already assigned intervals, split it into two parts and assign one of them to slave 3. In the scenario of Fig. 4.2, the master chooses the interval assigned to slave 2 and shares it with slave 3. However, at this point of the execution, slave 2 is not aware of its newly assigned subinterval $[\frac{p!}{2}, \frac{3p!}{4}[$. As depicted in Fig. 4.2, it may explore the solutions belonging to interval $[\frac{3p!}{4}, p![$, that is, the interval assigned to slave 3, leading to *"redundancy."* This issue is handled in [19] as follows. The master and the slaves continuously checkpoint together and update their intervals each fixed period of time. Depending on search speed and on whenever the checkpoint is done, redundancy may or may not occur. In our example, slave 1 has updated its work unit, whereas slave 2 has not. However, in [19] this solution was shown to be efficient. More precisely, experimental results have shown that the redundancy rate is of 0.39%. While this rate may appear to be low, as we are dealing with large-scale instances, it represents a huge number of nodes.

More importantly, the master-slave model clearly induces a bottleneck around the master. In fact, assume that after some steps of computation, where the master maintains a long list of subintervals, many slaves simultaneously request their Master for a work interval. Then, for a huge number of requests, this will either induce a huge response delay or lead to the master crashing. The scalability and the parallel efficiency of the master-slave approach is hence limited when trying to handle a huge amount of computational resources.

4.3 A PURE PEER-TO-PEER B&B APPROACH

4.3.1 Preliminaries

The communication graph induced by the master-slave model can be viewed as a star graph. In other words, computational nodes are organized according to a star overlay where the center of the star is the master and leaves are slaves. Since the center (master) has a global view of remaining intervals and can communicate directly with the leaves (slaves), it is rather easy to coordinate the parallel B&B tree exploration. As pointed earlier, a star overlay, however, fails to scale efficiently when a huge number of computational resources are available. In order to gain in scalability, the general idea of our approach is to use a fully decentralized communication topology, that is to say, a pure peer-to-peer overlay. In addition, since our primary goal is to speed up the B&B search process, we shall provide distributed algorithms ensuring two main features:

- First, we want to guarantee that the parallel search process *terminates* and effectively computes the optimal solution. This is straightforward using a star overlay because the center has a global view of intervals being explored.
- Second, we want to gain not only in *scalability* but also in *parallel efficiency*. In fact, in a fully distributed scheme, balancing the workload (intervals) cannot be handled by a unique center node. Hence, nodes have to self-coordinate the B&B search process and distribute the load efficiently while having a local view of intervals being explored. Moreover, handling an increasing number of computational nodes organized according to a pure peer-to-peer overlay implies more communications and message exchanges, which could lead to efficiency loss if not managed very carefully.

In the remainder, we describe how to guarantee these two properties in a static environment, that is, when computational nodes are fully available and do not crash. Let us assume that the computational nodes are organized according to a pure peer-to-peer overlay. In other words, each computational node can communicate with only a subset of other computational nodes called its neighbors. We assume that the considered overlay can be any connected graph $G = (V, E)$, that is, a node $v \in V$ designates a computational node and an edge (u, v) designates the fact that u and v are neighbors in the overlay. A high-level description of our approach is given in Algorithm 4.1. Through lines 26 to 39, we define the behavior of a node upon receiving a message. Through lines 3 to 25, we give the main set of instructions executed by a node in order to coordinate the search process with its neighbors in a local manner. This is, in fact, the core of our distributed P2P approach. In the following sections, we describe the main issues we face and give a general overview of the different techniques we use. In this following, we shall discuss the important algorithmic and technical implementation issues.

Algorithm 4.1 General overview of our *B&B* distributed algorithm for a node $v \in V$

```
   /* Initial conditions                                                    */
 1  For one of the nodes: count_v := −1; sol_v := ⊥; [x, y[:= [0, N[,ready_v = true;
 2  For all the others: count_v := 0; sol_v := ⊥; [x, y[:= ∅, ready = true;
 3  High level code executed by node v (in parallel with receive triggers below):
 4      while count_v ≤ X do
 5          increment_v := true; ready_v := true; Q_v := ∅;
 6          while [x, y[ ≠ ∅ do
 7              Explore [x, y[ using the B&B algorithm;
 8              As soon as a better solution sol_v is found Send New_Sol(sol_v) to all neighbors;

 9          if count_v = −1 then count_v := 0;
10          Send Count_Request to all neighbors;
11          Wait Upon Reception of Count_Reply(count_w) from every neighbor w :
12              if count_w = −1 then
13                  increment_v := false; count_v := 0; Q_v := Q_v ∪ {w};
14                  if [x, y[ = ∅ then
15                      Send Work_Request to w;
16                      Upon Reception of Work_Reply([z', y'[) from a neighbor w do :
17                          if [z', y'[ ≠ ∅ then [x, y[ := [z', y'[;

18          ready_v := false;
19          if [x, y[ ≠ ∅ then count_v := −1;
20          Send Safe(count_v) to every neighbor w ∉ Q_v;
21          Wait Upon Reception of Safe(count_w) from every neighbor w ∉ Q_v :
22              if count_w < count_v then increment_v := false;
23          If increment_v then count_v := count_v + 1;

24      Send Terminated to all neighbors;
25      Wait Upon Reception of Terminated from all neighbors;
26  High level code for receive triggers executed by node v (in parallel):
27      Upon Reception of Count_Request from a neighbor w do :
28          if ready_v ∧ w ∉ Q_v then Send Count_Reply(count_v) to w;
29          else
30              /* Inqueue the Count_Request and delay the response (v waits until
                 it is ready for the next round) */
31              Send Count_Reply(count_v) to w later as soon as ready_v ∧ w ∉ Q_v is verified;

32      Upon Reception of Get_Work from a neighbor w do :
33          if [x, y[ is not yet entirely explored then
34              Let z ∈ [x, y[ be the integer corresponding to the solution being explored last;
35              [x, y[ := [z, (z+y)/2 [ ; Send Work([(z+y)/2 , y[) to w;
36          else Send Work(∅) to w;

37      Upon Reception of New_Sol(sol_w) from a neighbor w do :
38          if sol_w is better than sol_v then
39              sol_v := sol_w; Send New_Sol(sol_v) to all neighbors w' ≠ w;
```

4.3.2 Information Sharing and Work Distribution

Following the interval-based approach of [20], there are two main issues to handle when exploring the B&B tree in parallel. First, each computational node should be assigned an interval to explore. To guarantee that the optimal solution will be effectively computed, we must ensure that an interval is assigned to at least one computational node. In addition, two intervals assigned to two computational nodes should not intersect to avoid redundancy and thus efficiency loss. Second, each computational node should be aware of the best solution found so far during the search process to avoid exploring unwanted branches (i.e., branches not leading to the optimal solution). The faster a computational node is aware of the best solution, the more the B&B branching is efficient. Having these issues in mind, we now describe our distributed algorithms.

4.3.2.1 Best Solution Sharing Mechanism. The following simple rules are used:

- If a solution sol_v improving the previous best-known solution is found locally by computational node v, then v sends a **New_Sol**(sol_v) message to its neighbors (line 8).
- If a node w receives a **New_Sol**(sol_u) message from neighbor u then it updates its current best solution sol_w. If sol_u is better than sol_w, then w also forwards **New_Sol**(sol_u) to its neighbors (line 37).

One may think that forwarding new solutions to neighbors could slow down the B&B search in two ways. First, the network may be flooded, leading to congestion problems. Second, the time needed to forward the best found solution may be non-negligible for an increasing number of computational nodes, hence slowing down the B&B pruning process. We later argue, in Section 4.4, that the above simple rules are sufficient to handle these two issues.

4.3.2.2 Work Sharing. A work unit corresponds to an interval $[x, y[$, where $x < y$, that is, a work consists of in exploring the region of the search space corresponding to interval $[x, y[$. We assume that initially there exists one computational node in the network holding the interval $[0, N[$ where N is the size of the problem being solved, that is, for a permutation of size p, $N = p!$. Then, computational nodes having initially no interval to explore or those that have finished exploring an interval ask their neighbors for a piece of interval. This is done by sending a **Work_Request** message (line 15). Upon receiving a **Work_Request** message, a node v holding an interval $[x, y[$ halts the searching process and sends a **Work_Reply**($[x', y'[$) message answering the neighbor's request (line 32). Here, subinterval $[x', y'[$ is chosen in such a way $[x', y'[\subset [x, y[$ and $[x', y'[$ have not been explored by node v yet. To make the management of the remaining intervals simple, interval $[x', y'[$ is chosen as follows. If node v is exploring the branch corresponding to integer $z \in [x, y[$ when receiving a **Work_Request** message, then it replies with interval $[\frac{z+y}{2}, y[$[3] and continues its local exploration process using interval $[z, \frac{z+y}{2}[$. This mechanism can be compared to the work-stealing mechanism designed in

---

[3] If many requests are received simultaneously from more than one neighbor, then node v could share its interval equally depending on the number of requests.

Cilk [6]. In Cilk, each processor p handles a set of tasks and it processes them one at a time. When another processor p' asks for a new task, processor p sends one of the tasks it is not processing to processor p'. In our mechanism, work units are handled differently. Each peer handles a unique work unit and splits it into two equal parts whenever another peer asks for a new work unit.

4.3.2.3 Load Balancing. Dividing an interval equally when receiving a neighbor's requests may appear inefficient from a dynamic load balancing point of view. However, one should keep in mind that the length of an interval does not reflect how difficult it is to explore. In fact, we may have a long interval that will be explored very quickly by the B&B process, for example, typically when the B&B pruning mechanism works very efficiently. Conversely, we may have a short interval that actually needs an extensive exploration and thus an increasing processing time. This is a well-understood problem due to the irregularity of the B&B search tree. Thus, one cannot say in advance which interval is harder to explore than another. In other words, different policies taking into account the length of intervals according to the power of nodes will fail to give strong guarantees on the load. However, we argue that the simple policy described above still enables a good dynamic load balancing. In fact, we can reasonably assume that the more powerful a computational node is, the faster it will go when exploring an interval and the more it will send work requests to neighbors. Therefore, even if some powerful nodes are assigned some easy-to-explore intervals at a given time, they will perform fast and quickly become more difficult intervals. Nodes with powerful computational resources actually act like a black hole to which work intervals are spontaneously attracted.

Notice also that our work sharing mechanism guarantees that no kind of redundancy can occur during the search (an interval cannot be explored by two processors at the same time). However, it may happen that, at the time a computational node v sends a Work_Request message, none of its neighbors has an interval to share with it. As we will see in the next section, this issue is to be handled closely with to the termination detection of the B&B search process.

4.3.3 Distributed Termination Detection

4.3.3.1 Basic Observations. As pointed out previously, a Work_Request message sent by node v cannot always be satisfied because v's neighbors could not have an interval to explore. From a local point of view, all that v can learn at this point is that its neighbors (in the logical overlay) have finished exploring their own intervals. Nevertheless, v could not say yet whether (i) some other intervals are being explored by other nodes farther away in the overlay or (ii) all nodes have finished exploring their intervals. In the former case, we would like node v to get a subinterval and enter again the exploration process. In the latter case, we would like node v to stop computing and to detect locally that the B&B exploration is terminated.

To handle this termination detection issue, we make use of the following key observation, which reflects the local nature of our work-sharing mechanism: If a node v sends a request message to its neighbors and none of them holds an interval, then this means that neighbors are symmetrically requesting a work interval from their own neighbors.

Thus, a simple solution would be as follows: (i) every node having an interval being explored and receiving a request answers with a subinterval as explained previously, and (ii) every other node requesting a work from neighbors waits until effectively receiving an interval from one neighbor. However, this solution will lead to a deadlock. To see this, consider, for instance, the situation where all nodes finish exploring their intervals simultaneously and hence no more intervals remain to explore. Then, all nodes will send request messages to their neighbors. Hence, no node will respond since the search process is actually terminated but no node can locally detect this global situation.

To correctly detect the global termination of the B&B search process, we use another more advanced technique. In fact, suppose that node v has made a first request to all its neighbors without receiving any interval. Then, node v resubmits its request. If node v does not receive an interval in this second round then node v concludes that its neighbors did not receive an interval during their first round. Thus, no node at distance two from v (in the overlay graph) owns an interval. Roughly speaking, by repeating the local request/response process t rounds, then a node can detect that no intervals are available in the ball of radius t around it. Therefore, after $\Theta(D)$ unsuccessful rounds[4] where D is the diameter of the overlay graph, a node can locally conclude that no interval is being explored by any node in the network and termination can thus be detected.

Remark 4.1

At this point, we recall that a large amount of the literature is devoted to termination detection [9, 22] in distributed systems. All existing termination detection techniques (wave-based, tree-based, snapshot, channel counting, etc.) have a cost [18]: delays and/or message overhead. Roughly speaking, distributed detection in our approach mimics a snapshot-based one (coupled with wave techniques) while using the computation proper messages. In fact, to detect termination we only have to detect in a ball of radius D (the diameter) that there remain no work intervals. Conversely, if in a ball B_t of radius $t < D$ the property $\mathcal{P}$="some work remains" holds, then termination cannot be announced. Counting (in a consistent manner) the number of times a node has performed unsuccessful work requests to neighbors is then sufficient to answer whether property $\mathcal{P}$ holds or not. In addition, this idea is both symmetric[5] and topology independent (meaning, for instance, that when switching to a dynamic environment, there is hope that it could still work under additional assumptions regarding overlay connectivity). For the sake of scalability, we thus use the basic messages of our algorithms, and we deliberately reduce the amount of required control/signal information and simplify at most the detection process to avoid congestion and delays. In other words, termination detection is carefully embedded in the work sharing mechanism. However, for our termination detection to work correctly, we need knowledge about the diameter D of the overlay. Actually, even a rough upper bound will do correctly and efficiently. In Remark 4.2, we argue why, in practice, the knowledge of D is not a requirement.

---

[4]That is, after $\Theta(D)$ local requests without getting an interval to explore.

[5]It is initiated symmetrically by all nodes.

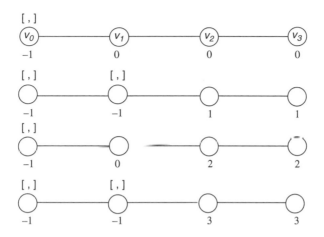

Figure 4.3 Interval vaporization

4.3.3.2 Technical Details Sketch. Technically speaking, we use an adaptation of the termination detection idea sketched in the previous section in order to take into account the specificity of our B&B exploration process. More specifically, every node v owns a variable $count_v$ counting the number of times v asks its neighbors for an interval. This request is performed by sending Count Request messages and receiving Count_Reply messages containing neighbors' counters values. Initially, if node v is exploring an interval, $count_v$ is set to -1. If v does not hold any interval or has just finished exploring an interval, $count_v$ is set to 0 and a work request round is started (lines 9 and 23). An unsuccessful round, meaning that none of v's neighbors holds an interval, makes v increment $count_v$ by one and start a new request round until reaching $\Theta(D)$. However, since a node can possibly terminate exploring the whole piece of work interval before being able to share it with a neighbor,[6] incrementing $count_v$ can lead to a situation where v increments its counter in an inconsistent manner (i.e., too fast). To illustrate this issue, let us consider the simple example of Fig. 4.3, where the overlay is a simple path of four nodes.[7] Suppose that initially node v_0 owns an interval, that is, all nodes but v_0 have their counters set to 0. After a first work request round, only node v_1 gets an interval. Nodes v_2 and v_3 increment their counters to 1. Suppose that during the second work request round, node v_1 terminates exploring its interval before receiving the request of its neighbor v_2. We term this situation as an "*interval vaporization.*" Then, after the second request round, node v_2 does not receive any work interval. Thus, if node v_2 increments its counter, as depicted in Fig. 4.3, then after the third request round, nodes v_2 and v_3 will set their counters to 3, reaching the diameter of overlay path. This interval

---

[6]For instance, this may happen when a request message takes a long time to be delivered.

[7]We choose a line topology for this example only for the sake of simplicity. The reasoning can be applied for *any* overlay topology. In particular, the path of the example can be thought of as a subgraph of a more general overlay. An example with a grid topology is given in Appendix 4.B to summarize our work-sharing algorithms.

vaporization situation can then occur further in future rounds as we can imagine that the intervals that node v_1 gets from node v_0 are always explored/pruned very quickly.

When an interval vaporization occurs at some node v, the counter of v is first set to -1 then to 0. Thus, a neighbor u of v, having a counter set to some value $x > 0$ in previous rounds, can detect that actually an interval vaporization has occurred at node v. Therefore, when detecting such a situation, node u does not increase its counter until v's counter reaches value x. This rule is implemented by lines 21 and 22 using the received Count_Reply(*count*) messages.

4.3.4 Asynchrony Issues

The previous work-sharing and termination detection mechanisms are based on request/response *rounds*. At each round, every node asks for neighbors' counters and possibly asks for some work interval, if any. This clearly implies a kind of synchronism between nodes in order to perform efficiently. However, in a fully *asynchronous* distributed environment, we cannot have any guarantees about the time it takes to deliver a message from a node to its neighbors, that is, link latencies could be arbitrary but finite. To illustrate these issues, let us consider the simple example of Fig. 4.4.

Assume that we have three nodes, u, v, and w, connected by a path somewhere in the network overlay. Assume that the network latency is high between v and u, whereas it is low between v and w. Suppose that nodes v and w have set their counters to x, while node u has executed a successful round and thus has a counter set to -1. Then, the request message sent from v to u will take much time, while node w will in the meanwhile perform a large number of requests. These requests are obviously useless as node v has not yet received the piece of information that can make it update its counter.

In addition, we remark that, due to network latencies, whenever a piece of information (e.g., a counter value) is exchanged between two nodes, this information may become incoherent with the sender status before it is actually received. For instance, using the example of Fig. 4.4, one can imagine the situation where node v performs a

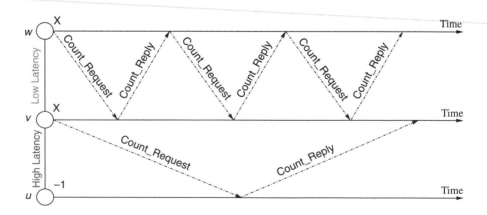

Figure 4.4 Synchronization issues

request round by sending **Count_Request** messages to its neighbors, including node w. Node w shall receive this message and send back a **Count_Reply**($count_w = x$) message to v. Meanwhile, node w may have symmetrically done the same process. Thus, during the time the **Count_Reply**(x) message is transmitted from node w to v, node w may set its counter to -1 (if it gets work from another neighbor), 0 (if it detects an interval vaporization), or $x + 1$.

To avoid these situations and allow nodes to operate correctly and efficiently under unknown network latencies,[8] we use an adaptation of a well-known technique, called α synchronizer [3, 23, 27]. This technique allows us to abstract away the problems induced by network latencies and to efficiently coordinate request rounds. Generally speaking, each time a work request round is started by some node v, node v performs the following local actions. First, it waits for neighbors' responses, that is, **Count_Reply** messages. This allows node v to detect that its requests were actually received by neighbors and to receive neighbors' counters. If node v detects that some neighbor owns an interval, then it asks to share it, that is, **Work_Request** and **Work_Reply** messages. After finishing this work request round, a node then sends a **Safe** message to neighbors (line 20) and symmetrically waits for their **Safe** messages before starting a new round (line 21) and so on until termination is detected or a piece of interval is received. Notice that nodes exploring some intervals do not send any **Safe** messages (line 6). Symmetrically, a node that has detected that a neighbor is exploring an interval (by receiving a **Count_Reply**(-1) message) does not send any **Safe** message to it (line 13). The same reasoning is applied for a node that claims termination (lines 24-25).

4.4 COMPLEXITY ISSUES

Because our distributed algorithms were designed to work under a fully asynchronous environment and due to irregularity/nondeterminism of the B&B tree exploration process, it is difficult to provide a rigorous complexity analysis of our P2P approach. The goal of this section is rather to highlight the main complexity issues of our approach by emphasizing the scalability and network congestion issues.

For our analysis, we will make the following assumptions:

- A *message* is an infrangible piece of information that is sent along a logical link between two nodes (peers) in the overlay, independently from the number of physical equipments required to transmit it over the physical network.

- During one *time unit*, a node in the network may send to each neighbor at most one message. Equivalently, this means that a message sending induces a delay of one time unit. We emphasize the fact that time units are introduced for the sake of analysis only. In other words, our algorithms do not assume any shared global

---

[8] Actually, in our distributed algorithm, we only assume that messages are received in the same order they are sent (i.e., asynchronous FIFO model).

clock or any known bound on the time needed to transmit a message over the network.

Let us denote by D the diameter of the network overlay $G = (V, E)$ and d_v the degree of node $v \in V$. From a message complexity point of view, we can then state the following:

Proposition 4.1

Whenever a new best solution is found by a node during the B&B local search process, it costs at most $O(|E|)$ messages until all other nodes in the network update their local solutions. In addition, assuming that sending a message to neighbors costs one time unit, it takes at most D time units to update the local solutions of all nodes.

Proof. When a node v discovers or is informed about a better solution, it broadcasts a New_Sol message containing this solution to its neighbors, costing one time unit. As these neighbors will also forward this solution to their neighbors, and so on, the new solution is spread up to distance t around w within t time units. Because, a new solution is forwarded only if it improves the best known one, it is clear that after at most $t = D$ time units, all nodes are informed and the new solution is not forwarded any more. In addition, by the algorithm description (line 8 and line 37), for any pair of neighbors (u, v), in the worst case node u sends the new solution spread by v to w and w sends it to v at the same time only once. Hence, it costs at most two messages per edge to spread the new solution and the proposition holds.   □

Proposition 4.2

Consider that, at a given time, a node v has no work interval to explore. Assume that no interval vaporization occurs during any work request round. In the worst case, node v sends at most $O(d_v \cdot D)$ messages within at most $O(D)$ time units until either it receives a work unit or it detects the termination of the B&B algorithm.

Proof. First, we argue that interval vaporization may make nodes perform additional rounds of work requests. However, this phenomenon is hardly predictable. The purpose of this proposition is to abstract away this issue and to focus on the efficiency of our work sharing and termination detection phase.

The bound claimed in the proposition then holds easily from the description of our algorithm. In fact, by abstracting away interval vaporization, there are two situations that may occur at any point of the algorithm execution:

- There remain no intervals to explore in the network. Thus, node v will make at most $\Theta(D)$ successive unsuccessful rounds and then terminate.
- There exists at least one node u holding an interval somewhere in the network. Node u is, by definition of D, at distance at most D from v. Thus, it takes at most $O(D)$ rounds before a piece of u's interval reaches v.

The proposition then holds by remarking that each round lasts $O(1)$ time units and costs $O(d_v)$ Count_Request messages plus $O(d_v)$ Safe messages.   □

Although, our approach can properly operate whatever the logical network topology is, it becomes clear from the previous analysis that it requires specific properties for the overlay graph to perform efficiently.

We first remark that when tackling large instance problems, the B&B process is initialized with some good solution (computed, for instance, using a given heuristic[9]). Thus, it is rare that too many new solutions are found by many peers at the same time. Equivalently, most of the time peers just prune the explored intervals without finding new solutions. Therefore, we can reasonably state that the communication complexity of our approach is dominated by the work-sharing mechanism. Thus, to gain in efficiency, the overlay graph should have a good balance between node degrees (i.e., each peer must have a low number of neighbors) and network diameter (i.e., peers must stay relatively close in the logical overlay). In fact, spreading a piece of information (intervals) over the network must be performed quickly while keeping the communication load of the peers at a low level to avoid bottlenecks around peers.

To satisfy these constraints, we make use of existing overlay constructions [10, 21, 25]. More precisely, we chose to use the well-known Pastry-like overlay [25]. In fact, both the diameter of the graph and the average degree are guaranteed to be order of $\log(n)$ with n being the number of nodes.

Assuming the latter overlay properties, and using Proposition 4.2, the combined work sharing and termination detection distributed algorithm described above costs roughly $O(\log(n)^2)$ messages per node. To illustrate how this could improve the scalability of the master-slave approach, let us first abstract away the congestion/delays created at the network due to communication cost. In other words, let us assume that the limitation of the master-slave approach is only due to the bottleneck created around the master, that is, to the number of slaves or equivalently to the degree of the star overlay induced by such an architecture. Let n be the maximum number of slaves that can be handled simultaneously by the master, that is, n is now the maximum number of slaves that leads to a bottleneck around the master. Then we can reasonably assume that n would be also the maximum number of neighbors before a communication bottleneck around a given peer can be observed. Thus, consider a P2P overlay with size $n' = \Theta(\exp(n))$. Then, we obtain a mean node degree of $\Theta(\log n') = \Theta(n)$. This means that while the Master-Worker model can handle only up to n computational nodes before breaking down, the P2P approach scales up to $\Theta(\exp(n))$ nodes. Of course, exponentially more computational resources does not straightforwardly mean exponential gain in load balancing/parallel efficiency nor in search speed-up, since handling more resources has a communication cost. In the master-slave approach, in order to share work or to announce termination, the master sends $O(1)$ messages to each slave. Overall, the number of messages sent is thus $\Theta(n)$, with the master having a degree equal to n. Assume now that it can be proven that $\Theta(n)$ is the maximum number of messages that can be sent simultaneously over the network before network delays/congestion can lead to the system breaking down. Thus, under the assumption that no work vaporization occurs, which is a reasonable assumption for large-scale and difficult instancesâĹš and using Proposition 4.2, our P2P

---

[9]It is generally admitted that starting a B&B from scratch is rather costly.

approach can still handle up to $n' = \Theta(n/\log^2 n)$, which is asymptotically better than $\Theta(n^{1-\epsilon})$ for an *arbitrary small* positive constant $\epsilon < 1$. Thus, overall, we obtain a better balance between scalability in terms of number of peers and scalability in terms of communication cost that is in parallel efficiency. As our experimental results show in Section 4.5, we even obtain lower communication overheads than expected theoretically while being more efficient in terms of space exploration and in parallel efficiency.

Remark 4.2
Notice that, for the sake of termination detection, we have assumed that the diameter D of the graph is known. This may appear as a strong and penalizing assumption. However, we argue that an upper bound on D is sufficient. In addition, using an upper bound instead of the exact value of D does not affect the communication cost as long as some work interval remains somewhere in the network, that is, message overhead will only occur when the search space is fully explored. According to the previous discussion, the overlay graph should be chosen such that $D = \Theta(\log n)$. Thus, in practice, for n around, let us say, 10^{10}, even an over estimated upper bound of, let us say, 100 is perfectly plausible.

4.5 EXPERIMENTAL RESULTS

Several experiments have been conducted to evaluate the scalability of our fully distributed P2P approach for the exact optimization branch-and-bound algorithm. The problem considered is an instance of the well-known flow-shop scheduling problem. This instance is denoted "Ta057" [28] and is reputed to be difficult to solve (50 jobs on 20 machines). In fact, a similar instance ("Ta056") was solved optimally for the first time in [20] using more than 1000 physical machines and over more than 25 days of cumulated computation time. In this section, we compare several measures with the state-of-the-art master-slave approach [20]. This comparison best suits our work, as we kept the same representation of the solutions and the same coding for the branch-and-bound algorithm. For our experiments, we choose to run our approach during a limited amount of time. This allows us to perform a higher number of runs and to compare both approaches at various scales within a reasonable amount of time. Extensive simulations involving up to 150,000 computational processes have been conducted. Our experimental results are reported and discussed in the following sections.

4.5.1 Experimental Testbed

The experiments have been conducted on the French nationwide Grid'5000 Experimental Grid [12]. Our objective is to study the performances of our approach at various scales and compare it to the MS approach proposed in [19]. Our experiments are conducted in a *static* environment. That is, the machines are supposed to be reliable and no failure of any type can occur. No entities can join or leave the network at any time. We use the exact combinatorial optimization branch-and-bound algorithm on an instance of the

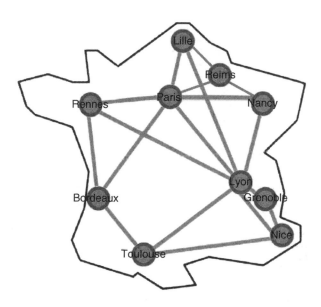

Figure 4.5 Grid'5000 geographical sites.

flow-shop scheduling problem (Ta057). The available instances for this problem are various in terms of size (from 10! up to 500! feasible solutions) and time needed to solve them. On a sequential machine, it can vary from some minutes to several years to solve such an instance. Thus, we choose to set the running time of *each* entity to 10 minutes. One may think at first sight that this value may be low. However, this value is relevant as some instances can be solved sequentially within this amount of time. Moreover, since we will consider P2P networks managing several thousands of entities, the overall running time from the B&B optimization point of view is huge. Secondly, considering such a value allows one to conduct a larger number of tests within a reasonable amount of time.

Our goal is to study the behavior of our approach at various scales during a fixed amount of time. These scales range from 1000 entities up to 150,000 entities. For that purpose, a fixed set of machines is used on Grid'5000, namely 569 physical nodes (consisting in 2046 computational cores) distributed on 8 geographical sites (all sites except Nancy and Reims) (Fig. 4.5). All the obtained results are an average of three separate runs. The characteristics of the physical machines used in our experiments are described in Table 4.1. Depending on the size of the overlay graph we want to experiment, each physical machine can hold a well-defined number of processes, each process modeling a node in the overlay. Each process then runs our distributed algorithms as described in previous sections. In particular, exploration of intervals is done using the classical sequential B&B algorithm and communication between processes is implemented using C++ sockets. The way these processes are dispatched is described in subsection 4.5.2.2. We first start by the parallel efficiency results of our P2P approach.

TABLE 4.1 Physical Machines' Characteristics

Name	CPU	Quantity	Total of cores	Core Frequency
SGI Altix Xe 310	Intel Xeon E5440 QC	136	1088	2.83 Ghz
IBM eServer 326m	AMD Opteron 252	30	60	2.6 Ghz
IBM eServer 326	AMD Opteron 248	8	16	2.2 Ghz
IBM eServer 326	AMD Opteron 246	275	550	2.0 Ghz
Sun Fire X2200 M2	AMD Opteron 2218	92	368	2.6 Ghz
Dell PowerEdge R410	Intel Xeon E5520	8	64	2.26 Ghz
	Total	569	2046	

4.5.2 Experiments on Large-Scale Networks

4.5.2.1 Parallel Efficiency. As pointed out earlier, the main drawback of a parallel application designed upon a master-slave model is the use of a central entity that coordinates all other entities in the network. In a large-scale scenario, this central entity, the master, must process an increasing number of requests from slave entities. Consequently, the mean delay taken to process a work request gets longer and the overall performances of the network degrades. Concretely, Fig. 4.6 depicts the parallel efficiency

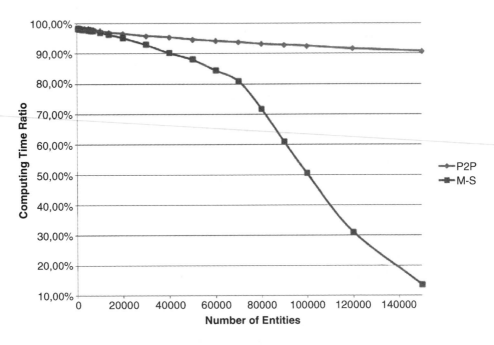

Figure 4.6 Parallel efficiency rates with the number of entities.

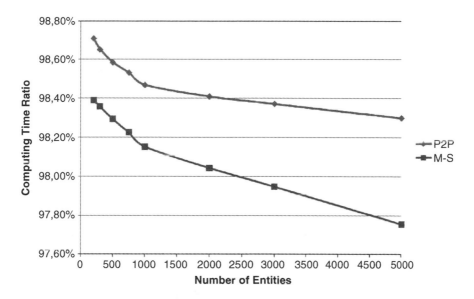

Figure 4.7 Parallel efficiency rates for small-scale networks.

(PE) rate along with the number of entities involved in the network. Parallel efficiency is obtained by comparing, for each computational entity, the amount of time spent on performing the B&B algorithm (i.e., exploring solutions in the search space) to the overall execution time. Around about 60,000 entities involved in the network, the PE of the Master-Worker approach begins to drop significantly. In addition, around about 70,000 and 80,000 entities, the master-slave curve does not go down as smoothly as for smaller values and breaks down quickly to reach considerably low levels when involving more than 100,000 entities (around 10%). This was expected in theory due to the increasing synchronization operations and the increasing computational load on the master entity. On the opposite, in our peer-to-peer approach, work requests are processed locally since a peer only communicates with its immediate neighbors. In fact, the load is somehow "distributed" among the peers. Thus, the mean delay for processing a request is kept low. This is why the PE rate for the P2P approach remains high, namely above 90%, even for large scale-simulations, involving more than 100,000 entities.

However, one may legitimately wonder if the gain in terms of PE also exists while evolving at very low scales. The graph provided in Fig. 4.7 confirms this idea although the numerical difference is quite low.

4.5.2.2 Network Congestion and Simulation Scenarios.
While performing large-scale simulations, as the number of processes increases, the amount of communications made through the physical network increases. Thus, for such a simulation to make sense, it is crucial to make sure that the network does not undergo congestion/overload. As this possible congestion will be due to massive network operations, we have to focus on whether or not a computational entity involved in our simulations

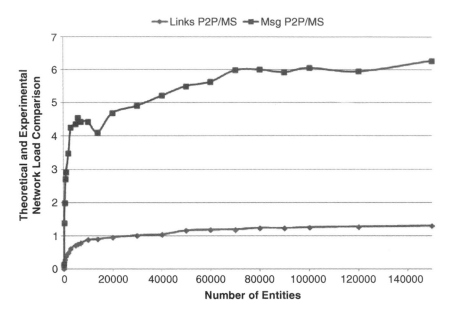

Figure 4.8   Theoretical and experimental network load ratios

(the process that simulates a peer) uses the physical network to communicate with another entity. Indeed, since the number of physical machines remains constant throughout our experiments, the number of processes deployed on each machine grows higher and higher. Thus, it may happen that two processes communicating with one another are located on the same physical machine. In this case, communications remain local and do not make use of the physical network. In Fig. 4.8, we report two important measures:

- The ratio $r_1 = \frac{L_{P2P}}{L_{M-S}}$ where L_{P2P} (resp. L_{M-S}) is the number of logical links connecting two nodes (processes) deployed on two different physical machines in the P2P (resp. master-slave) approach. (See the bottom curve.)
- The ratio $r_2 = \frac{Msg_{P2P}}{Msg_{M-S}}$ where Msg_{P2P} (resp. Msg_{M-S}) is the number of messages exchanged through logical links connecting two processes deployed on two different physical machines in the P2P (resp. master-slave) approach. (See the top curve.)

In a master-slave architecture, it can be easily predicted that most processes will use the physical network as they will communicate with the same central entity (master process). Consequently, we pay attention to deploy our P2P approach in such a way that the physical network is also used in the same manner as in the master-slave architecture. More precisely, we have deployed the peers randomly on the machines such that (i) the previous property is satisfied for every simulation run, and (ii) the properties of the resulting logical topology are similar to a Pastry-like network, in terms of both average

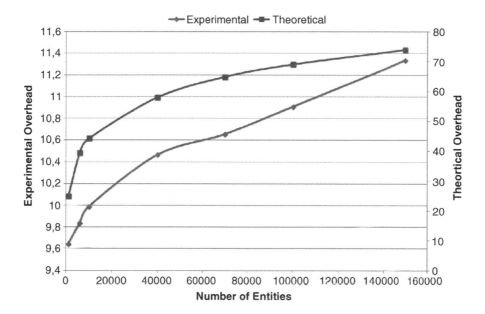

Figure 4.9 Messages overhead

node degree and graph diameter.[10] In Fig. 4.8, one can see that the network is expected to be used by our P2P overlay topology in the same way as by the master-slave star overlay. In other words, this indicates that, in our simulation scenarios, none of the two approaches is penalized by network congestion issues than the other.

Furthermore, when looking at the number of messages sent over the physical network (bottom curve in Fig. 4.8), we see that our P2P approach costs more messages than the master-slave approach. Thus, we can reasonably state that the PE of the master-slave approach goes down because of the bottleneck created around the master and not due to network congestion issues. In contrast, our P2P PE remains good even for large-scale simulations intensively using the physical network. In fact, although the network is solicited up to 6.5 times more in the P2P approach, the PE rate remains high, namely above 90%.

4.5.2.3 Message Overhead. In Fig. 4.9 (red/bottom curve with the left Y axis), we compare the number of messages sent by all processes (including local communications on the same physical machine) in both approaches. One can see that for our P2P approach, peers send about 11 times more messages than the master-slave approach. This also explains why in Fig. 4.8, when comparing the number of sent messages that actually use the physical network in both approaches, we obtain a ratio of around 6.5.

---

[10]More precisely, the constructed overlay is a hypercube having a well defined dimension that guarantees the low degree low diameter property.

In Fig. 4.9 (blue/top curve with the right Y axis), we also notice that the *experimental* message overhead factor is significantly lower than the ratio that could be expected according to the complexity analysis presented earlier. Indeed, one can see that as the experimental overhead factor remains between 9 and 11, the theoretical overhead (a very worst-case scenario) expected according to the constructed logical topology is much higher, namely starting at 20 and rising up to 75. We thus can state that the theoretical analysis of Section 4.4 is pessimistic compared with what happens in practice.

With the discussion in the previous section, we can thus conclude that the message overhead cost we paid in order to design our fully distributed scheme is perfectly negligible from a PE point of view.

4.5.2.4 *Search Space Exploration Speed-Up.* In previous sections, we

showed that the loss of performance of the master-slave approach is not due to a possible network congestion, as our P2P approach induces a network load several times more important in terms of messages exchanged, without losing in PE. However, designing an efficient and scalable parallel technique avoiding network congestion and handling more computational resources may not be sufficient to claim that, dealing with combinatorial optimization problems, it enables exploration of the search space more quickly. In Fig. 4.10, we focus on the average number of solutions of the search space explored by each computational node in both approaches. One can see that our fully distributed approach explores up to 7 times more solutions than the master-worker approach of [20]. More importantly, to understand the obtained curve, we should keep in mind that the space search speed-up is guided by two factors: the degree of parallelism (PE as depicted in Fig. 4.6) and the B&B pruning itself, which is theoretically

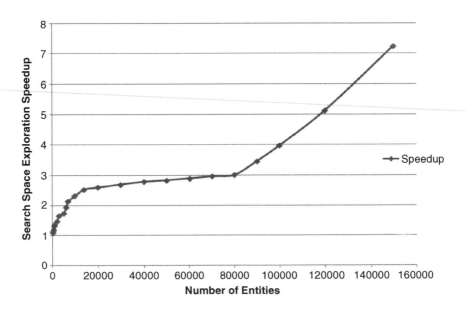

Figure 4.10 Speed-up, in terms of solutions explored.

unpredictable. Observed at low scales, the communication cost in both approaches is too low to have a significant impact on the global search speed up. In fact, we claim that at low scales the speed-up is mostly dominated by the pruning since PE of both approaches are comparable âŁšÃ„Ã¬with of course still an advantage for our P2P approach. However, when involving about 70000 computational nodes, the PE of the master-slave model is no longer competitive and it starts dropping significantly, as described previously in Fig. 4.6. Hence, we observe a breakpoint around 80,000 entities in Fig. 4.10. This break-point can be interpreted as the network size where the impact of PE on search speed-up becomes critical and the pruning cannot balance the loss in PE. We can thus state the gain in terms of PE of our P2P approach has a major impact when involving large-scale deployment of parallel B&B experiences on large instances.

4.5.2.5 *Combinatorial Speed-Up.*

Up to now, we studied the performances of our approach by comparing it with the master-slave based approach. Here, we propose to study its intrinsic performances. In Fig. 4.11, for a given number N of entities in the network, we compute the ratio $\frac{s_N}{s_1}$ where s_N represents the number of nodes explored in the search tree by the N entities and s_1 the same number but for only one entity. For the sake of clarity, we also represented the curve $y \mapsto x$, the case of the linear speed-up. We can see that our P2P approach has a good ratio, close to the linear one, whereas the master-slave ratio remains very low. The master-slave approach is not able to take advantage of an increasing amount of computational resources because of the communication bottleneck around the master entity, whereas the P2P approach deals easily with the induced communication overhead. Practically, the P2P approach obtains

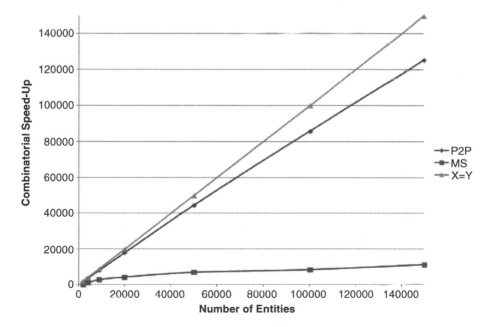

Figure 4.11 Speed-up, in terms of solutions explored.

a ratio up to 130,000 when involving 150,000 entities, while the master-slave approach reaches a ratio of 12,000. In addition to performing better than the master-slave approach, our approach provides an efficient parallelization of the B&B algorithm as its intrinsic performances are good.

4.5.3 Lower Scales' Results

In the previous section, we focused on the behavior of our approach when evolving at extreme scales. We noticed that, in spite of a greater communication overhead, our approach obtains better results in terms of parallel efficiency than the master-slave approach, that is, the entities spend less time communicating with each other than in the master-slave approach. However, the results obtained so far focus only on the B&B execution over a fixed period of time; the considered instance was not fully solved. Thus, one may wonder whether the termination detection mechanism, based on the work sharing mechanism, has a major impact on the performances of our P2P approach. In this section, we analyze, at lower scales, the performances of our approach when solving entirely small instances of the flow-shop scheduling problem. In the following, we focus on instances from Ta021 to Ta030 [28], which consists of scheduling 20 jobs on 20 machines. Those instances require about one day to be solved from scratch using B&B on a single computing peer. We then deploy the B&B algorithm in a "*real-case*" fashion, that is, we use a number of physical cores varying from 200 to 1000 and we run exactly one peer on each core. We use the same computing nodes as in the previous section.

In Fig. 4.12, left, we draw the execution time (in seconds) according to the number of peers in the network, that is, the duration between the first peer starting its execution

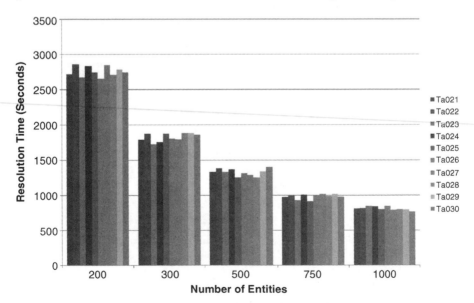

Figure 4.12 Execution time for small instances with the P2P approach using a Pastry-like topology.

and the last peer claiming the termination of the B&B algorithm. In Fig. 4.12, right, we draw the parallel efficiency obtained with our P2P approach for the different B&B instances. One can remark that the execution time decreases smoothly as we scale the network up to 1000. We observe that at the higher scales (1000), the peer-to-peer starts to scale worse than the lower scales (200 to 800). This is attributed to the size of the experimented B&B instances. In fact, the B&B work granularity becomes so small that work can no more be shared among peers. This is expected since the considered instance becomes so relatively small with the considered 1000 peer scale. However, we observe that for lower scales, our P2P approach scales almost linearly, which is consistent with the previous large-scale experiments. In particular, this confirms the fact that the designed termination detection mechanism does not impact the overall performance.

4.6 CONCLUSION

In this chapter, we proposed a new peer-to-peer approach for the tree-based B&B algo-rithm. This approach is based on fully distributed algorithms dealing with work sharing and termination detection in an asynchronous FIFO message passing communication model. Using a small-degree, small-diameter network overlay, we argued that this ap-proach allows us to improve the scalability of the state-of-the art master-slave approach by controlling the overhead in terms of message exchanged and increasing the over-all parallel efficiency. We also show by extensive experiments that our P2P approach effectively scales well and induces significant improvements to the the master-slave approach.

Although our algorithms were discussed in the specific context of permutation-based problems and parallel B&B, it is not difficult to see that it can be extended to other contexts. Roughly speaking, for that purpose one must define the following features depending on the application context: (i) an encoding of work units (intervals), (ii) the processing of work units (sequential B&B), and (iii) the global information that needs to be shared (best B&B solution).

The study conducted in this chapter also raises many ongoing issues. For instance, it would be challenging to find another overlay allowing us to obtain the same paral-lel efficiency rates as ours while having lower message overhead. Another hot issue is to extend our distributed algorithms in a dynamic environment where peers may join, leave, or crash at any time during the distributed parallel search process. This work can, in fact, be viewed as the basis for a future real-life scheme involving volatile and unpredictable resources available from both computational grids and personal computers.

ACKNOWLEDGMENT

We thank the technical staffs of the French Grid'5000 experimental grid for making their clusters accessible and fully operational.

REFERENCES

[1] K. Aida and Y. Futakata, High-performance parallel and distributed computing for the bmi eigenvalue problem. In: 16th International Parallel and Distributed Processing Symposium, (IPDPS'02), pp. 71–78 (2002).

[2] K. Aida and T. Osumi, A case study in running a parallel branch and bound application on the grid. In: SAINT '05: The 5th IEEE Symposium on Applications and the Internet, pp. 164–173. Washington, DC (2005).

[3] B. Awerbuch, Complexity of network synchronization. Journal of the ACM **32**(4), 804–823 (1985).

[4] A. Bendjoudi, N. Melab, and E.G. Talbi, P2P design and implementation of a parallel branch and bound algorithm for grids. *International Journal of Grid and Utility Computing* **1**(2), 159–168 (2009).

[5] A. Bendjoudi, N. Melab, and E.G. Talbi, Fault-tolerant mechanism for hierarchical branch and bound algorithm. In: Workshop on Large-Scale Parallel Processing (2011).

[6] R.D. Blumofe, C.F. Joerg, B.C. Kuszmaul, C.E. Leiserson, K.H. Randall, and Y. Zhou, Cilk: An efficient multithreaded runtime system. *Journal of Parallel and Distributed Computing* **37**(1), 55–69 (1996).

[7] A. Cabani, S. Ramaswamy, M. Itmi, and J.P. Pécuchet, Phac: An environment for distributed collaborative applications on p2p networks. In: 6th International Conference on Distributed Computing and Internet Technology (ICDCIT), pp. 240–247 (2007).

[8] A. Di Constanzo, Branch-and-bound with peer-to-peer for large-scale grids. Ph.D. thesis, Ecole doctorale STIC, Sophia Antipolis, France (2007).

[9] E.W. Dijkstra and C.S. Scholten, Termination detection for diffusing computations. *Information Processing Letters* **11**(1), 1–4 (1980).

[10] L. Garcs-Erice, E. Biersack, P.A. Felber, K.W. Ross, and G. Urvoy-Keller, Hierarchical peer-to-peer systems. In: Proceedings of ACM/IFIP 9th International Conference on Parallel and Distributed Computing (EuroPar'03), pp. 643–657 (2003).

[11] B. Gendron and T.G. Crainic, Parallel branch-and-bound algorithms: Survey and synthesis. *Operations Research* **42**(6), 1042–1066 (1994).

[12] Grid'5000. http://www.grid5000.fr/ (last accessed 18 Jun 2013).

[13] A. Iamnitchi and I. Foster, A problem-specific fault-tolerance mechanism for asynchronous, distributed systems. In: Proceedings of the 29th International Conference on Parallel Processing, pp. 4–13 (2000).

[14] J.M. Jansen and F.W. Sijstermans, Parallel branch-and-bound algorithms. *Future Generation Computer Systems* **4**(4), 271–279 (1989).

[15] V. Kumar and L.N. Kanal, Parallel branch-and-bound formulations for and/or tree search. *IEEE Transactions on Pattern Analysis and Machine Intelligence*, **PAMI-6**(6), 768–778 (1984).

[16] H. Liu, X. Jia, P.J. Wan, X. Liu, and F.F. Yao, A distributed and efficient flooding scheme using 1-hop information in mobile ad hoc networks. *IEEE Trans. Parallel Distrib. Syst.* **18**, 658–671 (2007). DOI http://dx.doi.org/10.1109/TPDS.2007.1023.

[17] B. Mans, T. Mautor, and C. Roucairol, A parallel depth first search branch and bound algorithm for the quadratic assignment problem. *European Journal of Operational Research* **81**(3), 617–628 (1995). DOI: 10.1016/0377-2217(93)E0334-T.

[18] F. Mattern, Algorithms for distributed termination detection. *Distributed Computing* **2**(3), 161–175 (1987).

[19] M. Mezmaz, N. Melab, and E.G. Talbi, A grid-enabled branch and bound algorithm for solving challenging combinatorial optimization problems. In: 21st International Parallel and Distributed Processing Symposium, 2007. (IPDPS'07), pp. 1–9 (2007).

[20] M. Mezmaz, N., M., and E.G. Talbi, Towards a coordination model for parallel cooperative p2p multi-objective optimization. In: European Grid Conference (EGC'2005), pp. 305–314 (2005).

[21] D.S. Milojicic, V. Kalogeraki, R. Lukose, K. Nagaraja, J. Pruyne, B. Richard, S. Rollins, and Z. Xu, Peer-to-peer computing. Tech. rep. (2008). http://citeseer.ist.psu.edu/milojicic02peertopeer.html (last accessed 18 Jun 2013).

[22] N. Mittal, S. Venkatesan, and S. Peri, Message-optimal and latency-optimal termination detection algorithms for arbitrary topologies. In: Proceedings of the 18th Symposium on Distributed Computing (DISC, pp. 290–304 (2004).

[23] S. Moran and S. Snir, Simple and efficient network decomposition and synchronization. *Theoretical Computer Science* **243**(1-2), 217–241 (2000).

[24] A. Prieditis, Depth-first branch-and-bound vs. depth-bounded ida. *Computational Intelligence* **14**(2), 188–206 (1998).

[25] A. Rowstron and P. Druschel, Pastry: Scalable, decentralized object location and routing for large-scale peer-to-peer systems. In: *Lecture Notes in Computer Science*, pp. 329–350 (2001).

[26] F. Saffre and R. Ghanea-Hercock, Beyond anarchy: self organized topology for peer to peer networks. *Complexity* **9**(2), 49–53 (2003).

[27] L. Shabtay and A. Segall, Low complexity network synchronization. Proceedings of the 8th International Workshop on Distributed Algorithms (WDAG '94) pp. 223–237 (1994).

[28] E. Taillard, Benchmarks for basic scheduling problems. *European Journal of Operational Research* **64**(2), 278–285 (1993).

[29] W. Zhang, Depth-first branch-and-bound versus local search: A case study. In: *Proc. 17th National Conf. on Artificial Intelligence* (AAAI-2000), pp. 930–935 (2000).

5

DATA DISTRIBUTION
MANAGEMENT

Azzedine Boukerche and Yunfeng Gu

CONTENTS

Large Scale Network-Centric Distributed Systems, First Edition. Edited by Hamid Sarbazi-Azad and Albert Y. Zomaya.
© 2014 John Wiley & Sons, Inc. Published 2014 by John Wiley & Sons, Inc.

In general, DDM (data distribution management) deals with two basic problems: how to distribute data generated at the application layer among underlying nodes in the distributed system and how to retrieve data whenever it is necessary. Alternatively, these two problems can also be described as partitioning of the application data space and mapping from the application data space into the system identifier space. The concept of DDM can also be found in HLA/RTI (high-level architecture/run-time infrastructure) under IEEE Standard 1516. It is one of seven service APIs provided by RTI. HLA is a general-purpose architecture for real-time distributed interactive simulation systems. It is used to support the portability and interoperability of a large number of distributed simulations across various computing platforms. RTI is the implementation of the HLA interface specification. It manages the interaction between simulations and coordinates operations inside the simulation. The goal of DDM defined in HLA/RTI is to establish simulation interconnectivity to send relevant data on request with a minimum of excess or irrelevant data.

In our work, DDM is addressed in two different network environments: peer-to-peer (P2P) overlay networks and cluster-based network environments. Although DDM provides the same data indexing service in both distributed network environments, it serves upper-layer applications for very different purposes, and it is supported by underlying networks with distinctive infrastructures. In P2P overlay networks, peers share part of their resources. Both computing load and data load are distributed to peers across the entire overlay network. The network size may expand to the Internet scale. However, peers might have different capacities to share the load; some might join or leave the system, or even fail, and the connectivity between them is unstable. DDM in P2P overlay networks is more feasible for massive data sharing systems or massively parallel computing. On the other hand, all peers in a cluster network are dedicated resources for the distributed environment. The cluster network might have very limited size, but the status of a peer is highly reliable, and the connectivity is always stable. DDM in such a network environment has been commonly used to support more intensive interactive simulations.

Because of the fundamental differences at both the application layer and the underlying network layer, the study of DDM must follow very different methodologies, which in turn diverts our interests and objectives in each area significantly.

5.1 ADDRESSING DDM IN DIFFERENT NETWORK ENVIRONMENTS

There are many differences between DDM in P2P overlay networks and cluster-based network environments. The only common feature shared by both is that they are all proposed to provide the data indexing service to the distributed environment. However, DDM in P2P overlay networks is considered more as a complete concept of building and maintaining P2P overlay architecture (e.g., CAN [1, 2] and Chord [1, 3]) than a simple technique of data fetching, and it is an open area that has received a great deal of interest in the literature since the 1960s. DDM in P2P overlay networks is commonly called associative searching or queries, which include key queries, semantic key queries, range queries, multi-attribute queries, joined queries, aggregation queries, and so on. For DDM in the cluster-based network environment, we choose HLA/RTI-based simulation systems. DDM is one of the important services APIs provide by RTI. HLA/RTI is a publish/subscribe system. In HLA/RTI, all components are packed and provided as services to the higher-layer simulation scenario. The detail of the DDM implementation is implementation dependent, and it is not publicly known.

Table 5.1 lists important features of DDM in both environments. In a P2P overlay network, the study object of DDM is the application data in data space. All peers in the system share part of their resources to participate in system-wide activities, and they are organized in either a tightly controlled topology (structured P2P networks) or a random graph (unstructured P2P networks). Therefore, the main challenge of DDM in the P2P overlay network is to build a robust and reliable P2P search network that is not only efficient in retrieving data from multiple peers but also inherently scalable, self-organizing, fault tolerant, and load balancing. Nevertheless, in the P2P overlay network, data is distributed and retrieved by following the same partitioning and mapping strategy, and retrieving data is basically a request-based transmission involving a series of routing operations. The data producer distributes data to the data owner, the data owner is responsible for storing data and responding to queries, and the data consumer retrieves data from the data owner. The destination node (data owner) is computed progressively at each intermediate node on the route. The main trade-off of DDM in the P2P overlay network is the decentralization of the application data and computation load versus the global awareness of system-wide operations.

Similarly, DDM in the cluster-based network environment studies the simulation data (simulation objects) in *routing space*. However, all underlying nodes in the cluster are fully connected to each other, and they are dedicated resources to the higher layer simulation scenario. Retrieving data is a subscription-based process involving a considerable amount computation load at the data owner. The *publisher* (Subsection 5.3.1.4) and *subscriber* (Subsection 5.3.1.4) register their interests (instead of distributing data) to the data owner. The data owner is responsible for detecting the *matching* (Subsection 5.3.1.4), which means computing the intersection region in *routing space* that has been both published and subscribed by some objects. Once a *matching* is detected, the data owner notifies corresponding *publisher*s and *subscriber*s, and the relevant data is sent from *publisher*s to *subscriber*s directly. Therefore, the main challenge of DDM in the cluster-based network environment is to detect *matching*. Because detecting *matching* can be done either exactly in a exhaustive manner or with a certain degree of tolerance by the data owner, the main trade-off of DDM in the cluster-based network environment is the communication overhead versus the computation complexity.

TABLE 5.1 Comparison of DDM in P2P and Cluster-Based Network Environments

	DDM in P2P	DDM in Cluster
Context	P2P overlay architecture – structured P2P – unstructured P2P	Simulation middle-ware (publish/subscribe system) – HLA / RTI
Applications	– Distributed directory system – P2P domain name services – Network file systems – Massive-scale fault-tolerant system, etc.	Real-time distributed interactive simulations
Study object	Application data in data space	Simulation data in routing space
Resources	Shared resources	Dedicated resources
Service provided	Data indexing	Data indexing
Underlying topology	– Structured P2P tightly controlled structure – Unstructured P2P random graph	Complete connection
Partitioning and mapping	– Structured P2P DHT Space-filling curves – Unstructured P2P duplicating popular contents	Implementation-dependent (not publicly known)
Retrieving data	Request-based	Subscription-based
Main challenges	Building distributed data structure	Matching detection
Main trade-off	Decentralization vs. global awareness	Communication overhead vs. computation complexity
Research focuses	Scalability, self-organizing, fault tolerance, load balancing	DDM performance

5.2 DDM IN P2P OVERLAY NETWORKS

5.2.1 Background

P2P is a potentially disruptive technology with numerous applications, like distributed directory system, P2P domain name services, network file systems, massively parallel systems, distributed e-mail systems, and massive-scale fault-tolerant systems. However, these applications will not be realized without a robust and reliable P2P search network.

The most popular P2P overlay networks that have been well studied or deployed so far can be categorized into two classes: structured P2P overlay networks [2–7] and unstructured P2P overlay networks [8–20]. Structured P2P overlay networks are also called DHT-based systems, in which the data space is partitioned and mapped into the identifier space by using a randomization function—the distributed hash table (DHT) [29–31]. The DHT-based system normally must maintain a tightly controlled topology. Some of the well-known DHT-based systems include CAN [1, 2], Chord [1, 3], Pastry [1, 4], Tapestry [1, 5], Kademlia [1, 6], and Viceroy [1, 7].

Unlike DHT-based P2P systems, unstructured P2P overlay networks, like Gnutella [1, 8, 9], Freenet [1, 10], FastTrack/KaZaA [1, 11–14], BitTorrent [1, 15, 16], and eDonkey [1, 17–20], are often organized in a flat, random, or simple hierarchical manner. The unstructured P2P network replicates the frequently visited data objects among the system, and the queries are often made by using flooding or random walks. It appears to be more effective at finding the very popular content. However, because of its ad hoc nature and flooding-based queries, the correctness and performance of the routing, the scalability of the system, and the consumption of network bandwidth are all uncertain.

The main challenge is how to locate data requested from the application data space in the P2P identifier space. This problem was solved by using DHT [29–31]. However, it is only applicable for the exact key query. Unstructured P2P networks can be used for more complex queries, but they do not guarantee that data will be located.

A multidimensional range queries is a more generalized form of many other queries. It provides efficient index services in P2P environments. It is the primitive service over which all other complex services can be built. It has many applications in large-scale distributed environments, such as grid computing, publish/subscribe systems, multiplayer games, group communication and naming, P2P data sharing, and global storage. Many of these applications collect, produce, distribute, and retrieve information from and into distributed data space. The scale of such data space can be extremely large and its dimensionality varies. The distribution and management of such data space, even the index part, appears to be a great challenge to the distributed environment. The very features that make DHT-based systems, good, like load balancing and random hashing, work against the range query. How data space is partitioned and mapped into the P2P identifier space needs to be considered.

In addition to concerns regarding the basic efficiency of the data query, there are more fundamental issues, like scalability, self-organizing, fault tolerance, and load balancing, which must be addressed properly in a distributed environment. In order to better resolve these problems, there are two interconnected parts of a process that must be done cooperatively. The first part of this process is related to how data space is partitioned and mapped into the identifier space in the distributed environment, or, in other words, how to distribute data into the P2P system so that specific data objects can be retrieved with a reasonable computation and communication cost. This is called *application constraint*. The second part of the process concerns how to organize peers in the distributed system or how to design and maintain a certain topology of the P2P system. This ensures that properties of the data object (like the semantic meaning of data) and the relationship among data objects (like the data locality) in the original data space preserved in the first part of the work are able to be easily managed and maintained in the identifier space. We call this *system constraint*. The *application constraint* determines what kind of space partitioning strategy should be used and hence what kind of pattern for the information query can be supported by the system. The *system constraint* determines the performance of the basic routing and maintenance operations, the computation complexity, and, if the system is scalable, error resilientce, self-organizing, and load balancing.

5.2.2   Data Space Partitioning and Mapping

The *application constraint* determines that both the structured and unstructured P2P overlay systems are well suited for exact key queries and might be adapted to even more complex queries. None of them is able to provide efficient support for the multidimensional range query, because the multidimensional range query (associative searching) adds additional requirements into both the *application constraint* and the *system constraint* over the P2P overlay layer. These requirements can be briefly stated as follows:

- Preserving the data locality in the process of data space partitioning.
- Maintaining the data locality at the P2P overlay layer.

The main concern in multidimensional space partitioning is how to preserve data localities. Many works have already addressed this concern. Among them, Quad-tree [21, 22, 28], K-d tree [22, 23], Z-order [24, 25], and Hilbert curve [26] are four well-known proposals. Although these works provide different solutions, they all share a common feature: using recursive decomposition for partitioning, which is a tree structure in nature.

Quad-tree and K-d tree provide solutions using hierarchical data structures, whereas Z-order and Hilbert curve provide solutions by linearizing points in multidimensional space using the space filling curves. The performance of these decomposition schemes are all bound by $O(lg(n))$. It has been found that the processing of Z-order and Hilbert curve has a natural connection with Quad-tree.

In addition to these standard decomposition schemes, locality-preserving hashing [42] was proposed in order to retain the range query in the DHT-based systems; however, random sampling [41] is another effort that does not scale well. No matter which decomposition scheme is used, two direct observations about partitioning in the multidimensional data space can be observed:

Fact 5.2.1 *Data localities expand exponentially as the dimensionality of data space increases.*

Because the total number of neighboring range data in p dimensional data space at the first order of decomposition is $k = 2^p$.

Fact 5.2.2 *Data localities extend exponentially as the order of decomposition increases.*

Because the total number of neighboring range data in p dimensional data space at the $d - th$ order of decomposition is k^d.

5.2.3 Corresponding Overlay Network Support

Preservation of data localities in data space partitioning is the *application constraint* enforced by the range query. Solutions include using recursive decomposition and the locality-preserving hashing. Correspondingly, the *system constraint* requires that the underlying P2P network layer must possess a certain inherent nature in order to accommodate and maintain data localities with exponentially expanding and extending rates. Existing P2P overlay networks, either DHT-based or unstructured, are originally designed to meet a specific demand, such as the exact key query. The very features that make them good, like random hashing and load balancing or replicating the popular contents, work against the range query.

Although the work in multidimensional space partitioning can be traced back to the 1960s, and the results and performance have been widely accepted ($O(lg(n))$), little effort has been made to study the corresponding P2P overlay network to provide comparable support for the multidimensional range query. Table 5.2 shows a comparison of current P2P systems supporting the multidimensional range query.

In Table 5.2, as we have discussed in the previous section, we do not consider DHT-based systems. SkipNet [39] and P-Grid [40] were designed and have been claimed to support the range query, but no experimental results have been found so far. Mercury [41] uses random sampling for data distribution, and its experimental results show a maximum of 0.1% selectivity in a three-dimensional data space (10% at each dimension). MAAN [42] employs locality-preserving hashing, and the maximum selectivity is about 1% in a two-dimensional data space (10% at each dimension). Other systems, like SCARP [32], MURK [32], ZNet [33], Skipindex [34], Squid [35], and SONAR [36], use recursive decomposition for partitioning and have underlying architectures that are either adapted structures from DHT-based systems (like Chord) CAN, or skip graphs [37], the only structure proposed for the range query. No system has direct mapping. They all must manage a tree-like structure internally. Their experimental results show very limited

T A B L E 5.2 Comparison of P2P Overlay Systems I

P2P Systems	Space Partitioning	Underlying Architecture	Direct Mapping
DHT-based	DHT	CAN/Chord/...	No
SkipNet	Naming sub-tree	Skip graphs	No
P-Grid	Virtual distributed search tree	Flat graphs	No
Mercury	Random sampling	Ring	No
SCARP	Z-order/Hilbert SFC	Skip graphs	No
MURK	K-d tree	d-torus (CAN)	No
ZNet	Z-order/Quad tree	Skip graphs	No
Skipindex	K-d tree	Skip graphs	No
Squid	Hilbert SFC	Ring (Chord)	No
SONAR	K-d tree	d-torus (CAN)	No
MAAN	Locality-preserving hashing	Ring (Chord)	No
BATON	Binary search tree	Balanced binary tree	Yes
VBI-Tree	SFC	Balanced binary tree	Yes

TABLE 5.3 Comparison of P2P Overlay Systems II

Underlying Architecture	P2P Systems	Routing Table Size	Routing	Join/Leave	Load Balancing	Fault Tolerance
Ring	Chord	$O(\log(n))$ [3]	$O(\log(n))$ [3]	$O(\log^2(n))$ [3]	Static [3]	Background stabilization routine [3]
	Squid					
	MAAN					Problem remains open [38]
	Mercury					
d-torus	CAN	$O(d)$ [2]	$O(dn^{1/d})$ [2]	$2d$ [2]	Static [2]	Background stabilization routine [2]
	MURK					Problem remains open [38]
	SONAR					
Skip Graphs	SkipNet	$O(n\log(n))$ [38]	$O(\log(n))$ [37]	$O(\log(n))$ [37]	Static [37, 38]	Inherently support [37]
	ZNet					Problem remains open [38]
	SCARP					
	Skipindex					
Flat Graph	P-Grid	N/A	$O(\log(n))$ [40]	N/A	Dynamic [40] Static [38]	Replication [40]
Balanced Binary Tree	BATON	3 [43, 44]	$O(\log(n))$ [43, 44]	$O(\log(n))$ [43, 44]	Dynamic [43, 44]	Redundant links [43, 44]
	VBI-Tree					

n: total number of peers; d: d-torus; k: k-ary tree

selectivity. A complete view of how the P2P system behaves in high-dimensional range queries with a wide range of selectivity is not available. However, BATON [43] and VBI-tree [44] are the only two systems that have been proposed with a tree-like structure at the overlay layer. High dimensional range queries (up to 20) with the same selectivity at each dimension are evaluated in these two systems, but without any regard for the size of selectivity.

One drawback that has been commonly shared in experimental results from all these systems is worth mentioning: when the dimensionality of data space is increased without varying selectivity at each dimension, the overall selectivity has been exponentially decreased, and the comparison of range queries presented in this way is not very convincing.

Comparisons of basic distributed operations in existing P2P overlay networks are summarized in Table 5.3. These comparisons are made by grouping P2P systems that have the same underlying architecture. Table 5.3 shows that the routing table size in tree-based structures does not depend on the network size, and their basic distributed operations are all bound by $O(log(n))$. Moreover, it is straightforward to conduct dynamic load balancing operations in a tree-based structure. In comparison, P2P systems built over a ring, d-torus, or skip graphs assume each peer has the same capacity to participate in the system-wide operations; although P Grid proposed a dynamic load balancing scheme in [40], it is considered to be static in [38] However, most of these P2P overlay structures were not built in favor of supporting fault tolerance: P2P systems built over a ring or d torus depend on a background stabilization routine to maintain the correctness of the routing table, but the challenge is when and with what frequency the stabilization routine needs to run [1]. In the flat graph structure, which has been commonly adopted by unstructured P2P networks, replication is so far the best solution for dealing with node's failures; and tree-based structures need to build redundant links in order to survive error-prone environments. Perhaps skip graph is the only structure that claims to be able to support fault tolerance inherently [37], but it is considered as an open problem according to [38].

We conclude that multidimensional range queries are sensitive to underlying topology. Although it is feasible to adapt existing P2P overlay structures that were originally designed for the exact key query, their inherent nature shows no consistency in accommodating data localities that have been well preserved using decomposition schemes employed at a higher layer. This inconsistency not only involves a considerable routing and maintenance cost, but also, at the architectural level, makes a simple, scalable, and reliable P2P solution for multidimensional range queries very difficult, or even impossible.

5.3 DDM IN CLUSTER-BASED NETWORK ENVIRONMENTS

5.3.1 Basic Concepts in DDM

In this section, we introduce some basic concepts that are widely used in the HLA/DDM-based distributed simulations community [46–48, 66]. In order to understand these concepts more thoroughly, we incorporate their different representations as used by two major DDM systems: the region-based system and the grid-based system.

5.3.1.1 Routing Space.

Routing space is a virtual area in which a simulation runs [45, 52, 53]. In the region-based DDM system, *routing space* is represented using a multidimensional coordinate system, while in the grid-based DDM system, it is divided into a certain number of grid cells. Therefore, a target area in *routing space* can be denoted either by a set of extents from the multidimensional coordinate system when the region-based DDM system is employed, or by a set of cell IDs when the grid-based DDM system is employed. We call the first representation of *routing space* the region-based DDM environment and the second representation the grid-based DDM environment. Because our interest lies in the grid-based DDM environment, we consider a two-dimensional, grid-based, square *routing space* in order to simplify our analysis. However, our results can also be extended for more general situations.

5.3.1.2 Objects, Federates, and Federation.

In a distributed environment, a *federate* is considered to be a distributed physical entity or a node in the network. Each *federate* can manage multiple virtual entities, called *objects*. Indeed, each *federate* is the owner of the *objects* it manages. Finally, *federation* is used to represent all of the *federates* involved in a simulation. We thus have three levels: *object* level, *federate* level, and *federation* level. Our main problem is resolved recursively by solving smaller problems at each lower level. When our focus is on the *object* level, we are interested in the behavior of each *object* owned by a *federate;* when our focus moves to the *federate* level, our interest is in the overall behavior of all *objects* owned by a single *federate*; and when our focus is on the *federation* level, we are interested in the overall behavior of all *federates*. Normally, we use f to denote the total number of *federates*, n to denote the total number of *objects*, and n_i to denote the total number of *objects* at a *federate* i.

5.3.1.3 Behavior of Entities

DISTRIBUTION OF OBJECTS. Initially, the *objects* owned by each *federate* are distributed to certain locations inside the *routing space*. In our work, this is the first distribution pattern that needs to be defined explicitly.

MOVEMENT OF OBJECTS. After their initial distribution, the *objects* move in one of four directions (east, west, south, and north) in each *timestep*. An *object* stops at the border of *routing space* until a different direction is chosen. DDM messages are generated because the movement of *objects* leads to the state change of cells in the grid-based DDM environment: thus, choosing the direction of movement for each *object* in each *timestep* is the second distribution pattern that needs to be defined explicitly.

PUBLISHING AND SUBSCRIBING. Publishing occurs when an *object* wants to provide information about itself to a certain area inside *routing space*, while subscribing occurs when an *object* needs to obtain information that is being published by other *object*s within a certain area inside *routing space*. A key fact to note about these two behaviors is that they are always bounded to a certain area. Any information published by an *object* is published into a specific area (publication region) in *routing space*, while any subscribing action is an effort made by an *object* to see if any information can be obtained from a specific area (subscription region). The movement of *object*s in *routing space* results in a considerable amount of publishing/subscribing requests being sent to the new target area, and in unpublishing/unsubscribing requests to the area to which the *object*s have previously published or subscribed.

5.3.1.4   Other Important Concepts

TIMESTEP.   There has been no exact definition of *timestep* thus far. According to our previous work, we can understand it as the distance of movement of an *object* within a constant time, after which a new direction should be chosen for the movement in the next *timestep*. Our study shows that *timestep* is of great value in the grid-based DDM system.

PUBLISHER AND SUBSCRIBER.   At the *object* level, a *publisher* or *subscriber* to an area is an *object* that is currently publishing or subscribing to that area. At the *federate* level, a *publisher* or *subscriber* to an area is a *federate* that has at least one *object* publishing or subscribing to that area. When an *object* has both publishing and behaviors, it can be either the *publisher* of one area or the *subscriber* of another depending on which behavior we are studying. In our analysis, we assume that the *object*s have both the publishing and subscribing behaviors.

PUBLICATION AND SUBSCRIPTION REGION.   A publication or subscription region is an area of limited size to which an *object* is able to publish or subscribe. As we have mentioned previously, in the region-based system, a region is denoted by a set of extents from the multidimensional coordinate system; and in the grid-based system, it is denoted by a set of cell IDs. Because we are interested in the grid-based system, and because an *object* has the symmetric behavior of publishing and subscribing, we use $s \times s$ to represent the size of a publication region or subscription region, where s is the number of cells in each dimension. However, we must also keep in mind that $s \times s$ is the *object* publication region size ($s = s_p$) when we study the publishing behavior, and it becomes the *object* subscription region size ($s = s_s$) when we study subscribing behavior. These two sizes are not necessarily identical.

MAXIMUM PUBLICATION AND SUBSCRIPTION REGION.   An important fact that we have to mention is that, in the grid-based system, an *object* with $s \times s$ publication or subscription region size normally publishes or subscribes to $(s + 1) \times (s + 1)$ cells. The reason for this is that a published or subscribed region tends to fall outside the boundaries of grid cells, and in the grid-based system a region is counted in an integer number of cells. This effect is the main drawback introduced by the grid-based DDM system. In addition, when an *object* is in the border area, it might not be able to publish or subscribe to the desired area, because the publication or subscription region may fall outside the boundary of *routing space*. This is the main reason for publication and subscription loss when we try to scale a simulation.

MATCHING. We have mentioned that publishing and subscribing are two behaviors that are bounded to certain areas inside *routing space*. Thus, whenever there is an intersection between the publication region and the subscription region of different *object*s, the information published by any *object*s in the intersection area becomes visible to any other *object*s that are subscribing to that area, meaning that information bounded to the intersection area needs to be transmitted from the *publisher*s to the *subscriber*s. In this case, the state of the intersection area is called *matching*.

In our study, because *federate*s are the physical entities that are responsible for exchanging information in the network, *matching* is a concept at the federation level [45, 54, 56, 64, 65]. It describes an important state of an area in *routing space*, specifically, that which occurs when different *federate*s are publishing and subscribing to it during the same *timestep*. After *matching* is detected, user level information needs to be transmitted from the *publisher*s to the *subscriber*s.

Therefore, the main functionality of DDM can be summarized as detecting *matching*, distributing *matching* information, and arranging the transmission of information in *matching* from *publisher*s to *subscriber*s. In DDM, this work is done by allocating a MGRP (multicast group) to the area in *matching*, and by sending triggering messages to all *publisher*s and *subscriber*s of that area and asking them to join that MGRP. Correspondingly, a reverse operation should be carried out once the *matching* condition is broken. All of this work is done by exchanging DDM messages within the *federation*.

5.3.1.5 Performance of DDM Implementations.
As a simulation middleware, the performance of the HLA/DDM implementation has a direct effect on the overall simulation performance. Traditionally, we use DDM time, DDM messages, and MGRP allocated as three main parameters to evaluate the performance of a DDM implementation.

DDM time is the total time used by the DDM system in a simulation. It includes the time spent on the registration of publishing and subscribing requests and its reverse process, *matching* detection, MGRP allocation and deallocation, and triggering *publishers/subscribers* to join or leave a MGRP. DDM time is regarded as the total response time of a DDM implementation to its higher-level applications.

DDM messages refers to the messages transmitted by the DDM system. DDM messages are different from the user messages transmitted by higher-level applications in that they are used to fulfill the goal of the DDM of a simulation.

MGRP allocated refers to the multicast groups allocated by the DDM system [45, 56, 57]. These multicast groups are used by higher-level applications for multicasting user messages, and they depend on the *matching* performance of a simulation.

5.3.2 Background

HLA/DDM is one of the most critical issues regarding large-scale distributed simulations [46–48]. Many HLA/DDM approaches have been devised in recent years to address this problem [45, 49–51]. In general, these designs can be classified into five categories: (i) the region-based DDM approach [45, 50]; (ii) the grid-based DDM approaches, examples of which include the fixed grid-based DDM approach [61, 62] and the dynamic grid-based DDM approach [45]; (iii) the agent-based DDM approach [51]; (iv) the hybrid DDM approach [49]; and (v) the sort-based DDM approach [63], an example of which is the grid-filtered region-based DDM approach [50].

In practice, these implementations demonstrate different focuses regarding the DDM performance issue. In the region-based DDM approach, a *region* in *routing space* is represented by a set of extents. Exact *matching* (sending the exact data required and only upon request) can be detected by computing these sets of extents of regions published or subscribed exhaustively. However, computing *matching* has to be performed by a central coordinator. In the grid-based DDM approach, *routing space* is divided into a certain number of grid cells, known as *grid*. The ownership of grid cells is distributed to each *federate*, and an additional registration process has to be performed because the *publisher/subscriber* may not be the owner of the cell. In the grid-based system, computing *matching* is performed by the owner of cells, and *matching* is detected based on each unit of the cell. Therefore, the central coordinator is not necessary. However, exact *matching* cannot be achieved.

If we compare these two approaches, the region-based approach achieves exact *matching* with considerable computation and communication overhead at the central coordinator, whereas the grid-based DDM approach sacrifices accuracy and distributes load in order to reduce processing time and communicational load. In order to compensate for the loss of *matching accuracy* introduced by the grid-based system, the agent-based and grid-filtered region-based approaches have been proposed. In these two approaches, a filtering mechanism has been used to filter out unnecessary data transmitted at the sender side and a higher *matching accuracy* can be obtained when compared to the grid-based DDM system, with a lower computation and communication overhead than the region-based DDM system [50, 51, 58, 59].

5.3.3 Data Distribution Management Schemes

Matching detection is the main computing problem in finding a pair of senders and receivers in the same area in a DDM system, while MGRP allocation is the main resource management problem. Existing DDM systems have solved these problems very differently depending on their various performance concerns. In this section, we will give a quick review of these DDM systems based on a comparison of their solutions to these two problems.

5.3.3.1 Region-Based DDM Approach. In the region-based DDM approach, a region in *routing space* is represented by a set of extents using the multidimensional coordinate system, *matching* is computed exhaustively, and the exact *matching* region can be found. However, since no single *federate* has a complete knowledge of how many other *federate*s are publishing or subscribing to a target region, a central coordinator must be chosen to perform the *matching* detection. Therefore, whenever there is a change to the publication or subscription regions in a *federate*, a notification must be sent to the central coordinator. Because a simulation will normally have a large number of simulated *object*s, and the movement of each *object* can cause frequent changes in the publication and subscription regions, a considerable amount of communicational load towards the central coordinator will be added to the network. In addition, an extremely large amount of computation work will be loaded onto the central coordinator.

One advantage of the region-based DDM approach is that the exact *matching* region can be found. Therefore, the MGRP is allocated whenever it is necessary, and the *publisher* multicasts the exact information that is required by the *subscribers*.

5.3.3.2 Grid-Based DDM Approaches.

In the grid-based DDM system, *routing space* is divided into a certain number of grid cells, and publication and subscription regions are represented by a set of cell IDs. In place of exhaustive computing, *matching* is found by checking a pair of *publishers* and *subscribers* within each cell. However, since a region that is represented using the multidimensional coordinate system tends to fall outside the boundaries of grid cells, a region represented using a set of grid cells normally appears larger than its region-based representation. Depending on what kind of MGRP allocation strategy is used, the grid-based DDM approaches have two different implementations.

FIXED GRID-BASED DDM APPROACH. The fixed grid-based approach is a simple solution for DDM. In this approach, *matching* detection is not implemented, and MGRPs are preallocated and bounded to each grid cell in the initialization phase of the simulation. All *federate*s have a complete knowledge of the MGRP information of each cell. Once a *publisher* is interested in a cell, it joins its MGRP and starts publishing regardless of whether there is a *subscriber*; correspondingly, once a *subscriber* arrives at a cell, it joins the cell's MGRP and starts listening regardless of whether there is a *publisher*.

Obviously, the fixed grid-based approach is not as feasible in a real simulation because it generates too many aimless messages and consumes a large amount of resources. Right after the work of this fixed approach was completed, an improved dynamic approach with *a matching* detection mechanism was carried out. This approach is based on distributing the ownership of grid cells to each *federate* and implementing a triggering mechanism for joining the MGRP.

DYNAMIC GRID-BASED DDM APPROACH. Two new mechanisms are employed by the dynamic grid-based DDM approach:

Cell's ownership distribution mechanism. In the dynamic grid-based DDM approach, grid cells have their ownerships uniformly distributed to each *federate*. Any publishing or subscribing request to a target cell needs to be registered to the owner of the cell. Therefore, each *federate* has complete knowledge of all publishing and subscribing activities that occur in the cells it owns. Depending on the cell's ownership distribution pattern, *matching* computing can be distributed evenly or with some other pattern within the *federation*, thus eliminating the need for a central coordinator.

Triggering mechanism. Since each *federate* has only part of the *matching* information *federation*-wide, once the *matching* of a cell has been detected, the owner is responsible for allocating a MGRP for this cell. The triggering mechanism is used to notify all *publishers* and *subscribers* to join the MGRP and prepare to multicast user messages.

By employing the cell's ownership distribution mechanism, the dynamic grid-based DDM scheme distributes the work of *matching* computing to each *federate*. All publishing and subscribing activities and their reverse operations need not only to be processed locally at each *federate*, but also to be registered with the owner of the target cell. Thus, each *federate* performs part of the *matching* detection *federation*-wide. When the *matching* of a cell is detected by its owner, the MGRP is dynamically allocated and the triggering mechanism is used to trigger all *publishers* and *subscribers* to join this MGRP. In response to the triggering message, *publishers* and *subscribers* register themselves to the MGRP at the owner and begin multicasting user messages.

The advantages of the dynamic grid-based DDM approach are obvious: the resource allocation is more efficient because the multicast groups are dynamically allocated when necessary; the communicational overhead is distributed within the *federation* because the cells' ownership has been distributed to each *federate* and the central coordinator has been removed; the computation overhead has been reduced because exhaustive *matching* computing is not necessary in the grid based system; and the total workload is distributed to each *federate*.

The weakness of this approach is the reduced accuracy introduced by the grid-based DDM system. As we mentioned in the beginning of this section, the publication/subscription region normally appears larger when using grid-based representation than when using region-based representation. Specifically, this means that the *publisher* may send more user messages than are actually required by the *subscribers*. Therefore, the performance gain of the dynamic grid-based DDM approach is obtained with a trade-off in additional traffic at the user level.

5.3.3.3 *Other DDM Schemes.*
As we have seen, the region-based DDM approach achieves exact *matching* with considerable computation and communication overhead, while the dynamic grid-based DDM approach sacrifices accuracy to obtain a gain in DDM performance. However, several other schemes, such as the grid-filtered region-based DDM approach and the agent-based DDM approach, have been devised to balance this trade-off. The main idea is to filter user messages at the sender side to avoid transmitting unnecessary data to the *subscribers*.

REFERENCES

[1] K. Lua, J. Crowcroft, M. Pias, R. Sharma, and S. Lim, "A survey and comparison of peer-to-peer overlay network schemes." *Communications Surveys and Tutorials*, IEEE (2005), pp. 72–93.

[2] S. Ratnasamy, et al., "A scalable content addressable network." *Proc. ACM SIGCOMM*, 2001, Vol. 31, No. 4. (Oct. 2001) pp. 161–172.

[3] I. Stoica, R. Morris et al., *"Chord: A Scalable Peer-to-Peer Lookup Protocol for Internet Applications."* IEEE/ACM Trans. Vol. 11, No. (Feb, 2003), pp. 17–32.

[4] A. Rowstron and P. Druschel, "Pastry: Scalable, distributed object location and routing for large-scale peer-to-peer systems." In IFIP/ACM Int. Conf. on Distributed Systems Platforms (Middleware) (Nov. 2001), pp. 329–350.

[5] B.Y. Zhao, et al., "Tapestry: A resilient global-scale overlay for service deployment." *IEEE Journal on Selected Areas in Communications* (IEEE JSAC), Vol. 22, No. 1. (2004), pp. 41–53.

[6] P. Maymounkov and D. Mazieres, "Kademlia: A peer-to-peer information system based on the XOR Metric." *Proc. IPTPS*, Cambridge, MA, Feb. 2002, pp. 53–65.

[7] D. Malkhi, M. Naor, and D. Ratajczak, "Viceroy: A scalable and dynamic emulation of the butterfly." *Proc. ACM PODC 2002*, Monterey, CA, July 2002, pp. 183–92.

[8] Gnutella Development Forum, http://groups.yahoo.com/group/the gdf/files/ (accessed Jan. 2010).

[9] Gnutella Ultrapeers, http://rfcgnutella.sourceforge.net/Proposals/Ultrapeer/ (accessed Jan. 2010).

[10] I. Clarke et al., "Freenet: A distributed anonymous information storage and retrieval system." *Lecture Notes in Computer Science*, Vol. 2009 (2001), pp. 46–66.

[11] Fasttrack P2P Technology, http://developer.berlios.de/projects/gift-fasttrack/ (accessed Jan. 2010).

[12] Fasttrack from Wiki, http://en.wikipedia.org/wiki/Kazaa (accessed Jan. 2010).

[13] Kazaa Media Desktop, http://www.kazaa.com/ (accessed Jan. 2010).

[14] Kazaa from Wiki, http://en.wikipedia.org/wiki/Fasttrack/ (accessed Jan. 2010).

[15] BitTorrent, http://www.bittorrent.com/ (accessed Jan. 2010).

[16] BitTorrent specification, http://www.bittorrent.org/ (accessed Jan. 2010).

[17] Overnet File-sharing Network, http: //www.overnet.com/ (accessed Jan. 2010).

[18] Overnet from Wiki, http://en.wikipedia.org/wiki/Overnet/ (accessed Jan. 2010).

[19] eDonkey200, http://www.edonkey2000.com/ (accessed Jan. 2010).

[20] eDonkey2000 from Wiki, http://en.wikipedia.org/wiki/EDonkey_network/ (accessed Jan. 2010).

[21] R.A. Finkel and J.L. Bentley, "Quad trees: A data structure for retrieval on composite keys." *Acta Informatica*, Vol. 4, No. 1. (1 Mar. 1974), pp. 1–9.

[22] H. Samet, "The quadtree and related hierarchical data structures." *ACM Computing Surveys* (CSUR), Vol. 16, No. 2 (Jun. 1984), pp. 187–260.

[23] J.L. Bentley, "Multidimensional binary search trees used for associative searching." *Commun. ACM*, Vol. 18, No. 9. (Sep. 1975), pp. 509–517.

[24] G.M. Morton, *A Computer Oriented Geodetic Data Base and a New Technique in File Sequencing*. Technical report, Ottawa, Canada, IBM Ltd. 1966.

[25] J.A. Orenstein and T.H. Merrett, "A class of data structures for associative searching." In PODS '84: Proc. of the 3rd ACM SIGACT-SIGMOD Symposium on Principles of Database Systems (1984), pp. 181–190.

[26] H.V. Jagadish, "Linear clustering of objects with multiple attributes." In SIGMOD '90: Proc. of the 1990 ACM SIGMOD Int. Conf. on Management of Data (1990), Vol. 19, No. 2, pp. 332–342.

[27] H.V. Jagadish, "Linear clustering of objects with multiple attributes." In SIGMOD '90: Proc. of the 1990 ACM SIGMOD Int. Conf. on Management of Data (1990), Vol. 19, No. 2, pp. 332–342.

[28] http://www.itl.nist.gov/div897/sqg/dads/HTML/kdtree.html (accessed Jan. 2010).

[29] D.R. Karger et al. "Consistent hashing and random trees: Distributed caching protocols for relieving hot spots on the world wide web." In ACM Symposium on Theory of Computing (1997), pp. 654–663.

[30] F. Dabek et al., "Towards a common API for structured peer-to-peer overlays." *Peer-to-Peer Systems II* (IPTPS 2003), Berkeley, CA, Feb. 2003, pp. 33–44.

[31] B. Karp et al., "Spurring adoption of DHTs with OpenHash, a public DHT service." *Peer-to-Peer Systems III* (IPTPS 2004), Berkeley, CA, Feb. 2004, pp. 195–205.

[32] P. Ganesan et al., "One Torus to rule them all: Multi-dimensional queries in P2P systems." In WebDB '04: Proc. of the 7th Int. Workshop on the Web and Databases (2004), pp. 19–24.

[33] Y. Shu et al., "Supporting multi-dimensional range queries in peer-to-peer systems." In 5th IEEE Int. Conf. on Peer-to-Peer Computing, 2005. P2P 2005, pp. 173–180.

[34] C. Zhang et al., *SkipIndex: Towards a Scalable Peer-to-Peer Index Service for High Dimensional Data.* Vol. TR-703 04, Princeton University, 2004.

[35] C. Schmidt et al., "Flexible information discovery in decentralized distributed systems." Proc. of the 12th IEEE Int. Symposium on High Performance Distributed Computing (HPDC'03) pp. 226–235.

[36] T. Schütt et al., "A structured overlay for multi-dimensional range queries." Euro-Par 2007, Parallel Processing (2007), pp. 503–513.

[37] J. Aspnes and G. Shah, "Skip graphs." In Proc. SODA, 2003., pp. 384–393.

[38] J. Risson and T. Moors, "Survey of research towards robust peer-to-peer networks: Search methods." *Computer Networks*, Vol. 50, No. 17, (Dec 2006), pp. 3485–3521.

[39] N. Harvey, M.B. Jones, S. Saroiu, M. Theimer, and A. Wolman, "SkipNet: A scalable overlay network with practical locality properties." In Proceedings of the 4th USENIX Symposium on Internet Technologies and Systems USITS'03, Mar. 2003, pp. 9–23.

[40] K. Aberer, P. Cudre-Mauroux, A. Datta, Z. Despotovic, M. Hauswirth, M. Punceva, and R. Schmidt, "P-Grid: A self-organizing structured P2P system." *ACM SIGMOD Record*, 2003, Vol. 32, No. 3, pp. 29–33.

[41] A. Bharambe, M. Agrawal, and S. Seshan, "Mercury: Supporting scalable multi-attribute range queries." *SIGCOMM*, Vol. 34, 2004, pp. 353–366.

[42] M. Cai, M. Frank, J. Chen, and P. Szekely, "MAAN: A multiattribute addressable network for grid information services." In Proceedings of the 4th International Workshop on Grid Computing, Nov. 2003, pp. 184–191.

[43] H.V. Jagadish, B.C. Ooi, and Q.H. Vu, "BATON: A balanced tree structure for peer-to-peer networks." Proceedings of the 31st International Conference on Very Large Data Bases, 2005, pp. 661–672.

[44] H.V. Jagadish, B.C. Ooi, Q.H. Vu, R. Zhang, and A.Y. Zhou, "VBI-Tree: A peer-to-peer framework for supporting multi-dimensional indexing schemes." The 22nd IEEE International Conference on Data Engineering (ICDE), 2006, pp. 34–44.

[45] A. Boukerche and A. Roy. "Dynamic grid-based approach to data distribution management." *JPDC*, 2002, Vol. 62, No. 3, pp. 366–392.

[46] DMSO. *Data Distribution and Management Design Document V. 0.2.* Department of Defense, Washington, DC, Dec. 1996.

[47] DMSO. *High Level Architecture Interface Specification, V. 1.3.* Department of Defense, Washington, DC, 1998. http://hla.dmso.mil.

[48] J.S. Dahmann and K.L. Morse. "High level architecture for simulation: An update." In 3rd IEEE DS-RT, 1998, pp. 32–40.

[49] G. Tan, Y. Zhang, and R. Ayani. "A hybrid approach to data distribution management." In IEEE (DS-RT), 2000, p. 55.

[50] A. Boukerche, N.J. McGraw, C. Dzermajko, and K. Lu. "Grid-filtered region-based data distribution management in large-scale distributed simulation systems." In 38th ANSS'05 Proceeding 1080-241X/05.

[51] G. Tan, L. Xu, F. Moradi, and Y. Zhang. "An agent-based DDM filtering mechanism." In 8th MASCOTS, 2000, p. 374.

[52] R. Fujimoto, T. Mclean, K. Perumalla, and I. Tacic. "Design of high performance RTI software." In IEEE DS-RT, 2000, pp. 89–96.

[53] M. Moreau. *Documentation for the RTI.* George Mason Univ., 1997.

[54] K. Morse. *Interest Management in Large Scale Distributed Simulations.* Technical Report, Univ. of California, TR 96–27, 1996.

[55] M. Macedonia, M. Zyda, D. Pratt, and P. Barham. "Exploiting reality with multi-cast groups: A network architecture for large scale virtual environments." In Virtual Reality Annual International Symposium, 1995, p. 2.

[56] H. Abrams, K. Watsen, and M. Zyda. *"Three-tiered interest management for large-scale virtual environments."* ACM Symposium on Virtual Reality Software and Technology, 1998, pp. 125–129.

[57] A. Berrached. "Alternative approaches to multicast group allocation in HLA data distribution management." In SIW, 98S-SIW-184, March 1998.

[58] A. Boukerche. "Time management in parallel simulation." In: B. Rajkumar Ed., *High Performance Cluster Computing.* Prentice Hall, Englewood Cliffs, NJ, 1999, Vol. 12, pp. 375–394.

[59] J.O. Calvin and D.J. Van Hook. "Agents: An architectural construct to support distributed simulation." In 11th Workshop on Standards for the Interoperability of DIS, 94-11-142, Sept. 1994.

[60] S.J. Rak, "Evaluation of grid based relevance filtering for multicast group assignment." 96-14-106. In 14th DIS, 1996.

[61] D.J. Van Hook, S.J. Rak, and J.O. Calvin. "Approaches to RTI implementation of HLA data distribution management services." 96-14-084, In 15th DIS, 1996.

[62] F. Weiland. "An empirical study of data partitioning and replication in parallel simulation." In Proceedings of the 5th Distributed Memory Computing Conference, Vol. II, 1990, pp. 915–921.

[63] K. Pan, S.J. Turner, W. Cai, and Z. Li. "An efficient sort-based DDM matching algorithm for HLA applications with a large spatial environment." In Proceedings of the

21st International Workshop on Principles of Advanced and Distributed Simulation, 2007, pp. 70–82.

[64] R. Minson and G. Theodoropoulos. "Adaptive interest management via push-pull algorithms." In Proceedings of the 10th IEEE International Symposium on Distributed Simulation and Real-Time Applications, 2006, pp. 119–126.

[65] E.S. Liu, M.K. Yip, and G. Yu. "Scalable interest management for multidimensional routing space." In Proceedings of the ACM on Virtual Reality Software and Technology, 2005, pp. 82–85.

[66] A. Boukerche, C. Dzermajko, and K. Lu. "Alternative approaches to multicast group management in large-scale distributed interactive simulation systems." *Future Generation Comp. Syst.* (2006), Vol. 22, No. 7, pp. 755–763.

6

MIDDLEWARE SUPPORT FOR CONTEXT HANDLING AND INTEGRATION IN UBIQUITOUS COMPUTING

Frederico Lopes, Paulo F. Pires, Flávia C. Delicato, Thais Batista, and Luci Pirmez

CONTENTS

Large Scale Network-Centric Distributed Systems, First Edition. Edited by Hamid Sarbazi-Azad and Albert Y. Zomaya.
© 2014 John Wiley & Sons, Inc. Published 2014 by John Wiley & Sons, Inc.

6.1 INTRODUCTION

The term *ubiquitous computing* (UC) denotes a recent, post-desktop, model of human–computer interaction in which information processing has been thoroughly integrated into everyday objects and activities in a way that the computational elements become invisible to the user.[1] Ubiquitous computing [1] encompasses sensor-instrumented environments, which are often endowed with wireless network interfaces, in which devices, software agents, and services are integrated in a seamless and transparent way and cooperate to meet high-level goals of human users. Ubiquitous environments may range from small-scale systems, comprising only applications and devices involved in a personal area network (PAN), to large-scale systems, encompassing physically distributed devices and applications and heterogeneous networks, based on different communication protocols and standards. Because UC always aims at satisfying user needs, it is typically a *user-centric* system. Moreover, since all the computational elements (devices, applications, etc.) must communicate and collaborate with each other in order to reach this goal, communication plays a key role in such environments. Therefore, ubiquitous systems are essentially *network-centric* systems as well.

Applications for UC hold specific features and requirements that pose several challenges for their development and execution. One key feature is the intrinsically high heterogeneity of ubiquitous environments, since typically a multitude of devices, sensors, and networks are integrated and work together to satisfy the user goals. Another feature is the dynamicity of the execution context. Devices can be mobile, frequently moving in and around the environment; wireless connectivity is subject to disruptions and oscillations in the strength of the transmitted signal; physical parameters such as temperature and light frequently change; the user activities, mood, and needs are also variable, and so on. Applications that run in ubiquitous environments must cope with their dynamic features and preferably exploit such characteristics to provide services of better quality and added value to the final user. Therefore, two important requirements of ubiquitous applications are (i) the capability of being aware of the surrounding context (*context awareness*) and (ii) the inherent support to adapt their behavior according to the changes in this context (*adaptation*).

Context is "any information that can be used to characterize the situation of an entity (person, local or object) that is considered important for the interaction between

---

[1]According to Mark Weiser, the author who first envisioned the ubiquitous computing paradigm, "the most profound technologies are those that disappear."

the user and the application, including the own user and the application itself" [2]. Context awareness refers to the ability of an application to perceive characteristics of its surrounding environment, to detect changes in those characteristics, and to trigger adaptations (whenever needed) according to different execution conditions. There are several challenges to be circumvented in order to suitably handle value-added information to ubiquitous applications, thus enabling them to dynamically and efficiently adapt to different execution contexts. The main challenges to be addressed are (i) the high degree of heterogeneity and distribution of the context sources, (ii) the different abstraction levels in which contextual data may be represented, and (iii) the inherent diversity and ambiguity in representing contextual data.

It is neither efficient nor desirable that such challenges are addressed at the level of the application business logic, since this approach tends to be tiresome, repetitive, and error prone, and it hinders the application development. Instead, a more promising approach is to delegate functionalities for handling contextual information to underlying infrastructures such as platforms or *middleware for context provision* [3–8]. Therefore, ubiquitous computing environments strongly rely on the use of middleware to tackle all their requirements and features.

Several context provision middleware are currently available, each one addressing different types of context and adopting different models for handling and representing contextual information (known as context model). Each middleware is often more suitable to meet different requirements of ubiquitous applications. For instance, some middleware platforms [4] focus on handling geographic location data (addressing mobility issues and location awareness requirement), while others focus on managing network properties and others are more concerned with user activities and preferences (focusing on user profile adaptations [5, 8]). Moreover, several existing platforms for context provision are only suitable to support simple applications, as, for instance supporting applications based on sensors that trigger alarms or systems that identify a person and load their personal preferences.

More complex, context-aware ubiquitous applications use context information provided by distinct context provision middleware. In general, those specific middleware do not interact to each other, imposing a new challenge to the application developers. They must choose between either building applications tied to a specific context middleware or knowing the details of more than one platform to programmatically handle the integration among them. The second option raises complex environments composed of several infrastructures, in order to build a more complete perception of the ubiquitous environment. In these scenarios, the application developer is unburdened of dealing with the heterogeneity of context sources but instead must deal with the middleware heterogeneity. In this case, developers will have to deal with a wide range of service discovery mechanisms, programming models, context models, APIs, and protocols. This feature configures a conceptual paradox once UC considers environments in which applications are able to access context information provided by distributed underlying infrastructures in a transparent and seamless way. Therefore, UC environments pose a new challenge, namely the *integration of context provision middleware*, in order to allow the use of several (contextual and traditional) services, provided by the underlying platforms, that could be composed to reach a high level user goal.

In this chapter, we first introduce some background concepts on UC and then present the state-of-the-art for the field of middleware for UC. Then, the requirement of the integration of UC middleware is addressed and an existent solution that addresses this requirement is described—the OpenCOPI (*Open COntext Platform Integration*) platform [9, 10]. OpenCOPI is a platform for UC that integrates context provision services and provides a unified environment that supports an easy context-aware application development. OpenCOPI allows the integration of services provided by distinct service sources, from services offered by simple ad-hoc sources to more complex services, as context provision middleware platforms. OpenCOPI design is based on Service-Oriented Architecture (SOA [11]) and its implementation is based on web services technologies, using open XML-based standards and languages. The use of standardized context models and mechanisms are important to provide a unified environment in which applications only need to deal with OpenCOPI models, making the applications independent on the distribution environment and on the underlying context information environment. In short, OpenCOPI provides (i) an automatic service composition, (ii) a standardized context and communication model, and (iii) a fault tolerance mechanism that handles service failures.

Another important feature of OpenCOPI is the use of semantic workflows. A workflow describes the order of a set of goals to be performed by several services to complete a given procedure [12]. This technology was chosen because it is useful in environments in which many services provided by different sources are available, where some of such services have similar functionality. The composition model adopted by OpenCOPI is based both on service functionality and on service metadata, enabling a better choice between available services with similar functionality.

This chapter is organized as follows. Section 6.2 presents some background on ubiquitous computing. Section 6.3 discusses the requirements of middleware for ubiquitous computing and illustrates existing UC middleware. Section 6.4 presents a new integration platform for ubiquitous computing. Finally, Section 6.5 presents our final remarks.

6.2 UBIQUITOUS COMPUTING

This section gives an overview of the ubiquitous computing paradigm, including its concepts, and describes the main requirements of ubiquitous applications.

Ubiquitous computing is a paradigm in which computing has been transparently and deeply integrated into users' everyday objects and activities. One major feature of ubiquitous systems is the dynamicity of the environment in the presence of multiple and heterogeneous devices. According to [13], "Ubiquitous computing represents a powerful shift in computation, where people live, work and play in a seamless computer-enabled environment, interleaved into the world. Ubiquitous computing postulates a world where people are surrounded by computing devices and a computing infrastructure that supports us in everything we do."

In [13], the author mentions the three core requirements of Weiser's vision of ubiquitous computing: (i) computers need to be networked, distributed, and transparently accessible; (ii) the human-computer interaction needs to be hidden; and (iii) the systems need to be context-aware in order to optimize their operations in the dynamic environment they operate. Moreover, the author considers that there are two additional core requirements: (iv) computers should operate autonomously; and (v) computers should handle a multiplicity of dynamic actions. Thus, the purpose of ubiquitous computing is to facilitate the interaction between users and interconnected computers in a way that such users do not perceive they are inputting commands in computers spread around in the environment. Furthermore, ubiquitous systems capture information about the environment to dynamically and automatically adapt themselves to perform the appropriate actions

Many of the ubiquitous computing requirements are described in the literature. Following, we present a compilation of reported requirements that we consider the most significant ones to be provided by UC middleware platforms:

- *Context-awareness:* Ubiquitous computing software is integrated with its environment. It must draw on context information to provide an adapted behavior and tailored functionality [14]. Thus, this feature allows the system to know its surrounding environment (that includes personal details about the user, details about locations, environment, objects, computational entities, etc.) and automatically self-adjust according to the context without the user being aware of it.

- *Interoperability:* Ubiquitous environments are composed of heterogeneous devices that offer different capabilities and use different technologies. Considering this argument, ubiquitous systems must be able to operate across different ubiquitous environments, in which heterogeneous devices are involved, allowing seamless integrations of these devices.

- *Coordination:* Ubiquitous environments are highly dynamic. Interactions (synchronous or asynchronous) among various computational entities can be realized over time. These interactions need to be realized in a coordinated way.

- *Transparency:* According to the principle of transparency, each system acts as a single virtual system even though it is physically distributed, enabling cross-platform interoperability across a set of hardware resources [13]. In such systems, the access to specific computational entities is hidden, and the services are transparently embedded and integrated into the environment.

- *Mobility:* Users, devices, and services may move in or around the environment. Thus, it is necessary to provide service discovery mechanisms to learn about all services available in a given moment in the vicinity of the user.

- *Adaptation and fault tolerance:* Considering the aforementioned high dynamicity of ubiquitous computing, ubiquitous systems must actively adapt their configuration in runtime and according to the changes. These systems must consider not only context changes but also faults in the available services, network, and devices and adapt to these failures to avoid a system crash.

- *Autonomy:* According to this feature, ubiquitous systems should able to control their own actions, that is, they should be self-governing. This characteristic reduces the complexity of managing the system from the user point of view. Autonomic systems can be goal-oriented so that users only need to interact by specifying high-level tasks to the system. So, the complexity from the user's standpoint is reduced since the systems themselves will automatically configure and reconfigure themselves in order to achieve continuous and reliable execution (but with minimal user intervention).

Many middleware platforms are emerging, based on in the literature, to provide (some of) the aforementioned requirements. Such platforms are described in the next section.

6.3   MIDDLEWARE FOR UBIQUITOUS COMPUTING

According to Emmerich et al. [15], the term *middleware* was (probably) coined in 1968 by Alex d'Agapeyeff at the NATO Conference on Software Engineering to refer to software that sits between the application programs and the operational system and is used to adapt generic file system functionality to specific application functionality needs. More recently, with the widespread use of client-server architectures, middleware has gained a network-centric meaning and is used to define a wide range of infrastructure software, such as web services, distributed transaction processing, message oriented, distributed object, and remote procedure call systems. In this context, middleware can be generically viewed as a reusable, customizable, and expandable set of functions, program abstractions, and services that are usually needed by applications in a networked environment. According to [16], "Using middleware has many benefits, most of which derive from abstraction: hiding low-level details, providing language and platform independence, reusing expertise and possibly code, easing application evolution. As a consequence, one may expect a reduction in application development cost and time, better quality (since most efforts may be devoted to application specific problems), and better portability and interoperability" [16]. Thus, the adoption of middleware platforms makes applications simpler to define since these platforms can handle the complexity of dealing with the heterogeneous services available in the environment.

In the same way that middleware is used in traditional distributed system to support the development of such systems, middleware can be used in ubiquitous computing to additionally provide context awareness for ubiquitous applications. Thus, middleware for ubiquitous systems (context provision middleware) must support context acquisition from different context sources (sensors, devices, etc.), infer higher-level context information by reasoning machines from low-level sensed context information, share and deliver context information between different applications, and self-adjust applications according to the context, in addition to other context-related functionalities.

The next section presents current approaches and techniques used by UC middleware to support the requirements of ubiquitous applications. Some middleware platforms that have been recently reported in the literature are also described.

6.3.1   Approaches and Techniques

To support context-awareness, middleware platforms for ubiquitous computing should (i) provide a context model and (ii) supply a mechanism for context management. The context model is important because it defines how to represent, manipulate, and exchange context information in a machine processable way. There are several approaches to representing context information, ranging from the simplest one (a key-value-based model) to more complex and expressive approaches such as ontology-based models. In the latter approach, the context information is represented through concepts and relationships between concepts. Ontologies are extensible, have high expressiveness, and allow the application of reasoning techniques to context inference. Ontologies avoid ambiguity. This characteristic makes them the best option to represent context information provided by heterogeneous services. More details about context model approaches can be found in [17].

SOA [11] has been considered as a promising paradigm to help meet the requirements of interoperability, mobility, and transparency. SOA is independent of any specific technology and it focuses on defining services as autonomous and heterogeneous computational components running on different platforms [13]. SOA specifies standardized communications protocols and provides a service description language to specify discoverable services offered by service providers and consumed by service consumers. SOA only defines the fundaments of service orientation; therefore, it is necessary to use a technology that implements SOA fundamentals. The most widely disseminated technology for service implementation is web services. In this technology, the software units are identified by a *Uniform Resource Identifier* (URI), in which the interfaces are described, published, and discovered through a contract (of use) and interaction with other systems uses messages transported by Internet protocols [18]. Web service technology is based on open standards to describe and discover services and to define the communication protocol. Together, these standards allow web services to be implemented and accessed through (virtually) any platform and programming language.

To achieve coordination and adaptation, a UC middleware platform can employ a workflow-based composition processes [12]. Workflows describe the order of a set of tasks performed by several services to complete a given procedure. They are useful in environments in which several services provided by different sources are available, where some of such services have similar functionality. In workflow-based approaches, users only specify which tasks they require but not which services should be used nor where the resources are. Moreover, workflows can handle faults at runtime according to resource availability, service quality, and context changes. They can specify ways of undoing previous operations and returning to a legal state from when a another path can be taken to reach the goal. This is essential in ubiquitous environments, which are characterized by uncertainties and faults, and also may offer multiple ways of reaching the same goal [19]. The workflow approach can be combined with web services technology in order to create new value-added services through *web services compositions*. Web service composition consists of synthesizing new *composite services* from atomic services to achieve an application goal. A composite service can be defined as a service whose implementation calls other services (as opposed to an atomic service, whose implementation is self-contained). Therefore, a composite service acts as both a service provider (from the aspect of the composite service) and as a service consumer of its child services [20]. Service composition increases service reuse, provides aggregated functionality, and promotes a higher level of abstraction.

The use of the web semantic approach combined with workflows and web services can help UC middleware platforms to provide adaptation and autonomy as well to improve transparency. Because web services standards do not allow the semantic description of services, the power of automation of service discovery, invocation, and composition is limited with such an approach. The combination of web services and workflows with semantic web technologies overcomes this limitation because it enables leveraging the web service description with semantic descriptions [21]. The use of semantic descriptions allows the employment of inference machines to automatically discover and compose services through service inputs, outputs, preconditions, and effects. Thus, the application developer does not need to directly choose the services needed by the application at development time, allowing greater flexibility and promoting on-demand service access.

Recently, the requirements of interoperability and transparency were shifted from the service level to the platform level. The current trend in ubiquitous computing is the emergence of complex and value-added context-aware applications in which middleware platforms based on heterogeneous networks, interfaces, and services technologies are used to provide user-centric applications. The big issue is that most complex pervasive platforms are composed of technology-dependent islands, that is, domain-specific platforms that employ heterogeneous protocols for discovering, communication and context representation. This aspect violates the transparency requirement and increases the complexity of the application development. For example, grid applications, mobile ad hoc networks, legacy systems, and sensor networks all use their own protocols such that they cannot interoperate with each other [22]. Achieving interoperability between independently developed systems has been one of the fundamental goals of middleware researchers and developers to allow the development of complex ubiquitous applications. A possible solution for this problem is to provide one-to-one bridges for mapping the middleware platforms. Another solution is to provide a new layer of middleware platform to support transparent interoperability between a myriad of underlying middleware for UC.

6.3.2 Existing Middleware Platforms

This section describes examples of existing context-provision middleware platforms starting with those providing only context-awareness followed by platforms that provide other requirements, as presented in Section 6.3.1.

Context Toolkit (CT) [3] is a framework for building and rapid prototyping context-aware services. It adopts a context model based on key value, in which the key-value pairs are used to describe the capabilities of a service. This context model does not include features for context reasoning and context sharing. CT provides a library with concrete components used to build the context-aware systems, allowing the separation of the context acquisition, representation, and interpretation processes. The acquisition of context information is performed by *widgets*, which are the architectural components of CT responsible for abstracting the data acquisition by sensors, thus constituting reusable components for sensing the context information. The context information acquired by many widgets is aggregated by *aggregator* components before being delivered to applications. The *interpreters* are components responsible for transforming low-level context information into high-level context information. However, the power of interpreters is limited by the simplicity of the CT context model. CT's *services* components are actuators' abstraction to execute actions in the environment (e.g., turn on a lamp, send a message, etc.).

MiddleWhere [4] is a middleware that provides location data and incorporates multiple location sensing techniques (e.g., GPS, fingerprint, RF badges, desktop login, etc.). Because each technique provides location information in different formats and different quality (e.g., resolution, confidence, freshness), this middleware implements an algorithm to fuse the location-data sensed by various techniques to derive the spatial probability distribution of people or devices they carry. MiddleWhere stores the location information in a spatial database and maintains the physical layout model of the environment. Its context model is hierarchical and supports a limited level of context reasoning. However, it allows deduction of various spatial relationships between objects (mobile and static objects) and their physical environment. Some examples of spatial relationships that are deduced by MiddleWhere include "proximity to another object, collocation of two objects in a certain region, containment of an object within a region and so on" [4]. MiddleWhere uses CORBA to communicate with applications and location services. Each location service abstracts a sensing technique and has an adaptor component for mapping the location information acquired by sensors into a common representation. Moreover, such adaptors can be programmed to trigger events to the MiddleWhere system.

MUSIC [5] is a plug-in-based context provision middleware platform that offers a dynamic environment for creation of context-aware applications. MUSIC is built following OSGi [23] and its services are described through Java interfaces. In this platform each plug-in provides some context information (as services), which can be shared with multiple applications. It provides an ontology context model and a methodology for realizing the plug-in's selection and composition, easing the application development. In MUSIC middleware, applications are modeled as a component framework and application functionalities can be dynamically configured conforming component implementations. The MUSIC's composition mechanism uses a planning algorithm based on the utility function determined by the applications' required properties and current execution state. Such algorithm uses QoS values to directly negotiate with service provider during planning. In MUSIC, the context changes can start the adaptation process, evaluating alternative configurations to select the best configuration for the current context to adapt the application.

ESCAPE [6] is a peer-to-peer and web service–based context provision framework specifically for emergency situations, such as disasters, in ubiquitous environments. The ESCAPE context model is XML based. Its architecture is divided into mobile devices (front-end) and high-end systems (back-end). The front-end side consists of an ad hoc network and it includes services for context sensing and sharing, which are based on web services. The back-end infrastructure includes web services for storing and sharing context information among different front-ends. In case of disaster events, many teams can cooperatively operate in both sides (front-end and back-end).

According to the authors, FollowMe middleware [7] is the first platform to adopt semantic workflow composition in context-aware systems. This characteristic allows one to discover and compose semantic web services through inference machines. FollowMe consists of a runtime environment and a software library to context-aware applications.

FollowMe uses OSGi as its lower platform to manage services in a more flexible and secure way and adopts an ontological context model based on OWL. The business process of FollowMe applications is described using high-level declarative specifications rather than explicit programming. This approach can simplify and speed up the development of complex applications. FollowMe workflows are built through a combination of elements, in which such elements can be automatic activities, manpower activities, events, and connectors (AND, XOR).

ALLOW [8] is an adaptable, pervasive flow paradigm, supporting context-aware runtime changes and deviations in the application execution flow. ALLOW has a set of useful adaptation modeling constructs to add dynamicity and flexibility to flow models. For example, the ALLOW context handlers support the automatic reaction to context condition violations during workflow execution. Other constructs enable specifying alternative flows and, in case of context violation, the workflow can jump, at runtime, from current flow to another application flow. ALLOW has its own language (Adaptable Pervasive Flow Language—APFL) for describing the application flows. APFL is based on BPEL and divides the activities into two categories: basic activities (abstract activity, message sending, message receiving, human interaction, data manipulation, and context event) and structured activities (scope or flow, exclusive decision or if, pick, and parallel fork/join). ALLOW supports rollback in the adaptation process, however, all possible workflow paths and adaptation plans should be planned at design time.

All context provision middleware previously presented do not address interoperability between different middleware platforms. Next paragraphs present platforms that focus on providing interoperability between different generic middleware that employ heterogeneous communication and middleware protocols. In general, these interoperable platforms provide drivers (or bridges) for each middleware platform to reach interoperability.

ReMMoC (Reflective Middleware for Mobile Computing) [24] dynamically adapts binding (IIOP, SOAP, and publish-subscribe) and discovery protocols (SLP and UPnP) to allow interoperation with heterogeneous services. The aim of ReMMoC is to "allow mobile clients to be developed independently from the underlying middleware implementations that may be encountered at different locations" [25]. ReMMoC is composed of two components: (i) a binding framework for interoperation with services implemented upon different middleware and different transport protocols types and (ii) a service discovery framework for discovering services advertised by service discovery protocols of all integrated middleware.

uMiddle [26] is a bridging mechanism that provides interoperability between devices over diverse middleware platforms and network domains. It enables platform-independent applications development. uMiddle translates communication protocols and data types from middleware platforms protocols to uMiddle protocols. This platform creates a semantic space in which services provided by different middleware can be aggregated independently from the underlying technology. Thus, applications built on top of uMiddle are free of platform dependencies and "can avail of all the devices from the various other platforms" [26]. uMiddle realizes the interoperability layer via mappers and translators. Mappers are components that discover native devices and services via a platform-specific discovery protocol and import them into the common semantic space by instantiating the translator for the specific protocol used by the integrated middleware.

Each translator acts as a proxy for a specific device or service. uMiddle uses a proprietary XML-based description language (USDL). This language enables the abstract description of services provided by the integrated middleware and enables mappers to configure translators for different device types from a generic implementation.

GridKit [27] is a self-configuring and self-adapting middleware that can be deployed for applications that run on environments with a high degree of heterogeneity. GridKit architecture is composed of four layers. The lower layer is the component model (OpenCOMJ). It is a runtime kernel that supports the loading and binding of lightweight software components at runtime [27]. The second layer is the *overlays framework*, which is a distributed framework for the deployment of multiple overlay networks (set of distributed overlay middleware instances and per-overlay plug-in components). The third layer consists of a set of GridKit frameworks that provide services such as service discovery, resource discovery, resource management, resource monitoring, and security. Finally, the upper layer abstracts the services provided by overlay middleware instances into web services. Thus, these web services can be used by applications to call the heterogeneous services in a transparent and integrated way.

The aforementioned middleware platforms deal with a different subset of the UC application requirements presented in Section 6.3.1. However, none of them simultaneously meet all these requirements. In particular, the existent proposals lack from a comprehensive solution to deal with interoperability issues at the middleware platform level. In the next section we present OpenCOPI, an example of middleware platform that tackles such issues.

6.4 A SOLUTION TO INTEGRATING CONTEXT PROVISION MIDDLEWARE FOR UBIQUITOUS COMPUTING

This section presents OpenCOPI [10], an example of a software system developed to integrate different context provision middleware, with the goal of facilitating the task of developing context-aware ubiquitous applications. To achieve this goal, OpenCOPI integrates different service providers required by such applications. These providers include, but are not limited to, several context-provision middleware. OpenCOPI enables different service providers to collaborate and complement functionalities offered by each one to reach a high-level goal: supplying value-added services and contextual data to ubiquitous applications.

6.4.1 Overview

OpenCOPI is a workflow-based, service-oriented platform, which integrates context provision services in a transparent and automatic way and provides an environment that facilitates the development of context-aware applications. OpenCOPI allows the integration of services provided by distinct sources, ranging from services offered by simple ad hoc systems (e.g., sensor devices from a wireless sensor network) to more complex services, for example services provided by context provision middleware. OpenCOPI architecture is based on SOA and on web services technologies, using open XML-based standards and languages. The use of a standardized context model and mechanisms is important to provide a unified environment in which applications only need to deal with OpenCOPI models. In short, OpenCOPI provides (i) an automatic service composition based on user preferences and service metadata, (ii) a standardized context and communication model, and (iii) an adaptation mechanism to be triggered in the event of service failures or changes in the delivered service quality.

OpenCOPI provides its own API and an OWL ontology-based context model, in which context is handled by adopting the semantic web services perspective [28]. Under this perspective, (i) service providers (including, but not restricted to, context provision middleware) publish their services using OWL-S, (ii) ubiquitous applications are services consumers, and (iii) OpenCOPI is a mediator that provides uniform access to services used by UC applications. Moreover, OpenCOPI offers automatic service composition, orchestration, execution, and adaption to support these applications. Such composition and orchestration are performed through a goal-oriented workflow, which decouples applications from the underlying services that accomplish a given workflow goal.

The composition model adopted by OpenCOPI is based both on services' functionality and on service metadata, enabling a better choice between available services with similar functionality, for example, different services that provide the same set of inputs and outputs. Such compositions are performed by choosing context services that offer context data matching with applications needs through QoS and QoC (quality of context) attributes. QoC means "any information that describes the quality of information that is used as context," for instance, precision, probability of correctness, resolution, up-to-dateness, and so on [29].

OpenCOPI provides an adaptive mechanism that deals with service failures in ubiquitous environments. Whenever a service failure happens, this mechanism automatically replaces the failing service with another equivalent (and available) one. Thus, OpenCOPI supports the fault-tolerance requirement of ubiquitous environments, increasing the availability of such systems.

6.4.2 Terminology

This subsection presents important terms and features necessary to fully understand OpenCOPI operation.

6.4.2.1 Services. Services are the basic elements in the OpenCOPI architecture and their features and functionality are described using OWL-S. There are two types of services in OpenCOPI: traditional services and context services. Such classification is not necessarily visible to final users, but it is important to OpenCOPI service composition process. Traditional services are services provided by databases, legacy systems, and message (SMS, e-mail, Twitter) systems, among others. In order to perform service selection and composition with context services, additional quality metadata is required, for example, the values of QoC [29] provided by the service.

6.4.2.2 Semantic Workflow. This is an abstract representation of a workflow described in terms of goals, representing the application execution flow, that is, a workflow defines the sequence in which these goals must be executed. Goals are composed of tasks, which are described in terms of semantic web services descriptions. Workflows are used to perform automatic service selection, composition, and orchestration. In an OpenCOPI environment, each application has its own workflow and each workflow goal is a high-level description of an application goal. A workflow is independent of specific concrete services. This approach, separating the abstract goal from the concrete services that are able to achieve it, is useful mainly in cases where there are several similar services available, offered by different providers. In such cases, the service that best meets the user requirements can be chosen to be executed based on a given high-level workflow goal.

6.4.2.3 Execution Plan. In order to execute a semantic workflow, it is necessary to create at least one concrete specification for the workflow, which is called an *execution plan*. Such an execution plan contains a set of concrete web services that are orchestrated through the execution of services in a particular order. Execution plans are built through an *on-the-fly* process of service discovery and composition, according to the semantic enriched interface of the selected services and the semantic workflow specification.

6.4.3 Context Model

The OpenCOPI context model is specified as an ontology. Such a context model was inspired by the CONON [31] ontology, but it includes extensions to allow the execution of our workflow-based strategy. Similar to the CONON approach, OpenCOPI ontology is implemented using OWL. The OpenCOPI ontology is organized in two layers in order to deal with the fact that, in ubiquitous environments, applications and services are commonly grouped as a collection of subdomains. There are common concepts that can be modeled using a generic context model, which is shared by all the subdomains of ubiquitous computing. Such concepts are represented in the first layer using the *generic context ontology*. However, there are particularities of each subdomain, which are detailed in different and extensible ontologies, encouraging the reuse of generic concepts and providing a flexible interface for defining domain-specific knowledge. Therefore, each second-layer ontology in OpenCOPI describes a different ubiquitous environment, for instance, home domain, office domain, petroleum exploration domain, and so on.

Figure 6.1 shows a representation of OpenCOPI Generic Context ontology. The model is structured around *objects* and *tasks* classes. *Objects* are physical or conceptual things, including *Person, Equipment, Computer Entity, Message*, and *Location*. *Tasks* are used to represent an activity implemented by web service(s). *Objects* can be used to describe *inputs, outputs*, and *preconditions* related to a task. Furthermore, associations among *objects* and *tasks* should be defined.

Figure 6.2 presents a partial definition of the health-care domain ontology. This (second-layer) ontology describes the specific subclasses (objects and tasks) for health-care environments. Moreover, this ontology shows several relationships between object-object and/or task-object. An example of an object-object relationship is the *locatedIn* relationship between *Equipment* and *Location* objects, which means that a given equipment is located in a particular location. An example of a task-object relationship is the

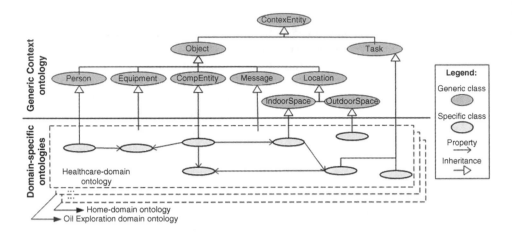

Figure 6.1 Partial description of the OpenCOPI generic context ontology.

relationship between the task *Send* and the object *Message*, which means that a message (e-mail, sms, or audio message) can be sent (using some communication channel).

6.4.4 Architecture

OpenCOPI architecture encompasses two layers (*ServiceLayer* and *UnderlayIntegrationLayer*) and two major interfaces (*IApp* and *IUnderlayIntegration*), as depicted in Fig. 6.3. *ServiceLayer* is responsible for managing the abstractions (OWL-S descriptions) of services supplied by service providers. The components of the *ServiceLayer* use such abstractions to support workflow creation and execution, service selection, service composition, and adaptation. Such components also support context reasoning and context storing, among other functionalities related to ubiquitous applications. *IApp*

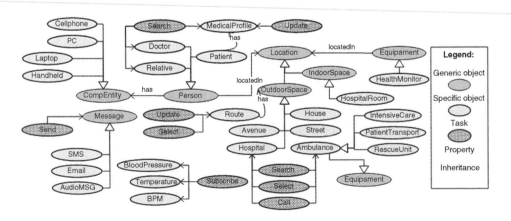

Figure 6.2 Partial description of OpenCOPI's health-care context ontology.

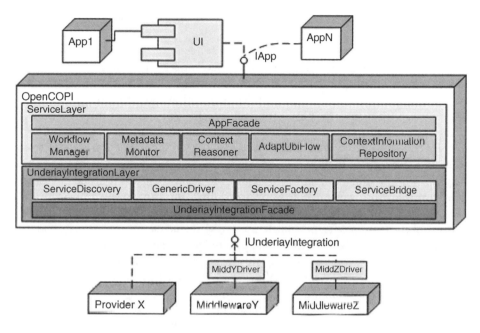

Figure 6.3 OpenCOPI architecture.

interface links applications with the OpenCOPI *ServiceLayer*. The *UnderlayIntegration Layer* is responsible for integrating service providers, mainly (but not only) the context provision middleware, performing context conversion whenever needed (from middleware context model to OpenCOPI context model) and communication protocol conversion. This latter type of conversion is required to integrate middleware that is not compliant with web services protocols and standards, but instead adopt different protocols as, for example, Sockets, RMI, and CORBA. The *IUnderlayIntegration* interface links service providers and OpenCOPI's *UnderlayIntegrationLayer*.

The *WorkflowManager* component manages the abstraction of available context services provided by context provision middleware. It is composed of four (sub)components that provide support for the specification of semantic workflows and for the generation of execution plans (EPs). The *ServiceManager* component is responsible for importing OWL-S descriptions from service providers to OpenCOPI and validating such descriptions. The *ServiceManager* also provides capabilities to search for basic concepts in the knowledge base (ontology) using inputs and outputs of available semantic web services. The *Semantic-Composer* component is responsible for discovering and composing web services according to semantic workflow specifications, that is, it makes the mapping between workflow goals and web services. First, it tries to discover (among a range of services available in the *SemanticServicesRepository*), those that can be used to compose the execution plan, given the goals specified in the application request. After this, it tries to combine the discovered services in order to consume all inputs and preconditions and produce all outputs specified in the request. The combined services are organized by the *SemanticComposer* according to the message flow between outputs of a service and inputs of the subsequent service.

The *SemanticServicesRepository* stores both the ontologies that describe the web services and the execution plans. The *WorkflowExecutor* component supports the workflow execution. It receives execution plans generated by the *SemanticComposer* for a specific workflow and chooses a plan to run (taking into account the QoS/QoC of the service providers included in the plan). At runtime, this component performs remote calls to the underlying context provision middleware, represented as web services operations and included in the EP. In case of failure in one execution plan, the *WorkflowExecutor* chooses another execution plan (if any) in an attempt to successfully execute the workflow. The function of the *MetadataMonitor* is to acquire metadata about services and context provided by context provision middleware to feed the *ContextInformationRepository* with metadata information. OpenCOPI adopts an SLA (*Service Level Agreements*) approach in which the service providers publish the quality metadata of their services and these metadata are used to select the services to be provided to the consumers. The techniques for acquisition and transformation of quality metadata (QoS/QoC deduction, filtering, or extrapolation) are beyond the scope of our work, but possible implementations for this component can be found in [32].

The *ContextReasoner* component makes inferences about context data (low-level context), acquired through the several context provision middleware, to supply high-level and consistent context information for the applications. The *Context- InformationRepository* component stores context data and context metadata. It supplies context data to both the *WorkflowManager* and the *ContextReasoner* components.

The *AdaptUbiFlow* component is responsible for the adaptation process in Open-COPI. As was previously mentioned, ubiquitous computing environments are highly susceptible to changes, several of them unpredictable. AdaptUbiFlow was specifically designed to deal with the requirement of adaptation. In AdaptUbiFlow, an adaptation of an application means the replacement of the running execution plan by another execution plan (that achieves the same stated goals). This component works directly with the *MetadataMonitor* and *WorkflowManager* components to identify a fault and automatically change the execution flow to use another execution plan in the presence of fault.

The components of *UnderlayIntegrationLayer* are in charge of integrating service providers. *ServiceDiscovery* is the component that discovers services in the environment and registers them in OpenCOPI. When discovered, traditional web services can be directly added in the *SemanticServiceRepository* since these services do not deal with context information and consequently do not require additional service handling. However, services provided by context provision middleware need additional steps to be integrated. For each context provision middleware, it is necessary to build a driver to implement the context model transformation (from the middleware context model to the OpenCOPI context model). For context provision middleware that *does not* provide APIs complaint to the web services technology, it is necessary to build drivers in order to abstract away the different APIs and allow transparent access to the context data provided by these context provision middleware. So, the driver is also responsible for issuing context queries and subscriptions from OpenCOPI to the underlying context provision middleware. Each driver should extend the *GenericDriver* component. This component implements the OpenCOPI side of the interface and defines operations for context model transformation and communication between a specific context provision middleware and OpenCOPI.

The *ServiceFactory* component is responsible for creating context services that encapsulate the specific middleware APIs, while the *ServiceBridge* component makes the link between these context services and the *WorkflowManager* component. Thus, each service provided by the middleware API is represented by a web service, created by Open-COPI, to represent the respective service API. Each OpenCOPI Web service created by the *ServiceFactory* uses the driver tailored for the specific underlying middleware.

6.4.5 Service Metadata

The service selection is based not only on the workflow created by the user but also on several metadata parameters. These parameters are described in OpenCOPI service metadata ontology and they are categorized (for didactical purposes) in two types: QoC and QoS. The possible values each parameter can assume are represented as ontology concepts. While QoC describes the quality of the context information provided by a service, QoS describes the quality of the service. Figure 6.4 presents the current version of OpenCOPI service metadata ontology, however, this ontology can be extended and other parameters can be added.

The meaning of each parameter is shown below, separated by category. OpenCOPI considers some QoC parameters proposed by [29]. These QoC parameters are:

- *Precision:* denotes the level of accuracy of the information provided by a given technology/technique for context provision. For example, a GPS receiver or a RFID reader can provide the location of a person with a precision of a few centimeters, while a triangulation algorithm based in 802.11 signal strength can provide a precision of few meters.
- *Correctness:* denotes the probability that a piece of context information is correct. As an example, consider a temperature sensor sensing a room. Internal problems in such a sensor can generate incorrect temperature values (e.g., measuring 30 °C, while the correct temperature would be 20 °C). Thus, the parameter correctness

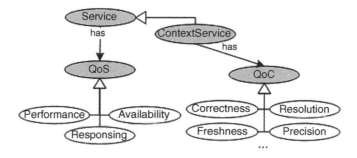

Figure 6.4 Ontology describing service's and context's quality parameters.

estimates how often context information provided by a source will be unintentionally wrong due to internal problems.

- *Resolution:* describes the granularity of the context information. For example, two temperature sensors (sensors a and b) may have different resolutions: while sensor of manufacturer a has resolution of $0.1\,°C$, sensor of manufacturer b can have resolution of $1.0\,°C$. If both sensors are placed in the same room with the current temperature around $15.4\,°C$, sensor a will show $15.4\,°C$ and sensor b will show $15°C$.
- *Freshness:* represents the time elapsed between the generation of the context data and the retrieval of this data by applications. So, a particular context data may be prioritized if it is newer than other similar data.

QoS parameters considered in our work are:

- *Response time:* represents the time between sending a service request to a service provider and receiving the response.
- *Availability:* represents the probability that the service provider is up and the service is running, that is, the service is ready for immediate use.
- *Performance:* describes the number of service requests fulfilled by the service provider at a given period of time.

OpenCOPI categorizes each parameter in levels to make it easier for users to express the desired QoC and QoS parameters. The possible levels are *high*, *medium*, *low*, or the special level *not relevant*, used whenever the user does not want to specify a particular parameter.

6.4.6 Workflow Specification

In OpenCOPI, a workflow is represented by a direct acyclic graph (DAG) in which each intermediary node represents a specific service and each directed edge represents the execution direction between two services. Each graph begins with an *initial node* and ends with a *final node*. *Initial* and *final nodes* do not represent any service but they are used to indicate, respectively, the beginning and the end of the graph. Each complete path between *initial node* and *final node* is an *execution route*, and an *execution route* represents a possible *execution plan* in the workflow. So, the graph represents the workflow with all possible execution plans. Figure 6.5 shows a graph with some possible execution routes, for example, (i) S1 → S2 → S3 → S4 → S5, (ii) S1 → S2' → S3 → S4" → S5, (iii) S1 → S6 → S4" → S5, etc.

6.4.7 Execution Plan Selection

The UML sequence diagram of Fig. 6.6 shows the steps of execution plan selection. On receiving a request for workflow execution, the OpenCOPI *WorkflowManager* component builds the possible execution plans that fulfill the request through the semantic composition of available services. Then, this component retrieves the current quality

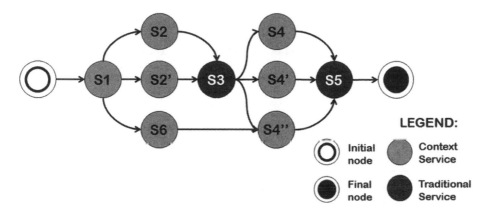

Figure 6.5 Example of graph representation.

parameters of the services that compose the generated execution plans (QoS and QoC) from *MetadataMonitor*. Following, *WorkflowManager* component calculates the quality of services of each execution plan through the quality parameters values of individual services that are part of such plan. Finally, all execution plans are ranked based on their

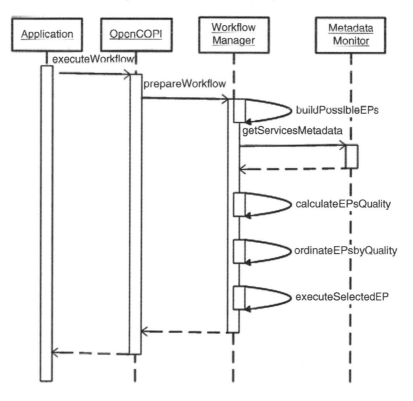

Figure 6.6 Sequence diagram of execution plan selection.

calculated quality and the best option is chosen to be executed. By default, the best option is the plan that presents the highest quality; however, the user can influence this decision at the moment of the abstract workflow definition by choosing the quality required for each service Details about execution plan selection are presented in [10].

6.5 CONCLUSION

Several recent technological advances have made the Mark Weiser view of ubiquitous computing a reality in our daily lives. However, in order to reach the full potential of this new scenario, it is crucial to reduce the efforts of developing ubiquitous applications. Applications for ubiquitous environments have a set of requirements that pose new important challenges to developers. An example of requirement is context-awareness. Context data is gathered from distributed, heterogeneous sources spread over the ubiquitous environment and applications need timeless and value-added information extracted from contextual raw data in order to behave accordingly and meet the user goals. The provision of context-awareness to applications is preferably left in charge of underling context provision middleware to unburden application developers. In this chapter, we highlighted the main requirements of ubiquitous applications that need to be fulfilled by context provision middleware and also described existent context middleware with different approaches and technologies. The growing emergence of context provision middleware, addressing different types of contextual information, which often do not interact with each other, imposes the need for integration and interoperability among those systems in order to fully meet the transparency requirement of UC. In this context, we introduced OpenCOPI, an example of existent platform that provides unified ontology-based context services for the development of ubiquitous applications and integrates services provided by distinct sources. Concerning the programming model, we consider that SOA provides a good metaphor for the type of interaction that takes place in ubiquitous systems. Therefore, OpenCOPI adopts an SOA-based approach, decoupling applications from the underlying context provision middleware. Moreover, OpenCOPI builds on semantic web services technology, providing value-added functionalities of discovering, selecting, and composing services that fulfill the application needs. It also relies on the concept of semantic workflow to provide the coordination and autonomy required by ubiquitous applications. In short, OpenCOPI provides: (i) an automatic service composition; (ii) a standardized context and communication model; and (iii) an adaptive mechanism to support adaptation in ubiquitous applications and deal with services failures, increasing the availability of such systems.

We believe that platforms such as OpenCOPI can effectively contribute to the leverage of ubiquitous computing, allowing that the full benefits of such environments can be widespread.

ACKNOWLEDGMENTS

This work was partially supported by the Human Resources Program of National Agency of Petroleum, Natural Gas and Biofuels (PRH/ANP), National Network on Teaching and Research (RNP), Coordination for Improvement of Higher Education Personnel (CAPES), and National Council for Scientific and Technological Development (CNPq). We would like to thank Paulo Ferreira (IST/Portugal), Everton Cavalcante, and Reginaldo Mendes for their contribution and collaboration in this work. We also want to express our gratitude to Albert Zomaya and Hamid Sarbazi-Azad, who kindly invited us to contribute to this book.

REFERENCES

[1] G. Judd and P. Steenkiste, "Providing contextual information to pervasive computing applications." In *International Conference on Pervasive Computing and Communications* 2003, Washington, DC.

[2] A. Bottaro and A. Gérodolle, "Home SOA: Facing protocol heterogeneity in pervasive applications." In *International Conference on Pervasive Services*, 2008, Sorrento, Italy: ACM.

[3] A.K. Dey, G. Abowd, and D. Sauber, "A conceptual framework and a toolkit for supporting the rapid prototyping of context-aware applications." *Human-Computer Interaction* 2001, 16(2).

[4] A. Ranganathan, J. Al-Muhtadi, S. Chetan, R. Campbell, and M. Dennis Mickunas, "MiddleWhere: A middleware for location awareness in ubiquitous computing applications." In *Middleware Conference*. 2004. Toronto, Canada.

[5] R. Rouvoy, P. Barone, Y. Ding, F. Eliassen, S. Hallsteinsen, J. Lorenzo, A. Mamelli, and U. Schols, "MUSIC: Middleware support for self-adaptation in ubiquitous and service-oriented environments." In *Software Engineering for Self-Adaptive Systems*, 2009, Springer, p. 164–182.

[6] H. Truong, L. Juszczyk, A. Manzoor, and S. Dustdar, "ESCAPE—An adaptive framework formanaging and providing context information in emergency situations." In *Second European Conference on Smart Sensing and Context*, 2007: Kendal, UK, p. 207–222.

[7] J. Li, Y. Bu, S. Chen, X. Tao, and J. Lu, "FollowMe: On research of pluggable infrastructure for context-awareness." In 20th *International Conference on Advanced Information Networking and Applications*. 2006, Vienna, Austria.

[8] A. Marconi, M. Pistore, and A. Sirbu, "Enabling adaptation of pervasive flows: Built-in contextual adaptation." *Lecture Notes in Computer Science*, 2009, 5900/2009, pp. 445–454.

[9] F. Lopes, F. Delicato, T. Batista, and P. Pires, "Context-based heterogeneous middleware integration." In *Workshop on Middleware for Ubiquitous and Pervasive Systems* (WMUPS'09). 2009.

[10] F. Lopes, T. Pereira, E. Cavalcante, T. Batista, F.C. Delicato, P.F. Pires, and P. Ferreira, "AdaptUbiFLow: Selection and adaptation in workflows for ubiquitous computing." In *International Conference on Embedded and Ubiquitous Computing* (EUC), 2011, Melbourne, Australia.

[11] D. Sprott and L. Wilkes, Understanding SOA. 2003.

[12] A. Abbasi and A. Shaikh, "A conceptual framework for smart workflow management." In *International Conference on Information Management and Engineering*, 2009.

[13] S. Poslad, *Ubiquitous Computing—Smart Devices, Environments and Interactions*, 2009, Wiley. p. 502.

[14] P. Tandler, "Synchronous collaboration in ubiquitous computing environments." In *Vom Fachbereich Informatik*, 2004, Technischen Universität Darmstadt, Darmstadt.

[15] W. Emmerich, M. Aoyama, and J. Sventek, "The impact of research on middleware technology." In *ACM SIGSOFT Software Engineering Notes*, 2007, pp. 89–112.

[16] S. Krakowiak, *Middleware Architecture with Patterns and Frameworks*, 2009.

[17] M. Baldauf, S. Dustdar, and F. Rosenberg, "A survey on context-aware systems." *International Journal of Ad Hoc and Ubiquitous Computing*, 2007, 2(4), pp. 263–277.

[18] Web Services Architecture. W3C Recommendation 2004, http://www.w3.org/TR/ws-arch/, (accessed August 2009).

[19] A. Ranganathan and S. McFaddin, "Using workflows to coordinate web services in pervasive computing environments." In *IEEE International Conference on Web Services*, 2004.

[20] A. Arsanjani, "Service-oriented modeling and architecture—How to identify, specify, and realize services for your SOA," 2004, http://www.ibm.com/developerworks/library/ws-soa-design1/, (accessed April 17, 2011).

[21] T. Berners-Lee, J. Hendler, and O. Lassila, "The semantic web." *Scientific American*, 2001.

[22] A. Bennaceur, G. Blair, F. Chauvel, et al., "Towards an architecture for runtime interoperability." In *4th International Conference on Leveraging Applications of Formal Methods, Verification and Validation*, 2010, Berlin.

[23] OSGi Alliance. OSGi. http://www.osgi.org/.

[24] P. Grace, G. Blair, and S. Samuel, "ReMMoC: A Reflective Middleware to support Mobile Client Interoperability." In *Proc. International Symposium of Distributed Objects and Applications Interoperability*, 2003.

[25] P. Grace and G. Blair, "Interoperating with heterogeneous mobile services." In *ERCIM News—Special: Applications and Services Platforms for the Mobile Users*, 2003. pp. 24–25.

[26] J. Nakazawa, H. Tokuda, W. Keith Edwards, and U. Ramachandran, "A bridging framework for universal interoperability in pervasive systems." In *International Conference on Distributed Computing Systems*, 2006.

[27] P. Grace, G. Blair, C. Cortes, and N. Bencomo, "Engineering complex adaptations in highly heterogeneous distributed systems." In *Proceedings of the Second International ICST Conference on Autonomic Computing and Communication Systems*, 2008.

[28] D. Martin, M. Paolucci, et al. "Bringing semantics to web services: The OWL-S approach." In *International Workshop on Semantic Web Services and Web Process Composition*, 2004, California.

[29] T. Buchholz, A. Küpper, and M. Schiffers, "Quality of context: What it is and why we need it." In *Workshop of the HP OpenView University Association*, 2003, Geneva, Switzerland.

[30] K. Sheikh, M. Wegdam, and M. van Sinderen, "Middleware support for quality of context in pervasive context-aware systems." In *IEEE International Conference on Pervasive Computing and Communications Workshops*, 2007, White Plains, NY.

[31] X.H. Wang, D. Zhang, T. Gu, and H. Pung, "Ontology based context modeling and reasoning using OWL." In *Second IEEE Annual Conference on Pervasive Computing and Communications Workshops*, 2004, Orlando, FL, pp. 18–22.

[32] H.-L. Truong, R. Samborski, and T. Fahringer, "Towards a framework for monitoring and analyzing QoS metrics of grid services." In *International Conference on e-Science and Grid Computing*, 2006.

Part 3

WIRELESS/MOBILE NETWORKS

7

CHALLENGES IN THE USE OF WIRELESS SENSOR NETWORKS FOR MONITORING THE HEALTH OF CIVIL STRUCTURES

Flávia C. Delicato, Igor L. dos Santos, Luci Pirmez, Paulo F. Pires, and Claudio M. de Farias

CONTENTS

Large Scale Network-Centric Distributed Systems, First Edition. Edited by Hamid Sarbazi-Azad and Albert Y. Zomaya.
© 2014 John Wiley & Sons, Inc. Published 2014 by John Wiley & Sons, Inc.

7.1 INTRODUCTION

Recent advances in wireless technologies and microelectromechanical systems (MEMS) have enabled the emergence of wireless sensor networks (WSNs). WSNs represent a new domain of distributed computing that has attracted great research interest. A WSN is composed of a large number of tiny battery-powered devices equipped with one or more sensing units and a processor, memory, and wireless radio. Such devices, named sensor nodes, smart sensors, or motes, have limited capabilities due to their size and energy constraints. Thus, energy consumption is an important issue in the design of protocols and algorithms for wireless sensor networks. Several protocols for WSNs are designed in an energy efficient way, thus reducing power consumption and maximizing the WSN lifetime. Recently, there has been interest in the use of WSNs [1] in different applications from several industry sectors.

Among such applications, structural health monitoring (SHM) is considered a promising field for the usage of WSNs, with several potential benefits not provided by traditional techniques for monitoring structures. SHM denotes the monitoring of physical structures that are in the civil engineering domain, enabling the prediction of damage and, therefore, proper scheduling of the required maintenance procedures, avoiding accidents of larger proportions. Damage, in the SHM domain, can be defined as the presence of an unnoticeable (with the naked eye) amount of microcracks on a structural element. The presence of microcracks causes changes in the material and/or geometric properties of the structure, affecting its performance [2]. Such microcracks tend to grow slowly in the early stages of damage emergence, but tend to grow faster immediately before a complete rupture of the structural element is about to happen, which may cause a catastrophic failure. Thus, the early stages of damage emergence are the best for performing damage detection and localization. In these early stages, there is still enough time to take repair actions. Precision equipment must be used to detect the small changes in the structural properties in the early stages of the damage emergence, a suitable requirement for the deployment and usage of a WSN in this context. In addition, in the late stages of damage emergence, close to a catastrophic failure moment, WSNs may be used to trigger actuators that can sound alarms, close gates, or perform an emergency procedure.

In WSN solutions built for the purpose of SHM, sensing devices are used to perform analog measurements of properties from many different positions in the structure, as well as from the external events that may affect such properties. For this reason, a large-scale wireless network of sensing devices should be considered. The sensing devices that are most frequently used in solutions of WSNs for SHM are strain gages and accelerometers, for collecting measurements of the structural properties, as well as thermometers and hygrometers, for collecting environmental properties. The sensor nodes then convert the measurements collected by such sensing devices into digital measurements and, through wireless communication, deliver them to a data collection station, often called the *sink node*. Traditionally, WSNs are used only as a communication infrastructure for delivering the collected measurements to the sink node, where further processing is done to assess structural integrity, as described, for instance, in [3] and [4].

Obviously, using WSNs as the communication infrastructure for SHM systems brings several advantages but poses a series of new challenges as well. One of the key challenges is how to adapt signal processing techniques, already available in the structural engineering domain, to perform as much data compression within the network as possible, reducing the need for transmissions, thus extending the WSN lifetime. One of the benefits is that, because the sensor nodes are endowed with processing capability (although limited), an immediate advantage of using WSNs is that the nodes can be used not only as passive data collectors but also to perform part of the required computing for detecting damage in the structure. In this context, a second key challenge is developing new decentralized techniques that allow a network-centric determination of the physical integrity of the structure. In other words, this challenge entails allowing the sensor nodes of the WSN themselves to detect, localize, and define the damage extension or severity without the help of the processing power of the sink node. In addition, the prediction, within the network, of the damage evolution is of great importance for structural prognosis. Surpassing this second challenge is the key to developing SHM systems that present a faster response in the case of damage, as well as a longer lifetime.

Indeed, such challenges are of great importance in most WSN applications beyond SHM. But in the SHM domain the volume of data generated per node is much greater than in other application domains, especially when using accelerometers for vibration monitoring. Due to this feature, the recent evolution of WSN solutions in the SHM domain was mainly driven by data compression, aggregation, and fusion techniques, which are presented in [5] for surpassing such challenges. In a previous work by our research team [6], the techniques described in [5] were applied in the context of WSNs for SHM. We presented a decentralized approach for damage detection, localization, and extension determination. The key idea of our proposal was to distribute the monitoring procedures among the nodes of a WSN organized in a hierarchical (cluster-based) topology in such a way that, only through the collaboration of the leaders of the clusters, was it possible to detect, localize, and determine the damage extension. When the sensor nodes process the information on the damage and make a decision, they may send messages for the related actuators that perform controlling actions such as triggering relays or sounding alarms.

The recent evolution of WSN solutions in the SHM domain seems to be driven in the direction of surpassing both challenges. Thus, it is possible to understand such evolution through the concept of "generations of sensor networks for SHM." This concept, explained in this chapter, relies on the idea that we can identify three different generations of sensor networks for SHM, whose degrees of data compression, aggregation, and fusion presented are continuously greater. In addition, the processing required to perform a physical integrity characterization is increasingly more distributed among the sensor nodes, relying less on the sink node along each generation of sensor networks for SHM.

The main focus of this chapter is thus to provide an overview of the challenges faced in the design of new techniques for enabling new decentralized solutions of large-scale WSNs in the SHM domain. As background concepts, this chapter first introduces the definition of SHM along with the concept of WSNs, after a brief overview concerning each subject separately. We cite several challenges and solutions found in the literature that we consider to be of importance for understanding the context of this domain of WSN applications, guiding further studies in it. This chapter might be a useful reference for anyone who wishes to begin their studies in this novel domain of WSN applications.

The remainder of this chapter is divided as follows: Sections 7.2 and 7.3 provides respectively, background concepts of SHM and WSNs. Section 7.4 presents both concepts together and mentions several solutions in which different challenges are faced in the design of new decentralized techniques for monitoring structures with WSNs. Finally, Section 7.5 concludes this chapter and suggests future research directions.

7.2 STRUCTURAL HEALTH MONITORING

In this section, the concept of SHM is introduced, the requirements for this kind of application are presented, with a focus on modal-based techniques, and the concept of "generations of sensor networks for SHM" is described. The approach of this section is to present the concept of SHM by itself, regardless of the concept of WSNs. Historically, SHM solutions relied only on wired sensor networks long before the advent of WSNs. Therefore, because there is not a direct dependence among SHM and WSN, it is not necessary to present examples using networks of wireless sensing devices (smart sensors) to accomplish the goal of introducing the concept of SHM. Thus, as a didactic choice, the examples in this section consider only networks of wired sensing devices, referred to here as "sensor networks." For the sake of the comprehension of the core concepts of this chapter, only in Section 7.4 are the examples of WSNs for SHM presented.

7.2.1 The Concept of Structural Health Monitoring

The concept of SHM is a relatively recent one in the literature. There are several works that present different viewpoints on SHM. Therefore, in this chapter, we will present this concept from our own point of view, which is mainly based on one of the most widely accepted points of view in the researched literature, that from [2]. The work in [2] presents an extensive review on traditional SHM techniques. This chapter focuses on the modal-based techniques, which are explained further in this section, since most of the experience of the authors in the SHM domain was acquired in the use of such techniques. The work in [7] presents a review focused on such modal-based techniques for SHM. In spite of the fact that modal-based techniques can also be used to monitor the health of mechanical systems, as, for instance, rotating machinery, the main focus of this chapter is on monitoring civil engineering structures.

Based on [2], SHM is defined as a strategy for assessing structural integrity. According to our experience [6], such a strategy may comprise (i) damage *detection*, which means detecting the presence of damage regardless of its position in the structure, (ii) damage *localization*, which aims at defining the exact position of the damage site, and (iii) damage *extension* definition, whose intention is to define the number of damage sites and/or their severity. The assessment of damage severity may be the focus of damage prediction, which aims to find out the exact moment where critical damage will occur. Critical damage is defined as damage of larger proportions (possibly larger than microcracks) that will critically prevent the structure from functioning or cause catastrophic failures, considering that critical damage begins as a small set of microcracks. Critical damage is, therefore, one of the last stages in the damage in the structure. Every damage site tends to evolve to this stage, and, to lower the cost of replacement of the structural components, it is important to perform damage prediction to discover the exact time such components require replacement.

There are also global monitoring and local monitoring strategies. Global monitoring strategies are centered on global parameters of the structure, such as, modal frequencies and shapes, whereas local monitoring strategies are centered on local inspections that make use of techniques based on infrared, acoustic emissions, or ultrasonic measurements. Global and local strategies for monitoring the health of structures are also mentioned as global health monitoring and local health monitoring in [8]. Local monitoring strategies are more expensive and time consuming than global monitoring strategies. Moreover, human access to the position chosen for the assessment is not always possible in local monitoring strategies. Thus, global monitoring strategies are widely used for monitoring the health of structures. Nevertheless, in global monitoring strategies it is relatively easy to detect the presence of damage but it is hard to define the damage's location and extent, which are easier to define using local monitoring strategies. Ideally, both kinds of strategies are necessary, but due to technical, financial, and safety constraints, it is usually preferable to define a global monitoring strategy only. Since global monitoring strategies are the ones most widely applied in the researched literature, most of the related works focus on damage detection, and some of such works also perform damage localization.

Damage can be defined as the presence of an unnoticeable (with the naked eye) amount of microcracks on a structural element, when the damage is at its early stages. These microcracks cause a change in the mass of the structure, altering its moment of inertia and making its current dynamic response different from its original response in the previous undamaged state. Thus, there is one basic principle for defining a strategy for monitoring the health of a structure: damage can only be assessed when comparing two different states of the structure [2]. Therefore, the use of a state where the structure is considered healthy for comparison is unavoidable.

There are different techniques for acquiring the information needed for such comparison. The values of the healthy reference state may be extracted from (i) an analytical or theoretical model as, for instance, the ones developed through finite element modeling (FEM) [9]; (ii) a first-time sensing at the early stages of the existence of the structure, when it is visually fully operational; and (iii) a statistical analysis of a long-term sensing period. Each technique has its own drawbacks. The FEM, for instance, requires a large amount of computational power, relies on the intricacy of the modeling performed by an engineer, and may not consider environmental variables and noise that may affect the real structure. Concerning the first-time sensing, it considers such environmental variables and any issue that did not follow the plans during the construction of the structure, and it is computationally inexpensive; but it may not consider all the possible events that may happen during the structure's existence (since it is not feasible to foresee all of them). Statistical analysis has similar drawbacks as both previous techniques, but it provides a more accurate estimate of the average healthy values of the variables because a longer period is considered for analysis; thus, a larger set of different events and noise interferences may be considered in the evaluation. Nevertheless, this technique is the most time consuming and may not be suitable for the fast development of a SHM system.

7.2.2 Requirements of Modal-Based Techniques in SHM Solutions

Most of the works in the researched literature focus on global strategies for monitoring structures, since the techniques that deal with global variables can be easily standardized. Techniques that deal with local variables usually require inspections, which demand a large amount of work and a more specific, per case analysis, which is preferably performed by a human.

Modal-based techniques [7] are among the techniques applied in global strategies. Such modal-based techniques are based on the premise that the presence of damage in a structure causes changes in the material and/or geometric properties of the structure, affecting its modes of vibration, thus causing a change in the structural dynamic response under excitation. Therefore, damage can be assessed through the changes in the parameters of the modes of vibration of the structure, such as modal frequencies and mode shapes. A large civil engineering structure, such as bridges and buildings, usually has different modes of vibration that can be excited. Such modes vibrate in different frequencies and present different shapes. Most global health monitoring techniques are centered on either finding shifts in resonant modal frequencies or changes in structural mode shapes.

In a vibration analysis, with the use of shakers and accelerometers, it is possible to acquire measurements from different points of the structure in order to define the resultant shape of the perceived mode of vibration. This perceived mode of vibration is most similar to the mode of vibration that has the modal frequency more similar to the excitation frequency. Thus, the perceived modes of vibration are the ones that get into resonance with the excitation frequency. The premise that changes in the dynamic characteristics of a structure indicate damage is compromised by the fact that temperature, moisture, and other environmental factors change, producing changes in the perceived mode shapes and dynamic characteristics of the structure in general. Such changes may be considered as noises in the measurements and must be dealt with in order to make these techniques work properly.

The assessment of mode shapes requires the sensing of the acceleration of several different points in the structure, requiring a large-scale network of sensors to be deployed. The assessment of shifts in the modal frequencies usually requires fewer sensors if there is only interest in lower modal frequencies, which usually can be detected from any point of the structure and are named global frequencies. However, higher modal frequencies also carry important information about the health of structures, but can usually be perceived only at specific points of the structure, being named local frequencies. In the case where the analysis of local frequencies is required to monitor the integrity of the structure, a large-scale network is suitable, because the deployment of sensors in several points of the structure allows the sensing of more local frequencies that are not detected by all sensors.

The assessment of modal frequencies requires the sensing of the acceleration of at least one point of the structure. This acceleration signal must be acquired with a certain sampling rate. The sampling rate must be at least twice the value of the highest frequency of interest in the power spectrum to meet the Nyquist criterion. A fast Fourier transform (FFT) must be applied on this acquired acceleration signal, and the resulting power spectrum can be then analyzed. The modal frequencies can be retrieved from this spectrum. The set of modal frequencies of the structure is called the signature of the structure. The amount of data collected during one sampling must be enough to generate a good resolution of the spectrum at the defined sampling rate. For this reason, when there is interest in local frequencies, which are higher and require a higher sampling rate, the amount of collected data is much larger.

The large amount of data collected in SHM applications inspired the development of several techniques for data fusion, which are based on signal processing, and on the employment of techniques for data fusion and aggregation [5]. Such techniques, which can be associated with the degree of decentralization and in-network processing, are the main inspiration for the concept of generations of sensor networks for SHM. The terminology in [5] points to three different abstraction levels of the data handled during the fusion process, defined by the fusion inputs and outputs: (i) *measurement*, where raw data is provided as input to the fusion process and is combined into a new piece of more accurate data, possibly with lower noise (thus a higher accuracy); (ii) *feature*, where attributes and characteristics of individual data samples are fused to obtain a feature map that describes the whole sensor field; and (iii) *decision*, where decisions or symbolic representations are taken as inputs to provide a more reliable or global decision on the data samples. Also, considering the relationship among the data sources, information fusion can be classified into (i) *complementary*, when information provided by the sources represents different portions of a broader scene, and the obtained information is more complete (than individual sources); (ii) *redundant*, if two or more independent sources provide the same piece of information, for increasing confidence; and (iii) *cooperative*, when the information provided by the sources is fused into new information that, from the application perspective, better represents the reality.

We consider that a SHM solution can be (i) *centralized*, where all the processing for assessing the structural integrity is made on the sink node; (ii) *partially decentralized*, where part of the processing for assessing the structural integrity is made within the network, collaboratively by the sensor nodes; and (iii) *decentralized*, where all the processing is made only by the sensor nodes, which refers to fully network-centric approaches.

7.2.3 The Generations of Sensor Networks for SHM

We suggest a classification for the works found in the researched literature about SHM solutions. This classification is based on the concept of "generations of sensor networks for SHM." This classification is an expansion to the concept of a "first-generation wireless structural monitoring system," briefly mentioned in [3]. The whole classification relies on the idea that three different generations of sensor networks for SHM existed, whose degrees of data compression and decentralization of techniques presented are increasingly greater. We state that the first generation of sensor networks for SHM concerns wired devices, while the second and third generations of sensor networks for SHM are related to wireless devices. These generations are numbered consecutively, according to the degree of decentralization and in-network processing presented by their related works. These generations have emerged in the order they were numbered, but works from both generations have chronologically evolved in parallel. Such works tend to evolve towards larger levels of decentralization and in-network processing [3], which suggests that subjects from the second generation of WSNs for SHM will remain a potential research field for a longer time than the subjects from the first generation.

The works in [10–12] were developed relying on the use of wired sensors and pertain to the first generation of sensor networks for SHM. In this generation, the use of wired devices was the only way to acquire measurements of the sensed structures. Energy and communication capabilities were not constraints in this scenario but the monitoring was costly and inflexible. These works present practical results of the application of correlation-based techniques for locating damage. Such correlation-based techniques make use of modal parameters of the structure. Therefore, they are also modal-based techniques. By the chronological order in which these works appear, an evolution of the correlation-based techniques for locating damage can be observed. The essence of such techniques is to correlate sets of theoretical ideal frequencies with a set of experimentally obtained frequencies. The modal-based techniques allow damage detection, localization, and extent determination in structures. Damage detection through such techniques is relatively simple, whereas localization and extent determination are not always easy. The correlation-based techniques aim at localizing damage through the analysis of the linear correlation between the variation rates of collected modal frequencies and theoretical modal frequencies.

In [10], one of the first studies based on the concept of linear correlation to detect damage in structures was developed, in which metrics to locate damage based on the variation of the natural frequencies of the structure were presented. An application of the principles of the technique developed in [10] is found in [11], in which a similar technique, called the damage location assurance criterion (DLAC), is presented. This technique measures the degree of correlation between an experimental vector with the variation rates of the frequencies and several vectors with analytical variation rates of the frequencies. These vectors, both experimental and those obtained through analytical models, contain information on the frequencies of the first modes of vibration of the structure. The number of modes of vibration depends on the depth of the performed analysis. These analytical vectors come from a finite element model of the structure, each of them relative to damage present in different positions. The most perfect correlation between the experimental vector and an analytic vector reveals the location of damage in the structure. This technique allows localization of only one site of damage on the structure, being the damage site represented by a loss of mass, through a cross-sectional area reduction to an element that composes the basic structure used in the experiment. To locate multiple damage sites in the structure, a technique called the multiple damage location assurance criterion (MDLAC) is proposed in [12].

With the advent of WSNs, the so-called smart sensors influenced the SHM domain in such a way that a second generation of sensor networks for SHM started. There are several motivations for the use of WSNs in SHM solutions: (i) a reduction of the need for humans to perform tasks of *in situ* verification about the structural state; (ii) the possibility of dynamically changing the layout of the WSN to monitor different positions and properties; (iii) the ease and flexibility in the installation of wireless sensor nodes, which becomes possible in areas where wired access is difficult or expensive; (iv) the easy and fast WSN reconfiguration after node failures as well as after changes in the environment; and (v) the lower hardware cost of the monitoring system.

In this section we introduced the concept of SHM, the modal-based techniques, and the first generation of sensor networks for SHM, which comprises wired sensor solutions. In order to present the last two generations in Section 7.4, the concept of WSNs must be introduced, which is done in Section 7.3.

7.3 WIRELESS SENSOR NETWORKS

This section introduces the concept of wireless sensor networks (WSNs). Wireless sensor networks are distributed systems composed of hundreds to thousands of low-cost, battery-powered, and reduced-size devices, endowed with processing, sensing, and wireless communication capabilities. Typical WSNs are composed of one or more sink nodes (also called base stations) and several sensor nodes deployed over a large geographic area of interest (the sensing field). Data are collected by sensor nodes from the sensing field and transmitted to the sink node, typically using a multi-hop communication protocol. Each sensor node encompasses software and hardware components. Sensor hardware has four main components: (i) a sensing subsystem including one or more sensors (with associated analog-to-digital converters) for data acquisition, (ii) a processing subsystem including a microcontroller and memory for local data processing, (iii) a communication subsystem for wireless data communication, and (iv) a power supply subsystem. Software comprises the application logic, protocols, and operating systems.

A major reason for the increasing interest in WSNs is their potential application in areas where traditional networks are unsuitable. Instead of a deployment scenario in which a few powerful sensing devices are linked by either wired connections or single-hop wireless connections, in WSNs multiple tiny nodes self-organize to compose a wireless ad-hoc network to meet application demands, so that it is much easier to install, configure the network, and change its topology after deployment. Examples of applications that can benefit from the use of WSNs are structural monitoring [20], habitat [21], wildlife [22], and environmental [23] monitoring, machine condition monitoring [24], surveillance systems [25], medical monitoring [26], and location tracking [27], among others.

The topic of WSNs can be considered as one of the truly multidisciplinary research efforts, bringing together researchers from a wide range of fields: from electronic experts to structural engineers (in the context of this chapter about SHM), and many others in the several other WSN application domains. However, a number of challenges remain to be overcome so that WSNs can be widely employed and reach their full potential. One major challenge is the highly limited energy capacity of the sensor nodes. Such constraint requires the adoption of strategies to achieve energy efficiency throughout the whole network, from the design of individual components of the node hardware to the entire protocol stack, including the application layer.

WSN nodes are endowed with limited power supply, usually provided by a non-rechargeable battery. A key feature of such networks is their capacity to operate unattended, without human intervention, for large periods of time. Considering that WSNs often have hundreds or thousands of sensors and that they should work unattended, once the node battery is depleted, battery or node replacement is nondesirable or even unfeasible. One possible way to minimize this drawback is using strategies for harvesting energy from the environment, that is, from natural sources [13]. However, the energy obtained from natural sources is often unreliable and unstable over time. Therefore, it is essential that WSNs are aware of their own energy and smartly handle their consumption in order to maximize their operational lifetime.

Current techniques for improving energy efficiency include conventional low-power hardware designs [14], which focus on the energy consumption at the circuit and architecture level of the single node [15] and energy-efficient strategies and protocols [16–18], which act on a network-wide level, in different layers of the WSN stack, such as routing, scheduling, medium access control, and application, among others. At the node level, since a large amount of energy is consumed by node components even if they are idle, power management techniques can be used to power off node components that are not temporarily needed. Moreover, techniques of dynamic reconfiguration, like dynamic modulation scaling (DMS) (used to reconfigure modulation schemes in communication) and dynamic voltage scaling (DVS) (used to reconfigure voltages and operating frequency of processors), allow dynamic reconfiguration of the sensor hardware to adapt to external dynamics, providing further savings in energy consumption [19].

At the network-wide level, policies for energy efficiency exploit the knowledge on the WSN behavior as a whole to achieve more significant energy savings than only considering individual nodes. These policies are implemented as software programs that actuate at the different protocol layers (data link, MAC, routing, and application) of the WSN stack. At the application layer, the use of algorithms for data fusion and/or aggregation is a possible strategy for energy saving. This strategy is relevant to the subject of this chapter. Algorithms for data fusion or aggregation exploit the in-networking processing capability of sensor nodes and the inherent redundancy in the sensor-generated data with the purpose of minimizing data transmissions, thus trading computation for communication costs. In addition to reducing energy consumption, in applications like SHM data fusion can also contribute to increasing the accuracy and reliability of the sensor-generated data. Therefore, such strategies play an important role in WSNs applied to the SHM domain.

In this section we introduced the concept of WSNs. In the next section, we will focus on the employment of WSNs for SHM solutions. The second and third generations of sensor networks for SHM refer to wireless sensor networks and, therefore, are the focus. Besides presenting the advantages of using WSNs to provide an efficient solution for this type of application domain, in comparison to other existent approaches, we will discuss open issues in this context. An open issue is, for instance, the development of techniques applied at the application layer to extend the network operational lifetime, while assuring high confidence/quality in the information about the structural integrity delivered by the network. As we previously mentioned, one example of such techniques is data fusion [5], and we will use this concept as one of the guidelines to present the literature review on WSNs for SHM.

7.4 APPLYING WIRELESS SENSOR NETWORKS FOR STRUCTURAL HEALTH MONITORING

In Section 7.2.3, we presented the concept of SHM and the first generation of sensor networks for SHM. This first generation is represented by wired sensor networks, and comprises centralized proposals with no in-network processing for assessing the structural integrity. The common approach of the solutions in the first generation is completely opposite the concept of network-centric solutions, and the presence of wires forbids large-scale deployments due to technical and economical issues.

In this section, we present the second and third generations of sensor networks for SHM. Both generations are represented by WSNs, and the approaches classified in each of them present increasing levels of data compression, aggregation, and fusion, with more distributed processing aimed at physical integrity characterization (of the structures). The second generation of sensor networks for SHM comprises solutions that are still centralized. The focus is on the reduction of the collected data to minimize transmissions and save energy from the wireless sensors, and the processing required by the structural engineering techniques for assessing the structural integrity is still mainly performed by the sink node. The third generation of sensor networks for SHM points towards fully network-centric approaches, comprising many partially decentralized solutions and few fully decentralized solutions. In the third generation, the focus is on distributing, among the sensor nodes, the processing required by techniques that are already established in the structural engineering domain for assessing the physical integrity of the structure. To the best of our knowledge, a proposal of our research team, called Sensor-SHM [6], is the only work in the researched literature that presents a fully decentralized approach, according to the definition of "decentralized" we stated in Section 7.2.2. Sensor-SHM will be described in Section 7.4.3 and used for comparison with each of the works presented in the following generations.

7.4.1 The Second Generation of Sensor Networks for SHM

In this section, we present the second generation of sensor networks for SHM. Examples of works that fit this generation are [3, 4, 28]. In [3] and [28], a system called Wisden is discussed. The authors of both works classify Wisden as a structural data acquisition system, which has a small degree of in-network processing. Wisden focuses on dealing with the issue of transporting raw acceleration signals to the base station (sink) for further centralized structural analysis. For that purpose, Wisden focuses on (i) *reliable data transport* (topology management, routing, and error recovery); (ii) *Compression* (surpassing periods of inactivity and performing wavelet compression techniques); and (iii) *data synchronization* [3]. Wisden faced resource constraints like the low sampling rate of 100 Hz, achievable by the vibration cards, and also the low network bandwidth available [29]. Originally, Wisden relied on MICA2 motes, but in [28], a comparison is made between the implementation of Wisden using MICA2 and MICAz platforms, showing a better performance for the MICAz mote.

In [4], the authors describe a WSN for remote monitoring of the Golden Gate Bridge, in the United States. The "46-hop network," as denominated by the authors, monitors the bridge's structural state through the measurement and interpretation of ambient vibrations and strong motion. The previously mentioned requirements of reliable data transport, compression, and data synchronization are also comprised by the six major requirements of WSNs for SHM defined in [4]. Beyond the three previously mentioned requirements, other major requirements are a high sampling rate (1 kHz was chosen) and a minimization of the effect of the sources of distortion over the acquired data. It is also worth mentioning that the work described in [4] presented the largest WSN testbed (46-hop network) that was ever deployed at the time. The authors also noticed that Wisden is not capable of sampling higher than 160 Hz, which is far below the requirements defined in [4].

7.4.2 The Third Generation of Sensor Networks for SHM

Works classified in the third generation of sensor networks for SHM are characterized by some degree of decentralization in its proposals. Some of these works aim at the calculation of "damage indexes," which have valuable meaning for damage characterization and can be efficiently transmitted among the motes in the network. Also, few levels of information fusion are presented by these works.

In [29], the authors discuss the issues around Wisden and present a new algorithm for SHM using WSNs. In spite of being designed in the context of Wisden (classified in the second generation), we classified this algorithm in the third generation of sensor networks for SHM because this work relies on more in-network processing in a partially decentralized approach for assessing damage, going further than Wisden, which relies only on data transport. The sensing technique defined in [29] uses electrodynamic shakers to generate vibrations on the structure and uses accelerometers in the sensor nodes to collect data for a few seconds in order to capture these vibrations. In order to perform a structural analysis, a FFT is applied over the acceleration data collected in each sensor node, converting the signal in time domain to a signal in frequency domain. Then, the power spectrum is analyzed and the frequencies of the structural modes of vibration, whose values correspond to the peaks of the power spectrum, are extracted. Then, one sensor node is elected among all the sensors to be responsible for obtaining a more accurate result by aggregating all measures of modal frequencies and their associated energies extracted from all the network nodes. Finally, this aggregated result is sent to the sink and then the frequency variation analysis can be done.

There are other different SHM techniques that can be used along with WSNs that also inspire decentralized processing. Some of these techniques are presented by the authors of [30], where three techniques for detecting damage on structures are discussed. The first is a technique that performs data compression within the network, and it is based on a time series of acceleration signals. In this technique, the response of a structure is modeled using linear auto-regressive (AR), or auto-regressive moving average (ARMA) time series. The damage is detected by a significant variation in the AR/ARMA coefficients, relative to the intact (healthy) structure coefficients. Each sensor node can locally compute these coefficients and forward them, instead of requiring that all sensors transmit their collected acceleration data. So, if each sensor node forwards 40 sets of AR/ARMA coefficients instead of 5,000 samples of acceleration data, more than 99% in communication overhead is saved. The second technique detects and locates structural damage using ratios of modal frequency changes between two different modes of vibration, a modal-based technique. Variations in the mode shapes may be more sensitive to damage, depending on the analyzed structure. The latter technique makes use of a neural network to detect the possibility of damage. We found several studies in the literature that were inspired by the second technique (including our previous work, Sensor-SHM [6]).

The proposal described in [31] makes use of a WSN to monitor structural conditions. The performed study resulted in the emergence of new challenges for WSNs, since these networks are used in the proposal not only as an infrastructure to carry information from the SHM solution, but the sensor nodes also incorporate part of the solution core. The mentioned work proposes a partially decentralized algorithm to be used along with the damage location assurance criterion (DLAC) method. In the algorithm, data is collected and partially processed by the sensor nodes inside the network (the so-called in-network processing). In the sink node, the frequency values that compose the signature of the structure are extracted by solving a mathematical equation expressing a curve that fits the resultant curve of a FFT. Afterwards, the DLAC algorithm runs on the sink, taking data relative to two sources as input to detect and locate damage: (i) the sensed data related to the structural frequency response and (ii) data related to the responses of an analytical model to the same scenario. The analytical model is developed through a finite element modeling. The partial decentralization of the procedure for damage detection, allowing the sensor nodes to act on the collected data, significantly reduces energy consumption because it minimizes the number of required transmissions. However, damage detection and localization through the use of the DLAC method was still centrally performed in the sink node.

In the SHM literature, the widespread use of damage coefficients similar to the DLAC is noticeable. In general, the numerical values of these coefficients are extracted from raw data through information fusion techniques, and their value indicates how intense an occurrence of damage is, if it exists, or how close a site is to the damage site. In [32] the authors analyze the design requirements of WSN-based SHM solutions and discuss the related challenges dealt with in distributed processing. Two algorithms are presented in [32]. The first algorithm, distributed damage index detection (DDID), is based on a centralized algorithm proposed in [33]. In [32], this centralized algorithm is revised into a distributed version. The second algorithm, collaborative damage event detection (CDED), uses the results provided by the DDID algorithm and aims to improve the reliability and accuracy of the damage report by exchanging data among the sensor nodes. The distributed damage index detection is, in fact, a measure for the possibility of damage occurrence, that is, a measure of how the raw data collected by the sensors deviates from its normal state, as stated in [34].

So, in [32], every sensor node inspects the collected raw data and determines the damage candidates by using the DDID algorithm. Once the candidates are defined, the sensor nodes will use the CDED algorithm to cooperatively create the damage report containing the information about the location, scale, and index of the damage. CDED and DDID are complementary algorithms in which information fusion is performed in different data abstraction levels. In DDID, the measurement and feature levels are more evident, whereas in CDED the decision level is more evident, which characterizes a multilevel data fusion as a whole. In the proposal described in [32], the sensors are clustered, and the network is comprised of two tiers, one containing the sensor nodes and another containing the cluster-head nodes.

Still, in the context of damage coefficients, there is the possibility of performing information fusion techniques over raw data from different sources to calculate a damage coefficient. This is the case of the damage factor presented in [35], a work in which distributed SHM technology for large-scale engineering structures is discussed. The damage factor in the aforementioned work is calculated by multiplying the differences between the healthy value and the current value of two different sources: the amplitude and the time of flight of the signal captured by piezoelectric sensors. This type of information fusion technique is classified as cooperative fusion [5].

Infrastructures like NetSHM [36] and Tenet [37] aim at allowing the use of different SHM techniques in one single solution. In fact, Tenet goes even farther, by supporting application domains other than only SHM. Both these infrastructures are not complete SHM solutions, but mainly act on lower WSN layers like transport and network layers, below the application layer, for supporting the development of general solutions over them. NetSHM is a programmable software system for implementing SHM techniques in general, as seen in the works previously described in the last two generations. Such a system allows civil engineers to employ SHM techniques along with WSNs, without having to understand the specificities of wireless sensor networking [36]. The principle called "the Tenet" by the authors in [37] can greatly simplify the development of sensor network solutions. This principle encompasses the existence of two tiers in the network. One tier contains master nodes and the other tier contains slave nodes. Master nodes are responsible for encompassing the main application logic. Multi-node data fusion functionality and complex application logic should be implemented only on masters. Slave nodes are responsible for data acquisition and are accessed through a simplified interface by the master nodes. Although NetSHM and Tenet present a similar approach to Wisden, they allow the use of data fusion techniques for extracting indexes from the raw data collected. Therefore, signal processing techniques, such as FFTs, can be performed in-network. This explains the classification of NetSHM and Tenet in the third generation of sensor networks for SHM.

Finally, a full SHM system based on a WSN must provide all the capabilities of both second and third generations of sensor networks for SHM. In SHM solutions, gathering the sampled acceleration signals at a sink node is useful for logging data and performing visual and custom analysis. Yet, the decision over the damage is better suited to be made autonomously, over simple indicators (numbers) built through information fusion techniques, speeding up the alarm/reaction at a damage occurrence. Thus, reliable and efficient data transport, based on compression of acceleration signals, as well as the use of information fusion techniques on a decentralized approach are important features to be considered in a full SHM system based on a WSN.

7.4.3 A Fully Decentralized, Network-Centric Approach: Sensor-SHM

Sensor-SHM [38] is a distributed algorithm in which each node of the network has only a partial view of the global situation and nodes collaborate by sharing their views to achieve the final goal (of characterizing damages). Sensor-SHM can be classified as a multilevel information fusion algorithm, because it encompasses a sequence of information fusion procedures, each of which acts in one or more of the three data abstraction levels seen in [5]. Sensor-SHM considers a hierarchical (clustered) network topology comprised of two layers. The lower layer contains sensor nodes, organized in clusters. The higher layer contains the leaders of clusters, also called cluster-heads (CHs). Sensor nodes perform sensing tasks only; CHs do not perform sensing tasks and are responsible for coordinating the communication and processing inside their respective clusters.

In short, the Sensor-SHM algorithm aims at generating a damage index. During a data collection stage (the common operation cycle of the algorithm), the sensors synchronously collect acceleration samples from the structure at a given sampling rate and duration. The sensors then perform a FFT over the collected sample, followed by a method for extracting the values from the given number of modal frequencies of interest in the power spectrum (the peaks of the power spectrum). Therefore, each sensor obtains a frequency vector named $\omega_{i,t}$, defined for every sensor i at a data collection stage t, whose size is equal to the number of modal frequencies of interest in the analysis. Thus, these vectors are transmitted for the respective CHs.

The CH is responsible for comparing the received vectors at the data collection stage t ($\omega_{i,t}$) with the respective vector of expected healthy frequencies ($\omega_{i,0}$), which was previously informed for each CH during a setup process. Also in the setup process, the CHs receive vectors with the values of the tolerable deviations for each sensor, and if one of the modal frequencies suffers a deviation larger than these tolerable values, the CHs calculate a damage index named $D_{i,t}$. All the values required at the setup procedure must be informed by a specialist in the structure. The values of ($\omega_{i,0}$) for each sensor are considered to be the values collected at the beginning of the operation of the structure in our work [6]. But they can also be obtained by other methods, as discussed in Section 7.3 (FEM or statistical analysis).

The $D_{i,t}$ index denotes how close to a damaged site the sensor i is at a data collection stage t. For acquiring this index, the vector with the deviations of each modal frequency named $\Delta\omega_{i,t} = |\omega_{i,0} - \omega_{i,t}|$ is multiplied by a vector A_i, which is also stored in the CHs at the setup process and comprises weights associated to each modal frequency shift. In as much as changes in the higher modal frequencies mean there are changes in the local modes of vibration, the A_i vector, also defined by a specialist in the structure, is responsible for identifying the sensor nodes that are closest to the damage position. Therefore, at the network startup process, the highest weight values are associated with the highest modes of vibration and are stored in the CH of each sensor node i. Thus, the sensor nodes that are closest to the damage position have the highest Di,t coefficients of the whole network.

In the following step, $D_{i,t}$ coefficients are aggregated in each cluster j by summing their values for all k sensors in the cluster, resulting in a $C_{j,t}$ coefficient. By its mathematical definition, $C_{j,t}$ coefficient is an indicator of how close to the damage the cluster as a whole is. The algorithm uses this indicator to locate and determine the damage extent. Damage detection is concluded in a previous step, when the vector $\Delta\omega_{i,t}$ surpasses the tolerance values. Ideally, a healthy structure should present null $\Delta\omega_{i,t}$ vectors, and damage is detected when one of the values of $\Delta\omega_{i,t}$ has a value different than zero, considering a given tolerance in the respective position of the tolerance vector.

In our algorithm of damage localization and extent determination, each CH node compares its $C_{j,t}$ coefficient with a L_j tolerance value. When the $C_{j,t}$ coefficient exceeds L_j, the CH sends a message informing of its $C_{j,t}$ coefficient to its neighbor CHs. The L_j tolerance is defined for each CH, in a similar way to the determination of the values of the Ti tolerance vector. After the CH j transmits its $C_{j,t}$ value to its immediate CH neighbors, it is expected that some of these neighbors also have exceeded their L_j tolerance value and thus have sent their respective $C_{j,t}$ coefficients to their neighbors. CHs then compare received $C_{j,t}$ values with their own and the CH that has the greatest $C_{j,t}$ value in a given neighborhood assumes the role of a "collector." The collector node is responsible for two tasks: (i) aggregating the information about the $\omega_{i,t}$ values from all its neighboring CHs and building a report to be sent to the sink, to issue a warning and (ii) acting on the environment around it by triggering a relay, aimed at preventing the progression of damage and avoiding further problems in the locality. At the sink, the damage localization can be reproduced through the unique identifiers and positions of the reporting sensors, and the extent is determined by the area covered by these sensors. Through the values contained in the report, it is possible to reproduce the situation that occurred within the network and take the appropriate decisions about the structural predictive maintenance.

Sensor-SHM differs from Wisden, as well as from all the works of the second generation of sensor networks for SHM, in the use of decentralized processing, because such a processing approach imposes new challenges. Reliable data transport and data synchronization are still challenges to be dealt with in all generations, as in every use of WSNs for SHM, but solutions to these challenges are different in a decentralized scenario because the amount of data is considerably smaller. Another difference is that in Sensor-SHM we rely on information fusion techniques instead of simple data compression.

Regarding the third generation of sensor networks for SHM, Sensor-SHM differs from [29] because the frequency variation analysis is performed within the network, with the collaboration of cluster-heads. Sensor-SHM is mainly inspired by the work presented in [31]. One of the differences between our proposal and this work is that, in our solution, the whole procedure of extracting the frequency values from the power spectrum is performed on the sensors, whereas in [31] it is conducted by the curve fitting stage, which is partially performed in the sensors and partially in the sink node. Unlike other algorithms proposed in the literature, all the SHM processing of our algorithm is performed on the sensor and cluster-head nodes, without the help of the sink node. And through collaboration among cluster-head nodes, it is possible detect, localize, and determine the extent of damage.

Similar to the work described in [32], our proposal, Sensor-SHM, is also based on a multilevel information fusion technique to generate damage indexes, and we have also adopted a network organization into two tiers. Moreover, the work in [32] points towards two main issues: (i) how much information should be sent back to the server in order to ensure both energy efficiency and precision of results, and (ii) how to automate the decision on the existence, location, and extent of damages that is originally made through human interference. Effectiveness around these issues was demonstrated in [32], and both issues are also dealt with in Sensor-SHM. The main points at which our work differs from the proposal of [32] are (i) the way in which the damage coefficient is calculated, since our damage coefficient is based on the analysis of modal frequencies and this feature is not exploited in DDID, which makes use of raw acceleration signals; (ii) the Sensor-SHM algorithm proposes more operations of information fusion in different levels to calculate the damage coefficients; and (iii) in Sensor-SHM the cluster meaning and the nodes' behavior are different.

The damage factor from [35] is calculated by multiplying the differences between the healthy value and the current value of two different sources: the amplitude and the time of flight of the signal captured by piezoelectric sensors. Although this is a feasible possibility, in Sensor-SHM only one feature is extracted from the raw data to calculate the damage coefficient. Future works may cover the aspect of cooperative fusion [5] in our proposed algorithm, Sensor-SHM. The information fusion techniques presented in [6] are considered complementary fusion [5], in the case of information fused among cluster-heads, and redundant fusion [5], in the case of information fusion within the sensors pertaining the same cluster.

Finally, Sensor-SHM differs from Tenet and NetSHM primarily because we propose a solution that deals with all the WSN layers, also comprising the application layer and throwing a focus on it, whereas in Tenet and NetSHM the focus is on the lower layers of the network.

7.5 CONCLUSION

In this chapter, the concepts of SHM and WSNs were briefly discussed apart from one another, and existent solutions employing WSNs in the context of SHM were explored and classified. The concept of "generations of sensor networks for SHM" was used for such classification. Each generation was presented by describing respective examples of works found in the current literature. It is important to mention that all the works presented and classified in this chapter focus on SHM techniques based on the use of accelerometers; but in further investigations, this classification can be expanded to works that use other kinds of sensing devices, for example, strain gauges, following the same logic of higher degrees of decentralization and in-network processing. This chapter also presented different examples of large-scale networks inside this classification, and showed evidence that the works are evolving towards network-centric approaches in which higher levels of decentralization and in-network processing are being pursued through an increased use of information fusion techniques. Indeed, Sensor-SHM is a first step toward the possibile creation of a fourth generation of sensor networks for SHM, in which the works present fully decentralized approaches, since the third generation encompasses only partially decentralized solutions by this time.

It was not our goal to exhaust the theme of the entire SHM domain; the range of SHM solutions is huge and encompasses distinct possibilities, involving knowledge from different fields of expertise. New SHM solutions using WSNs are constantly arising and existent ones are being enhanced. The WSN hardware is also in constant evolution, enabling higher sampling rates and processing/storage capabilities, thus surpassing many open issues in the use of WSNs for SHM.

ACKNOWLEDGMENTS

This work is partly supported by the National Council for Scientific and Techno-logical Development (CNPq) through processes 481638/2007-5 for Luci Pirmez and Flávia C. Delicato; 4781174/2010-1 and 309270/2009-0 for Luci Pirmez; 311363/2011-3, 470586/2011-7 and 201090/2009-0 for Flávia C. Delicato; 480359/2009-1 and 311515/2009-6 for Paulo F. Pires; by the Financier of Studies and Projects (FINEP) through processes 01.10.0549.00 and 01.10.0064.00 for Luci Pirmez; and by the Foundation for Research of the State of Rio de Janeiro (FAPERJ) through processes E26/101.360/2010 for Luci Pirmez; E-26/100.428/2010 for Claudio M. de Farias.
    We also want to express our gratitude to Albert and Hamid, who kindly invited us to contribute to this Book.

REFERENCES

[1] M. Hatler, D. Gurganious, and C. Chi, "Industrial wireless sensor networks—A market dynamics report." *On World* (2010), p. 157.

[2] H. Sohn, C. R. Farrar, F. M. Hemez, D. D. Shunk, D. W. Stinemates, B. R. Nadler, et al. A Review of Structural Health Monitoring Literature: 1996–2001. Los Alamos National Laboratory Report No. LA-13976-MS, 2004.

[3] N. Xu, S. Rangwala, K. K. Chintalapudi, D. Ganesan, A. Broad, R. Govindan, and D. Estrin, "A wireless sensor network for structural monitoring." In *Proceedings of the ACM Conference on Embedded Networked Sensor Systems*, ACM Press, Nov. 2004, pp. 13–24.

[4] S. Kim, S. Pakzad, D. Culler, J. Demmel, G. Fenves, S. Glaser, and M. Turon, "Health monitoring of civil infrastructures using wireless sensor networks." In *Proceedings of the 6th International Conference on Information Processing in Sensor Networks*, ACM Press, Cambridge, MA, 2007, pp. 254–263.

[5] E. F. Nakamura, A. A. F. Loureiro, and A. C. Frery, "Information fusion for wireless sensor networks: methods, models, and classifications." *ACM Computing Surveys* 2007, 39(3), pp. 9/1–9/55.

[6] I. L. Santos, L. Pirmez, E. T. Lemos, L. A. V. Pinto, F. C. Delicato, and J. N. Souza, "Resource consumption analysis for a structural health monitoring algorithm using wireless sensor networks." In *XXVIII SBRC*, 2010, Gramado. Anais. Porto Alegre: SBC, 2010. Vol. 1. pp. 263–276.

[7] C. R. Farrar and S. W. Doebling, "An overview of modal-based damage identification methods." *EUROMECH 365 International Workshop: DAMAS 97, Structural Damage Assessment Using Advanced Signal Processing Procedures*, 1997.

[8] P. C. Chang, A. Flatau, and S. C. Liu, "Health monitoring of civil infrastructure." *Structural Health Monitoring*, 2003, 2(3), pp. 257–267.

[9] K. H. Huebner, *The Finite Element Method for Engineers.* 1975, John Wiley & Sons.

[10] P. Cawley and R. D. Adams, "The localization of defects in structures from measurements of natural frequencies." *J Strain Anal* 1979, 14, pp. 49–57.

[11] A. Messina, A. I. Jones, and J. E. Williams, "Damage detection and localization using natural frequency changes." *Proceedings of Conference on Identification in Engineering Systems,* Swansea, UK, 1996, pp. 67–76.

[12] T. Contursi, A. Messina, and E. J. Williams, "A multiple-damage location assurance criterion based on natural frequency changes." *Journal of Vibration and Control,* 1998, No. 4, pp. 619-633.

[13] S. Roundy and L. Frechette, "Energy scavenging and nontraditional power sources for wireless sensor networks." In I. Stojmenović, Ed. *Handbook of Sensor Networks, Algorithms and Archtectures.* 2005, Wiley Interscience.

[14] J. Hill, R. Szewczyk, and A. Woo, et al. "System architecture directions for networked sensors." *Proceedings of the 9th ASPLOS;* Nov. 2000, Cambridge, MA.

[15] D. D. Wentzloff, B. H. Calhoun, and R. Min, et al. "Design considerations for next generation wireless power-aware microsensor nodes." *Proceedings of the 17th International Conference on VLSI Design* (VLSID'04), 2004, Mumbai, India. pp. 361–367.

[16] I. Akyildiz, W. Su, Y. Sankarasubramaniam, and E. Cayiric, "A survey on sensor networks." *IEEE Communications Magazine,* Aug. 2002, pp. 102–114.

[17] J. Al-Karaki and A. Kamal, "Routing techniques in wireless sensor networks: A survey." *IEEE Wireless Communications* Dec. 2004, Vol. 11, No. 6, pp. 6–28.

[18] I. Demirkol, C. Ersoy, and F. Alagoz, "MAC protocols for wireless sensor networks: A survey." *IEEE Communications Magazine,* Apr. 2006, Vol. 44, No. 4, pp. 115–121.

[19] C. Yeh, *Dynamic Reconfiguration Techniques for Wireless Sensor Networks.* Master's thesis, University of Massachusetts, 2008.

[20] N. Xu, S. Rangwala, and K. K. Chintalapudi, et al. "A wireless sensor network for structural monitoring." *Proceedings of the ACM SenSys,* Nov. 2004, Baltimore, MD.

[21] A. Mainwaring, D. Culler, and J. Polastre, et al. "Wireless sensor networks for habitat monitoring." *Proceedings of the 1st ACM international Workshop on Wireless Sensor Networks and Applications,* Sept. 2002, Atlanta, GA, pp. 88–97.

[22] T. Liu, C. M. Sadler, P. Zhang, and M. Martonosi, "Implementing software on resource-constrained mobile sensors: Experiences with Impala and ZebraNet." *Proceedings of the International Conference on Mobile Systems, Applications, and Services,* 2004, Boston, MA.

[23] G. Werner-Allen, K. Lorincz, and J. Johnson, et al. "Fidelity and yield in a volcano monitoring sensor network." *Proceedings of the 7th Symposium on Operating Systems Design and Implementation,* Nov. 2006, Seattle, WA, pp. 381–396.

[24] R. Gao and Z. Fan, "Architectural design of a sensory-node-controller for optimized energy utilization in sensor networks." *IEEE Transactions on Instrumentation and Measurement,* Apr. 2006, Vol. 55, No. 2, pp. 415–428.

[25] A. Arora, P. Dutta, and S. Bapat, et al. "A line in the sand: A wireless sensor network for target detection, classification, and tracking." *Computer Networks,* Dec. 2004, Vol. 46, No. 5, pp. 605–634.

[26] V. Shnayder, B. Chen, and K. Lorincz, et al. *Sensor Networks for Medical Care.* Technical Report TR-08-05, Division of Engineering and Applied Science, Harvard University, 2005.

[27] M. Chen, C. Hu, and W. Weng, "Dynamic object tracking tree in wireless sensor network." *EURASIP Journal on Wireless Communications and Networking*, Mar. 2010.

[28] J. Paek, K. Chintalapudi, J. Caffrey, R. Govindan, and S. Masri, "A wireless sensor network for structural health monitoring: Performance and experience." In *Proceedings of the Second IEEE Workshop on Embedded Networked Sensors* (EmNetS-II), May 2005.

[29] J. Caffrey, et al. *Networked Sensing for Structural Health Monitoring.* Center for Embedded Network Sensing. Paper No. 524, 2004.

[30] K. Chintalapudi, T. Fu, J. Paek, N. Kothari, S. Rangwala, J. Caffrey, R. Govindan, E. Johnson, and S. Masri, "Monitoring civil structures with a wireless sensor network." *IEEE Internet Computing* 2006, Vol. 10, No. 2, pp. 26–34.

[31] G. Hackmann, F. Sun, N. Castaneda, C. Lu, and S. Dyke, "A holistic approach to decentralized structural damage localization using wireless sensor networks." *Proceedings of 29th IEEE Real-Time Systems Symposium*, 2008.

[32] M. Wang, J. Cao, B. Chen, Y. Xu, and J. Li, "Distributed processing in wireless sensor networks for structural health monitoring." *LNCS*, 2007, Vol. 4611, pp. 103–112.

[33] B. Chen and Y. L. Xu, "A new damage index for detecting sudden stiffness reduction." In *Proc.1st International Conference on Structural Condition Assessment, Monitoring and Improvement*, Perth, Western Australia, 2005, pp. 63–70.

[34] C. Park, J. Tang, and Y. Ding, "Aggressive data reduction for damage detection in structural health monitoring." *Structural Health Monitoring*, Jan. 1, 2010, Vol. 9, No. 1, pp. 59–74.

[35] F. Yuan, D. K. Liang, and L. H. Shi, et al. "Recent progress on distributed structural health monitoring research at NUAA." *Journal of Intelligent Material Systems and Structures*, 2008, Vol. 19, No. 3, pp. 373–386.

[36] K. Chintalapudi, J. Paek, O. Gnawali, and T. Fu, et al. "Structural damage detection and localization using NetSHM." In *Proceedings of 5th International Conference on Information Processing in Sensor Networks: Special Track on Sensor Platform Tools and Design Methods for Networked Embedded Systems* (IPSN/SPOTS'06), Apr. 2006.

[37] O. Gnawali, B. Greenstein, K. Jang, A. Joki, and J. Paek, et al. "The tenet architecture for tiered sensor networks." In *Proceedings of the 4th ACM Conference on Embedded Networked Sensor Systems* (Sensys '06). ACM Press, Nov. 2006.

[38] I. L. Santos, L. Pirmez, E. T. Lemos, L. A. V. Pinto, F. C. Delicato, J. N. Souza, and A. Zomaya, "A localized algorithm for structural health monitoring using wireless sensor networks." *Information Fusion*, Available online 16 Feb. 2012, DOI: 10.1016/j.inffus.2012.02.002.

8

MOBILITY EFFECTS IN WIRELESS MOBILE NETWORKS

Abbas Nayebi and Hamid Sarbazi-Azad

CONTENTS

8.1 INTRODUCTION

In recent years, wireless sensor networks (WSNs), mobile ad hoc networks (MANETs), and wireless mesh networks have sparked much research interest. These wireless

Large Scale Network-Centric Distributed Systems, First Edition. Edited by Hamid Sarbazi-Azad and Albert Y. Zomaya.
© 2014 John Wiley & Sons, Inc. Published 2014 by John Wiley & Sons, Inc.

networks offer promising technologies and are anticipated to make a great difference in everyday life in the near future.

Mobile ad hoc networks are comprised of mobile nodes communicating via wireless links. Wireless sensor networks consist of a large number of small sensor nodes distributed over a vast field to obtain fine-grained sensing data. Mobility is an important factor that affects performance of wireless networks [1, 2], including wireless sensor networks [3, 4], mobile ad hoc networks, and wireless mesh networks. In fact, topology of a mobile wireless network is subject to continuous changes, which considerably affects the performance of routing protocols [5]. Mobility might be controlled by network management [6, 7] and hence is useful for achieving sensing coverage, data gathering, or balancing energy consumption.

In a typical delay-tolerant network (DTN), mobility of nodes is used to deliver data. However, in a majority of applications, especially in mobile ad hoc networks and wireless mesh networks, mobility of nodes is not a desirable characteristic of the network in terms of performance. Mobility may degrade the performance of such networks due to route cache misses, frequent calls for route discovery procedures, or misplacing the destination. In these cases, analysis and design of reliable wireless networks in the presence of node mobility is called *mobility tolerance study*. Mobility tolerance study can be experimental or analytical. Analytic mobility tolerance study, as a field of analytic performance evaluation, has its own advantages over simulation approach. However, analytical performance evaluation of wireless networks, even without considering mobility is not a trivial task.

In order to ease the analysis of mobility effects on the performance of wireless networks, a possible approach, called *intermediate performance modeling* (IPM), can divide the analysis into two steps:

Step I: Analysis of the effects of mobility on some intermediate performance measures (e.g., link lifetime).

Step II: Analysis of the effects of the intermediate performance measures on some final performance measures (e.g., packet loss ratio).

The first step is actually an issue of geometry, probability theory, radio signal propagation models, and mobility traces. The second step is more specialized and relates to particular protocols. Thus, using IPM, one may reuse results of the first step, for several evaluations. Moreover, given the results of the first step, for several mobility conditions a particular protocol can be evaluated for all of them.

In the rest of the chapter, we first discuss the effect of mobility on the link lifetime of the wireless networks. Then we study the effect of mobility on the topology of wireless networks.

8.2 THE EFFECT OF NODE MOBILITY ON WIRELESS LINKS

Link lifetime can be considered an intermediate performance measure. Link lifetime is already used for performance evaluation of wireless networks (i.e., step II) in some studies [8–12]. Residual link lifetime can be easily sampled from network logs without additional software/hardware components such as GPS, which make the application of the IPM method more practical. In comparison, performance evaluation using trace-based mobility simulations [13] requires special network setup and GPS devices, which limits applicability of these methods. For example, GPS devices cannot function at indoor environments. Moreover, the set of people who carry GPS devices is limited to particular groups such as students, employees of a laboratory, or attendees of a conference [13, 14]. In contrast, link lifetime measurements can be performed on actually functioning networks without interruption of the network operation.

The importance of the study of link lifetime has drawn much attention [5, 8, 15–28]. The analysis of link/route stability is justified in [27] for its importance in

- evaluating quality of service,
- establishing stable routes to maximize throughput and reduce traffic latency,
- devising efficient route repair strategies, and
- studying network connectivity and performance.

Here, we review a probabilistic approach to studying residual link lifetime (RLL) and link lifetime (LL). LL is defined as the time interval in which one node stays in the transmission area of another node and RLL is the remaining lifetime of a link established at a random point in time. In this context, one of the crucial aspects to be addressed is the stability of the established routing paths (also called path duration) that is the time interval from when the route is established until one of the links along the route becomes unavailable. Indeed, this metric significantly affects the performance of on-demand routing protocols. When a link is broken, all the paths using this link are torn down, too, and new paths must be checked for availability, which is a resource consuming task. Hence, the performance of mobile wireless networks mainly depends on the residual lifetime of individual links. Link availability is another metric that is defined as the probability that a wireless link between two mobile nodes exists at time $t + t_0$, given that a link existed at time t_0.

RLL is an important parameter in topology control [29, 30] in mobile networks. Some topology control protocols are highly sensitive to link breakages and some can tolerate it [31]. However, the more knowledge we have about the RLL, the more precise the evaluation and design of a topology control protocol can be done. Much work has been done to investigate the link lifetime and RLL in different scenarios [19, 23, 32, 33]. Some of the studies on link lifetime can be categorized as below:

- Analytic studies with different mobility models: In [9, 10, 22, 24, 25], and [15], analytic models for link lifetime under Brownian motion mobility model, random waypoint mobility model, random direction, and the random ad hoc mobility model are proposed, respectively.
- Using different models: Although many of the studies used a geometric model, authors in [17] tried to model route lifetime by a complex Markov chain, and

authors in [28] provided an approximation model for link lilfetime based on a
two-state Markov chain.

- Pure simulation-based or experimental studies: Link lifetime evaluations in
[5, 16, 19] are based only on simulation experiments. An experimental study
of link statistics for a mobile network in a laboratory environment is reported in
[26]. Authors in [16] experimentally investigate the link stability.

Here, we will review a geometrical model used to obtain a closed-form expression
for the residual link lifetime PDF (probability density function). Then, we will study
some aspects of RLL and link lifetime.

8.2.1 Geometric Modeling

Several geometric models are proposed to study RLL or link lifetime [9, 10, 18, 23].
However, modeling of RLL or link lifetime is a delicate probabilistic/geometric issue.
For example, a small mistake in assumptions in [8] led to large errors in the results, which
is commented on in [34]. Here, we review a sample geometric model for RLL analysis.

Consider two wireless nodes WN_1 and WN_2 with velocity vectors $\vec{V_1}$ and $\vec{V_2}$,
respectively (Fig. 8.1). β is defined as the random angle between the x axis and $\vec{V_r}$.
At time t_0, node WN_1 visits node WN_2 at distance r. Now, we try to evaluate the time
interval in which WN_2 remains in the transmission region of WN_1, that is the RLL of
the active link between WN_1 and WN_2. The RLL is obtained by

$$T = P/V_r, \qquad (8.1)$$

where P is the distance that WN_2 must travel relatively to WN_1 to reach the boundary
of the transmission range of WN_1. Using this model, the pdf of T is obtained as [32]

$$f_T(\tau) = \int_{V_r} f_{v_r}(v_r) \int_r f_r(r) \, v_r \, f_{P|r}(\tau \, v_r|r) \, dr \, dv_r, \qquad (8.2)$$

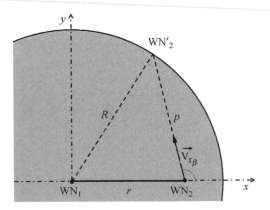

Figure 8.1 Relative motion of two wireless nodes.

where

$$f_r(r) = \frac{2r}{R^2}, \quad 0 \le r \le R \tag{8.3}$$

and

$$f_{P|r}(p|r) = \frac{1}{\pi} \frac{\frac{R^2 + p^2 - r^2}{p^2 r}}{\sqrt{4 - \frac{(R^2 - p^2 - r^2)^2}{p^2 r^2}}}, \quad R - r \le p \le R + r. \tag{8.4}$$

This relation is applicable for centro-symmetric mobility models. Using this relation, the distribution of RLL is obtained given the distribution of relative velocity. For example, for constant velocity mobility model [23], in which nodes move with a constant velocity ($|\vec{V}| = v_c$) in a random direction, the pdf of relative velocity is obtained [9, 10] as

$$f_{V_r}(v_r) = \frac{2}{\pi \sqrt{4v_c^2 - v_r^2}} \times [U(v_r) - U(v_r - 2v_c)], \tag{8.5}$$

where U is the unit step function. Therefore, the pdf of RLL is obtained as

$$f_T(\tau) = \frac{1}{\pi^2 R^2 \tau} [4\tau v_c R + 2(R - \tau v_c)(R + \tau v_c) \ln(\frac{R + \tau v_c}{|R - \tau v_c|})]. \tag{8.6}$$

Expression (8.6) can be used as a tight approximation of the distribution of RLL for the traditional random direction mobility model as well. According to [32], the pdf of link lifetime is obtained by

$$f_D(\tau) = -\frac{df_T(\tau)}{d\tau} \times \frac{\pi^2 R}{8 v_c}. \tag{8.7}$$

8.2.2 LL and RLL Properties

Based on the model in [32], it is shown that the expected value of RLL is infinite while the average of LL is finite. That is why LL is proposed as a performance or connectivity metric in the literature [23, 35], while RLL is never used as a metric. Maybe it looks like a paradox that the expected value of whole link lifetime is finite and the expected value of residual link lifetime (a portion of link lifetime) is greater. One may think that, because link establishment is performed at a random point of time (over the link lifetime) the average of the residual link lifetime must be half of the average of total link lifetime and consequently could not be greater than the average of the link lifetime. However, the case is analogous to the inspection paradox [36]. Briefly, when a node tries to establish a link, the neighbors with larger LL are more likely to be detected. In other words, average link lifetime is directly affected by the *frequency* of visiting (entrances to the transmission range) different nodes with different velocities, whereas average residual link lifetime is directly affected by the *density* of different nodes with different link lifetimes in the vicinity of a particular node [34].

Another interesting outcome of the closed-form expression for the pdf of RLL is that we can easily show RLL has a long-tailed distribution [33] and thus is heavy-tailed since every long-tailed distribution is also heavy-tailed [37]. RLL has no finite mean or any higher moment. LL in the case of the constant velocity model has also a long-tailed distribution. However, LL has a finite mean but no higher moments. These results reveal important facts about the behavior of LL and RLL random variables. Intuitively, these two random variables take small values frequently and very large values rarely. This can be of help to network designers in avoiding false heuristic assumptions. For example, a network designer may measure the average and variance of RLL from the logs of an actual network and estimate some RLL based on that. However, the results here confirm that, firstly, the average of RLL is not a stable measure and cannot provide only concrete facts about RLL distribution. Secondly, as RLL takes small values frequently and very large values rarely, most of the realistic samples of RLL are not close to the calculated average from the logs.

Other outcomes of the model are the investigation of the effect of the number of stationary nodes on the LL and RLL, investigation of the effect of buffer zone on the LL and RLL, and study of the behavior of LL and RLL in multivelocity mobility models [33].

In the next section, we will investigate the effect of mobility on network topology. As delivering pure analytic methods for this case are very complicated, we will use some facts obtained through simulation to ease the study.

8.3 THE EFFECT OF NODE MOBILITY ON NETWORK TOPOLOGY

It is a widely accepted fact that the limited energy available at the nodes of a wireless mobile network must be used as efficiently as possible [38]. If energy conservation techniques are used at different levels, the functional lifetime of both individual nodes and the network can be extended considerably. For this reason, energy conserving protocols at the MAC, routing, and upper layers have been proposed [39, 40]. Further energy can be saved if the network topology itself is energy-efficient, that is, if transmission ranges of the nodes are set in such a way that a target property (e.g., connectivity) of the resulting network topology is guaranteed, while the global energy consumption is reduced. Decreasing the nodes' transmission power with respect to the maximum level potentially has two positive effects: (i) reducing nodes' energy consumption, and (ii) increasing the spatial reuse, with a positive overall effect on network capacity [41].

Here, we will study a phase transition phenomenon in connectivity of topologies made by *homogeneous topology control* and *k-Neigh topology control protocol*, and based on that we find a relation between topology update time and transmission range.

The simplest form of topology control is *homogeneous topology control*, where a fixed value of transmission range is used for all nodes [29]. In the case that mobile nodes do not have a mechanism to adjust their transmission power adaptively at run time, it is the only possible solution. Thus, determining a proper global transmission range for this kind of topology control is of great importance [29, 42–45].

The topology constructed by the TC protocol is called *logical topology*. Each node keeps a list of logical neighbors in the logical topology and only communicates with them.

The logical topology is required to be connected. Several protocols could be executed on top of the logical topology and could construct a subgraph (e.g., a broadcast tree) out of it. Connectivity of the logical topology is a necessary condition for connectivity of such structures. The connectivity is ensured under all localized topology control protocols when the network is static. However, due to node mobility, there is no guarantee that a logical neighbor is within the transmission range at a later time. In this case, some logical neighbors are no longer reachable while others are still reachable (reachable neighbors are called *effective neighbors*). The union of the effective neighbor sets of all nodes forms an *effective topology* [31].

In case of homogeneous topology control, all the physical neighbors within critical transmission range are listed as logical neighbor list upon receiving a "hello" message from each other. An important problem in application of TC protocols under mobility conditions is the evaluation and determination of "hello" interval in order to conserve more energy while preserving connectivity. Obviously, setting a small value for "hello" interval leads to frequent execution of TC and more energy consumption. On the other hand, setting a high value for this important parameter may lead to a disconnected *effective topology* in a portion of the network lifetime unless the transmission range of the nodes is increased to keep the network connected, which will increase power consumption of the network in another way. Therefore, there is an optimal setting for transmission range and "hello" interval. To obtain such an optimal point, we need to have the relation between the transmission range and the "hello" interval that keeps the network connected.

The k-Neigh [46] topology protocol is based on the construction of a logical topology through connecting each node to its K nearest neighbors. Unidirectional links are either removed or converted into bidirectional edges. k-Neigh is a simple, fully distributed, asynchronous, and localized protocol that relies only on distance estimation, a technique that can be implemented at a reasonable cost in many realistic scenarios, and it does not need location information or angle of arrival (AoA) data to construct the topology.

In order to study mobility tolerance of a topology, we need to first define the connectivity requirement as a quantitative metric. In the next section, we will provide a formal definition of connectivity for the sake of this study.

8.3.1 Definitions of Connectivity

Below, some of the connectivity terms introduced in the literature are reviewed.

- *Strict connectivity (SCON):* Strict connectivity [31] is defined as traditional mathematical connectivity.
- *Weak connectivity (WCON):* There are different definitions for the weak connectivity. In several cases, the main goal behind defining a weak connectivity condition is for practical considerations. The rationale is that the network designer could be interested in maintaining only a certain fraction of the nodes connected, if this would result in significant energy savings. In [31], the weak connectivity is defined in terms of capability of completing a connectivity related

task, such as global flooding, measured in terms of the percentage of nodes that receive the message. In [46], a network is called weakly connected when at least 95% of network nodes belong to the same connected component with probability of at least 0.95.

In [12], the following *statistical connectivity requirements* are defined:

- *Statistical strict connectivity, SSC(α)*, is satisfied if the network is strongly connected with probability at least α.
- *Mean largest connected component ratio, MLCCR (α)*, is satisfied if *MLCCR* $\geq \alpha$ where *MLCCR* is the ratio of the mean size of the largest connected component to the size of whole network and α is a parameter over [0,1] (size of a network or a component is defined as the number of nodes included in it). For example, a random graph satisfies *MLCCR*(0.95) if the average of largest connected component covers at least 95% of the nodes. In practice, we can measure MLCCR on a large set of topologies.
- *Weak connectivity probability, WCP (α, β)*, is satisfied if *WCP* $\geq \alpha$ where *WCP* is the probability of observing a weakly connected network and α and β are parameters over [0,1]. A network is considered weakly connected if the ratio of the size of the largest connected component to the size of network is greater than or equal to β. For example, a random graph satisfies *WCP*(0.8,0.95) if the largest connected component covers at least 95% of nodes with probability of 0.8 or higher. Obviously, *WCP*(α, 1) is equivalent to *SSC*(α).

Now, we can formalize the problem of determining "hello" interval as the evaluation of statistical topology lifetime.

- *Statistical topology lifetime (STL):* Statistical topology lifetime is the maximum time interval after construction of the topology in which a specific *statistical connectivity requirement* is met.

8.3.2   Phase Transition Phenomenon in Connectivity and Disconnection Degree

A phase transition is a phenomenon where a system undergoes a sudden change of state: small changes of a given parameter in the system induce a great shift in system global behavior. This abrupt transition occurs at a specific value pc, called the *critical point* or *critical threshold*. Below pc, the system is said to be in a subcritical phase — the global behavior is nonexistent. Above pc the system is in a supercritical phase and the global property may be almost surely observed [47]. Connectivity phase transition is reported by several studies in random graphs [48, 49] and static wireless networks with respect to critical transmission range [43], number of neighbors [50], and probability of rebroadcasting [47]. For mobile networks, authors in [12] study the phase transition in connectivity of mobile networks with respect to time after construction of the topology.

Figures 8.2 and 8.3 depict the change of different connectivity metrics (MLCCR and WCP) with time for homogeneous and K-neigh topology control protocols, respectively. For consistency, we used the average number of neighbors for homogeneous case as an indicator of transmission range. As illustrated in the figures, as the number of nodes in the network or the average number of neighbors (K) is increased, a sharper reduction is observed. These figures clearly show a phase transition phenomenon in connectivity metrics with time.

Another phenomenon that has a crucial role in the proposed method concerns the average node degree at the time of phase transition, which is defined as the time instance

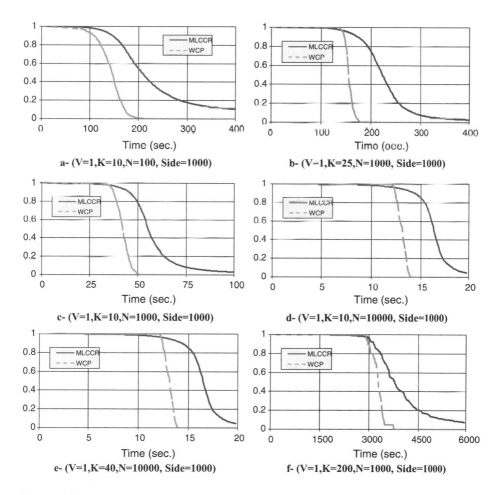

Figure 8.2 Phase transition in different scenarios with increasing time for homogeneous topology control. Simulation scenarios [9, 10] are mentioned below the curves, where V, K, N, and Side are node speed (m/s), average number of neighbors, number of nodes, and the side of square simulation area, respectively.

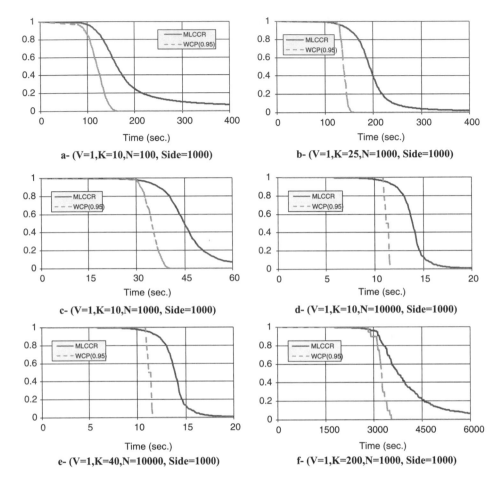

Figure 8.3 Phase transition in different scenarios with increasing time (after topology construction) for k-Neigh topology control. Simulation scenarios [12] are mentioned below the curves, where V, K, N, and Side are node speed (m/s), parameter K of the protocol, number of nodes, and the side of square simulation area, respectively.

in which the connectivity metric reaches its threshold and will be called *disconnection degree*.

Figure 8.4 depicts the value of disconnection degree for homogeneous topology control for two typical connectivity requirements: WCP(0.95,0.95) and MLCCR(0.95) and different values of N for scenario ($V = 1$, $K = 10$, N, $Side = 1000$). As depicted in the figures, disconnection degree is almost fixed. Figure 8.5 depicts the disconnection degree for k-Neigh topology control for various scenarios. Surprisingly, the disconnection degree is almost fixed. Even in the case that the initial degree is very large (K=200), disconnection occurs when the degree reaches around 4.5. Thus, regardless of the initial density of the graph and number of nodes, disconnection degree is almost fixed.

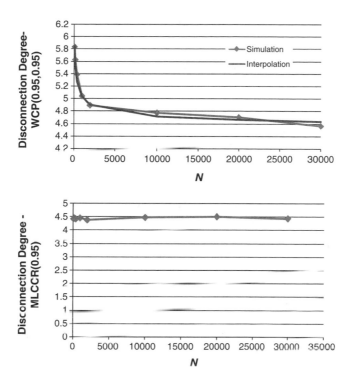

Figure 8.4 The value of disconnection degree for scenarios ($V = 1$, $K = 10$, N, Side $= 1000$) and different values of N using two connectivity requirements: WCP(0.95,0.95) at left and MLCCR(0.95) at right. For WCP(0.95, 0.95) the points can be interpolated with $4.5 + 8.5/N^{0.4}$ for better accuracy.

Based on these two phenomenon in [9, 10] and [12,] two methods are provided to accurately evaluate STL or "hello" interval. Indeed, using the results from LEL computation, we can obtain the amount of time required for average degree of the effective topology to reach to 4.5, and that is an estimation of STL. Comparison of the estimation results with simulation results confirms applicability of the estimation.

8.4 CONCLUSION

In this chapter, the effect of mobility on link and topology of wireless networks was studied. A common approach for analysis of the effect of mobility on the link lifetime and residual link lifetime of wireless networks is geometrical modeling. Using the geometric model, probability density function of link lifetime or residual link lifetime can be obtained for simple synthetic mobility models. For analysis of the effect of mobility on topology of wireless networks, a phase transition phenomenon was observed for different scenarios for two well-known topology control protocols, homogeneous topology

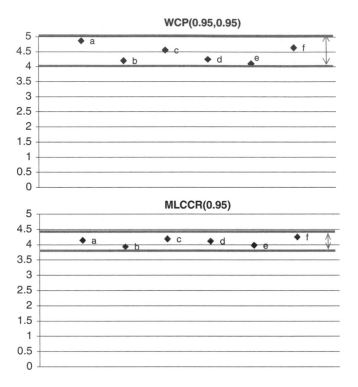

<u>Figure 8.5</u> The value of disconnection degree for different scenarios in Fig. 3 using two connectivity requirements: WCP(0.95,0.95) at left and MLCCR(0.95) at right. Letter marks are corresponding to scenarios in Fig. 3.

control and k-Neigh topology control. We observed that disconnection occurs suddenly in the networks rather than gradually. Another observation was that the degree of the effective topology was almost fixed around 4.5 at the time of disconnection. Using these facts, one can evaluate the lifetime of the topologies which could be directly used for optimizing the "hello" interval in topology control protocols.

REFERENCES

[1] M. M. Zonoozi and P. Dassanayake (1997). "User mobility modeling and characterization of mobility patterns." *IEEE Journal of Selected Areas in Communications* **15**: 1239–1252.

[2] T. Camp and J. Boleng, et al. (2002). "A survey of mobility models for ad hoc network research." *Wireless Comm. & Mobile Computing (WCMC)* **2**(5): 483–502.

[3] L.F. Akyildiz and W. Su, et al. (2002). "Wireless sensor networks: A survey." *Computer Networks* **38**: 393–422.

[4] K. Akkaya and M. Younis (2005). "A survey on routing protocols for wireless sensor networks." *Journal of Ad Hoc Networks*, **3**: 325–349.

[5] N. Sadagopan and F. Bai, et al. (2003). *PATHS: Analysis of Path Duration Statistics and the Impact on Reactive MANET Routing Protocols.* ACM MobiHoc, Annapolis (MD).

[6] G. Cao and G. Kesidis, et al. (2005). "Purposeful mobility in tactical sensor networks." *Sensor Network Operations*, IEEE Press, Piscataway, NJ, pp. 113–126.

[7] D. Johnson and T. Stack, et al. (2006). "TrueMobile: A Mobile Robotic Wireless and Sensor Network Testbed." INFOCOMM.

[8] P. Samar and S. B. Wicker (2006). "Link dynamics and protocol design in a multihop mobile environment." *IEEE Transactions on Mobile Computing* 5(9).

[9] A. Nayebi and H. Sarbazi-Azad (2007a). "Lifetime analysis of the logical topology constructed by homogeneous topology control in wireless mobile networks." *The 13th International Conference on Parallel and Distributed Systems (ICPADS)*, Taiwan, IEEE Publishing.

[10] A. Nayebi and H. Sarbazi-Azad (2007b). "A model for link excess life in mobile wireless networks." Technical report 2007-118, HPCAN lab., Sharif University of Technology, Tehran, Iran.

[11] A. Nayebi and G. Karlsson (2008). Neighbor Discovery in Mobile Wireless Networks. Stockholm, Sweden, Royal Institute of Technology (KTH), Technical report: TRITA-EE_2008:066.

[12] A. Nayebi and H. Sarbazi-Azad (2009). "Analysis of k-Neigh topology control protocol for mobile wireless networks." *Computer Networks* 53(5): 613–633.

[13] I. Rhee and M. Shin, et al. (2007). "Human mobility patterns and their impact on routing in human-driven mobile networks." Sixth Workshop on Hot Topics in Networks (HotNets-VI).

[14] P. Hui and A. Chaintreau, et al. (2005). "Pocket switched networks and human mobility in conference environments." ACM SIGCOMM Workshop on Delay-Tolerant Networking (WDTN '05), Philadelphia, PA.

[15] A. B. McDonald and T. Znati (1999). "A path availability model for wireless ad hoc networks." IEEE WCNC.

[16] M. Gerharz and C. de Waal, et al. (2002). "Link stability in mobile wireless ad hoc networks." IEEE LCN.

[17] Y.-C. Tseng, Y.-F. Li, et al. (2003). "On route lifetime in multihop mobile ad hoc networks." *IEEE Transactions on Mobile Computing* 2(4).

[18] D. Yu and H. Li, et al. (2003). "Path availability in ad-hoc network." Int'l Conf. on Telecomm. (ICT 2003), Tahiti, France.

[19] F. Bai, and N. Sadagopan, et al. (2004). "Modeling path duration distributions in MANETs and their impact on reactive routing protocols." *IEEE Journal on Selected Areas of Communications (JSAC)* 22(7).

[20] Z. Cheng and W. B. Heinzelman (2004). "Exploring long lifetime routing (LLR) in ad hoc networks." 7th ACM International Symposium on Modeling, Analysis and Simulation of Wireless and Mobile Systems (MSWIM 2004).

[21] P. Samar and S. B. Wicker (2004). "On the behavior of communication links of a node in a multi-hop mobile environment." 5th ACM international symposium on Mobile ad hoc networking and computing (MobiHoc), Roppongi, Japan.

[22] G. Carofiglio and C. Chiasserini, et al. (2005). *Analysis of Route Stability in MANETs.* Second EuroNGI Workshop on New Trends in Modelling, Quantitative Methods and Measurements, Aveiro, Portugal.

[23] S. Cho and J. P. Hayes (2005). "Impact of mobility on connection stability in ad hoc networks." IEEE WCNC.

[24] Y. Han and R. J. La (2006). "Maximizing path durations in mobile adhoc networks." 40th Annual Conference on Information Sciences and Systems, Princeton, NJ.

[25] Y. Han and R. J. La, et al. (2006). "Distribution of path durations in mobile ad-hoc networks— Palm's Theorem to the rescue." *Computer Networks* **50**(12): 1887–1900.

[26] V. Lenders and J. Wagner, et al. (2006). *Analyzing the Impact of Mobility in Ad Hoc Networks.* REALMAN06, Florence, Italy.

[27] G. Carofiglio and C. Chiasserini, et al. (2009). "Route stability in MANETs under the random direction mobility model." *IEEE Transactions on Mobile Computing* **8**(9): 1167–1179.

[28] X. Wu and H. R. Sadjadpour, et al. (2009). "From link dynamics to path lifetime and packet-length optimization in MANETs. *Computer Networks* **15**(5): 637–650.

[29] P. Santi (2005). "The critical transmitting range for connectivity in mobile ad hoc networks." *IEEE Transactions on Mobile Computing* **4**(3).

[30] P. Santi (2005). *Topology Control in Wireless Ad Hoc and Sensor Networks*, John Wiley and Sons.

[31] J. Wu and F. Dai (2006). "Mobility-sensitive topology control in mobile ad hoc networks." *IEEE Transactions on Parallel and Distributed Systems* **17**(6).

[32] A. Nayebi and A. Khosravi, et al. (2007). "On the link excess life in mobile wireless networks." International Conference on Computing: Theory and Applications ICCTA, IEEE Computer Society.

[33] A. Nayebi and H. Sarbazi-Azad (2012). "Analysis of link lifetime in wireless mobile networks." *Ad Hoc Networks* **10**(7): 1221–1237.

[34] A. Nayebi (2011). "A comment on link dynamics and protocol design in a multi-hop mobile environment." *Wireless Sensor Network* **3**(3): 114–116.

[35] F. Bai, and N. Sadagopan, et al. (2003). "The IMPORTANT framework for analyzing the impact of mobility on performance of routing for ad hoc networks." *Ad Hoc Networks* **1**(4): 383–403.

[36] S. M. Ross (1985). *Introduction to Probability Models*, Academic Press.

[37] S. Asmussen (2003). *Applied Probability and Queues.* Berlin, Springer.

[38] M. Ilyas and I. Mahgoub (2004). *Handbook of Sensor Networks: Compact Wireless and Wired Sensing Systems*, CRC Press.

[39] L. Demirkol and C. Ersoy, et al. (2006). "MAC protocols for wireless sensor networks: a survey." *IEEE Communications Magazine* **44**(4): 115–121.

[40] J. Ben-Othman and B. Yahya (2010). "Energy efficient and QoS based routing protocol for wireless sensor networks." *Journal of Parallel and Distributed Computing* **70**(8): 849–857.

[41] V. Kawadia and P. R. Kumar (2003). "Power control and clustering in ad hoc networks." IEEE INFOCOM 03.

[42] M. D. Penrose (1997). "The longest edge of the random minimal spanning tree." *The Annals of Applied Probability* **7**(2): 340–361.

[43] P. Gupta and P. R. Kumar (1998). "Critical power for asymptotic connectivity." 37th IEEE Conference on Decision and Control.

[44] P. Santi and D. M. Blogh (2002). "An evaluation of connectivity in mobile wireless ad hoc networks." International Conference on Dependable Systems and Networks (DSN'02).

[45] P. Santi and D. Blough (2003). "The critical transmitting range for connectivity in sparse wireless ad hoc networks." *IEEE Transactions on Mobile Computing* **2**(1): 25–39.

[46] D. M. Blough and M. Leoncini, et al. (2006). "The k-Neighbors Approach to Interference Bounded and Symmetric Topology Control in Ad Hoc Networks." *IEEE Transactions on Mobile Computing* **5**.

[47] Y. Sasson and D. Cavin, et al. (2002). Probabilistic Broadcast for Flooding in Wireless Mobile Ad hoc Networks Swiss Federal Institute of Technology (EPFL).

[48] P. Erdos and A. Rényi (1960). "On the evolution of random graphs." *Publications of the Mathematical Institute of the Hungarian Academy of Sciences* **5**: 17–61.

[49] B. Bollobas (1985). *Random Graphs*. New York, Academic Press.

[50] U. N. Raghavan and H. P. Thadakamalla, et al. (2005). "Phase transitions and connectivity in distributed wireless sensors networks." 13th International Conference on Advanced Computing & Communications.

9

ANALYTICAL MODEL OF TIME-CRITICAL WIRELESS SENSOR NETWORK: THEORY AND EVALUATION

Kambiz Mizanian and Amir Hossein Jahangir

CONTENTS

Large Scale Network-Centric Distributed Systems, First Edition. Edited by Hamid Sarbazi-Azad and Albert Y. Zomaya.
© 2014 John Wiley & Sons, Inc. Published 2014 by John Wiley & Sons, Inc.

9.1 INTRODUCTION

Wireless sensor networks (WSNs) are self-organized ad hoc networks, which are equipped with limited computing and radio communication capabilities [2]. Nodes are capable of sensing, gathering, processing, and communicating data, especially the data pertaining to the physical medium in which they are embedded. It is envisioned that a typical WSN consists of a large number of nodes [2, 24, 26]. A typical network configuration consists of sensors working unattended and transmitting their observed or sensed values to some processing or control center, the so-called sink or base-station node, which serves as a user interface. Due to the limited transmission range, sensors that are far away from the sink deliver their data through *multihop* communications, that is, using intermediate nodes as relays. In this case, a sensor may be both a data source and a data router.

This enables sensing and actuation at a fine-grained level, both spatially and temporally. Though significant on their own, WSNs play a central role in achieving the goal of truly ubiquitous computing and smart environments. By interfacing the data collection and dissemination infrastructure of WSN with external networks and devices, control and automation of physical entities like houses, factories, farms, and so on can be achieved at a level that was not possible before.

Although energy efficiency is usually the primary concern in WSNs, the requirement of low latency communication is becoming increasingly important in emerging applications. Out-of-date information will be irrelevant and even leads to negative effects to the system monitoring and control. Real-time (RT) sensor systems have many applications, especially in intruder tracking, medical care, fire monitoring, and structural health diagnosis.

WSN differs dramatically from the traditional RT systems due to its wireless nature, limited resources (power, processing, and memory), low node reliability and dynamic network topology. Thus, developing real-time applications over WSN should consider not only resource constraints but also the node and communication reliability and the globally time-varying network performance.

This chapter establishes a probabilistic fundamental quantitative notion for time-critical applications on real-time information transfer in multihop wireless networks. Those wireless sensor networks that are capable of providing bounded delay guarantees on packet delivery are referred to as real-time wireless sensor networks (RT-WSN). A vast majority of WSN applications are real-time. However, bounded delay latency is extremely impressed in path reliability when any lost packet must be retransmitted and it can cause to additional delivery delay. Here, the packet loss probability is the probability of one path's link failure when a node's buffer in the end point of the link is full and there is no space for new packets or the probability of one path's node failure when a node's energy is depleted and the node does not have any energy for taking more transmissions. The analysis of RT-WSN is the focus of this chapter. In the following, we describe applications of "deadline aware" intelligent sensors in smart systems for areas such as healthcare and environmental monitoring.

Environmental applications of sensor networks include tracking the movements of birds, small animals, and insects; or monitoring environmental conditions such as pollution or forest fire detection. Imagine that a WSN is deployed to detect a forest fire. The sensor nodes must report the exact origin of the fire to the end users before the fire spreads uncontrollably. The network should be able to detect the outbreaks of wildfire at any location within the monitored region with a high probability, and report this event to a sink node within a time deadline. In the case of intrusion, a failure of timely tracking will allow the intruder to escape. Application of WSN to monitor the health of senior citizens and patients is an actively pursued area of research. Typically, the nodes of the network report to a collector node, which is connected to the health-care provider through an external network. The health-care provider's server monitors the WSN data for alarms, and alerts health-care personnel upon alarm detection. The network is of little use if, during emergencies, doctors are not alerted soon enough to save patients' lives.

In this chapter a new probabilistic analytical model for calculating RRT (reliable real-time) degree in multihop WSNs is shown, where RRT degree describes the percentage of real-time data that the network can reliably deliver on time from any source to its destination. Analytical expressions for reliable real-time degree facilitate the process of designing a WSN that is guaranteed to meet specified throughput and delay requirements. These expressions describe values of a set of variables that will enable the network to meet anticipated soft real-time requirements. In other words, they define the feasibility region in the space of such variables. In the event of a dynamically changing network, which is expected in WSN, in addition to planning and designing, the feasibility region allows optimization of the operation of the network.

Thus, the purpose of this chapter is to perform a probabilistic analysis of reliable real-time degree in a wireless sensor network, which considers the packet loss and packet delay as real-time measures, and node failure and link failure as reliability metrics. The effect of network load is also examined.

The rest of this chapter is organized as follows: in Section 9.2, a literature survey is presented. In Section 9.3, the preliminaries and assumption of the problem are clarified and a model for evaluating the reliable real-time degree is derived. Section 9.4 presents the model validation and Section 9.5 provides some conclusions and future work.

9.2 REAL-TIME WIRELESS SENSOR NETWORK: AN OVERVIEW

Here is an overview of the prior work that has been done in different areas relevant to traffic modeling.

9.2.1 Previous Work on a Related Analytical Model

A large amount of research on sensor networks has already been reported, ranging from studies on network capacity and signal processing techniques to algorithms for traffic routing, topology management, and channel access control.

With regard to analytical studies, results on the capacity of large stationary ad hoc networks are presented in [11] (note that sensor networks can be viewed as large ad hoc networks, but WSNs almost are stationary and all nodes send messages to a few sinks). In [11], two network scenarios are studied: one including arbitrarily located nodes and traffic patterns, the other one with randomly located nodes and traffic patterns. The case of tree-like sensor networks is studied in [9], where the authors present optimal strategies for data distribution and data collection, and analytically evaluate the time performance of their solution. An analytical approach to coverage and connectivity of sensor grids is introduced in [25]. The sensors are unreliable and fail with a certain probability, leading to random grid networks. Results on coverage and connectivity are derived as functions of key parameters such as the number of nodes and their transmission radius.

Some researchers have looked at latency issues from different perspectives. For instance, the approach of Intanagonwiwat et al. [16] exploits latency and credibility trade-off in order to propose a solution to the problem of how long a node should wait before aggregating and sending its data to its parent, where a parent denotes the next hop.

Another in-network data aggregation scheme that aims at minimizing the end-to-end delay is proposed in [12]. This scheme does not consider any latency bound but tries to minimize the average end-to-end delay by concatenating multiple packets into one at the MAC layer. The idea is to limit the medium access contention so that the packet queuing delay be reduced. Moreover, they use a feedback mechanism at each sensor node to adjust the number of concatenated packets based on the current traffic conditions.

In [1] Abdelzaher et al., a sufficient condition for schedulability under fixed-priority scheduling allows capacity planning to be employed prior to deployment so that real-time requirements are met at run-time. The bound is derived for load balanced networks, as well as networks where all traffic congregates at a number of sinks.

The approach of Chiasserini et al. [5] exploits several performance metrics, among which the distributions of the data delivery delay. They consider that the information sensed by a network node is organized into data units of fixed size and can be stored at the sensor in a buffer of infinite capacity. They assume that wireless channel is error-free.

In [6] Chiasserini et al. present a methodology to analyze the behavior of large-scale sensor networks. Their approach was based on a fluid representation of all quantities that depend on the specific location within the network topology and on probabilistic functions to characterize the behavior of individual nodes. They did not consider the battery discharge of the sensors and the behavior of the nodes dependent on their residual energy.

In [22], the authors propose a quantitative real-time model for WSNs and describe real-time degree by considering the packet loss and packet delay as real-time measures. However, this model does not consider the probability of node failure due to node energy depletion and its effect on path reliability and real-timeliness in WSNs.

9.2.2 Previous Work on the Real-Time Communication Protocols

Real-time communication is a critical service for future sensor networks to provide distributed microsensing in physical environments. Wireless sensor networks need novel communication protocols to support higher-level services and should also be adaptive to avoid unpredictable congestion and holes in wireless sensor networks.

RAP [21] is a multilayer, real-time communication architecture for wireless sensor networks. It provides a set of convenient, high-level query and event services. It is based on novel location-addressed communication models supported by a lightweight network stake, which integrates a transport layer location addressed protocol (LAP), a geographic routing protocol, a velocity monotonic scheduling (VMS) layer, and a contention-based MAC that supports prioritization. VMS is a concept of novel packet-requested velocity that reproduces both distance and timing constraints of sensor networks. Two versions of this algorithm are implemented. The static VMS computes a fixed, requested velocity at the sender of each packet. The requested velocity is $V = dis(x_0, y_0, x_d, y_d)/D$, where $dis(x_0, y_0, x_d, y_d)$ is the geographic distance between a sender and a destination, and D is an end-to-end deadline. The requested velocity of a packet is fixed in the networks. The dynamic VMS recalculates the requested velocity of a packet upon its arrival at each intermediate node. The requested velocity is then set to $V_i = dis(x_i, y_i, x_d, y_d)/(D - T_i)$. The requested velocity of a packet will be adjusted based on its actual velocity.

SPEED [13] is an adaptive, location-based real-time routing protocol that aims to reduce the end-to-end, deadline-miss ratio in a wireless sensor network and is a real-time communication protocol for wireless sensor networks. It supports soft communication based on feedback control and stateless algorithms. It also provides three types of real-time communication services: uncast, multicast, and anycast. SPEED utilizes geographic locations to make localized routing decisions. In addition, it is capable of handling congestion and provides soft real-time communication, which location-based protocols do not offer. Route discovery broadcasts in reactive routing algorithms can lead to significant delays in sensor networks. SPEED maintains only immediate neighbor information. It requires neither a routing table, as in DSDV, nor predestination states, as in AODV. SPEED does not use any information related to deadlines. However, it provides real-time guarantees by providing a uniform packet delivery speed across the wireless sensor network so that the end-to-end delay of the packet is proportional to the distance between the source and destination. SPEED does not require specialized MAC support and can work with existing best MAC protocols due to the feedback control scheme that it employs. All distributed operations in SPEED are highly localized, meaning that any action invoked by a node will not affect the whole system.

MMSPEED [8] is a packet-delivery mechanism for wireless sensor networks to grant service differentiation and probabilistic QoS guarantees in timeliness and reliability domains. For the timeliness domain, MMSPEED provides multiple network-wide speed options so that various traffic types can dynamically choose the proper speed options. Both SPEED and MMSPEED use fixed transmission power.

RPAR [7] varies from the previously mentioned protocols in several ways. First, RPAR is the only protocol that combines power control and real-time routing to support energy-efficient, real-time communication. Moreover, RPAR allows the application to control the trade-off between energy utilization and communication delay by specifying packet deadlines. In addition, RPAR is designed to handle faulty links. RPAR also utilizes a novel neighborhood management mechanism that is more efficient than the periodic beacons scheme adopted by LAPC [10], SPEED, and MMSPEED. The main aspect of this protocol is a dynamic transmission power adjustment and routing decision in order to minimize miss ratios. The transmission power has a large impact on the delivery ratio, as it improves wireless link quality and decreases the required number of transmissions to deliver a packet. However, transmitting a packet at a high power level has a side effect of decreasing throughput due to increased channel contention and interference.

9.3 REAL-TIME DEGREE

When WSNs are used for real-time applications, real-time constraints should be defined for network communications. One of these parameters is the real-time degree [22] that shows the percentage of packets that are delivered to the destination before the deadline; this parameter is also a supplement for the rate of data loss. The related analytical relations are obtained and provided in [22].

In the following, we present these equations with detailed descriptions for clarity.

9.3.1 Basic Assumptions

To calculate the average percentage of packets delivered to the destination before the deadline, each node in a wireless sensor network is assumed as in Fig. 9.1.

As can be seen in Fig. 9.1 each node has a buffer with a length of B packets and receives data from the previous node and transmits it to the next node. Each node can also generate data to be transmitted. Hence, it is assumed that the data received or generated has a Poisson distribution [5, 6] with an average rate of λ. In addition, this data leaves the node with an average rate of μ and with an exponential distribution, so we can model it as an M/M/1/k queue.

Moreover, it is assumed that the wireless sensor network consists of a number of such nodes that have an undefined topology. A sample network is shown in Fig. 9.2 where each node is presented as a router.

As can be seen in this figure, different routes exist between the source and the destination, so if any of the paths fails, the other routes can be used. For example, if route $\{a,b,c,d\}$ is created and is later cut for any reason, it can be replaced by another route. For instance, if link c is destroyed, routes $\{m,h\}$ or $\{i,l,o,h\}$ can be used.

If nodes i and j are, respectively, the sender and receiver nodes ($1 \leq i \leq N$ and $0 \leq j \leq N$ and if 0 stands for a sink), information transmission process will be successful when [5, 11]:

1. The distance between i and j is not more than tr (transmission range),

$$d_{i,j} \leq tr \tag{9.1}$$

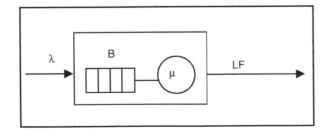

Figure 9.1   The structure of wireless sensor network nodes.

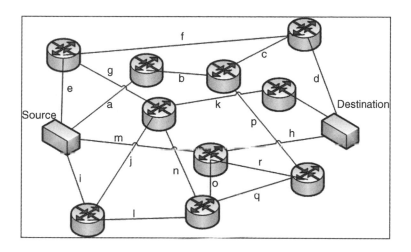

Figure 9.2   A sample network consisting of m/m/1/k nodes.

2. For any other node like k that receives information simultaneously,

$$d_{i,k} > tr \qquad\qquad (9.2)$$

3. For any other node like l that transmits information simultaneously,

$$d_{l,j} > tr. \qquad\qquad (9.3)$$

In this network it is assumed that, at the beginning, the initial procedures are run and thus each node is aware of its neighbor nodes. In addition, routings are also carried out and routes are available from the source to the destination.

We consider a network of stationary nodes performing, for instance, environmental monitoring and surveillance. Therefore, after this phase we assume slight changes to be made to the paths because in the wireless sensor networks the nodes are usually fixed [5].

It is assumed that in the MAC layer the CSMA/CA mechanism is available, thus MACA or MACAW [3, 5, 18] can, for example, be chosen as the MAC and tr can be considered to be the radial radius of the transmission.

Wireless sensor networks usually have undefined topologies, so we should assume all things to happen randomly. Hence, in order to do more mathematical operations, network parameters are assumed to be random variables and the following assumptions are taken into account regarding the network and its nodes:

1. All of the network nodes have identical statistical attributes.
2. The routing algorithm chooses all alternative routes with an equal probability.
3. Network links fail independently.
4. If one of the links along a path fails, it is assumed that the entire path is destroyed.

5. All network routes have the same statistical attributes.
6. The number of the nodes along a route is shown by N, which is a random variable and $E[N]$ stands for its average value.
7. LF is the probability of failure of each link.
8. The length of packets has an exponential distribution with an average of L.
9. The buffer length of each node is equal to b byte or B packets length.
10. The rate of data arrival to each node has a Poisson distribution with an average of λ (this assumption also includes the packets generated by the node itself).
11. Service rate for the nodes is shown by μ and has an exponential distribution.
12. At the beginning R routes are available from each source to the sink.
13. t_r denotes the transmission rate of the nodes.
14. r stands for network load.

On the basis of the above assumptions and the explanations provided, the results of the analytic model are as follows (details are provided in [22]).

9.3.2 Evaluation of the Real-Time Degree

In this section, we define real-time degree by considering node failure and link failure as reliability measures.

Phase 1: In this phase the probability of packet loss is calculated for a normal route. The probability of the loss of the packets of one route, PL_{path}, depends on the probability of the loss of packets in each node of that particular route, PL_{node}. Thus:

$$PL_{path} = 1 - (1 - PL_{node})^{E[N]} \qquad (9.4)$$

Therefore, we should calculate the mean probability of packet loss in each node. We assume the probability of the loss of each packet in each node to be equal to the probability of overloading of the node buffer and lack of free space in that buffer for new packets. Therefore, according to the queuing theory PL_{node} is equal to [20]:

$$PL_{node} = P_{B+1} = \frac{(r)^{B+1}(1 - r)}{1 - (r)^{B+2}}. \qquad (9.5)$$

where r is the average network load at a sensor node and you can find it by equation (9.8). Also B is calculated by:

$$B = \frac{b\mu}{t_r} \qquad (9.6)$$

Now, if we assume S to be the traffic generated in each node for each pair of source-destination routes, since the packets can be re-sent in case they are lost, G can show the total traffic of a node (sum of the new traffic and re-sent traffic). Therefore, the following relation is true:

$$S = G\left(1 - PL_{path}\right) \qquad (9.7)$$

Now we have to calculate the value of r. To compute the network load at a sensor node, we note that, because of packet loss probability at the sensor node, the load will be reduced at each successive node from source to a destination. For example, in the ith node, $i = 0, 1, 2, \ldots, E[N] - 1$; this traffic exists in the case of traversing all previous i-1 nodes without packet loss. Therefore, the probability of traffic existence in node i is equal to $(1 - PL_{node})^i$ and because of similarities between nodes and paths statistical properties, we have:

$$r = \left(\frac{G}{E[N]} \right) \sum_{i=0}^{E[N]-1} (1 - PL_{node})^i = \frac{G[1 - (1 - PL_{node})^{E[N]}]}{PL_{node}{}^* E[N]} \tag{9.8}$$

By comparing relations (9.5) and (9.8), we find that in order to calculate PL_{node} we need to obtain the value of r and in order to obtain r we need to calculate PL_{node}. Usually in calculating the blocking probability for circuit-switched networks with fixed routes we also face such problems, which can be solved using the Erlang fixed-point method [19, 27]. To solve this problem, we use the iterative calculation method with enough calculation times. Calculations are repeated to the point that the results are made convergent.

Phase 2: In this phase, the mean path delay is calculated, or, actually, the time duration that it takes for a packet to successfully be delivered to the base station.

A packet that moves from the source to the sink has a delay of W in each node and has a propagation delay of t_p in each link. There are N nodes and N-1 links in each path, so for path delay we have:

$$Delay_{path} = \sum_{i=1}^{E[N]} W + (E[N] - 1) E[t_p]$$

$$= \sum_{i=1}^{E[N]} W + \frac{E[Len_{path}]}{C} \tag{9.9}$$

And, according to the queuing theory equations, we have:

$$L = \frac{r'}{1 - r'} - \frac{(B + 2) r'^{B+2}}{1 - r'^{B+2}} \tag{9.10}$$

$$r' = \frac{r}{\beta} \tag{9.11}$$

$$W = \frac{L}{\bar{\lambda}} \tag{9.12}$$

$$\bar{\lambda} = \lambda (1 - \pi_{B+1}) = \lambda \left(1 - \frac{(r')^{B+1} (1 - r')}{1 - (r')^{B+2}} \right) \tag{9.13}$$

And, based on the above equations, we have:

$$W = \frac{r' \left[1 + (B+1) r'^{B+2} - (B+2) r'^{B+1}\right]}{\lambda (1 - r') \left(1 - r'^{B+1}\right)} \tag{9.14}$$

In the relations above, Len_{path} is a random variable that denotes the cumulative distribution of links' length; C is the radio velocity, or in other words, the propagation speed of radio waves in the space; β is the probability of data transmission during a time slot that the buffer is not empty, which is discussed in detail in the next phase along with its associated relations.

Phase 3: In this phase, the probability of data transmission during a time slot is studied. The amount of this probability depends on the channel contention. For example, if no contentions or conflicts occur in the wireless medium, this probability will be equal to one ($\beta = 1$).

We define β as the probability of data transmission during a time slot. As was discussed in the previous section, data transmission by a node is carried out if conditions (9.1) to (9.3) are true. To calculate β, interference in the nodes adjacent to the node under study should be examined (details are provided in [5]). Therefore, to estimate the probability, β, for a general sensor like i we proceed as follows.

First, we calculate probability, $I^i(n)$, for each node n, $(1 \leq n \leq N)$. $I^i(n)$ means that during a transmission node, n, whether as the sender or receiver, may be involved and the transmission may totally block transmissions of i.

This probability is calculated based on the average transmission rate between node n and the general node m (i.e., $r_{n,m}$), thus we have [5]:

$$I^i(n) = \sum_{m=1}^{N} r_{m,n} \, 1_{\{d_{(n,i)} \leq tr\}} + \sum_{m=0}^{N} r_{n,m} \, 1_{\{d_{(m,i)} > tr\}} \, V^i(n), \tag{9.15}$$

where $m = 0$ is the sink, and $1_{\{.\}}$ is the indicator function. The first sum to the right of this equation is for transmissions that violate condition (9.2) or transmissions with i as their target, whereas the second sum is for transmissions for which condition (9.2) is true, but condition (9.3) is violated. If there exists at least one next-hop of i within the transmission range of n, with n being different from i, then component $V^i(n)$ will be equal to one, otherwise it will be equal to zero.

Thus,

$$V^i(n) = \begin{cases} 1 & \exists k \in H^i : d_{(n,k)} \leq tr , \, n \neq i \\ 0 & \text{otherwise} \end{cases}, \tag{9.16}$$

where H^i stands for a set of next-hops of node i. Hence, β^i is obtained as below [5]:

$$\beta^i = \prod_{n=1}^{N} \left[1 - I^i(n)\right] \tag{9.17}$$

And

$$\beta = \frac{\sum_{i=1}^{E[N]} \beta^i}{E[N]} \tag{9.18}$$

Now, in order to calculate the real-time degree of a route, the following considerations should be taken into account.

If the path is not destroyed and packet loss is not observed as well, and if packets delay in reaching the destination is less than the specific threshold time, then the real-time degree will be equal to one; otherwise, the real-time degree will be in an inverse relationship with packet loss and packet delivery after expiration of the specific threshold time.

If the path fails, then an alternative route can be selected based on a probability and the real-time degree can be calculated for the new route.

Since packet loss and packet delay have different units of measure and thus they cannot be simultaneously substituted in computational formulas, we express the delay caused by packet loss with the unit of time. Thus, if the sender receives a NACK packet or if it does not receive an ACK after a while and the time also expires, then the sender waits for a random period of time (the back-off period) between I to K and then re-sends that particular packet. We can show the average back-off period as $\frac{K+1}{2}$. So a value equal to $T\left(2\left(E[N] - 1\right)E[t_p] + \frac{K+1}{2}\right)$ should be added to the path delay, where $T = \frac{(G-S)}{S}$ is the ratio of re-sent packets to newly generated packets. Therefore, according to the probability of packet loss and packet retransmission the total route delay will be equal to

$$Delay_{path} = \sum_{i=1}^{E[N]} W + \frac{E\left[Len_{path}\right]}{C} + T\left(\frac{2E\left[Len_{path}\right]}{C} + \frac{K+1}{2}\right) \tag{9.19}$$

or

$$Delay_{path} = \sum_{i=1}^{E[N]} W + \frac{(2T+1)E\left[Len_{path}\right]}{C} + \frac{(K+1)T}{2} \tag{9.20}$$

According to the above relations and also the similar statistical attributes of the paths, the following relations are obtained:

$$Real - time\ degree = \frac{1 - P_{path\_failure}}{1 + Max\left(\left(Delay_{path} - T_{Delay}\right)/T_{Delay}, 0\right)}$$
$$+ P_{path\_failure} \times P_{existence\_of\_backup\_path} \times Real - time\ degree \tag{9.21}$$

$$\Rightarrow Real - time\ degree =$$
$$\frac{1 - P_{path\_failure}}{\left(1 + Max\left(\frac{Delay_{path}}{T_{Delay}} - 1, 0\right)\right) \times \left(1 - P_{path\_failure} \times P_{existence\_of\_backup\_path}\right)} \tag{9.22}$$

In the above relations, $P_{path\_failure}$ denotes path failure and is equal to the probability of failure of at least one link along the path. Thus,

$$P_{path\_failure} = 1 - (1 - LF)^{E[N]-1} \qquad (9.23)$$

$P_{existence\_of\_backup\_path}$ shows the probability of existence of a backup path.

According to the problem assumption, R routes exist between the source and the destination, thus only if all the R-1 routes are destroyed will no backup paths be available:

$$P_{existence\_of\_backup\_patht} = 1 - P_{path\_failure}^{R-1} \qquad (9.24)$$

T_{Delay} is the threshold delay of packets. That is to say, if a packet delay exceeds this T_{Delay}, the real-time degree decreases in inverse proportion.

Now we prove that the range of real-time degree is between 0 and 1.

$$Let: P_1 = P_{path\_failure}, \ P_2 = P_{existence\_of\_backup\_path}$$

$$0 \le P_1 \le 1, \ 0 \le P_2 \le 1 \quad \Rightarrow \quad P_1 \ge P_1 P_2$$

$$\Rightarrow \quad 1 - P_1 \le 1 - P_1 P_2 \quad \Rightarrow \quad \frac{1 - P_1}{1 - P_1 P_2} \le 1 \qquad (9.25)$$

$$1 + Max\left((Delay_{path} - T_{Delay})/T_{Delay}, 0\right) \ge 1$$

$$\Rightarrow \quad \frac{1}{1 + Max\left((Delay_{path} - T_{Delay})/T_{Delay}, 0\right)} \le 1 \qquad (9.26)$$

$$\Rightarrow \quad \frac{1 - P_1}{1 - P_1 P_2} \times \frac{1}{1 + Max\left((Delay_{path} - T_{Delay})/T_{Delay}, 0\right)} \le 1 \qquad (9.27)$$

$$\Rightarrow \quad Real - time \ degree \le 1 \qquad (9.28)$$

On the other hand, it is clear that the real-time degree is larger than 0, thus,

$$0 \le Real - time \ degree \le 1 \qquad (9.29)$$

In this section we proposed a quantitative real-time model for WSNs and calculated real-time degree by considering the packet loss and packet delay as real-time measures. However, this model does not consider the probability of node failure due to node energy depletion and its effect on path reliability and real-timeliness in WSNs. In next section you can find the reliable real-time quantitative model.

9.4 RELIABLE REAL-TIME DEGREE

The ultimate goal of this section is an analytical model of reliable real-time (RRT) degree. It describes the percentage of real-time data that the network can reliably deliver on time from any source to its destination. Having the above relations in the mind and the similarity of the statistical properties of the paths helps us to obtain RRT degree.

Because a real-time system requires accurate and on-time deliverance of information and since energy is one of the important variables in the wireless sensor networks, we expand the previous relations and put energy as a parameter in them.

One of the changes made is the probability of packet loss that is modeled as the probability of link failure along the path, which is equal to the probability of packet loss due to buffer overload or the probability of failure of a node due to consumption of its energy. Thus,

$$PL_{path} = 1 - \left((1 - PL_{node})^{E[N]} \times R_{path} \right) \qquad (9.30)$$

where R_{path} is the reliability of the path; and it is probable that none of the nodes along the path will fail until the deadline. This probability is calculated in equation (9.34).

As is shown in [23], after calculating the $Delay_{path}$, based on equations in the previous section, we can calculate the reliable real-time degree according to following equations.

According to the definition of the reliable real-time degree [23] that suggests the percentage of the real-time data, the network is capable of sending accurately and on-time from each source to its specific destination, we have:

$$RRT\_degree = (1 - PL_{node})^{E[N]} \times (1 - MissRatio) \times (1 - P_{failure}) \qquad (9.31)$$

We have assumed that the rate of packet arrival to each node has a Poisson distribution with an average of λ, so we can assume that the interval between the arrivals of packets has an exponential distribution and thus the $MissRatio$ is calculated as below:

$$MissRatio = e^{-\frac{1}{Delay_{Path}} \times T_{Delay}} \qquad (9.32)$$

where T_{Delay} is the threshold delay of packets. Thus, if $Delay_{path}$ is larger than T_{Delay} (threshold delay) the miss ratio will increase and the reliable real-time degree will decrease in inverse proportion.

Since we have assumed that R non-failed paths exist between each source and the sink, and if one path fails, it is substituted by another path and this action is repeated to the point that no other nonfailed paths remain. $P_{failure}$ suggests that R paths are failed and no other spare paths are available. Hence,

$$R_{Total} = 1 - P_{failure} = 1 - (1 - R_{path})^R \qquad (9.33)$$

Phase 4: In this phase, we calculate the reliability of a path. Path reliability or *Rpath* is the probability of a occurrence of a condition when none of the path nodes fail before the deadline (T_{Delay}). Thus,

$$R_{path} = e^{-\left(\frac{1}{Path\ Lifetime}\right) \times T_{Delay}} \qquad (9.34)$$

where the failure rate, $\frac{1}{Path\ Lifetime}$, is equal to the average number of failures during the path lifetime.

Now we should calculate the average lifetime of a path. According to [5], the energy consumed by a node is calculated as below:

$$E_{i,j} = E_{i,j}^{(tx)} + E_{j}^{(rx)} \qquad (9.35)$$

where $E_{i,j}$ is the amount of energy consumed by a node to transmit a unit of data from node i to the next-hop in the path (i.e., j). This includes the total amount of energy consumed by node i at the time of sending data ($E_{i,j}^{(tx)}$) and the amount of energy consumed by node j at the time of receiving data ($E_{j}^{(rx)}$).

When transmitting data, the radio transmitter amplifier, the electronic circuits of the transmitter, the receiver, and the processor of the node, which is responsible for signal generation and processing operations, consume energy. When receiving data, the electronic circuits of the transmitter, the receiver, and the processor, which performs processing operations such as demodulation and decoding, consume energy. Therefore, $E_{j}^{(rx)}$ includes the energy consumed by the circuits of the transmitter and the receiver ($E^{(ele)}$) and the energy consumed by the processing functions ($E^{(proc)}$); whereas $E_{i,j}^{(tx)}$ includes the energy consumed by the radio transmitter amplifier along with $E^{(ele)}$ and $E^{(proc)}$, which is directly proportional to the square of the distance between the transmitter and the receiver. Thus [5, 14]:

$$E_{i,j} = \left[2\left(E^{(ele)} + E^{(proc)}\right) + d_{i,j}^{2}E^{(amp)}\right] \qquad (9.36)$$

where $E^{(amp)}$ is a constant and $d_{i,j}$ is the distance between i and j based on the circular radius. Thus, the average amount of power consumption along the path is calculated as:

$$p(path) = \sum_{i=0}^{E[N]} (\lambda E_{i,i+1}) \qquad (9.37)$$

So, the average power consumption along the path is equal to

$$p(node) = \frac{p(path)}{E[N]} \qquad (9.38)$$

The network lifetime is defined as the shortest period of time that is required for at least one node in the network to lose its energy [4]. Thus,

$$Path\ Lifetime = \frac{\min\ \{B_i,\ i \in (0,\ E[N]-1)\}}{p(node)} \qquad (9.39)$$

where B_i is the remaining power of node i along the path during the transmission of a new packet.

9.5 MODEL VALIDATION

In this section we use GloMoSim [28] to study the reliable real-time degree of wireless sensor networks. GloMoSim is a scalable discrete-event simulator developed by UCLA. This software provides a high-fidelity simulation for wireless communication with detailed propagation, radio, and MAC layers. Table 9.1 describes the detailed setup for our simulator. The communication parameters are mostly chosen in reference to the Berkeley Mote [15] specification.

There are two typical traffic patterns in sensor networks: a base station pattern and a peer-to-peer pattern. In our evaluation, we use a base station scenario, where six nodes, randomly chosen from the left side of the terrain, send data to the base station at the middle of the right side of the terrain. The average hop count between the node and base station is about eight or nine hops. Each node generates flow with a rate of 1 packet/second. In order to evaluate the end-to-end delay, we increase the rate of this flow step by step from 1 to 100 packets/second over several simulations.

Figure 9.3 shows the end-to-end delay. At each point, we average the end-to-end delays of all the packets from the 96 flows (16 runs with 6 flows each). As can be seen in Figure 9.3, by increasing the packet transmission rate, end-to-end delay increases as well. As the rate increases, the buffer full probability increases as well and the lost packets must be retransmitted until they are successfully delivered to the sink.

Fig. 9.4 shows the miss ratio. We assume that T_{Delay} is 150 ms., and as can be seen in Fig. 9.4, by increasing the packet transmission rate, miss ratio increases as well. The reason is that when the rate increases, then the average end-to-end delays will also increase.

The reliable real-time degree is metrics in soft real-time systems. We set the buffer size to 50 packets. In the simulation, some packets are lost due to a full buffer. We also consider these situations as a deadline miss. The result shown in Fig. 9.5 is the summary of 16 randomized runs. When the packet rate increases, the buffer full probability and node failure probability increase as well. Hence, the packet loss also increases. Another

TABLE 9.1 Simulation Settings

MAC layer	MACA [18]
Routing layer	DSR [17]
Radio layer	RADIO-ACCNOISE
Propagation model	TWO-RAY
Bandwidth	200Kb/s
Payload size	32 Byte
Terrain	(200m, 200m)
Node number	100
Node placement	Uniform
Radio range	40m
R	2
Transmit power consumption	26.7 mw
Receive power consumption	22.6 mw

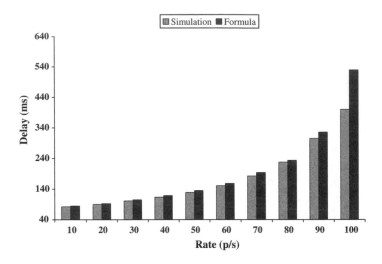

Figure 9.3   End-to-end delay under different network load.

consequence of the rate increase is the end-to-end delay augmentation. So the packet rate increase yields a decrease of reliable real-time degree (percentage of on-time successfully delivered data).

Figure 9.6 shows the node energy consumption rate versus data rate. When the packet transmission rate increases, the node energy consumption rate increases as well.

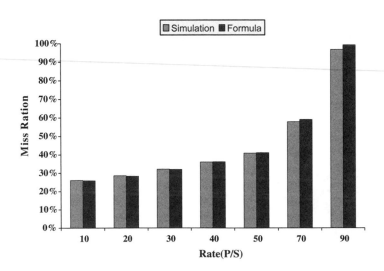

Figure 9.4   Miss ratio under different network load.

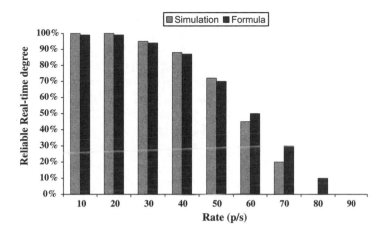

Figure 9.5 Reliable real-time degree under different network load.

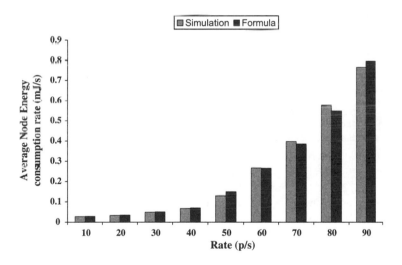

Figure 9.6 Node energy cost under different network load.

9.6 CONCLUSION

We introduced in this chapter a metrics, real-time degree, and reliable real-time degree, based on a queuing-theory model for general-case wireless sensor network in which the nodes are M/M/1/k queues. Parameters such as packet loss, packet delay, and path lifetime were considered as important factors in determining the reliable real-time degree of such a network. We have analyzed a semi-qualitative phenomenon so that we can predict the real-time behavior of network in the case of stochastic events. Simulation results are in accordance with the model.

The model could be modified to take into account some aspects that have not been addressed in this work and that may be an interesting subject for future research. For instance, a model of other queuing policy or firm real-time can be included and some of the assumptions that we made while developing the analytical model, such as those where all the nodes are active and none of them in sleep mode, can be modified. Furthermore, we point out that the model can be extended to describe various aspects in the design of sensor networks, such as data aggregation or backpressure traffic mechanisms. Finally, cluster-based network architectures as well as the case where the network topology varies could be studied.

REFERENCES

[1] T. F. Abdelzaher, K. S. Prabh, and R. Kiran, "On real-time capacity limits of multihop wireless sensor networks," In Proceedings of the 25th IEEE Real-Time Systems Symposium (RTSS) (2004), pp. 359–370.

[2] F. Akyildiz, W. Su, Y. Sankarasubramaniam, and E. Cayirci, "A survey on sensor networks," *IEEE Comm. Mag* (2002), 102–114.

[3] V. Bharghavan, A. Demers, S. Shenkar, and L. Zhang, "MACAW: A media access protocol for wireless LANs," ACM SIGCOMM'94 (1994), pp. 212–225.

[4] K. Chen, Y. Qin, and F. Jiang, "A probabilistic energy-efficient routing (PEER) scheme for ad-hoc sensor networks," 3rd Annual IEEE SECON Conference, Reston, VA, (2006), pp. 964–970.

[5] C. F. Chiasserini and M. Garetto, "Modeling the performance of wireless sensor networks," IEEE INFOCOM 1 (2004), pp. 7–14.

[6] C. F. Chaiasserini, R. Gaeta, M. Gribaudo, D. Manini, and M. Sereno, "Fluid models for large-scale wireless sensor networks," *Performance Evaluation* (2007), 64 (7-8) 715–736.

[7] O. Chipara, Z. He, G. Xing, Q. Chen, X. Wang, C. Lu, J. Stankovic, and T. Abdelzaher, "Real-time power aware routing in wireless sensor networks," in 14th IEEE International Workshop on Quality of Service (IWQoS 2006), New Haven, CT, June (2006), pp. 83–92.

[8] E. Felemban, C.-G. Lee, E. Ekici, R. Boder, and S. Vural, "MMSPEED: Multipath multi-SPEED protocol for QoS guarantee of reliability and timeliness in wireless," *IEEE Transactions on Mobile Computing*, (2006), 5(6) 738–754.

[9] C. Florens and R. McEliece, "Packet distribution algorithms for sensor networks," IEEE INFOCOM (2003), pp. 1063–1072.

[10] M. R. Fouad, S. Fahmy, and G. Pandurangan, "Latency-sensitive power control for wireless ad-hoc networks," in Q2SWinet '05 (2005), pp. 31–38.

[11] P. Gupta and P. R. Kumar, "The capacity of wireless networks," *IEEE Transaction on Information Theory* 46(2) (2000), 388–404.

[12] T. He, B. M. Blum, J. A. Stankovic, and T. F. Abdelzaher, "AIDA: Adaptive application independent aggregation in sensor networks," *ACM Trans on Embedded Computing System*, (2003), 3(2) 426–457.

[13] T. He, J. Stankovic, C. Lu, and T. Abdelzaher, "SPEED: a stateless protocol for real-time communication in sensor networks," in Proceedings of IEEE International Conference on Distributed Computing Systems, (2003), pp. 46–55.

[14] W. R. Heinzelman, A. Chandrakasan, and H. Balakrishnan, "Energy-efficient communication protocol for wireless micro sensor networks," 33rd International Conference on System Sciences (HICSS '00) (2000) 10 pp.

[15] J. Hill, R. Szewczyk, A. Woo, S. Hollar, D. Culler, and K. Pister, "System architecture directions for network sensors," ASPLOS (2000), 93–104.

[16] C. Intanagonwiwat, D. Estrin, R. Govindan, and J. Heidemann, "Impact of network density on data aggregation in wireless sensor networks, Proceedings of the 22nd International Conference on Distributed Computing Systems (2002), pp. 457–458.

[17] D. B. Johnson and D. A. Maltz, "Dynamic source routing in ad hoc wireless networks," *Mobile Computing* (1996), 153–181.

[18] P. Karn, "MACA: A new channel access method for packet radio," 9th Computer Networking Conference (1990), pp. 134–140.

[19] F. P. Kelly, "Loss networks," *The Annals of Applied Probability* (1991), 1(3) 319–378.

[20] L. Kleinrock, *Queuing Systems, Volume I: Theory*. John Wiley & Sons (1975).

[21] C. Lu, B. Blum, T. Abdelzaher, J. Stankovic, and T. He, "RAP: A real-time communication architecture for large-scale wireless sensor networks," in Eighth IEEE Real-Time and Embedded Technology and Applications Symposum (RTAS '02), (2002), pp. 55–66.

[22] K. Mizanian and A. H. Jahangir, "A quantitative real-time model for multihop wireless sensor networks," Third International Conference on Intelligent Sensors, Sensor Networks and Information Processing (ISSNIP'07) (2007), pp. 79–84.

[23] K. Mizanian, H. Yousefi, and A. H. Jahangir, "Modeling and evaluating reliable real-time degree in multi-hop wireless sensor networks," Sarnoff 2009, 32nd IEEE Sarnoff Symposium 2009, (2009), pp. 1–6.

[24] G. J. Pottie and W. J. Kaiser, "Wireless integrated network sensors," *Communications of the ACM* (2000), 43(5) 51–58.

[25] S. Shakkottai, R. Srikant, and N. B. Shroff, "Unreliable sensor grids: coverage, connectivity and diameter," IEEE INFOCOM 2 (2003), pp. 1073–1083.

[26] J. A. Stankovic, T. F. Abdelzaher, C. Lu, L. Sha, and J. Hou, "Real-time communication and coordination in embedded sensor networks," *Proceedings of the IEEE* (2003), 91(7) 1002–1022.

[27] W. Whitt, "Blocking when service is required from several facilities simultaneously," *AT&T Technical Journal* (1975), 64(8) 1807–1856.

[28] X. Zeng, R. Bagrodia, and M. Gerla, "GloMoSim: A library for parallel simulation of large-scale wireless networks," In Proceedings of the 12th Workshop on Parallel and Distributed Simulations (PADS '98) (1998), pp. 154–161.

10

MULTICAST TRANSPORT PROTOCOLS FOR LARGE-SCALE DISTRIBUTED COLLABORATIVE ENVIRONMENTS

Haifa Raja Maamar and Azzedine Boukerche

CONTENTS

Large Scale Network-Centric Distributed Systems, First Edition. Edited by Hamid Sarbazi-Azad and Albert Y. Zomaya.
© 2014 John Wiley & Sons, Inc. Published 2014 by John Wiley & Sons, Inc.

10.1 INTRODUCTION

The aim of this chapter is to give an overview of multicast transport protocols. The
first section provides an introduction to multicasting and the features that can be added
to satisfy each application's requirements, while the second section describes multicast
protocols by classifying them according to several features.

Collaborative virtual environments (CVEs) require that geographically distributed
users collaborate in closely coupled and highly synchronized tasks to manipulate shared
objects. In order to keep users up-to-date with the changes, and to maintain the synchronization between them, an efficient transport protocol to deliver data is needed.
The traditional unicast model that Transport Control Protocol (TCP) [1] offers is inefficient for such applications. In fact, it is not useful to transmit the same data to each
receiver across the network. CVE applications use large-scale distributed simulations
where hundreds or even thousands of distributed users intercommunicate in real time.
For this reason, it is necessary to use the multicast approach to deliver data.

Several multicast protocols have been proposed by many researchers in the last
decade. This interest was mainly due to the numerous communication applications, such
as multipoint data dissemination or conferencing tools, which use multicast as a solution
to deliver information to different users of the application.

10.2 DEFINITION AND FEATURES

10.2.1 Definition

Multicast is being chosen more often by several communication applications as a solution
for delivering data to a large number of receivers simultaneously. During the last decade,
research on multicasting received a great deal of interest. Many definitions of multicasting
have been given in the literature. Multicasting can be defined as "the delivery of information to a group of destinations simultaneously using the most efficient strategy to deliver
the messages over each link of the network only once, creating copies only when the links

to the destinations split" [2]. Sahasrabuddhe et al. [3] also defined multicasting as follows: "Multicasting is the ability of a communication network to accept a single message from an application and to deliver copies of the message to multiple recipients at different locations" [3]. Forouzan [4], in his book TCP/IP Protocol Suite, stated, "In multicasting routing, there is one source and a group of destinations. The relationship is one-to-many. In this type of communication, the source address is a unicast address, but the destination address is a group address. The group address defines the members of the group."

Multicasting requires less bandwidth and delays than multiple unicasting [4]. In fact, the sender in multicasting sends only one packet that is duplicated by the routers. However, in multiple unicasting, several packets are sent from the source, which requires more bandwidth to handle all of the messages sent. Multicasting has been proven to be the best delivery solution for many applications.

During recent years, several protocols, mechanisms, and techniques were designed in order to ensure multicasting. Multicast transport protocols have been the subject of active research since. This research has been specially supported by both the Internet Engineering and Internet Research Task Forces (IETF and IRTF) that were coordinating the development and standardization of multicast transport protocols [5]. To provide multicast services, a large number of protocols have been designed. However, these protocols were designated to satisfy the requirement of a special class of applications and were then applied in different environments. Among these applications are multimedia conferencing systems, distributed interactive simulations [6], chat groups, distance learning [7], media applications, multi-player games [8], distributed whiteboard tools, and collaborative applications, just to mention a few.

Each proposed protocol has its own features to satisfy the requirement of its application. And each protocol has its own technique to ensure reliability, quality of service (QoS), error recovery, ordering, congestion control, and flow control. Since there are several applications, the requirements and environments may differ from one application to another. As a consequence, the design of a multicast protocol that satisfies all the requirements is a challenging problem and most likely impossible. In the following section, we will present the features of the multicast protocols.

10.2.2 Features

A number of multicast protocols have been designed to address a variety of problems for different types of applications [5]. Most of these protocols must acquire certain features to satisfy the application's requirement. In the following, we will present and discuss the different features that most multicast protocols need.

10.2.2.1 Reliability. A protocol is said to be "reliable" if it guarantees that data transmitted by the sender is delivered to the intended receivers in order and without duplication. Both the sender and receiver can test if the reliability is satisfied. For a unicast transmission, the reliability is easy to satisfy since there is only one receiver that either receives or does not receive all the data transmitted by the sender. However, for a multicast transmission, it is not always the case, and protocols need strong reliability properties to be able to deliver data to the intended receivers.

There are many techniques to ensure reliability. Usually, unicast transport protocols such as TCP use ACK messages to ensure reliability and detect packet losses: Receivers must send ACK messages to the sender to inform it about the packet received. By checking the packet's sequence number, the sender can detect a lost packet. This approach is referred to as *sender-initiated*, because the sender is responsible for detecting lost packets. However, this approach is not efficient for multicast protocols. In fact, if each receiver sends an ACK message, then this may create an ACK implosion problem.

Another approach commonly used is the *receiver-initiated* one, where it is the responsibility of the receiver to detect packet losses. This approach is used to solve the ACK implosion problem. Receivers must check the packet's sequence number when they receive messages. If a missing packet is detected, the receiver must send a NACK message to the sender, to inform it about the missing packet.

Most of the multicast transport protocols use the receiver-initiated technique, and a study done by Pingali et al. [9] shows that the receiver-initiated approach performs better than the sender-initiated one. In order to ensure reliability, and depending on the requirement, some protocols, such as RMP or RBP, described in the next sections, combine both approaches.

10.2.2.2 Congestion and Flow Control. Congestion control deals with controlling the traffic in the network, by reducing, most of the time, the rate of sending packets. Congestion control is important for a wide number of applications [10]. For this reason, many techniques and algorithms are used to control the congestion. Protocols control the congestion by checking the type and the amount of feedback received from the network. This feedback is composed especially of the delay and loss of packets. In order to avoid congestion, multicast protocols either require that receivers maintain the same speed [10], or allow certain receivers to bring down their rate requirement when they detect congestion.

10.2.2.3 Ordering. Several applications require that packets are received in order because out-of order packets may lead receivers to a different state. To that end, many protocols are designed in a way to provide a mechanism to ensure complete ordering. This feature is realized via the use of sequence numbers. Ordering is an important feature for multicast protocols. In fact, ordering allows receivers to have the same and correct execution. It also helps them to detect duplicate messages and discard them when necessary. There are different types of ordering [6, 10]:

1. Total order means that all of the receivers have the same order of packets.
2. Causal ordering means that, if sending a message m causally precedes sending message m', then no receiver delivers the message m' before the message m.

Collaborative applications necessitate that messages are totally ordered delivered [5].

10.2.2.4 Error Recovery. An error recovery mechanism is important for reliable multicast protocols. Many approaches and algorithms exist in order to select a repair server to perform error recovery. If a single server is used to ensure the responsibility of error recovery, then this leads to the well-known implosion problem [11] caused by the ACK and NACK messages sent by the receivers. For this reason, some protocols use the receiver-based reliability where the receiver is responsible for detecting lost packets and asking for the repair. In some protocols, such as Scalable Reliable Multicast (SRM) [10], described later, every user can participate in the repair process if it holds the repair message. In fact, when a member detects a lost packet, it multicasts a retransmission request for the entire group. Any user that has the correct message can multicast the repair to the entire group. In order to avoid duplicate requests and repairs, a back-off algorithm is used. In other protocols, like tree-based protocols such as the Reliable Multicast Transport Protocol (RMTP) [7], described later, it is the responsibility of the group's master to recover an error and retransmit the missing packet. In fact, in this class of protocols, receivers are grouped into local groups based on their geographic position. A designated receiver is selected in each group and is responsible for ensuring error recovery for all the receivers in its group. By using this technique, multicast protocols avoid the implosion problem at the sender side. However, since the error recovery is only concentrated on one server, this class of protocols still suffers from several problems [11]. In fact, tree-based protocols can still suffer from implosion problems, since all the requests for a retransmission in a specific group are sent to the same designated receiver. Moreover, if the server that is responsible for the error recovery fails, then receivers cannot get the repair until a new designated receiver is elected [11].

10.2.2.5 Group Management. Some multicast protocols do not need knowledge of group membership. The sender does not keep track of the receivers in the multicast group. Receivers can join and leave the application without informing the sender. In this case, the sender just transmits its data to a multicast group address and receivers join to get the data [5]. This technique is based on IP multicast and is used by many protocols because it facilitates scalability [5]. However, other protocols require knowledge of group membership. In this case, group management is either controlled by the sender or hierarchically by a designated receiver or a group master [10]. Receivers have to make the one who is responsible for group management aware of their status and inform it before leaving or joining a session.

Most of the multicast transport protocols ensure scalability. In fact, the multicast transport of data is a good solution for applications that need to scale since they do not keep a track of users in the group; the sender just multicasts the message and receivers join the group and get the message [5].

In the next section, we will classify the multicast transport protocols designed in the literature and describe the most important protocols widely used.

10.3 CLASSIFICATION OF MULTICAST PROTOCOLS

Several transport protocols have been designed in the literature [5, 10]. However, not all of these protocols were designed to be applied in the same class of applications and to satisfy the same objective. In her survey, "Multicast Transport Protocols: A

Survey and Taxonomy" [5], Katia Obraczka classified the multicast transport protocols as follows:

1. general-purpose protocols
2. multicast interactive applications
3. data distribution services

Most multicast transport protocols have been designed for a specific class of applications: interactive applications and data distribution services. However, some of the techniques designed earlier did not target a specific class of application and they are therefore general purpose. This classification is elaborated in the next section.

10.3.1 General-Purpose Protocols

This category represents protocols that have been designed at the early stage. These protocols were not conceived for a specific class of application and they are therefore under the general-purpose class of protocols. These protocols are all message oriented. Among the protocols designed in this class are Reliable Broadcast Protocol (RBP), Multicast Transport Protocol (MTP), Reliable Multicast Protocol (RMP), and Xpress Transport Protocol (XTP).

10.3.1.1 Reliable Broadcast Protocol (RBP). This protocol [5] was designed in the early 1980s. It offers multipoint communication between sites connected by a local area broadcast network [5]. In order to broadcast all the messages to receivers, the sender transmits the message to a primary receiver called a token site. The primary receiver gets and stores the message transmitted by the source, which continues to retransmit the broadcast message until it gets an ACK message from the token site confirming that it received the complete message. This ACK message contains a global timestamp that the receivers use to order and find a lost message. The token site sends the message to the broadcast group. When a receiver detects a lost message, it sends a NACK message to the token site, which retransmits the missing message. The role of token site rotates among receivers in the broadcast group in order to reduce storage costs. A member can be a token site only if it has all the messages sent earlier than the timestamp of the current token site. In order to ensure the reliability and ordering, RBP mixes the negative acknowledgment (NACK) with the positive acknowledgment (ACK).

10.3.1.2 Multicast Transport Protocol (MTP). This protocol [12] was influenced by RBP [5]. It offers reliable and ordered delivery of data [5]. As described in RBP, MTP has a group master, which ensures that the data is delivered reliably and in order. In addition to the reliable and ordered delivery of data, MTP ensures the synchronization among the receivers to agree on the order of receipt of all messages [13]. Users in this protocol can have one of the following roles:

1. The *group master* ensures that data is delivered reliably and in order. It gives the token to the member who wants to transmit data. Moreover, it checks the membership and performance of the group members. In fact, if a group member

that has the token disconnects, then the master removes it from the group and rejects the member's outstanding messages.

2. The *producer* is allowed to send messages to the entire group and to consume data sent from other producers. Before transmitting the message, the producer has to get the token from the group master.

3. The *consumer* is allowed to only receive messages from the sender.

If a new member wants to join the group, it has to send an adhesion message to the group master, which will decide whether the new member can join the group. Before allowing the new member to join the group, the group master must have all the transmit tokens in order to ensure that the new member gets only the complete messages. The group master then informs its client application about the new member. When a lost message is detected, MTP uses the NACK messages. In fact, as soon as a consumer detects a lost message, it sends a NACK to the message's producer that multicasts the missing message to the entire group [5]. In terms of flow control, MTP is based on a fixed-size transmission window, which defines the maximum number of data packets that the member can send to the group within a period of time. Every member of the group must accept the actual window size when it joins the group [5].

10.3.1.3 Reliable Multicast Protocol (RMP).

This protocol [14] offers a totally ordered and reliable multipoint transport on top of an unreliable multicast service such as IP multicasting [5, 10]. Note that RMP [5, 10] is inspired from RBP [5]

The flow and congestion control mechanisms for RMP are based on the algorithms by Van Jacobson that were designed for TCP. These mechanisms allow RMP to offer high performance over LANs and WANs [10]. Like in RBP, the sender transmits the message to a primary receiver, a *token site*, which sends an ACK message to the sender to confirm that it received the entire message. The token site, which rotates among the members of the group, is responsible for managing new members and those that want to leave the session. In order to accelerate error recovery, RMP uses NACK messages. A small number of ACK messages are used to guarantee the delivery [10]. To implement the flow control and when a lost packet is detected, the receiver does not send a request to the token site but it multicasts a NACK to the entire group. When the sender gets the NACK message, it backs off exponentially and retransmits the missing packet.

10.3.1.4 Xpress Transport Protocol (XTP).

XTP [10, 15], which is an enhanced version of the Xpress Transfer Protocol, is a network-and-transport-layer protocol [10]. It unifies unicast and multicast features. XTP is a one-to-many protocol, designed to serve small and medium groups. For each association established between the sender and a receiver, XTP associates a state information packet. This packet contains important information such as the sequence number, size of the transmission window, an estimated round-trip time, and rate of transfer [6]. The sending application controls the group membership by deciding which member can join the application. To that end, the sending application uses the Multicast Group Management (MGM) service offered by XTP [5]. XTP ensures the reliable delivery of data by the use of TCP. For data that do not need to be transferred reliably, UDP is used as best effort transfer.

XTP is a sender reliable protocol. In fact, the *Loss Estimation System* (LES) resides with the sender, and receivers must send information about the packets received periodically. When a receiver detects a lost packet, it sends a NACK message to the sender, which multicasts the missing message to the entire group. The sender can choose when the receivers should produce ACK messages. Depending from the sender's choice, receivers can either always send ACK messages, sometimes, or never [5]. XTP provides both rate and window-based flow control.

10.3.2 Multicast Interactive Applications

Interactive application refers to a human–computer interaction application. These applications support one or more users and one or more computers. Multipoint interactive applications have seen growing interest in the last decade. These applications include multiparticipant multimedia conferencing services, distributed whiteboard application, and circuit-switched and gigabit network environments. Reliability in these applications is important, but interactive applications are willing to relax on the reliability in favor of real-time delivery. In this section, we will present the most important protocols designed to satisfy the requirement of interactive applications. Among protocols developed in this category are Multicast Transport Protocol-2 (MTP-2), Real-Time Transport Protocol (RTP), Scalable Reliable Multicast (SRM), and Reliable Adaptive Multicast Protocol (RAMP).

10.3.2.1 Multicast Transport Protocol-2 (MTP-2). This protocol [16], which is an enhanced version of MTP described above, was designed by C. Bormann et al. to satisfy the requirement of collaborative applications [5]. The changes applied to MTP-2 are as follows [5]:

1. *Immediate joins*: In MTP, if a new user wants to join a session, it has to wait until the master gets all the transmitted tokens. In MTP-2, new users can join the multicast group by ignoring all the messages sent before the join message.

2. *Master recovery*: MTP did not study the failure of the master and did not thus propose any solution for this problem. To that end, MTP-2 studied the master's failure problem and addressed it by allowing the group members to detect the failure and to select a new master.

3. *Dynamic group parameter adjustment*: Unlike in MTP, where the transmission window size is fixed, the MTP-2 allows the master to dynamically change the transmission size according to the network state.

4. *Differentiated services*: MTP-2 allows the sender to choose whether it needs an atomic message delivery for every message sent. If atomicity is not required, the receiver will send an atomic message when it gets the entire message.

The reliability is ensured on the receiver side. In fact, when the receiver detects a lost packet, it sends a NACK message to the sender, which multicasts the missing packet to the entire group [6].

10.3.2.2 Real-Time Transport Protocol (RTP). This protocol [17] was developed by the Audio-Video Transport Working Group of the IETF in 1996. RTP was designed in order to be applied in multiparticipant multimedia conferencing services over the internet [5]. It delivers audio and video packets over the Internet with real-time characteristics, without ensuring any reliable or order delivery. To that end, RTP applies User Datagram Protocol (UDP) [18] to deliver data and uses the sequence numbers to re-order the packets. RTP tries to prevent packet loss and does not tolerate jitter. In fact, if a packet is lost in a real-time application, then there is no need to retransmit it again.

RTP uses Real Time Control Protocol (RTPC) [19] in order to control information and monitor quality of service (QoS). In fact, RTCP provides three types of reports exchanged between the source and receivers: the Sender report, Receiver report, and Source description [20]. These reports have important information such as the number of packets sent, number of packets lost, an estimation of delay, and an estimation of jitter. All this information allows the sender to have an idea of the network state and to adapt according to the transmission rate.

10.3.2.3 Scalable Reliable Multicast (SRM). SRM [10] is a framework that has been designed in a distributed whiteboard application, which has been used on a global scale with sessions having few hundred participants [6]. This protocol is efficient [21], robust, and scales well when it is used for large networks and large sessions. SRM [10] is designed to deliver all the data to all the group members, not including any particular delivery order. The transport method is the best effort, but the reliability is built on an end-to-end basis. For the delivery, SRM is based on the IP multicast, but it added a special feature; SRM forces all the members that want to receive the data sent to the group to announce themselves by sending a "join" message, multicasting it to all the members of the group. When a member generates new data, it sends it to the multicast group. In order to keep track of the packets received, every member must periodically send a session message that contains the highest sequence number received from each member [10]. It also allows users to know the current participants of the session.

Each receiver is individually responsible for detecting lost packets and does this by finding a gap in the sequence space [10]. Should a gap be found, a request is made for a retransmission of the lost packet. First, a *negative acknowledgment* (NACK) is sent to all members. Everyone can then participate and send the repair. This is important since the original sender does not have to make the repair, especially if the distance[1] between it and the NACK sender is large [10]. With the involvement of every member, SRM makes the repair process faster [6, 10]. The members that participate in the repair process use the slotting-damping technique. In fact, when a member requests a retransmission, it sends it to the multicast group. The closest member (the one who has the right packet) times out first and multicasts the repair packet. The other members that were supposed to send a request, and hear the request already sent, suppress their own request and wait for the repair. Similarly, the members that heard the request, that have the right packet and

---

[1]The distance is calculated using the session messages and the round-trip time it takes for a packet to travel between two members.

scheduled the answer, suppress their repair packet from their buffer when they hear the answer of the first member. The main concern of SRM is congestion control. To avoid it, SRM uses the *exponential backoff* before the NACKS and repairs. This means that the user, who is going to send a NACK or a repair, sends its packet and sets a timer t. If it does not receive an answer before the timeout, it sends again the same packet and waits for 2t. The main issue that SRM encounters is the important delay during the transmission of the message.

10.3.2.4 Reliable Adaptive Multicast Protocol (RAMP). RAMP [22] was designed to be applied in all-optical, circuit-switched, and gigabit network environments [5]. This protocol is a transport layer protocol that runs over network layer protocols such as IP multicast [22]. RAMP [22] ensures reliable and ordered delivery of all data sent. RAMP also offers sender-based reliability—the sender can choose to send the data either reliably or unreliably.

A session can start when the sender sends a *connect* message to an IP multicast address and receives an *accept* message from at least one receiver. The receiver can detect a lost packet by checking the sequence numbers in the packet. When such is the case, the receiver sends (unicasts) a NACK message to the sender to inform it about the missing packet. Depending on the number of NACK messages received, the sender either unicasts or multicasts the repair packet [5]. Depending on transmission rate and the number of receivers, the sender can shift between two modes: idle or burst [5]. In the burst mode, the sender requires a reliable transfer: receivers must acknowledge the receipt of the messages. If the sender does not receive an ACK message from a receiver, it keeps retrying for a certain time and then deletes it from its membership list. The sender is in the idle mode and sends idle messages, either when it accepts the first *accept* message or when it has no data to transfer. In this protocol, the sender controls the group membership information that is necessary for the setup of circuits in the circuit-switched networks. RAMP does not scale well. To control the flow, RAMP [22] uses a simple technique that allows the sender to adapt the transmission rate depending on the network state.

10.3.3 Data Distribution Services

Many applications, such as those for news and business, need to distribute data to their clients. If the information to be sent is the same for each customer, then dissemination of data will be easier if it is sent through multicasting. For this reason, several protocols have been designed in order to satisfy the requirement of data dissemination class of applications. In what follows, we will describe some of the protocols that were designed in this category. Among these protocols, we mention. Tree-Based Multicast Transport Protocol (TMTP), Reliable Multicast Transport Protocol (RMTP), Multicast File Transfer Protocol (MFTP), and Tree-Based Reliable Multicast Protocol (TRAM).

10.3.3.1 Tree-Based Multicast Transport Protocol (TMTP). TMTP [23] was designed to offer reliable communication for interactive collaborative applications such as distributed shared whiteboards, distributed games, or simulations [23]. It takes advantage of the efficient best effort delivery of IP multicast to deliver data. To improve the flow and error control, TMTP organizes users in a hierarchical control tree and this by the use of an expanding ring search. Each sub-tree is represented by a Domain Manager that takes care of the local retransmission when its local receivers detect lost packets. This protocol does not need to have a receiver to start transmitting data. Users can join the application in the middle of the simulation. The sender uses IP multicast to transmit data to the entire multicast group. The error control is distributed among several nodes, Domain Managers [23], which lead to the participation of these nodes in the error recovery. To this end, TMTP uses a limited number of NACK messages with NACK suppression mechanism. When the receiver detects a lost packet, it multicasts a NACK message combined with NACK suppression, and when its parent receives the NACK message, it multicasts the missing packet.

TMTP also provides dynamic group membership, without assuming any knowledge of it. A session directory offers primitives [5] to create, delete, join, and leave the multicast group. In order to control the flow and during the creation of the group, members accept a predefined transmission rate to be applied during the application. Yavatkar et al. claimed that, when implemented and tested, TMTP was able to scale well, reduce the load on the sender, and minimize the end-to-end latency [23].

10.3.3.2 Reliable Multicast Transport Protocol (RMTP).

RMTP [7] can be built on top of either virtual-circuit networks or datagram networks. The main characteristic of this protocol is its architecture. In fact, RMTP is based on a hierarchical structure forming a multicast tree, with the sender as the root node and the receivers as the leaf nodes [7]. In order to have the tree, receivers are grouped into local regions or domains based on their proximity in the network. In each domain there is a special receiver (representative) called a designated receiver (DR), who is responsible for [7] sending acknowledgments periodically to the sender, processing acknowledgments from receivers in its domain, and retransmitting lost packets to the corresponding receivers. RMTP is composed of three components: the master that controls the sessions and the communications; the DRs, which can be the senders and the receivers; and, finally, the receivers that are only capable of receiving the messages sent by the DRs. The receivers choose their representative DR. In fact, each sender or DR sends a special packet called the SEND_ACK_TOME that contains a value of the time to live (TTL). The receiver will then check the TTL of each packet and choose the one that has the largest value of TTL. This chosen node will be the DR of that receiver.

RMTP also supports a multilevel hierarchy of local regions [7]. In such a case, the sender will receive only as many status messages as there are DRs in the highest level of the multicast tree. RMTP assumes that there is a session manager who takes care of the connection parameters and provides them to the sender and the receivers. The connection parameters are the packet size, the interval T_{send}, and Ws, the number of packets transmitted, which varies depending on the network state. This session manager is not a part of RMTP but is used to manage the RMTP session.

The protocol works as follows [7]: The sender sends the message to all the DRs (of the highest level), who will be responsible of transmitting the data to their local receivers. The message transferred by the sender is divided into fixed-size data packets, with the exception of the last one. The first packets are referred to as DATA and the last one is called DATA_EOF. For each packet DATA there is a corresponding sequence number that allows the receivers to order the packets and to detect if there are any lost packets [7]. The receivers must send periodically their status packets to their DRs, indicating which packets have been successfully received, in order to enable them to check whether there is a lost packet. In this case, if the number of receivers asking for a retransmission exceeds a certain threshold, then the lost packet is multicast; otherwise DRs just perform an end-to end transmission of the right packet to the desired receiver and reduce by that the *end-to-end delay* significantly. The DRs, from their side, will send their own status to the sender indicating which packets they have received and which packets they have not received. By using this technique, there is only one ACK message sent to the original sender per local region. This prevents the problem of ACK implosion. By reducing the unnecessary retransmission that the original sender has to send, in case of a lost packet, this protocol achieves *high throughput* and a*low end-to-end delay* [7].

To avoid network congestion, the source sends the data at a variable rate, which is based on the feedback from the group [11]. RMTP is designed to facilitate scalability [7] and, based on [21], RMTP has been shown via an analysis model to be the most scalable choice. RMTP is based on the IP-multicast technique. In fact, the sender does not have to keep track of the receivers, and this gives *a high degree of scalability*. Receivers can join and leave the session when they want to without informing the sender.

Since RMTP allows users to join the group at any time, it has two features that allow late users to catch up with the rest [7]:

1. *Immediate transmission request*: When the user finds out that it joined the group in the middle of the transmission, it requests all the packets that it missed. It sends to its DR a special packet ACK_TXNOW, asking for the missing packets. The DR sends these packets using unicast.
2. *Data cache in the sender and the DRs*. The DRs and the sender should have a buffer that contains the message sent during the session. This feature allows the receivers to request a retransmission of a lost packet from the corresponding DR or sender.

To provide reliable delivery to all receivers, and because the sender does not keep an explicit list of receivers, termination of an RMTP session is timer based [7]. In fact, after the transmission of the last packet, the sender starts a timer that expires after T_{dally} seconds. This interval T_{dally} is set to be twice the lifetime of a packet in an Internet. When the timer expires, the sender deletes all state information associated with the connection. Any ACK message from a receiver resets the timer to its initial value. Once the receiver gets all the packets, it stops sending ACK messages.

The main disadvantage of this protocol is that the sender and DRs have an additional cache. In fact, as discussed above, RMTP provides a high degree of scalability because the sender does not keep a track of the receivers in the multicast tree. But in order to be able to retransmit the lost packets, the sender and the DRs must buffer the message sent during the session and need then an additional cache. Another disadvantage, discussed in [7], is that the DRs are chosen by the receivers based on the TTL of the SEND_ACK_TOME packet, and a big number of receivers can choose the same DR, which result in an unbalanced tree.

10.3.3.3 Multicast File Transfer Protocol (MFTP). MFTP [24], developed
by StarBurst Communications, runs over UDP in the application layer and offers a reliable transfer of files from one sender to multiple receivers. The MFTP source switches between three modes, unicast, multicast, or broadcast, depending on the type of data transmitted and the transmission mode supported by the network [5]. This protocol has two components:

1. *Administrative protocol*: used for the group management and for the creation and rupture of the group.
2. *Data transfer protocol*: used for the transmission of the file reliably to all the users in the multicast group.

Using the second component, the MFTP server informs (via an announcement) a file transfer session and clients join the session to receive the file transmitted. The file is sent in passes. First, the sender sends the entire file in the first pass and then retransmits lost packets in the succeeding passes [5]. When a receiver detects a lost packet, it sends a NACK message to the sender, which retransmits the missing packet. Receivers must acknowledge reception of the packets only when they are asked to. Announcements are sent to a *public group* supported by the administrative protocol. However, data is sent on a private group address [5]. Clients can join the public group and listen to the announcements, however, only those allowed by the source can join the private group.

The MFTP server is responsible for multicast group management, file transfer, and transfer operation. Only when requested do receivers acknowledge the reception of the file transmitted.

10.3.3.4 Tree-Based Reliable Multicast Protocol (TRAM). TRAM [25] is
a scalable transport protocol implemented for the transfer of bulk data from a single sender to multiple receivers [26]. This protocol has been a part of the JAVA Reliable Multicast Service (JRMS) project [26]. Similar to RMTP [7] and TMTP [23], TRAM is a tree-based protocol, where the tree design is dynamic, as in TMTP [23]. TRAM offers different types of trees to satisfy the applications' requirement. The tree is composed of the sender at the root and the receivers at the leaf nodes. Some receivers are designated to be repair heads and are responsible for the repair process of their group members [26]. TRAM is dynamic and allows the redesign of the tree by enabling receivers to find a better head repair.

TRAM is designed, in a way, to guarantee data delivery for all of the receivers of the multicast tree [26]. Reliability is ensured via the use of ACK messages. Upon the reception of data, receivers send ACK messages to their repair head. The latter is able to detect lost messages and to send the missing packets to the required receivers. In order to be able to retransmit data, the head repair must have a cache memory that contains the data transmitted [26]. Receivers check the reachability periodically. If there is no answer from one receiver, it is then deleted from the repair tree. Similarly, if there is no answer from a head repair, then it is abandoned and its group members are assigned to an active head repair [26]. Depending on the network congestion, the sender transmits data at a variable rate in order to control the flow.

10.4 CONCLUSION

Multicasting refers to the simultaneous delivery of information to a large number of destinations. Multicasting is the first choice of several communication applications because it requires less bandwidth and delays than a multiple unicasting. To that end, many multicast transport protocols have been designed. However, not all of them have been able to satisfy different applications' requirement and they must have their own features to meet these requirements. Among the features that the multicast protocol need to have are reliability, congestion and flow control, ordering, error recovery, and group management.

As the number of applications using multicasting has grown, the number of multicast transport protocols has increased as well. The latter can be classified into three categories, depending on the type of applications:

1. General-purpose protocols: RBP [5], MTP [12], RMP[14], and XTP [10,15]
2. Multicast interactive applications: MTP-2 [16], RTP [17], SRM [10], and RAMP[22]
3. Data distribution services: TMTP [23], RMTP [7], MFTP [24], and TRAM [25]

REFERENCES

[1] A. Striegel and G. Manimaran, "A survey of QoS multicasting issues," *IEEE Communications Magazine*, 2002, Vol. 40, No. 6, pp. 82–87.

[2] IETF Multicast and Anycast Group Membership (magma) Working Group [IETF Multicast & Anycast Group Membership (magma) Working Group], http://datatracker.ietf.org/wg/magma/charter/ (Accessed April 2012).

[3] L. H. Sahasrabuddhe and B. Mukherjee, "Multicast routing algorithms and protocols: A tutorial," *IEEE Network*, 2000, pp. 90–102.

[4] B. A. Forouzan, TCP/IP Protocol Suite, *McGraw-Hill Science/Engineering/Math*; 2nd edition (June 27, 2002).

[5] K. Obraczka, "Multicast transport mechanisms: A survey and taxonomy," *IEEE Communications Magazine*, 1998, Vol. 36, No. 1, pp. 94–102.

[6] E. Frécon, "A survey of CVE technologies and systems," *SICS Technical Report*, T2004-03, ISSN 110-3154, 2004.

[7] C. Bouras, E. Giannaka, A. Panagopoulos, and T. Tsiatsos "A platform for virtual collaborative spaces and educational communities: the case of EVE." *Multimedia Systems Journal, Special Issue on Multimedia System Technologies for Educational Tools*, 2006, Vol. 11, No. 3, pp. 290–303.

[8] F. Santos, B. Fonseca, P. Martins, and L. Morgado, "Negotiation of spatial configurations in collaborative virtual environments," *m-ICTE 2006*, Sevilla, Spain, FORMATEX, November 2006.

[9] D. Towsley, J. Kurose, and S. Pingali, "A comparison of sender-initiated and receiver-initiated reliablemulticast protocols", *IEEE Journal on Selected Areas in Communications*, 1997, Vol. 15, No. 3, pp. 398–406.

[10] J. W. Atwood, "Classification of reliable multicast protocols," *IEEE Network*, 2004, Vol. 18, No. 3, pp. 24–34.

[11] Z. Xiao and K. P. Birman. "A randomized error recovery algorithm for reliable multicast," *IEEE Proceedings Twentieth Annual Joint Conference of the IEEE Computer Societies and Communication Societies (INFOCOM'01)*, 2001, pp. 239–248.

[12] S. Armstrong, A. Freier, and K. Marzullo, "Multicast transport protocol," *Internet RFC 1301*, February 1992.

[13] Multicast Transport Protocol, ftp://ftp.rfc-editor.org/in-notes/rfc1301.txt (Accessed April 2012).

[14] B. Whetten, T. Montgomery, and S. Kaplan, "A high performance totally ordered multicast protocol," *Selected Papers from the International Workshop on Theory and Practice in Distributed Systems*, Vol. 938 Lecture Notes in Computer Science, Springer Verlag, pp. 33–57.

[15] Xpress Transport Protocol, http://www.ccii.co.za/products/xtp.html (Accessed April 2012).

[16] C. Bormann, J. Ott, H.C. Gehrcke, T. Kerschat, and N. Seifert, "MTP-2: Towards achieving the S.E.R.O. properties for multicast transport," International Conference on Computer Communications Networks, San Francisco, California, September 1994.

[17] H. Schulzrinne and S. Casner. "RTP: A transport protocol for real-time applications." *Internet Engineering Task Force, Internet Draft*, October 20, 1993.

[18] RTP: A Transport Protocol for Real-Time Applications, http://www.ietf.org/rfc/rfc1889.txt (Accessed April 2012).

[19] Real Time Control Protocol, http://www.freesoft.org/CIE/RFC/1889/13.htm (Accessed April 2012).

[20] Real Time Protocol, http://icapeople.epfl.ch/thiran/CoursED/RTP.pdf (Accessed April 2012).

[21] P. Parnes, "The mStar Environment Scalable Distributed Teamwork Using IP Multicast," Master's thesis, Luleå University of Technology, Sweden, September 1997.

[22] A. Koifman and S. Zabele, "RAMP: A Reliable Adaptive Multicast Protocol," *IEEE Proceedings Fifteenth Annual Joint Conference of the IEEE Computer Societies (INFOCOM'96)*, San Francisco, CA, March 1996, pp. 1442–1451.

[23] R. Yavatkar, J. Griffioen, and M. Sudan, "A reliable dissemination protocol for interactive collaborative applications." In *Proceedings of the ACM Multimedia '95 Conference*, November 1995, pp. 333–344.

[24] K. Miller, K. Robertson, A. Tweedly, and M. White, "Starburst Multicast File Transfer Protocol (mftp) Specification," *Internet draft, IETF, draft-miller-mftp-spec-02.txt*, January 1997.

[25] D. Chiu, et al., "TRAM: A Tree-based Reliable Multicast Protocol," Sun Microsystems Laboratory Technical Report, SML TR-98-66, Sun Microsystems, July 1998, pp. 1–22.

[26] D. M. Chiu, S. Hurst, M. Kadansky, and J. Wesley, "TRAM: A Tree-based Reliable Multicast Protocol," Sun Microsystems Laboratories Technical Report, SMLI TR-98-66, September 1998.

11

NATURE-INSPIRED COMPUTING FOR AUTONOMIC WIRELESS SENSOR NETWORKS

Wei Li, Javid Taheri, Albert Y. Zomaya, Franciszek Seredynski, and Bjorn Landfeldt

CONTENTS

Large Scale Network-Centric Distributed Systems, First Edition. Edited by Hamid Sarbazi-Azad and Albert Y. Zomaya.
© 2014 John Wiley & Sons, Inc. Published 2014 by John Wiley & Sons, Inc.

11.1 INTRODUCTION

Millions of years of evolution created a large spectrum of highly organized forms of life on Earth, including plants, animals, and eventually humans. Today, society has reached a state of organization that requires new, powerful, and efficient mechanisms to solve complex real-life problems in the economy, engineering, and science. Economists, engineers, and scientists look into the future hoping to mimic and deploy already existing mechanisms in nature in the form of nature-inspired computational paradigms to efficiently solve many real-life problems. Through the observation of various natural phenomena, people have imitated the complete appearance and/or borrowed many ideas from several functions of plants and animals to produce effective materials, structures, tools, mechanisms, processes, algorithms, and methods in current man-made systems. One area that has, to a large extent, grown out of these aspirations is sensor network technology [1], which fundamentally borrows the ability to sense and communicate information among large populations from nature.

A sensor can be viewed as a device to measure an environmental stimulus and convert it into an electronic signal to be read by an observer or an instrument. Although the capability of man-made sensors is usually not as broad as bio-sensors, they still preserve the analogy with their direct biological ancestors. Besides sensing, man-made sensors may also have extra functions such as data storage, wireless communication, and even a limited amount of computation. A single sensor, however, is only capable of covering a limited area of interest that might not be large enough for many applications. On the other hand, because improving resolution and accuracy of sensor devices has resulted in increasing their prices, making them unviable for mass production, a network/group of them is used instead. Here, relatively simple sensors work together to form a larger system, namely a wireless sensor network (WSN), which alleviates many difficulties facing each of them individually.

The fundamental concept of a WSN is to perform networked sensing using a number of relatively cheap and unsophisticated sensors, instead of the conventional approach of deploying expensive and sophisticated sensing devices. This approach has the potential benefit of achieving greater coverage, accuracy, and reliability at a lower cost than using a single high-capability sensor. These benefits make WSNs attractive to a wide range of applications, and, therefore, this technology is identified as one of the most important advancements of the 21st century [2, 3]. To date, WSNs have been applied to many domains, including military, commercial, civilian, healthcare, industrial, and scientific applications. For example, WSNs are used to monitor water environments [4], wildlife habitats [5], and military applications [6]. Further applications are listed in [7, 8].

Most current WSN deployments use less than 1000 sensors [9–11]. In these designs, the system behavior is generally predetermined, the data collected from the interesting area of and will be sent back to a central authority, called sink. Under these centralized control schemes [12–13], sensors closer to the sink serving as routers (to forward information to sink) for most of the time experience a more rapid energy consumption than the others. Sensors are also designed to work together in the system, though only in simple ways: multihop networks are formed and clocks are synchronized. Existing networking technologies still appear to be hardly extended to such systems with the number of sensors is significantly increased [14, 15]. This results in extreme difficulty in managing each sensor and maintaining the overall system efficiency. Furthermore, many other issues, such as energy efficiency, scheduling, topology control, routing, and collaboration, must also be addressed in designing and implementing large-scale WSNs. Therefore, viable WSN solutions must reduce management complexity and allow their users to mainly focus on the application function itself. Toward this end, it is necessary to design and implement autonomic mechanisms on WSNs to add self-governance capability to these systems.

In natural systems with self-governance capability, each entity makes its own decision through cooperating with others and adjusts its functions without any external instruction. In information technology, most nature-inspired works are focused on optimization problems where further nature-inspired characteristics, such as scalability, adaptability, robustness, and self-properties [16], are also considered in implementing autonomic WSNs.

In this chapter, we present how nature-inspired algorithms can affect the underlying design principles, enabling technologies, implementation, and management issues of autonomic WSNs. Section 11.2 explains how WSN can benefit from autonomic mechanisms. In Section 11.3, we present a brief introduction to nature-inspired computing. We further review several current nature-inspired techniques to construct autonomic WSN in Sections 11.4–11.8 and also present the state-of-the-art techniques in those areas. Section 11.9 introduces several works in which multiple biological principles are used to build fundamental frameworks for implementing autonomic WSNs. Finally, conclusions are provided in Section 11.10.

11.2 AUTONOMIC WSNs

Inspired by the autonomic nervous system of a human body, IBM initiated a project to relieve humans of the burden of managing complex computer systems. This project aimed to build autonomic computing by designing computers that can manage themselves [17]. Therefore, it was necessary to provide a computing element with enough knowledge about its environment and actions. Two frameworks were proposed as solutions in this work. The first framework was an autonomic element equipped with a number of functional modules to monitor, analyze, plan, execute, sensor, and actuate. The second framework was a prototype to build and learn environments. This framework was partially implemented and a toolbox of components was provided to manipulate and use acquired information. When these models are applied to a complex computing system, four properties of a self-managing system emerge. These are self-configuration, self-optimization, self-healing, and self-protecting [18]. These frameworks and their properties are major breakthroughs for achieving the long-term goal of designing fully unsupervised complex systems.

The autonomic computing model proposes a general architecture as guidance to achieve self-governed systems. In practice, each model needs to be implemented using an enabling technology. One possible solution is the use of multiagent systems (MASs) in which a set of autonomous entities, agents, interact with each other to effectively construct a collaborative system [18, 19]. MASs can also provide additional functions such as autonomy, social ability, reactivity, and proactivity [20]. The core idea in MASs is to enable an agent or a software-based entity (capable of displaying autonomous and cooperative behavior) to respond to external stimuli based on its local knowledge. Hence, agents demonstrate an important characteristic of decentralization [21]; no agents control or instruct other agents, such as the case in cooperative systems. These properties in MASs inspired researchers to implement analogous autonomic computing ideas into WSNs to solve several large-scale and complex problems. In WSNs, a sensor passes through the three distinct phases of birth, work, and death with specific characteristics for each stage.

In the birth phase, sensors become fully functional. In most cases, because sensor nodes are usually assumed to be randomly deployed without advance knowledge of their physical location/position, they cannot be equipped with preprogrammed configuration to handle diverse unexpected scenarios. Hence, sensor nodes need to be equipped with several autonomic mechanisms (e.g., self-localization and/or self-configuration) to handle many situations. Therefore, after power-up initialization, each node starts detecting whether it is inside an already-operational network or not. With the capability of self-localization, a sensor node is able to establish and dynamically update a reference system to identify positions of other sensors. With the help of self-configuration, a sensor can also configure itself based on the environment it is operating in. These procedures are followed by exchange of information with neighbors so that each sensor eventually becomes a part of a holistic system (either from a networking or from a sensing point of view). Furthermore, because internal environments of WSNs appear to be dynamic, each sensor also needs to adapt itself to these changes and procedures to establish sensing and communication schedules without manual intervention.

In the work phase, an organized structure has been set up and the network is ready to operate [7, 22]. In this phase, sensor nodes are distributed within the sensing space and each sensor has the capability to sense and forward its data to a sink—through multi- or single-hop routing schemes. The sink may process the received data and return results to the sender or forward the data to a task manager node via wire/wireless connections.

For many applications, prolonging lifetime of the WSN is the most important aspect, as recharging or manually changing sensors' batteries is almost impossible. The lifetime of each sensor greatly depends on tasks it executes and the amount of data it transmits. In fact, because the energy used to execute a few thousand instructions is in the same order as transmitting a single bit of data over 100 meters, limiting each sensor's activity is the most direct solution to increase lifespan of WSNs [23, 24]. In these works, the overall activity schedule of nodes is designed so that several sensors remain active to maintain connectivity of the network and retain the quality of service, while other nodes are switched to semiactive mode with an operating sensing unit and/or transceiver, and others are switched to sleep mode with only partial monitoring or even deep sleep without any working unit [25]. This power management mechanism highlights classical problems of topology control, network routing, and sensing coverage in WSNs. Several particular applications require sensors to be deployed in unattended areas, such as underwater [26, 27], hostile environments [28, 29], or even physically unreachable areas such as inside human bodies [30, 31] or inside a wall [32–34]. These particular examples show that using a centralized controller can be at best very difficult, as the operational environment requires distributed control and management. Furthermore, because collected data in WSNs might be affected by ambient noise [35] and collected false information could disturb a system's well-balanced states, sensors must be able to recognize and eliminate false information before sending the data to other sensors or to the sink. In addition, enabling such autonomic principles will (1) help sensors to avoid wasting energy on transferring all information to the central controller to process, and (2) assist in detecting a network's path breaks and gaps inside the covered area caused by damaged or exhausted sensor nodes. In fact, because the communication range of sensors is limited in most WSNs, sensor nodes tend to interact with their neighboring nodes. Therefore, by applying autonomic principles to WSNs, central controllers are weakened. In this case, through interaction with neighbors, autonomic principles bring functionality to the entire system without global coordinators. These principles are referred to as self-organization and emergence and they help centralized controlled WSNs to overcome some inherent weakness and achieve better energy efficient to prolong the system lifetime.

In the death phase, one or more sensor nodes exhaust their energy and the network topology changes. Although it is necessary to remove depleted nodes from local knowledge bases, other nodes may not immediately respond to the death of their neighbors. Therefore, an autonomic mechanism should be designed to restore connectivity after several nodes in the network are lost. Sample solutions here include renegotiating network routes, activating redundant nodes to replace lost nodes, or rebuilding the logical topology.

As explained earlier, autonomic computing principles can be incorporated into WSNs through proper deployment of MAS technologies. However, because MASs are mostly used in rich platforms such as semantic webs, web services, service-oriented computing, data centers, clusters, grid computing systems, and others [18, 36, 37], it is often difficult to adjust these principles to operate within the resource-constrained sensor network platforms. Therefore, bringing autonomic techniques to WSNs without overspending limited resources has been widely questioned. In the following section, we further discuss nature-inspired computing as an alternate solution to implement autonomic WSNs, mainly because (1) most natural systems need to work autonomously without external intervention, and (2) most elements in such systems are employed to perform a dedicated or a very narrow range of functions [38].

11.3 PRINCIPLES OF NATURE-INSPIRED COMPUTING

Nature-inspired computing takes its inspiration from natural systems and consists of a set of schemes that solve complex computational problems. The nature-inspired paradigm can be divided into three main categories [39]: (1) biologically inspired computing, (2) simulation and emulation of nature by means of computing, and (3) computing with natural materials. Through observation and study of many natural systems and the existence of a large number of individual autonomous entities, it is easy to detect the natural tendency for individual entities to be able to autonomously process tasks. In nature, overall systems are formed through interactions of these individual entities with the capability of sending/receiving information, performing actions, and modifying their states based on several local rules. An entity receives several pieces of information (e.g., sharable knowledge from its neighbors, environmental stimulus, and/or state of its neighbors) and uses its local rules to respond [40]. These responses can change the internal state of an entity, its external display for certain behaviors, or even its inhabiting environment. Furthermore, to adapt to varying circumstances without prior external instructions, an autonomous entity must also modify its local rules over time. These fundamental attributes of natural systems, discriminate them from other systems as elaborated on in the following sections.

Autonomy: In natural systems, entities act independently with bounded rationality [41–43]. Each entity senses its local living environment and autonomously takes action or interacts with others accordingly (without any explicit external instruction) [44].

Decentralization: There are many examples (e.g., ant colonies) in nature with no central controller to instruct and coordinate individual entities [43, 45, 46]. This property can be thought of as dissemination of the decision-making authority of a system among its individual entities. Compared with a centralized control mechanism, a decentralized scheme not only makes the system easier to expand [47], but also avoids a single point of failure as the most well-known performance bottleneck in all systems [48].

Adaptivity: Because natural systems may reside in complicated environments, their entities need to be resilient to unpredictable changes. Therefore, once an entity realizes its fitness no longer adapts to the rest of the system, it adjusts its states accordingly. This property helps each entity to stabilize itself, even in case of frequent external environmental changes.

Self-organization: Elementary components of both natural and nature-inspired computing-based systems are interacting autonomous entities. Therefore, through local interactions among entities, a system can retain its harmony, stay organized, and maintain its functional structure without the need for external control. Increasingly, in order of importance [49–51]: robustness [52, 53], and dynamism [52] are additional characteristics that may influence the self-organization processes.

Emergence: The micro-macro effect is the most important attribute of the emergence behavior [49, 54–57]. An emergence is defined as a phenomenon in which global behavioral patterns of higher macro-levels of a system are altered or influenced by actions in the lower micro-levels. The other characteristics of emergence are novelty [49, 58, 59], irreducibility [58, 60], and coherence [49, 61].

Unlike centralized systems in which a controller exercises its influence over a system, entities of natural systems tend to work distributed, in environments filled with fluctuation and randomness. In fact, decentralized control mechanisms provide the general characteristics of robustness and resilience for a system [52]. As a result, natural systems are less sensitive compared with man-made systems, and, thus, damages have a limited impact on these systems. In addition, natural systems are assumed to be highly nonlinear, as cause and effect in such systems are not linearly related to each other [62–65]. That is, small causes may induce large effects, and large causes may only produce small effects.

The feedback mechanism has another important role in natural systems, to control systems' fluctuations. Two basic types of feedback exist: positive and negative. A positive feedback results in amplification effects of initial changes; a negative feedback stabilizes systems' states by preventing them from overreacting to external stimuli. Several interlocking positive and negative feedback loops exist in natural systems, during which beneficial information is amplified and deviations are suppressed. Therefore, natural systems cannot immediately operate at an ideal performance level; instead, such systems use their feedback mechanisms and take several adaptation steps through small, controlled fluctuations to slowly approach their expected performance levels. Although reaching equilibrium, robustness, and reliability are among many products of such complex mechanisms, they still greatly suffer from many drawbacks that limit applicability of nature-inspired computing algorithms (e.g., reduced determinism and controllability of the system behavior [66–68]). Furthermore, although nature-inspired algorithms will eventually result in the desired solution or behavior in many cases, there is usually very limited knowledge of when such states will be reached [68]. Thus, a proper trade-off must be set to balance scalability, controllability, and performance in such systems. Figure 11.1 shows a symbolic performance comparison between optimized systems and natural systems.

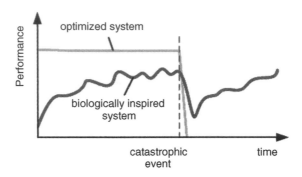

<u>Figure 11.1</u>   Performance comparison between biologically inspired systems and optimized systems [66].

11.4   CELLULAR AUTOMATA

In an attempt to create self-replicating machines, Cellular automata (CA) were first proposed by von Neumann in the early 1950s [69]. CA exhibit several fundamental properties in natural systems; for example, they are massively parallel, homogeneous, and only use local interactions. From a static point of view, CA consist of a number of cells in an infinitely large n-dimensional lattice in which each cell is associated with a specific value, called state value. State values are taken from a finite set of possible values to present the overall system's state at any particular time. To determine the state of different cells in different time frames, transition rules are added to CA models. Transition rules are designed to calculate the next state for a particular cell based on its current state as well as the states of its neighbor(s).

Because, for computer simulations, CA models need to be run on a finite number of cells, the following boundary conditions are set: null boundary, periodic boundary [70], reflective boundary [71], and constant boundary [72]. In a null boundary, the top-bottom-left-right-most cell of the lattice is connected to logical state of '0'; in periodic boundary (primary selection for most simulations), the modeled lattice is folded so that border cells become adjacent; in reflective and constant boundary conditions, border cells are assumed connected to a group of cells with a predetermined state.

CA models preserve favorable characteristics in building autonomic WSNs. Among these characteristics are: operating on discrete cells, operating on homogenous nodes, operating on local interactions, operating with discrete states, operating on asynchronous events, and operating on decentralized control schemes [73]. In WSN approaches based on CA models, sensors are considered as cells placed on one or two-dimensional lattices that update their states based on their current state as well as received state information from their neighbours and the environment.

11.4.1   One-Dimensional Cellular Automata and Its Applications in WSNs

One-dimensional cellular automata (1D-CA) is an array of cells distributed on a straight line. Because of its inherent simplicity, 1D-CA with only two cell states is the most studied variant of CA [74]. In numerous 1D-CA applications, the size of a neighborhood (including the center cell) is usually equal to three [69, 75], five [76], or seven cells [77] for neighborhood radius of one, two, and three, respectively.

For example, a design called Eemca [78] used a neighborhood size of three with periodic boundary condition to monitor efficiency of sensor nodes' energy spending. In this approach, nodes running Eemca have only two states, either active for elected coordinators or standby otherwise. In any particular moment, Eemca aimed to minimize the number of active sensors (coordinators) to minimize energy consumption of the whole network, while still covering maximum network area to process a global task. Here, after a certain amount of time, unused nodes in the standby state may become active based on their local rules. Designers of Eemca examined system performance under three selected rules: rule 95, rule 5, and rule 23. Rule 95 changes the next state of a node to active when at most one of its two neighbors is active and changes to standby when both neighbors are active. Rule 5 means the next state of a node will be active only if both its neighbors are in standby. Rule 23 indicates that the next state of a node will be in standby only if both neighbors (including itself) are active. The experimental results show that rule 5 gives the best trade-off between life span and coverage for a generic system.

11.4.2 Two-Dimensional Cellular Automata and Its Applications in WSNs

A two-dimensional CA (2D-CA) with several identical characteristics to 1D-CA needs further configurations and has more complexity. 2D-CA cells are formed by different types of lattices and neighborhood structures. Depending on the geometry of an individual cell in 2D-CA, triangle, square, or hexagon lattices might be used for different applications. The most commonly studied lattice of 2D-CA is the regular square with two fundamental types of neighborhoods: von Neumann and Moore. In von Neumann, a neighborhood is defined as horizontal and vertical cells of a central cell only, while in a Moore neighborhood all cells around a central cell are considered. As an instance, a 2D-CA von Neumann and Moore neighborhood with radius of one has five and nine cells, respectively. Figure 11.2 shows a graphical representation of these neighborhood types for a sample radius of one.

Renan et al. developed a CA-based simulator called CASim [79] to verify several issues regarding topology control algorithms in WSNs. They modeled a WSN as a

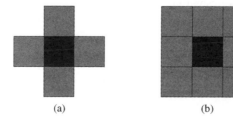

(a)   (b)

Figure 11.2 Examples of two types of neighbors of the central cell in a two-dimensional CA: (a) von Neumann neighborhood, (b) Moore neighborhood

2D-CA with null boundary condition and Moore neighborhood with neighborhood radius of one. In their approach, each sensor has two states, active and standby. At the very beginning, all nodes are set to the active state and have initial random timer values. Once a sensor's timer is expired, it checks its neighbors' states. If more than one, its neighbors are active and it switches to the standby mode and reinitiates its timer to another random value. The process lasts until all nodes are depleted or the network connectively fails.

Jones et al. [10, 11, 80] presented a communal sensor network scheme in which operation of most existing sensor networks is conceived as organisms in an ecosystem. In their approach, autonomous sensor nodes function asynchronously and cooperatively to achieve a common goal. These sensor nodes only sense data and forward to the sink without knowledge of other nodes in the system. 2D-CA is used to simulate a WSN operation as an ecosystem of individual sensors. Here, cells are assigned different values for their neighbor's radius (however fixed during the whole time of simulation). Based on these conditions, an algorithm is presented to perform the full data aggregation in a scalable fashion. The assumption is made that data collected by these sensors can be mapped onto a real number in the range of [0, 255]. In any particular time slot, sensors exchange information with their neighbors. If all neighbors of a selected cell have the same value as itself, the selected cell switches its status to inactive and does not participate until it is reactivated; otherwise, the selected cell computes the average of its neighbors' values and updates itself and all its neighbors to this value.

2D-CA is also used to solve other types of problems in WSNs. Teymorian et al. [81] presented a key management scheme for WSN, called CAB, with simple bitwise OR and XOR rules. Song et al. [82] proposed a 2D-CA model to investigate and analyze the process of malware propagation over WSNs by using multihop broadcast protocols. Allegretti et al. [83] implemented their "MASS" algorithm on a continuous 2D-CA model. In this work, unlike traditional 2D-CA models, the state of each cell could be set to finite discrete values to store continuous value ranges.

11.5 SWARM INTELLIGENCE

Swarm intelligence (SI) is based on the collective ability of social insects (or other animal species) that interact according to a set of local rules and exhibit collective intelligence at a system level to solve a common problem. Classical examples of such intelligence include a group of ants foraging for food, a school of fish swimming together, or birds flying as a flock. In SI, entities within a swarm system are assumed to have fairly limited capabilities by themselves [84–87]. Swarm systems should follow five basic principles that lead to an intelligent behavior as an emergent property of the whole system. These principles are proximity, quality, diversity, stability, and adaptability [88, 89]. SI imposes new ways to control a system with a large number of simple homogeneous agents. Three successful examples of SI are an ant colony, firefly synchronization, and particle swarm optimization. Ant colony optimization focuses on discrete optimization problems; firefly synchronization provides solutions for discrete synchronization of individual entities; and particle swarm optimization proposes an efficient and general approach to solve nonlinear optimization problems with constraints [90].

11.5.1   Ant Colony Optimization

Ant colony optimization (ACO) [85, 87, 90–92] is a meta-heuristic optimization algorithm inspired by the way ants find the shortest path from their nest to a food source. ACO algorithms can provide reasonable solutions to hard combinatorial optimization problems [93] (e.g., the traveling salesman problem, quadratic assignments problem, graph coloring, job-shop scheduling, or vehicle routing problem) in a reasonable amount of computation time. Moreover, because of many similarities between ants foraging and routing, ACO also showed reasonable performance in solving dynamic and distributed routing problems [94] as well as other stochastic time-varying problems.

11.5.1.1   Basic Concepts.   Ants' foraging process consists of several steps, from sending out the first group of forager ants to building a solid path for other ants to follow and bring food to the nest. At the beginning, several forager ants randomly wander around until they discover a food source. Through a mass recruitment process [95] "recruiter" ants pass their food location knowledge to other ants by laying a chemical low-molecular-weight substance (pheromone) on the road to form a trail. Other ants may follow the trail to reach the same food source and become "recruiter" ants, or they may decide to ignore the trail and search for other locations. During this self-reinforcement positive feedback process, the more "recruiter" ants lay pheromone on the road, the stronger the pheromone becomes, and therefore, the more ants may follow the path. In this process, because pheromone is a volatile material, pheromones on the unsuccessful paths will disappear over time and become obsolete to others. Figure 11.3 illustrates how ants find the shortest path between their nests to a food location by releasing pheromone.

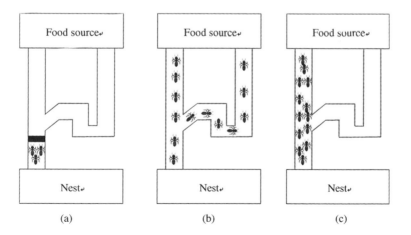

Figure 11.3   Illustration of how ants find food by releasing pheromone and establishing a shortest path. (a) The path to destination is blocked originally. (b) Initial ant movement when the block is removed. (c) The ants' movement after some time has passed, as they have found the food and released enough pheromone on a path.

The ACO algorithm is inspired by these trail-laying and trail-following behavioral patterns. Pheromone update and probabilistic transition rules are used to mathematically model these patterns in an ACO algorithm. The pheromone update rule specifies how an ant can probabilistically decide a path to follow, while pheromone updating rule determines how the strength of pheromone on a path is modified (either increased or decreased). The probability for ant k to select a path from location i to location j at iteration t can be described as:

$$
p_{ij}^k(t) = \begin{cases} \dfrac{[\tau_{ij}(t)]^\alpha \cdot [\eta_{ij}]^\beta}{\sum_{j \in J_i^k} [\tau_{il}(t)]^\alpha \cdot [\eta_{ij}]^\beta}, & if \ j \in J_i^k \\[4mm] 0, & otherwise \end{cases}
$$

where $\tau_{ij}(t)$ is the strength of pheromone from location i to j, η_{ij} is the heuristic desirability for choosing location j when ant k is located at location i, and J_i^k is the possible list of locations still to be visited/discovered by ant k from node i. The parameters α and β are two user-defined coefficients to control the relative weight of trial intensity $\tau_{ij}(t)$ and heuristics η_{ij}. In this case, the differential amount of pheromone released by ant k in each iteration can be expressed as: $\tau_{ij}(t) \leftarrow (1 - \rho)\tau_{ij}(t) + \Delta\tau_{ij}(t)$, where $\rho \in (0, 1]$ is the pheromone decay rate, and $\Delta\tau_{ij}(t) = \sum_k \Delta\tau_{ij}^k(t)$, where $k = 1, 2, 3, \cdots\cdots, N$ is the index of ants.

11.5.1.2 Applications in WSNs.
ACO-based routing algorithms have been studied by many researchers. Ant-based [96] or ant-like [97] algorithms were proposed and applied to circuit-switching and voice-application networks [98], wired networks [99], and mobile ad hoc networks (MANET) [100]. Although these ant-inspired algorithms follow the common ACO mechanisms, small variations are applied to their pheromone updating and transition rules to match their different objectives. For example, to design ACO-based routing algorithms for WSNs, several other constraints, like scalability, QoS, and energy [101], must also be considered. The following algorithms are among many ACO-based approaches proposed for WSNs.

Qkdem et al. [102] proposed a routing scheme based on the standard ACO algorithm with further concern for nodes' energy levels. In their algorithm, heuristic value of η_{ij} (transition rules to calculate the probability of the next route) for node j is expressed by equation $\eta_{ij} = \dfrac{e_j}{\sum_{n \in N_i} e_n}$, where e_j is the energy level of node j. Based on the energy level of surrounding nodes, each ant uses this equation to choose a node to forward its packet. After all ants have finished their tours, each ant deposits an amount of pheromone as $\Delta\tau_k(t) = w(1/J_w^k(t))$, where $J_w^k(t)$ is the length of tour $w^k(t)$ laid by ant k at iteration t, and w represents the effecting weight of this rule. Ants update trails according to this formula on the way back to the source. In their implementation, however, pheromone decaying is not considered in the pheromone updating rule.

Aghaei et al. [103] designed an ACO-inspired routing algorithm to optimize several metrics, including energy consumption, latency, throughput, and packet survival rate, and make their algorithm more suitable for WSNs. They used two types of ants (forward and backward) to perform different tasks. Forward ants [99] are used to choose a route from source to destination. Every forward ant is able to generate a list of its visited nodes.

This list is then used to help subsequent forwarding ants to avoid visited nodes. Backward ants, on the other hand, treat every intermediate node as an independent destination. They calculate data collected by forward ants and use a reinforcement learning algorithm [104, 105] to ensure that forward ants have chosen the optimum path. With a certain probability of $\Delta p = e^{-\gamma \cdot d_{i,d}^k}$, where γ is an arbitrary value between 0 and 1, backward ants may change the route formerly found/established by forward ants.

Huang et al. [106] proposed a many-to-one routing algorithm to solve a multi-objective optimization problem (MOP) [107] in WSNs. In their design, heuristic desirability of η_{ij} is a set based on a combination of energy cost and utilization efficiency of network sources. Here, each ant uses the formal equation to update a pheromone trail on its way to the destination.

11.5.2 Firefly Synchronization

An individual firefly can solely decide its flashing rate at night. However, if it meets a group of fireflies, it observes their flashing rate and adjusts its frequency to harmonize with the group. This phenomenon [108] shows how interactions among individual self-organized entities can result in distributed synchronization without any centralized control unit.

Mathematical models were designed to capture firefly synchronization behavior as a set of pulse-coupled oscillators [109]. A pulse-coupled oscillator is denoted as a phase function $\phi(t)$. If the oscillator is separated, its function value varies from 0 to 1 over time. Once this value reaches 1, the oscillator releases a pulse and resets itself to the initial state. If a separated oscillator is coupled with other oscillators, it not only releases a pulse in each round based on its own rate, but also receives pulses from its neighbors. For each firefly, if an expected pulse is received from one of its neighbors, its oscillator will immediately recalculate the value of its phase function and immediately produces a pulse. This will lead the oscillator to fire earlier than its predetermined rate. Thus, all oscillators in a group will eventually reach a synchronized state (after several iterations).

11.5.2.1 *Applications in WSNs.* Time synchronization aims to provide a common notion of time for all nodes in a network. Limiting factors of time synchronization in WSNs [110], such as energy efficiency, scope, and scalability, make traditional synchronization schemes' network time protocol (NTP) and global positioning system (GPS) inapplicable for WSNs. Although, several specific time synchronization schemes are proposed for WSNs, only a few of them are applicable, mainly because they usually depend on a central control unit (root node or cluster head) and are, therefore, not robust enough when nodes start to fail. For example, approaches in [111, 112] are constructed based on a rooted spanning tree structure, or the design in [113] is based on a clustering approach. Inspired by the mechanism of firefly synchronization, Geoffrey et al. [114] proposed a fully decentralized algorithm, reach back firefly algorithm (RFA), to synchronize nodes. In this algorithm, each node periodically broadcasts a synchronization message, and whenever a node receives such message, it calculates its increment value. Unlike the conventional firefly algorithm, RFA sums up the increments and stores it in

the node. This value is then used to reset oscillator values, despite original resetting to 0 in the original approach. Through these interactions, all nodes will eventually advance their phases and become synchronized.

Hong and Scaglione [115] used the introduced model in [109] to design their synchronization protocol for large-scale WSNs. To avoid the avalanche effect of propagation delays in their system (which usually occurs between two pulse-coupled oscillators), they used a refractory period. During the refractory period, the phase function of a node is always set to 0 and no signal is received from other nodes. In other times (outside of the refractory period), their algorithm works as normal pulse-coupled oscillators.

11.5.3 Particle Swarm Optimization

Another type of swarm intelligence, particle swarm optimization (PSO), is inspired by bird flocking and fish schooling. PSO is a population-based algorithm in which swarm particles correspond to individuals in a population. In PSO, every particle is supposed to use knowledge of its own past experiences as well as past experience of its neighbors to supervise/control its behaviour. For a given problem, through a global value called *pbest*, each particle is always aware of the best known solution already found. In PSO, particles communicate within each other using two variables: *lbest* and *gbest*. *lbest* (*l* for local) represents the best local solution for each particle and its *k*-nearest neighbors; *gbest* (*g* for global) represents the best solution for all particles, that is, all particles are assumed to be neighbors. Figure 11.4 shows symbolic representations of these solutions. During PSO's iterative searching process, particles change their velocities based on their available information (*pbest, lbest,* and *gbest*) step by step and continue searching until they reach the optimal solution.

PSO has been successfully applied to solve many nonstochastic and stochastic optimization problems in different research areas [115]. PSO also showed great potential to solve clustering and other optimization problems in WSNs. PSO is applicable to WSNs, as its implementation code uses primitive mathematical operations, occupies a small size of memory, and uses limited computational resources for execution [89].

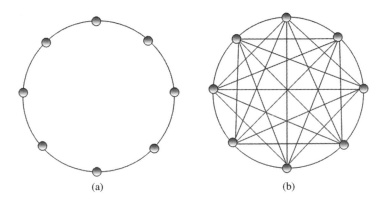

(a)   (b)

Figure 11.4 Figure 4: Examples of gbest and lbest neighborhoods, (a) lbest for k = 2, (b) gbest.

11.5.3.1 Applications in WSNs. Following on the weighted clustering algorithm (WCA) [116], Ji et al. [117] revised the WCA to solve the problem of when a node becomes a cluster head, and, therefore, its surrounding nodes can no longer participate in the cluster head election. They proposed a new algorithm, called divided range particle swarm optimization (DRPSO), to further optimize the minimum number of cluster heads in a mobile ad hoc network. In DRPSO, particles are divided into different groups and sorted based on their focused objective functions' values (e.g., weighting factor in WCA). In each group, standard PSO is executed several times until a terminal condition is met. After k iterations, all generated solutions are collected to find/elect the best number of cluster heads in the system. PSO is also used to solve another cluster-head identification problem in [118]. In this approach, the aim was to solve the following multiobjective optimization problems: (1) maximizing total gathered data, and (2) minimizing energy consumption of all nodes. Guru et al. [119] also used PSO to solve a cluster formation problem by formulating it as a minimization problem. They adopt four different PSO methods (PSO-TVIW [120], PSO-TVAC [121], HPSO-TAVC [121], and PSO-SSM [122]) to group sensor nodes in WSNs based on their clustering criteria and reduce total communication distances.

11.6 ARTIFICIAL IMMUNE SYSTEMS

The primary feature of a vertebrate immune system is to protect the organism against invasion of pathogens [123] such as viruses, bacteria, fungi, and parasites. Such immune systems can be classified into two types: innate and adaptive. Innate immune systems serve as the first line of defense and respond/react to pathogens entering the body. This response is not limited to particular invaders [124]. If one of the innate immune system's cells is able to recognize/detect a pathogen, it immediately releases signals to inform other innate immune system's cells, as well as the adaptive immune system, to strike against the recognized/detected pathogen. Although the innate immune system plays a major role in initiating an immune responses and provides co-stimulatory signals [39, 125] the adaptive immune system cannot eliminate all invading pathogens. In such scenarios, the organism needs to activate the adaptive immune system to recognize other invaders and launch a direct attack against them. To complete this task, two types of lymphocytes (B- and T- white blood cells) play vital roles here. These cells, which are generated from bone marrow and thymus, are capable of learning from the infection and provoke an immune response accordingly.

Negative selection, clonal selection, the immune network, and danger theory are among many immunological theories proposed to explain how immune systems work. These theories are used to develop several artificial immune systems (AISs).

11.6.1 Negative Selection

In negative selection, immature T-cells are moved from bone marrow to the thymus after generation. In thymus glands, T-cells that do not bind to self-proteins either become mature and then are released into the lymphatic system, or they die. The principle of negative selection inspired Forrest et al. [126, 127] to develop an algorithm to detect abnormal data manipulations in computer systems. This algorithm is composed of detector generation and anomaly monitoring phases. In the detector generation phase, a shape-space string with length l, namely "self", is defined and then used to randomly generate other strings. The algorithm then continues by calculating affinity between random strings and the self-strings by adopting a metric such as r-contiguous bits or r-chunk. Random strings with low affinity will be used as detectors after the affinity check. Using these detectors in the anomaly monitoring phase, the algorithm continually matches detectors with the protected string to monitor changes.

11.6.2 Danger Theory

In danger theory, "danger" occurs when a cell dies abnormally, such as injury, infection, and inflammation. Here, a danger signal is triggered to activate the immune system and fight harmful pathogens accordingly. The remaining part of this theory is the same as the negative selection theory. Danger theory is defined because negative selection that is based on self-non-self-discrimination does not properly fit all experimental observations. For example, self-changing in an organism, such as puberty, pregnancy, or harmless foreign bacteria in foods, should not be treated as threats and therefore should not alert the immune system. Matzinger [128] even proposed a theory that immune systems do not response to all non-self-cells; in fact, they only react to those that cause danger to the host.

11.6.3 Clonal Selection

Clonal selection was proposed by Burnet in 1959 [129] to describe basic properties of how an adaptive immune system reacts to invading pathogens. Although B- and T-cells are both capable of performing clonal selections, most researches only focus on B-cells as they can mutate and therefore have further enhanced adaptability [130]. When a pathogen enters an organism, it is first recognized by cells of the adaptive immune system. These cells are then proliferated at a very controlled high rate to work as long-lived memory cells and are distributed to blood, lymph, and other tissues. In fact, the controlled mutation mechanism here cause cells with high affinity to undergo low mutation (and vice versa) during the complicated process of proliferation.

Clonal selection theory inspired many researchers to develop different kinds of population-based algorithms to solve optimization problems [131, 132], design supervised learning algorithms [133, 134], and many more. From the computation point of view, all these algorithms are based on the well-known CLONALG algorithm and involve the following three basic steps to solve optimization problems: population initialization, antigenic presentation, and iteration. In the first step, the algorithm creates an initial population of antibodies (P). In the second step, antigenic presentation can be further divided into four phases: fitness evaluation, clonal selection and expansion, affinity maturation, and meta-dynamics. Fitness evaluation is used to determine the fitness of each element of P. In the clonal selection and expansion phase, "N" highest fitness elements of P are selected and used to generate clones of these antibodies proportionally to their fitness. The affinity maturation phase mutates all the duplications generated from the previous phase with a rate that is inversely proportional to their fitness and adds these mutated individuals to population P. In the last phase, meta-dynamics, "M" number of individuals are replaced by new ones. In the third step, the algorithm repeats the second step until a certain stopping criterion is met.

11.6.4 Immune Networks

Immune networks were proposed by Jerne [135] based on several shortcomings of traditional self-non self-discrimination theories. The theory of immune networks is based on the fact that immune cells and molecules compose an adaptive network to interact with each other and their surrounding environments. In fact, from the classical point of view, immune cells will only naturally perish if they do not receive any stimulation in their lifetime. In Jerne's theory, however, immune cells interact not only with epitopes or antigens but also with idiotopes on other antibodies. Here, when no pathogen invades, this network treats system perturbations (over a certain threshold) as a foreign stimulus and responds to it. This mechanism contributes to retain cells' states and forms a stable immunological memory structure.

Although this theory is not verified by adequate experimental evidence, it has already been applied to solve difficult problems in many research areas. For example, properties such as adaptation, self-organization, and plasticity are extracted from such systems and used to construct decentralized, controlled man-made systems [136, 137].

11.6.5 Applications in WSNs

Drozda, Schaust, and co-workers [138–140] applied AIS principles to detect misbehaviors in WSNs. In their approach, a negative selection algorithm is designed to consider limitation of power supply, computation resource and memory for sensors, and route packets in a WSN. Here, five different metrics are used to detect abnormal MAC and routing level changes/behavior in a system. Their scheme had two phases: learning and detection. In the learning phase, each node produces and maintains its own detectors to learn normal behaviors in a misbehavior-free period [141]; a detector is defined as a bit sequence produced by a negative selection algorithm that only matches against non-self-antigens using the r-contiguous matching rule. In the detecting phase, all nodes ignore their own generated detector lists and use a common detector list to compute affinity between detectors and testing strings. Although by using this method, individual nodes cannot recognize their misbehaving neighbors, a group of sensors can detect misbehaving nodes if they cooperate and exchange anomaly information with each other.

Atakan et al. [142] proposed a method called Distributed Node and Rate Selection (DNRS), based on AIS, to construct an effective WSN communication system. In their approach, a minimum number of sensors are activated to form a functional network with appropriate frequency to report events. In DNRS, a B-cell stimulation model is used to select designated sensor nodes. Immune network theory was then used to determine reporting frequency of designated nodes. During node selection, sensor nodes, event sources, and sensor data were treated as B-cells, antigens, and antibodies, respectively. Designated node selection was also based on three factors: (1) affinity between a sensor node and an event source, (2) affinity between a sensor node and its uncorrelated neighbor nodes (stimulating B-cells), and (3) affinity between a sensor node and its correlated neighbor nodes (suppressing B-cells). Thus, if the sum of these influences for a sensor node was over a certain threshold, the node was selected as a designated node. After the step of designated node selection, DNRS regulates the reporting frequency rate of each node to provide the event detection reliability with minimum energy consumption in a distributed way. Based on the immune network models, DNRS selects the appropriate reporting frequencies of sensor nodes according to the congestion in the forward paths, while the event estimation distortion is periodically calculated at the sink node.

11.6.6   The Cognitive Immune Model

Cognitive immune models were initially proposed by Cohen [143–145] to model a holistic immune system as a complex, adaptive, and reactive system. Such systems are assumed to be capable of cognition and, thus, have become popular in immunological research. This theory, with a completely different viewpoint from conventional immunology theories, claims that the primary function of immune systems is maintenance, not protection. Therefore, the entire immune system is considered as a computational system [146].

Although cognition in biology is usually defined as the brain's awareness or conscious thinking, Cohen has defined his model to integrate three basic elements to implement the same function without consciousness. The first element is the ability of the system to evaluate options and make decisions based on a number of choices. The second element is the internal image of its environment the system lives in. Two types of images are considered in this model [147]: innate and acquired. Innate images are inherited from parents, while acquired images are obtained from life experiences. Acquired images are gained through interactions among entities as well as each entity's self-organization process. Interaction among entities not only helps exchange new information in a system, but it also helps retain formerly useful information to form a complete set of knowledge for individuals within a system. System components, in turn, are able and free to make suitable decisions based on a number of available options. Such a decision-making process depends on the information each individual has. These interactions result in choices, and therefore, the emergence of cognition. Cohen also described three important mechanisms that contribute to the emergence of cognition: co-respondence, pleiotropia, and redundancy. The fundamental role of co-respondence is that of maintenance and protection, where the immune system itself maintains different classes of immune cells (T cells, B cells, macrophages). These cells individually examine different aspects of objects that might be of interest and trigger them, either from inside or outside of the body. By expressing co-response signals, each type of immune cell notifies other immune cells about what it has examined. Pleiotropia denotes the ability of a single immune component to produce various diverse effects. Depending on existing conditions, immune agents react differently and perform different executions (sometimes even contradictory). For example, in the natural immune system, a T cell can kill a specific cell and stimulate the growth of another. Redundancy can be simple or degenerate. Simple redundancy indicates multiple copies of the same element, while degenerate redundancy describes the situation in which many different immune components perform the same action.

11.6.6.1 Application in WSNs.
SpeckNets [148] is a new type of WSN that is composed of thousands of nodes (called specks) with the size of approximately five millimeters [149]; excluding base station. Inspired by Cohen's cognitive immune system model, SpeckNets are designed so that individual specks can regulate their operations and prolong their lifetime to fulfil their application goals [151]. These networks are also designed to consider functional requirements such as self-regulation, easy scalability, perturbation tolerance, and many other challenges, such as the existing large number of individually weak and unreliable entities during their deployment phase. Figure 11.5 illustrates a simple mapping between the Cohen's model and the SpeckNet immune-based architecture.

As shown Fig. 11.5, nodes in SpeckNet perform three basic functions based on Cohen's model: (1) they sense the information from their living environment, (2) they process received data, and (3) they communicate with each other. During the active state, nodes can continuously gather information from both internal and external sources. In this architecture, internal states represent specks' current status (e.g., battery level, malfunction or node's failure, relative positions of other specks, etc.). Depending on the working environment of the network, any external stimulus, such as humidity, light, pressure, or temperature, can be considered as external information for SpeckNets. Upon collection of all information, collected data is filtered, aggregated, and processed by

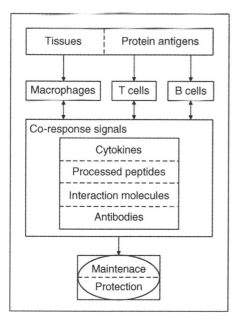
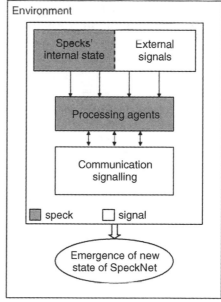

Figure 11.5 The relationship between Cohen's cognitive immune system model and a Speck-Net, from [150].

different specks' functional modules. This process is similar to how different stimuli are handled by different cell types (macrophages, T cells, and B cells) in immune systems. For example, specks collect information unsorted and interact/communicate asynchronously. Specks can also switch to idle or even sleeping state to save more energy. Integration of all these functional mappings allows SpeckNet to efficiently maintain system states and react/respond to environmental changes.

11.7 EVOLUTIONARY COMPUTING

In biology, evolution is a complex process of organisms' adaptation to the living environment from one generation to the next. Darwin's theory points out two major mechanisms of evolution: natural selection and genetic variation. Individuals of each population measure their fitness values (adaptability) in their living environments where fitness value of each individual depends on its personal gene composition. As a result of natural selection, individuals with higher fitness values (better adapted to the environment) have higher chances of survival, and, consequently, have more chances to reproduce. As a result, less-adapted individuals will be eliminated over generations.

During reproduction of fit parents, new offspring are created by a genetic variation mechanism; this will result in improving gene composition of new individuals (children). The genetic basis of inheritance was discovered by Gregor Mendel and completed by several researchers. The genetic study proves that genes carry the inherited information to the next generation and control the characteristics of individuals. Influenced by the environment, genes adjust themselves by deviating in the genetic material or by exchanging genetic material between chromosomes. Therefore, evolution can be considered a result of reproducing populations of individuals' genetic variation followed by selection [125].

11.7.1 Basic Concepts

Inspired by evolutionary biology, evolutionary computing (EC) was developed to provide search, optimization, and learning techniques to solve complex problems [39, 86]. The standard evolutionary algorithm is a generic, iterative, and stochastic procedure to generate tentative solutions for a certain problem. Initially, a representation scheme is constructed to define the set of solutions that form the search space for a given problem. A population of individuals is either randomly generated or heuristically seeded. Each individual evaluates its fitness value based on the problem being solved. Then the following steps are executed iteratively until the termination condition is met. Firstly, based on fitness values, simulated natural evolution is performed to select individuals from the current population and reproduce offspring using different methods, sexually or asexually. Secondly, in the reproduction process, genetic variation is performed through different genetic operators. Survivors and their offspring form the new population of the next generation. Most evolutionary algorithms involve the basic concepts of the standard algorithm but differ in the representation, selection, reproduction, genetic variation, and sequence in which these processes are applied. The following four main strands of

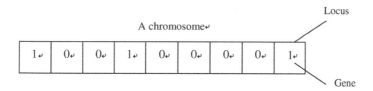

Figure 11.6   An example of a chromosome in a GA.

EC are genetic algorithms, genetic programming, evolution strategies, and evolutionary programming.

11.7.2   Genetic Algorithms

The most well-known algorithm in the area of evolutionary computing is the genetic algorithm (GA) [151]. In a GA, a data structure representing an individual of a population is usually called a chromosome. A chromosome is denoted as a fixed-length string of binary digits (0,1), or bitstring. Similar to the biological source, each unit of the bitstring can be considered as a gene located in a certain location, called the locus, and presents a particular feature of an individual. An example is given in Fig. 11.6.

The fitness of every bit string is evaluated, in the sense of the quality of a solution for a particular problem, to promote individuals with higher fitness values. This selection process is often employed as an algorithm called fitness proportional selection, also known as roulette wheel selection [152]. After this, selected strings act as parents to create their offspring using reproduction operators: crossover and mutation. Crossover swaps a subsequence between two parent strings and recombines them to generate new strings. Mutation is a bit-flipping operation performed on offspring, where each bit is changed with some predefined probability value to the opposite value. These selection and reproduction steps are continually performed until the termination criterion is reached.

11.7.3   Genetic Programming

Genetic programming (GP) is an evolutionary optimization technique proposed by Cramer [153] and further developed and formalized by Koza [154]. The distinctive feature of GP is a possibility of searching for solutions to a problem as a function or a program. GP is similar to GA, but the main differences between these two techniques are the representation of individuals and the sequence of selection for genetic operators. In the standard GP, the representation uses a variable-sized tree to provide a flexible way of describing functions in a variable length of computer program in the LISP language. The entire tree corresponds to a single function or a program and each node in the tree denotes a value or a functional label. The tree usually expresses a function in a left-most, depth-first manner. After calculating fitness value of each tree, selection and genetic operators are applied. Unlike GA, the selection and genetic operators in GP are performed in parallel with a certain value of probability for each operation, the sum of these probability values is equal to 1. Besides the selection operator, the most commonly used genetic operator in GP is subtree crossover to creates new trees by swapping sub-trees of their parents. Mutation is rarely used here. The selection and genetic operators are continually used until the termination condition is satisfied.

11.7.4 Evolution Strategies

Evolution strategies (ES) represent a number of evolutionary algorithms independently developed by Rechenberg [155], Schwefel [156], and their colleagues to solve the practical optimization problems in engineering. The representation of an ES uses a fixed-length, real-valued vector in the search space. Similar to GA, each position in its attribute vector presents a feature of an individual. An individual usually contains an attribute vector and a set of strategy parameters. This representation dedicates great potential benefits in the evolutionary search process to make strategy parameters cooperate with the attribute vector; this process is known as self-adaptation.

The order of applying operators and their importance in ES are different than those in GA. Here, operators are applied in the following order: recombination, mutation, and deterministic selection. After generating an initial population and evaluating its individuals' fitness, the recombination operator is applied. This operator that is similar to the crossover operator in GA, where a pair of parents creates not two but one offspring. Similar to GA, there exists a number of recombination operators, among which are discrete and intermediate ones. In discrete recombination, the attribute vector of a single offspring is created by selecting its components from its parents' vectors with the same probability (0.5). The intermediate recombination averages two parent vectors, element by element, to construct a new offspring vector. When the recombination is finalized, the mutation operator starts. Mutation plays an important role in ES, as opposed to GA, where it plays a secondary role. A widely applied mutation in ES is a Gaussian mutation. This operator obtains a random value from a Gaussian distribution function and adds it to each element of all offspring obtained during recombination. The last applied operator is a deterministic selection.

Two deterministic selection mechanisms are usually used in the standard ES algorithm: $(\mu + \lambda)$ selection and (μ, λ) selection. Here, μ denotes the size of parent population, and λ denotes the number of offspring received by recombination. In the $(\mu + \lambda)$ selection, the population consisting temporarily of parents and offspring is reduced to μ of the best individuals from the whole population. In the (μ, λ) selection, the next generation of individuals is created by selecting μ of the best individuals from the population of offspring only. The evolutionary process is terminated when the stop condition is met.

11.7.5 Evolutionary Programming

L.J. Fogel et al. [157] proposed evolutionary programming (EP) as an evolutionary computing algorithm to develop alternative forms of artificial intelligence using finite state machines. Several decades later, Fogel [158, 159] extended this work by using a representative fixed-length, real-valued vector. Spears et al. [160] showed that type of representation in EP is greatly dependent on the problem domain. The selection mechanism adopted by EP is similar to the tournament selection [161], occasionally used in GA. A stochastic tournament selects μ individuals based on their fitness from the total of 2μ individuals (μ parents and μ offspring). The major difference between EP and ES is that no crossover takes place between individuals in EP; only mutation occurs. Similar to other evolutionary computation algorithms, EP ends up with the loop in which a stop condition is satisfied.

11.7.6 Applications in WSNs

Jourdan and Weck [162] used a GA to optimize sensor placement to determine the best system layout considering two competing objectives: total sensor coverage and lifetime of the network. In their approach, sensors are assumed to be deployed into a flat square area of interest. The initialized network layout is randomly generated, where N sensor placements (individuals) are presented as bit strings with their horizontal and vertical coordinates presented as genes. An individual randomly mates with another individual in a population to produce two offspring using crossover. After the children strings are created, the newly generated individuals are mutated with a certain probability. The coverage and lifetime of the children are evaluated by the method called Pareto dominance, where fitness values are assigned to parents and children. The N individuals with best fitness form the next generation; the process continues until the maximum number of generations is reached.

Hussain et al. [163] employed a GA to produce energy-efficient clusters for routing in WSNs. In the beginning, a hierarchical cluster-based routing (HCR) protocol was used to generate the initialized population. Sensor nodes are considered as genes of a chromosome where nodes elected as cluster heads are denoted by "1" and "0" otherwise. The fitness value of a chromosome is designed to minimize the energy consumption as well as to extend the network lifetime; it is usually a function of five parameters: direct distance to sink, cluster distance, the standard deviation of cluster distance, transfer energy, and number of transmissions. The fitness value of each chromosome is calculated and continually updated in each generation. Eventually, the best fit chromosome is determined and helps the cluster protocol to reach the minimized energy consumption for a given number of transmissions.

EQSC is a GA-based algorithm, proposed by Youssef et al. [164], to construct a self-organized system to respond to queries. The whole system's topology involves an optimal subset of sensors that are sufficient to process a query; this query is subject to constraints of connectivity, coverage, energy consumption, coverage size, and communication overhead. The algorithm aims to select a minimum number of sensors to cover the maximum sensing area of the entire geographical region and also to form a logical routing topology for data-gathering and transmission to the query source. Furthermore, query processing must take the energy consumption into consideration to extend the lifetime of the system. An initial population composed of K chromosomes is randomly generated. Each chromosome is a combination of sensors satisfying the requirement of a query. They use the total energy consumption of the selected sensors as the fitness function; that is, the higher fitness values represent selected sensors that consume less energy. Unlike traditional GAs, EQSCs [165] directly select distinct chromosomes from the current generation to form the next generation. In their scheme, the new population is usually composed of the best chromosomes from the original population (50%), chromosomes obtained by crossover (30%), and chromosomes generated by mutation (20%). This algorithm is terminated when a fixed number of iterations are performed with no further improvement in the query cover.

11.8 MOLECULAR BIOLOGY

Molecular biology aims to develop a strong understanding life at all scales, beginning from the structure of a biological cell, through mechanisms of interactions among cells (including how these interactions are regulated), up to the issue of how various cells work together to create organisms. The organism can be seen as a hierarchical organization that contains a large number of autonomous entities and exhibits dynamic functioning relying on enzymes, motor proteins, and other macromolecules involved in intracellular trafficking and signaling [166]. Comparing organisms to computer networks, similar features and a highly hierarchical structure can be found in both systems [167, 168], especially for information exchanges between entities. In cellular environments, information exchange among cells called signaling pathways follows a similar principle—a message is transferred to a destination using multiple hops. For example, small molecules like steroid hormones reach a destination cell via blood flows. The remote information exchange works as follows: a signal is released into the blood and carried to remote cells, the hormone can then penetrate a cell's membrane and enter it. Within the cell, the receptor binds the hormone. The ligand receptor complex can now enter the nucleus of a cell and initiate gene transcription to trigger a corresponding reaction.

Dressler and his colleagues concentrated on how to pass the principles from molecular biology, particular the signaling pathway, to sensor networks. They first proposed a new communication method called a feedback loop [169], inspired by the angiogenesis-based process for blood pressure in an organism, to transfer information over unreliable communication paths in WSNs. Here, priorities are initially assigned to messages that need to be immediately transferred. Based on their priorities, each message is sent to its immediate neighbors as well as several remote nodes with different percentages. This process is repeated until the desired job is confirmed as running or the job is globally cancelled. This work was followed by extending their work to construct a rule-based self-organized sensor and actor network (SANET) to improve scalability and support real-time applications [170, 171]. Messages of a rule-based sensor network (RSN) contain all requisite information to allow data-centric communication as well as network-centric operations without the need of further knowledge. When a node of RSN receives messages, these messages are stored in a message buffer and then the rule interpreter uses specific syntaxes to distribute messages into different working sets. The following corresponding actions are applied to messages in different working sets: rule execution, node control, and simulation control. Even though the message handling in RSN is not comparable to biological cells, the proposed process still models the basic principle of DNA processing instructions and is able to generate cellular responses.

11.9 BIO-NETWORKING ARCHITECTURE

In the previous sections, several nature-inspired techniques to construct autonomic communication systems are introduced; most of them are used to implement one or several specific functions in WSNs. To obtain more advantages from nature-inspired techniques, researchers started to apply multiple technologies to design computer network architectures.

Suda et al. presented a framework called bio-networking architecture to design network systems [172] based on several biological principles and mechanisms from swarm intelligence. In their design, the entity of a system is represented as an autonomous object called a cyber-entity. Cyber-entities implement different functions and provide them to other entities inside the network or human being. Autonomous actions such as migration, replication, reproduction, and death are also implemented here. Natural selection and evolution is performed in the system and a cyber-entity must manage its energy to be persistent for as long as possible. These cyber-entity agents act autonomously based on local information and interactions to produce advantageous behavioral patterns that cannot be achieved by a single individual. As a result, such systems are able to meet key requirements of a complex adaptive system, including scalability, adaptability, and availability.

BiSNET (Biologically-Inspired architecture for Sensor NETworks) [173, 174] is a middleware platform that addresses several challenges of designing WSNs, including autonomy, scalability, adaptability, self-healing and simplicity. It models a middleware platform as a hive where [175] each sensor node operates on top of a TinyOS to provide applications. Each application consists of multiple software entities called agents. Various biological principles, including decentralization, autonomy, food gathering/storage, and natural selection, are adopted in designing BiSNET agents. The actions that each agent performs are based on its remaining energy.

Agoulmine et al. [176] proposed a biologically inspired architecture to meet several challenges for autonomic network management. In their scheme, the core idea of implementing an autonomic system is to map different biological principles into local rules within system elements. These local rules are used to form autonomic elements (AEs) that can cohesively cooperate and support high-level objectives. To be more specific, the homeostatic model inspired by blood glucose is employed to provide equilibrium of the overall system and to handle stimulus from internal or external environments; internal stimulus such as change in loads due to the increase of network traffic, and external stimulus such as node/link failures, or new nodes join the system. This mapping provides self-management to the system. The reaction diffusion model is used to implement the self-organization function by using peer-to-peer interaction among nodes through exchange of local messages. Each node may receive a message (known as morphogens in biology) from neighboring devices with regard to their states and change its state accordingly. In conjunction with the reaction diffusion model, they map chemotaxis into their model to determine routing paths of a packet using chemical gradients, calculation of node loads, and information of hop counts to the destination.

To implement the self-learning capability in this framework, they adopt principles from neural systems to enable their system elements to decide what behavior to take based on past experiences. Past experiences could involve different network traffic types and/or different profiles of traffic. Finally, to endow the system with self-protection ability, the properties of immune systems are invoked. Through the interactions, all of these principles are converted into local behavioral rules for autonomic elements. Here, interactions among these elements also cause emergence of system-level behavior and the purpose of autonomic communication is to minimize/alleviate human interventions.

11.10 CONCLUSION

Nature-inspired models present several attractive features such as self-organization and emergence, good scalability, adaptation, and resilience to changes in the environment. This survey showed that these attributes can bring great benefits to design and implementation of self-organized, large-scale WSNs. Self-organized mechanisms alleviate the dependence of sensors on a central controller and therefore help sensors to consume energy more efficiently in reaching the primary goal of WSNs to prolong their lifetime. Furthermore, because of the inherent limitations/characteristics of natural systems, nature-inspired models usually reach their expected performance level more slowly than conventional control-based systems. Here, interactions among entities within a system may also remain subtle, and more precise characterization is required to describe them. Therefore, better understanding of specific functions of natural systems is required to design and implement appropriate nature-inspired models. In fact, simple mimicking of biological functions is not enough in many cases.

REFERENCES

[1] Y. Bar-Cohen, "Biomimetics - Using nature to inspire human innovation." *Bioinspir Biomim*, 2006. **1**: p. 1–12.
[2] P. Coy, "21 ideas for the 21st century." *Business Week*, 1999. **30**: p. 81–162.
[3] T. Editors, "10 emerging technologies that will change the world." *MIT Technology Review*, February, 2003.
[4] Jiang Peng, et al., Research on Wireless Sensor Networks Routing Protocol for Wetland Water Environment Monitoring, in Proceedings of the First International Conference on Innovative Computing, Information and Control (ICICIC'06). 2006.
[5] S. Robert, et al., "An analysis of a large scale habitat monitoring application," in *Proceedings of the 2nd International Conference on Embedded Networked Sensor Systems*. 2004, ACM: Baltimore, MD.
[6] C. Thomas, et al., "Sensor deployment strategy for target detection," in *Proceedings of the 1st ACM International Workshop on Wireless Sensor Networks and Applications*. 2002, ACM: Atlanta, Georgia.
[7] I.F. Akyildiz, et al., "Wireless sensor networks: a survey." *Computer Networks*, 2002. **38**(4): p. 393–422.
[8] M. Kuorilehto, M. Hannikainen, and T.D. Hamalainen, "A survey of application distribution in wireless sensor networks." EURASIP *J. Wireless Communication Network*, 2005. **5**(5): p. 774–788.

[9] L. Dehni, F. Krief, and Y. Hermani, "Power Control and Clustering in Wireless Sensor Networks." Challenges in Ad Hoc Networking: Fourth Annual Mediterranean Ad Hoc Networking Workshop, June 21-24, 2005, de Porquerolles, France, 2006.

[10] K.H. Jones, et al., "Biology Inspired Approach for Communal Behavior in Sensor Networks," in *System Sciences, 2006. HICSS'06. Proceedings of the 39th Annual Hawaii International Conference.* 2006.

[11] K.H. Jones, et al., "Biology-inspired distributed consensus in massively-deployed sensor networks," in *Proc. 4th International Conference on Ad hoc Networks and Wireless.* 2005.

[12] A. Wadaa, et al., "Training a Wireless Sensor Network." *Mobile Networks and Applications,* 2005. **10**(1): p. 151–168.

[13] S. Olariu and I. Stojmenovic. Design guidelines for maximizing lifetime and avoiding energy holes in sensor networks with uniform distribution and uniform reporting. 2006.

[14] G.M.P. O'Hare, et al., "Autonomic wireless sensor networks: Intelligent ubiquitous sensing." In Proceeding of ANIPLA 2006, International Congress on Methodologies for Emerging Technologies in Automation, 2006.

[15] D. Ganesan, et al., "Complex behavior at scale: An experimental study of low-power wireless sensor networks." UCLA Computer Science Technical Report UCLA/CSD-TR, 2003: p. 02-0013.

[16] S. Dobson, et al., "A survey of autonomic communications." *ACM Transactions on Autonomous and Adaptive Systems* (TAAS), 2006. **1**(2): p. 223–259.

[17] J.O. Kephart and D.M. Chess, "The vision of autonomic computing." *Computer,* 2003: p. 41–50.

[18] M.C. Huebscher and J. McCann, "A survey of Autonomic Computing - degrees, models and applications." *ACM Computing Surveys,* 2008, Vol. 40, No. 3, pp. 1–28.

[19] W.F. Truszkowski, et al., "Autonomous and autonomic systems: a paradigm for future space exploration missions." *Systems, Man, and Cybernetics, Part C: Applications and Reviews, IEEE Transactions on,* 2006. **36**(3): p. 279–291.

[20] M. Wooldridge and N.R. Jennings, "Intelligent agent: Theory and practice." *Knowledge Engineering Review,* 1995. **10**: p. 115–152.

[21] M. Woolridge and M.J. Wooldridge, *Introduction to Multiagent Systems.* 2001, John Wiley & Sons, Inc. New York, NY.

[22] M. Ilyas, I. Mahgoub, and I. NetLibrary, *Handbook of Sensor Networks: Compact Wireless and Wired Sensing Systems.* 2005; CRC Press.

[23] G.J. Pottie and W.J. Kaiser, "Wireless integrated network sensors." *Communications of the ACM,* 2000. **43**(5): p. 51–58.

[24] F. Ye, et al., "PEAS: a robust energy conserving protocol for long-lived sensor networks." *Distributed Computing Systems, 2003. Proceedings. 23rd International Conference on,* 2003: p. 28–37.

[25] L. Wang and Y. Xiao, "A survey of energy-efficient scheduling mechanisms in sensor networks." *Mobile Networks and Applications,* 2006. **11**(5): p. 723–740.

[26] I.F. Akyildiz, D. Pompili, and T. Melodia, "Underwater acoustic sensor networks: research challenges." *Ad Hoc Networks,* 2005. **3**(3): p. 257–279.

[27] J. Cui, et al., "The challenges of building scalable mobile underwater wireless sensor networks for aquatic applications." *IEEE Network,* 2006. **20**(3): p. 12.

[28] C.Y. Chong and S.P. Kumar, "Sensor networks: evolution, opportunities, and challenges." *Proceedings of the IEEE*, 2003. **91**(8): p. 1247–1256.

[29] K. Martinez, R. Ong, and J. Hart. Glacsweb: A Sensor Network for Hostile Environments. 2004.

[30] C. Otto, et al., "System architecture of a wireless body area sensor network for ubiquitous health monitoring." *Journal of Mobile Multimedia*, 2006. **1**(4): p. 307–326.

[31] I.F. Akyildiz, T. Melodia, and K.R. Chowdhury, "A survey on wireless multimedia sensor networks." *Computer Networks*, 2007. **51**(4): p. 921–960.

[32] L.C. Zhong, et al., "An ultra-low power and distributed access protocol for broadband wireless sensor networks." IEEE Broadband Wireless Summit, 2001.

[33] L.C. Zhong, et al. Data Link Layer Design for Wireless Sensor Networks. 2001.

[34] C. Guo, L.C. Zhong, and J.M. Rabaey, "Low power distributed MAC for ad hoc sensor radio networks." *GLOBECOM-NEW YORK*, 2001. **5**: p. 2944–2948.

[35] V.S. Petrovic and C.S. Xydeas, "Sensor noise effects on signal-level image fusion performance." *Information Fusion*, 2003. **4**(3): p. 167–183.

[36] N. Gibbins, S. Harris, and N. Shadbolt, "Agent-based semantic web services." *Web Semantics: Science, Services and Agents on the World Wide Web*, 2004. **1**(2): p. 141–154.

[37] M.N. Huhns, et al., "Research directions for service-oriented multiagent systems." *IEEE Internet Computing*, 2005: p. 65–70.

[38] W. Elmenreich, "Intelligent methods for embedded systems." In the First Workshop on Intelligent Solutions for Embedded Systems. 2003. Vienna, Austria.

[39] L.N. de Castro, "Fundamentals of natural computing: an overview." *Physics of Life Reviews*, 2007. **4**(1): p. 1–36.

[40] J. Liu and K.C. Tsui, "Toward nature-inspired computing." *Commun. ACM*, 2006. **49**(10): p. 59–64.

[41] A. Moreno, A. Etxeberria, and J. Umerez, "The autonomy of biological individuals and artificial models." *BioSystems*, 2008. **91**(2): p. 309–319.

[42] C. Boutilier, Y. Shoham, and M.P. Wellman, "Economic principles of multi-agent systems." *Artificial Intelligence*, 1997. **94**(1-2): p. 1–6.

[43] P. Champrasert and J. Suzuki. *SymbioticSphere: A Biologically-Inspired Autonomic Architecture for Self-Adaptive and Self-Healing Server Farms.* 2006. IEEE Computer Society Washington, DC.

[44] T. Froese, N. Virgo, and E. Izquierdo, "Autonomy: A review and a reappraisal." *Lecture Notes in Computer Science*, 2007. **4648**: p. 455.

[45] M. Resnick, "Decentralized modeling and decentralized thinking." *Modeling and Simulation in Precollege Science and Mathematics*, 1999: p. 114–137.

[46] E. Merelli, et al., "Agents in bioinformatics, computational and systems biology." *Briefings in Bioinformatics*, 2007. **8**(1): p. 45.

[47] A.M. Mahdy, J.S. Deogun, and J. Wang. "Towards scalable clustering of infrastructured mobile ad hoc networks." In *Advances in Wired and Wireless Communication, 2005 IEEE/Sarnoff Symposium on*. 2005.

[48] R. Albert, H. Jeong, and A.L. Barabasi, Error and attack tolerance of complex networks. Arxiv preprint cond-mat/0008064, 2000.

[49] T. De Wolf and T. Holvoet, "Emergence versus self-organisation: Different concepts but promising when combined." *Engineering Self Organising Systems: Methodologies and Applications*, 2005. **3464**: p. 1–15.

[50] H.V.D. Parunak, "Entropy and self-organization in multi-agent systems." *Proceedings of the Fifth International Conference on Autonomous Agents*, 2001: p. 124–130.

[51] N. Foukia and S. Hassas, "Towards self-organizing computer networks: A complex system perspective." *Proceedings of the International Workshop on Engineering Self-Organizaing Applications*, 2003.

[52] F. Heylighen, "The science of self-organization and adaptivity." *The Encyclopedia of Life Support Systems*, 2002.

[53] R. Nagpal, "A catalog of biologically-inspired primitives for engineering self-organization." *Lecture Notes in Computer Science*, 2004: p. 53–62.

[54] J. Fromm, *On Engineering and Emergence*. Arxiv preprint nlin/0601002, 2006.

[55] G.D.M. Serugendo, M.P. Gleizes, and A. Karageorgos, "Self-organisation and emergence in MAS: An overview." *Informatica*, 2006. **30**(1): p. 45?4.

[56] T. De Wolf and T. Holvoet, "Emergence and self-organisation: A statement of similarities and differences." *Proc. of the 2nd Int. Workshop on Engineering Self-Organising App*, 2004.

[57] J.H. Holland, *Emergence: From Chaos to Order*. 1998: Perseus Books.

[58] G. Di Marzo Serugendo, M.P. Gleizes, and A. Karageorgos, "Self-organization in multi-agent systems." *The Knowledge Engineering Review*, 2006. **20**(2): p. 165–189.

[59] L. Rue, "A guide to thinking about emergence." *Zygon* (r), 2007. **42**(4): p. 829–835.

[60] R.C. Richardson and A. Stephan, "Emergence." *Biological Theory*, 2007. **2**(1): p. 91–96.

[61] J.G. Restrepo, E. Ott, and B.R. Hunt, "Emergence of coherence in complex networks of heterogeneous dynamical systems." *Physical Review Letters*, 2006. **96**(25): p. 254103.

[62] J.W. Haefner, *Modeling Biological Systems: Principles and Applications*. 2005: Springer.

[63] S. Camazine, *Self-Organization in Biological Systems*. 2001: Princeton University Press.

[64] J. Walleczek, *Self-Organized Biological Dynamics and Nonlinear Control: Toward Understanding Complexity, Chaos and Emergent Function in Living Systems*. 2000: Cambridge University Press.

[65] W.H. Steeb, Y. Hardy, and R. Stoop, *The Nonlinear Workbook*. 2002; World Scientific River Edge, NJ.

[66] N.W.M.M. Kenji Leibnitz, "Biologically inspired networking, in Cognitive Networks," H.M. Qusay, Editor. 2007. p. 1–21.

[67] F. Dressler, "A study of self-organization mechanisms in ad hoc and sensor networks." *Computer Communications*, 2008.

[68] F. Dressler, *Self-Organization in Sensor and Actor Networks*. 2007, Wiley.

[69] A. Ilachinski, *Cellular Automata: A Discrete Universe*. 2001, World Scientific.

[70] W.G. Weng, et al., "Cellular automaton simulation of pedestrian counter flow with different walk velocities." *Physical Review E*, 2006. **74**(3): p. 36102.

[71] J.V. Rodriguez, et al., "Spatial stochastic modelling of the phosphoenolpyruvate-dependent phosphotransferase (PTS) pathway in *Escherichia coli*. *Bioinformatics*, 2006. **22**(15): p. 1895.

[72] C. Grelck, F. Penczek, and K. Trojahner, "CAOS: A domain-specific language for the parallel simulation of cellular automata." *Lecture Notes in Computer Science*, 2007. **4671**: p. 410.

[73] I. Wokoma, L. Sacks, and I. Marshall, "Biologically inspired models for sensor network design." The London Communications Symposium, University College London, September, 2002.

[74] N. Ganguly, et al., A survey on cellular automata. Project BISON (IST-2001-38923), 2001.

[75] P.P. Chaudhuri, *Additive Cellular Automata: Theory and Applications.* 1997: Wiley-IEEE Computer Society Pr.

[76] W. Li, N.H. Packard, and C.G. Langton, "Transition phenomena in cellular automata rule space." *Physica D*, 1990. **45**(1-3): p. 77–94.

[77] M. Mitchell, P. Hraber, and J.P. Crutchfield, *Revisiting the Edge of Chaos: Evolving Cellular Automata to Perform Computations.* Arxiv preprint adap-org/9303003, 1993.

[78] I. Banerjee, et al., "An energy effilcient monitoring of ad-hoc sensor network with cellular automata." *Systems, Man and Cybernetics, 2006. ICSMC'06. IEEE International Conference on*, 2006. **6**.

[79] O.C. Renan, et al., "Simulating large wireless sensor networks using cellular automata. In *Proceedings of the 38th annual Symposium on Simulation*. 2005, IEEE Computer Society.

[80] K.H. Jones, et al., "Energy usage in biomimetic models for massively-deployed sensor networks." *Lecture Notes in Computer Science*, 2005. **3759**: p. 434.

[81] A.Y. Teymorian, L. Ma, and X. Cheng. "CAB: A cellular automata-based key management scheme for wireless sensor networks." In *Military Communications Conference, 2007. MILCOM 2007.* IEEE, 2007.

[82] S. Yurong and J. Guo-Ping. "Modeling malware propagation in wireless sensor networks using cellular automata." In *Neural Networks and Signal Processing, 2008 International Conference on*. 2008.

[83] D.G. Allegretti, G.T. Kenyon, and W.C. Priedhorsky, "Cellular automata for distributed sensor networks." *International Journal of High Performance Computing Applications*, 2008. **22**(2): p. 167.

[84] G. Beni and J. Wang, "Swarm intelligence in cellular robotic systems." *NATO ASI Series F Computer and Systems Sciences*, 1993. **102**: p. 703–703.

[85] E. Bonabeau, M. Dorigo, and G. Theraulaz, *Swarm Intelligence: From Natural to Artificial Systems.* 1999: Oxford University Press, New York.

[86] J. Taheri, and A.Y. Zomaya, "An overview of neural network models," in *Handbook of Bioinspired Algorithms and Applications* S. Olariu and A.Y. Zomaya, editors. 2006, Chapman&Hall/CRC Press, Boca Raton, FL.

[87] J.F. Kennedy, et al., *Swarm Intelligence.* 2001: Springer.

[88] M.M. Millonas, Swarms, *Phase Transitions, and Collective Intelligence.* 1994, Addison-Wesley Publishing.

[89] J. Kennedy and R. Eberhart. "Particle swarm optimization." In *Neural Networks, 1995. Proceedings., IEEE International Conference on*. 1995.

[90] S. Olariu and A.Y. Zomaya, *Handbook of Bioinspired Algorithms and Applications.* 2006: Chapman & Hall/CRC.

[91] M. Dorigo and G. Di Caro. "Ant colony optimization: A new meta-heuristic. In *Evolutionary Computation, 1999. CEC 99. Proceedings of the 1999 Congress on*. 1999.

[92] M. Dorigo and T. Stützle, Ant Colony Optimization. 2004, MIT Press.

[93] E.L. Lawler, *Combinatorial Optimization: Networks and Matroids.* 2001, Courier Dover Publications.

[94] K.M. Sim and W.H. Sun, "Ant colony optimization for routing and load-balancing: Survey and new directions." *Systems, Man and Cybernetics, Part A, IEEE Transactions on*, 2003. **33**(5): p. 560–572.

[95] D. Sumpter and S. Pratt, "A modelling framework for understanding social insect foraging." *Behavioral Ecology and Sociobiology*, 2003. **53**(3): p. 131–144.

[96] S. Ruud, H. Owen, and B. Janet, "Ant-like agents for load balancing in telecommunications networks," In *Proceedings of the First International Conference on Autonomous Agents.* 1997, ACM: Marina del Rey, CA.

[97] D. Camara and A.A.F. Loureiro. "A GPS/ant-like routing algorithm for ad hoc networks." In *Wireless Communications and Networking Conference, 2000. WCNC. 2000 IEEE.* 2000.

[98] M. Heissenbuttel and T. Braun, "Ants-based routing in large scale mobile ad-hoc networks." *Kommunikation in verteilten Systemen (KiVS03)*, March, 2003.

[99] G. Di Caro and M. Dorigo. "AntNet: Distributed stigmergetic control for communications networks." *Journal of Artificial Intelligence Research*, 1998. **9**(2): p. 317–365.

[100] M. Gunes, U. Sorges, and I. Bouazizi. "ARA-the ant-colony based routing algorithm for MANETs." In *Parallel Processing Workshops, 2002. Proceedings. International Conference on.* 2002.

[101] J.N. Al-Karaki and A.E. Kamal, "Routing techniques in wireless sensor networks: A survey." *Wireless Communications, IEEE [see also IEEE Personal Communications]*, 2004. **11**(6): p. 6–28.

[102] S. Okdem and D. Karaboga. "Routing in wireless sensor networks using ant colony optimization." In *Adaptive Hardware and Systems, 2006. AHS 2006. First NASA/ESA Conference on.* 2006.

[103] R. GhasemAghaei, et al. "Ant colony-based reinforcement learning algorithm for routing in wireless sensor networks." In *Instrumentation and Measurement Technology Conference Proceedings, 2007. IMTC 2007. IEEE.* 2007.

[104] D. Subramanian, P. Druschel, and J. Chen. *Ants and Reinforcement Learning: A Case Study in Routing in Dynamic Networks.* 1997, *Lawrence Erlbaum.*

[105] L.P. Kaelbling, M.L. Littman, and A.W. Moore, *Reinforcement Learning: A Survey.* Arxiv preprint cs.AI/9605103, 1996.

[106] H. Ru, et al. "The ant-based algorithm for the optimal many-to-one routing in sensor networks." In *Communications, Circuits and Systems Proceedings, 2006 International Conference on.* 2006.

[107] K. Deb, *Multi-Objective Optimization Using Evolutionary Algorithms.* 2001, Wiley.

[108] U. Wilensky and K. Reisman, "Thinking like a wolf, a sheep, or a firefly: Learning biology through constructing and testing computational theories-an embodied modeling approach." *Cognition and Instruction*, 2006. **24**(2): p. 171–209.

[109] R.E. Mirollo and S.H. Strogatz, "Synchronization of pulse-coupled biological oscillators." *SIAM J. Appl. Math*, 1990. **50**(6): p. 1645–1662.

[110] F. Sivrikaya and B. Yener, "Time synchronization in sensor networks: A survey." *Network, IEEE*, 2004. **18**(4): p. 45–50.

[111] G. Saurabh, K. Ram, and B.S. Mani, "Timing-sync protocol for sensor networks," in *Proceedings of the 1st International Conference on Embedded Networked Sensor Systems.* 2003, ACM: Los Angeles, CA.

[112] Mikl, et al., "The flooding time synchronization protocol." In *Proceedings of the 2nd International Conference on Embedded Networked Sensor Systems*. 2004, ACM: Baltimore, MD.

[113] E. Jeremy, G. Lewis, and E. Deborah, "Fine-grained network time synchronization using reference broadcasts." *SIGOPS Oper. Syst. Rev.*, 2002. 36(SI): p. 147–163.

[114] W.-A. Geoffrey, et al., "Firefly-inspired sensor network synchronicity with realistic radio effects." In *Proceedings of the 3rd International Conference on Embedded Networked Sensor Systems*. 2005, ACM: San Diego, CA.

[115] C. Hyeong Soo, "An adaptation of particle swarm optimization for Markov decision processes." In *Systems, Man and Cybernetics, 2004 IEEE International Conference on*. 2004.

[116] M. Chatterjee, S.K. Das, and D. Turgut, "WCA: A weighted clustering algorithm for mobile ad hoc networks." *Cluster Computing*, 2002. 5(2): p. 193–204.

[117] J. Chunlin, et al. "Particle swarm optimization for mobile ad hoc networks clustering." In *Networking, Sensing and Control, 2004 IEEE International Conference on*. 2004.

[118] J. Tillett, R. Rao, and F. Sahin. "Cluster-head identification in ad hoc sensor networks using particle swarm optimization." In *Personal Wireless Communications, 2002 IEEE International Conference on*. 2002.

[119] S.M. Guru, S.K. Halgamuge, and S. Fernando. "Particle swarm optimisers for cluster formation in wireless sensor networks." In *Intelligent Sensors, Sensor Networks and Information Processing Conference, 2005. Proceedings of the 2005 International Conference on*. 2005.

[120] Y. Shi and R.C. Eberhart. "Empirical study of particle swarm optimization." In *Evolutionary Computation, 1999. CEC 99. Proceedings of the 1999 Congress on*. 1999.

[121] A. Ratnaweera, S.K. Halgamuge, and H.C. Watson, "Self-organizing hierarchical particle swarm optimizer with time-varying acceleration coefficients." *Evolutionary Computation, IEEE Transactions on*, 2004. 8(3): p. 240–255.

[122] L. Yu, Q. Zheng, and H. Xingshi. "Supervisor-student model in particle swarm optimization." In *Evolutionary Computation, 2004. CEC2004. Congress on*. 2004.

[123] C.A. Janeway, et al., *Immunobiology: The Immune System in Health and Disease*. 1999.

[124] C.A. Janeway Jr and R. Medzhitov, "Innate immune recognition." *Science's STKE*, 2002. 20(1): p. 197.

[125] L.N. De Castro, *Fundamentals of Natural Computing: Basic Concepts, Algorithms, and Applications*. 2006: Chapman & Hall/CRC.

[126] S. Forrest, et al. "Self-nonself discrimination in a computer." In *Research in Security and Privacy, 1994. Proceedings., 1994 IEEE Computer Society Symposium on*. 1994.

[127] S. Forrest and C. Beauchemin, "Computer immunology." *Immunological Reviews*, 2007. 216(1): p. 176.

[128] P. Matzinger, "Tolerance, danger, and the extended family." *Annual Reviews in Immunology*, 1994. 12(1): p. 991–1045.

[129] F.M. Burnet, *The Clonal Selection Theory of Acquired Immunity*. 1959: Vanderbilt University Press, Nashville, TN.

[130] Y.C. Lee and A.Y. Zomaya, "Immune system support for scheduling." *Advances in Applied Self-organizing Systems*, 2007.

[131] L.N. de Castro and F.J. Von Zuben, "Learning and optimization using the clonal selection principle." *Evolutionary Computation, IEEE Transactions on*, 2002. 6(3): p. 239–251.

[132] S.M. Garrett, "Parameter-free, adaptive clonal selection." In *Evolutionary Computation, 2004. CEC2004. Congress on.* 2004.

[133] A. Watkins and J. Timmis, "Exploiting parallelism inherent in AIRS, an artificial immune classifier." *Lecture Notes in Computer Science,* 2004: p. 427–438.

[134] A. Watkins, X. Bi, and A. Phadke, "Parallelizing an immune-inspired algorithm for efficient pattern recognition." *Intelligent Engineering Systems through Artificial Neural Networks: Smart Engineering System Design: Neural Networks, Fuzzy Logic, Evolutionary Programming, Complex Systems and Artificial Life,* 2003: p. 224–30.

[135] N.K. Jerne, "Towards a network theory of the immune system." *Ann Immunol (Paris),* 1974. **125**(1-2): p. 373–89.

[136] L.N. de Castro and F.J. Von Zuben, "aiNet: An artificial immune network for data analysis." *Data Mining: A Heuristic Approach,* 2001: p. 231–259.

[137] L.N. De Castro and J. Timmis, *Artificial Immune Systems: A New Computational Intelligence Approach.* 2002, Springer.

[138] M. Drozda, S. Schaust, and H. Szczerbicka. "Is AIS based misbehavior detection suitable for wireless sensor networks?" In *Wireless Communications and Networking Conference, 2007.WCNC 2007. IEEE.* 2007.

[139] M. Drozda, S. Schaust, and H. Szczerbicka. "AIS for misbehavior detection in wireless sensor networks: Performance and design principles." In *Evolutionary Computation, 2007. CEC 2007. IEEE Congress on.* 2007.

[140] S. Schaust, M. Drozda, and H. Szczerbicka. "Impact of packet injection models on misbehaviour detection performance in wireless sensor networks." In *Mobile Adhoc and Sensor Systems, 2007. MASS 2007. IEEE Internatonal Conference on.* 2007.

[141] U. Aickelin, et al., "Danger theory: The link between AIS and IDS?" *Lecture Notes in Computer Science,* 2003: p. 147–155.

[142] Bari, et al., "Immune system based distributed node and rate selection in wireless sensor networks." In *Proceedings of the 1st International Conference on Bio Inspired Models of Network, Information and Computing Systems.* 2006, ACM, Cavalese, Italy.

[143] I.R. Cohen, *Discrimination and Dialogue in the Immune System.* 2000, Elsevier.

[144] I.R. Cohen and ScienceDirect, *Tending Adam's Garden: Evolving the Cognitive Immune Self.* 2000, Academic Press San Diego, CA.

[145] I.R. Cohen, "Antigenic mimicry, clonal selection and autoimmunity." *Journal of Autoimmunity,* 2001. **16**(3): p. 337–340.

[146] I.R. Cohen, "Real and artificial immune systems: Computing the state of the body." *Nature Reviews Immunology,* 2007. **7**(7): p. 569.

[147] P. Andrews and J. Timmis, "In silico immunology." In *Alternative Inspiration for Artificial Immune Systems: Exploiting Cohen's Cognitive Model.* 2007, Springer.

[148] Speckled Computing Consortium. Retrieved Nov 10, 2008; Available from: http://www.specknet.org.

[149] H. Emma, D. Despina, and M. Chris, "Immunological inspiration for building a new generation of autonomic systems," in *Proceedings of the 1st International Conference on Autonomic Computing and Communication Systems.* 2007, ICST (Institute for Computer Sciences, Social-Informatics and Telecommunications Engineering): Rome, Italy.

[150] D. Davoudani, E. Hart, and B. Paechter, "An immune-inspired approach to speckled computing." *Lecture Notes in Computer Science,* 2007. **4628**: p. 288.

[151] J.H. Holland, "Genetic algorithm." *Scientific American*, 1992. **4**(1): p. 44–50.

[152] D.B. Fogel, N.S. Inc, and C.A. La Jolla, "An introduction to simulated evolutionary optimization." *Neural Networks, IEEE Transactions on*, 1994. **5**(1): p. 3–14.

[153] N.L. Cramer, *A Representation for the Adaptive Generation of Simple Sequential Programs*. 1985, Lawrence Erlbaum Associates, Mahwah, NJ.

[154] J.R. Koza, *Genetic Programming: On the Programming of Computers by Means of Natural Selection*. 1992, MIT Press.

[155] I. Rechenberg, *Cybernetic Solution Path of an Experimental Problem. Royal Aircraft Establishment*. Library Translation, 1965. **1122**.

[156] H.P. Schwefel, *Kybernetische Evolution als Strategie der experimentellen Forschung in der Stromungstechnik*. Master's thesis, Technical University of Berlin, 1965.

[157] L.J. Fogel, A.J. Owens, and M.J. Walsh, *Artificial Intelligence Through Simulated Evolution*. 1966, John Wiley & Sons Inc.

[158] D.B. Fogel, "Applying evolutionary programming to selected traveling salesman problems." *Cybernetics and Systems*, 1993. **24**(1): p. 27–36.

[159] D.B. Fogel, "A comparison of evolutionary programming and genetic algorithms on selected constrained optimization problems." *Simulation*, 1995. **64**(6): p. 397.

[160] W.M. Spears, et al., "An overview of evolutionary computation." *Lecture Notes in Computer Science*, 1993: p. 442–442.

[161] T. Blickle and L. Thiele. *A Mathematical Analysis of Tournament Selection*. 1995, Morgan Kaufmann.

[162] D.B. Jourdan and O.L. de Weck. "Layout optimization for a wireless sensor network using a multi-objective genetic algorithm." In *Vehicular Technology Conference, 2004. VTC 2004-Spring. 2004 IEEE 59th*. 2004.

[163] S. Hussain, A.W. Matin, and O. Islam. "Genetic algorithm for energy efficient clusters in wireless sensor networks." In *Information Technology, 2007. ITNG '07. Fourth International Conference on*. 2007.

[164] S.M. Youssef, M.A. Hamza, and S.F. Fayed, "EQOWSN: Evolutionary-based query optimization over self-organized wireless sensor networks." *Expert Systems With Applications*, 2007.

[165] Z. Michalewicz, *Genetic Algorithms+ Data Structures= Evolution Programs*. 1996, Springer.

[166] J.A. Tuszynski and M. Kurzynski, *Introduction to Molecular Biophysics*. 2003, CRC Press.

[167] F. Dressler, "Efficient and scalable communication in autonomous networking using bio-inspired mechanisms—an overview." *Informatica*, 2005. **29**(2): p. 183–188.

[168] B. Kruger and F. Dressler, "Molecular processes as a basis for autonomous networking." *Wisdom of Education for Globalization*.

[169] F. Dressler, et al. *Self-Organization in Sensor Networks Using Bio-Inspired Mechanisms*. 2005.

[170] D. Falko, et al., "Efficient operation in sensor and actor networks inspired by cellular signaling cascades," in *Proceedings of the 1st International Conference on Autonomic Computing and Communication Systems. 2007*, ICST (Institute for Computer Sciences, Social-Informatics and Telecommunications Engineering): Rome, Italy.

[171] F. Dressler, et al., "A rule-based system for programming self-organized sensor and actor networks." *Computer Networks*, 2008.

[172] T. Suda, T. Itao, and M. Matsuo, "The bio-networking architecture: The biologically inspired approach to the design of scalable, adaptive, and survivable/available network applications." *The Internet as a Large-Scale Complex System*, 2004.

[173] P. Boonma and J. Suzuki, "BiSNET: A biologically-inspired middleware architecture for self-managing wireless sensor networks." *Computer Networks*, 2007. **51**(16): p. 4599–4616.

[174] P. Boonma, P. Champrasert, and J. Suzuki, "Bisnet: A biologically-inspired architecture for wireless sensor networks." *Proceedings of The Second IEEE International Conference on Autonomic and Autonomous Systems*, 2006.

[175] P. Levis, et al., "TinyOS: An operating system for sensor networks." *Ambient Intelligence*, 2005: p. 115–48.

[176] N. Agoulmine, et al., "Challenges for autonomic network management." *Proc. of 1st IEEE Workshop on Modelling Autonomic Communication Environments (MACE06)*, Dublin, Ireland, October, 2006: p. 25–26.

Part 4

GRID AND CLOUD COMPUTING

12

SMART RPC-BASED COMPUTING IN GRIDS AND ON CLOUDS

Thomas Brady, Oleg Girko, and Alexey Lastovetsky

CONTENTS

Large Scale Network-Centric Distributed Systems, First Edition. Edited by Hamid Sarbazi-Azad and Albert Y. Zomaya.
© 2014 John Wiley & Sons, Inc. Published 2014 by John Wiley & Sons, Inc.

12.1 INTRODUCTION

The remote procedure call (RPC) paradigm [1] is widely used in distributed computing. It provides a straightforward procedure for executing parts of an application on a remote computer. To execute a RPC, the application programmer does not need to learn a new programming language but merely uses the RPC API. Using the API, the application programmer specifies the remote task to be performed, the server to execute the task, the location of the input data on the user's computer required by the task, and the location on the user's computer where the results will be stored. The execution of the remote call involves transferring input data from the user's computer to the remote computer, executing the task on the remote server and, delivering output data from the remote computer to the user's computer.

GridRPC [2] is a standard promoted by the Open Grid Forum, which extends the traditional RPC. GridRPC differs from the traditional RPC in that the programmer does not need to specify the server to execute the task. When the programmer does not specify the server, the middleware system, which implements the GridRPC API, is responsible

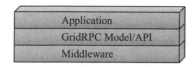

Figure 12.1   Overview of GridRPC model/API.

for finding the remote executing server. When the program runs, each GridRPC call results in the middleware mapping the call to a remote server and then the middleware is responsible for the execution of that task on the mapped server. Another difference is that GridRPC is a stubless model, meaning that client programs do not need to be recompiled when services are changed or added. This facilitates the creation of interfaces from interactive environments like Matlab, Mathematica, and IDL. A number of Grid middleware systems have recently become GridRPC compliant, including GridSolve [3], Ninf-G [4], and DIET [5].

12.1.1   GridRPC Programming Model and API

The aim of the GridRPC model is to provide a standardized, portable, and simple programming interface for a RPC. The intent is to unify client access to existing Grid computing systems (such as GridSolve, Ninf G, DIET, and OmniRPC). This is done by providing a single standardized, portable, and simple programming interface for a RPC (Figure 12.1).

This standardization provides portability of the programmers' source code across all GridRPC implemented platforms. Since the GridRPC model specifies the API and the programming model but does not dictate the implementation details of the servers, which will execute the remote procedure call, there may be multiple different middleware implementations of the GridRPC model in which the source code could be executed.

12.1.1.1   Design of the GridRPC Programming Model. The functions presented in this section are shared by all the implementations of the GridRPC model. However, the mechanics of these functions differ in each implementation.

REGISTER DISCOVERY.   The servers of the Grid environment register the tasks, which they can execute with a "registry." This involves sending information such as how the client should interface with the task and what type of arguments the server expects when the task is called (the calling sequence). In this chapter, the registry will be an abstract term for the entity/entities that stores the information about the registered tasks and the underlying network. This may be a single entity, such as the Agent in GridSolve, or several entities, such as the MDS (or LDIF), running on servers in Ninf-G, or the Global Agents and Local Agents, running in the DIET system.

RUN-TIME OF CLIENT APPLICATION.   When the GridRPC call `grpc_function_handle_default()` is invoked, the client contacts the registry to look-up a desired task and receives a handle, which is used by the client to interface with the remote task. A task handle is a small structure that describes various aspects of the task and its arguments, such as:

- The task name (`dgesv`, `dgemm` etc.)
- The object types of the arguments (scalars, vectors, matrices, etc.)
- The data type of the arguments (integer, float, double, complex, etc.)
- Whether the arguments are inputs or outputs

The client then uses the handle to call the task, which eventually returns the results. Each GridRPC call gets processed individually, where each task is discovered (task look-up) and executed separately from all the other tasks in the application.

Currently, a task is discovered by explicitly asking the registry for a known function through a string look-up. For applications that are run using the GridSolve middleware, the discovery mechanism is done via the GridSolve agent. In Ninf-G, discovery is done via the Globus MDS, which runs on each server; in DIET, discovery is done via the Global Agent. The GridRPC model does not dictate the mechanics of resource discovery since different underlying GridRPC implementations may use vastly different protocols.

GridSolve and DIET are GridRPC systems that can perform dynamic mapping of tasks. Discovery for dynamic mapping also involves discovery of performance models, which are used by the mapping heuristics.

12.1.1.2 GridRPC: API and Semantics.
Now we will introduce the fundamental objects and functions of the GridRPC API and explain their syntax and semantics. The two fundamental objects in the GridRPC model are the task handles and the session IDs. The task handle represents a mapping from a task name to an instance of that task on a particular server.

Once a particular task-to-server mapping has been established by initializing a task handle, all GridRPC calls using that task handle will be executed on the server specified in that binding. In GridRPC systems, which perform dynamic resource discovery and mapping, it is possible to delay the selection of the server until the task is called. In this case, resource discovery and mapping is done when the GridRPC task call is invoked with this initialized handle. In theory, there is more chance to choose a "better" server in this way, since at the time of invocation more information regarding the task and network is known, such as the size of input/outputs, complexity of task, and dynamic performance of client-server links.

The two types of GridRPC task call functions are blocking calls and non-blocking calls. The `grpc_call()` function makes a blocking remote procedure call with a variable number of arguments. This means the function does not return until the task has completed and the client has received all outputs from the server.

The `grpc_call_async()` function makes a non-blocking remote procedure call with a variable number of arguments. When this call is invoked, the remote task and data transfer of the input are initiated and the function returns. This means that either the client computation or server computation can be done in parallel with the `grpc_call_async()` call.

The `grpc_wait()` function waits for the result of the asynchronous call with the supplied session ID. The `grpc_wait_all()` function waits for all preceding asynchronous calls.

12.1.2 GridRPC: A GridRPC Application

Table 12.1 is a simple application that uses the GridRPC API. It comprises three task handles and three corresponding remote calls. The task handles are set up so that the remote call is bound to a server at call time by passing "bind_server_at_call_time"[1] as a parameter. This string could be substituted with a server host name, or the user could assign it to the default server by calling `grpc_function_handle_default()`.

The task "mmul" takes four arguments: the size of the matrices, the two input matrices, and the one output matrix. In this application, the sizes of the matrices are not known prior to run-time as they can only be established by executing the local functions (initMatA and initMatB). Therefore, it is impossible for a user to decide which servers to assign which tasks since the size of inputs and outputs and complexity are not known until the application is run. This is a difficult decision even if the sizes of the matrices are known before run-time as the performance of underlying networks are dynamic and difficult to predict in Grid environments.

It is also impossible for a dynamic GridRPC system such as GridSolve, which can discover resources and map tasks at run-time, to optimally map the tasks in this application. This is due to the current GridRPC model only permitting a single task to be processed at any one time. Therefore, when the system maps the GridRPC task call executing handle h1, it has no knowledge of what tasks are executing in parallel with this task and the computation load of the tasks executing in parallel.

Consider the following scenario: M is initialized to 1000 and N is initialized to 100. Therefore, the computational load of the first task will be far less than that of the second task. In this circumstance, when the system maps the function handle h1, it will map this to the fastest server as this will yield the lowest execution time for this task. Then, when the system maps the function executing handle h2, it will map it to the second fastest server as the fastest server is currently heavily loaded with the first task. This is poor load balancing of computation and will affect the overall performance of the parallel execution of both tasks.

In addition, since tasks are processed individually in the GridRPC model, it is impossible for systems, which implement this model, to know the dependencies between tasks. Since dependencies between tasks are not known and the communication model of GridRPC model is based on the client-server model, bridge communication between remote tasks is forced. With the GridRPC model, this dependent argument would have to be sent from the source task to the destination task via the client, which is two communication steps. This necessity for the client to buffer intermediate data may also cause memory paging on the client. In this application, the third task, h3, is dependent on argument F from the second task h2 and argument C from task h1. In this case, the only way

---

[1] This special string is a GridSolve-specific workaround to enable lazy binding in GridRPC.

T A B L E 12.1 GridRPC Model: Example Application

```
main()
{
    int N;
    int M;
    double A[N*N], B[N*N], C[N*N];
    double D[M*M], E[M*M], F[M*M], G[M*M];

    grpc_function_handle_t h1, h2, h3;
    grpc_session_t s1, s2;
    grpc_initialize(argv[1]);

    /* initialize */
    char * hndl_str= "bind_server_at_call_time";

    grpc_function_handle_init(&h1, hndl_str,"mmul/mmul");
    grpc_function_handle_init(&h2, hndl_str, "mmul/mmul");
    grpc_function_handle_init(&h3, hndl_str, "mmul/mmul");

    N=getNSize();
    initMatA(N, A);   initMatB(N, B);
    if(grpc_call_asnc(&h1,&s1, N, A, B, C)!= GRPC_NO_ERROR) {
        fprintf(stderr, "Error in grpc_call\n");
        exit(1);
    }

    M=getMSize();
    initMatD(M, D);   initMatD(M, E);
    if(grpc_call_async(&h2, &s2, M, D, E, F)!=GRPC_NO_ERROR){
        fprintf(stderr, "Error in grpc_call\n");
        exit(1);
    }

    grpc_wait(s1);
    grpc_wait(s2);

    if (grpc_call(&h3, M, C , F, G) != GRPC_NO_ERROR) {
        fprintf(stderr, "Error in grpc_call\n");
        exit(1);
    }

    grpc_function_handle_destruct(&h1);
    grpc_function_handle_destruct(&h2);
    grpc_function_handle_destruct(&h3);
    ...
    grpc_finalize();
}
```

to send F from the server executing h2 and C from the server executing h1 to the server executing h3 is via the client, which is two communication steps. Mapping tasks individually in this application has forced bridge communication and increased the amount of memory used on the client. This will affect the overall volume of communication and may cause paging on the client, which would significantly affect the performance of the application. In addition, since tasks are mapped individually onto a star network, parallelism of remote communication cannot be employed. In this case, if dependencies were known, argument C could be sent from the server executing h1 to the server executing h3 in parallel with computation and communication of task h2 (permitting that task h2 has been assigned a different server than h3).

From this application, it is evident that the potential for higher-performance applications would be increased if we could map tasks collectively as a group on to a network, which is fully connected. This is the premise of the SmartGridRPC model.

12.1.3 Implementing the GridRPC Model in GridSolve

The GridSolve agent, which is the focal point of the GridSolve system, has the responsibility of performing discovery and mapping of tasks. The GridSolve agent is implementation of the registry entity, which was outlined in the Section 1.1.

In order to map a task on the client-server network, the agent must discover performance models, which can be used to estimate the execution time of individual tasks on different servers on the network. These performance models include functions for each task, which calculate the computation/communication load of tasks, and parameters, which specify the dynamic performance of the network. These performance models are sent from each server in the network to the agent before run-time of the client application (Agent discovery).

12.1.3.1 GridSolve: Agent Discovery. The section outlines the GridSolve implementation of the "Register discovery" part of the GridRPC model. The agent maintains a list of all available servers and their registered tasks. This list is incremented when each new server registers with the agent. In addition, the agent stores performance models required to estimate the execution time of available tasks on the servers.

This includes the dynamic performance of each server and functions/parameters, which are used to calculate the computational/communication load of tasks. These performance models are implemented by executing the LINPACK benchmark on each server when they are started, running the CPU load monitor on the server and using descriptions of the task provided by the person that installed the task to generate functions for calculating the computation and communication load of the tasks (Fig. 12.2).

The server may optionally be configured to maintain a history of execution times and use a non-negative least squares algorithm to predict future execution times. At run-time of the client application, when each GridRPC task call is invoked, these performance models are used to estimate the execution time of the called task on each server.

12.1.3.2 Run-time GridRPC Task Call. In practice, from the user's perspective the mechanism employed by GridSolve makes the GridRPC task call fairly transparent.

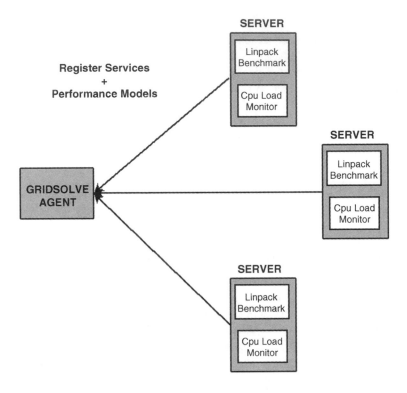

Figure 12.2 GridSolve: agent discovery.

However, behind the scenes, a typical GridRPC task call involves the following operations:

- The discovery operation
- The mapping operation
- The execution operation

THE DISCOVERY OPERATION. When the GridRPC call is invoked, the client queries the agent for an appropriate server that can execute the desired function. The agent returns a list of available servers, ranked in order of suitability.

This ranked list is sorted based only on task computation times. Normally, the client would simply submit the service request to the first server on the list, but if specified by the user it is resorted according to its overall computation and communication time. If this is specified, the bandwidth from the client to the top few servers is measured. This is done using a simple 32KB ping-pong benchmark. The time required to do the measurement will depend on the number of servers, which have the requested task, and the bandwidth and latency from the client to those servers. When the data is relatively small, the measurements are not performed because it would take less time to just send the data than it would take to do the measurements. Also, since a given service may be available on many servers, the cost of measuring network speed to all of them could be prohibitive. Therefore, the number of servers to be measured is limited to those with the highest computational performance.

THE MAPPING OPERATION. As previously described, the agent sends a server list, which is ordered according to their estimated computation time. In GridSolve, there are a number of mapping heuristics that can be employed to generate the mapping solution. Among the mapping heuristics is the minimum completion time (MCT) mapping heuristic, which bases its execution time on the performance models and the dynamic network performance of each server. Also included is a set of mapping heuristics that rely on the other performance model in GridSolve called the Historical Trace Manager (HTM).

THE EXECUTION OPERATION. The client attempts to contact the first server from the list. It sends the input data to the server; the server then executes the task on behalf of the client and returns the results. If at any point the execution fails, the client automatically moves down the list of servers.

12.1.4 GridRPC Limitations

GridRPC has some limitations affecting the performance of Grid applications. When using the traditional GridRPC to execute tasks remotely, the mapping and execution of the task is one atomic operation, which cannot be separated. As a result, each task is mapped separately and independently of other tasks of the application.

Another important aspect of the GridRPC model is its communication model. The communication model of GridRPC is based on the client-server model or star network topology. This means that a task can be executed on any of the servers and inputs/outputs can only traverse the client-server links.

Mapping tasks individually on to the star network results in mapping solutions that are far from optimal. If tasks are mapped individually, the mapping heuristic is unable to take into account any of the tasks that follow the task being mapped. Consequently, the mapping heuristic does not have the ability to optimally balance the load of computation and communication. Another consequence of mapping tasks in this way is that dependencies between tasks are not known at the time of mapping. Therefore this approach forces bridge communication. Bridge communication occurs when the output of one task is required as an input to another task. In this case, using the traditional GridRPC model, the output of the first task must be sent back to the client and the client then subsequently sends it to the server executing the second task when it is called.

Also, since dependencies are not known and the network is based on the client-server model, it is impossible to employ any parallelism of communication between the tasks in the group. For example, this can be implemented if there is a dependency between two tasks and the destination task is not executed in parallel or immediately after the source task. In theory, this dependent data could be sent to the destination task in parallel with any computation or communication on any other machine (client or other servers) that happens in the intervening time. However, since tasks are mapped individually onto a star network, this parallelism of communication cannot be realized using the GridRPC model.

12.2 SMARTGRIDRPC AND SMARTGRIDSOLVE

SmartGridRPC [6] is an enhancement of the traditional GridRPC model that allows a group of tasks to be mapped collectively onto a fully connected network. This would remove each of the limitations of the GridRPC model already described. The Smart-GridRPC model has extended the GridRPC model to support collective mapping of a group of tasks by separating the mapping of tasks from their execution. This allows the group of tasks to be mapped collectively and then executed collectively.

In addition, the traditional client-server model of GridRPC has been extended so that the group of tasks can be collectively executed onto a network topology, which is fully connected. This is a network topology where all servers can communicate directly or servers can cache their outputs locally.

12.2.1 SmartGridRPC Programming Model and API

The aim of the SmartGridRPC model is to enhance the GridRPC model by providing functionality for collective mapping of a group of tasks on a fully connected network.

The SmartGridRPC programming model is designed so that when it is implemented it is interoperable with the existing GridRPC implementation (Fig. 12.3). Therefore, if any middleware has been extended to be made SmartGridRPC compliant, the application programmer has the option regarding whether their application is implemented for the SmartGridRPC model, where tasks are mapped collectively onto a fully connected network, or for the standard GridRPC model, where tasks are mapped individually onto a client-server star network.

In addition, the SmartGridRPC model is designed so that when it is implemented it is incremental to the GridRPC system. Therefore, if the SmartGridRPC model is installed only on the client side, the system will be extended to allow for collective mapping. If the SmartGridRPC model is installed on the client side and on only some of the servers in the network, the system will be extended to allow for collective mapping on a partially connected network. If it is installed on all servers, the system will be extended to allow for collective mapping on the fully connected network.

Figure 12.3 Overview of SmartGridRPC model/API.

12.2.1.1 SmartGridRPC Programming Model. The SmartGridRPC model
provides an API, which allows the application programmer to specify a block of code
in which a group of GridRPC task calls should be mapped collectively. Then, when the
application is run, the specified group of tasks in this block of code is processed collectively. Namely, all tasks in the group are discovered collectively, mapped collectively,
and executed collectively on the fully connected network. In the discovery phase, performance models are generated for estimating the execution time of the group of tasks
on the fully connected network. In the mapping phase, the performance models are used
by the mapping heuristic to generate a mapping solution for the group of tasks. In the
execution phase, the group of tasks is executed on the fully connected network according
to the mapping solution generated.

In the context of this chapter, a performance model is any structure, function, parameter, etc., used to estimate the execution time of tasks in the distributed environment.
The SmartGridRPC performance model refers to performance models that are used to
estimate the time of executing a group of tasks on the fully connected network. The
GridRPC performance model refers to performance models that are used to estimate
the execution time of an individual task on a star network. A mapping heuristic is an
algorithm that aims to generate a mapping solution that satisfies a certain criterion,
for example, minimum completion time or minimum perturbation. The SmartGridRPC
mapping heuristics refer to mapping heuristics that map a group of tasks onto a fully
connected network. The GridRPC mapping heuristics refer to mapping heuristics that
map an individual task on to a client-server network. Furthermore, a mapping solution
is a structure that outlines how tasks should be executed on the distributed network. The
SmartGridRPC mapping solution outlines both a task-to-server mapping of each task
in the group to a server in the network and the communication operations between the
tasks in the group. The GridRPC mapping solution outlines the server list that specifies
where the called task should be executed and the backup servers that should execute the
task should the execution fail.

The collective mapping of the SmartGridRPC model allows the mapping heuristics
to estimate the execution time of more mapping solutions than if these tasks were
mapped individually and, therefore, have greater potential of finding a more optimal
solution.

The job of generating the performance models is divided between the different
components of GridRPC architecture (i.e., client, server, and registry). The components
may only be capable of constructing part of the performance model required to estimate
the groups' execution time. Therefore, the registry accumulates these parts from the
different components and generates the required performance models.

There are numerous methods for estimating the execution time of the group of
tasks on a fully connected network, so the implemented performance models are not
specified in the SmartGridRPC model. Examples of performance models would be the
ones currently implemented in SmartGridSolve, which have extended the performance
models used in GridSolve. In the future, SmartGridSolve will implement performance
models such as the Functional Performance Model, which is described in [7, 8]. Other
possible implementations could include the Network Weather Service [9], the MDS

directories (Globus, Ninf) [4], and the Historical Trace Manager (GridSolve) [10]. In general, in the SmartGridRPC model, the performance models are used to estimate:

- The execution time of a task on a server
- The execution time of multiple tasks on a server and the effect the execution each task has on the other (perturbation)
- The communication time of sending inputs and outputs between client and server
- The communication time of sending inputs and outputs between different servers

Mapping heuristics implement a certain methodology that uses these performance models to generate a mapping solution, which satisfies a certain criterion. Examples of mapping solutions include the greedy mapping heuristic and the exhaustive mapping heuristics, which have been implemented in SmartGridSolve. There has been extensive research done in the area of mapping heuristics [11], so this is not the focus of our study.

The following sections describe the programming model of SmartGridRPC in the circumstance where the performance models are generated on the registry and the group of tasks is mapped by a mapping heuristic on the registry. However, the SmartGridRPC model could have an alternative implementation. These performance models could be generated on the client and the group of tasks could also be mapped by a mapping heuristic on the client. This may be a more suitable model for systems, such as Ninf-G, that have no central daemon like the GridSolve Agent or the DIET Global Agent.

The SmartGridRPC map function separates the GridRPC call operations into three distinct phases so they can be done for all tasks collectively:

- Discovery phase – The registry discovers all the performance models necessary for estimating the execution time of the group of tasks on a fully connected network.
- Mapping phase – The mapping heuristic uses the performance models to generate a mapping solution for the group of tasks.
- Execution phase – The group of tasks is executed on the fully connected network according to the mapping solution.

There are two types of discovery mechanisms used to determine the execution time of a group of tasks on a fully connected network:- "Registry" discovery and "Client Application Run-Time" discovery.

REGISTER DISCOVERY. The servers provide the part of the performance model that facilitates the modeling of the execution of its available tasks on the underlying network. This partial model can either be automatically generated by the server or has to be explicitly specified or both. This partial model is referred to as the *server PM*.

As previously mentioned, the SmartGridRPC model does not specify how to implement the *server PM*, as there are many possible implementations. Exactly when the *server's PM* is sent to the registry is also not specified by the SmartGridRPC model, as this depends on the type of performance model implemented.

For example, the *server PM* could be sent to the registry upon registration and then updated after a certain event has occurred (i.e., when the CPU load or communication load has changed beyond a certain threshold) or when a certain time interval has elapsed. Or it may be updated during the run-time of the application when actual running times of tasks are used to build the performance model. Suffice to say that the *server PM* is updated on the registry and is stored there until it is required during the run-time of a client application.

CLIENT APPLICATION RUN-TIME. The client also provides a part of the performance model that is sent to the registry during the run-time of the client application. This is referred to as the *client PM*. This part of the performance model is application-specific, such as the list of tasks in the group, their order, the dependencies between tasks, and the values of the arguments in the calling sequences. In addition, the *client PM* specifies the performance of the client-server links.

In order to determine the parts of the performance model of the group of tasks, which are application-specific, each task that has been requested to be mapped collectively will be iterated through twice. On the first iteration, each GridRPC task call is discovered but not executed. This is the *discovery phase*. After all tasks in the group are discovered, the client determines the performance of the client-server links and sends the *client PM* to the registry. The registry then generates the performance models based on the stored *server PM* and the *client PM*. Based on these performance models, the mapping heuristic generates a mapping solution. This is the *mapping phase*. On the second iteration through the group of tasks, each task is then executed according to the mapping solution generated. This is the *execution phase*. This approach of iterating twice through the group tasks to separate the discovery, mapping and execution of tasks into three distinct phases is the basis that allows the SmartGridRPC model to collectively map and then collectively execute a group of tasks.

The run-time map function, grpc_map(), is part of the SmartGridRPC API and allows the application programmer to specify a group of GridRPC calls to map collectively.

This is done by using a set of parentheses, which follows the map function, to specify a block of code, which consists of the group of GridRPC task calls that should be mapped collectively:

```
grpc_map(char * mapping_heuristic_name){
     ...
     //group of GridRPC calls to map collectively
     ...
}
```

When this function is called, the code and GridRPC task calls within the parentheses of the function are iterated through twice, as previously described.

DISCOVERY PHASE. On the first iteration through the group of tasks, each GridRPC task call within the parentheses is discovered but not executed, so therefore all tasks in the group can be discovered collectively. This is different from the GridRPC model, which only allows a single task to be discovered at any one time. The client can therefore look up and retrieve handles for all tasks in the group at the same time. In addition to sending the handles, the registry also sends back a list of all the servers that can execute each task. The client then determines the performance of the client-server links to the servers in the list. The client may only determine the performance of some of these links, depending on how many servers are in this list, or may not determine the performance of any of the links if the arguments being sent over the links are small. Exactly how the client determines the performance of these links is not specified by the SmartGridRPC model. This could be implemented using NWS sensors, ping-pong benchmarks, MDS directory, or any other conceivable method for determining the performance of communication links.

The client now sends the *client PM* to the registry. The *client PM* specifies the order of tasks in the group, their dependencies, and the values of each argument in the calling sequence of each task and the performance of the client-server links. This does not involve sending nonscalar arguments, such as matrices or vectors, but just the pointer value as this will be used to determine the dependencies between tasks. The registry then uses the *server PM* and *client PM* to generate the performance models for estimating the time of executing a group of tasks on the fully connected network. These performance models are then used in the mapping phase to generate a mapping solution.

MAPPING PHASE. Based on the performance models, the mapping heuristic then produces a mapping solution, which satisfies a certain criterion, for example, minimizing the execution time of tasks. The implemented mapping heuristic is chosen by the application programmer using the SmartGridRPC API.

There is an extensive number of possible mapping heuristics that could be implemented and therefore the mapping heuristics implemented are not bound by the SmartGridRPC model. However, the SmartGridRPC framework allows different mapping heuristics and different performance models to be added and therefore provides an ideal framework for testing and evaluating these performance models and mapping heuristics.

EXECUTION PHASE. The execution phase occurs on the second iteration through the group of tasks. In this phase, each GridRPC call is executed according to the mapping solution generated by the mapping heuristic on the previous iteration. The mapping solution not only outlines the task to-server mapping but also the remote communication operations between the tasks in the group.

12.2.1.2 *SmartGridRPC: API and Semantics.* The SmartGridRPC API allows a user to specify a group of tasks that should be mapped collectively on a fully connected network. The SmartGridRPC map function is used for specifying the block of code, which consists of the group of GridRPC tasks calls that is to be mapped collectively.

When the `grpc_map()` function is called, the code within its parenthesis will be iterated through twice, as previously described. After the first iteration through the group of tasks, the mapping heuristic specified by the parameter "mapping_heuristic_name" of the `grpc_map()` function generates a mapping solution.

The mapping solution outlines a task to server mapping and also the communication operations between tasks. These communication operations include:

- Client-server communication: standard GridRPC communication
- Server-server communication: server sends a single argument to another server

- Client broadcasting: client sends a single argument to multiple servers
- Server broadcasting: server sends a single argument to multiple servers
- Server caching: server stores an argument locally for future tasks

As a result, the network may have:

- A fully connected topology, where all the servers are SmartGridSolve enabled servers (SmartServers) that can communicate directly with each other.
- A partially connected topology, where only some of the servers are *SmartServers* that can communicate directly. The standard servers can only communicate with each other via the client.
- A star connected topology, where all servers are standard servers and they can only communicate with each other via the client.

During the second iteration through the code, the tasks will be executed according to the generated mapping solution.

The SmartGridRPC model also requires a method for identifying code that will be executed on the client. There are many possible approaches that could be implemented to identify client code. For example, a preprocessor approach could be used to identify the client code transparently. Where the client code cannot be identified, we provide a grpc_local() function call, which the application programmer can use to explicitly specify client computation:

```
grpc_map(char * mapping_heuristic_name) {

    //reset variables which have been updated
    // during the discovery phase

    grpc_local(list of arguments){
        //code to ignore when generating task graph
    }
    ...
    // group of tasks to map collectively
    ...
}
```

The grpc_local() function is used to specify the code block that should be ignored during the first iteration through the scope of grpc_map(). The function is also used to specify remote arguments that are required locally. This information is used to determine when arguments will be sent back to the client and also facilitates the generation of the task graph.

Any segment of client code that is not part of the GridRPC API should be identified using this function. There is one exception to this rule: when the client code directly affects any aspect of the task graph. For example, if a variable is updated on the client that determines which remote tasks get executed or the size of inputs/outputs of any task, then the operations on this variable should not be enclosed by the `grpc_local()` function. If any variables or structures are updated during the task discovery cycle then they should be restored to their original values before the execution cycle begins.

12.2.1.3 A SmartGridRPC Application.

Table 12.2 is the SmartGridRPC implementation of the GridRPC application in Section 12.1.2. There is only one extra call required to make this application SmartGridRPC enabled, which is the `grpc_map()` function. In this example, the user has specified that all three tasks should be mapped collectively.

Let us consider the same simple scenario as in Section 1.2, where task h2 has a larger computational load than h1 and the underlying network consists of two servers that have different performances. In this case, since all tasks are mapped together, the SmartGridRPC model will improve the load balancing of computation by assigning task h2 to the faster server and h1 to the slower.

In addition, task h3 has a dependency on the argument F, which is an output of task h2, and argument C, which is an output of task h1. Since the tasks are mapped as a group and therefore dependencies can be considered, this dependency can be mapped onto the virtual link connecting the servers executing both tasks, which will reduce the communication load. Or if the tasks are executing on the same server, then the output can be cached and retrieved from the same server, which would further reduce the communication load and further increase the overall performance of the group of tasks.

Also, since no intermediate results are sent back to the client, the amount of memory utilized on the client will be reduced and this will reduce the risk of paging on the client. This prevention of paging could also considerably reduce the overall execution time of the group of tasks.

In addition, since dependencies are known and the network is fully connected, the remote communication of argument C from server executing task h1 to server executing task h2 could be done in parallel with the communication and computation of h2.

12.2.2 SmartGridSolve: Implementing SmartGridRPC in GridSolve

SmartGridSolve [12] is an extension of GridSolve that makes the GridSolve middleware compliant with the SmartGridRPC model. SmartNetSolve [13] was previously implemented to make the NetSolve [14] middleware, which was the predecessor of GridSolve, compliant with the SmartGridRPC model.

The SmartGridSolve extension is interoperable with GridSolve. Therefore, if GridSolve is installed with the SmartGridSolve extension, the user can choose whether to implement an application using the standard GridRPC model or the extended SmartGridRPC model. In addition, SmartGridSolve is incremental to the GridSolve system. Therefore, if the SmartGridSolve extension is installed only on the client side, the system will be extended to allow for collective mapping. If SmartGridSolve is installed on the client side and on only some of the servers in the network, the system will be extended to allow for collective mapping on a partially connected network. If it is installed on all servers, the system will be extended to allow for collective mapping on the fully connected network.

T A B L E 12.2 SmartGridRPC Model: Example Application

```
main()
{
    int N=getNSize();
    int M=getMSize();

    double A[N*N], B[N*N], C[N*N];
    double D[M*M], E[M*M], F[M*M], G[M*M]
    grpc_function_handle_t h1, h2, h3;
    grpc_session_t s1, s2;
    grpc_initialize(argv[1]);

    /* initialize */
    initMatA(N, A);  initMatB(N, B);
    initMatD(M, D);  initMatD(M, E);


    grpc_function_handle_default(&h1, "mmul/mmul");
    grpc_function_handle_default(&h2, "mmul/mmul");
    grpc_function_handle_default(&h3, "mmul/mmul");

    grpc_map("greedy_map"){
      if(grpc_call_asnc(&h1,&s1,N,A,B,C)!= GRPC_NO_ERROR) {
        fprintf(stderr, "Error in grpc_call\n");
        exit(1);
      }
      if(grpc_call_async(&h2, &s2,M,D,E,F)!=GRPC_NO_ERROR){
        fprintf(stderr, "Error in grpc_call\n");
        exit(1);
      }
      grpc_wait(s1);
      grpc_wait(s2);

      if (grpc_call(&h3,M,C ,F,G) != GRPC_NO_ERROR){
        fprintf(stderr, "Error in grpc_call\n");
        exit(1);
      }
    }

    grpc_function_handle_destruct(&h1);
    grpc_function_handle_destruct(&h2);
    grpc_function_handle_destruct(&h3);
    ...
    grpc_finalize();
}
```

12.2.2.1 Agent Discovery. This section presents the SmartGridSolve implementation of the "register discovery" part of SmartGridRPC model outlined in Section 12.2.1.1. In addition to registering services, the servers also send the *server PM*. The *server PM* makes up part of the performance model used for estimating the execution time of the server's available tasks on the fully connected network. This along, with the *client PM*, is used to generate a performance model, which is used by the mapping heuristics to produce mapping solutions.

Currently, the *server PM* of SmartGridSolve extends that of GridSolve, which comprises functions for calculating the computation load and communication load and parameters for calculating the dynamic performance of the servers and client-server links.

However, the network discovery of GridSolve is extended to also discover the dynamic performance of each link connecting *SmartServers*. These are those servers, which can communicate directly with each other or store/receive data from their local cache. The dynamic performance of the server-server links are taken periodically using the same 32KB ping-pong technique used by GridSolve.

To achieve backward compatibility and to give server administrators full control over how the server operates, a server that has the SmartGridSolve extension enabled may be also started as a standard GridSolve server.

As a result, the network may have:

- A fully connected topology
- A partially connected topology
- A star connected topology

Also, to minimize the volume of data transferred around the network, every *Smart-Server* is given an ID. Each *SmartServer* then only sends ping-pong messages to those *SmartServers* that have an ID that is lower than their own. This prevents the performance of the same communication link being measured twice. Once determined, these values are sent to the agent to update the *server PM*. The *server PM* is stored on the registry and updated either periodically (every 5 minutes) or when the CPU load monitor records a change, which exceeds a certain threshold. This *server PM* is then used to generate the performance models during the run-time of a client application.

12.2.2.2 Run-time of Client Application. This section presents the Smart-GridSolve implementation of the "Client application run-time" part of the SmartGridRPC model. Each phase of the SmartGridRPC run-time map function (`grpc_map()`) will be described.

DISCOVERY PHASE. On the first iteration through the group of tasks, each GridRPC task call (`grpc_call()`) within the parentheses is discovered but not executed. This involves discovering the name of each task and the calling sequence of each task, which involves discovering the pointers to the nonscalar arguments (such as matrices, vectors, etc.) and the values of the scalar arguments.

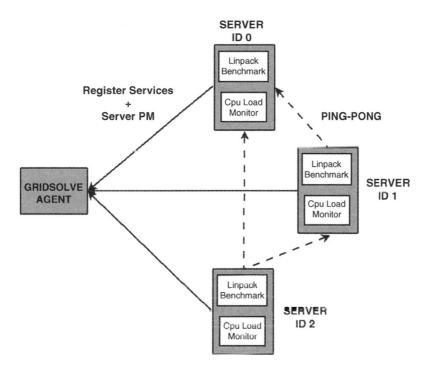

Figure 12.4 SmartGridSolve: Agent discovery.

After the first iteration through the group, the client contacts the agent and looks up the group of tasks, which involves sending the agent a list of the task names.

The agent then creates a handle for each task. The agent sends back the group of handles, one for each task. In addition, for each handle it sends a list of servers, which can execute each task.

The client then uses the list of servers to perform the ping-pong benchmark on each of the links from the client to each server that can execute a task in the group of tasks. Subsequent to this, the client will send the *client PM*, which is a structure that specifies application-specific information such as the list of tasks, the calling sequence, and the dependencies between the tasks. In addition, it specifies the performances of each client-server link.

The agent can now generate all the performance models necessary for estimating the execution time of the group of tasks on the fully or partially connected network. In SmartGridSolve, these performance models consist of a task graph, a network graph, and functions for estimating computation and communication times.

The task graph specifies the order of tasks, their synchronization (whether they are executed in sequence or parallel), the dependencies between tasks, the load of computation, and communication of each task in the group.

The network graph specifies the performance of each server in the network and the communication links of the fully connected, partially connected, or star network. These performance models will be used by the mapping heuristics in the mapping phase to generate a mapping solution for the group of tasks.

MAPPING PHASE. The mapping heuristic produces a mapping solution graph based on the task graph, the network graph, and the functions for estimating computation and communication time. The mapping heuristics currently implemented in SmartGridSolve are:

- Exhaustive mapping heuristic
- Random walk mapping heuristic
- Greedy mapping heuristic

The mapping solution generated by these heuristics is then used in the execution phase to determine how the group of tasks should be executed on the network.

EXECUTION PHASE. This execution phase occurs on the second iteration through the group of tasks. In this phase, each called GridRPC call is executed according to the mapping solution generated by the mapping heuristic. The mapping solution not only outlines the task-to-server mapping but also the communication operations between the tasks in the group. In addition to the standard GridRPC communication, the mapping solution can use the following communication operations:

- Server-server communication
- Client broadcasting
- Server broadcasting
- Server caching

12.2.2.3 Fault Tolerance. SmartGridSolve maps tasks to servers collectively and allows server-to-server communication, so a single server's failure can affect not only tasks running on that server, but also tasks dependent on those tasks.

There are two fault tolerance modes in SmartGridSolve.

ADVANCED MODE. The advanced mode is the default mode implemented in `grpc_map()` function in SmartGridSolve. If there is a problem communicating with a server running a task, or the server reports a failure during `grpc_call()` or `grpc_call_async()`, the library enters the fault mode. The agent is notified that the server is unavailable and should be removed from the list of available servers. All remaining `grpc_call()` and `grpc_call_async()` calls do nothing, `grpc_local()` blocks are skipped, and the `grpc_map()` loop is started over again in mapping phase.

The disadvantage of this mode is that even a single server's fault is expensive: it leads to all tasks inside `grpc_map()` block to be mapped and started over again. All results of computation done already inside `grpc_map()` block are lost.

The advantage of this mode is that it has no performance impact if there are no faults.

If several servers became unavailable during execution of a single `grpc_map()`, only the first fault is detected, all subsequent calls to `grpc_call()` and `grpc_call_async()` do nothing, and the remapping is performed before the next loop pass. At the moment of the next remapping the agent may have noticed some of the other failed servers, but it may take several mapping and execution attempts before the agent notices all failed servers.

SIMPLE MODE. The simple mode is implemented in `grpc_map_ft()` function. This function works the same way as `grpc_map()`, but with server-to-server communication disabled. As a result, a failure of a single GridRPC call does not affect other calls. The fault tolerance inside `grpc_map_ft()` is implemented the same way as in GridSolve: if there is any problem communicating with a server running a task, or the server reports a failure of that task, another server is selected, and the task is run again on that server.

The advantage of this approach is that each fault is relatively cheap: a server's fault affects only those tasks that are running on this server at the moment of the fault.

The disadvantage is that, although tasks are still mapped to servers collectively, the communication optimization is sacrificed: all communication goes through the client. This has a significant negative impact on performance in absence of faults.

If several servers became unavailable during execution of a single `grpc_map_ft()`, each fault is handled independently, and each failed task is retried on a different server.

ADDITIONAL CONSTRAINTS FOR FAULT TOLERANCE IN ADVANCED MODE. The current implementation of SmartGridSolve places additional constraints on the code inside `grpc_map()` block to work correctly in case of a task failure. The existing guideline is that all side effects should be done in `grpc_local()` block, which is skipped during discovery phase and is run only during the actual task execution phase (the last pass of the loop). However, in case of task failure, the task execution phase is not the the last: the loop will start over again for the mapping phase. This means that if there is `grpc_call()` or `grpc_call_async()` after the `grpc_local()` block, and this call has failed, `grpc_local()` block preceding it has been already executed, producing side effects, and there is no way to roll those side effects back. Hence, here is the additional guideline for `grpc_local()` block to work correctly in case of failure: If there are more remote task calls after the `grpc_local()` block inside `grpc_map()` loop, the code inside this `grpc_local()` block should be idempotent, that is, it produces exactly the same results if it is run more than once.

12.3 MAKING SMARTGRIDSOLVE SMARTER

12.3.1 SmartGridSolve Approach to Smart Mapping and Its Limitations

The current approach to smart mapping implemented by SmartGridSolve is the following. A block containing an algorithm to apply smart mapping to is marked by the `grpc_map()` directive before the block. So, if the original algorithm looks as follows:

```
grpc_call(task1,  ...);
grpc_call(task2,  ...);
grpc_call(task3,  ...);
```

after converting it to use smart mapping it will look like this:

```
grpc_map("heuristics_name") {
    grpc_call(task1,  ...);
    grpc_call(task2,  ...);
    grpc_call(task3,  ...);

}
```

The `grpc_map()` directive is actually a C preprocessor macro implemented as a `while` loop. The first pass of this loop discovers all GridRPC calls, but instead of executing them it just stores the information about calls and their arguments for building a dependency graph. Before the second loop pass, the dependency graph is built and sent to the agent for smart mapping. The agent responds with the suggested mapping, and the tasks are run on servers suggested by the agent during the second loop pass. If a fault happens during the execution of a task, the faulty server is excluded from the list of available servers, all subsequent task runs are skipped, and the loop is run once again, asking the agent for mapping and then running the tasks inside the loop pass.

This approach is very simple, but it has the following limitations.

- The current implementation of the `grpc_map()` directive puts significant restrictions on a code inside the block following it. Although the fact that `grpc_map()` is implemented as a loop should be hidden as an implementation detail, a user still must keep this in mind. In particular, all statements besides GridRPC calls should be written to yield the same result when run during the first and second loop pass. Users should keep in mind that the loop is run at least twice and avoid the statements with side effects inside the `grpc_map()` controlled block. A special `grpc_local()` block was introduced to allow all statements that should not be run during the discovery phase to be put there. However, this does not fully protect those statements from being run twice in case of the GridRPC call failure. This means that all statements inside the `grpc_map()` block should be idempotent: either having no side effects, or if they have one, the side effect should be exactly the same when the statement is performed for the second time (except statements inside `grpc_local()` blocks not followed by any GridRPC calls). See the last paragraph of section 12.2.2.3 for details. It is very easy to violate this restriction and there is no easy way to detect whether it has happened. A simple mistake can lead to unpredictable results. Or even worse, a program can silently produce incorrect results only if a server fault has happened during algorithm execution.

- The current implementation does not handle branching inside the `grpc_map()` block properly. If there is an if statement, the rules of C programming language dictate that only one branch is executed during the discovery phase. This means that no GridRPC calls in another branch will be taken into account when building the dependency graph.

- The implementation of `grpc_map()` block and GridRPC calls uses global state to determine which loop pass is taking place and what to do. This makes GridRPC implementation non re-entrant and thread unsafe.

- If a fault happens during GridRPC call, all the mapping, and the discovery, mapping and execution stages are performed again on the whole algorithm inside `grpc_map()` block, not taking into account that some tasks could have already successfully completed and their results are not lost.

12.3.2 A Better Approach to Smart Mapping

In order to achieve more correct smart mapping that puts less constraints on statements used inside the block to be mapped, other approaches are needed. Very few programming languages have facilities for introspection on the statement level, and those languages are not widely used for grid computing anyway, so in order to discover GridRPC calls dependency graph correctly without executing the block in a "special mode," some kind of additional tool is needed.

In order to discover the dependency graph, the algorithm should be analyzed somehow before it is run. As the algorithm does not contain self-modifying code, the dependency graph is the same during different algorithm runs, so it does not make sense to build it every time it is run. A better way to build the dependency graph is to analyze the algorithm during the compilation phase or even before. Hence, the preprocessor approach (discovery before compilation) is proposed.

The preprocessor approach can be implemented by a program that reads a program written in a programming language, analyzes it, finds all blocks marked for smart mapping, finds all GridRPC calls inside these blocks, builds dependency graph for all those blocks, and then outputs the program with blocks marked for smart mapping modified to contain dependency graph table, a call to the agent to get task-to-server mapping in the beginning of the block, and GridRPC calls that use this mapping.

The preprocessor approach can lift some restrictions on code inside the `grpc_map()` block because there will be no discovery phase during runtime, just the execution phase:

- There will be no need in `grpc_local()` blocks to keep some code from being executed during the discovery phase.

- All GridRPC calls in all branches of if statements will be taken into account when building the dependency graph, not just ones that happen to be executed during the discovery phase.

However, this approach makes the solution for fault tolerance used in the current implementation of SmartGridSolve even less optimal: placing restrictions on code inside `grpc_map()` block just for the rare case of task failure. A better approach to lifting remaining restrictions on code is proposed in Section 12.3.3.1.

12.3.3 Better Approaches to Fault Tolerance

The current implementation of fault tolerance in SmartGridSolve is very simple, and it is far from optimal. It has no performance overhead in case there are no faults, but if the fault happens the overhead is huge. The algorithm inside the `grpc_map()` block is being essentially restarted in this case.

There are three main directions to improve fault tolerance in SmartGridSolve:

- Lifting the restrictions on code inside `grpc_map()` block caused by fault-handling implementation
- Reducing the set of tasks to be restarted to only those tasks that have their results lost
- Reducing the set of tasks to be restarted by reducing the likelihood of their results being lost
- Improving reliability of mapping and graceful handling of mapping failures

12.3.3.1 Recovery from Task Failures. When the task-to-server mapping is found, everything else looks simple at first glance: just execute the algorithm, making GridRPC calls according to the mapping. However, things become complicated if there is a GridRPC call that has failed. The problem is what to do when this happened. Usually, it is not enough to re-run the failed GridRPC call on a different server; some of the previous GridRPC calls results are lost if server-to-server communication is involved. This means that a new mapping should be built and those GridRPC calls that have results lost have to be re-run as well.

All GridRPC tasks have an interesting property: they are independent of each other, return the same results when called with the same arguments, and have no side effects. This means that, in case of GridRPC failure, instead of rolling back the whole algorithm to a checkpoint, we can re-run all GridRPC calls that have results lost with exactly the same arguments as before, and we will have exactly the same result.

In this approach, each GridRPC call should store its arguments in some kind of redo log. Also, each GridRPC call should contain logic for fault recovery: ask an agent for another task-to-server mapping using the same dependency graph and re-run the redo log or its part in case of failure.

The redo approach has the advantage that it completely solves the problem with side effects inside and outside of program state: nothing has to be rolled back, no program state needs to be restored, no side effects need to be discovered. Combined with the preprocessor approach to discovering the dependency graph described in Section 12.3.2, it allows one to completely lift the constraints on code inside the `grpc_map()` block described in Sections 12.2.2.3 and 12.3.1.

12.3.3.2 *Restarting Only Relevant Tasks*

NOT REMAPPING COMPLETED TASKS. The current SmartGridSolve implementation remaps and executes again even those tasks that were successfully completed, and results were successfully retrieved by the client, even if there are no more tasks that need those results.

The simplest and most obvious improvement is to take completed tasks into account and exclude those that have final results retrieved by the client from the remapping in case of other tasks' failure. It is necessary to remap only those tasks that were not completed or have other tasks that are dependent (directly or indirectly) on their results.

The correct implementation of this improvement decreases performance penalty in case of a failure and has negligible performance impact if there are no failures.

INDIVIDUALLY RESTARTING TASKS NOT DEPENDENT ON OTHER ONES. The most difficult problem to solve in case of a fault during collective mapping is the loss of results that were produced by other tasks. But the simple case if there is no data from other tasks needed by the failed task can be handled without a complete remapping. If there is no data loss from other tasks, the failed task can be restarted individually.

The correct implementation of this improvement decreases performance penalty in case of a failure and has negligible performance impact if there are no failures.

12.3.3.3 *Losing Fewer Results*

KEEPING TASK RESULTS UNTIL ALL TASKS DEPENDENT ON THEM ARE FINISHED. Another direction of improvement of fault tolerance is to prevent losing the results of completed tasks. The current SmartGridSolve sends the results of tasks to the tasks dependent on those results directly. The sending server removes the results when the transmission is complete, so the results are lost in case of the receiving server's fault after the results were transmitted. This means that the failed task cannot be restarted individually: the data needed for this task are lost and have to be recalculated by running all the tasks necessary to produce those data again.

Recalculating lost results can be avoided if they were stored somewhere else, not only on a failed server. It can be implemented by caching data on the server that produced the results until all tasks that need those results are completed and have passed their results to the client or to other servers.

This approach has no additional overhead besides using storage for the results for a longer period of time. However, this still results in a high performance penalty if the server that keeps the results and the server running a task using those results failed simultaneously. In this case, the results are lost and must be recalculated by rerunning all tasks the lost data depend on.

REDUNDANT STORAGE FOR INTERMEDIARY RESULTS. To decrease probability of data loss even more, a more generic approach can be used for storing task results redundantly. For example, task results can be kept not only on the server where those results were produced and on the servers that run tasks that need those results, but also on some servers that are not supposed to run tasks that need those results. The agent can keep track of the servers where results are stored and instruct them to send the data to the servers where remapped tasks will be run in case of a failure. The number of servers to store the same data redundantly should be configurable.

This approach can be optimized further by sending results for redundant storage to those servers that are the most likely candidates for running tasks that use those results in case of a server failure, and by taking into account where data are stored when remapping tasks.

12.3.3.4 More Reliable Mapping

REDUNDANT AGENTS. There is a problem in the current SmartGridSolve implementation: the agent is a single point of failure, and there is no recovery in case of the agent's failure. Servers are redundant, and tasks running on a failed server can be retried on another server. However, the failed agent can make the whole grid unusable by making all clients unable to map or remap all further tasks.

This problem can be solved by running multiple synchronized instances of the agent. A server can register with any agent instance, and this information will be propagated among all instances. The protocol of server-agent and client-agent communication can be extended by allowing them to reconnect to another agent instance in case of communication error.

IMPROVED MAPPING ERROR HANDLING. There is another issue that is not directly related to performance in case of server failure, but it is related to the handling of agent failure. The current SmartGridSolve implementation has no way to handle task mapping failure gracefully. This is because the condition inside the `while()` loop in plain C has no way to communicate additional information besides being true or false. If there is an error during task mapping, the client falls back to individual mapping for all further tasks, and there is no way to switch to smart mapping for further task groups, even if the agent became available again. The handling of mapping failure can be improved in preprocessor approach by introducing syntax to handle such kind of failure.

12.4 SMART RPC-BASED COMPUTING ON CLOUDS: ADAPTATION OF SMARTGRIDRPC AND SMARTGRIDSOLVE TO CLOUD COMPUTING

Cloud computing allows users to have easy access to large distributed resources from data centers anywhere in the world. Moreover, by renting the infrastructure on a pay-per-use basis, they can have immediate access to required resources without any capacity planning and they are free to release them when resources are no longer needed. These resources can be dynamically reconfigured to adjust to a user's needs or the variable load of applications, allowing for optimum resource utilization. Hence, the computing infrastructure can be scaled up and down according to the application requirements or the budget of the user or a combination of both.

SmartCloudSolve (SCS) is a Platform as a Service (PaaS). PaaS are platforms that facilitate deployment of cloud applications without the cost and complexity of buying and managing the underlying hardware and software layers. SCS is based on SmartGridSolve [6], which is an extension to GridSolve [3], the middleware platform for Grids and Clusters. SCS allows application programmers to easily convert existing applications into high-performance scalable applications that will run on a number of cloud infrastructures. Other examples of PaaS include Google AppEngine [15], MicroSoft Azure [16], and Force.com [17].

The following are the advantages of using SCS over other PaaS:

- Increased performance: SCS can automatically generate a task graph for an application, and this task graph is used to improve the mapping of the application on the cloud infrastructure, thus increasing the performance of the application.
- Automation: SCS can improve the scaling up and scaling down of the cloud infrastructure by using the task graph. SCS can determine future levels of parallelism of the application from its task graph and therefore can scale the infrastructure up ahead of time to maximize performance. Since future levels of parallelism can be determined, SCS can also terminate servers if they are not required for future tasks and therefore reduce costs.
- Ease of use: With a few simple steps, an application programmer can change the existing serial applications into high-performance scalable applications that can execute in a cloud environment.
- Flexibility: The application programmer can choose from a number of programming languages, and their application is not restricted to run on a single public or private cloud.

12.4.1 Cloud Computing

In this section we will describe the three major catogories of cloud computing. These are Infrastructure as a Service (IaaS), Platform as a Service (PaaS), which is the catogory the SCS platform falls under, and Software as a Service (SaaS).

12.4.1.1 Infrastructure as a Service. Infrastructure as a Service (IaaS) or Hardware as a Service (HaaS) are terms that refer to the practice of delivering IT infrastructure based on virtual or physical resources as a commodity to customers. These resources meet the end user requirements in terms of memory, CPU type and power, storage, and, in most of the cases, operating system. Users are billed on a pay-per-use basis and must set up their system on top of these resources that are hosted and managed in data centers owned by the vendor. Amazon is one of the major players in providing IaaS solutions. Other providers include Rackspace [18], GoGrid [19], and FlexiScale [20].

12.4.1.2 Platform as a Service. Cloud systems can offer an additional abstraction level: instead of supplying a virtualized infrastructure, they can provide the software platform that systems run on. The sizing of the hardware resources demanded by the execution of the services is made in a transparent manner. This is denoted as Platform as a Service (PaaS). Platform as a Service solutions provide an application or development platform in which users can create their own application that will run on the cloud. PaaS implementations usually provide users with an application framework and a set of API that can be used by developers to program or compose applications for the cloud. The two major players adopting this strategy are Google and Microsoft. Google AppEngine is a platform for developing scalable web applications that will be run on top of the server infrastructure of Google. It provides a set of APIs and an application model that allow developers to take advantage of additional services provided by Google, such as Mail, Datastore, Memcache, and others. By following the provided application model, developers create applications in Python. These applications will be run within a sandbox and AppEngine will take care of automatically scaling when needed. Azure is the solution provided by Microsoft for developing scalable applications for the cloud. It is a cloud service operating system that serves as the development, run-time, and control environment for the Azure Services Platform. By using the Microsoft Azure SDK, developers can create services that leverage the .NET Framework. These services must be uploaded through the Microsoft Azure portal in order to be executed on top of Windows Azure. Additional services, such as workflow execution and management, web services orchestration, and access to SQL data stores, are provided to build enterprise applications.

12.4.1.3 Software as a Service. Software as a Service solutions are at the top end of the cloud computing stack and they provide end users with an integrated service comprising hardware, development platforms, and applications. Examples of the SaaS implementations are the services provided by Google for office automation, such as Google Document and Google Calendar, which are delivered for free to Internet users and for a charge for professional quality services. An example of a commercial solution is Salesforce.com [21], which provides an online customer relation management service.

12.4.2 SmartCloudSolve (SCS)

12.4.2.1 Overview. SCS is a PaaS that allows programmers to easily develop applications or convert their existing applications into high-performing scalable applications that will execute on a cloud infrastructure. SCS will give the application programmer the freedom to develop their application using any one of a number of languages and execute that application on any one of a number of cloud infrastructures. Therefore, programmers can focus on software development in their language of choice as opposed to focusing on managing the underlying cloud infrastructures (servers, network, storage, etc.) and determining how the application should be executed on that infrastructure.

By using the simple SmartGridRPC API, applications written in a number of languages can be easily converted into high-performing scalable cloud applications. Applications written using the SmartGridRPC API are interpreted by SCS, which then generates a task graph automatically for the application. The task graph is a directed acyclic graph representing the order, computational load, communication load of each task in the application, and the data dependencies between these tasks. This task graph is used to determine a close to optimal solution for executing the application on the cloud. The mapping outlines how tasks are mapped to the server and how communication will be sent between these tasks (inter-server communication). SCS design also takes advantage of the processing power of each individual CPU core in the underlying infrastructure by using the task graph to leverage message passing, process forking and threading. In addition, the task graph is used to determine ahead of time when to automatically scale up and scale down the cloud infrastructure and can thus minimize time and cost.

12.4.2.2 Advantages of the SCS Platform. The main advantages of SCS over existing cloud PaaS is that you can implement applications in any number of languages and these application can potentially achieve higher performance. The application programmer creates an application using their chosen language and the SmartGridRPC API. SCS applications can be developed in Fortran, C, Matlab, Mathematica, and Octave. The platform is extensible to include other languages. Therefore, the application programmer will not be locked-in to a specific development language, which is the case with most other PaaS. With Google, for example programmers must write their applications only in the Python programming language to Google-specific APIs. "Regular" applications that have been implemented to run on a single machine can be implemented for SCS to execute on a cloud infrastructure with only a few simple changes. In addition, higher performance can be achieved since the task graph of the application is automatically generated and is known prior to execution. This can be used to determine the scaling of the infrastructure and to implement a close-to-optimal execution of the application on that infrastructure.

The other advantage of SCS is there is no infrastructure lock-in. When an application is developed for SCS it will not be locked in to any one infrastructure. The application is "cloud neutral," which is not the case with other PaaS. For example, if you develop an application using Force.com, which is the SalesForce PaaS or Google AppEngine, it is impossible to move these applications to other cloud infrastructures. SCS will be developed so that applications can be easily moved from one cloud provider to another or even to a private cloud.

12.4.2.3 High-Level Design of the SCS Platform. Figure 12.5 shows a high-level view of the design of SCS. In the software layer, the application programmer creates an application using their chosen language and the SmartGridRPC API.

In the platform layer, SCS automatically generates a task graph when the application is run, which is then used to optimally map the application to the cloud infrastructure. The infrastructure is scaled up and down based on the level of parallelism in the task graph. In addition, using this graph the load of computation and communication is balanced over the network and inter-server communication is implemented to further increase the performance. The task graph could also be used to execute parallel fine-grain tasks on multiple processors on the same machine (OpenMP [22]/Pthreads [23]) or on multiple processors on different machines (MPI [24]).

In the infrastructure layer, SCS executes the application on the target infrastructure. The original target infrastructure for SmartGridSolve, which SCS is based on, is Grids and clusters. SCS supports many different architectures/platforms, such as Linux, Solaris, BSD, Windows, and Windows, Compute Cluster. This means that SCS can easily be extended so that applications can be executed across a number of public clouds or

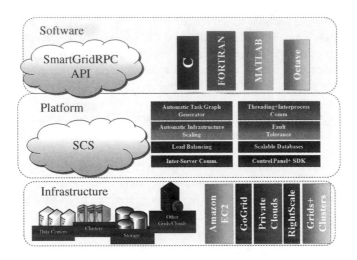

Figure 12.5   Overview of SmartCloudSolve.

even private clouds. Namely, SCS could be extended for other public clouds such as Rackspace, GoGrid, Flexiscale, and private clouds such as the Eucalyptus cloud [25].

12.4.2.4 *SCS API and Application Implementation.* This section will describe how a programmer can easily convert their serial application into a high-performance scalable application using the SmartGridRPC APIs. SmartGridRPC model is the programming model that the SCS platform is based on, which was described in Section 12.2.1.

Hydropad [26] is a real-life astrophysics application that simulates the evolution of clusters of galaxies in the Universe. Hydropad requires high-processing resources because it must simulate an area comparable to the dimensions of the Universe. The cosmological model, which this application is based on, has the assumption that the Universe is composed of two different kinds of matter. The first is baryonic matter, which is directly observed and forms all bright objects. The second is dark matter, which is theorized to account for most of the gravitational mass in the Universe. The evolution of this system can only be described by treating both components at the same time, looking at all of their internal processes, while their mutual interaction is regulated by a gravitational component. Figure 12.6 shows the serial implementation of the main loop of the Hydropad that simulates the evolution of the Universe. At each iteration of the loop, the *grav* function calculates the gravitational effect the matter has on each other. The *dark* function and the *bary* functions then use the result of the *grav* function to calculate their new respective positions. The *grav* function then uses the positions of the particles in the previous evolution step to calculate the gravitational result in this evolution step. This is done cyclically for each evolution step of the Universe that is simulated.

T A B L E 12.3 Hydropad Serial Application

```
t_sim=0;
while(t_sim < t_total){
    grav(phiold, ... .);
    if(t_sim==0){
        initvel(phi, ...);
    }
    dark(x1, ..);
    bary(n, ...);
    t_sim+=t_step;
}
```

Table 12.3 shows the same Hydropad application implemented as a serial application. Table 12.4 shows the same application implemented for SCS. When implementing a SCS application, there are three areas that the application programmer needs to identify. These are the remote computation part of the application, the local computation part of the application, and the part of the application that will be mapped collectively.

To convert a serial application into a cloud application, the application programmer must first identify functions for remote execution using the *gridrpc_call* function. In this example, the programmer has identified the *grav, initvel, dark,* and *bary* functions for remote execution. The SCS system may now execute these tasks locally or remotely in the cloud, depending on which gives higher performance. Secondly, the parts of the application executing local computation need to be identified. In this case, the local operation on *t_sim* has been identified using the *grpc_local* function. The region of the application that will be mapped and executed collectively is identified using the parenthesis of the *gridrpc_map* function.

T A B L E 12.4 Hydropad Cloud Application

```
#include "gridrpc.h"
t_sim=0;
gridrpc_map(){
    while(t_sim < t_total){
        gridrpc_call (grav , phiold, ... .);
        if(t_sim==0){
            gridrpc_call (initvel , phi, ...);
        }
        gridrpc_call (dark, x1, ..);
        gridrpc_call (bary , n, ...);
        gridrpc_local(){
            t_sim+=t_step;
        }
    }
}
```

This application is now a high-performance scalable cloud application. SCS can now generate a task graph for this application and can therefore scale up and down the cloud infrastructure, balance the load of computation and communication, and perform inter-server communication to maximize the performance of the application.

ACKNOWLEDGMENT

This publication emanated from research conducted with the financial support of Science Foundation Ireland under Grant Number 08/IN.1/I2054.

REFERENCES

[1] A. Birrell and B. Nelson, "Implementing remote procedure calls," *ACM Transactions on Computer Systems*, Vol. 1, No. 2, pp. 39–59, 1984.

[2] K. Seymour et al., "Overview of GridRPC: A remote procedure call API for grid computing," *Lecture Notes in Computer Science*, Vol. 2536, pp. 274–278, 2002.

[3] A. YarKhan, K. Seymour, K. Sagi, Z. Shi, and J. Dongarra, "Recent developments in Grid-Solve," *International Journal of High Performance Computing Applications*, Vol. 1, No. 20, p. 131, 2006.

[4] Y. Tanaka, H. Nakada, S. Sekiguchi, T. Suzumura, and S. Matsuoka, "Ninf-G: A reference implementation of RPC-based programming middleware for Grid computing," *Journal of Grid Computing*, Vol. 1, No. 1, pp. 41–51, 2003.

[5] E. Caron and F. Desprez, "DIET: A scalable toolbox to build network enabled servers on the Grid," *International Journal of High Performance Computing Applications*, Vol. 3, No. 20, p. 131, 2006.

[6] T. Brady, J. Dongarra, M. Guidolin, A. Lastovetsky, and K. Seymour, "SmartGridRPC: The new RPC model for high performance grid computing," *Concurrency and Computation: Practice and Experience*, Vol. 18, No. 22, pp. 2467–2487, 2010.

[7] R. Higgins and A. Lastovetsky, "Managing the construction and use of functional performance models in a Grid environment," *Proceedings of the 23rd International Parallel and Distributed Symposium (IPDPS 2009)*, 2009.

[8] A. Lastovetsky, R. Reddy, and R. Higgins, "Building the functional performance model of a processor," *Proceedings of the 21st Annual ACM Symposium on Applied Computing (SAC 2006)*, pp. 746–753, 2006.

[9] R. Wolski, N. Spring, and J. Hayes, "The network weather service: A distributed resource performance forecasting service for metacomputing," *Journal of Future Generation Computing Systems*, Vol. 5, No. 15, pp. 757–768, 1999.

[10] Y. Caniou and E. Jeannot, "Study of the behaviour of heuristics relying on the Historical Trace Manager in a (multi)client-agent-server system," *Technical Report 5168*, 2004.

[11] T. Braun et al., "A comparison of eleven static heuristics for mapping a class of independent tasks onto heterogeneous distributed computing systems," *Journal of Parallel and Distributed Computing*, Vol. 6, No. 61, pp. 810–837, 2001.

[12] T. Brady, M. Guidolin, and A. Lastovetsky, "Experiments with SmartGridSolve: Achieving higher performance by improving the GridRPC model," *Proceedings of the 9th IEEE/ACM International Conference on Grid Computing (Grid 2008)*, pp. 49–56, 2008.

[13] T. Brady, E. Konstantinov, and A. Lastovetsky, "SmartNetSolve: High level programming system for high performance Grid computing," *Proceedings of the 20th International Parallel and Distributed Symposium (IPDPS 2006)*, 2006.

[14] H. Casanova and J. Dongarra, "NetSolve: A network server for solving computational science problems," *International Journal of High Performance Computing Applications*, Vol. 11, No. 3, p. 212, 1997.

[15] E. Ciurana, *Developing with Google AppEngine*. Apress, 2009.

[16] R. Jennings, *Cloud Computing with the Windows Azure Platform*. Wrox, 2009.

[17] J. Ouellette, *Development with the Force.com Platform: Building Business Applications in the Cloud.*: Addison-Wesley, 2009.

[18] Rackspace cloud hosting company. [Online]. http://www.rackspace.com/

[19] GoGrid cloud infrastructure service. [Online]. http://www.gogrid.com/

[20] FlexiScale is the Utility Computing platform. [Online]. http://www.flexiscale.com/

[21] C. McGuire, C. Roth, D. Carroll, and N. Tran, *SalesForce.com Fundamentals: An Introduction to Custom Application Development in the Cloud*. SalesForce.com, 2008.

[22] L. Dagum and R. Mcnon, "OpenMP: An industry-standard API for shared-memory programming," *IEEE Computational Science and Engineering*, No. 5, pp. 46–55, 1998.

[23] B. Nichols and D. Buttlar, *Pthreads Programming*. O'Reilly Media, 1996.

[24] W. Gropp, E. Lusk, and A. Skjellum, *Using MPI: Portable Parallel Programming with the Message-passing Interface*. The MIT Press, 1999.

[25] D. Nurmi et al., "The Eucalyptus open-source cloud-computing system," in *International Symposium on Cluster Computing and the Grid*, 2009.

[26] M. Guidolin and A. Lastovetsky, "Grid-enabled Hydropad: A scientific application for benchmarking GridRPC-based programming systems," *Proceedings of the 23rd International Parallel and Distributed Symposium (IPDPS 2009)*, 2009.

13

PROFIT-MAXIMIZING RESOURCE ALLOCATION FOR MULTITIER CLOUD COMPUTING SYSTEMS UNDER SERVICE LEVEL AGREEMENTS

Hadi Goudarzi and Massoud Pedram

CONTENTS

Large Scale Network-Centric Distributed Systems, First Edition. Edited by Hamid Sarbazi-Azad and Albert Y. Zomaya.
© 2014 John Wiley & Sons, Inc. Published 2014 by John Wiley & Sons, Inc.

13.1 INTRODUCTION

Demand for computing power has been increasing due to the penetration of information technologies in our daily interactions with the world both, at personal and communal levels, encompassing business, commerce, education, manufacturing, and communication services. At the personal level, the wide-scale presence of online banking, e-commerce, SaaS (Software as a Service), social networking, and so on produce workloads of great diversity and enormous scale. At the same time, computing and information-processing requirements of various public organizations and private corporations have also been increasing rapidly. Examples include digital services and functions required by various industries, ranging from manufacturing to housing, and from transportation to banking. Such a dramatic increase in the computing resources requires a scalable and dependable IT (information technology) infrastructure comprising servers, storage, network bandwidth, physical infrastructure, an electrical grid, personnel, and billions of dollars in capital expenditure and operational costs, to name a few.

Datacenters are the backbone of today's IT infrastructure. The reach of datacenters spans a broad range of application areas, from energy production and distribution, complex weather modeling and prediction, manufacturing, transportation, entertainment, and even social networking. There is a critical need to continue to improve efficiency in all these sectors by accelerated use of computing technologies, which inevitably requires increasing the size and scope of datacenters. However, datacenters themselves face the major impediment of power consumption. The energy consumption of the datacenters is increasing and covers up to 2% of the total electrical energy consumption in the United States in 2010 [1]. Power consumption of datacenters will soon match or exceed many other energy-intensive industries such air transportation.

Apart from total energy consumption, another critical component is peak power; according to EPA report [2], the peak load on the power grid from datacenters is estimated to be approximately 7 Gigawatts (GW) in 2006, equivalent to the output of about 15 base-load power plants. This load is increasing as shipments of high-end servers used in datacenters (e.g., blade servers) are increasing at a 20–30% CAGR.

The environmental impact of datacenters is estimated to be 116.2 million metric tons of CO_2. Realizing the perils of spiraling carbon emissions growth, the Intergovernmental Panel on Climate Change (IPCC) has called for an overall greenhouse gas emissions reduction of 60–80%—below levels from 2000—by 2050 to avoid significant environmental damage. It is believed that the information and communication technology (ICT) industry can enable a large portion of that reduction. By providing actors with the information necessary to make better decisions about energy consumption, ICT solutions can reduce the carbon footprint of human activity while improving quality of life. ICT-enabled solutions may cut annual CO_2 emissions in the US by 13–22% from business-as-usual projections for 2020, which translates to gross energy and fuel savings of $140–240 billion [3]. To enable a sustainable ICT ecosystem both economically and environmentally, it is imperative that datacenters implement efficient methods to minimize their energy use, thus reducing their ecological footprint and becoming more "green."

A significant fraction of the datacenter power consumption is due to resource over-provisioning. For instance, an EPA report [2] predicted that if datacenter resources were managed with state-of-the-art solutions, the power consumption in 2011 could be reduced from 10 Gigawatts to below 5 Gigawatts. These solutions require well-provisioned servers in datacenters. More precisely, today's datacenters tend to be provisioned for near-peak performance since typical service-level agreements (SLAs) between clients and hosting datacenters discourage the development of significant performance bottlenecks during peak utilization periods. In order to achieve peak performance with minimum power dissipation under given SLAs, we need to design computing systems with the least energy consumption per instruction.

Optimal provisioning allows datacenter operators to use only the minimum resources needed to perform the tasks arriving at the datacenter. Optimal provisioning is complicated by the fact that, over time, datacenter resources become heterogeneous, even if a datacenter is initially provisioned with homogeneous resources. For instance, replacing nonoperational servers or adding a new rack of servers to accommodate demand typically leads to installing new resource types that reflect the advances in current state-of-the-art in server design.

System-wide power management is another huge challenge in the datacenter. First, restrictions on availability of power and large power consumption of the IT equipment make the problem of datacenter power management a very difficult one to cope with. Second, the physical infrastructure (e.g., the power backup and distribution system and the computer room air conditioning, or CRAC for short, systems) tends to account for over one third of total datacenter power and capital costs [4–6]. Third, the peak instantaneous power consumption must be controlled. The reason for capping power dissipation in the datacenters is the capacity limitation of the power delivery network and CRAC units in the datacenter facility. Fourth, power budgets in datacenters exist in different granularities: datacenter, cluster, rack, or even servers. A difficulty in the power capping is the distributed nature of power consumption in the datacenter. For example, if there is a power budget for a rack in the datacenter, the problem is how to allocate this budget to different servers and how to control this budget in a distributed fashion. Finally, another goal is to reduce the total power consumption. A big portion of the datacenter operational cost is the cost of electrical energy purchased from the utility companies. A trade-off exists between power consumption and performance of the system, and the power manager should consider this trade-off carefully. For example, if the supply voltage level and clock frequency of a CPU are reduced, the average power consumption (and even energy needed to execute a given task) is reduced, but the total computation time is increased.

In general, datacenters serve different (sometimes independent) applications or serve the same application for different clients. If a physical server is dedicated for each application, the number of applications that datacenter can support will be limited to the number of physical servers in the datacenter. Also, allocating one application to each server can be energy inefficient because of energy usage pattern of the applications.

Virtualization technology creates an application-hosting environment that provides independence between applications that share a physical machine together [7]. Nowadays, computing systems rely heavily on this technology. Virtualization technology provides a new way to improve the power efficiency of the datacenters: consolidation. Consolidation means assigning more than one virtual machine (VM) to a physical server. As a result, some of the servers can be turned off and power consumption of the computing system decreases. This is because servers consume more than 60% of their peak power in the idle state and turning off a server improves the power efficiency in the system. Again the technique involves a performance–power tradeoff. More precisely, if workloads are consolidated on servers, performance of the consolidated VMs may decrease because of the reduction in the available physical resources (CPU, memory, I/O bandwidth), but the power efficiency will improve because fewer servers will be used to service the VMs.

The IT infrastructure provided by the datacenter owners/operators must meet various service level agreements (SLAs) established with the clients. The SLAs include compute power, storage space, network bandwidth, availability, and security. Infrastructure providers often end up overprovisioning their resources in order to meet the clients' SLAs. Such overprovisioning may increase the cost incurred by the datacenters in terms of the electrical energy bill. Therefore, optimal provisioning of the resources is imperative in order to reduce the cost incurred by the datacenter operators.

The IT infrastructure provided by large datacenter owners/operators is often *geographically distributed*. This helps to reduce the peak power demand of the datacenters on the local power grid, allow for more fault tolerance and reliable operation of the IT infrastructure, and reduce cost of ownership. A datacenter, however, comprises thousands to tens of thousands of server machines, working in tandem to provide services to the clients; see, for example, [8] and [9]. In such a large computing system, energy efficiency can be maximized through system-wide resource allocation and server consolidation: this is in spite of non-energy-proportional characteristics of current server machines [10]. More precisely, computer servers suffer from significant imbalances in their energy proportionality. In particular, they consume 80% of the peak power even at 20% utilization [11]. Hence, it is insufficient to consider energy cost of operating a datacenter based on the number of active servers; in fact, it is critical to consider the energy cost as a function of server utilization.

This chapter provides a review of the important approaches and techniques for addressing power and performance management problems in a datacenter. The review is by no means comprehensive, but aims to present some key approaches and results. Next, a problem related to maximization of the profit in a hosting datacenter or cloud computing system is discussed and an efficient solution is proposed. The chapter is thus organized as follows. A review of some of the approaches and techniques addressing power management and performance management is presented in Sections 13.2 and 13.3. A system model for the profit maximization problem is presented in Section 13.4. The problem formulation and the proposed solution are presented in Section 13.5. Simulation results and conclusions are given in the Sections 13.6 and 13.7.

13.2 REVIEW OF DATACENTER POWER MANAGEMENT TECHNIQUES

Various approaches for power management in datacenters have been presented in the literature. Power management is strongly linked with job (VM) management (including job migration and consolidation) in a datacenter. As a result, most of the prior work

[12–20] considers power management along with job management. Some researchers use control theoretic approaches [12–14, 19, 21], while others rely on heuristic approaches for power management [11, 15–17]. From another perspective, some of the prior work focuses on average power reduction [11, 15], another group focus on the power capping problem [13, 15], and others consider both of these issues [12, 20].

Two main techniques in saving energy consumption for non-peak-workload conditions are (1) voltage and frequency scaling of CPUs in servers and (2) turning on and off servers. Individual and coordinated voltage and frequency scaling as well as turn on/off policy are compared with each other in terms of the resulting power saving potential [22]. According to this study, voltage and frequency scaling policy results in 18% power savings subject to meeting the performance constraints, whereas the policy that considers turning on/off servers produces 42% power savings. At the same time, 60% savings in power consumption can be achieved for a policy with coordinated voltage and frequency scaling along with turning servers on/off based on the workload intensity.

In another work, Raghavendra et al. [12] present a power management solution that coordinates different power saving approaches in order to avoid interference among these approaches. More precisely, the authors propose a hierarchical approach for power management. At the lowest level, an efficiency controller optimizes the average power consumption in each server by adjusting the P state of the CPU to match the future demand. Moreover, a server manager is used to prevent (thermal) power budget violation in the servers. At the top-most level, enclosure and group managers are used to control the (thermal) power in blade enclosures/racks and at the datacenter level, respectively. These controllers are designed in a coordinated fashion to avoid negative interference in the power and performance domains. A VM controller is deployed to decrease the average power consumption (operational cost) in the datacenter by consolidating the VMs into as few servers as possible and, subsequently, turning off any unused servers. Current server utilization information is used as the input to this controller, which decides about the VM to server assignments so as to decrease the power consumption at the rack or datacenter levels. Moreover, information about approximate power budget caps and any power violations in the previous decision making interval is used to implement an effective VM to server assignment. The authors use a greedy bin-packing heuristic as an approximation of the optimal solution in VM controller.

To evaluate their proposed architecture, a trace-based simulation approach for a datacenter is used that utilizes real-world enterprise traces for server simulation. Simulation results show that most of the powers savings comes from a VM controller, in the case of low-to-medium utilization of servers, while increasing the server utilization makes the local power optimizer more important.

Srikantaiah et al. [11] present an energy-aware consolidation technique for a cloud computing system. The authors report the performance, energy consumption, and resource utilization of the servers under different resource usages. Each server is considered to have two resource dimensions: disk and CPU. They notice that server utilization and performance are affected by consolidation in a nontrivial manner because of the contention for shared resources among consolidated applications. Based on these observations, they recommend doing consolidation carefully so as not to overutilize servers in one resource dimension. The task placement problem, which is a bin packing problem considering two-dimensional resources in the servers, is discussed and a greedy solution is proposed for that problem.

Wang and Wang [13] present coordinated control of power and application performance for virtualized server clusters. The authors present a coordinated approach based on feedback control theory to manage the (peak) power consumption and performance of the VMs in a server cluster. The proposed architecture includes a cluster-level power control loop and a performance control loop for every VM. The cluster-level power control loop measures the total power consumption of the cluster and, based on the difference of this value from the target power consumption, calculates the CPU frequency for each server and sends the frequency value to the dynamic voltage and frequency scalling (DVFS) controller in physical machines. For each VM, there is a performance controller to ensure satisfying a response time constraint. Based on the value of the average response time, this control loop adjusts the CPU resources allocated to a VM by changing its share from the CPU cycles. Moreover, a cluster-level resource coordinator is used to migrate the VMs if they are assigned to machines without sufficient resources. This migration is implemented by a first-fit greedy heuristic to find the first physical host for VMs.

13.3 REVIEW OF DATACENTER PERFORMANCE MANAGEMENT TECHNIQUES

Different definitions for datacenter performance have been used in the published work. Whenever we consider a private datacenter, maximizing the number of serviced applications in each time slot can be used to capture the datacenter performance [24]. This is especially true when all ready jobs can be executed in the given time slot by some server in the datacenter. For example, in Google's datacenters, the maximum number of serviced web queries in a unit of time denotes the datacenter performance. For these cases, the energy cost is proportional to the datacenter performance (energy proportionality is achieved in the aggregate). In public datacenters (i.e., the hosting datacenters or public cloud providers), performance can be defined as the total profit accrued by the datacenter owner by serving every client's requests [34]. For example, in the Amazon EC2 public cloud, the profit that the cloud provider can get by serving the clients while meeting their SLAs determines the system performance.

A datacenter's performance is strongly influenced by the resource management approach used in the datacenter. Job scheduling and job-to-server assignment (or virtual machine management and placement in virtualized datacenters) are two of the important techniques used in resource management to optimize performance, energy consumption, and profit in datacenters. These problems have extensively been considered in the literature. Some of the published work [20, 23–26] describes industrial platforms and solutions, whereas others [27–31] represents solutions presented by academia. From a different viewpoint, some of the publications [23–26, 32] focus on performance, while others [27–31] consider both performance and power dissipation.

In the following paragraphs, we explain a representative work by Verna et al. [28]. The work presents a framework, called pMapper, and an algorithm for solving power and migration cost-aware application placement in a virtualized datacenter. pMapper relies on an application placement controller with the objective of minimizing the power dissipation and migration cost subject to a performance requirement.

Various actions in the pMapper are categorized as (i) soft actions like VM re-sizing, (ii) hard actions such as DVFS, and (iii) server consolidation actions. These actions are implemented by different parts of the implemented middleware. There is a performance manager, which has a global view of the applications and their SLAs and commands the soft actions. A power manager issues hard actions whereas a migration manager triggers consolidation decisions in coordination with a virtualization manager. These managers communicate with an arbitrator as the global decision making part of the system to set the VM sizes and find a good placement of applications onto the servers based on the inputs of different managers. In particular, an efficient algorithm is presented for placing applications on the physical servers so as to minimize the total system cost assuming fixed VM sizes. Servers are ordered based on their power efficiency figures, and a first-fit decreasing heuristic is used to place the applications on the servers starting with the most power-efficient server.

To provide an acceptable quality of service or to meet negotiated service level agreement with the clients, datacenter performance should be estimated accurately. Different approaches have been proposed for performance modeling in datacenters. Queuing theoretic models are used in some works including [33–43]. Other work uses learning-based modeling [40] or control theory-based modeling [21] approaches. The average response time [34] and instantaneous response time [37] have been used to specify service level agreements. Similarly, hard deadlines [37] and utility functions (as a function of response time) [33] have been used to set SLAs. Energy consumption and power management are considered in some of the published works along with performance management [36, 40–46].

In the following paragraphs, a SLA-based resource management algorithm based on the queuing (proposed by Zhang and Ardagna in [34]) is explained in some detail. The authors have focused on a theoretical method to model performance and used it for a profit optimization problem in an autonomic computing system. In the considered system, a centralized dispatch and control unit distributes users' requests to various servers and determines the scheduling policy.

More precisely, an enterprise computing system with a number of heterogeneous server clusters is considered. Each server cluster comprises multiple servers of the same type. Each server offers only one type of resource, that is, computing resource (memory or I/O bandwidth are not considered). For each client, SLA is defined based on a utility function. This utility function, which is a discrete function, determines the price that client pays based on the average response time that he/she receives for its tasks. Generalized processor sharing is used as scheduling policy for each server. Using these models, an optimization problem to maximize the profit in the system is introduced. Profit is defined as the difference between the revenue gained from utility functions (defined based on the clients' SLAs) and the operational cost of the system (which is the energy consumption cost of the active servers). This problem is formulated as a mixed integer programming problem. It is shown that the multichoice Knapsack problem is reducible to the aforesaid problem and hence the problem is NP-hard.

Properties of the profit optimization problem are analyzed and an optimization algorithm is presented for this problem. A fixed-point iteration procedure is employed to determine the optimal scheduling policy, while a network flow problem is solved to determine the request forwarding policy between different servers. A simulation environment is used to evaluate the performance of the proposed solution. Comparison with the proportional sharing mechanism shows 25% energy reduction using the proposed solution for the case of a fixed number of active servers.

Ardagna et al. [35] extend the works in [34] to multitier application placement considering SLAs based on response time and present an optimization technique to optimize the profit. Local search, fixed point iteration, and greedy heuristics are deployed in the proposed solution.

13.4 SYSTEM MODEL OF A MULTITIER APPLICATION PLACEMENT PROBLEM

Modern internet applications are complex software implemented on multitier architectures [39]. Each tier provides a defined service to the next tiers and uses services from the previous tiers. The problem of resource allocation for multitier applications is harder than that for single-tier applications because tiers are not homogenous and a performance bottleneck in one tier can decrease the overall profit (gain from meeting a service level agreement, SLA), even if the other tiers have acceptable service quality.

In this section, a SLA-based multidimensional resource allocation scheme for the multitier services in a cloud computing system (e.g., a hosting datacenter) is presented to optimize the total expected profit. The profit is composed of the expected gain due to satisfying the SLA contracts of the clients, the expected penalty for violating the contracts, and the energy cost (in dollars) of serving clients' requests. In this chapter, we use terms "applications" and "clients" interchangeably.

A cloud computing system comprises potentially heterogeneous servers chosen from a set of known *server types*. Servers of a given type are modeled by their processing (rate of computational work performed by the server), communication (available bandwidth), and main memory capacities as well as their operational expense (cost), which is directly related to their average power consumption. We assume that the local (or networked) secondary (hard disk) storage is not a system bottleneck. The operational cost of a server is modeled as a constant power cost plus another variable power cost that is linearly related to the utilization of the server in the processing domain. Note that the power cost of communication resources in a datacenter is amortized over all servers and switching gear, assumed to be relatively independent of the clients' workload, and hence, not incorporated in the equation for power cost of a server. We assume that the cloud computing system has a central manager that has information about clients and servers.

Each client is identified by a unique ID, represented by index i. Each server is similarly identified by a unique ID, denoted by index j. There are often a set of application tiers that an application needs to complete. For each tier, requests of the application are distributed among some of the available servers. Each ON server is assigned to exactly one of these application tiers. This means that if a server is assigned to some tier, it can only serve the requests on that specified tier. Each application has a constraint on

TABLE 13.1 Notation and Definitions

Symbol	Definition
λ_i	Predicted average request rate of the ith client
λ_i^{max}	Agreed average request rate of the ith client per SLA
λ_i^{EPT}	Expected profitability threshold on average request rate of the ith client
cc_i	Client class of the ith client
sc_j	Server class type of the jth server
$U_i^b(R_i)$	Utility function value as a function of the response time for each request in
U_i^g	the Bronze SLA class
R_i^g, u_i^g, f_i^g	Contract response time target, utility and penalty values for each request in the Gold SLA class
a_i^b	Rate of increasing utility by decreasing the average response time for the ith client in the Gold SLA class
$s_{ij}^{pf,t}, s_{ij}^{cf,t}$	Average processing and communication service times of the jth server for
$s_i^{pb,t}, s_i^{cb,t}$	requests of the ith client in the tth tier for forward and backward directions (for communication, it is independent of server type)
m_i^t	Required memory for the tth tier of the ith client
C_j^p, C_j^c, C_j^m	Total processing, communication, and memory capacities of the jth server
$p_i^t = 1 - q_i^t$	Probability that requests of ith client do not go to the next tier and instead go back to the previous tier
P_j^0	Constant power consumption of the jth server operation. It is related to sc_j.
P_j^p	Power consumption of the jth server in terms of the processing resource utilization related to the $sc(j)$
T_e	Duration of the decision epoch in seconds
C_p	Cost of energy consumption
x_j	A pseudo-Boolean integer variable to determine if the jth server is ON (1) or OFF (0)
y_j^t	A pseudo-Boolean integer variable to determine if the jth server is assigned to the tth tier (1) or not (0)
α_{ij}^t	Portion of the ith client's requests that are in the tth tier and served by the jth server
$\phi_{ij}^{pf,t}, \phi_{ij}^{cf,t}$	Portion of processing, communication, and memory resources of the jth server
$\phi_{ij}^{pb,t}, \phi_{ij}^{cb,t}$	that is allocated to the tth application tier of the ith client (forward (f) or
$\phi_{ij}^{m,t}$	backward (b) directions)

memory allocation in each tier. This means that a constant amount of memory should be allocated to the ith client in each server that serves a portion of the client's requests in tier t. No hard constraints are imposed on the processing and communication resource allocations but these allocations determine the system profit.

To increase readability, Table 13.1 presents key symbols used throughout this chapter along with their definitions.

13.4.1 Multitier Service Model

Consider the ith client with an ordered set of application tiers, T_i. This ordered set is a subset of the available tiers in the cloud computing system. This is a simplified

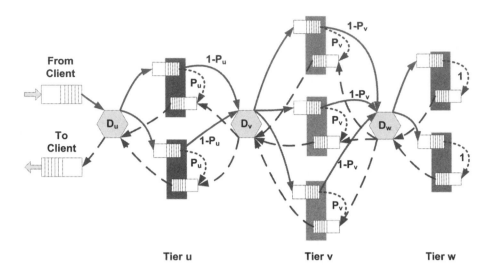

Figure 13.1 An example of a client with three application tiers.

model taken from [39]. The interarrival time of requests for the ith client is assumed to follow an exponential distribution with rate parameter λ_i. In addition, in each level of the application tier, the client's requests are distributed among a number of servers. For each tier, there is a probability p_i^t that the requests do not go to the next application tier and instead return to the previous tier. Therefore, there are requests moving in two different directions: forward and backward. Although the backward requests are served by those servers that previously served the requests in the forward direction, because the backward streams of requests may have different service times, they are put in different queues. In this model, the requests in the backward direction go to the previous tier with probability of one.

Figure 13.1 shows an example of a multitier system with three tiers. D* represent the request dispatchers in different tiers. In this figure, the solid lines represent forward requests while the dashed lines show backward requests. For this case, the ordered subset of tiers is $\{u, v, w\}$, which is a subset of T_i by fixing $order(u) < order(v) < order(w)$. Also, the probabilities are related to the specific client and the selected subset of tiers used by it.

The processing and communication queues in each server are assumed to be in series. This allows pipelining between processing and communication processes in the servers. In addition, we consider *generalized processor sharing* (GPS) at each queue since GPS approximates the scheduling policy used by most operating systems, for example, weighted fair queuing and the CPU time sharing in Linux.

Based on the queuing theory, the output of each queue with this characteristic has an exponential distribution with a mean value of $1/(\mu - \lambda)$. The *average response time* of the requests in the queues of a resource (the μ parameter) can be calculated by dividing the percentage of allocated resource (ϕ_{ij}^*) by the average service time of the client's request on that resource (s_{ij}^*) multiplied by the processing or communication capacity of the resource. The *average arrival rate* of the requests for a resource (the λ parameter) can in turn be calculated by multiplying the average arrival rate of the requests by the probability of receiving requests in a specific tier (calculated from probabilities, $p_i^t = 1 - q_i^t$), and the probability of assigning the requests to the server (α_{ij}^t).

We use f and b to denote forward and backward directions, whereas p and c denote the processing and communication parts of the application. With this notation, the average response time in the forward direction of processing and communication queues for the ith client in tier t is calculated as follows:

$$R_i^{pf,t} = \sum_j \alpha_{ij}^t \left(\frac{1}{C_j^P \phi_{ij}^{pf,t} / s_{ij}^{pf,t} - \alpha_{ij}^t Q_i^t \lambda_i} \right) \tag{13.1}$$

$$R_i^{cf,t} = \sum_j \alpha_{ij}^t \left(\frac{1}{C_j^c \phi_{ij}^{cf,t} / s_i^{cf,t} - \alpha_{ij}^t q_i^t Q_i^t \lambda_i} \right) \tag{13.2}$$

where Q_i^t is the probability of receiving a request in tier t, which is related to the product of the probability of moving in the forward direction in the previous tiers.

$$Q_i^t = \prod_{l \in T_i, order(l) < order(t)} q_i^l \tag{13.3}$$

In calculating average response time for the communication queue in the forward direction, the average arrival rate for this queue is similar to (13.1) multiplied by q_i^t. This is because only requests that are going to be served in the next tier are served in the communication queue of the forward direction of a tier. The average response times for processing and communication queues in the backward direction, which are omitted for brevity, are calculated from equations similar to (13.1) and (13.2).

To improve readablity, we use $\mathbf{M}_{ij}^t$ and Λ_{ij}^t to denote four-element vectors of the service rate and arrival rate of the ith client assigned to the jth server for different directions and different queues.

$$\mathbf{M}_{ij}^t = \left[\frac{\phi_{ij}^{pf,t}}{s_{ij}^{pf,t}}; \frac{\phi_{ij}^{cf,t}}{s_{ij}^{cf,t}}; \frac{\phi_{ij}^{pb,t}}{s_{ij}^{pb,t}}; \frac{\phi_{ij}^{cb,t}}{s_{ij}^{cb,t}} \right] \tag{13.4}$$

$$\Lambda_{ij}^t = Q_i^t \alpha_{ij}^t \lambda_i [1; q_i^t; 1; 1] \tag{13.5}$$

In the remainder of this chapter, the kth element of $\mathbf{M}_{ij}^t$ and Λ_{ij}^t will be denoted by $\mathbf{M}_{ij}^{t,k}$ and $\Lambda_{ij}^{t,k}$, respectively.

Based on the GPS technique and the model presented above, the average response time of the ith client is calculated as follows:

$$R_i = \sum_{t \in T_i} Q_i^t R_i^t \tag{13.6}$$

where

$$R_i^t = R_i^{pf,t} + q_i^t R_i^{cf,t} + R_i^{pb,t} + R_i^{cb,t} \tag{13.7}$$

13.4.2 SLA Model for This System

The service level agreement (SLA) is an important consideration in the system. There are different kinds of SLAs in literature, but we adopt two classes of SLAs: (i) the average-response-time-guaranteed SLA and (ii) the SLA that has a price prerequest based on the response time. The arrival rate of the requests is a random process, which may not even be stationary. If the cloud manager reacts to these changes by limiting the arrival rate of the clients, it is possible to violate the SLA constraints or pay large penalties during busy times. It is also possible that the cloud manager conservatively plans for the maximum arrival rate of the clients, which in turn leads to resource overbooking and increases in the cost of operation.

In this chapter, two models of the SLA are considered: (i) the *Gold SLA* class, which specifies an average response time target, a maximum arrival rate for the client's requests, a *utility* (reward) value for each serviced request (regardless of its response time), and a *penalty* if the average request response time is missed; and (ii) the *Bronze SLA* class, which specifies a maximum arrival rate and a *utility function* that specifies a profit per request based on the response time. The arrival rate of a client in the Gold SLA class is determined by a *probability distribution function* (PDF) dynamically profiled and predicted by a cloud-level monitor. This PDF is used to determine the proper amount of resources to allocate to the servers in this SLA class based on the penalty value set in the SLA for exceeding the response time bound. The expected client utility (per request) for the Gold SLA class is calculated as follows:

$$U_i^g = \left(u_i^g - \left(1 - CDF\left(\lambda_i^{EPT} \right) \right) f_i^g \right) \tag{13.8}$$

The first term in the parentheses is the constant price that the user pays for the service whereas the second term is the expected penalty for violating the constraint in the SLA. Based on the resources provided to the client, it is possible to calculate an *expected profitability threshold* (EPT) for the request arrival rate, that is, the maximum arrival rate of a client's requests that can satisfy the average response time constraint in the Gold SLA class. The Probability of violating the contract average response time constraint is $[1 - CDF\left(\lambda_i^{EPT} \right)]$, where CDF denotes the *cumulative distribution function* of the predicted average arrival rate of the ith client.

The utility function for the Bronze SLA class is a nonincreasing function of the average response time. It is possible that the average response time is higher than a predicted average response time, that is, there is no guarantee for the response time in this SLA class. We use the predicted average response time (based on the most probable average interarrival rate) as the model response time for the user associated with this SLA class.

13.4.3 Resource Management Problem

The goal of the resource management problem is to maximize the total profit for serving the clients. In this system, the decision-making interval (called a *decision epoch* from here on) can be defined based on dynamic parameters in the system. In particular, the frequency of changes in the request rates of the clients affects the acceptable decision time. This is because the solution found by the presented algorithm is acceptable only as long as the client behaviors remain stationary during the decision epoch. Although some small changes in the parameters can be effectively tracked and responded to by proper reaction of *request dispatchers*, large changes cannot be handled by the local managers.

In the following, the resource allocation problem in each decision epoch is presented, along with a solution. However, we do not discuss the characterization and prediction of clients' behavior and dynamic changes in system parameters, as these issues fall outside the scope of the discussion.

13.5 PROFIT MAXIMIZATION IN A HOSTING DATACENTER

13.5.1 Problem Formulation

The profit maximization problem in a hosting datacenter is formulated next.

$$Max \sum_{i=1}^{n} \lambda_i^{max} T_e U_i - C_p \sum_j \left[x_j P_j^0 + P_j^P \sum_t y_j^t \sum_i \left(\phi_{ij}^{p,f,t} + \phi_{ij}^{pb,t} \right) \right] T_e \quad (13.9)$$

Subject to:

$$\sum_t y_j^t \leq 1, \qquad\qquad \forall j \qquad (13.10)$$

$$x_j \geq \sum_t y_j^t \sum_i \alpha_{ij}^t, \qquad\qquad \forall j \qquad (13.11)$$

$$\sum_t y_j^t \sum_i (\phi_{ij}^{p,f,t} + \phi_{ij}^{pb,t}) \leq 1, \qquad\qquad \forall j \qquad (13.12)$$

$$\sum_t y_j^t \sum_i (\phi_{ij}^{cf,t} + \phi_{ij}^{cb,t}) \leq 1, \qquad\qquad \forall j \qquad (13.13)$$

$$\sum_t y_j^t \sum_i (\phi_{ij}^{m,t}) \leq 1, \qquad\qquad \forall j \qquad (13.14)$$

$$\sum_j \alpha_{ij}^t = 1, \qquad\qquad \forall i, t \qquad (13.15)$$

$$M_{ij}^t \geq \Lambda_{ij}^t, \qquad\qquad \forall i, j, t \qquad (13.16)$$

$$\phi_{ij}^{m,t} = z_{ij}^t m_i^t / C_j^m, \qquad\qquad \forall i, j, t \qquad (13.17)$$

$$z_{ij}^{t} \geq \alpha_{ij}^{t}, \ z_{ij}^{t} \leq \sum_{j} \alpha_{ij}^{t} + \alpha_{ij}^{t} - \varepsilon, \qquad\qquad \forall i, j, t \qquad (13.18)$$

$$x_{j} \in \{0, 1\}, \ y_{j}^{t} \in \{0, 1\}, \ z_{ij}^{t} \in \{0, 1\}, \qquad\qquad \forall i, j, t \qquad (13.19)$$

$$\mathrm{M}_{ij}^{t} \geq 0, \ \phi_{ij}^{m,t} \geq 0, \alpha_{ij}^{t} \geq 0, \qquad\qquad \forall i, j, t \qquad (13.20)$$

with addition of equations (13.1–13.8). Parameter ε denotes a very small positive value.

In this problem, α_{ij}^{t}, ϕ_{ij}, x_{j}, and y_{j}^{t} are the optimization parameters (cf. Table 13.1 for their definitions), whereas the other parameters are constant or functions of the optimization variables. In the objective function, the first part is the summation of the client's utilities. If a client has opted for the Gold SLA class, the utility is calculated from (13.8); otherwise, the Bronze utility function is used to calculate the utility. The second part of the objective function is the operation cost of the servers. The total power consumption of the servers is calculated by adding the fixed power consumption of the ON servers and variable (utilization-dependent) power consumption. Multiplying the total power consumption by the duration of the epoch produces the energy consumption. Clearly, the average price of a KWh of electrical energy can be used to convert the energy consumption to the operational cost in dollars.

Constraint (13.10) forces the servers to select only one of the tiers, whereas constraint (13.11) determines the ON servers based on the allocated resources. Constraints (13.12), (13.13), and (13.14) are used to limit the summation of the processing, communication, and memory resources in the servers. Constraint (13.15) ensures that *all* requests generated by a client during a decision epoch are served in the servers. Constraint (13.16) shows the lower limit of the processing and communication resources in the servers if the allocated client uses the Bronze SLA contract. Constraint (13.17) determines the amount of the memory allocated to the assigned clients. Assigned clients are determined by a pseudo-Boolean parameter, z_{ij}^{t}. If α_{ij}^{t} is not zero, the value of z_{ij}^{t} is set to one based on the first inequality in (13.18); otherwise the value of z_{ij}^{t} is zero as seen from the second inequality in (13.18). Finally, constraints (13.19) and (13.20) specify domains of the variables.

It can be seen that the problem formulation is a mixed integer nonlinear programming problem, which cannot be solved by any commercial software because of the huge input size (in terms of the number of clients and servers). A heuristic solution for this problem inspired from the force-directed scheduling is presented in Section 13.5.

In this section, a heuristic, called *force-directed resource assignment* or FRA, to find a solution for the optimization problem in (13.9) is presented. In this heuristic algorithm, a constructive initial solution is generated. To generate the initial solution, clients are processed based on a greedy order and resources are assigned to them one by one. Next, distribution rates are fixed and resource sharing is improved by a local optimization step. Finally, a resource consolidation technique, inspired by the force-directed search, which is one of the most important scheduling techniques in the high-level synthesis [48], is applied to consolidate resources, determine the active (ON) servers, and further optimize the resource assignment. The pseudo code for this heuristic is shown in Algorithm 13.1.

Algorithm 13.1 Force_directed_resource_assignment ()

```
// Find an initial solution
mᵢ = metric for ranking clients;
For (index = 1:number of clients){
     i = argmax (Mᵢ);
     nᵢᵗ = metric for ranking tiers in client i;
        For (temp = 1 to |Tᵢ|){
            t = argmax (Nₜ);
            Initial_Assingmnent (i);
            Update resource availability;}
        Remove client I from mᵢ;}
// Update resource shares
For i = 1 to num_servers{
        (Mᵢⱼᵗ) = Adjust_ResourceShares (αᵢⱼᵗ);}
// Force-Directed Search
Resource_Consolidate ();
        P = total profit;
```

13.5.2 Initial Solution

To generate the initial solution, a constructive approach is used. In this constructive approach, resource allocation for clients is done one by one. It means that clients are picked based on an order, resources are allocated to that client, and resource availabilities are updated. The goal of the resource allocation part in this approach is to maximize the profit that can be earned from each client considering resource availability. This process continues until all clients are processed. Details of this constructive approach are presented in the following paragraphs.

The order of resource assignment to the clients and tiers affects the quality of the solution, especially when the total computation and communication resources in the system are only just enough to meet the client's requirements.

A greedy technique to rank the clients and the application tiers for each client is used to determine the order of resource assignment processing in our constructive approach. For each client, the following equation is used as its ranking metric:

$$
m_i = \sum_j \sum_{t \in T_i} \left(\frac{1}{s_{ij}^{pf,t}} + \frac{q_i^t}{s_{ij}^{cf,t}} + \frac{1}{s_{ij}^{pb,t}} + \frac{1}{s_{ij}^{cb,t}} \right) \tag{13.21}
$$

Clients are ordered in nondecreasing order of this metric and processed in that order (going from low to high metric values). This allows us to assign resources to the clients that need more resources (clients' requests give rise to fairly low service rates) or the number of available resources is lower (clients' requests can be served only on a relatively small number of available servers).

For the selected client, tiers are ordered using a similar metric:

$$n_i^t = \sum_j \left(\frac{1}{s_{ij}^{pf,t}} + \frac{q_i^t}{s_{ij}^{cf,t}} + \frac{1}{s_{ij}^{pb,t}} + \frac{1}{s_{ij}^{cb,t}} \right) \tag{13.22}$$

For example after selecting a client for resource allocation, the required tiers for this client are ordered based on the summation of the available servers multiplied by the service rate of that server for that specific tier (ordered from low to high).

To generate the initial solution, Clients are picked based on the ranking metric in (13.21). The picked client is assigned to available servers to optimize the total profit earned from serving the client. After finding the solution, resource availabilities are updated and the next client is picked for the next assignment. The formulation below describes the profit maximization problem for a picked client (i^{th} client).

$$Max \quad \lambda_i^{max} T_e U_i - C_p \sum_j \left[P_j^0 \sum_t (\phi_{ij}^{cf,t} + \phi_{ij}^{cb,t}) + P_j^p \sum_t (\phi_{ij}^{pf,t} + \phi_{ij}^{pb,t}) \right] T_e \tag{13.23}$$

Subject to:

$$\phi_{ij}^{pf,t} + \phi_{ij}^{pb,t} \leq 1 - \phi_j^p, \qquad \forall i, j, t$$

$$\phi_{ij}^{cf,t} + \phi_{ij}^{cb,t} \leq 1 - \phi_j^c, \qquad \forall i, j, t$$

$$C_j^m / m_i^t \leq 1 - \phi_j^m, \qquad \forall i, j, t$$

with addition of constraints (13.10), (13.15), (13.16), and (13.20) with consideration of previous tier-server assignments.

ϕ_j^p, ϕ_j^c, and ϕ_j^m denote the previously committed portion of the processing, communication, and memory resources to the jth server, respectively.

To eliminate the effect of fixed power consumption of servers on the complexity of the problem, we replaced the constant energy cost with a cost linearly proportional to the utilization of the server in communication domain in (13.23). Even with this relaxation, it can be shown that the Hessian matrix of the objective function in (13.23) is not negative definite or positive definite, and, therefore, it is not possible to use the convex optimization method for this problem. To address this last difficulty, α_{ij}^t is fixed in order to make the problem a concave optimization problem with respect to $\phi_{ij}^{p,t}$ and $\phi_{ij}^{c,t}$. This means that we examine different assignment parameters (α_{ij}^t) for different servers, and the complete solution can be found by selecting the best set of assignment and allocation parameters.

To solve the problem with fixed α_{ij}^t using the Karush-Kuhn-Tucker (KKT) conditions, we need to obtain the derivatives of the profit with respect to the optimization parameters. Taking this derivative for the Bronze class is straightforward and omitted here for brevity. The derivation of the profit function (Pr) with respect to $\phi_{ij,t}^{pf}$ for a client in the Gold class is given below:

$$\frac{\partial Pr}{\partial \phi_{ij,t}^{pf}} = T_e f_i^g \lambda_i^{max} \frac{\partial CDF(\lambda_i)}{\partial \lambda_i} \frac{\partial \lambda_i^{EPT}}{\partial \phi_{ij}^{pf,t}} - T_e C_p P_j^p \qquad (13.24)$$

Note that all calculations are done in $\lambda_i = \lambda_i^{EPT}$ From the definition of λ_i^{FPT}, $\partial \lambda_i^{EPT} / \partial \phi_{ij,t}^p$ is calculated as:

$$\frac{\partial \lambda_i^{EPT}}{\partial \phi_{ij}^{pf,t}} = \frac{Q_i^t \alpha_{ij}^t / s_{ij}^{pf,t} \left(M_{ij}^{t,1} - \Lambda_{ij}^{t,1} \right)^2}{\sum_{t \in T_i} Q_i^t \left[\left(R_i^{pf,t} \right)^2 + q_I^t \left(R_i^{cf,t} \right)^2 + \left(R_i^{pb,t} \right)^2 + \left(R_i^{cb,t} \right)^2 \right]} \qquad (13.25)$$

where λ_i in Λ_{ij}^t is set to λ_i^{EPT} for this calculation. The other derivatives of profit have the same form as (13.25) except that the superscripts are appropriately modified. This equation shows that, the total profit is more sensitive to the amount of resources allocated to a client that imposes a higher penalty value for violating its response time constraint.

The complete solution of problem (13.23) in the case of the Bronze SLA class can be found by applying *dynamic programming* (DP) as explained next. The solution of the problem for constant α_{ij}^t and for each server is calculated applying KKT conditions. Using this solution, the partial profit of assigning an α_{ij}^t portion of the ith client's requests from tier t to the jth server is calculated. Then the DP method is used to find the best case of assigning the client's requests to the servers so that constraint (13.25) for each tier is satisfied. To control the complexity of dynamic programming we used only up to five inactive servers from each server type and up to five active servers from each server type with least resource usage up to that point.

In the case of the Gold SLA class, because the derivatives of the profit with respect to optimization parameters include all of the optimization parameters in a server, it is not possible to find the solution of the problem in one step. Instead, iteration on the solution found by the KKT conditions is used to reach an acceptable γ_{ij}^t for the servers. More precisely, we start with the γ_{ij}^t value obtained for the Bronze SLA class and perform iterations (using numerical techniques [49]) on the solution of the problem calculated applying KKT conditions. These iterations continue until the profits of two consecutive iterations are nearly the same. The pseudo code for this step for i^{th} client is shown in Algorithm 13.2.

Resource allocation in this constructive approach is not final because some servers are turned ON and resource can indeed be allocated better. By solving the problem of resource adjustment for each server, the solution is optimal by considering a fixed client to server assignment. This procedure is called *Adjust_ResourceShares(α_{ij}^t)* in the pseudo code.

Algorithm 13.2 Initial Assignment (i)

```
Stable = 0 and Profit = 0;
While (Stable == 0){
// Find Optimal Resource Allocation for each server type
For (t ∈ Tᵢ){
        For (servers considered for resource assignment to
            tier t){
        For (αᵗᵢₖ = 1/granularity of alpha to 1)
            Find resource shares from KKT conditions ;}}
// Find the Best way to combine resources
    For (t ∈  Ti  (picked based on the ranking metric)){
        X = granularity of alpha;
        Y = number of server considered for resource assignment
            to tier t;
        For (y =1 to Y){
          For (x = 1 to X){
            D[x,y] = −infinity;
            For (z = 1 to x){ //portion of request assignment
                D[x,y]=max(D[x,y],D[x-1,y-z]+partial profit from
                    alloc (yᵗʰ server and αᵗᵢₖ=z));}
            D[x,y]=max(D[x,y], D[x-1,y]);}}
        Back track to find the best solution from D[X,Y];}
    IF (class client type is Gold){
        Find EPT arrival rate and Calculate eqn (13-24) for each
            server;
        IF (no changes from previous step) Stable = 1;}
    Else
        Stable =1;}
```

13.5.3 Resource Consolidation Using Force-Directed Search

To search the solution space, a method inspired by the force-directed search is used. This search technique is not only a local neighborhood search but also acts like a steepest ascent method. This characteristic makes this searching technique less dependent on the initial solution.

This algorithm is based on defined forces between servers and clients. A client that has the highest *force difference* toward a new server (difference of forces toward a new server and the server that the client is already assigned to) is picked and if the required server is available, the load replacement is done. After this replacement, forces are updated and the new maximum force differential client-to-server assignment is made. This algorithm continues until there are no positive force differentials for any clients. Because the total profit in this system is not monotonically increasing, the best solution is saved in each step. Algorithm 13.3 shows the pseudo code of this technique.

Algorithm 13.3 Resource_Consolidate ()

```
// Search the solution space to find better profit
TP = total profit;
Initialize the forces between clients and servers;
// calculate force differentials
```
$D_{i,j \to k}^{\alpha,t} = F_{ik}^{\alpha,t} - F_{ij}^{\alpha,t} ; \forall j, i, t, \alpha$
$\Delta F = 1;$
```
While (ΔF>0) {
        ΔF = max (D_{ij→k}^{α,t});   // client i and α
        j = selected source server;
        k = selected destination server type;
        g = selected destination server;
        If (ΔF is toward an ON server in server type k) {
                g = find the least busy server in k, assigned to
                    tier t;
                If (lower bound constraints satisfied)  goto Re-Assign;
                Else goto skip Re-Assign; }
        Else If (ΔF is toward an OFF server in server type k) {
                g = find an OFF server in k;
                If (found an OFF server)  goto Re-Assign;
                Else goto skip Re Assign; }
        Else If (ΔF is toward a server serving client i)  goto
            Re Assign;
Re-Assign:      Re-assign α portion of the requests to g from j;
                Update force related to j, g and client i;
                P = total profit;
                If (P>TP)  TP = P; save the state; }
        Skip Re-Assign: Update the move limit; }
```

In this search technique, a definition of force is used that is based on the partial profit gained from allocating each portion of the clients' request in a specific tier to a server with specific type. For example, if there are K different server types that can execute tier t of the applications, the force toward each server type (for the ith client) is calculated according to (13.26) for the Gold SLA class and according to (13.27) for the Bronze SLA class:

$$F_{ik}^{\alpha,t} = \frac{\alpha_{ij}^t}{|T_i|} \lambda_i^{max} f_i^g CDF \left(\lambda_i^{EPT} \right) - C_p P_j^p (\phi_{ij}^{pf,t} + \phi_{ij}^{pb,t}) \tag{13.26}$$

$$F_{ik}^{\alpha,t} = -a_i^b \lambda_i Q_i^t \alpha_i \left(R_i^{pf,t} + q_i^t R_i^{cf,t} + R_i^{pb,t} + R_i^{cb,t} \right) - C_p P_j^p (\phi_{ij}^{pf,t} + \phi_{ij}^{pb,t}) \tag{13.27}$$

where k denotes the server type k and ϕ's are the results of the optimal resource allocation problem. Also, λ_i^{EPT} is the expected profitability threshold on λ_i based on the new resource allocation. To account for the cost of turning on a server that is off, $T_e C_p P_j^0 \left(\phi_{ij}^{cf,t} + \phi_{ij}^{cb,t} \right)$ must be subtracted from these forces. These values show the partial improvement in the total profit if a portion of the clients' requests in tier t is assigned to a server from a specific server type.

For each client, forces toward servers having some resources allocated to that client are calculated from other formulas to keep different parts of the application together. This is because splitting a client's requests among servers reduces the total profit in case of equal resources. Also, some time, merging parts of a client's request increases the total profit without increasing the resources used. Details are omitted for brevity.

Based on these forces, the client replacement and reassignment of the resources are done. In each step, the highest force differential is picked. If the selected destination server is not one of the servers that the client is already assigned to and is an ON server, among all the ON servers assigned to the selected tier on the selected server type, the one with the lowest utilization is picked. If there is any available server to pick, the reassignment is done only if the available resources on that server satisfy the lower bound constraints on the required resource shares.

After replacement, forces for the selected client are updated. Also, forces that are related to the selected source and destination servers are updated. To limit the number of tries in the algorithm and avoid loops and lockouts, we apply the following rules:

- After reassigning a portion of a client's request, forces toward destination of this reassignment are updated as a weighted average of the expected partial profit and resulting partial profit.
- The reassignment of a portion of the client's requests to a server type is locked after some reassignment in order to avoid loops.
- For a server with utilization less than a threshold, clients are rewarded to depart from the server (i.e., there will be less force to keep the clients on the server) so that we can eventually turn off the server.
- We limit the number of reassignments to control the complexity of the search method.

13.6 SIMULATION RESULTS

In this section we present the simulation results of the proposed solution to evaluate its effectiveness. The number of server types is varied between 2 and 10. For each server type, an arbitrary, but fixed, number of servers exist as explained below. We consider 10 to 100 clients in the system and for each client the processing power and memory capacity requirements are set as random variables with known probability distribution functions (PDFs) to model clients with different computational and memory requirements. Ten different application tiers in the system are considered. The number of application tiers for each client is selected randomly to be between 3 and 5 and the probabilities of moving in the corresponding tier graph are randomly set with an average of 80% for going forward and 20% going backward. Service times for clients with different application tiers on different server types are also modeled with random variables. Each client is assumed to have Gold or Bronze SLA class with probability of 50%.

To model the PDF for the arrival rate of the client requests in the Gold SLA classes, we use a linear function between zero and the maximum arrival rates.

The power dissipation cost of different server types is determined as random variables. The mean of these random variables is set based on the actual server power measurements. Also, for the memory capacity of the server types, random variables based on actual server configurations are used. The processing and communication capacities of the server types are selected arbitrarily based on the actual available servers such as Intel Xeon processors and Gigabyte communication ports.

We used two different *scenarios* in terms of the number of servers. In the first scenario (low server to client ratio), the average number of servers is $5n$, where n denotes the number of clients. In the second scenario (high server to client ratio), the average number of servers is set to $10n$. Recall that from the distribution of tiers per client, there are (on average) $4n$ client-tiers in both scenarios system.

The proposed force-directed resource assignment algorithm (called FRA) is against a baseline iterative method (IM), which first fixes the resource shares and optimizes the task distribution rates and, subsequently, uses the derived distribution rates and then optimizes the resource shares. This is similar to the iterative improvement approach of [34] and [35]. We also compare our results with the upper bound solution (UB) that can be found from relaxing the capacity constraints in the problem. In particular, FRA/UB and FRA/IM columns in Table 13.2 report the quality (expected total system profit) of our solution with respect to the upper bound solution and the IM solution, respectively.

As can be seen, the quality of our solution compared to the upper bound is quite different for the first and second scenarios. This is because this upper bound solution does not worry about the resource availability in the system and only finds the best possible profit for the case of no competition among clients to reserve the resources. Also this table shows that FRA generates a better solution with respect to the IM method.

TABLE 13.2 Quality of the Final Solution

Client count, n	First Scenario (low server count – high workload)		Second Scenario (high server count = low workload)	
	FRA/UB	FRA/IM	FRA/UB	FRA/IM
10	58%	114%	80%	140%
20	54%	116%	71%	117%
30	57%	120%	69%	139%
40	52%	117%	76%	142%
50	57%	109%	76%	110%
60	55%	107%	80%	109%
70	53%	107%	77%	120%
80	50%	113%	76%	108%
90	49%	115%	77%	107%
100	49%	110%	84%	105%

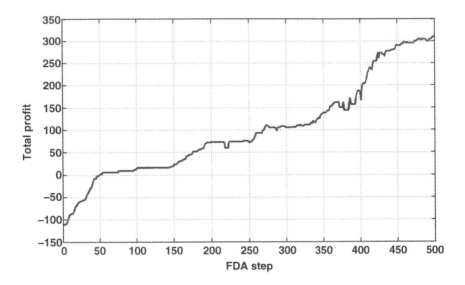

Figure 13.2 An example of Resource Consolidation Improvement in case of a poor initial solution.

To show the effectiveness of the server consolidation technique proposed above, a solution based on the proposed initial solution with the constraint of $\alpha_{ij}^t \leq 0.2$ is generated, and then the force-directed search is used to find the final solution. The trace of the execution for this setup is shown in Figure 13.2. Here the numbers of clients and servers are set to 50 and 250, respectively. This corresponds to the first (low server to client) ratio scenario.

The upper bound profit in this case is 2000. It can be seen that the resource consolidation method based on the force-directed search gradually increases the total profit. Also, some decrease in the total power dissipation can be observed, which is due to the nature of the force-directed search.

Figure 13.3 shows the average run time of the proposed heuristic for different number of clients and servers. Although the average number of servers for the second scenario is double this number for the first scenario, the run time does not increase much because the force-directed search is based on the server types, not the actual servers. It can be seen that, in case of having an average of 400 client-tiers and 1000 servers, the solution is found in less than 1.5 minutes, which is acceptable for cases with decision epoch lengths in the order of half an hour.

To show the characteristic of the proposed solution, Figure 13.4 shows the average ratio of $\lambda_i^{EPT}/\lambda_i^{max}$ for the clients with the Gold SLA class for different ratios of f_i^g/u_i^g. As expected, the ratio of the EPT arrival rate is increased to compensate for the increase in the penalty value. For some penalty values, the EPT arrival rate, is more than the contract arrival rate, which is due to the iterative nature of the resource allocation in the case of the Gold SLA.

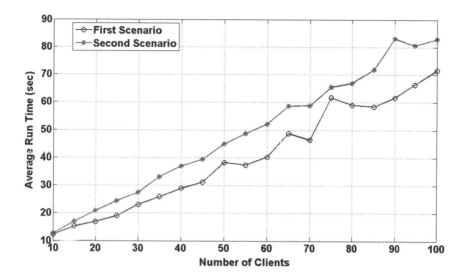

Figure 13.3   Average run time of FRA algorithm on 2.8GHZ E5550 server (Intel) for different numbers of clients.

Figure 13.5 shows the average utilization factor of the servers in case of different P_j^p / P_j^0 values. Lowering the value of P_j^p / P_j^0 means that the idle energy cost accounts for a bigger portion of the total energy cost in the case of full utilization, which tends to result in more consolidation in servers and thus fewer ON servers.

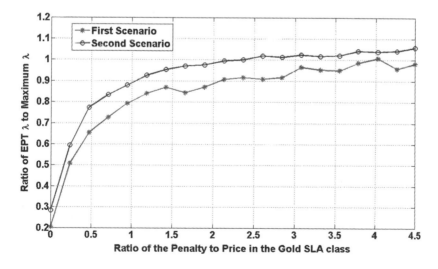

Figure 13.4   Ratio of EPT interarrival rate to maximum interarrival rate for different penalty values for Gold SLA class.

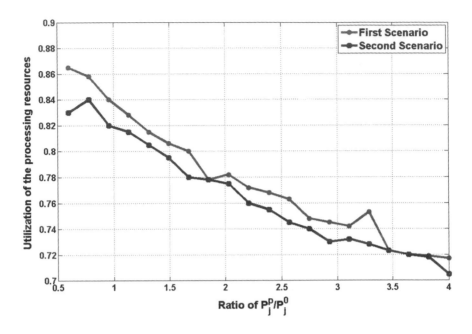

Figure 13.5 Utilization of the servers for different P_j^p/P_j^0 values.

13.7 CONCLUSION

In this chapter, we reviewed important approaches and techniques for addressing the power and performance management problems in hosting datacenters. Then, we considered the problem of the resource allocation to optimize the total profit gained from the SLA contracts. A model based on the multitier applications was presented and the guarantee-based SLA was used to model the profit in the system. A solution based on generating a constructive initial solution and a resource consolidation technique based on the force-directed search was subsequently presented. The quality of the solution is compared with the upper bound solution found by relaxing the resource capacity constraints and the iterative improvement approach proposed in the previous work.

REFERENCES

[1] J. G. Koomey, "Growth in data center electricity use 2005 to 2010," 2011.
[2] Report to Congress on Server and Datacenter Energy Efficiency. http://www.encrgystar.gov/index.cfm?c=prod_development.server efficiency#epa. Retrieved Oct. 2009.
[3] The Climate Group on behalf of the Global eSustainability Initiative (GeSI), "SMART 2020: Enabling the low carbon economy in the information age," 2008.
[4] D. Meisner, B.T. Gold, and T.F. Wenisch, "PowerNap: Eliminating server idle power," 14th Intl. Conf. on Architectural Support for Programming Languages and Operating Systems, 2009.

[5] S. Pelley, D. Meisner, T.F. Wenisch, and J. VanGilder, "Understanding and abstracting total datacenter power," Workshop on Energy-Efficient Design, 2009.

[6] EPA Conf. on "Enterprise Servers and Datacenters: Opportunities for Energy Efficiency," Lawrence Berkeley National Laboratory. 2006. Available at http://hightech.lbl.gov/DCTraining/presentations.html.

[7] P. Barham, B. Dragovic, K. Fraser, S. Hand, T. Harris, A. Ho, R. Neugebauer, I. Pratt, and A. Warfield. "Xen and the art of virtualization." Presented at 19th ACM Symposium on Operating Systems Principles, 2003.

[8] M. Armbrust, A. Fox, R. Griffith, A.D. Joseph, R. Katz, A. Konwinski, G. Lee, D. Patterson, A. Rabkin, I. Stoica, and M. Zaharia. "A view of cloud computing." *Commun ACM* 53(4), pp. 50–58, 2010.

[9] R. Buyya. "Market-oriented cloud computing: Vision, hype, and reality of delivering computing as the 5th utility." The 9th IEEE/ACM Symposium on Cluster Computing and the Grid, 2009.

[10] L.A. Barroso and U. Hölzle, "The case for energy-proportional computing," *IEEE Computer*, 2007.

[11] S. Srikantaiah, A. Kansal, and F. Zhao. "Energy aware consolidation for cloud computing." In Proceedings of the 2008 Conference on Power Aware Computing and Systems (HotPower'08). 2008.

[12] R. Raghavendra, P. Ranganathan, V. Talwar, Z. Wang, and X. Zhu. "No "power" struggles: Coordinated multi-level power management for the datacenter." *ACM SIGPLAN Notices* 43(3), pp. 48–59, 2008.

[13] X. Wang and Y. Wang. "Co-con: Coordinated control of power and application performance for virtualized server clusters." Presented at 2009 IEEE 17th International Workshop on Quality of Service (IWQoS), 2009.

[14] Y. Chen, A. Das, W. Qin, A. Sivasubramaniam, Q. Wang, and N. Gautam. "Managing server energy and operational costs in hosting centers." Presented at SIGMETRICS 2005, 2005.

[15] K. Le, R. Bianchini, T.D. Nguyen, O. Bilgir, and M. Martonosi. "Capping the brown energy consumption of internet services at low cost." Presented at 2010 International Conference on Green Computing (Green Comp), 2010.

[16] A. Beloglazov and R. Buyya. "Energy efficient resource management in virtualized cloud datacenters." Presented at 2010 10th IEEE/ACM International Conference on Cluster, Cloud and Grid Computing (CCGrid), 2010.

[17] R. Nathuji and K. Schwan. "VirtualPower: Coordinated power management in virtualized enterprise systems." *Operating Systems Review* 41(6), pp. 265–78, 2007.

[18] L. Liu, H. Wang, X. Liu, X. Jin, W. He, Q. Wang, and Y. Chen. "Greencloud: A new architecture for green datacenter." Presented at 6th International Conference Industry Session on Autonomic Computing and Communications Industry Session, ICAC-INDST'09, June, 2009.

[19] Y. Wang, X. Wang, M. Chen, and X. Zhu. "Power-efficient response time guarantees for virtualized enterprise servers." Presented at 2008 IEEE 29th Real-Time Systems Symposium, 2008.

[20] S. Kumar, V. Talwar, V. Kumar, P. Ranganathan and K. Schwan. "Vmanage: Loosely coupled platform and virtualization management in datacenters." Presented at 6th International Conference on Autonomic Computing, ICAC'09, June 15–19, 2009.

[21] D. Kusic, J.O. Kephart, J.E. Hanson, N. Kandasamy, and G. Jiang. "Power and performance management of virtualized computing environments via lookahead control." Presented at 2008 International Conference on Autonomic Computing (ICAC '08), 2008.

[22] E.N. Elnozahy, M. Kistler, and R. Rajamony, "Energy-Efficient Server Clusters," *Proc. 2nd Workshop Power-Aware Computing Systems, LNCS 2325*, Springer, 2003.

[23] Xiaobo Fan, Wolf-Dietrich Weber, and Luiz Andre Barroso. "Power provisioning for a warehouse-sized computer." *SIGARCH Comput. Archit. News* 35, 2 (June 2007), 13–23.

[24] C. Tang, M. Steinder, M. Spreitzer, and G. Pacifici. "A scalable application placement controller for enterprise datacenters." Presented at 16th International World Wide Web Conference, WWW2007, May 8–12, 2007.

[25] T. Kimbrel, M. Steinder, M. Sviridenko, and A. Tantawi. "Dynamic application placement under service and memory constraints." Proceedings of the 4th International Conference on Experimental and Efficient Algorithms. 2005.

[26] A. Karve, T. Kimbrel, G. Pacifici, M. Spreitzer, M. Steinder, M. Sviridenko, and A. Tantawi. "Dynamic placement for clustered web applications." Presented at 15th International Conference on World Wide Web, WWW'06, May 23, 2006 - May 26. 2006.

[27] J.S. Chase, D.C. Anderson, P.N. Thakar, A.M. Vahdat, and R.P. Doyle. "Managing energy and server resources in hosting centers." Presented at 18th ACM Symposium on Operating Systems Principles (SOSP'01), October 21–24, 2002.

[28] A. Verrna, P. Ahuja, and A. Neogi. "pMapper: Power and migration cost aware application placement in virtualized systems." Presented at ACM/IFIP/USENIX 9th International Middleware Conference. 2008.

[29] I. Goiri, F. Julia, R. Nou, J.L. Berral, J. Guitart, and J. Torres. "Energy-aware scheduling in virtualized datacenters." Presented at 2010 IEEE International Conference on Cluster Computing (CLUSTER 2010). 2010.

[30] B. Sotomayor, R.S. Montero, I.M. Llorente, and I. Foster. "Virtual infrastructure management in private and hybrid clouds." *IEEE Internet Comput.* 13(5), pp. 14–22, 2009.

[31] M. Mazzucco, D. Dyachuk, and R. Deters. "Maximizing cloud providers' revenues via energy aware allocation policies." Presented at 2010 IEEE 3rd International Conference on Cloud Computing (CLOUD 2010), 2010.

[32] F. Chang, J. Ren, and R. Viswanathan. "Optimal resource allocation in clouds." Presented at 3rd IEEE International Conference on Cloud Computing, CLOUD 2010, July 5–10, 2010.

[33] A. Chandra, W. Gongt, and P. Shenoy. "Dynamic resource allocation for shared data centers using online measurements." Presented at International Conference on Measurement and Modeling of Computer Systems ACM SIGMETRICS 2003.

[34] L. Zhang and D. Ardagna. "SLA based profit optimization in autonomic computing systems." Presented at ICSOC '04: Proceedings of the Second International Conference on Service Oriented Computing, November 15–19, 2004.

[35] D. Ardagna, M. Trubian, and L. Zhang. "SLA based resource allocation policies in autonomic environments." *Journal of Parallel and Distributed Computing* 67(3), pp. 259–270, 2007.

[36] D. Ardagna, B. Panicucci, M. Trubian, and L. Zhang. "Energy-aware autonomic resource allocation in multi-tier virtualized environments." *IEEE Transactions on Services Computing*, Vol. 5, No. 1, pp. 2–19, 2010.

[37] Z. Liu, M.S. Squillante and J.L. Wolf. "On maximizing service-level-agreement profits." Presented at Third ACM Conference on Electronic Commerce, 2001.

[38] B. Addis, D. Ardagna, B. Panicucci, and L. Zhang. "Autonomic management of cloud service centers with availability guarantees." Presented at 2010 IEEE 3rd International Conference on Cloud Computing (CLOUD 2010), 2010.

[39] B. Urgaonkar, G. Pacifici, P. Shenoy, M. Spreitzer, and A. Tantawi. "An analytical model for multi-tier internet services and its applications." Presented at SIGMETRICS 2005: International Conference on Measurement and Modeling of Computer Systems, June 6–10, 2005.

[40] X. Wang, Z. Du, Y. Chen, and S. Li. "Virtualization-based autonomic resource management for multi-tier web applications in shared data center." *J. Syst. Software* 81(9), pp. 1591–608, 2008.

[41] H. Goudarzi and M. Pedram. "Maximizing profit in the cloud computing system via resource allocation." Int'l Workshop on Datacenter Performance, 2011.

[42] H. Goudarzi and M. Pedram. "Multi-dimensional SLA-based resource allocation for multi-tier cloud computing systems." In Proceedings of IEEE International Conference on Cloud Computing (CLOUD), 2011.

[43] H. Goudarzi, M. Ghasemazar, and M. Pedram. "SLA-based optimization of power and migration cost in cloud computing." In Proceedings of IEEE/ACM International Conference on Cluster, Cloud and Grid Computing (CCGrid), 2012.

[44] G. Tesauro, N.K. Jong, R. Das, and M.N. Bennani. "A hybrid reinforcement learning approach to autonomic resource allocation." Presented at 3rd International Conference on Autonomic Computing, 2006.

[45] A. Gadafi, D. Hagimont, L. Broto, and J. Pierson. "Autonomic energy management of multi-tier clustered applications." Presented at 2009 10th IEEE/ACM International Conference on Grid Computing, Grid 2009, October 13–15, 2009.

[46] M. Pedram and I. Hwang. "Power and performance modeling in a virtualized server system." Presented at 39th International Conference on Parallel Processing Workshops (ICPPW), 2010.

[47] S. Martello and P. Toth, *Knapsack Problems: Algorithms and Computer Implementations.* John Wiley and Sons, 1990.

[48] P.G. Paulin and J.P. Knight. "Force-directed scheduling for the behavioral synthesis of ASICs." *IEEE Transactions on Computer-Aided Design of Integrated Circuits and Systems*, Vol. 8, No. 6, pp. 661-679, 1989.

[49] J. Nocedal and S.J. Wright. *Numerical Optimization.* Springer-Verlag, 1999.

14

MARKET-ORIENTED CLOUD COMPUTING AND THE CLOUDBUS TOOLKIT

Rajkumar Buyya, Suraj Pandey, and Christian Vecchiola

CONTENTS

Large Scale Network-Centric Distributed Systems, First Edition. Edited by Hamid Sarbazi-Azad and Albert Y. Zomaya.
© 2014 John Wiley & Sons, Inc. Published 2014 by John Wiley & Sons, Inc.

14.1 INTRODUCTION

In 1969, Leonard Kleinrock, one of the chief scientists of the original Advanced Research Projects Agency Network (ARPANET) project, which seeded the Internet, said [26]: "As of now, computer networks are still in their infancy, but as they grow up and become sophisticated, we will probably see the spread of, 'computer utilities', which, like present electric and telephone utilities, will service individual homes and offices across the country." This vision of computing utilities, based on a service-provisioning model, anticipated the massive transformation of the entire computing industry in the 21st century whereby computing services will be readily available on demand, like water, electricity, gas, and telephony services available in today's society. Similarly, computing service users (consumers) need to pay providers only when they access computing services, without the need to invest heavily or encounter difficulties in building and maintaining complex IT infrastructure by themselves. They access the services based on their requirements without regard to where the services are hosted. This model has been referred to as utility computing, or recently as Cloud computing [10].

Cloud computing delivers infrastructure, platform, and software (applications) as services, which are made available as subscription-based services in a pay-as-you-go model to consumers. In industry, these services are referred to as Infrastructure as a Service (IaaS), Platform as a Service (PaaS), and Software as a Service (SaaS), respectively. The Berkeley Report [3], released in 2009, notes: "Cloud computing, the long-held dream of computing as a utility has the potential to transform a large part of the IT industry, making software even more attractive as a service."

Clouds aim to power the next generation data centers by architecting them as a network of virtual services (hardware, database, user-interface, application logic) so that users are able to access and deploy applications from anywhere in the world on demand at competitive costs, depending on users' Quality of Service (QoS) requirements [10]. It offers significant benefit to IT companies by freeing them from the low-level tasks of setting up basic hardware (servers) and software infrastructures and thus enabling them to focus on innovation and creating business value for their services.

The business potential of Cloud computing is recognized by several market research firms, including IDC (International Data Corporation), which reported that worldwide spending on Cloud services would grow from $16 billion in 2008 to $42 billion in 2012. Furthermore, many applications making use of Clouds emerge simply as catalysts or market makers that bring buyers and sellers together. This creates several trillion dollars of business opportunity to the utility/pervasive computing industry, as noted by Bill Joy, co-founder of Sun Microsystems [10].

Cloud computing has high potential to provide infrastructure, services, and capabilities required for harnessing this business potential. In fact, it has been identified as one of the emerging technologies in IT, as noted in "Gartner's IT Hype Cycle" (see Fig. 14.1). A "Hype Cycle" is a way to represent the emergence, adoption, maturity, and impact on applications of specific technologies.

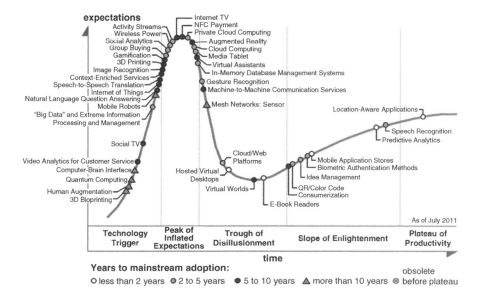

Figure 14.1   Gartner 2011 Hype Cycle of Emerging Technologies.

Cloud computing is definitely at the top of the technology trend, reaching its peak of expectations in just three to five years. This trend is enforced by providers such as Amazon (http://aws.amazon.com), AT&T, Google, SalesForce (http://www.salesforce.com), IBM, Microsoft, and Sun Microsystems, who have begun to establish new data centers for hosting Cloud computing applications such as social networks (e.g., Facebook, http://www.facebook.com), gaming portals (e.g., BigPoint, http://www.bigpoint.com), business applications (e.g., SalesForce.com), media content delivery, and scientific workflows. It is predicted that within the next two to five years, Cloud computing will become a part of mainstream computing; that is, it enters into the plateau of productivity phase.

Currently, the term Cloud computing mostly refers to virtual hosting solutions with some or no added value for customers. This market segment is known as Infrastructure-as-a-Service (IaaS) and concentrates the majority of the big companies operating in Cloud computing. The technology and the general concepts that characterize IaaS solutions are now largely developed and well established, and many companies and users have already adopted the Cloud option to save in infrastructure costs and access huge computing power on demand. The new challenges for what concerns the mainstream adoption of Cloud computing are more concentrated on how to make a profitable use of this technology and how to simplify the development of Clouds aware applications. In particular, there is an entire market related to the delivery of platforms and tools for building applications that are hosted in the Cloud or that leverage Cloud services for many of their tasks. In this sense, the Cloudbus Toolkit for Market Oriented Cloud Computing provides a set of tools and technologies that, taken together, contribute to realize the vision of Cloud computing. It approaches this challenge from a market-oriented perspective, which is one of the driving factors of this technology.

The rest of the chapter is organized as follows: Section 14.2 presents a high-level definition of Cloud computing followed by open challenges and a reference model; Section 14.3 presents Cloudbus vision and architecture in conformance with the high-level definition; Section 14.4 lists specific technologies of the Cloudbus toolkit that have made the vision a reality; Section 14.5 discusses the integration of the Cloudbus toolkit with other Cloud management technologies; and Section 14.6 presents experimental results demonstrating market-oriented resource provisioning within a Cloud and across distributed resources along with hosting of ECG analysis as SaaS on Amazon IaaS (EC2 and S3) services. Finally, Section 14.7 concludes by providing insights into future trends in Cloud computing.

14.2   CLOUD COMPUTING

Cloud computing [3, 10] is an emerging paradigm that aims at delivering hardware infrastructure and software applications as services, which users can consume on a pay-per-use-basis. As depicted in Fig. 14.1, Cloud computing is now at the peak of its hype cycle and there expectations are high for this technology. To fully understand its potential, we first provide a more precise definition of the term, introduce a reference model for

Cloud computing, provide a brief review of the state of the art, and briefly sketch the challenges that lie ahead.

14.2.1 Cloud Definition and Market-Oriented Computing

The Cloud computing paradigm means different things to different people. As a result, there are several definitions and proposals [42]. Vaquero et al. [42] have proposed a definition that is centered on scalability, a pay-per-use utility model, and virtualization. According to Gartner, Cloud computing is a style of computing where service is provided across the Internet using different models and layers of abstraction. The cloud symbol traditionally represents the Internet. Hence, Cloud computing refers to the practice of moving computing to the Internet. Armbrust et al. [3] observe that "Cloud computing refers to both the applications delivered as services over the Internet and the hardware and system software in the data centers that provide those services." This definition captures the real essence of this new trend, where both software applications and hardware infrastructures are moved from private environments to third-party data centers and made accessible through the Internet. Buyya et al. [10] define a Cloud as a type of parallel and distributed system consisting of a collection of interconnected and virtualized computers that are dynamically provisioned and presented as one or more unified computing resources based on service-level agreements. This definition puts Cloud computing into a market-oriented perspective and stresses the economic nature of this phenomenon.

The key feature emerging from the above characterizations is the ability to deliver both infrastructure and software as services that are consumed on a pay-per-use-basis. Previous trends were limited to a specific class of users, or specific kinds of IT resources; the approach of Cloud computing is global and encompasses the entire computing stack. It provides services to the masses, ranging from the end-users hosting their personal documents on the Internet to enterprises outsourcing their entire IT infrastructure to external data centers. Service level agreements (SLAs), which include QoS requirements, are set up between customers and Cloud providers. An SLA specifies the details of the service to be provided in terms of metrics agreed upon by all parties, and penalties for violating the expectations. SLAs act as a warranty for users, who can more comfortably move their business to the Cloud. As a result, enterprises can cut down on maintenance and administrative costs by renting their IT infrastructure from Cloud vendors. Similarly, end-users leverage the Cloud not only for accessing their personal data from everywhere, but also for carrying out activities without buying expensive software and hardware.

Figure 14.2 shows the high-level components of the service-oriented architectural framework consisting of clients brokering and coordinator services supporting utility-driven management of Clouds: application scheduling, resource allocation, and migration of workloads. The architecture cohesively couples the administratively and topologically distributed storage and compute capabilities of Clouds as parts of a single resource leasing abstraction [10]. The system will ease the cross-domain integration of capabilities for on-demand, flexible, energy-efficient, and reliable access to the infrastructure based on emerging virtualization technologies [1, 4].

Market-oriented computing in industry is becoming a reality, as evidenced by developments from companies such as Amazon. For example, EC2 started with flat pricing

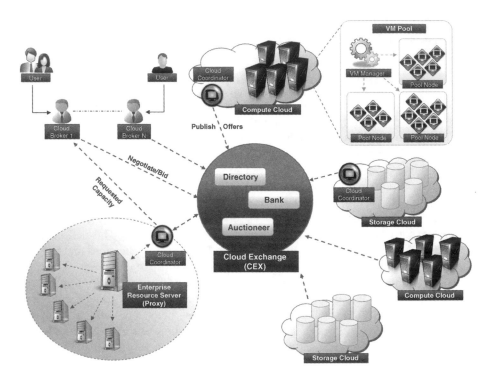

Figure 14.2 Utility-oriented Clouds and their federated network mediated by Cloud exchange.

then moved to pricing based on service difference and later introduced auction based models, using spot instances (http://aws.amazon.com/ec2/spot-instances).

The Cloud Exchange (CEx) acts as a market maker for bringing together service producers and consumers. It aggregates the infrastructure demands from the application brokers and evaluates them against the available supply currently published by the Cloud Coordinators. It aims to support trading of Cloud services based on competitive economic models such as commodity markets and auctions. CEx allows the participants (Cloud Coordinators and Cloud Brokers) to locate providers and consumers with fitting offers. Such markets enable services to be commoditized and, thus, can pave the way for the creation of a dynamic market infrastructure for trading based on SLAs. The availability of a banking system within the market ensures that financial transactions pertaining to SLAs between participants are carried out in a secure and dependable environment. Every client in the Cloud platform will need to instantiate a Cloud brokering service that can dynamically establish service contracts with Cloud Coordinators via the trading functions exposed by the Cloud Exchange.

This is a broad vision about how a future market-oriented Cloud computing system should be structured. The available technologies for Cloud computing are components that can be used to realize this vision. Before exploring them, we will introduce a Cloud computing reference model that provides an organic view of a Cloud computing system and will be used to classify the state of the art.

14.2.2 Cloud Computing Reference Model

Figure 14.2 provides a broad overview of the scenario envisioned by Cloud computing. This scenario identifies a reference model into which all the key components are organized and classified. As previously introduced, the novelty of this approach encompasses the entire computing stack: from the system level, where IT infrastructure is delivered on demand, to the user level, where applications transparently hosted in the Cloud are accessible from anywhere. This is the revolutionary aspect of Cloud computing that makes service providers, enterprises, and users completely rethink their experience with IT.

The lowest level of the stack is characterized by the physical resources, which constitute the foundations of the Cloud. These resources can be of a different nature: clusters, data centers, and desktop computers. On top of these, the IT infrastructure is deployed and managed. Commercial Cloud deployments are more likely to be constituted by data centers hosting hundreds or thousands of machines, while private Clouds can provide a more heterogeneous environment, in which even the idle CPU cycles of desktop computers are used to handle the compute workload. This level provides the "horse power" of the Cloud.

The physical infrastructure is managed by the core middleware, whose objectives are to provide an appropriate runtime environment for applications and to best utilize the physical resources. Virtualization technologies provide features such as application isolation, quality of service, and sand boxing. Among the different solutions for virtualization, hardware-level virtualization and programming-language-level virtualization are the most popular. Hardware-level virtualization guarantees complete isolation of applications and a fine partitioning of the physical resources, such as memory and CPU, by means of virtual machines. Programming-level virtualization provides sand boxing and managed executions for applications developed with a specific technology or programming language (e.g., Java, .NET, and Python). Virtualization technologies help create an environment in which professional and commercial services are integrated. These include negotiation of the quality of service, admission control, execution management and monitoring, accounting, and billing.

Physical infrastructure and core middleware represent the platform where applications are deployed. This platform is made available through a user-level middleware, which provides environments and tools simplifying the development and the deployment of applications in the Cloud. They are Web 2.0 interfaces, command line tools, libraries, and programming languages. The user-level middleware constitutes the access point of applications to the Cloud.

At the top level, different types of applications take advantage of the offerings provided by the Cloud computing reference model. Independent software vendors (ISV) can rely on the Cloud to manage new applications and services. Enterprises can leverage the Cloud for providing services to their customers. Other opportunities can be found in the education sector, social computing, scientific computing, and Content Delivery Networks (CDNs).

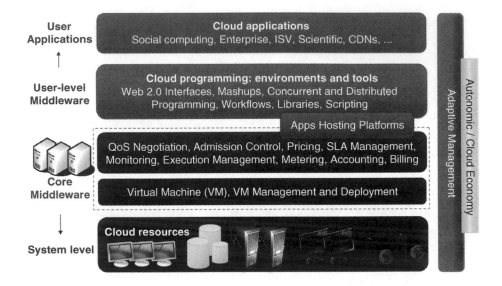

Figure 14.3   Cloud computing reference model.

14.2.3   State of the Art in Cloud Computing

It is uncommon for a single solution to encompass all the services described in the reference model. More likely, different vendors focus on providing a subclass of services addressing the needs of a specific market sector while research projects are more interested in facing the challenges of a specific aspect of Cloud computing, such as scheduling, security, privacy, and virtualization. In this section, we will review the research and the most prominent commercial solutions for delivering Cloud computing–based software systems. By following the previous reference model it is possible to classify the available options into three main categories: Software-as-a-Service (SaaS), Platform-as-a-Service (PaaS), and Infrastructure/Hardware-as-a-Service (IaaS/HaaS), as depicted in Fig. 14.3. Table 14.1 summarizes the main characteristics of these categories and provides some examples of organizations offering services.

14.2.3.1   Infrastructure as a Service. Infrastructure-as-Service (IaaS) or Hardware-as-a-Service (HaaS) solutions deliver IT infrastructure based on virtual or physical resources as a commodity to customers. These resources meet end-user requirements in terms of memory, CPU type and power, storage, and, in most of the cases, operating system as well. It is possible to identify two different approaches: pure IaaS solutions that provide both a management infrastructure and the physical hardware where the infrastructure is deployed, and IaaS implementations that concentrate only on providing a management infrastructure and are meant to be deployed on top of a physical existing infrastructure provided by the user.

The idea of using hardware virtualization technologies for providing executing environments on demand is not new. The first attempts to provide a virtual machine–based

T A B L E 14.1 Cloud Computing Services Classification

Category	Characteristics	Product Type	Vendors & Products
SaaS	Customers are provided with applications that are accessible anytime and from anywhere	Web applications and services (Web 2.0)	SalesForce.com (CRM), Clarizen.com (project management), Google Mail (automation)
PaaS	Customers are provided with a platform for developing applications hosted on the Cloud	Programming APIs and frameworks; deployment system.	Google AppEngine, Microsoft Azure, Manjrasoft Aneka
IaaS/HaaS	Customers are provided with virtualized hardware and storage on top of which they can build their infrastructure	Virtual machines management infrastructure, storage management	Amazon EC2 and S3; GoGrid; Nirvanix

execution environment for applications found in the Denali project [47]. The focus of Denali was to provide a scalable infrastructure able to support the management of a large number of server applications by using lightweight virtual machines. Figuereido et al. [17] investigated the use of virtual machine images for customizing the execution environments in Grids. VMPlant [27] is a framework that embodies these concepts and provides a management infrastructure of a virtual machine within a computing Grid. On the same line, Virtual Workspaces [22] provide configurable execution environments that are dynamically deployed by means of virtual machine images in a Grid infrastructure. An evolution of these concepts is Nimbus [23], which constitutes a complete realization of the IaaS model for science clouds. It is a set of open source tools, which, when put together, contribute to deliver an Infrastructure-as-a-Service solution mostly focused on scientific applications. OpenNebula [41] and Eucalyptus [33] constitute a complete platform for delivering IaaS solutions. Eucalyptus is an open-source framework that turns a collection of clusters into a computing and storage cloud. It provides interface compatibility with, and constitutes an alternative to, Amazon EC2 and S3 allowing users to build an Amazon-like private cloud and to migrate naturally to the public infrastructure later. OpenNebula is a virtual machine manager that can be used to deploy virtualized services on both a local pool of resources and on external IaaS clouds. Together with Haizea [41], a resource lease manager that can act as a scheduling backend for OpenNebula, it provides advanced features such as resource reservation and preemption. OpenNebula and Haizea have been developed under the RESERVOIR project [39], aimed at defining an advanced system and service management approach that will serve as infrastructure for cloud computing implementations.

Pure IaaS solutions are more likely to be found in industry: Amazon is one of the major players in this field. Amazon Elastic Compute Cloud (EC2) provides a large computing infrastructure and a service based on hardware virtualization. By using

Amazon Web Services, users can create Amazon Machine Images (AMIs) and save them as templates from which multiple instances can be run. It is possible to run either Windows or Linux virtual machines, for which the user is charged per hour for each of the instances running. Amazon also provides storage services with the Amazon Simple Storage Service (S3); users can use Amazon S3 to host large amounts of data accessible from anywhere. Joyent provides customers with infrastructure, hosting, and application services. It has been particularly successful in scaling collaborative applications such as LinkeDin (http://www.linkedin.com) and Facebook. Facebook, for example, hosts nearly 300 million users that are seamlessly using Amazon Cloud services. Other relevant implementations of pure IaaS solutions are GoGrid, ElasticHosts, Rackspace, and Flexiscale. Some vendors are focused on providing a software management infrastructure that allows users to best exploit existing virtual infrastructure. Commercial solutions of this kind rely on existing pure IaaS vendors and provide added value on top of them. RightScale provides a management layer aiming to eliminate the vendor lock-in by letting the user to choose the specific virtual infrastructure (Amazon, VMWare, etc.) and software stack to compose for their virtual environment (SkyTap). Other vendors, such as CloudCentral and Rejila, add specific features such as facilities for composing one's own virtual infrastructure or automated application packaging and deployment. Other solutions are completely specialized in providing a flexible and full-featured virtual infrastructure design environment and do not provide bare metal virtual servers or storage (Elastra, CohesiveFT).

14.2.3.2 *Platform as a Service.* Platform as a Service solutions provide an application or development platform in which users can create their own application that will run on the Cloud. More precisely, they provide an application framework and a set of APIs that can be used by developers to program or compose applications for the Cloud. Currently, most of the research and the industrial effort have been put into providing IaaS solutions, which are commonly identified as Cloud computing. PaaS solutions are more likely to be explored in the coming years, once the technologies and the concepts of infrastructure provisioning are fully established. For this reason there are a limited number of implementations for this approach in both the academy and the industry. We can categorize the PaaS approach into two major streams: those that integrate an IT infrastructure on top of which applications will be executed as a part of the value offering and those that do not. Solutions that include an IT infrastructure are most likely to be found in the industry, while the other ones are more common in the academy.

MapReduce [14] has gained considerable success as a programming model for the Cloud. Google has proposed it for processing massive quantities of data on large-scale distributed infrastructures. It is characterized by a programming model expressing distributed applications in terms of two computations, map and reduce, and a fault-tolerant distributed file system that is optimized for moving large quantities of data. Hadoop [48] is an open source implementation of MapReduce and has been utilized as a Cloud programming platform on top of the Amazon EC2 (Elastic MapReduce) and the Yahoo Cloud Supercomputing Cluster. Other research and commercial implementations adopting the PaaS approach are mostly focused on providing a scalable infrastructure for developing web applications. AppEngine (http://code.google.com/appengine) is a PaaS solution proposed by Google for developing scalable web applications executed on its the large server infrastructure. It defines an application model and provides a set of APIs that allow developers to take advantage of additional services such as Mail, Datastore, Memcache, and others. Developers can develop their application in different languages (Python, Java, and other JVM based languages) and upload it to AppEngine, which will execute it in a sandboxed environment and automatically scale up and down. AppScale [11] is an open-source implementation of AppEngine, developed at the University of California, Santa Barbara. It enables the execution of AppEngine applications on local clusters and can utilize Amazon EC2 or Eucalyptus-based clouds to scale out applications. It is meant to provide a framework for scientists to do research on programming cloud applications.

Heroku (http://www.heroku.com) is a Cloud computing platform that automatically scales web applications based on Ruby on Rails (http://rubyonrails.org). Very few implementations propose a platform for developing any kind of application in the Cloud.

Azure (http://www.microsoft.com/windowsazure) is a Cloud service operating system that serves as the development, run-time, and control environment for the Azure Services Platform. By using the Microsoft Azure SDK, developers can create services that leverage the .NET Framework. These services must be uploaded through the Microsoft Azure portal in order to be executed on top of Windows Azure. Additional services, such as workflow execution and management, web services orchestration, and access to SQL data stores, are provided to build enterprise applications.

Extreme Application Platform (XAP) (http://www.gigaspaces.com/xap) commercialized by GigaSpaces, is a middleware for developing ultra-fast, scalable, distributed applications. It is based on the concept of space, representing a shared environment that can be used as a fast in memory distributed store, execution runtime for applications, and message bus. By using XAP it is possible to define policies for elastically scaling applications according to their needs.

SaaSGrid (http://apprenda.com), commercialized by Apprenda, is a software development platform specifically designed for developing SaaS applications.

The Granules [2] project is a lightweight streaming-based runtime for cloud computing. It orchestrates the concurrent execution of applications on multiple machines. The runtime manages an applications execution through various stages of its lifecycle: deployment, initialization, execution, and termination. Force.com (http://www.salesforce.com/platform) and CloudHarbor.com (http://www.cloudharbor.com) are similar examples but mostly focused on the development of Business Process Modeling (BPM) applications.

As part of the Cloudbus Toolkit, Aneka [43], commercialized by Manjrasoft, is a pure PaaS implementation for developing scalable applications for the Cloud. The core value of Aneka is a service-oriented runtime environment that is deployed on both physical and virtual infrastructures and allows the execution of applications developed by means of various programming models. More details will be given in Section 14.4.1.

14.2.3.3 *Software as a Service.* Software as a Service solutions are at the top end of the Cloud computing stack and they provide end users with an integrated

service comprising hardware, development platforms, and applications. Users are not allowed to customize the service but get access to a specific application hosted in the Cloud. The SaaS approach [5] for delivering IT services is not new, but it has been profitably integrated into the Cloud computing stack by providing an on-demand solution for software applications. Examples of SaaS implementations are the services provided by Google for office automation, such as Google Mail, Google Documents, and Google Calendar, which are delivered for free Internet users and for a charge for professional-quality services. Examples of commercial solutions are SalesForce.com (http://www.salesforce.com) and Clarizen.com (http://www.clarizen.com), which provide online CRM (Customer Relationship Management) and project management services, respectively. Appirio (http://www.appirio.com) is an integrated solution that provides complete support for any management aspect of modern enterprises, from project management to resource planning. The peculiarity of Appirio is the ability of integrating into the platform additional services exposed by other Clouds such as Amazon EC2, SalesForce.com, Google AppEngine, and Facebook.

14.2.3.4 Alliances and Standardization Initiatives. Research and activities on Cloud computing have also investigated other aspects, which are transversal to the classification previously introduced. These aspects include security, privacy, standardization, and interoperation.

Security and privacy are a major research area in Cloud computing, in addition to the development of frameworks. In particular, trust has been reported to be one of the most important issues when considering moving to the Cloud. On this topic, Li and Ping [30] developed a trust model for enhancing security and interoperation among Clouds. Pearson et al. investigated the management from the perspective of Cloud services design [36] and data encryption [38], while other research focused on access control to the Cloud and identity management [20, 29, 37]. Security is of interest not only in academia but among IT practitioners. For example, the Cloud Security Alliance is an initiative whose mission is to promote the use of best practices for providing security assurance within Cloud computing and to provide education on the uses of Cloud computing to help secure all other forms of computing.

Standardization and interoperability is another important area of research in Cloud computing. Currently only a few studies have been investigated these topics and the most relevant outcomes are the Open Cloud Manifesto (http://www.opencloudmanifesto.org) and the Open Virtualization Format (OVF).[1] The Open Cloud Manifesto represents an initiative, supported by the major players in Cloud computing, for the promotion of Open Clouds characterized by interoperability between providers and true scalability for applications. The Open Virtualization Format is an open standard for packaging and distributing virtual appliances or, more generally, software to be run in virtual machines. These initiatives are still at an early stage and more research has to be pursued in this field.

---

[1] http://www.dmtf.org/standards/published documents/DSP0243 1.0.0.pdf

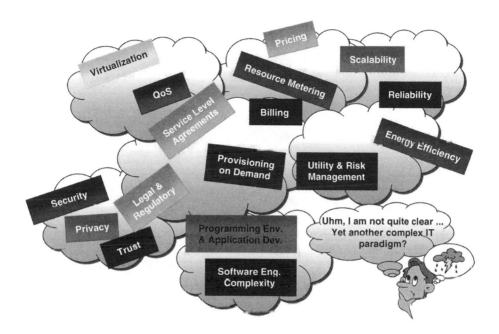

Figure 14.4   Open challenges in Cloud computing.

14.2.4 Open Challenges

Cloud computing introduces many challenges for system and application developers, engineers, system administrators, and service providers [3, 10, 12]. Figure 14.4 provides an overview of the key challenges. In this section, we will discuss some of them.

14.2.4.1 Virtualization. Virtualization enables consolidation of servers for hosting one or more services on independent virtual machines in a multitenancy manner. When a large number of VMs are created they need to be effectively managed to ensure that services are able to deliver quality expectations of users. That means VMs need to be migrated to suitable servers, to ensure that the agreed-upon QoS is delivered, and consolidated later to a fewer number of physical servers when the demand decreases. These capabilities raise challenging questions:

- How does the service provider guarantee scalability to its users?
- How does one make profitable use of virtualization technology to satisfy customer requirements and infrastructure capabilities?

It is a customary practice not to disclose the amount of computer/storage resources a service provider has to its customers. In this setting, a customer may choose a particular provider solely based on its reputation and advertised capabilities. When the service provider receives a large number of requests, it may have to overload its hardware to fulfill them. The challenge here is the capability to manage a sheer number of requests for VMs and the load on the infrastructure [40]. Even though, theoretically, it may be possible to scale out replicate VMs [28], practically any service provider may limit its resources for several reasons: managerial, cost, risk, etc. There are software and hardware barriers when trying to instantiate large number of VMs in a data center [21]. In such cases, when service brokers overprovision resources across data centers with an aim to accommodate a large number of user requests, virtualization limitation may result in violation of contracts. This is always a challenge when trying to balance overprovisioning using virtualization techniques.

A service provider must adopt a technology that suits its customers, needs and matches its infrastructure capabilities. A perfect matching has a long-term effect on revenues, market impact, and sustainability. For example, different Cloud vendors may choose to adopt any of the hypervisors (e.g., Xen, Citrix, Hyper-V, VMware, etc.) as per their service characteristics and requirements. This creates a divide between the interoperability of VM images between Cloud providers. The co-existence of competitive technologies tends to lower the effectiveness of each of them until one becomes a common standard.

14.2.4.2 Security, Privacy, and Trust. One of the major concerns when moving to Clouds is related to security, privacy, and trust. Security, in particular, affects the entire Cloud computing stack [36]. The Cloud computing model promotes massive use of third-party services and infrastructures to host important data or perform critical operations. In this scenario, trust in providers is fundamental to ensuring the desired level of privacy for applications hosted in the Cloud. The obvious questions are:

- How to secure the data and computation on the VMs managed by a Cloud service provider.
- What is the role of a VM management software in ensuring security from both providers' and users' points of view and isolation from application and users' data? In particular, what are the restrictions on obtaining and using statistical data out of hosted services?
- How to manage access to VM images, track the provenance of images, and provide users and administrators with efficient image filters and scanners that detect and repair security violations [46].
- How do we trust third-party software that is a part of the Cloud infrastructure? What are the boundaries/restrictions for engaging third parties in the service provider management chain?
- What are the standards of security, privacy, and trust in computation, data, and identity of Cloud users [36]?

One of the major concerns for the end users of Cloud computing services is the risk of leakage of data deployed to Cloud computing services. A virtual machine manager/resource allocator manages the VM nodes in a data center. As these virtual nodes are deployed on top of physical hardware, there is always a super user (privileged user) from the provider's side who has access to the VM state and the physical node. Any accidental or intentional access/leak of data processed by the VMs cannot be completely ruled out. Even encrypting data would not be of much help as the raw data are processed in the memory. Both data and computations are susceptible to attacks resulting from any intruder's VM inspection or unauthorized VM migrations to any physical nodes. The other side of this problem can be analyzed from the provider side. Currently, any Cloud user can use any software on the VM as long as the user pays for the usage of the services. This user might be running a spamming network/software in the Cloud. Cloud service providers face an unabated challenge to identify and restrict malicious attempts by users of its services. This issue defines a new boundary on the capabilities of the VM management software. If the underlying hypervisor is allowed to transparently monitor the processes a VM is running, the use of malicious software could be restricted. In this process, a service provider may choose to offload part of its responsibilities (monitoring, identifying, and accounting) to third-party application vendors. In such cases, customer privacy is directly or indirectly affected by the functionality and terms of operation of those tertiary units.

Cloud service providers expose operating systems, applications, and utilities as images for public as well as private use. A user can lease these images to instantiate a VM or use the application/s bundled in the instantiated image. Users may customize the image and then store them for future usage. These public/private images are shared images with access rights managed by the service provider upon the user's request. The responsibility of checking the integrity of these images in terms of security risks to other VMs running in the data center lies on the service provider's side. It is a challenge to continuously maintain provenance of images, their composition, and access rights in a large, public Cloud computing infrastructure.

Trusting a Cloud service provider to secure user data, computation, and the compliance terms laid out in the SLA is now a matter of innovation. The tools and capabilities provided by providers to monitor QoS satisfactions need to be audited by a third party that both provider and end user trust. Organizing such a trust network in Cloud computing by not compromising its utility, flexibility, and economy is a challenge.

The lack of and insufficiency of standards in maintaining privacy of computation, data, and identity of end users elevates the challenges in using Cloud computing services. At present, traditional tools and models used to enforce a secure and reliable environment from a security point of view are the only ones available. As previously discussed in Section 14.2.3.4, this area is interesting from a research point of view, and some early work has already been done. These could be used as a starting point for building the security infrastructure of the Cloud for the future.

14.2.4.3 Legal and Regulatory.

Besides security, there are legal and regulatory issues that need to be addressed. Cloud service providers may choose to host user application data anywhere on the planet. The physical location of data centers and clusters determines the set of laws that can be applied to the management of data. For example, specific cryptography techniques could not be used because they are not allowed in some countries. Simply, specific classes of users, such as banks, would not be comfortable putting their sensitive data into the Cloud, in order to protect their customers and their business. At present, a conservative approach is taken regarding hosting sensitive data. An interesting initiative is the concept of availability zones promoted by Amazon EC2. Availability zones identify a set of resources that have a specific geographic location. There are four regions grouping the availability zones: US, Europe, Asia-Pacific, South America. Although this initiative is mostly concerned with providing better service in terms of isolation from failures, network latency, and service down-time, it could be an interesting example for exploring legal and regulatory issues.

14.2.4.4 *Service Level Agreements and Quality of Service.* Service Level Agreements define the functional and nonfunctional characteristics of Cloud services that are agreed by both the customer and the provider. The common parameters that define a SLA are pricing model, usage model, resource metering, billing, and monitoring. In most cases, the desired level of security is also established within a SLA. When a service provider is unable to meet the terms stated in the SLA, a violation occurs. For example, an IaaS Cloud service provider may guarantee a minimum response time from a VM, minimum storage space, reliability of data, etc. However, if a customer does not get the desired response time, runs out of virtual disk space, or is met with frequent errors, the SLA is violated. The SLA also defines a penalty model to compensate the customer in case of violations. At present, the adopted solution for pricing falls into the pay-as-you-go model and users are charged according to the usage of the Cloud services. With constant changing of customer requirements, providers face the following challenges:

- How to guarantee QoS satisfactions and prevent SLA violations.
- How to manage Cloud services to meet the SLA terms for increasing customers and for their ever-increasing demands.
- How to manage SLA in a Cloud computing environment.

The notion of QoS satisfaction varies across customers as every user has its own requirements. Some general metrics from the user's perspective are amount of aggregate CPU power for the VMs instantiated, minimum bandwidth available, number and size of input/output devices (e.g. storage volumes, virtual hardware, etc.), and average response time. Typically, a customer is more inclined to request a statistical bound on most of these parameters than an average [50]. At the moment, no Cloud service providers guarantee the minimum QoS for any of these metrics. From a provider's point of view, it still remains a challenge to provision, manage, and predict the use of its Cloud services in the long run. That difficulty obstructs it to state concrete SLA terms in writing with its customers. With the increasing number of users, most violations are likely to happen during load fluctuations due to the lack of either sufficient resources or weakness in managing VMs at the provider's side. In this direction, Patel et al. [35] have proposed a mechanism for managing SLAs in a Cloud computing environment using the Web Service Level Framework (WSLF) [24]. They propose using dynamic schedulers for measuring parameters, enabling measurements through third parties, and modeling penalties as financial compensations (moderated via a third party) to adapt web SLA to a Cloud environment.

More sophisticated and flexible pricing policies that take into account SLA violations have to be developed and put in place in order to devise an efficient pricing model for the Cloud computing scenario. As services are offered on a subscription basis, they need to be priced based on users' QoS expectations that vary from time to time. The complexity of enabling a SLA is higher in a multitenancy environment [49], where many businesses (i.e., tenants) have varying QoS requirements. It is also important to ensure that whenever service providers are unable to meet all SLAs, their violation needs to be rectified so that customers do not have to bear the loss resulting from service providers' incompetence.

14.2.4.5 Energy Efficiency.
Data centers are expensive to operate as they consume huge amount of power [31]. The combined energy consumption of all data centers worldwide is equivalent to the power consumption of the Czech Republic. As a result, their carbon footprint on the environment is rapidly increasing. In order to address these issues, energy efficient resource allocation and algorithms need to be developed. The challenges are as follows:

- How to balance energy consumption and optimal performance of data centers so that users can be charged at a nominal rate.
- How to choose locality of data centers so that data security, operation cost, and energy consumption meet the terms in the SLA signed with users.

The performance of data centers depends on the provisioning and usage of its hardware devices by the VM management software depending on user needs. As more CPUs are used, the temperature of the hardware increases. This requires cooling of the data center. Hence, performance of the data center and energy consumption are directly related to each other. For every increase in energy consumed, the cost of operation of the data center grows. This cost may be transferred to the users unless the provider balances the performance and energy consumption. Placing the data centers in cold regions such as Iceland is seen to be a viable option. However, there are concerns about the locality of data as users may restrict where their data is placed. Placement and sizing of data centers presents a challenging optimization problem, involving several factors [19].

14.2.4.6 Programming Environments and Application Development.
Cloud computing introduces practical and engineering problems to solve. Cloud computing infrastructures need to be scalable and reliable. In order to support a large number of application service consumers from around the world, Cloud infrastructure providers (i.e., IaaS providers) have been establishing data centers in multiple geographical locations to provide redundancy and ease of access and to ensure reliability [15]. Cloud environments need to provide seamless/automatic mechanisms for scaling their hosted services across multiple, geographically distributed data centers in order to meet QoS expectations of users from different locations. The scaling of applications across multiple-vendor infrastructures requires protocols and mechanisms needed for the creation of inter-Cloud environments.

From the perspective of applications, the development of platforms and services that take full advantage of the Cloud computing model constitute an interesting software engineering problem. The immediate challenges are:

- Should the application logic and its scalability be handled by the application itself or be entrusted to a third-party middleware?
- How to provide application developers the technical know-how and the intricacies of multiple data centers, platforms and services.
- How to define the terms and conditions for licensing the usage and interoperability between numerous SaaS in Clouds.

Numerous middleware are being designed to handle the scalability of applications so that application designers are isolated from the intricacies of Cloud platforms. However, this practice results in (a) applications having to rely on a generic middleware to scale their logic, and (b) developers are usually restricted in following a confined set of APIs to use the middleware, which instead limits the features of applications. If application developers were to know the details of the data center they would deploy their application in, it would make the application custom designed for high performance in specific data centers. This duality is a challenge as Cloud providers would not want to disclose their hardware details and application developers are limited using APIs from third-party middleware. For SaaS providers, licensing has become a major issue. Moving an application to a public Cloud would make proprietary software accessible to millions. This is a challenge as software vendors are wondering how to respect the boundaries of Open Source technologies and licensed software in Clouds, while making them interoperable.

14.2.4.7 Applications on Clouds. At present there are numerous real-world applications that are running on distributed clusters around the world. However, only a few of them would be able to utilize Cloud resources with minor modifications. This is due to the fact that legacy applications were designed to operate on physical hardware with heavy optimizations targeting storage, input/output, communication, and so on. Cloud computing offers a different paradigm where traditional assumptions about hardware devices and software models may not always work. Input/output throughput, for example, may be different depending upon the location of the VM instance allocated for an application and the storage hardware used. Similarly, other attributes of an application, such as user experience, distribution, and maintenance, have new issues when applications are moved to Clouds. The questions that are important to ask before moving applications to Clouds are:

- How does one map application attributes to Cloud attributes [13]?
- Are all applications "Cloud ready"?
- Should an application use multiple Cloud services or a single Cloud service provider?

Application attributes, such as data requirements, platform, communication, distribution, and security, may be related to different layers of the Cloud stack. It may satisfy the requirements by combining services from different Cloud vendors. However, combining different service providers brings with it higher cost, risks, managerial difficulties, and interoperation issues. Applications need to be "Cloud ready" before they can reap the benefit of what Cloud computing has to provide.

14.2.4.8 Standardization. As the Cloud is becoming a commonly used environment for hosting applications, numerous tools and services are available for use from each vendor. Due to a lack of standardization, these tools are not fully compatible with each other. This only accelerates the divide between Cloud service providers, limiting the interoperability between services hosted by each provider. For example, an application may need to implement ad hoc connectors to utilize IaaS solutions from different vendors.

As already introduced in Section 14.2.3.4, an effort towards standardization is the Open Virtualization Format (OVF), an open standard for packaging and distributing virtual appliances or more generally software to be run in virtual machines. Although major representative companies in the field (Microsoft, IBM, Dell, HP, VMware, and XenSource) are supporting the initiative, which resulted in a preliminary standard by the Distributed Management Task Force, the OVF specification only captures the static representation of a virtual instance. Hence, it is mostly used as canonical way of distributing virtual machine images. Many vendors and implementations simply use OVF as an import format and convert it into their specific runtime format when running the image. In the management layer of the Cloud computing stack, the OGF Open Cloud Computing Interface (OCCI) is working towards specifications for remote management of Cloud computing services. Their specification would help standardize the development of tools that govern the functionality of deployment, scaling, and monitoring of VMs and/or workloads running as part of elastic Cloud services.

Standardizing every aspect of IaaS, PaaS, or SaaS is challenging. Vendors try to make their products different from their competitors' to gain a better market share. Having a unique and highly regarded capability usually draws lots of customers initially. However, after many companies evolve and the capability is common among all vendors, it becomes a standard. But until that happens, users may not be able to utilize existing capabilities across all Cloud service providers. Standardizing on a single Cloud provider can lead to data lock-in or application architecture or application development lock-in [32]. Additional effort has to be put toward defining and enforcing standards for both customers' and service providers' satisfaction.

These are some of the key challenges that need to be addressed for a successful adoption of the Cloud computing paradigm into the mainstream IT industry. R&D initiatives in both academia and industry are playing an important role in addressing these challenges. In particular, the outcome of such research in terms of models, software frameworks, and applications constitute the first tools that can be used to experience Cloud computing. The Cloudbus Toolkit is a step towards this goal.

14.3 CLOUDBUS: VISION AND ARCHITECTURE

Figure 14.5 provides a glimpse of the future of Cloud computing. A Cloud marketplace, composed of different types of Clouds such as computing, storage, and content delivery Clouds, will be available to end users and enterprises.

Users can interact with the Cloud market either transparently, by using applications that leverage the Cloud, or explicitly, by making resource requests according to application needs. At present, it is the responsibility of the users to directly interact with the Cloud provider. In the context of a real Cloud marketplace, users will indirectly interact with Cloud providers, but they will rely on a market maker or meta-broker component, which is in charge of providing the best service according to the budget and the constraints of users. A Cloud broker client, directly embedded within applications, or available as a separate tool, will interact with the market maker by specifying the desired Quality of Service parameters through a Service Level Agreement. As a result of the query, the meta-broker will select the best option available among all the Cloud providers belonging to the Cloud marketplace. Such interaction will take place through native interfaces exposed by the provider or via standardized brokering services.

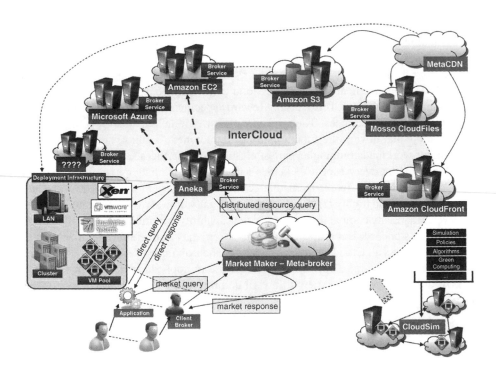

Figure 14.5   Cloud computing marketplace.

In order to increase their chances of providing a better service to customers, different Cloud providers could establish peering arrangements among themselves in order to off-load to (or serve from) other providers service requests. Such peering arrangements will define a Cloud federation and foster the introduction of standard interface and policies for the interconnection of heterogeneous Clouds. The integration of different technologies and solutions into a single value offering will be the key to the success of the Cloud marketplace. PaaS solutions, such as Aneka [43], could rely on different providers for leveraging the workload and balance the use of private resources by provisioning virtual resources from public Clouds. This approach applies for compute intensive, storage, and content delivery. MetaCDN [6], which is a Content Delivery Cloud, aims to provide a unified access to different storage Clouds in order to deliver better service to end-users and maximize its utility.

The scenario projected by using the Cloud marketplace has its own challenges. Some of them have been already discussed in Section 14.2.4. In order to make this vision a reality, a considerable amount of research needs to be carried out through vigorous experiments. Simulation environments will help researchers in conducting repeatable and controllable experiments, while devising new policies and algorithms for resource provisioning or new strategies for an effective and energy-efficient use of physical resources. A simulation toolkit should support modeling of any possible scenario and any layer of the Cloud computing reference model: from the fundamental components of the infrastructure, such as physical nodes, data centers, and virtual machines, to the high-level services offered to end users. This will help researchers to finely reproduce the problem frame they want to solve and to obtain reliable results.

The Cloudbus Toolkit is a collection of technologies and components that comprehensively try to address the challenges involved in making this vision a concrete reality. Figure 14.6 provides a layered view of the entire toolkit and puts it into the context of a real Cloud marketplace. At the top of the stack, real-life applications belonging to different scenarios (finance, science, education, engineering, multimedia, and others) leverage the Cloud horsepower. Resources available in the Cloud are acquired by means of third-party brokering services that mediate the access to the real infrastructure. The Cloudbus toolkit mostly operates at this level by providing a service brokering infrastructure and a core middleware for deploying applications in the Cloud. For what concerns the brokering service, the Market maker is the component that allows users to take full advantage of the Cloud marketplace. The Market maker relies on different middleware implementations to fulfill the requests of users: these can be Cloudbus technologies or third-party implementations. Figure 14.6 provides a breakdown of the components that constitute the Cloudbus middleware. Technologies such as Aneka and Workflow Engine provide services for executing applications in the Cloud. These can be public Clouds, private intranets, or data centers that can all be uniformly managed within an InterCloud [16] realm.

In the following sections, we will present more details about the Cloudbus toolkit initiative and describe how they can integrate with each other and existing technologies in order to realize the vision of a global Cloud computing marketplace.

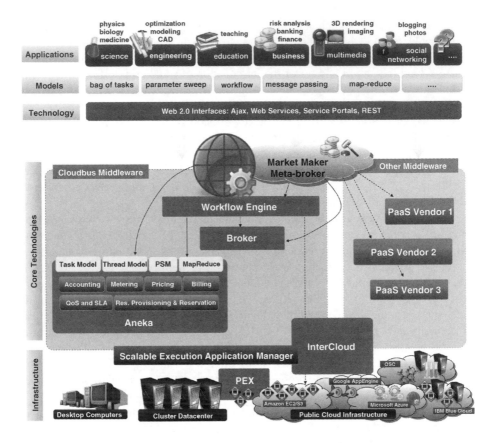

Figure 14.6 The Cloudbus Toolkit: A layered view of technologies and components for market oriented Cloud computing available within the Cloudbus toolkit.

14.4 CLOUDBUS AND CLOUDS LAB TECHNOLOGIES

The CLOUDS Lab designs and develops Cloud computing technologies to support science, engineering, business, creative media, and consumer applications. A summary of various Cloudbus technologies is listed in Table 14.2. In this section, we briefly describe each of these technologies.

14.4.1 Aneka

Aneka [43] is a Platform-as-a-Service solution for Cloud computing and provides a software platform for developing and deploying applications in the Cloud. The core features of Aneka are (a) a configurable software container constituting the building blocks of the Cloud; (b) an open-ended set of programming models available to developers to express distributed applications; (c) a collection of tools for rapidly prototyping and porting ap-

T A B L E 14.2 Components of the Cloudbus Toolkit

Technology	Description
Aneka	A software platform for developing and deploying Cloud computing applications.
Broker	A middleware for scheduling distributed applications across Windows and Unix-variant distributed resources.
Workflow Management System	A middleware that handles dependent tasks, implements scheduling algorithms, and manages the execution of applications on distributed resources.
Market Maker/ Meta-Broker	A matchmaker that matches users' requirements with service provider's capabilities at a common marketplace.
InterCloud	A model that links various Cloud providers through peering arrangements to enable inter-Cloud resource sharing.
MetaCDN	A system that intelligently places users' content onto "Storage Cloud" resources based on their QoS and budget preferences.
Data Center Optimization	Adaptive allocations of compute, storage, and network resources to virtual machines and appliances.
Energy Efficient Computing	Research on developing techniques and technologies for addressing scalability and energy efficiency.
CloudSim	A simulation toolkit that helps users model compute, storage, network, and other related components of Cloud data centers.

plications to the Cloud; and (d) a set of advanced services that put the horse power of Aneka in a market oriented perspective.

One of the elements that makes Aneka unique is its flexible design and high level of customization, allowing it to target different application scenarios: education, engineering, scientific computing, and financial applications. The Aneka container, which is the core component of any Aneka-based Cloud, can be deployed into any computing resource connected to the Internet, whether it be physical or virtual. This makes the integration with public and private Clouds transparent; and specific services for dynamic provisioning of resources are built into the framework in order to exploit the horse power of the Cloud. A collection of standardized interfaces, such as web services, make Aneka completely integrable with client applications and third-party brokering services that can negotiate the desired QoS and submit applications to Aneka Clouds.

14.4.2 Brokers: Harnessing Cloud and Other Distributed Resources

The Gridbus Resource Broker [44] is a market-oriented meta-scheduler for Computational and Data Grids, with support for a wide range of remote resource access services offered via various traditional middleware technologies such as Aneka [43], PBS, Globus, and SGE. It has been extended to provide compute and storage services offered by public Clouds such as Amazon EC2. The broker supports various application models such as parameter sweep, workflow, parallel tasks, and bag of tasks.

The broker takes care of many functions that distributed applications require, including discovering the right resources for a particular user application, scheduling jobs in order to meet deadlines, and handling faults that may occur during execution. In particular, the broker provides capabilities such as resource selection, job scheduling, job management, and data access to any application that requires distributed Grid resources for execution. The broker handles communication with the resources running different middleware, job failures, varying resource availability, and different user objectives such as meeting a deadline for execution or limiting execution within a certain budget.

The broker also provides QoS parameters in its service description for applications requiring a mix of public and private Cloud resources. Users specify QoS values for their applications at the broker's interface. The broker schedules the applications onto distributed resources comprising of local resources and Cloud resources to meet users QoS requirements. It facilitates dynamic provisioning policies where part of application workload can be moved to public Clouds and the remaining can be executed in the local resources. The division of workload is, however, dependent on the budget/deadline of the application and the capabilities of local resources to execute the application.

14.4.3 Workflow Engine

The Workflow Management System (WMS) [34] aids users by enabling their applications to be represented as a workflow and then executed on the Cloud from a higher level of abstraction. The WMS provides an easy-to-use workflow editor for application composition, an XML-based workflow language for structured representation, and a user-friendly portal with discovery, monitoring, and scheduling components. It can leverage Aneka [43] as well as the Gridbus Broker [44] to manage applications running on distributed resources. These tools, put together, enable users to select distributed resources on Clouds, upload/download a huge amount of data to/from selected resources, execute applications on distributed resources using various scheduling algorithms, and monitor the progress of applications in real-time.

A typical scenario is when the workflow engine is hosted as a PaaS and is using various other Cloud services, such as storage, content distribution, and so forth. In this case, users may submit applications via a web application running on Google App Engine, which delegates the requests to the workflow engine running in Amazon EC2. The application is billed using a SaaS application hosted by Salesforce.com. Other enterprise networks could use the workflow engine and submit jobs to Aneka Enterprise Cloud.

Our recent focus has been on managing data-intensive applications using the workflow engine in Clouds. We have developed several heuristics for scheduling workflow applications by leveraging distributed data retrievals. In contrast to using a single data source, we transfer segments of data from all available sources (to a compute resource for processing) in proportion to the cost of data transfer from the data storage locations. Hence, we schedule workflow tasks to resources and transfer data in order to minimize the total data transfer cost. We have particle swarm optimization (PSO-based), nonlinear programming (NLP-based), and probe-based heuristics for data retrieval and task scheduling.

Reliability of service providers is also one of the parameters that needs attention when using Cloud services. We have developed scheduling heuristics for workflow applications based on reliability. The WMS has been used for several real-world applications such as fMRI brain imaging analysis [34], evolutionary multi-objective optimizations using distributed resources, and intrusion detection systems with various models.

14.4.4 Market Maker/Meta-broker

Market Maker/Meta-broker [18] is a part of Cloud infrastructure that works on behalf of both Cloud users and Cloud service providers. It mediates access to distributed resources by discovering suitable Cloud providers for a given user application and attempts to optimally map the requirements of users to published services. The Market Maker is part of a global marketplace where service providers and consumers join to find suitable matches for each other. It provides various services to its customers such as resource discovery, meta-scheduler, reservation service, queuing service, accounting, and pricing services.

User application brokers send requests for resources using the Cloud Exchange User Interface. The meta-broker discovers available resources and starts matching users' requirements (application broker for the meta-broker) to resource providers' capabilities. Upon suitable matching and reservation of resources, the user is notified of the available time slots. Users can directly use these resources to execute their jobs.

14.4.5 InterCloud

In the coming years, users will be able to see a plethora of Cloud several providers around the world desperate to provide resources such as computers, data, and instruments to scale science, engineering, and business applications. In the long run, these Clouds may require sharing their loads with other Cloud service providers as users may select various Cloud services to work on their applications, collectively. Therefore, dispersed Cloud initiatives may lead to the creation of disparate Clouds with little or no interaction between them. The InterCloud model [16] will (a) promote interlinking of islands of Clouds through peering arrangements to enable inter-Cloud resource sharing; (b) provide a scalable structure for Clouds that allow them to interconnect with one another and grow in a sustainable way; and (c) create a global Cyber infrastructure to support e-Science and e-Business applications.

14.4.6 MetaCDN

MetaCDN [6] is a system that exploits "Storage Cloud" resources offered by multiple IaaS vendors, thus creating an integrated overlay network that provides a low-cost, high-performance CDN for content creators. It removes the complexity of dealing with multiple storage providers by intelligently matching and placing the content provided by users onto one or many storage providers based on their quality of service, coverage, and budget preferences. By using a single unified namespace, it helps users to harness the performance and coverage of numerous "Storage Clouds".

In the MetaCDN service, users can use the web portal or the SOAP and RESTful Web Services to deploy content to geographically distributed locations as per their requirements, manage replica distribution according to their storage and data communication budget, and view and modify existing distributed content.

14.4.7   Data Center Optimization

Data centers form the core part of any Cloud infrastructure. They host compute, storage, and network hardware where virtual machines are instantiated and leased to the users on demand. When allocating hardware to real-time/reserved requests, it becomes absolutely critical to use an adaptive algorithm such that the total cost of allocation is minimized. For instance, instantiating VMs in random machines may lead to too many machines being turned ON with least resource utilization. Likewise, if VMs are targeted to only few racks, a "hot spot" could lead to higher power consumption or hardware overload. Thus allocation should take into account the QoS requirements of users and not overprovision resources on any single hardware. Allocation of virtual machines onto physical machines with multiobjective optimization is a challenging problem [45].

14.4.8   Energy-Efficient Computing

In order to support elastic applications, Cloud infrastructure providers are establishing Data Centers in multiple geographic locations. These Data Centers are expensive to operate since they consume significant amount of electric power. For instance, the energy consumption of Google Data Center is equivalent to the power consumption of cities such as San Francisco. This is not only increasing the power bills, but also contributing to global warming due to its high carbon footprint. Indeed, the ICT sector is currently responsible for about 2% of global greenhouse gas emissions.

In our current research, we are investigating and developing novel techniques and technologies for addressing challenges of application scalability and energy efficiency with the aim of making a significant impact on industry, producing service-oriented green ICT technologies. As part of this, we explored power-aware scheduling [25], which is one of the ways to reduce energy consumption when using large data centers. Our scheduling algorithms select appropriate supply voltages of processing elements to minimize energy consumption. As energy consumption is optimized, operational cost decreases and the reliability of the system increases.

In a typical scenario, users send requests for VM provisioning to the global managers. The global managers exchange information for energy-efficient VM allocation and migration. This information is shared with the local managers, which in turn control the VMs in the physical nodes.

14.4.9   CloudSim

The CloudSim toolkit [9] enables users to model and simulate extensible Clouds as well as execute applications on top of Clouds. As a completely customizable tool, it allows extension and definition of policies in all the components of the software stack. This makes it suitable as a research tool as it can relieve users from handling the complexities arising from provisioning, deploying, and configuring real resources in physical environments.

CloudSim offers the following novel features: (i) support for modeling and simulation of large-scale Cloud computing infrastructure, including data centers on a single physical computing node; and (ii) a self-contained platform for modeling data centers, service brokers, scheduling, and allocations policies. To enable the simulation of data centers, CloudSim provides (i) virtualization engine, which helps the creation and management of multiple, independent, and co-hosted virtualized services on a data center node; and (ii) flexibility to switch between space-shared and time-shared allocation of processing cores to virtualized services. These features of CloudSim would speed up the development of new resource allocation policies and scheduling algorithms for Cloud computing.

14.5 EXPERIMENTAL RESULTS

14.5.1 Aneka Experiment: Application Deadline-Driven Provisioning of Cloud Resources

The Cloud provides a market where compute resources can be leased by paying the usage cost. We used this concept and combined local and Cloud resources when executing an application with varying deadlines. Cloud resources were provisioned only when the local resources could not meet the application deadline. As a test application we used a bag of task application, submitting 200 tasks with a variable deadline, each task taking 5 seconds to complete. We submitted this application with varying deadlines, as depicted in Table 14.3.

Table 14.3 clearly shows the advantage of using Cloud resources to meet the deadline when applications require tighter deadlines that cannot be fulfilled by local resources. Our scheduling algorithm estimated the total time the application would take when using local resources and only provisioned extra Cloud resources when this deadline could not be met. As we relaxed the deadline, from 60 seconds to 1200 seconds, the number of additional resources provisioned decreased from 18 to 1, and the cost of usage of EC2 resources fell from $US 0.765 to $US 0.085, respectively. Using Cloud as a readily

TABLE 14.3 Using Cloud Resources when Required

Deadline (Seconds)	Execution Time	Deadline Met?	Cloud Nodes Provisioned	Tasks on Local Resources	Tasks on Cloud (EC2)	Budget Spent (US$)
60	144	No	18	115	85	0.765
120	118	Yes	9	112	88	1.530
180	170	Yes	5	125	75	0.425
1200	225	Yes	1	181	19	0.085

available market, where compute resources are traded, we could meet the deadline for our test application.

14.5.2 Broker Experiment: Scheduling on Cloud and Other Distributed Resources

The Gridbus broker's architecture and operational model is shown in Fig. 14.7. As noted earlier, it supports market-oriented leasing of distributed resources depending on application and user's QoS requirements. At present, the broker can accommodate compute, storage, network, and information resources with prices based on compute time and bandwidth usage. It can also accommodate user objectives such as the fastest computation within the budget (time optimization), or the cheapest computation within the deadline (cost optimization) for both compute and data-intensive applications. The compute-intensive algorithms are based on those developed previously in Nimrod/G [7].

We have created a synthetic parameter sweep application (PSA) that executes a CPU intensive program with 100 different parameter scenarios or values. It led to the creation of an application containing 100 jobs, each job is modeled to execute ~5 minute with variation of (+/-20 sec.).

We have set the deadline of 40 minutes and budget of $6 for completing execution of the application; and conducted DBC (Deadline and Budget-Constrained) experiments for two different optimization strategies:

- Time optimization—this strategy produces results as early as possible, but before a deadline and within a budget limit.

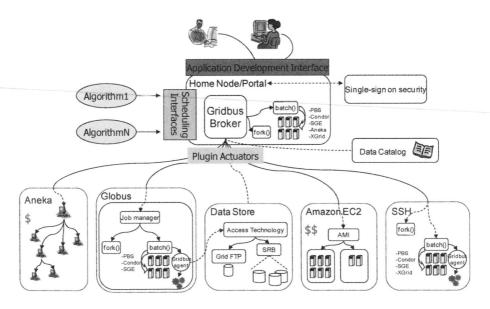

Figure 14.7 A Resource Broker Architecture and Operational Model.

- Cost optimization—this strategy produces results by deadline, but reduces cost within a budget limit.

We have used Grid and Cloud resources from Australia, Europe, and the United States in these scheduling experiments. Table 14.4 shows resource details such as architecture, location, access price, and the number of jobs processed by them. These are shared resources and hence application scheduling has to be adaptive in nature. In the case of Amazon resources, the Broker on assigning jobs to them, created appropriate VM instances on EC2 resources and managed the execution of jobs on them. The access price (as Rate, indicated in cents/second; for readability purpose, it is multiplied by 1000) is based on a commodity market model. The access price used for EC2 resources is the actual price Amazon charges; whereas it is artificial for other resources. However, they are assigned to reflect the offering of differentiated services at different costs as in the real-world marketplace.

The results of scheduling experiments carried out using the Gridbus broker in May 2009 are summarized as follows:

	Time Optimization	Cost Time Optimization
Budget Consumed	5.04$	3.71$
Time to Complete	28 min	35 min

In the case of time optimization, the broker has scheduled jobs across all the available resources based on their completion rate, even if they are costly, as the as the job execution price is within the limit of budget available for each job. Many jobs are sent to powerful resources (such as one located at Georgia State University), even if they are expensive, as long as they are affordable and able to complete jobs quickly. For example, the Georgia cluster is leased to process 32 jobs as it is the most powerful resource. As a result, the broker is able to complete the application in 28 minutes (much earlier than the deadline) and spent $5.04.

In the case of cost optimization, the broker has preferred resources that are cheaper, such as Amazon EC2, as long as they can complete assigned jobs within the deadline. It also scheduled jobs to other slightly more expensive resources, just to make sure that the deadline can be met. For example, the expensive Georgia cluster is used to process only 11 jobs to ensure application execution by the deadline. As a result, the broker is able to complete the application by 35 minutes (very close to the deadline) and spent $3.71, which is less the amount spent by the time optimization strategy.

These two experiments demonstrate that Cloud and Grid consumers can choose an appropriate strategy for execution of their applications depending on the timeframe by which results are needed. If the task at hand is an urgent one, they can choose the time instead of the cost optimization strategy. In addition, they can control the amount they are willing to invest for processing applications on market-oriented grid and cloud computing resources.

TABLE 14.4 Grid and Cloud Resources Used in Brokering Experiments

Organization	Resource Details	Rate (Cents per second*1000)	Total Jobs Time-Opt	Total Jobs Cost-Opt
Georgia State University, US	snowball.cs.gsu.edu 8 Intel 1.90GHz CPU, 3.2 GB RAM, 152 GB HD, Linux	90 (0.09)	32	11
H. Furtwangen University, Germany	unimelb.informatik.hs-furtwangen.de 1 Athlon XP 1700+ CPU, 767 MB RAM, 147 GB HD	3 (0.003)	4	5
University of California-Irvine, US	harbinger.cali2.uci.edu 2 Intel P III 930 MHz CPU, 503 MB RAM, 32 GB HD	2	8	10
University of Melbourne, Australia	billabong.csse.unimelb.edu.au 2 Intel(R) 2.40GHz CPU, 1 GB RAM, 35 GB HD	6	8	10
University of Melbourne, Australia	gieseking.csse.unimelb.edu.au 2 Intel(R) 2.40GHz CPU, 1 GB RAM, 71 GB HD	6	8	10
Amazon EC2*	ec2-Medium instance 5 EC2 Compute Units*, 1.7 GB RAM, 350 GB HD	60	14	16
Amazon EC2*	ec2-Medium instance 5 EC2 Compute Units, 1.7 GB RAM, 350 GB HD	60	13	16
Amazon EC2*	ec2-Small instance 1 EC2 Compute Unit, 1.7 GB RAM, 160 GB HD	30	7	11
Amazon EC2*	ec2-Small instance 1 EC2 Compute Unit, 1.7 GB RAM, 160 GB HD	30	6	11
	Total Price / Budget Consumed Time to Complete Execution		5.04$ 28 min	3.71$ 35 min

14.5.3 Deploying ECG Analysis Applications in Cloud Using Aneka

Advances in sensor technology, personal mobile devices, wireless broadband communications, and Cloud computing are enabling real-time collection and dissemination of personal health data to patients and health-care professionals anytime and from anywhere. Personal mobile devices, such as PDAs and mobile phones, are becoming more powerful in terms of processing capabilities and information management and play a major role in people's daily lives.

We designed a real-time health monitoring and computing system for people who suffer from cardiac arrhythmias. We implemented a personal health monitoring solution using real-time electrocardiogram (ECG) data to perform ECG beat and episode detection and classification. We developed a prototype system that collects people's electrocardiogram (ECG) data, disseminates them to an information repository, and facilitates analysis of these data using software services hosted in Clouds. We collected ECG data via sensors attached to a person's body, used a mobile device to communicate this data to the ECG analyzer (hosted as SaaS in Clouds), and disseminated the analyzed data to the person's mobile phones when requested.

Figure 14.8 shows the components of the system. The environment hosting the health monitoring application must be able to handle large number of users, maintain user information, and disseminate them as and when requested by them, as users pay for the services. The users possess a mobile device that is connected to a sensor device,

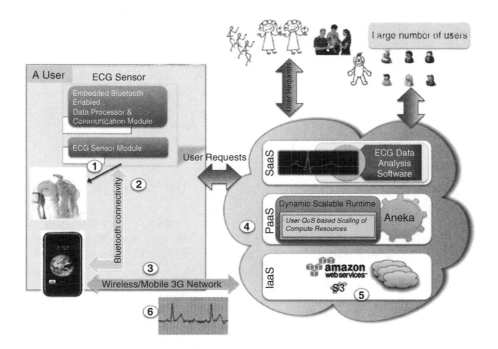

Figure 14.8 Scaling applications using Aneka Cloud computing technology.

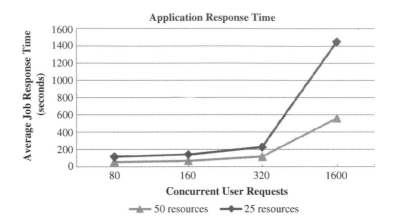

Figure 14.9 Response time of ECG application for varying number of EC2 compute resources.

which monitors the user's heartbeat. This mobile device communicates with the ECG data analysis service hosted in the Cloud to upload data and download the results in user-readable format (e.g., graphs, statistical data, alerts, etc.). The computation is carried out in the Cloud using services that can scale out depending on the number of user requests.

The time taken by a system to respond to each user is of paramount importance in applications such as ECG monitoring. As the number of requests grows, the system suffers from increasing response time, as we show in Figure 14.9. When the maximum number of resources that can be used is limited to 25 resources, the response time for the ECG application, depicted in Fig. 14.8, increases as compared to the scenario when a maximum of 50 resources were used. This was mainly due to the queuing of user requests waiting for resources to be free. Even though the Cloud resources were instantiated dynamically, limiting the number of total resources used has a significant effect on mission critical applications. Thus, Cloud computing provides a platform for dynamically provisioning as many resources as and when required.

14.6 RELATED TECHNOLOGIES, INTEGRATION, AND DEPLOYMENT

The Cloudbus toolkit provides a set of technologies completely integrated with each other. More importantly, they it supports integration with third-party technologies and solutions. Integration is a fundamental element in the Cloud computing model, where enterprises and end-users offload their computation to third-party infrastructures and access their data anytime from anywhere in a ubiquitous manner.

Many vendors provide different solutions for deploying public, private, and hybrid Clouds. At the lowest level of the Cloud computing reference model, virtual server containers provide a management layer for the commodity hardware infrastructure: VMware, Xen [4], and KVM (Kernel-based Virtual Machine) are some of the most popular hypervisors available today. On top of these, Infrastructure-as-a-Service solutions such as Amazon EC2, Eucalyptus [33], and OpenNebula provide high-level service to end-users. Advanced resource managers such as OpenPEX and Haizea complete the picture by providing an advance reservation–based approach for provisioning virtual resources on such platforms. Technologies such as Aneka and the Workflow Engine can be readily integrated with these solutions in order to utilize their capabilities and scale on demand. This applies not only for compute-type workloads, but also for storage Clouds and CDNs, as demonstrated by the MetaCDN project. At a higher level, the Market maker and the Grid Service Broker are able to provision compute resources with or without a SLA by relying on different middleware implementations and to provide the best suitable service to end-users.

The Cloudbus toolkit is a work in progress, but several Cloudbus technologies have already been put into action in real scenarios. A private Aneka Cloud has been deployed at GoFront (GoFront Group, Zhuzhou Electric Locomotive Works, is China's premier and largest nationwide research and manufacturer of rail electric traction equipment), in order to increase the overall productivity of product design and the return on investment of existing resources. The Workflow Engine has been used to execute complex scientific applications such as functional Magnetic Resonance Imaging (fMRI) workflows on top of hybrid Clouds composed of Amazon EC2 and physical clusters from labs worldwide. Various external organizations, such as HP Labs, use CloudSim for Industrial Cloud computing research.

Furthermore, Aneka has been extended to support dynamic pooling of resources from public Clouds. This capability of Aneka enables creation of hybrid Clouds by leasing additional resources from external/public Clouds such as Amazon EC2 whenever the demand on private Cloud exceeds its available capacity. In addition, Aneka supports federation of other private Clouds within an enterprise, which are managed through Aneka or other vendor technologies such as XenServer and VMWare.

Moreover, some of our Cloudbus technologies have been utilized by commercial enterprises and they are demonstrated at public international events such as the 4th IEEE International Conference on e-Science, held in Indianapolis, Indiana, in the U.S., and the 2nd IEEE International Scalable Computing Challenge hosted at the 9th International Conference on Cluster Computing and Grid (CCGrid 2009) held in Shanghai, China. These demonstrations included fMRI brain imaging application workflows, and gene expression data classification on Clouds and distributed resources.

14.7 CONCLUSION

In this chapter, we introduced the fundamental concepts of market-oriented Cloud computing. We studied the building blocks of Cloud computing systems (IaaS, PaaS, and SaaS) and presented a reference model. The model, together with the state-of-the-art technologies presented in this chapter, contribute significantly towards the mainstream adoption of Cloud computing technology. However, any technology brings with it new challenges and breakthroughs. We detailed the major challenges faced by the industry when adopting Cloud computing as a mainstream technology as part of the distributed computing paradigm. We presented a utility-oriented Cloud vision that is a generic model for realizing market-oriented Cloud computing vision. Cloudbus realized this by developing various tools and platforms that can be used individually or together as an integrated solution. We also demonstrated via experiments that our toolkit could provide applications based on deadline, optimize cost and time of applications, and manage real-world problems via an integrated solution.

Market-oriented computing in industry is becoming a reality, as evidenced by the plethora of vendors that provide Cloud computing services. For example, EC2 started with flat pricing, then moved to pricing based on service difference, and recently introduced auction-based models. In the next two decades, service-oriented distributed computing will emerge as a dominant factor in shaping the industry, changing the way business is conducted and how services are delivered and managed. This paradigm is expected to have a major impact on service economy, which contributes significantly to the GDP of many countries. The service sector includes health services (e-health), financial services, and government services. With increased demand for delivering services to a larger number of users, providers are looking for novel ways of hosting their application services in Clouds at lower cost while meeting users' quality of service expectations. With increased dependency on ICT technologies, major advances are required in Cloud computing to support elastic applications offering services to millions of users simultaneously.

Software licensing will be a major hurdle for vendors of Cloud services when proprietary software technologies have to be made available to millions of users via public virtual appliances (e.g., customized images of OS and applications). Overwhelming use of such customized software would lead to seamless integration of enterprise Clouds, with public Clouds for service scalability and greater outreach to customers. More and more enterprises would be interested in moving to Clouds for cooperative sharing. In such scenarios, security and privacy of corporate data could be of paramount concern. One of the solutions would be to establish a globally accredited Cloud service regulatory body that would act under a common statute for certifying Cloud service providers; standardizing data formats, enforcing service level agreements, handling trust certificates, and so forth.

On one hand, there are technological challenges; on the other, there are issues with balancing usage cost and services delivered. Cloud service providers are already tussling by advertising attractive pricing policies to lure users of all kinds to use their services (e.g., Amazon, SalesForce, Google, etc.). As the market condition are determined through intense competition between many vendors, dynamic negotiations and SLA management will play a major role in determining the amount of revenue to be generated for service providers. Similarly, users will be able to choose better services that fit their requirements and budget. They will evaluate services based on their level of QoS satisfaction so that they get the right value for the price paid.

As the price for commodity hardware and network equipment for a data center is already becoming less expensive, a significant part of the total cost of operating Cloud services on an industrial scale is determined by the amount of energy consumed by the data center. To conserve energy and save cooling costs, data centers could adopt energy-efficient resource allocation policies. Moreover, they could use renewable sources of energy to power their centers and create the smallest carbon footprint, in the long run. A daunting task for any vendor is to keep its Cloud services alive and running for as long as it takes. As users gradually become dependent on Cloud services, a sudden disruption

expectations

Platform as a Service
(PaaS)
Cloud Security
Cloud Email
Application PaaS (aPaaS)
Multitenancy
Elasticity
Cloud Collaboration Services
Browser Client OS
Database Platform as a Service (dbPaaS)
Cloud-Enabled BPM Platforms
Cloud-Parallel Processing
Cloud-Application Development Services
"Big Data" and Extreme Information
Processing and Management
Hybrid Cloud Computing
Cloud Services Brokerage
Cloud-Optimized Application Design

Private Cloud Computing
Cloud Computing
Infrastructure as a Service (IaaS)
Public Cloud Computing/the Cloud

Real-Time Infrastructure

Public Cloud Storage

Dedicated Email Services
Cloud Advertising
Sales Force Automation SaaS

Cloudbursting
Community Cloud

Cloud/Web
Platforms

Virtualization
Software as a Service (SaaS)

Private PaaS

IT Infrastructure Utility

Cloud Security and Risk Standards

Enhansed Network Delivery

DevOps

As of July 2011

| Technology Trigger | Peak of Inflated Expectations | Trough of Disillusionment | Slope of Enlightenment | Plateau of Productivity |

time

Years to mainstream adoption:

obsolete

○ less than 2 years ◎ 2 to 5 years ● 5 to 10 years ▲ more than 10 years ⊗ before plateau

Source: Gartner (July 2011)

Figure 14.10   Gartner 2011 Hype cycle of Cloud computing.

of any of the services will send a ripple effect around the world that could destabilize markets (e.g., financial institutions such as banks depending on Clouds), paralyze IT services (e.g., email services), and so forth. To prevent these effects arising from vendor "lock-in," interoperability issues between Cloud service providers should be adequately addressed. Nevertheless, Cloud computing is the technology for realizing a long-awaited dream of using distributed compute, storage resources, and application software services as commodities (computing utilities).

As the hype of Cloud computing matures and the technology is adopted in main-stream industry, the challenges and misunderstandings gradually will be mitigated. The state of various capabilities of Cloud computing noted in the Gartner hype cycle released in July 2011 is shown in Figure 14.10. Overall, Cloud computing is still at the peak of the hype. Cloud application development tools, Cloud service integration and others have overcome the hype to reach the highest level of expectation in the last two to five years. This hype curve represents a trend in the industry and Cloudbus as an academic R&D project continues to advance the field of Cloud computing much earlier than what is predicted in the hype curve. Hence, we believe that Cloudbus technologies are at the forefront of innovation in Cloud computing and its results will aid the industry in rapid progression of the Cloud computing paradigm from technology trigger to plateau of productivity.

ACKNOWLEDGMENTS

This work is partially supported through an Australian Research Council (ARC) Discovery Project grant and the International Science Linkages (ISL) program of the Department of Innovation, Industry, Science and Research. All members of our CLOUDS Lab have been actively contributing towards various developments reported in this chapter. In particular, we would like to thank Srikumar Venugopal, Xingchen Chu, Rajiv Ranjan, Chao Jin, Michael Mattess, William Voorsluys, Dileban Karunamoorthy, Saurabh Garg, Marcos Dias de Assunção, Alexandre di Costanzo, Mohsen Amini, James Broberg, Mukaddim Pathan, Chee Shin Yeo, Anton Beloglazov, Rodrigo Neves Calheiros, and Marco Netto. We also thank Mohsen Amini for providing us with experimental results of execution of Broker on Clouds. This chapter is a substantially extended version of the CloudCom 2009 conference paper [8].

REFERENCES

[1] VMware: Migrate Virtual Machines with Zero Downtime, http://www.vmware.com/products/vmotion.

[2] "An overview of the granules runtime for cloud computing." *Proceedings of the 2008 Fourth IEEE International Conference on eScience*, pp. 412–413, Indianapolis, Indiana, USA, 2008.

[3] M. Armbrust, A. Fox, R. Griffith, A.D. Joseph, R. Katz, A. Konwinski, G. Lee, D. Patterson, A. Rabkin, I. Stoica, and M. Zaharia. "A view of cloud computing." *Communications of the ACM*, 2010, 53, 50–58.

[4] P. Barham, B. Dragovic, K. Fraser, S. Hand, T. Harris, A. Ho, R. Neugebauer, I. Pratt, and A. Warfield. "Xen and the art of virtualization." *Proceedings of the Nineteenth ACM Symposium on Operating Systems Principles*, pp. 164–177, New York, NY, USA, 2003.

[5] K. Bennett, P. Layzell, D. Budgen, P. Brereton, L. Macaulay, and M. Munro. "Service-based software: The future for flexible software." *Proceedings of the Seventh Asia-Pacific Software Engineering Conference*, pp. 214–221, Singapore, 2000, IEEE.

[6] J. Broberg, R. Buyya, and Z. Tari. "Metacdn: Harnessing 'storage Clouds' for high performance content delivery." *Journal of Network and Computer Applications*, 32(5):1012–1022, 2009.

[7] R. Buyya, D. Abramson, and J. Giddy. "A case for economy Grid architecture for service-oriented Grid computing." Proceedings of the 10th Heterogeneous Computing Workshop, In conjunction with the 15th International Parallel and Distributed Processing Symposium, San Francisco, USA, 2001.

[8] R. Buyya, S. Pandey, and C. Vecchiola. "Cloudbus toolkit for market-oriented cloud computing." *Proceedings of the 1st International Conference on Cloud Computing*, Vol. 5931 of LNCS, pp. 24–44, Beijing, China, 2009.

[9] R.N. Calheiros, R. Ranjan, A. Beloglazov, C.A. F. De Rose, and R. Buyya, "CloudSim: A toolkit for modeling and simulation of cloud computing environments and evaluation of resource provisioning algorithms," *Software: Practice and Experience (SPE)*, Vol. 41, No. 1, pp. 23–50, 2011.

[10] R. Buyya, C.S. Yeo, and S. Venugopal. "Market-oriented cloud computing: Vision, hype, and reality for delivering it services as computing utilities." *Proceedings of the 10th IEEE International Conference on High Performance Computing and Communications*, pp. 5–13, DaLian, China, 2008, IEEE.

[11] N. Chohan, C. Bunch, S. Pang, C. Krintz, N. Mostafa, S. Soman, and R. Wolski. "AppScale: Scalable and open AppEngine application development and deployment." Proceedings of

the First International Conference on Cloud Computing, LNICST, Munich, Germany, 2009, Springer-Verlag.

[12] R. Chow, P. Golle, M. Jakobsson, E. Shi, J. Staddon, R. Masuoka, and J. Molina. "Controlling data in the cloud: Outsourcing computation without outsourcing control." *Proceedings of the 2009 ACM Workshop on Cloud Computing Security*, pp. 85–90, Chicago, IL, USA, 2009, ACM.

[13] D. Chantry. Mapping applications to the cloud. Microsoft Corporation, January 2009. http://msdn.microsoft.com/en-us/library/dd430340.aspx (accessed: January 2010).

[14] J. Dean and S. Ghemawat. "MapReduce: Simplified data processing on large clusters." In *Operating Systems Design and Implementation*, Vol. 6, San Francisco, CA, 2004. USENIX.

[15] G. DeCandia, D. Hastorun, M. Jampani, G. Kakulapati, A. Lakshman, A. Pilchin, S. Sivasubramanian, P. Vosshall, and W. Vogels. "Dynamo: Amazon's highly available key-value store." *SIGOPS Oper. Syst. Rev.*, 41(6):205–220, 2007.

[16] R. Buyya, R. Ranjan, and R.N. Calheiros. "InterCloud: Utility-oriented federation of Cloud computing environments for scaling of application services." *Proceedings of the 10th International Conference on Algorithms and Architectures for Parallel Processing*, pp. 13–31, LNCS 6081, Busan, South Korea, 2010, Springer.

[17] R.J. Figueiredo, P.A. Dinda, and J.A.B. Fortes. "A case for grid computing on virtual machines." *Proceedings of the 23rd International Conference on Distributed Computing Systems*, pp. 550–559, Providence, RI, USA, 2003, IEEE.

[18] S.K. Garg, S. Venugopal, and R. Buyya. "A meta-scheduler with auction based resource allocation for global grids." *Proceedings of the 4th International Conference on Parallel and Distributed Systems*, pp. 187–194, Melbourne, Australia, 2008, IEEE.

[19] A. Greenberg, J. Hamilton, D.A. Maltz, and P. Patel. "The cost of a cloud: Research problems in data center networks." *SIGCOMM Comput. Commun. Rev.*, 39(1):68–73, 2009.

[20] L. Hu, S. Ying, X. Jia, and K. Zhao. "Towards an approach of semantic access control for cloud computing." *Proceedings of the 1st International Conference on Cloud Computing*, Vol. 5931 of LNCS, pp. 145–156, Beijing, China, 2009.

[21] M.H. Jamal, A. Qadeer, W. Mahmood, A. Waheed, and J.J. Ding. "Virtual machine scalability on multi-core processors based servers for cloud computing workloads." *Proceedings of the Fifth International Conference on Networking, Architecture, and Storage*, pp. 90–97, Macau, China, 2009, IEEE.

[22] K. Keahey, I. Foster, T. Freeman, and X. Zhang. "Virtual workspaces in the Grid." *Proceedings of the 11th International Euro-Par Conference*, Vol. 3648 of LNCS, pp. 421–431, Lisbon, Portugal, 2005, Springer.

[23] K. Keahey, R.J. Figueiredo, J. Fortes, T. Freeman, and M. Tsugawa. "Science clouds: Early experiences in cloud computing for scientific applications." *Cloud Computing and Its Applications*, Chicago, IL, USA, 2008.

[24] A. Keller and H. Ludwig. "The WSLA framework: Specifying and monitoring service level agreements for web services." *Journal of Network and Systems Management*, 11(1):57–81, 2003.

[25] K.H. Kim, R. Buyya, and J. Kim. "Power aware scheduling of bag-of-tasks applications with deadline constraints on dvs-enabled clusters." *Proceedings of the Seventh International Symposium on Cluster Computing and the Grid*, pp. 541–548, Rio de Janeiro, Brazil, 2007, IEEE.

[26] L. Kleinrock. "An Internet vision: The invisible global infrastructure." *AdHoc Networks Journal*, 1(1):3–11, 2003.

[27] I. Krsul, A. Ganguly, J. Zhang, J.A.B. Fortes, and Figueiredo. "VMPlants: Providing and managing virtual machine execution environments for Grid computing." *Proceedings of the 2004 ACM/IEEE Conference on Supercomputing*, Pittsburgh, PA, USA, 2004, IEEE.

[28] H.A. Lagar-Cavilla, J.A. Whitney, A.M. Scannell, P. Patchin, S.M. Rumble, E. de Lara, M. Brudno, and M. Satyanarayanan. "Snowflock: Rapid virtual machine cloning for cloud computing." *Proceedings of the 4th ACM European Conference on Computer systems*, pp. 1–12, Nuremberg, Germany, 2009, ACM.

[29] H. Li, Y. Dai, L. Tian, and H. Yang. "Identity-based authentication for cloud computing." *Proceedings of the 1st International Conference on Cloud Computing*, Vol. 5931 of LNCS, pp. 157–166, Beijing, China, 2009.

[30] W. Li and L. Ping. "Trust model to enhance security and interoperability of cloud environment." *Proceedings of the 1st International Conference on Cloud Computing*, Vol. 5931 of LNCS, pp. 69–79, Beijing, China, 2009.

[31] L. Liu, H. Wang, X. Liu, X. Jin, W.B. He, Q.B. Wang, and Y. Chen. "Greencloud: A new architecture for green data center." *Proceedings of the 6th International Conference Industry Session on Autonomic Computing and Communications Industry Session*, pp. 29–38, Barcelona, Spain, 2009, ACM.

[32] E.M. Maximilien, A. Ranabahu, R. Engehausen, and L.C. Anderson. "Toward cloud-agnostic middlewares." *Proceedings of the 24th ACM SIGPLAN Conference Companion on Object Oriented Programming Systems Languages and Applications*, pp. 619–626, Orlando, FL, USA, 2009, ACM.

[33] D. Nurmi, R. Wolski, C. Grzegorczyk, G. Obertelli, S. Soman, L. Youseff, and D. Zagorodnov. "The Eucalyptus open-source cloud-computing system." *Proceedings of the 9th IEEE/ACM International Symposium on Cluster Computing and the Grid*, pp. 124–131, Shanghai, China, 2009, IEEE.

[34] S. Pandey, W. Voorsluys, M. Rahman, R. Buyya, J. Dobson, and K. Chiu. "A grid workflow environment for brain imaging analysis on distributed systems." *Concurrency and Computation: Practice & Experience*, 21(16):2118–2139, 2009.

[35] P. Patel, A. Ranabahu, and A. Sheth. "Service level agreement in cloud computing." *Proceedings of the 24th ACM SIGPLAN Conference Companion on Object Oriented Programming Systems Languages and Applications*, Orlando, FL, USA, 2009, ACM.

[36] S. Pearson. "Taking account of privacy when designing cloud computing services." *Proceedings of the 2009 ICSE Workshop on Software Engineering Challenges of Cloud Computing*, pp. 44–52, Vancouver, Canada, 2009, IEEE.

[37] L. Yan, C. Rong, and G. Zhao. "Strengthen cloud computing security with federal identity management using hierarchical identity-based cryptography." In *CloudCom '09: Proceedings of the 1st International Conference on Cloud Computing*, Vol. 5931 of LCNS, pp. 167–177. Springer-Verlag, December 2009.

[38] S. Pearson, Y. Shen, and M. Mowbray. "A privacy manager for cloud computing." *Proceedings of the 1st International Conference on Cloud Computing*, Vol. 5931 of LNCS, pp. 90–106, Beijing, China, 2009.

[39] B. Rochwerger, A. Galis, E. Levy, J.A. Càceres, D. Breitgand, Y. Wolfsthal, I.M. Llorente, M. Wusthoff, R.S. Montero, and E. Elmroth. "RESERVOIR: Management technologies and requirements for next generation Service Oriented Infrastructures." *Proceedings of the 11th*

IFIP/IEEE *International Conference on Symposium on Integrated Network Management*, pp. 307–310, Long Island, NY, USA, 2009, IEEE.

[40] A. Singh, M. Korupolu, and D. Mohapatra. "Server-storage virtualization: integration and load balancing in data centers." *Proceedings of the 2008 ACM/IEEE Conference on Super-computing*, pp. 1–12, Austin, TX, USA, 2008, IEEE.

[41] B. Sotomayor, R.S. Montero, I.M. Llorente, and I. Foster. "Resource leasing and the art of suspending virtual machines." *Proceedings of the 11th IEEE International Conference on High Performance Computing and Communications*, pp. 59–68, Seoul, Korea, 2009, IEEE.

[42] L.M. Vaquero, L. Rodero-Merino, J. Caceres, and M. Lindner. "A break in the clouds: towards a cloud definition." *SIGCOMM Comput. Commun. Rev.*, 39(1):50–55, 2009.

[43] C. Vecchiola, X. Chu, and R. Buyya. "High speed and large scale scientific computing." In *Aneka: A Software Platform for .NET-based Cloud Computing*, pp. 267–295. IOS Press, 2009.

[44] S. Venugopal, R. Buyya, and L. Winton. "A grid service broker for scheduling e-science applications on global data grids." *Concurrency and Computation: Practice & Experience*, 18(6):685–699, May 2006.

[45] W. Voorsluys, J. Broberg, S. Venugopal, and R. Buyya. "Cost of virtual machine live migration in clouds: A performance evaluation." *Proceedings of the 1st International Conference on Cloud Computing*, Vol. 5931 of LNCS, pp. 254–265, Beijing, China, 2009

[46] J. Wei, X. Zhang, G. Ammons, V. Bala, and P. Ning. "Managing security of virtual machine images in a cloud environment." *Proceedings of the 2009 ACM Workshop on Cloud Computing Security*, pp. 91–96, Chicago, IL, USA, 2009, ACM.

[47] A. Whitaker, M. Shaw, and S.D. Gribble. "Denali: A scalable isolation kernel." *Proceedings of the 10th Workshop on ACM SIGOPS European Workshop*, pp. 10–15, Saint-Emilion, France, 2002, ACM.

[48] T. White. *Hadoop: The Definitive Guide.* O'Reilly Media, June 2009.

[49] E. Wustenhoff. Service level agreement in the data center. Sun BluePrints OnLine, Sun Microsystems, USA, April 2002. http://www.sun.com/blueprints/0402/sla.pdf.

[50] K. Xiong and H. Perros. "Service performance and analysis in cloud computing." *Proceedings of the 2009 Congress on Services—I*, pp. 693–700, Los Angeles, CA, USA, 2009, IEEE.

15

A CLOUD BROKER ARCHITECTURE FOR MULTICLOUD ENVIRONMENTS

Jose Luis Lucas-Simarro, Iñigo San Aniceto, Rafael Moreno-Vozmediano, Ruben S. Montero, and Ignacio M. Llorente

CONTENTS

Large Scale Network-Centric Distributed Systems, First Edition. Edited by Hamid Sarbazi-Azad and Albert Y. Zomaya.
© 2014 John Wiley & Sons, Inc. Published 2014 by John Wiley & Sons, Inc.

359

15.1 INTRODUCTION

In the last few years the cloud computing market [1] has experienced important growth. With the market expansion, the complexity is also increasing as users must deal with different cloud providers and their particular features (e.g., virtual machine (VM) types, pricing schemes, and cloud interfaces).

The cloud computing market provides users with different cloud providers, such as Amazon EC2 [2], CloudSigma [3], ElasticHosts [4], Flexiant [5], GoGrid [6], and Rackspace [7], which offer users a wide range of options to cover their needs using cloud technology. In general, cloud providers present some features in common: virtual machine instances with identical technical specifications, a friendly proprietary interface for managing the offered virtual resources, and some similar pricing models like pay-as-you-go or long time reservation models.

However, there are more differences than similarities among them: different cloud provider interfaces, both in functionality and usability; incompatible image types, due to different packing systems; diverse capability to change features online (e.g., add more computer power or disk capacity); variant pool of instances; and, obviously, different price and charging time periods (within any pricing model) are different from one to another.

In this complex cloud market, where the use of federated clouds [8, 9] and multi-cloud deployments [10] have emerged, a cloud broker is a useful tool to avoid the difficulty of dealing with so many cloud providers and their particular features. A cloud broker provides a uniform interface to different cloud provider technology, and also collects information from providers (instance availability, prices, etc.). Moreover, users can take advantage of the cloud broker for deploying their virtual infrastructure among multiple clouds using different optimization algorithms [30]. Section 15.2 describes the current state of cloud brokers and their features.

Some benefits of the use of cloud brokering mechanisms are the following:

- Usability: A cloud broker provides users a uniform interface to manage their infrastructures, not having to deal with different particular interfaces. This interface makes the multiple interaction with clouds transparent for users.

- Optimization: The cloud broker can provide several optimization algorithms for user service deployment in order to optimize different variables like overall infrastructure cost, service performance, or others, depending on the strategies selected by the user.
- Advanced service management: The broker can provide some advanced tools, like auto-scaling policies. With the auto-scaling policies, the users do not have to worry about the escalation of their infrastructure. Instead, the cloud broker will select the optimum size for each moment, avoiding both performance degradation and over provisioning.
- Adaptability: The cloud broker can be configured for adapting user services with different workloads and restrictions.

However, the implementation of cloud brokering mechanisms represents several challenges that are analyzed in Section 15.3.

In this chapter we propose a cloud broker architecture oriented to manage the deployment of multitier and elastic services among available cloud providers. Thus, the broker is able to interact with different cloud providers and their own particular features (instance types, pricing schemes, etc.). Moreover, the broker is able to provision elastic services dynamically with the resources needed at every moment. Section 15.4 depicts the cloud broker architecture and its components, specially focused on the service description.

The management of a particular service by a cloud broker not only involves the infrastructure deployment but also the optimization of some of its parameters (e.g., cost, performance, etc.). The broker we propose offers scheduling policies guided by different optimization criteria (e.g., cost optimization, performance optimization, resource consumption, etc.) and several restrictions (e.g., resource consumption, cost threshold, etc.) to help users to adapt the broker functionalities to their services. Section 15.5 explains the scheduling policies used by the broker. Then, Section 15.6 describes the obtained scheduling results in a single cloud scenario, presenting a use case in which the broker reduces the overall cost: deployment of a grid in a single cloud, and in a multi-cloud scenario, showing the benefit of using the broker in two use cases: a Web server and a virtual classroom. Finally, Section 15.7 provides some conclusions.

15.2 STATE OF THE ART ON CLOUD BROKERING

In the current cloud market there are several companies offering brokering solutions, such as RightScale [11], SpotCloud [12], Kavoo [13], and CloudSwicht [14], among others. In this section, we review some of the current commercial solutions as well as research attempts.

RightScale [11] offers a cloud management platform for control, administration, and lifecycle support of cloud deployments. It has an adaptable automation engine that automatically adapts the deployment to certain events in a pre-established way. In addition, it includes a multi-cloud engine that interacts with cloud infrastructure APIs and manages the unique requirements of each cloud. The broker architecture we propose offers similar functionality, but it includes certain utilities like load planning techniques that are not implemented in RightScale.

Spot Cloud [12] provides a structured cloud capacity marketplace. In this marketplace, the service providers sell the extra capacity they have and the buyers can take advantage of cheap rates, selecting the best service provider at each moment. The broker proposed in this work makes something similar but in an automated way. With our solution, the user does not have to check the price of each cloud provider at each moment; instead, an optimization algorithm can be used to select the best way to place the VM according to the actual rates of all the cloud service providers.

Kavoo [13] provides application-centric management of virtual resources in the cloud. It takes all the information that somehow affects the application and allows changing the operating system in which the application runs dynamically. Our architecture is not application centric; the cloud broker manages the VM in different clouds but it does not alter the applications inside the instances.

Finally, CloudSwitch [14] offers the possibility to run the applications in the best fitting instance among several cloud providers by comparing different instances with the requirements of the VM to be deployed. The main idea is to offer a solution to the heterogeneous and constantly expanding system that does not have an instance that fits all the necessities. To do so, it creates a comparison of different instances, taking into account business and technical requirements, and creates a fitting percentage that compares the VM necessities with the instances. Our broker is similar to CloudSwitch in the sense that it fits the VM needs in the smallest instance that can support it. The difference is that our broker intends to do that dynamically and without user interaction.

These commercial solutions still present some deficiencies for cloud adoption and hence many researchers continue to focus on the obstacles and opportunities that cloud brokering presents today.

Some of this research is taking place in Europe and is attempting to solve some of the problems commercial solutions have. There are two research projects that deserve mention. The first is Mosaic [15], which offers an open-source cloud application programming interface that targets the development of a multi-cloud oriented application to offer simple and transparent access to heterogeneous cloud computing resources and avoids lock-in into proprietary solutions. It is still a work in progress and, unlike our broker, it is not an application but an application programming interface. The second research project is Optimis [16], which offers a framework and a toolkit to simplify service construction, support deployment and runtime decisions of hybrid clouds, and support service brokerage via interoperability and architecture independence.

Apart from these projects, R. Moreno-Vozmediano [10] analyzed the cost per job with different multi-cloud cluster configurations. K. Keahey et al. [17] analyzed the actual challenges for multi-cloud service deployment: image compatibility, contextualization compatibility, and API-level compliance. They explains possible solutions for each of the challenges and create a virtual cluster interconnected with ViNe.

R. Buyya et al. [18] proposed a federated intercloud environment to avoid the actual obstacles and to be able to achieve all the Quality of Service (QoS) targets under variable workload, resource, and network conditions. The redundancy and reliability needed to meet the QoS targets are obtained thanks to clouds in multiple geographical locations, and the performance targets are met, dynamically resizing the resources. The difference with our proposal is that our broker does not need a federation-driven market. To the best of our knowledge, the federation does not exist today and the negotiation protocols are not standard. Hence, our proposal can work in the actual cloud market while the federated intercloud only works in simulations.

15.3 CHALLENGES OF CLOUD BROKERING

Cloud computing usage is increasing both in breadth, as the number of resource types offered grows, and in depth, as the number of cloud providers increases. From a user perspective, access to multiple cloud providers involves several challenges [19, 20] that make cloud usage difficult (e.g., different cloud interfaces, instance types, pricing schemes, and image types). The use of a cloud broker would cope with some of these challenges as follows:

- Different *cloud interfaces*. Each cloud provider exhibits its proprietary interface, but some efforts have been made to standardize an interface for accessing any cloud provider, such as *Open Cloud Computing Interface (OCCI)* [21, 22], or APIs with various adaptors for accessing different clouds, such as *DeltaCloud* [23].

  OCCI is a protocol and API that comprises a set of open community-lead specifications delivered through the Open Grid Forum [24]. OCCI was originally initiated to create a remote management API for IaaS-model, based services, allowing for the development of interoperable tools for common tasks-including deployment, autonomic scaling, and monitoring. It has since evolved into a flexible API with a strong focus on integration, portability, interoperability, and innovation while still offering a high degree of extensibility. The current release of the OCCI is suitable to serve many other models in addition to IaaS, including PaaS and SaaS.

  DeltaCloud is an API developed by Red Hat that abstracts the differences between clouds. Each particular cloud is controlled through an adaptor. Some clouds supported by DeltaCloud are Amazon EC2, GoGrid, and OpenNebula[25]-built clouds [26].

  The cloud broker we propose uses DeltaCloud to communicate with different clouds.

- Different *instance types*. Apart from standard instances, there are special high-CPU or high-memory instances for high computing applications, along with clustered instances, if needed, or live-changeable instances, depending on the provider. Today, it is not easy to compare the performance of different instances in different clouds, which makes the optimization of cost or performance difficult. The cloud broker handles generic and service-adapted performance metrics (see Section 15.5.2), which are based on data provided by the user.

- Different *pricing schemes*. In the early phase of cloud adoption, the price model was dominated by fixed prices [27]. Today, the cloud market trend shows that dynamic pricing scheme utilization is increasing, in which prices change according to demand for each cloud provider. Currently, no pricing interface is available, so users find it difficult to search cloud prices and decide where to put their resources. The cloud broker we propose includes a Cloud manager, which collects information from providers and works as a pricing interface.

- Different *image types*. Each cloud provider uses a particular image format, packaged in its own way. Thus, an image type created, for example, in Amazon EC2 (Amazon Machine Image, AMI) does not work in every provider, so users need to create an image type in almost each cloud provider. One possible solution is to contextualize the image, using in each cloud provider a predefined image and giving it a post-configuration script that will prepare the image to work properly. The cloud broker supports image contextualization by adding this post-configuration script in the service description. Moreover, with this solution users do not need to save the image into a storage system, thus avoiding additional storage fees.

- Network latencies. In a multi-cloud environment the challenge of how to cope with a large amount of network communications among several virtual machines has to be addressed. Some user services can be critical in network communications having low tolerance to delays (e.g., live video streaming or parallel applications). Thus, the service will not get any benefit from a multi-cloud environment unless the VMs that need to communicate between them are deployed in the same location. The cloud broker permits the indication of location restrictions for deploying part of the infrastructure in the same cloud location, which is a partial solution to the high network latencies problem.

- Network across clouds. Resources running on different cloud providers are located in different networks. However, some kinds of services require all their components to be located on the same local network to communicate the different service components. This challenge can be addressed by adopting the Virtual Private Network (VPN) technology to interconnect the different cloud resources in a secure way.

15.4 PROPOSAL OF A BROKER ARCHITECTURE FOR MULTICLOUD ENVIRONMENTS

In this chapter, we propose a cloud broker architecture for managing and scheduling services as introduced in Section 15.1.

The main technical features of this cloud broker architecture are the following: modular, since it provides basic components but allows them to be easily replaceable by others (i.e., scheduling policies); open, since its code is planned to be available for developers and the scientific community; adaptable, since several use cases can be adapted using the cloud broker; and standard based.

The broker architecture proposed, shown in Fig. 15.1, has two main actors: the cloud broker administrator and the cloud broker user. The former configures the cloud broker options before the start of the broker execution. It includes the definition of a cloud provider list, with the corresponding accounting information, and an instance list that includes the available instance types in each cloud and their prices.

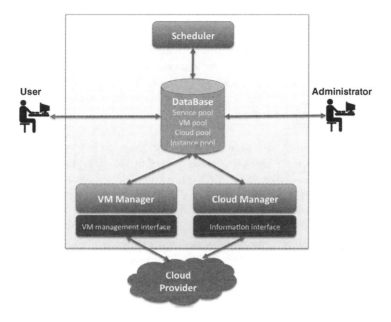

Figure 15.1 Cloud broker architecture.

The latter receives information of both cloud and instance lists and specifies a new service, describing it through a service description file. A service is a set of components, each one composed by a number of virtual machines, a common optimization criteria, and some particular restrictions. The service description options are detailed in Section 15.4.2.

The broker is supported by a central database and also has three main components: the scheduler, which reads the user description and invokes the selected scheduling module with its restrictions; the VM manager, which performs the deployment action; and the Cloud manager, which collects information from cloud providers. In the next section, the main functions of these components are exposed.

15.4.1 Broker Components

15.4.1.1 Database. The database back-end is the central component of this architecture. It stores the clouds, instances, services, and VM lists that are used by the rest of architecture components. The *cloud list* stores information about cloud providers. Each provider is linked to a file with information about accounting info (user name, passwords, public or private key paths, etc.).

The *instance list* stores information about the available type of instances in each cloud. Each instance belongs to a cloud and is defined by an instance type (e.g., small, large, etc.), with its price and the pricing model (e.g., on-demand, reserved, spot, etc.) to be applied.

The *service list* stores information about the services defined by the user. Each service is described in a service description file (see Section 15.4.2).

Finally, the *VM list* stores information about VMs managed by the cloud broker in different clouds. Each VM belongs to a service and is mapped to a particular instance type. It also includes a current status (pending, running, cancelled, shutdown, or failed) and some timing and resource consumption information (e.g., CPU, memory, or network usage).

15.4.1.2 Scheduler. The scheduler reads the service list, and uses the service description file as input to deploy each new service. It invokes to the particular scheduling module specified in the service description (once for static scheduling and periodically for dynamic scheduling), then it decides a set of VM to be deployed (or cancelled) in each cloud and updates the VM list to inform the VM manager which VM must be deployed or cancelled.

Before each scheduling action, the scheduler also reads the instance list to know the type of instances available in each cloud, the price of each instance, the number of instances available, and so on.

15.4.1.3 VM Manager. The VM manager periodically reads the VM list, submits the VMs in pending state, and shuts down the VMs in cancelled state. When a new submitted VM is deployed and running in the cloud, or a cancelled VM is shut down, the VM manager updates its state in the VM list. The VM manager also monitors periodically the deployed VM and collects data about CPU, memory, and network usage of each one. This information is updated in the VM list. The VM manager uses the accounting information in the cloud list to access each cloud in order to deploy, shut down, or monitor VMs.

15.4.1.4 Cloud Manager. The cloud manager periodically collects information about instance availability and instance prices for all the instances listed in the instance list. Then it updates the instance list with the information collected. It is especially useful in dynamic prices case, in which it is necessary to periodically update these prices.

15.4.2 Service Description

The service description is a file defined by the user in some standard language, which contains detailed information about the service to be deployed by the broker, such as the components of the service, an optimization criteria, scheduling policies to use, scheduling constrains, type of instances to use, and performance of each instance. The information sections of the service description are the following:

15.4.2.1 Service Components and Lifetime. This part of the service description include a list of components of the service, which is an enumeration of the components that will be deployed as VM in different clouds (e.g., Component 1: web server front-ends; Component 2: data-baser servers; Component 3: application servers (back-ends); Component 4: file server); a list of images (e.g., AMI in Amazon EC2) associated with each component in each cloud to use; a list of post-configuration files for each service component (if necessary); and timing information (e.g., service start and end times).

15.4.2.2   Scheduling Parameters. For each service component, we must specify the scheduling parameters used to schedule and deploy this component. These parameters are: scheduling strategy, which can be static or dynamic; scheduling period, which is the interval between consecutive scheduling decisions in dynamic scenarios; scheduling policy, driven by various optimization criteria that are detailed in Section 15.5.2; and different kinds of restrictions detailed in Section 15.5.3.

15.4.2.3   Cloud Instance Usage and Instance Performance. The user can define which clouds (among those available) it wants to use for deploying a given service component, and which kind of instances it wants to use. In addition, the user can also specify the performance that each instance type is offering for the particular service (notice that the performance analysis of each instance must be done off-line by the user, and provided as an input of the service description).

15.5 SCHEDULING POLICIES FOR EFFICIENT CLOUD BROKERING

The cloud broker allows users to choose among several scheduling policies. In this section, we describe some scheduling strategies, optimization criteria, and user restrictions that can be integrated with the broker. Some of them are used in the experiments described in following sections.

15.5.1   Static vs. Dynamic Scheduling

The cloud scheduling issue can be addressed using either a static or a dynamic approach. The static approach is suitable for situations where the number of required virtual resources does not change (e.g., a fixed-size service), and the cloud provider conditions remain unchanged throughout the service life-cycle (resource prices, resource availability, etc.). In this scenario, the resource selection can be done off-line, once only, and in advance of service deployment. Conversely, the dynamic approach is more suitable for variable size services (e.g., a web server with fluctuating resource requirements), or in the case of changing cloud provider conditions (variable prices, dynamic resource availability, etc.). In this case, the optimization algorithm should run periodically to adapt the resource selection to the variable service resource requirements and cloud conditions. Although most of current cloud providers exhibit static conditions (prices change very rarely, resource availability is unknown but assumed to be high, etc.), dynamic pricing schemes have started to be adopted.

15.5.2   Optimization Criteria

For each service component, the scheduler can handle different scheduling policies based on different cost functions to optimize. The cost function to optimize must be unique, while some restrictions could be indicated to depict the user service needs. Some of the optimization criteria that can be considered are the following:

- *Cost optimization.* The broker tries to optimize the total cost of the service's infrastructure by deploying its components in the most appropriate cloud provider in each case. This criterion can combine static and dynamic prices of different providers, and in case of dynamic prices, the use of prediction models for guessing which provider will offer the cheapest prices in the next scheduling period.
- *Performance optimization.* The broker tries to optimize the performance of each service component. The measurement of this performance can be done in different ways:
  - Based on service performance metrics: The user should measure, following an off-line procedure, the performance of the application deployed in different instance types and clouds. This measure, which must be provided in the service description as an input of the cloud broker, indicates the expected performance of each cloud instance type (e.g., requests per second, response time, etc.).
  - Based on HW generic performance metrics: If service performance metrics are not available, the performance can be measured using basic HW metrics, as, for example, the number of Compute Units offered by each instance, or the MIPS/MFLOPS performance of each instance.
- *Resource consumption optimization.* The broker tries to maximize the CPU (also memory or bandwidth) consumption without exceeding a certain critical threshold.
- *Energy consumption optimization.* In this case, the broker should know energy consumption data from each instance type of each cloud provider. The broker tries to minimize this consumption, deploying less instances or using the saver ones.
- *Combined criteria.* A scheduling policy can be based on combining some of the previous criteria. For example, an optimization criteria based on the performance/cost ratio; or an optimization criteria based on a function of CPU and energy consumption, assigning a weight to each component (e.g., 80% CPU and 20% energy consumptions).

In each scheduling decision of each case, the scheduler will try to optimize the criterion being applied in the following period.

15.5.3   User Restrictions

Apart from optimization criteria, users can indicate several restrictions to guide the particular scheduling policy in order to adapt the broker decisions to the user needs. Some restrictions that can be considered are the following:

- *Price restriction*, which indicates the maximum budget available for deploying the service (e.g., 10€ per hour).

- *Performance restriction*, which indicates the minimum performance to achieve for the service (e.g., 100 requests per second during the service execution).
- *Instance type restriction*, which allows users to indicate which instance types they want to use or not use, and the percentage of usage of each one (e.g., "only small instances" or "50% of large and 50% of xlarge instances").
- *Number of instances*, which specifies the maximum or minimum number of instances to be deployed (e.g., no more than 50 VMs).
- *Load balancing restriction*, which allows a user to specify the maximum (or minimum) percentage of instances that can be deployed in each cloud (e.g., "at least 10% VM's in each cloud," "between 20% and 40% in each one," or "at least 20% only in cloud X").
- *Reallocation restriction*, which allows a user to specify the percentage of VMs that the broker can reallocate in each scheduling period. It helps in case of services that need to have part of the infrastructure always available, but can afford the reallocation of the other part of this infrastructure if it is going to provide benefits. This reallocation causes some VMs to be stopped and started in another location and hence some delays are introduced to continue working. If this restriction is not used, the broker could reallocate the whole infrastructure in each scheduling decision.
- *Resource consumption restriction*, which sets the maximum and minimum CPU (also memory, bandwidth, or energy) consumption allowed in the service (e.g., no more than 90% of CPU usage).

These restrictions combined with the selected optimization criterion adjust the broker functionality to solve the user needs. For example, users could optimize their service total cost but maintain performance over 100 attended requests per second; or they could optimize the number of CPU cores available for their service, with a maximum budget of 6€ per hour.

15.6 RESULTS

In the previous sections the general idea of the cloud broker was introduced. Now we present some preliminary results of cost optimization we get using the cloud broker both in single and multiple-cloud environments.

In the first experiment, the cost optimization for a variable computation demand application will be obtained by focusing on different pricing schemes of reserved and on-demand instances in a single cloud. In the second experiment, the broker will follow an algorithm to select the best cloud location for two different infrastructures, taking advantage of dynamic prices in a multi-cloud environment.

15.6.1 Cost Optimization in a Single Cloud

The goal of the first experiment is to deploy a computing infrastructure with a dynamic workload (e.g., a grid) in a single cloud provider. The broker tries to optimize the cost of the infrastructure by using a combination of reserved and on-demand instances.

In addition, to adapt the infrastructure to the variable service demand, the user can specify a minimun and maximum CPU load threshold (e.g., 65-85%), and the broker monitors the CPU of all the deployed VMs so that, if the average CPU load exceeds 85%, it automatically launches more instances to avoid the cluster performance degradation. In a similar way, when the load is below 65%, some instances are withdrawn from the service and shut-down.

In order to reduce the cost of the infrastructure, the cost optimization algorithm tries to reserve an optimal number of instances, based on the historical profile of the service deployed so that the infrastructure is provisioned using a combination of reserved instances, and on-demand instances when needed, reducing the cost compared to the deployment using only on-demand instances.

The reserved instances usually require a one-time payment that is compensated with cheaper hourly rates [28]. Hence, to reduce the final price of a reserved instance, a minimum number of usage hours is necessary. So, the scheduling policy needs to predict the number of necessary instances that will be needed in the future and reserve only the number of instances that will be used more than the minimum number of usage hours.

With this cost optimization algorithm, the broker is able to offer a on-demand service at smaller cost than the service provider itself thanks to the mixture of reserved and on-demand resources.

To test the scheduling policy DAS2 [29], workload traces and the Amazon price configurations for the standard instances [28] were used. In Fig. 15.2, the number of required and reserved instances over a three-year period is presented, and in Fig. 15.3, the cost of the deploying the service with this cost optimization technique is compared with the cost of deploying the service in the cloud provider using only on-demand instances.

15.6.2 Cost Optimization in a Multicloud Environment

The multicloud scheduling strategy proposed offers the possibility of using several clouds to deploy a service, taking advantage of clouds' dynamic prices. The aim is to deploy the user's service in the more appropriate cloud location at every moment (dynamic prices vary due to cloud providers' demand and providers publish them hourly) in order to optimize the overall cost of the infrastructure.

For these experiments, three different locations within Amazon EC2 infrastructure have been considered: United States Wet, Europe, and Asia. Also, their prices have been collected from the Amazon EC2 web page. We have considered two different use cases: an infrastructure for a virtual classroom and an infrastructure for web servers.

15.6.2.1 Infrastructure for a Virtual Classroom. An investment in PCs for a classroom can be expensive when the PCs are idle most of the time. To avoid this problem, the classroom can be virtualized using cloud resources, so that the classroom administrator, using the cloud broker, can order the deployment of a given number of VMs according with the class necessities. In this example, we have decided to maintain a fixed number of VMs of the same instance type. The broker takes one scheduling decision

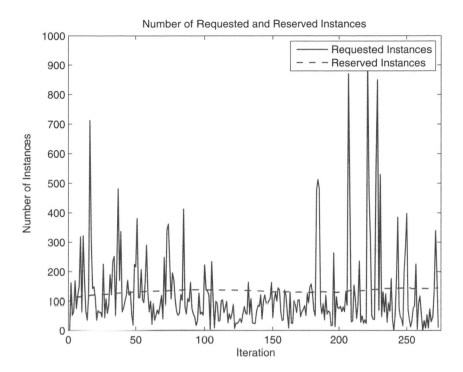

Figure 15.2   Number of reserved instances compared to the number of required instances.

per hour, and the whole infrastructure is reallocated to the cloud location that exhibits the lowest price. Thus, the broker takes advantage of dynamic prices to optimize the cost of the virtual infrastructure. Figure 15.4 shows the observed prices for the XL instance type from 8h to 20h obtained from the three locations of Amazon EC2 mentioned before. The black line shows the best prices of each scheduling decision and the cost reduction when the broker is used.

Figure 15.5 depicts the economic benefit obtained using the cloud broker in this fixed-size experiment, compared to a static deployment of the same infrastructure in every cloud provider.

15.6.2.2   *Infrastructure for a Web Server.*   A web server should be always online, allowing user access at every moment. In this example, we have a web cluster service composed by a front-end server, which will be deployed in a static way and will stay online for all the service life cycle, and 11 back-end servers, which will be deployed in a dynamic way. Here, reallocation restriction is attached to the model, maintaining part of the back-ends always online and reallocating the rest of them. Figure 15.6 represents the optimal deployment when 30% of the virtual infrastructure can be reallocated in each scheduling decision.

Figure 15.7 represents a cost comparison between deploying the virtual infrastructure in the same cloud location or deploying it in a dynamic way. The first three columns

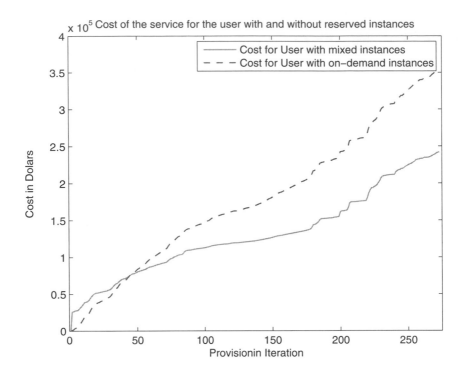

Figure 15.3   Cost for the user with the optimum reserved instances and no reserved instances.

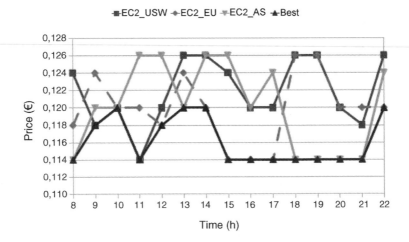

Figure 15.4   Dynamic prices.

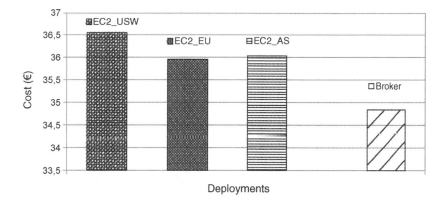

Figure 15.5 Cost of using the cloud broker against static deployments.

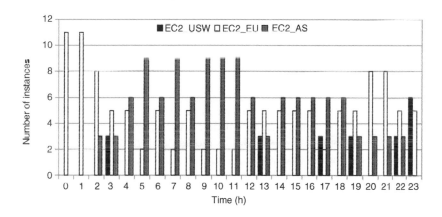

Figure 15.6 Hourly deployment reallocating up to 30% of virtual infrastructure.

refer to the static deployment in the three cloud locations that we have considered, while the last four columns refer to a dynamic deployment using the reallocation restriction of 10%, 30%, 50%, and 100% of the back-end infrastructure.

As a result, dynamic deployments present a lower cost than any static one. Moreover, the more VMs can be reallocated, the more economic benefits the broker can provide.

15.7 CONCLUSION

In this chapter, we present a cloud broker architecture for deploying virtual infrastructures belonging to different services across single or multiple clouds. The aim of the broker is to optimize a service parameter (e.g., cost, performance, resource consumption) following several optimization criteria. A discussion about cloud brokering challenges has been provided to illuminate the necessity of cloud brokering mechanisms.

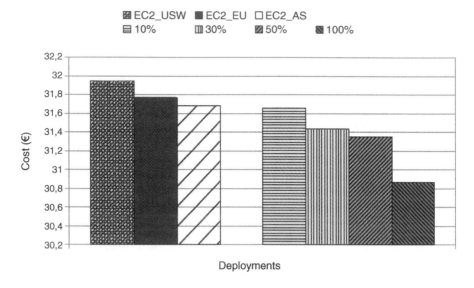

Figure 15.7   Cost comparison between static and dynamic deployments.

Inside the cloud broker architecture, we have defined the main actors, explaining their role in the broker. Also we define the main components of the architecture and their particular features, especially the scheduling module and the scheduling policies, with their optimization criteria and restrictions.

Finally, we present some preliminary results in single-cloud and multi-cloud scenarios. In the first scenario, we show that the use of the broker is beneficial when it is used in a single cloud using a cost optimization criteria that reserves the optimum number of instances to reduce the final cost.

To test this scenario, DAS2 [29] grid traces are used to simulate how the broker can deploy a grid service in the cloud. The results show that using the broker can reduce the cost of deploying the grid by 32%.

In the second scenario, we show that the use of several clouds can reap several benefits when part of or the entire infrastructure can be reallocated in each scheduling decision to the most favorable cloud.

We have studied two use cases: a virtual classroom and a web server. The main difference between them is the percentage of virtual infrastructure that can be reallocated in each scheduling decision. Results show that the more of a virtual infrastructure that can be reallocated, the more benefit the cloud broker provides.

ACKNOWLEDGMENTS

This research is funded, in part, by the European Union's Seventh Framework Programme ([FP7/2007-2013]) under grant agreement no 258862 (4CaaSt); by Consejería de

Educación of Comunidad de Madrid, Fondo Europeo de Desarrollo Regional, and from Ministerio de Economía y Competitividad of Spain through research grant TIN2012-31518 (ServiceCloud).

REFERENCES

[1] R. Buyya, C.S. Yeo, and S. Venugopal, "Market-oriented cloud computing: Vision, hype, and reality for delivering it services as computing utilities," in *High Performance Computing and Communications, 2008. HPCC '08. 10th IEEE International Conference on*, pp. 5 –13, Sept. 2008.

[2] Amazon Elastic Compute Cloud (EC2), http://aws.amazon.com/ec2/, (accessed June 2013).

[3] Cloud Sigma home page, http://www.cloudsigma.com/, (accessed June 2013).

[4] Elastic Hosts home page, http://www.elastichosts.com/, (accessed June 2013).

[5] Flexiant Cloud Computing Services, http://www.flexiant.com/, (accessed June 2013).

[6] Gogrid home page, http://www.gogrid.com/, (accessed June 2013).

[7] Rackspace Hosting, http://www.rackspace.com/, (accessed June 2013).

[8] B. Rochwerger, D. Breitgand, E. Levy, A. Galis, K. Nagin, I. M. Llorente, R. Montero, Y. Wolfsthal, E. Elmroth, J. Caceres, M. Ben-Yehuda, W. Emmerich, and F. Galan, "The reservoir model and architecture for open federated cloud computing," *IBM Journal of Research and Development*, Vol. 53, pp. 4:1–4:11, July 2009.

[9] E. Elmroth, F. Marquez, D. Henriksson, and D. Ferrera, "Accounting and billing for federated cloud infrastructures," in *Grid and Cooperative Computing, 2009. GCC '09. Eighth International Conference on*, pp. 268–275, Aug. 2009.

[10] R. Moreno-Vozmediano, R.S. Montero, and I.M. Llorente, "Multicloud deployment of computing clusters for loosely coupled mtc applications," *Parallel and Distributed Systems, IEEE Transactions on*, Vol. 22, pp. 924–930, June 2011.

[11] RightScale home page, http://www.rightscale.com/, (accessed June 2013).

[12] SpotCloud home page, http://www.spotcloud.com/, (accessed June 2013).

[13] Kavoo home page, http://www.kaavo.com/, (accessed June 2013).

[14] Cloud Switch home page, http://www.cloudswitch.com/, (accessed June 2013).

[15] M. Armbrust, A. Fox, R. Griffith, and A. Joseph, "mOSAIC," tech. rep., European Commission: Information Society and Media, May 2010. 2 pages.

[16] Optimis home page, http://www.optimis-project.eu/content/welcome-optimis, (accessed June 2013).

[17] K. Keahey, M. Tsugawa, A. Matsunaga, and J. Fortes, "Sky computing," *Internet Computing, IEEE*, Vol. 13, pp. 43–51, Sept.-Oct. 2009.

[18] R. Buyya, R. Ranjan, and R. Calheiros, "Intercloud: Utility-oriented federation of cloud computing environments for scaling of application services," *Algorithms and Architectures for Parallel Processing*, pp. 13–31, March 2010.

[19] M. Vouk, "Cloud computing–issues, research and implementations," *Journal of Computing and Information Technology*, Vol. 16, No. 4, pp. 235–246, 2004.

[20] T. Dillon, C. Wu, and E. Chang, "Cloud computing: Issues and challenges," *Advanced Information Networking and Applications, International Conference on*, Vol. 0, pp. 27–33, 2010.

[21] R. Nyrén, A. Edmonds, A. Papaspyrou, and T. Metsch, "Open Cloud Computing Interface—Core," tech. rep., OCCI Open Grid Forum, Apri 2011. 17 pages.

[22] T. Metsch and A. Edmonds, "Open Cloud Computing Interface—Infrastructure," tech. rep., OCCI Open Grid Forum, Apri 2011. 15 pages.

[23] Delta Cloud home page, http://deltacloud.org/, (accessed June 2013).

[24] Open Grid Forum home page, http://www.gridforum.org/, (accessed June 2013).

[25] B. Sotomayor, R. Montero, I. Llorente, and I. Foster, "Capacity leasing in cloud systems using the OpenNebula Engine," *Cloud Computing and Applications*, 2008.

[26] R. Moreno, R. Montero, and I. Llorente, "Elastic management of cluster-based services in the cloud," in *Proceedings of the 1st workshop on Automated Control for Datacenters and Clouds (ACDC09), held in conjunction with the 6th International Conference on Autonomic Computing and Communications*, pp. 19–24, ACM, Association for Computing Machinery, 2009.

[27] M. Mihailescu and Y. M. Teo, "Dynamic resource pricing on federated clouds," *10th IEEE/ACM International Conference on Cluster, Cloud and Grid Computing*, Vol. 0, pp. 513–517, 2010.

[28] Amazon Pricing Schemes, http://aws.amazon.com/ec2/pricing, (accessed June 2013).

[29] DAS2 workload trace, http://gwa.ewi.tudelft.nl/pmwiki/reports/gwa-t-1/trace_analysis_report.html_analysis_report.html, (accessed June 2013).

[30] J. L. Lucas-Simarro, R. Moreno-Vozmediano, R. S. Montero, and I. M. Llorente, "Scheduling strategies for optimal service deployment across multiple clouds," *Future Generation Computing Systems*, Vol. 29, pp. 1431–1441, August 2013.

16

ENERGY-EFFICIENT RESOURCE UTILIZATION IN CLOUD COMPUTING

Giorgio L. Valentini, Samee U. Khan, and Pascal Bouvry

CONTENTS

Large Scale Network-Centric Distributed Systems, First Edition. Edited by Hamid Sarbazi-Azad and Albert Y. Zomaya.
© 2014 John Wiley & Sons, Inc. Published 2014 by John Wiley & Sons, Inc.

16.1 INTRODUCTION

Data communications are an important element of our daily lives. Most of our interactions rely on gathering information through the client-server paradigm [7]. Over time, user demands have rapidly increased in terms of the number of requests. To cater to the consistent amount of requests, computational capacities and facilities must be constantly reviewed and improved. To remain competitive, the proportional nonnegligible amount of the required energy has been often left behind.

Recent advocacy of "green" or "sustainable computing" (tightly coupled with energy consumption) has received considerable attention. The scope of sustainable computing goes beyond the main computing components, expanding into a much larger range of resources associated with auxiliary equipment, such as the water used for cooling and the physical/floor space occupied by the resources.

In Cloud computing, energy consumption and resource utilization are strongly coupled. Specifically, resources with a low utilization rate still consume an unacceptable amount of energy compared to the energy consumption of a fully utilized or sufficiently loaded Cloud computing. According to recent studies [5, 23, 28, 44], average resource utilization in most data centers can be as low as 20%, and the average energy consumption of idle resources can be as high as 60% (or peak power). To increase resource utilization, task consolidation is an effective technique, greatly enabled by virtualization technologies, which facilitate the concurrent execution of several tasks and, in turn, reduce energy consumption.

Our study uses two energy-conscious heuristics for task consolidation presented by Lee and Zomaya in [46]: *MaxUtil*, which aims to maximize resource utilization, and

ECTC (acronym for Energy-Conscious Task Consolidation—an overview of the most common acronyms used in our study is provided in Table 16.1), which explicitly takes into account both active and idle energy consumption. For a given task, *ECTC* computes the energy consumption based on an objective function derived from findings reported

TABLE 16.1 Common Acronyms

Acronym	Description
a_j	Arrival time of a task
ETC	Energy-efficient Task Consolidation (algorithm)
d	Distance between two points
$\mathcal{D}$	Solution set in the two-dimension search space
d_j	Due date of a task
δ	Normalized complement of the distance result (d)
ECTC	Energy-Conscious Task Consolidation
e_j	Energy consumption of a task on a resource
ϵ_i	Minute energy factor of a resource
E_i	Energy consumption of a resource
$E_{\mathcal{R}}$	Energy consumption of the system
$\mathcal{F}$	Subset (of equivalents solutions) of $\mathcal{D}$
$f_{i,j}$	Generic cost function
f_x	Normalized result of the *ECTC* cost function
f_y	Result of the *MaxUtil* cost function
m	Number of resources
MaxUtil	Maximum (rate) Utilization
$m(p)$	Objectives vector
n	Number of tasks
$norm_x$	Normalization function
p_i	Point in the two-dimensional search space
p_{max}	Power consumption at peak load
p_{min}	Power consumption in the active mode
p_Δ	$p_{max} - p_{min}$
r_i	i^{th} resource
$\mathcal{R}$	Set of resources
t_j	j^{th} task
$\mathcal{T}$	Set of tasks
$u_{i,j}$	Resource usage of a task
U_i	Utilization rate of a resource
$U_{\mathcal{R}}$	Utilization rate of the system
τ	Generic time period
τ_x	Generic time periods of the *ECTC* cost function
τ_0	Total processing time of a task on a resource
τ_1	Time period where a task is run alone
τ_2	Time period where a task is consolidated
$\dfrac{\lambda}{\mu}$	Output / Input (ratio)
$[x_{min}:x_{max}]$	*ECTC* unit range
$[y_{min}:y_{max}]$	*MaxUtil* unit range

in the literature. As stated in the findings, the energy consumption can be significantly reduced while consolidating tasks instead of being executed stand alone. Consequently, the two heuristics reduce energy consumption without any performance degradation while assigning a given task to a selected resource.

To take advantage of both of the methods, while always considered separately, we propose to combine the heuristics in a complementarity approach. Identifying the resource offering the best compromise between the two heuristics will most likely truly maximize the utilization rate while minimizing the energy consumption. The main idea of the proposed approach is to execute the task on the optimal "energy-efficient" resource.

The remainder of this chapter is organized as follows. Section 16.2 overviews the related work. Section 16.3 details the Cloud computing, energy models, and task consolidation algorithms. The complementarity approach and the related mathematical model are described in Section 16.4, while the simulation results and the discussions are summarized in Section 16.5 and Section 16.6, respectively. Section 16.7 concludes our study.

16.2 RELATED WORK

Energy efficiency is an emerging research issue, recently addressed by several researchers. For example, Khan and Ahmad in [38] were the first to use game theoretical methodologies to simultaneously optimize system performance and energy consumption. Since then, several research works have used similar models and approaches, which have addressed a mix of research problems related to large-scale computing systems, such as energy proportionality, memory-aware computations, data intensive computations, energy-efficient, grid scheduling, and green networks [4, 8, 10, 13, 19, 25, 29, 37, 45].

Cloud computing and green computing paradigms are closely related and are gaining more attention. The energy efficiency of Cloud computing became one of the most crucial research issues. Advancements in hardware technologies [41], such as low-power CPUs, solid state drives, and energy-efficient computer monitors, have relieved the energy issue to a certain degree. Meanwhile, a considerable amount of software approach research has been conducted, such as scheduling and resource allocation [9, 18, 20, 22, 30, 32, 45] and task consolidation [21, 33, 35, 47].

Virtualization technologies are a key component within the task consolidation approach. Parallel processing has been greatly eased and boosted with the prevalence of many-core processors. That is, multiples tasks are often run on a single many-core processor. The parallel processing practice seems at a glance to inherently increase performance and productivity. But the trade-off between the aforementioned increase and the consequent energy consumption should be carefully investigated. For example, the load imbalance (especially in the many-core processors) is a major source of energy drainage that has motivated multiple task consolidation studies [21, 33, 35, 47].

Srikantaiah et al. [35] approached the task consolidation using the traditional binpacking problem with two main characteristics: (1) CPU usage and (2) disk usage. The proposed algorithm consolidates the tasks, relying on the Pareto front to balance the energy consumption and the performance. The algorithm incorporates two main steps:

(1) determination of the optimal points from the profiling data and (2) "energy-aware" resource allocation using the Euclidean distance between the current selection and the optimal point within each server.

Song et al. [47] proposed a utility analytic model for Internet-oriented task consolidation. The model considers a task's request for web services such as e-books database or e-commerce. The proposed model aims to maximize the resource utilization and to reduce the energy consumption, offering the same quality of services appropriate to the dedicated servers. The model also measures performance degradation of the consolidated tasks through the introduced "impact factor" metric.

The task consolidation mechanisms detailed by Torres et al. [21] and Nathuji et al. [33] deal with energy reduction using unusual approaches, especially in [21]. Unlike typical task consolidation strategies, the approach used in [21] adopts two interesting techniques: (1) memory compression and (2) request discrimination. The first enables the conversion of the CPU power into extra memory capacity to allow more (memory intensive) tasks to be consolidated, whereas the second blocks useless/unfavorable requests (coming from web crawlers) to eliminate unnecessary resource usage. The VirtualPower approach proposed in [33] incorporates task consolidation into the power management, combining "soft scaling" and "hard scaling" methodologies. The two methodologies (of [21] and [33]) are based on power management facilities equipped with virtual machines and physical processors, respectively.

More recently, several noteworthy efforts on energy-aware scheduling (in large-scale distributed computing systems as grids) using game theoretic approaches have been reported [34, 38]. Subrata et al. [34] propose a cooperative game model and the Nash Bargaining solution to address the grid load-balancing problem. The main objective is to minimize energy consumption while maintaining a specified service quality (i.e., time and fairness). Both [38] and [34] deal with independent jobs through the (semi-)static scheduling mode leveraging DVFS technique to minimize the energy consumption. (For recent literature reviews, the reader is referred to [1], [11], and [12].)

16.3 ENERGY-EFFICIENT UTILIZATION OF RESOURCES IN CLOUD COMPUTING SYSTEMS

16.3.1 Cloud Computing

The underlying system consists of a set $\mathcal{R} = \{r_0, \dots, r_{m-1}\}$ of m resources (processors) that are fully interconnected in the sense that a route exists between any two resources. It is assumed that resources are homogeneous in terms of computing capability and capacity. The aforementioned is achieved through the virtualization technologies as many-core processors and virtualization tools are commonplace [14]. The number of concurrent tasks on a single physical resource is loosely bounded and Cloud computing can span multiple geographical locations.

The Cloud computing model we consider is assumed to (a) be confined to a particular physical location, (b) have the inter-processor communications performing with the same speed on all links without substantial contentions, and (c) allow the flow of messages from one resource to another while a task is being executed on the recipient resource.

16.3.2 Energy Model

The energy model is based on the fact that processor utilization has a linear relationship with energy consumption. The proportional relationship means that, for a particular task, the information on the processing time and the processor utilization is sufficient to measure the energy consumption for the task.

At any given time, for a resource r_i, the utilization U_i is defined as

$$U_i = \sum_{j=0}^{n-1} u_{i,j}, \tag{16.1}$$

where n is the number of tasks running at the given time and $u_{i,j}$ is the resource usage of a task t_j.

The energy consumption E_i of a resource r_i at any given time is defined as

$$E_i = (p_{max} - p_{min}) \times U_i + p_{min}, \tag{16.2}$$

where p_{max} is the power consumption at the peak load (or 100% utilization) and p_{min} is the minimum power consumption in the active mode (or as low as 1% utilization).

Consequently, at any given time, the total utilization $(U_\mathcal{R})$ as the total energy consumption $(E_\mathcal{R})$ of the system are defined as

$$U_\mathcal{R} = \sum_{i=0}^{m-1} U_i \quad \text{and} \quad E_\mathcal{R} = \sum_{i=0}^{m-1} E_i, \tag{16.3}$$

respectively, where m represents the number of resources.

The resources in the underlying system are assumed to be incorporated with an effective power-saving mechanism for idle time slots. The mechanism results from the significant difference in energy consumption between active and idle resources states. Specifically, the energy consumption of an idle resource at any given time is set to 10% of p_{min}. Because the overhead to turn off and on a resource takes a nonnegligible amount of time, the option for idle resources was not considered in our study or by others [21, 33, 35, 46, 47].

16.3.3 Task Consolidation Problem

The task consolidation (also known as server/workload consolidation) problem is the process of assigning a set $\mathcal{T} = \{t_0, \ldots, t_{n-1}\}$ of n tasks (service requests or simply services) to a set $\mathcal{R} = \{r_0, \ldots, r_{m-1}\}$ of m Cloud computing resources, without violating time constraints. The main purpose remains to maximize resource utilization and ultimately to minimize energy consumption.

Time constraints are directly related to the resource usage associated with the tasks. More precisely, in the consolidation problem, the resources allocated to a particular task must sufficiently provide the resource usage of that given task. For example, a task with its resource usage requirement of 60% cannot be assigned to a resource for which the available resource utilization at the time of that task's arrival is 50%.

16.3.4 Task Consolidation Algorithm

16.3.4.1 Overview. Task consolidation is an effective means to manage resources, particularly in Cloud computing, both in the "short-term" and "long-term" [24, 31]. In the short-term case, volume flux on incoming tasks can be "energy-efficiently" dealt with by reducing the number of active resources and putting redundant resources into a power-saving mode, or even turning off some idle resources systematically. In the long-term case, cloud infrastructure providers can better supply power and resources, alleviating the burden of excessive operational costs due to overprovisioning. Lee and Zomaya [16] focused on the short-term case, even if the results delivered by the task consolidation algorithms could be used as an estimator in the long-term provisioning case.

Subsection 16.3.4.2 presents the energy conscious task consolidation heuristics (*ECTC* and *MaxUtil*), more commonly referred to as cost functions [46]. The two cost functions are described side-by-side to highlight the main differences, being whether the energy consumption is considered explicitly or implicitly. More precisely, *MaxUtil* makes task consolidation decisions based on resource utilization, which is a key indicator for energy efficiency.

16.3.4.2 Cost Functions (ECTC and MaxUtil). The cost function, termed *ECTC*, computes the actual energy consumption of the current task by subtracting the minimum energy consumption (p_{min}) required to run a task, if other tasks would be running in parallel with that task. That is, the energy consumption of the overlapping time period among the running tasks and the current task (t_j) is explicitly taken into account. The cost function tends to discriminate the task being executed in a stand-alone mode.

The value $f_{i,j}$ of a task t_j on a resource r_i obtained using the *ECTC* cost function [46] is defined as

$$f_{i,j} = [(p_\Delta \times u_j + p_{min}) \times \tau_0] - [(p_\Delta \times u_j + p_{min}) \times \tau_1 + (p_\Delta \times u_j \times \tau_2)],$$
(16.4)

where p_Δ is the difference between p_{max} and p_{min}, u_j is the utilization rate of t_j, and τ_0, τ_1, and τ_2 are the total processing time of t_j. That is, the time period t_j is running stand alone and that t_j is running in parallel with one or more tasks, respectively. For example, consider two tasks (t_0 and t_1) that are running in parallel on the same resource (r_0), with t_0 arriving first on the resource (see Fig. 16.1). While computing the result for $f_{0,1}$

$$\tau_0 = \text{the total execution time of } t_1,$$
$$\tau_1 = \tau_0 - \tau_2,$$
$$\tau_2 = \tau_0 - \tau_1,$$

where τ_1 is the time period where t_1 will be running stand alone on r_0, and τ_2 the time period where t_1 will be consolidated with t_0 in r_0 (the overlapping time).

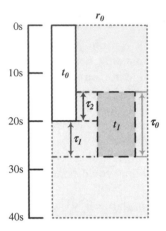

Figure 16.1 Time periods of the task t_1.

The rationale behind the *ECTC* cost function is that the energy consumption at the lowest resource utilization is far greater than that in idle state, and the additional energy consumption imposed by overlapping tasks contributes to a relatively low increase.

Alternatively, the *MaxUtil* cost function is derived with the average utilization during the processing time of the current task, as core component. The cost function aims to increase consolidation density and has a dual benefit. That is, (a) the implicit reduction of the energy consumption is directly related to (b) the decreased number of active resources. In others words, *MaxUtil* tends to intensify the utilization of a small number of resources.

Consequently, the value $f_{i,j}$ of a task t_j on a resource r_i using the *MaxUtil* cost function [46] is defined as

$$f_{i,j} = \frac{\sum_{\tau=1}^{\tau_0} U_i}{\tau_0}, \tag{16.5}$$

which is the utilization of a resource r_i, as defined in Equation (16.1), divided by the total execution time (τ_0) of task t_j.

16.3.4.3 Task Consolidation Algorithm. In essence, for a given task, the algorithm checks every resource and identifies the most energy-efficient resource for that task. The evaluation of the most energy-efficient resource is dependent on the used heuristic (*ECTC* or *MaxUtil*). More specifically, on the employed cost function (referred to as $f_{i,j}$). Algorithm 16.1 describes the main steps of the task consolidation procedure.

16.3.5 Application of the Model: A Working Example

As incorporated into the energy model, energy consumption is directly proportional to the resource utilization. In short, for any two task-resource matches, the one with a higher utilization may be selected. However, because the determination of the right match is

---

Algorithm 16.1 Task consolidation algorithm

---

input : $t_j \in \mathcal{T} = \{t_0, \ldots, t_{n-1}\}$, $\mathcal{R} = \{r_0, \ldots, r_{m-1}\}$
output: $r^* \in \mathcal{R}$
begin

     $r^*, f_{*,j} \longleftarrow \emptyset$
     forall $r_i \in \mathcal{R}$ **do**
         Compute the cost function value $f_{i,j}$ of t_j on r_i
         if $f_{i,j} > f_{*,j}$ **then**
             $r^* \longleftarrow r_i$
             $f_{*,j} \longleftarrow f_{i,j}$

     Assign t_j to r^*

---

not entirely dependent on the current task, *ECTC* makes its decisions based rather on the (sole) energy consumption of that task.

Table 16.2 details four tasks properties specifically selected (as the working example) to point out the divergent behavior of *ECTC* and *MaxUtil*. For each task (t_j) we specified the arrival time (a_j), processing time (τ_0), and utilization or resource usage requirement (u_j). For the working example it is assumed that p_{min} is set to 20 and p_{max} to 30. These values can be seen as rough estimates in actual resources and can be referenced as 200 *watt* and 300 *watt*, respectively. Conforming to the respective properties presented in, Table 16.2, each task (t_j) will be assigned to the more "energy-efficient" resource (r_i) selected through the cost functions.

Figure 16.2 depicts the allocation of the first three tasks, where task t_3 illustrates the divergence from the results obtained from the respective cost functions. Based on the (sole) energy consumption of the task, *ECTC* assigns t_3 to the resource r_1 (see Fig. 16.2(a)), while based on the available utilization rate of the resources, *MaxUtil* assigns t_3 to the resource r_0 (see Fig. 16.2(b)). The difference between the two functions becomes more prominent when task t_4 must be assigned to a resource. As illustrated in Fig. 16.3, *ECTC* can only assign t_4 to the empty resource r_2 (see Fig. 16.3(a)), while *MaxUtil* assigns t_4 to r_1 (see Fig. 16.3(b)). On our specific working example *MaxUtil* seems to be more "energy-efficient" than *ECTC*.

Reference [46] claimed that the performances of the algorithms can be slightly ameliorated incorporating task migration. At each computational time, the scheduler checks

T A B L E 16.2 Task Properties

Task (t_j)	Arrival Time (a_j)	Processing Time (τ_0)	Utilization (u_j)
0	00 (*sec.*)	20 (*sec.*)	40%
1	03 (*sec.*)	08 (*sec.*)	50%
2	07 (*sec.*)	23 (*sec.*)	20%
3	14 (*sec.*)	10 (*sec.*)	40%
4	20 (*sec.*)	15 (*sec.*)	70%

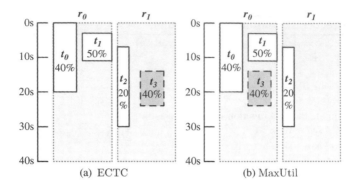

Figure 16.2 Depiction of the first three tasks.

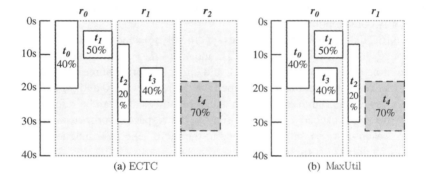

Figure 16.3 Final depiction for all the tasks

if some of the running tasks would be more "energy-efficient," when allocated to a different resource. If suitable, then the scheduler proceeds with the migration. Interestingly, the benefit of using migration is not apparent. Migrated tasks tend to be with short remaining processing times and these tasks are most likely to hinder the consolidation of new arriving tasks. Consequently, the incorporation of task migration increased the energy consumption.

16.4 COMPLEMENTARITY APPROACH

16.4.1 Main Idea

The algorithm described in Section 16.3.4 uses only one of the two cost functions at a time. In advance, it must be decided whether to use *ECTC* or *MaxUtil*. According to the working example described in Section 16.3.5, for a given task, the result of the two cost functions can diverge. The divergence comes from the two different considered aspects (energy consumption or resource utilization).

The idea behind the complementarity approach is to combine the two cost functions to only benefit from their advantages. The algorithm will then provide, as a result, the more "energy-efficient" resource based on both of the considered aspects. That is, the (sole) energy consumption as the resource utilization.

16.4.2 Motivation

We must note that *ECTC* computes the energy consumption of a given task on a selected resource, while *MaxUtil* looks after the more energy-efficient resource in terms of resource utilization. The *ECTC* cost function is designed to prioritize resource sharing. As stated in Subsection 16.3.4.2, for a given resource, the energy consumption of two tasks running in parallel is slightly superior than the energy consumption of a task ran alone [15–17].

To be accurate on the computation of the energy consumption, *ECTC* uses τ_1 and τ_2 (see Subsection 16.3.4.2). Based on the time periods (τ_x), the cost function gives priority to resources where concurrent tasks can be fully consolidated and tends to discard the resources offering only a partial consolidation. The aforementioned scenario is illustrated in Fig. 16.2. Task t_0 do not fully overlap task t_3 on resource r_0, then *ECTC* assigns t_3 on r_1 because t_3 can be fully consolidated with the task t_2.

The working example presented in Section 16.3.5 pointed out the main drawback of *ECTC*. Intuitively, the resulting divergence from the behavior of *MaxUtil* can be seen as a "domino effect" that will temporarily affect the system. Energy efficiency (see Fig. 16.3) being the main concern of the presented heuristics, the eventuality of a "domino effect" should not be neglected while considering the *ECTC* cost function for the task consolidation problem as defined in Section 16.3.3. Alternatively, *MaxUtil* always minimizes the total number of used resources without individually considering the energy consumption of the given task.

Because the objective of our study is to minimize the energy consumption as the total number of used resources, our proposal combines the two cost functions to select the resource that will most likely maximize the utilization rate and minimize the energy consumption.

16.4.3 Approach

The approach is geometrical and uses the two cost functions described in Equation (16.4) and Equation (16.5). The respective results are combined to build a "point" in a two-dimensional search space where *ECTC* gives the x coordinate and *MaxUtil* the y coordinate.

Originally, Equation (16.4) returns a value greater than zero only when applied on a resource allowing task consolidation. Among the collected results, the highest value identifies the most "energy-efficient" resource (if $\tau_1 \neq \tau_0$), while the null value identifies empty (non "energy-efficient") resources (if $\tau_1 = \tau_0$). Figure 16.4 illustrates the rationale behind the *ECTC* cost function.

To properly construct the point in the search space, the two cost functions must be slightly modified. Defining the energy consumption e_j of a task (t_j) on a given resource

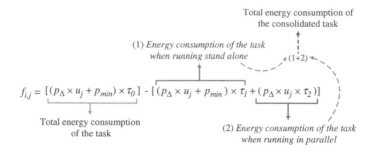

Figure 16.4   Structure of the *ECTC* cost function.

(r_i) as

$$e_j = (p_\Delta \times u_j + p_{min}), \tag{16.6}$$

the value $f_{i,j}$ of t_j on r_i obtained using the *ECTC* cost function is now defined as

$$f_{i,j} = \begin{cases} (e_j \times \tau_0) & ; \text{ if } \tau_1 = \tau_0 \\ ((e_j \times \tau_1) + (p_\Delta \times u_j \times \tau_2)) & ; \text{ otherwise.} \end{cases} \tag{16.7}$$

The value of $f_{i,j}$ obtained using the *MaxUtil* cost function during a specific time period (τ) as

$$f_{i,j} = \sum_{\tau=a_j}^{d_j} U_i, \tag{16.8}$$

where a_j is the arrival (or ready) time and d_j the due date (given by $a_j + \tau_0$) of the current task t_j.

16.4.4 Metric Normalization

To find the optimal point in a two-dimensional search space, the results of the two cost functions must be normalized to a homogeneous unit scale. Because the range of *MaxUtil* is defined in a continuous unit scale from 1 to 100, the result of *ECTC* will be normalized to the unit scale of *MaxUtil*, from now on formally referred to as $[y_{min} : y_{max}]$.

For a given task (t_j) the utilization on a selected resource (r_i) is directly dependent on the speed (operations per seconds) of the CPU on that resource. The amount of time needed for the resource to accomplish the task is derived from the speed of that CPU. Based on the above information (speed and time) of a selected resource, the maximum value (x_{max}) returned by the *ECTC* cost function can be then estimated and the *ECTC* unit range defined by the bounded interval going from 0 to x_{max}.

Defining x_{min} as the lower bound and x_{max} as the upper bound of the *ECTC* unit range, the normalization of the (*ECTC*) metric on the unit scale $[y_{min} : y_{max}]$ is given as

$$norm_x \; : \; [x_{min} : x_{max}] \longrightarrow [y_{min} : y_{max}],$$
$$norm_x = \left[\frac{(f_{i,j} - x_{min}) \times (y_{max} - y_{min})}{x_{max} - x_{min}} \right]. \tag{16.9}$$

As mentioned in the Section 16.4.3, for a set of resources ($\mathcal{R} = \{r_0, \ldots, r_{m-1}\}$) the highest value ($f_{i,j}$) returned by the cost functions identifies the most "energy-efficient" resource (see Algorithm 16.1). Because we modified the original *ECTC* cost function (see Equation (16.7)), the complement of $norm_x$, denoted as f_x, must be considered

$$f_x \; : \; [y_{min} : y_{max}] \longrightarrow [y_{min} : y_{max}],$$
$$f_x = y_{max} - norm_x, \tag{16.10}$$

to coherently build the normalized two-dimensional point in the evaluation space.

16.4.5 Evaluation Space

Renaming the respective returned value from the cost functions as f_x for (the normalized complement of) *ECTC* and f_y for *MaxUtil*, the coordinates of the point p_i for a selected resource r_i is defined as

$$p_i = (f_x; f_y),$$

and among all the points, the optimal will be the higher point giving the best compromise between the results of the two cost functions (f_x and f_y). The ideal optimal points must then belong to the domain space of the function

$$f(x) = y. \tag{16.11}$$

Therefore, the closer the p_i is to the line (given by Equation (16.11)), the more probable it is for that point to be the local optimal. For every p_i, the respective distance to the corresponding ideal optimal point will be computed and referred to as

$$d = |f_x - f_y|. \tag{16.12}$$

The smaller the value of d, the closer the p_i is to the respective ideal optimal point belonging to the domain space (of Equation (16.11)). This also will be the best compromise offered by the given point. The value of d will finally be the main estimator of the selection of the best candidate among the equivalent optimal solutions.

16.4.6 Selection of the Best Candidate

16.4.6.1 Mathematical Model. There exist many methodologies to find the optimal solution among the solution set [2, 6, 36]. The main idea would be to avoid having to compare all points within the solution space at every decision point.

The first step of our approach consists of constructing the solution search space based on the results of the two cost functions. The optimal solution will be identified and updated at the same time the solution set is constructed. By the time the solution set is built the optimal solution will be identified. The search operation will rely on the Pareto dominance criteria [40, 42, 43]. The first point of the solution space will be set as the "current" optimal solution. The "current" solution will then be compared to the next (new) created point and updated, if needed.

Formally, let $\mathcal{D}$ be a finite set. For a fixed natural k, a mapping

$$m \; : \; \mathcal{D} \longrightarrow \mathbb{R}^k,$$
$$m(p) = (m_1(p), \ldots, m_k(p)),$$

can be defined, whose components $m_i : \mathcal{D} \longrightarrow \mathbb{R}, \forall i : 1 \leq i \leq k$, are denoted as objectives and $\mathbb{R}^k$ is the evaluation (or measurement) space of the elements of $\mathcal{D}$. As already mentioned, our approach maximizes the considered objectives. Accordingly, given p and q, the two elements of $\mathcal{D}$, p dominates q, and it is represented as $p \succ q$, if and only if,

$$\bigl(\forall i : 1 \leq i \leq k : (m_i(p) \geq m_i(q)) \wedge (\exists j : 1 \leq j \leq k : m_j(p) \neq m_j(q))\bigr). \quad (16.13)$$

From our analysis and discussion of Section 16.4.5 it follows that

$$m(p) = (f_x, \; f_y),$$

where $m(p)$ belongs to the homogeneous unit scale $[y_{min} : y_{max}]$.

16.4.6.2 *Algorithm*. For each resource, the algorithm constructs the corresponding point in the evaluation space ($\mathcal{D}$) and verifies if the new created solution dominates the current optimal solution. If the aforementioned case is verified, then the algorithm updates the optimal solution. Algorithm 16.2 details the main steps of the procedure used to identify the optimal solution from the solution set $\mathcal{D}$.

Algorithm 16.2 Complementarity procedure.

---

input : $t_j \in \mathcal{T} = \{t_0, \ldots, t_{n-1}\}$, $\mathcal{R} = \{r_0, \ldots, r_{m-1}\}$
output: $r^* \in \mathcal{R}$
begin
    $r^*, optimal \longleftarrow \emptyset$
    forall $r \in \mathcal{R}$ **do**
        $x \longleftarrow f_x$
        $y \longleftarrow f_y$
        $result \longleftarrow (x, \; y)$
        if $result \succ optimal$ **then**
            $optimal \longleftarrow result$
            $r^* \longleftarrow r$

16.4.7 Processing of Equivalent Solutions

The design of Algorithm 16.2 does not identify equivalent solutions. A double dominance check must be introduced and the equivalent solutions added to a subset $\mathcal{F}$ ($\mathcal{F} \subseteq \mathcal{D}$). Because the optimal solution may change by the time the domain space ($\mathcal{D}$) is constructed, $\mathcal{F}$ must "reset" each time a new optimal point is identified. This will ensure that the subset only contains the equivalent solutions to the latest optimal point.

By the time the solution space is constructed, the equivalent optimal points will be identified. The selection among the equivalent solutions belonging to $\mathcal{F}$, if any, will rely on d. Because our approach maximizes the considered objectives, the complement of d, denoted as δ, will be considered according the formula

$$\delta : [y_{min} : y_{max}] \longrightarrow [y_{min} : y_{max}],$$
$$\delta = y_{max} - d. \tag{16.14}$$

The aforementioned selection process will sequentially compare each $f \in \mathcal{F}$ with the actual optimal point. The actual optimal will then be updated based on the δ parameter, or on the sum of the two coordinates $((f_x, f_y) \in p_i)$, if the pair share the same value for the x (energy consumption) or y (utilization) coordinate.

16.4.8 Energy-Efficient Task Consolidation Algorithm

The algorithm constructs, for each resource, the corresponding point in the evaluation space ($\mathcal{D}$) and verifies if the: (a) new created solution dominates the current optimal solution or (b) two solutions are equivalent, otherwise. If the fist aforementioned case is verified, then the algorithm updates the optimal solution and "reset" the equivalent solutions subset ($\mathcal{F}$). Otherwise the algorithm update $\mathcal{F}$ with the new created solution if suitable. Among the equivalent solutions of $\mathcal{F}$, the algorithm identifies the optimal solution through: (c) the δ parameter or (d) the sum of the two coordinates. Algorithm 16.3 describes the entire procedure that identifies the optimal solution from the solution set $\mathcal{D}$ and the related subset $\mathcal{F}$.

16.4.9 An Intuitive Example

Conforming to the data provided in Table 16.2, the problem will be now solved using the *ETC* algorithm, where for the normalization procedure into the *MaxUtil* unit scale, y_{min} is set to 1, y_{max} to 100, and x_{max} to 1000. Table 16.3 summarizes the numerical results of Equation (16.7), Equation (16.8), Equation (16.9), Equation (16.10), Equation (16.12), and Equation (16.14) presented in the previous subsections of section 16.4. For each task (t_j) a maximum number of three resources (r_i) are identified. *ECTC* and *MaxUtil* represent the values of the respective cost functions (see Equation (16.7) and Equation (16.8)) for a given task (t_j) on the selected resource (r_i). The normalized value of *ECTC* is given by $norm_x$ (see Equation (16.9)) and the coordinates of the constructed point in the two-dimensional search space are denoted by p_i (see Equation (16.10)). The value of d (see Equation (16.12)) illustrates the distance from the point (p_i) and the corresponding ideal optimal point for the selected resource (r_i), while δ_i (see Equation (16.14)) denotes

---

Algorithm 16.3 *ETC* algorithm

---

input : $t_j \in \mathcal{T} = \{t_0, \ldots, t_{n-1}\}$, $\mathcal{R} = \{r_0, \ldots, r_{m-1}\}$
output: $r^* \in \mathcal{R}$
begin

    $r^*, optimal, \mathcal{F} \longleftarrow \emptyset$
    forall $r \in \mathcal{R}$ **do**
        $x \longleftarrow f_x$
        $y \longleftarrow f_y$
        $\delta \longleftarrow (y_{max} - |x - y|)$
        $result \longleftarrow (x, y)$
        if $(result \succ optimal)$ **then**
            $optimal \longleftarrow result$
            $r^* \longleftarrow r, \mathcal{F} \longleftarrow \emptyset$
            $\mathcal{F} \longleftarrow \mathcal{F} \cup (result, r, \delta)$

        if $((result \not\succ optimal) \wedge (optimal \not\succ result))$ **then**
            $\mathcal{F} \longleftarrow \mathcal{F} \cup (result, r, \delta)$

    forall $(f, r, \delta) \in \mathcal{F}$ **do**
        if $((f_x \neq optimal_x) \wedge (f_y \neq optimal_y))$ **then**
            if $(\delta > \delta_{optimal})$ **then**
                $optimal \longleftarrow f$
                $\delta_{optimal} \longleftarrow \delta$
                $r^* \longleftarrow r$

        else
            if $((f_x + f_y) > (optimal_x + optimal_y))$ **then**
                $optimal \longleftarrow f$
                $\delta_{optimal} \longleftarrow \delta$
                $r^* \longleftarrow r$

---

the normalized complement of the aforementioned distance (d). If at the arrival time of a task (t_j) the selected r_i has not enough available resource utilization rate for the given t_j, then that resource will not be shown in the table. The double right arrow ($\Rightarrow$) identifies the optimal result selected by the algorithm.

For example, task t_0 requires: (a) 40% of available resource utilization, (b) 20 seconds to be executed by a selected resource, and (c) arrives at time t equal to zero. In line with the aforementioned task's properties, when evaluating the resource r_0, (d) *ECTC* returns a value equal to 480 (converted to 48 after normalization) and (e) *MaxUtil* a value equal to 40 (because run in stand alone mode). The coordinates of the corresponding point

TABLE 16.3 Results of the *ETC*'s Computations

Task (t_j)	Resource (r_i)	ECTC	$norm_x$	MaxUtil	p_i (f_x; f_y)	d	δ_i
t_0	⇒ r_0	480	48	40	(52; 40)	12	88
	r_1	480	48	40	(52; 40)	12	88
	r_2	480	48	40	(52; 40)	12	88
t_1	⇒ r_0	180	18	90	(82; 90)	8	92
	r_1	200	20	50	(80; 50)	30	70
	r_2	200	20	50	(80; 50)	30	70
t_2	⇒ r_1	506	50	20	(50; 20)	30	70
	r_2	506	50	20	(50; 20)	30	70
t_3	⇒ r_0	120	12	80	(88; 80)	8	92
	r_1	200	20	60	(80; 60)	20	80
	r_2	240	24	40	(76; 40)	36	64
t_4	⇒ r_1	205	20	90	(80; 90)	10	90
	r_2	405	40	70	(60; 70)	10	90

p_0 are given based on the result obtained in: (d) and (e). The x coordinate is computed subtracting 48 (result obtained from (d)) from 100 (value set as y_{max}), equal to 52 (f_x). The y coordinate is equal to 40 (f_y), as computed in (e). From the coordinates (f_x and f_y) of p_0 we compute (f) the distance ($d = |f_x - f_y|$), equal to 12. The value of δ_0 is then computed substracting the result obtained in (f) to y_{max} ($\delta_0 = 100 - 12$) and is equal to 88.

The resulting two-dimensional search space for the evaluation of task t_0 on the three considered resources is illustrated in Figure 16.5(a). For a given task (t_j), if at least two resources (r_i) share the same coordinates (e.g., task t_0 in Table 16.3), then that point is only represented once. In the aforementioned table and figure, the point p_0 identifies r_0 as the optimal (most "energy-efficient") resource evaluated through the *ETC* algorithm. Consequently, the algorithm assigns t_0 to r_0 as depicted in Fig. 16.6.

Figure 16.5 illustrates the two-dimensional search spaces for each task, in agreement with the informations contained in Table 16.3. Among the points within the evaluation space, the (black) full dot (within the subset $\mathcal{F}$) identifies the optimal point (resource) for the given task, while the line given by Equation (16.11) represents the ideal optimal points.

Throughout the numerical results summarized in Table 16.3 (visually reflected in Fig. 16.5), the *ETC* algorithm evaluates and identifies the optimal solution simultaneously considering two aspects: (a) the resource utilization rate and (b) the energy consumption implied by a given task. As a result, the solution selected by the algorithm is the "energy-efficient" optimal in terms of both (a) and (b).

Figure 16.6 depicts an additional representation of the optimal scenario provided by the algorithm after completing the evaluation of our intuitive example. The four tasks have been assigned only on two resources. As expected the algorithm maximized the resource utilization rate simultaneously minimizing the system's energy consumption. For each given task of our particular example, *ETC* selected the same solutions than *MaxUtil* (see Fig. 16.3(b)). The main difference being that *ETC* always guarantees Pareto optimality in terms of energy efficiency.

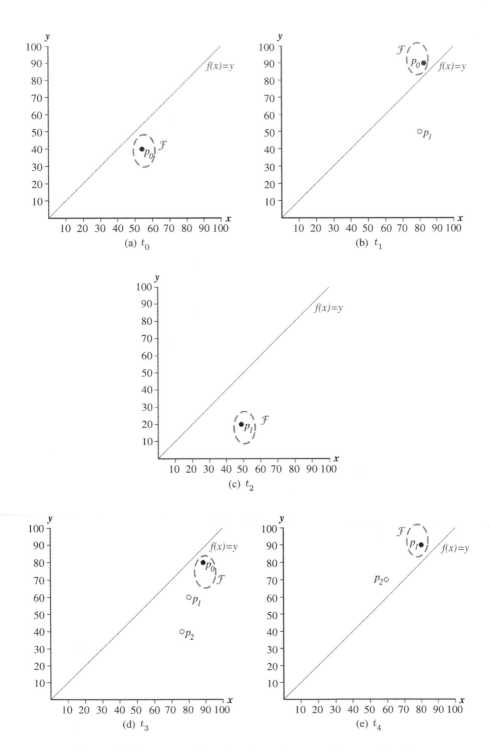

Figure 16.5 The two-dimensional search space of the *ETC* algorithm.

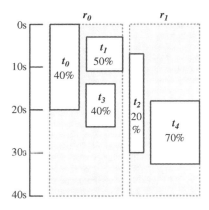

Figure 16.6   The final result identified by the *ETC* algorithm.

16.5   SIMULATION RESULTS

16.5.1   Simulation Setup

The simulations were carried out using the MPICH2 framework [27], a high-performance and widely portable implementation of the Message Passing Interface (MPI) standard [26]. MPICH2 has two main goals. First, to provide an MPI implementation that efficiently supports different computation and communication platforms (including commodity clusters, high-speed networks, and proprietary high-end computing systems). Second, to enable cutting-edge research in MPI through an easy-to-extend modular framework for other derived implementations.

Throughout the simulations, the resource usage of the generated tasks was random and uniformly distributed between 4% and 95% (or 0.04 and 0.95). The minimum utilization rate of 4% avoids generating processing times lower than 1 *millisecond* ($\tau_0 < 1\ ms$).

The architecture used to simulate the environment followed the Master-Slave scheme. One selected resource (the Master) was in charge of (a) dynamically generating the next task and (b) selecting the "optimal" resource (the Slave) to execute that task, according to the selected energy efficiency policy.

Because Cloud computing systems are always ready to perform the next incoming request, our problem becomes time and space dependent. That is, every future decision will be directly dependent on the previous decision.

To properly emulate the system, the simulation was divided into three steps: (1) the "seeding," (2) the "training" (or warm-up) period, and (3) the (window) "run". First, the resources are filled with "concurrent" tasks (seeding operation) generated on a nonlinear "time dependent" distribution, aiming to simulate some ongoing previous requests. Secondly, the new tasks were randomly generated and assigned to the "optimal" resource (training period) based on the current work-flow of the system. Finally, the run evaluates the heuristics based on a predefined interval of tasks. More precisely, the seeding operation creates the environment, the training period stabilizes the simulation, and the run evaluates the algorithm over a window consisting of one hundred thousand (10^5)

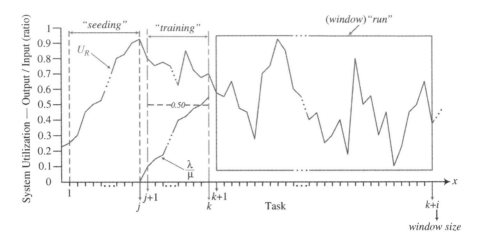

<u>Figure 16.7</u> The three steps of the simulation.

tasks dynamically generated and assigned among the system. Figure 16.7 illustrates the aforementioned steps.

The length of the warm up ("training") period needs to be evaluated, if the state of the model at starting time does not represent the steady state of the actual system. The point at which the model seems real for the first time could be estimated as the warm-up time. In our experiment, the warm-up period is the amount of (simulated) tasks that need to run before the data collection begins [3]. The switch from the "training" to "run" occurs dynamically based on the result given by the "output to input" ratio (λ/μ), also know as the system utilization. At each task assignment, λ and μ represent the number of outgoing and incoming tasks, respectively. The ratio (λ/μ) aids in the monitoring of the system, allowing a dynamic start to the evaluation of the selected heuristic in an environment secured from collapse. The "run" starts as soon as the simulation reaches the steady state. In our environment, we considered the steady sate from any value of the ratio (λ/μ) greater than 0.50.

The performance and behavior of the *ETC* algorithm were evaluated compared to the individual results obtained with Algorithm 16.1 presented in Section 16.3, initially setting *MaxUtil* and successively *ECTC* as the cost function.

Given that the main objective of our experiment was to maximize the utilization while minimizing the energy consumption, at each task assignment two global factors were logged: (a) the total rate of resources utilization $(U_{\mathcal{R}})$ and (b) the cumulated amount of the energy consumption $(E_{\mathcal{R}})$ of the system (see Equation (16.3)). Both (a) and (b) aim to observe the global behavior in terms of energy efficiency of the selected algorithms.

To compare the scalability of the different heuristics, at each task assignment, we observed the speed intended as the time (in *microseconds* (μs)) to select the "optimal" resource. The recorded computation relied on the MPICH2 time function (MPI_Wtime).

The simulation environment was developed based on four different topologies: (a) 10 and 20 resources of 4 cores and (b) 5 and 10 resources of 8 cores. The number of cores

TABLE 16.4 Parameters of the Simulation Environment

Type	Parameter	Value
General	CPU speed	2,048 GHz
	Window of tasks	100 000
	Resource usage	[0.04 : 0.95]
	$[x_{min} : x_{max}]$	[1 : 20 000]
	$[y_{min} : y_{max}]$	[1 : 99]
	p_{min}	20
	p_{max}	30
	$\frac{\lambda}{\mu}$	0.50
4 cores	Single core speed	512 MHz
	Number of resources	10, 20
	Number of operations per second	[1 : 9 400]
8 cores	Single core speed	256 MHz
	Number of resources	5, 10
	Number of operations per second	[1 : 4 700]

available on a resource bound the maximum number of tasks that can be concurrently executed on a selected resource. The experiment followed the specifications of the task consolidation problem as explained in Section 16.3.3.

For each resource a central processing unit (CPU) of 2,048 GHz was assumed and equally shared between the predefined numbers of cores. The process to randomly generate the tasks is as follows. Initially, a bounded number is generated corresponding to the number of operations (per second) needed to perform that given task. Being bounded, the aforementioned prevents the resulting generated task to overflow the computational capabilities of the available resources (i.e., $u_j > 100\%$ for a given task t_j). The bounded interval that generates the number of operations (per second) is directly dependent on: (a) the predefined CPU speed and (b) the number of cores. From (a) and (b) we compute the sole core speed. Successively, dividing the number of operations (per second) by the sole core speed we obtain the processing time (in milliseconds (ms)) needed for the given task to be executed on a selected resource. Finally, the utilization rate of that task is derived by dividing the processing time by the predefined CPU speed. Table 16.4 summarizes the parameters used to set our experiment.

16.5.2 Results

16.5.2.1 Energy Efficiency. The results presented in the following graphs aim to evaluate the energy efficiency of the three heuristics: (a) *MaxUtil*, (b) *ECTC*, and (c) the Energy-efficient Task Consolidation (*ETC*) algorithm.

For each of the heuristics we depicted four graphs (see Fig. 16.8, Fig. 16.9, Fig. 16.10, and Fig. 16.11) that showed the behavior, in terms of energy efficiency and task consolidation, among the four selected topologies: (a) 10 and 20 resources of 4 cores and (b) 5 and 10 resources of 8 cores. Within the aforementioned figures, the solid line represents the total utilization rate of the system while the dashed line the energy

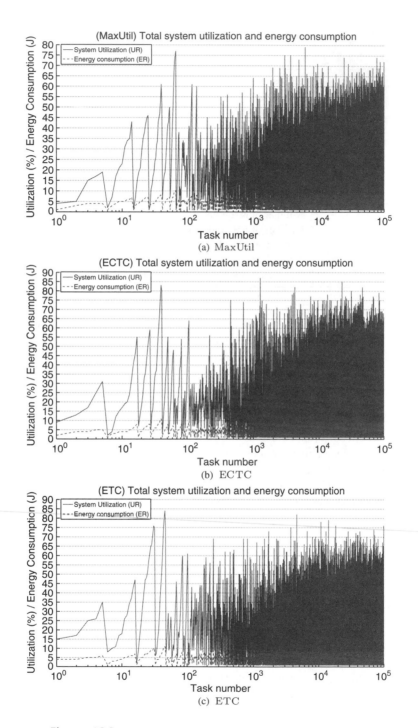

Figure 16.8   Results on the 4 cores and 10 resources topology.

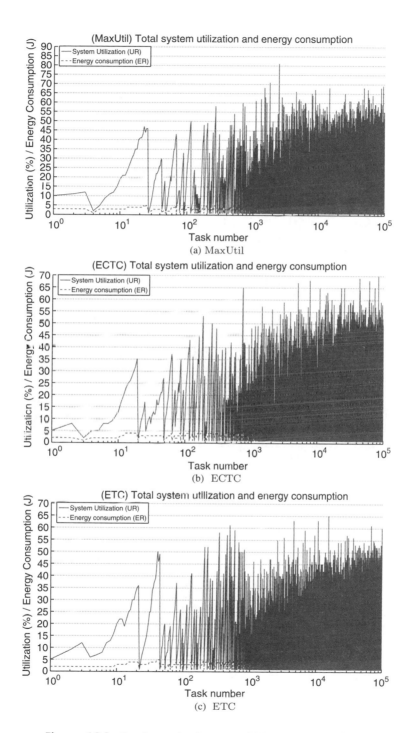

Figure 16.9 Results on the 4 cores and 20 resources topology.

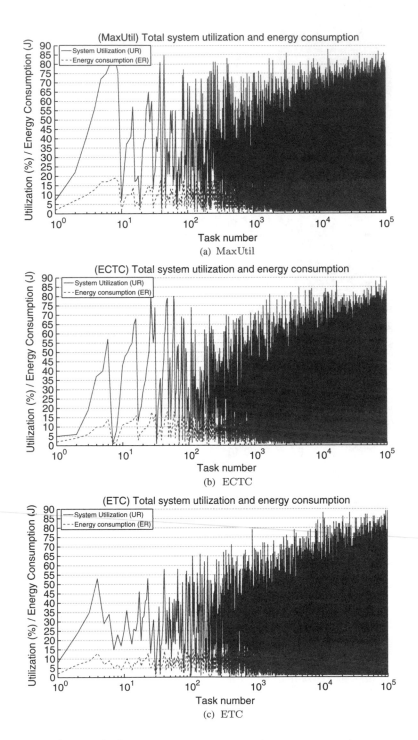

Figure 16.10   Results on the 8 cores and 5 resources topology.

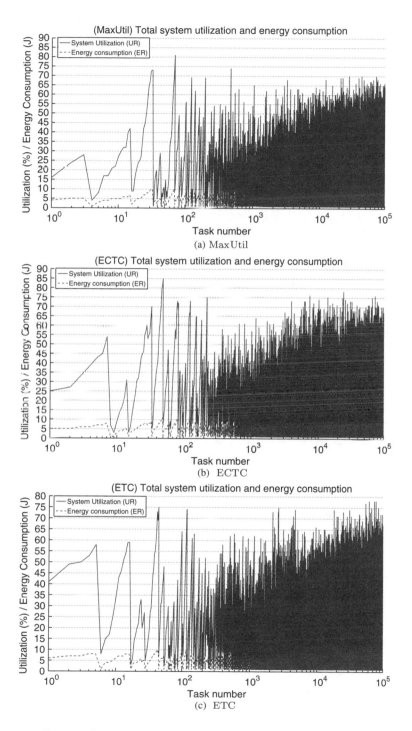

Figure 16.11 Results on the 8 cores and 10 resources topology.

consumption. The sampling rate for the collection of the system's status was performed at each task assignment. The y axis shows the utilization as the (normalized) energy consumption unit scale, while the task index was reported following a logarithmic scale in the x axis.

Among the four figures, the subfigures (a) and (b) correspond to *MaxUtil* and *ECTC*, respectively, while the subfigures (c) to the *ETC* algorithm. From our results, no significant differences can be pointed out among the three heuristics conforming to the task consolidation problem. Consequently, *MaxUtil*, *ECTC*, and the *ETC* algorithm can be considered equally "energy efficiently."

16.5.2.2 Speed Analysis. Figure 16.12 depicts the behavior of the heuristics in term of speed. The time needed to select the "optimal energy-efficient" resource among the system at each task assignment. The solid line represents the *ETC* algorithm, while the dashed and the dotted lines represent *MaxUtil* and *ECTC*, respectively. The data are represented following a logarithmic scale on both of the axis, where the task number is provided on the x and the time (in microseconds (μs)) on the y axis.

Among the considered aspects (utilization rate and energy consumption), *MaxUtil* only considers the available utilization rate, developed to maximize task consolidation. *ECTC* considers the available utilization rate (as *MaxUtil*) combined with the time periods (τ_x) to predict the energy consumption of the given task on a selected resource, designed to consolidate task energy-efficiently. When compared, *MaxUtil* proved to be faster than *ECTC*.

The *ETC* algorithm uses the solutions generated by *MaxUtil* and *ECTC* to construct the two-dimensional evaluation space, conferring to the algorithm the more complex election of the optimal solution. Consequently, our proposed algorithm was the slowest when compared, but resulted being the heuristic that provided the best "energy-efficient" solutions.

16.6 DISCUSSION OF RESULTS

Recalling Section 16.3, our study described two existing heuristics: (a) *MaxUtil* and (b) *ECTC*. The main difference between (a) and (b) being whether the energy consumption is implicitly or explicitly considered. *MaxUtil* proved to maximize task consolidation reducing in turns the number of used resources. Consequently, the decreased number of used resources directly reduces the energy consumption of the system. According to the aforementioned *MaxUtil* was defined as implicitly energy-efficient. Alternatively, *ECTC* was developed to consolidate tasks that can be fully overlapped, tending to discard the consolidation option for partial-overlapping tasks. The main concern of *ECTC* remains the energy consumption of the given task on the selected resource, that must be minimal. Consequently, the aforementioned property defined *ECTC* as explicitly energy-efficient.

The rationale behind the *ECTC* cost function relies on the energy consumption during the time periods (τ_x) and p_{min}, the minimum power consumption in the

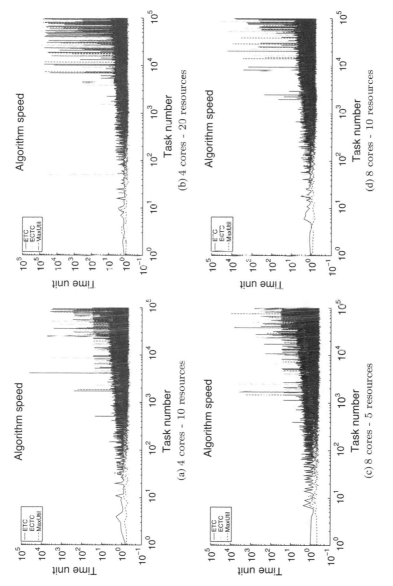

Figure 16.12 Computational speed of the heuristics.

active mode. Designed to consolidate only full overlapping tasks, *ECTC* allows the minimum power consumption p_{min} to be ignored for that given task, independently from the number of consolidated tasks. The estimation of the energy consumption of the given task will be fully dependent on the time period given by τ_2, the time period τ_1 being respectively null (see Fig. 16.4).

When the consolidated task can only be partially overlapped, for that task, *ECTC* considers the energy consumption as follows. The time period τ_1 with the implied power consumption in the active mode (p_{min}) is added to the energy consumption during the time period τ_2 (see Fig. 16.12). For example, if n tasks are consolidated based on partial overlap, p_{min} must be considered n times on n different (time periods) τ_1. Formally, let the time period (τ_1) corresponding to the task (t_j) on a selected resource (r_i) defined as τ_{1_j}, the total power consumption of that resource must then be increased by the minute energy factor

$$\epsilon_i = \left(p_{min} \times \sum_{j=0}^{n} \tau_{1_j} \right),$$ (16.15)

which is what *ECTC* tries to avoid.

Because the time periods constraints are strongly related to the minimum power consumption in the active mode, *ECTC* can "diverge" by taking decisions that generate the "domino effect" as mentioned in Section 16.4.2. From the energy efficiency point of view, *MaxUtil* saves energy minimizing (when possible) the number of used resources of the system, while *ECTC* prioritizes the consolidation of full overlapping tasks. More precisely, *ECTC* runs as much as possible concurrent tasks under the same p_{min} to save that energy consumption.

The proposed algorithm named *ETC* was built from the two heuristics (*MaxUtil* and *ECTC*). The *ETC* algorithm identifies the resource offering the best compromise between the results of the two cost functions, consolidating tasks energy-efficiently. The closer the normalized results (see Section 16.4), the more the offered solutions will be energy-efficiently converging. Consequently, divergent solutions will be dismissed by the *ETC* algorithm discarding the possibility of generating the domino effect as mentioned above.

16.7 CONCLUSION

Task consolidation, especially in Cloud computing systems, became an important approach to streamline resource usage that in turn improves energy efficiency. Two existing energy-conscious heuristics for task consolidation, offering different energy-saving possibilities, were analyzed in our study. For both heuristics we identified the corresponding drawback and proposed, as a (single) solution, the Energy-efficient Task Consolidation (*ETC*) algorithm. The aforementioned algorithm combines the two heuristics to construct the corresponding two-dimensional search space. Within the domain space, the optimal solution set and the corresponding optimal solution are selected through the Pareto dominance criteria and the Euclidean distance, respectively. The efficiency of the proposed algorithm was proved through the evaluation study, consisting of different simulations carried out using the MPICH2 framework. Concerned with the energy efficiency of the system and the scalability of the proposed algorithm, at each task assignment we observed three main aspects: the total energy consumption, the total resource utilization, and the time needed to select the optimal solution. To evaluate the performance of the *ETC* algorithm according to the aforementioned criteria, the two heuristics were individually implemented and used as key indicator for the energy efficiency and the scalability. Despite the more elaborate selection of the optimal solution, our study reported that the proposed *ETC* algorithm was the slowest, but was the heuristic that provided the best "energy-efficient" solution. The result of our study should not only contribute to the reduction of electricity bills of Cloud computing infrastructure providers, but also promote the combinations of existing techniques toward optimized models for energy efficient use, without performance degradation.

REFERENCES

[1] A. Beloglazov, R. Buyya, Y.C. Lee, and A.Y. Zomaya, "A taxonomy and survey of energy-efficient data centers and Cloud computing systems," *Advances in Computers*, 82, 2011, pp. 47–111.

[2] A. Ghosh and S. Dehuri, "Evolutionary algorithms for multi-criterion optimization: A survey," *International Journal of Computing & Information Sciences*, 2(1), April 2004.

[3] A. Mehta, "Smart modeling - Basic methodology and advanced tools," In *Proc 32nd Conference on Winter Simulation (WSC '00)*, Orlando, FL, USA, 1, 2000, pp. 241–245.

[4] A.Y. Zomaya, "Energy-aware scheduling and resource allocation for large-scale distributed systems," in *11th IEEE International Conference on High Performance Computing and Communications (HPCC)*, Seoul, Korea, 2009.

[5] C. Lefurgy, X. Wang, and M. Ware, "Server-level power control," in *Proc 4th IEEE International Conference on Autonomic Computing (ICAC '07)*, Jacksonville, FL, USA, June 2007, pp. 4.

[6] C.A. Coello Coello, "A comprehensive survey of evolutionary based multiobjective optimization techniques," *Knowledge and Information Systems*, 1(3), Citeseer, 1999, pp. 129–156.

[7] D. Grigoras, "Advanced environments, tools, and applications for cluster computing," *NATO Advanced Research Workshop, IWCC 2001*, Mangalia, Romania, September 2001, *Lecture Notes in Computer Science*, 2326, Springer, 2002.

[8] D. Kliazovich, P. Bouvry, and S.U. Khan, "DENS: Data center energy-efficient network-aware scheduling," in *ACM/IEEE International Conference on Green Computing and Communications (GreenCom)*, Hangzhou, China, December 2010, pp. 69–75.

[9] D. Zhu, R. Melhem, and B.R. Childers, "Scheduling with dynamic voltage/speed adjustment using slack reclamation in multiprocessor real-time systems," *IEEE Transactions on Parallel and Distributed Systems*, 14(7), pp. 686–700.

[10] F. Pinel, J. Pecero, P. Bouvry, and S.U. Khan, "Memory-aware green scheduling on multi-core processors," in *39th IEEE International Conference on Parallel Processing (ICPP)*, San Diego, CA, USA, September 2010, pp. 485–488.

[11] F. Pinel, J. E. Pecero, S. U. Khan, and P. Bouvry, "A review on task performance prediction in multi-core based systems," in *11th IEEE International Conference on Scalable Computing and Communications (ScalCom)*, Pafos, Cyprus, September 2011.

[12] G. L. Valentini, W. Lassonde, S. U. Khan, N. Min-Allah, S. A. Madani, J. Li, L. Zhang, L. Wang, N. Ghani, J. Kolodziej, H. Li, A. Y. Zomaya, C.-Z. Xu, P. Balaji, A. Vishnu, F. Pinel, J. E. Pecero, D. Kliazovich, and P. Bouvry, "An Overview of Energy Efficiency Techniques in Cluster Computing Systems," *Cluster Computing*, 16(1), 2013, pp. 3–15.

[13] G. Valentini, C.J. Barenco Abbas, L.J. Garcia Villalba, and L. Astorga, "Dynamic multi-objective routing algorithm: a multi-objective routing algorithm for the simple hybrid routing protocol on wireless sensor networks," *IET Communications*, 4(14), 2010, pp. 1732–1741.

[14] I. Menken and G. Blokdijk, *Virtualization - The Complete Cornerstone Guide to Virtualization Best Practices: Concepts, Terms, and Techniques for Successfully Planning, Implementing and Managing Enterprise IT Virtualization Technology*, Emereo Publishing, October 2008.

[15] J. Choi, S. Govindan, B. Urgaonkar, and A. Sivasubramaniam,"Profiling, prediction, and capping of power consumption in consolidated environments," in *16th International Symposium on Modeling, Analysis, and Simulation of Computer and Telecommunication Systems (MASCOTS 2008)*, Baltimore, MD, USA, September 2008, pp. 3–12.

[16] J. Choi, S Govindan, J. Jeong, B Urgaonkar, and A. Sivasubramaniam, "Power consumption prediction and power-aware packing in consolidated environments," in *IEEE Transactions on Computers*, 59(12), 2010, pp. 1640–1654.

[17] J.G. Koomey, "Estimating total power consumption by servers in the U.S. and the world," Lawrence Berkeley National Laboratory, Stanford University, 2007.

[18] J.J. Chen and T.W. Kuo, "Multiprocessor energy-efficient scheduling for real-time tasks with different power characteristics," in *Proc International Conference on Parallel Processing (ICPP '05)*, 2005, pp. 13–20.

[19] J. Kolodziej, S. U. Khan, and F. Xhafa, "Genetic algorithms for energy-aware scheduling in computational grids," in *6th IEEE International Conference on P2P, Parallel, Grid, Cloud, and Internet Computing (3PGCIC)*, Barcelona, Spain, October 2011.

[20] J. Moore, J. Chase, P. Ranganathan, and R. Sharma, "Making scheduling cool: temperature-aware workload placement in data centers," in *Proc USENIX Annual Technical Conference*, 2005.

[21] J. Torres, D. Carrera, K. Hogan, R. Gavalda, V. Beltran, and N. Poggi, "Reducing wasted resources to help achieve green data centers," in *Proc 4th workshop on High-Performance, Power-Aware Computing* (HPPAC '08), 2008.

[22] K.H. Kim, R. Buyya, and J. Kim, "Power aware scheduling of bag-of-tasks applications with deadline constraints on DVS-enabled clusters," in *Proc 7th IEEE International Symposium on Cluster Computing and the Grid (CCGrid '07)*, 2007, pp. 541–548.

[23] L. Barroso and U. Holzle, "The case for energy-proportional computing," *IEEE Computer*, 40(12), 2007, pp. 33-37.

[24] M.G. Jaatun, G. Zhao, and C. Rong, "Cloud computing: First International Conference, CloudCom 2009," China, December 2009, *Lecture Notes in Computer Science*, 5931, Springer.

[25] M. Guzek, J.E. Pecero, B. Dorrosoro, P. Bouvry, and S.U. Khan, "A cellular genetic algorithm for scheduling applications and energy-aware communication optimization," in *ACM/IEEE/IFIP International Conference on High Performance Computing and Simulation (HPCS)*, Caen, France, June 2010, pp. 241–248.

[26] Message Passing Interface (MPI), http://www.mpi-forum.org/ (accessed April 2011).

[27] MPICH2, http://www.mcs.anl.gov/research/projects/mpich2/, release 1.3.2p1 (accessed April 2011).

[28] P. Bohrer, E. Elnozahy, T. Keller, M. Kistler, C. Lefurgy, and R. Rajamony, "The case for power management in web servers," *Power Aware Computing*, Kluwer Academic Publishers, 2002, pp. 261–289.

[29] P. Ruiz, B. Dorronsoro, G. Valentini, F. Pinel, and P. Bouvry, "Optimization of the enhanced distance based broadcasting protocol for MANETs," *Journal of Supercomputing*, Springer, 55, 2011, pp. 1–28.

[30] Q. Tang, S.K. Gupta, and G. Varsamopoulos, "Energy-efficient thermal-aware task scheduling for homogeneous high-performance computing data centers: a cyber-physical approach," *IEEE Transactions on Parallel and Distributed Systems*, 19(11), 2008, pp. 1458–1472.

[31] R. Buyya, J. Broberg, and A.M. Goscinski, *Cloud computing: Principles and Paradigms*, John Wiley & Sons, 2011.

[32] R. Ge, X. Feng and K.W. Cameron, "Performance-constrained distributed DVS scheduling for scientific applications on power-aware clusters," in *Proc the ACM/IEEE conference on SuperComputing (SC '05)*, 2005, pp. 34–44.

[33] R. Nathuji and K. Schwan K, "VirtualPower: Coordinated power management in virtualized enterprise systems," in *Proc 21st ACMSIGOPS Symposium on Operating Systems Principles (SOSP '07)*, 2007, pp. 265–278.

[34] R. Subrata, A.Y. Zomaya, and B. Landfeldt, "Cooperative power-aware scheduling in grid computing environments," *Journal of Parallel and Distributed Computing*, 70(?), pp. 84–91.

[35] S. Srikantaiah, A. Kansal, and F. Zhao, "Energy aware consolidation for Cloud Computing," in *Proc USENIX HotPower'08: Workshop on Power Aware Computing and Systems in Conjunction with OSDI*, San Diego, CA, USA, December 2008.

[36] R.T. Marler and J.S. Arora, "Survey of multi-objective optimization methods for engineering," Published online: 23 March 2004, Springer.

[37] S.U. Khan, "A self-adaptive weighted sum technique for the joint optimization of performance and power consumption in data centers," in *22nd International Conference on Parallel and Distributed Computing and Communication Systems (PDCCS)*, Louisville, KY, USA, September 2009, pp. 13–18.

[38] S.U. Khan and I. Ahmad, "A cooperative game theoretical technique for joint optimization of energy consumption and response time in computational grids," *IEEE Transactions on Parallel and Distributed Systems*, 20(3), 2009, pp. 346–360.

[39] T. Kuroda, K. Suzuki, S. Mita, T. Fujita, F. Yamane, F. Sano, A. Chiba, Y. Watanabe, K. Matsuda, T. Maeda, T. Sakurai, and T. Furuyama, "Variable supply-voltage scheme for low-power high-speed CMOS digital design," *IEEE Journal of Solid-State Circuits*, 33(3), 1998, pp. 454–462.

[40] V. Pareto, *Manuale di Economia Politica*, Societa Editrice Libraria, Milano, Italy, 1906. Translated into English by A.S. Schwier, *Manual of Political Economy*, New York, Macmillan, 1971.

[41] V. Venkatachalam and M Franz, "Power reduction techniques for microprocessor systems," *ACM Computing Surveys*, 37(3), 2005, pp. 195–237.

[42] W. Stadler, "A survey of multicriteria optimization or the vector maximum problem, part I: 1776-1960." *Journal of Optimization Theory and Applications*, 29(1), 1979, pp. 1–52.

[43] W. Stadler, "Applications of multicriteria optimization in engineering and the sciences (A survey)," *in* M. Zeleny (ed.) *Multiple Criteria Decision Making—Past Decade and Future Trends*, Greenwich, CT, JAI, 1984.

[44] X. Fan, X.-D. Weber, and L.A. Barroso, "Power provisioning for a warehouse-sized computer," in *Proc 34th annual International Symposium on Computer Architecture (ISCA '07)*, 2007, pp 13–23.

[45] Y.C. Lee, and A.Y. Zomaya, "Minimizing energy consumption for precedence-constrained applications using dynamic voltage scaling," in 9th *IEEE/ACM International Symposium on Cluster Computing and the Grid (CCGrid)*, Shanghai, China, 2009, pp. 92–99.

[46] Y.C. Lee and A.Y. Zomaya, "Energy efficient utilization of resources in Cloud computing systems," published online: 19 March 2010, Springer.

[47] Y. Song, Y. Zhang, Y. Sun, and W. Shi, "Utility analysis for internet-oriented server consolidation in VM-based data centers," in *Proc IEEE International Conference on Cluster Computing (Cluster '09)*, 2009.

17

SEMANTICS-BASED RESOURCE DISCOVERY IN LARGE-SCALE GRIDS

Juan Li, Samee U. Khan, and Nasir Ghani

CONTENTS

Large Scale Network-Centric Distributed Systems, First Edition. Edited by Hamid Sarbazi-Azad and Albert Y. Zomaya.
© 2014 John Wiley & Sons, Inc. Published 2014 by John Wiley & Sons, Inc.

17.1 INTRODUCTION

The new generation of grids enables the sharing of a wide variety of resources, including hardware, software packages, knowledge information, licenses, specialized devices, and other grid services [1]. These resources are geographically distributed and owned by different organizations. The fact that users typically have little or no knowledge of the resources contributed by other participants in the grid poses a significant obstacle to their use. For this reason, resource discovery is a vital part of a grid system, and an efficient resource discovery infrastructure is crucial to make the distributed resource information available to users in a timely and reliable manner. However, resource discovery in large-scale grids is challenging due to the potential large number of resources, and their diverse, distributed, and dynamic nature. In addition, it is equally difficult to integrate the information sources with a heterogeneous representation format.

The provision of an *information service*, as currently envisaged by the grid community, is a first step towards the discovery of distributed resources. However, a large part of these efforts have been focused on "getting it to work," without directly addressing issues of scalability, reliability, and information quality [1]. For example, classical grids, such as the The Globus Toolkit [2], always use centralized or static hierarchical models to discover resources. To discover resources in a more dynamic, large-scale, and distributed environment, peer-to-peer (P2P) techniques have been used in resent research (e.g., [3, 4]). P2P systems offer many benefits, such as adaptation, self-organization, fault-tolerance, and load-balancing, but they also present several challenges that remain obstacles to their widespread acceptance and usage in grids: First, current P2P systems offer limited data management facilities; in most cases, searching information relies on simple identifiers or Information Retrieval (IR)-style string matching. This limitation is acceptable for file-sharing applications, but in order to support complex resource discovery in grids we need richer facilities for exchanging, querying, and integrating structured and semi-structured data. Second, most P2P systems specialize in a single functionality, for example, music sharing. More efforts are needed to support the sharing of varieties of resources in grids. Moreover, designing a good search mechanism is difficult in P2P systems because of the scale of the system and the unreliability of individual peers.

An effective grid resource discovery mechanism should support expressive query language. Most existing search systems use simple keyword-based lookups, which limit the searchability of the system. Our proposed framework improves search expressiveness from two directions: First, it uses a semantic metadata scheme to provide users with a rich and flexible representation mechanism, to enable effective descriptions of desired resource properties and query requirements. Second, we employ ontological domain knowledge to assist in the search process. The system is thus able to understand the semantics of query requests according to their meanings in a specific domain; this procedure helps the system to locate only semantically related results.

The more expressive the resource description and query request, however, the more difficult it is to design a scalable and efficient search mechanism. We ensure scalability by reconfiguring the network with respect to shared ontologies. This reconfiguration partitions the large unorganized search space into multiple well-organized semantically related subspaces that we call semantic virtual organizations. Semantic virtual organizations help to discriminatively distribute resource information and queries to related nodes, thus reducing the search space and improving scalability. To further improve the efficiency of searching the virtual organizations, we propose a semantics-based searching mechanism OntoSum. OntoSum utilizes the famous "small-world" theory to reorganize the virtual organization so that query can be answered efficiently by forwarding between neighboring nodes.

The remainder of this chapter is organized as follows: Section 17.2 provides a general overview of related work in resource discovery in grids. Section 17.3 describes our approach to the construction of semantic virtual organizations (VOs). Section 17.4 presents OntoSum, a framework for semantic resource discovery in virtual organizations. The implementation of a prototype system is detailed in Section 17.5. Finally, Section 17.6 presents our conclusions, a discussion of limitations, and suggestions for future work. This work has utilized our previous research results presented in [36–38].

17.2 RELATED WORK

Traditionally, a Grid Information Service is mainly based on a centralized or hierarchical model. In the Globus Toolkit 2 [2], the Monitoring and Discovery Service (MDS) [5] provides access to static and dynamic information about resources. MDS is based on the Lightweight Directory Access Protocol (LDAP) [6] and consists of two components: Grid Index Information Services (GIIS) and Grid Resource Information Service (GRIS). The resource information is obtained by the information provider and is passed on to GRIS. GRIS registers its local information with the GIIS, which registers with another GIIS, and so on. MDS clients can get the resource information directly from GRIS (for local resources) and/or a GIIS (for grid-wide resources). The MDS hierarchy mechanism is similar to DNS. GRIS and GIIS, at lower layers of the hierarchy, register with the GIIS at upper layers, realizing the large indexing and discovery. Globus Toolkit versions 3, 4, and 5 [2] provide a service-oriented information service, that is, the Index Service. The Index Service leverages service data defined in the Open Grid Services Architecture (OGSA) [7] specification to provide services. All services are described in a standardized XML schema, called Elements of Service Data (SDEs). The Index Service provides high-level API functionalities to register, aggregate, and query SDEs. Users can get a node's resource information by either directly querying a server application running on that node, or querying dedicated information servers that retrieve and publish the resource information of the organization. Techniques for associating information servers, and to construct an efficient, scalable network of directory servers, are left unspecified.

Other grid applications proposed similar information services. For example, Condor's Matchmaker [8] uses a centralized mechanism to locate desirable resources. Each node in the Condor system advertises its resources and reports resource status to a central manager. The central manager then matches resource requesters' queries with resource providers' advertisements. In another example, Legion [9] takes an object-oriented approach to resource management. It uses *Collections* to search and locate resources in the grid. When a user requests a resource, Legion will query resource information in multiple Collections; if it finds several such resources, Legion's resource scheduler will randomly choose one of them.

For small-to-medium-scale grids, these centralized or static hierarchical solutions work fine. However, for large-to-global-scale grids, these approaches are not efficient and do not scale. Additionally, even for smaller grids, a centralized solution will always be a performance bottleneck and a single point of failure. Presently, grids have moved from the obscurely academic to the highly popular. As the size of the grid grows from tens to thousands or even millions of nodes, the traditional server-based grid information service will not scale well. As a remedy, some researchers (e.g., [10]) advocate the use of P2P techniques for implementing scalable grid systems.

P2P systems offer many benefits over the traditional client-server model, including better scalability, automatic management, fault-tolerance, and load-balancing. Therefore, we use P2P as our underlying communication structure. At the same time, P2P systems also present several challenges that preclude their widespread acceptance and usage in grids. For example, current P2P systems often lack the ability to deploy production-quality services, persistent and multipurpose service infrastructure, complex services, robustness, performance, and security. Thus, one of the tasks of this chapter is suggest how to overcome these problems and make P2P systems better serve grid needs.

17.3 VIRTUAL ORGANIZATION FORMATION

17.3.1 Overview

If not properly organized, searching an Internet-scale grid for quality resources is like looking for a needle in a haystack – we have too large a space to explore. Therefore, as the first step of our discovery scheme, we organize and reduce the huge chaotic search space to multiple semantics-based subspaces. Participants in each subspace share similar semantic interests, forming semantics-based Virtual Organizations (VO). Searching can then be performed on VOs, and queries can be quickly propagated to many appropriate members in the VO. This procedure results in a higher precision and recall of search results.

17.3.2 Ontological Directories

In order to organize different interests and facilitate the construction of VOs, we propose an abstract generic ontological model that guides users in determining the desired ontological properties and choosing the "right" VOs to join. The ontology model defines most general categories of existence (e.g., existing item, spatial region, dependent part), which essentially form a hierarchy where each entry corresponds to a categorical domain. Here we provide a formal definition of this ontology model, which we call the ontology directory.

DEFINITION 17.1:   An ontology directory is a system $D = (L, H, r)$, which consists of:

- A lexicon: The lexicon L contains a set of natural language terms.
- A hierarchy H: Terms in L are taxonomically related by the directed, acyclic, transitive, reflexive relation H. ($H \subset L \times L$);
- A root term r ∈ L. For all l ∈ L, it holds: H(l,R).

The ontology directory essentially defines a hierarchy where each node corresponds to a lexicon or a categorical term. It is almost a rooted tree structure, with rare nodes having multiple parents. The subordination relationship between nodes is interpreted as the involvement (topic/subtopic) relationship, while the layers of nodes correspond to intuitively perceived levels of abstractness of topics. Each node is described by primitives that are generic concepts that include other concepts. An example of a primitive is *computer* that includes *software*, *hardware*, *networks*, and so forth. The hierarchical relationship, also called the IS-A relationship, is transitive, that is, whatever holds for a more general concept also holds for a more specific concept, for example, *music* is a type of *art*.

The ontology model allows users to choose the right VO to join, detect new trends, or find useful information they did not realize was available. Our ontology directory is different from those global web directories such as Google directory, Yahoo directory, and DMOZ [11], because it is not predefined, but created and extended automatically with network growth and the evolution of the ontology. Moreover, the ontology directory loosely defines domain categories; it does not expect different communities of users to conform to the same ontology to describe their resources and interests. Therefore, it is based on multiple ontologies as opposed to a global ontology.

To implement the ontology directory in a decentralized manner, we propose an efficient and scalable distributed hash table (DHT) structure [12] to index and lookup the hierarchical taxonomy. To index and retrieve the hierarchical ontology directory with a flat DHT structure, we extend the basic DHT API. The directory path starting from the root is used to represent the ontology domain (e.g., /computer/systems/network). One domain corresponding to a particular VO should include contact information for peers in this VO. A direct indexing scheme is to index the full directory path as a key, and users can locate a VO by providing the full directory path. However, like navigating in a UNIX file system, users rarely input an absolute directory path, but rather browse directories level by level and select the more interesting one at each level. Therefore, it is necessary to provide users an ontology browsing interface. Moreover, to automatically locate related VOs for nodes, we extract key concepts from the joining nodes' ontology

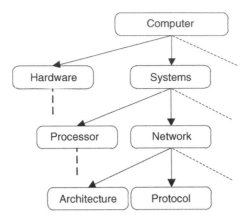

Figure 17.1   Fragment of an ontological directory model.

and then use them as keys to locate the right directory domain. Therefore, we should also provide a keyword-based lookup interface.

Consider the ontology model in Figure 17.1. It consists of taxonomy paths:

```
/computer
/computer/systems
/computer/hardware
/computer/systems/network
/computer/systems/processor
/computer/systems/network/architecture
/computer/systems/network/protocol
```

Some domains may relate to keywords, for example:

Keywords: *cluster, grid, P2P,* are related to taxonomy */computer/system/network/architecture*

Keywords: *protocol, TCP, IP* are related to taxonomy */computer/system/network/protocol*

For each path and keyword, a hash value (key) is computed in Pastry [13], a DHT implementation, using an SHA-1 algorithm. Table 17.1 shows keys for taxonomy paths and keywords of the model. To make the example simple, we use a 4-digit (8 bits) identifier space; in reality, a much larger identifier space is used, such as 160 or 128 bits. Each key is assigned to a node, which is the nearest node to the key in the key-space. For example, as listed in Table 17.1, the hashed key of directory path */computer/system* is *0230,* and the key is stored at node *0213,* as shown in Fig. 2, since node *0213*'s ID is closest to the key. Each owner node of a directory key maintains a Least Recently Used (LRU) cache storing contact information of peers that are interested in this directory. To implement the directory browser's functionality, an overlay node that is in charge of a directory entry also stores information about that directory's direct children. When the user chooses one directory, Pastry routes to that directory entry and retrieves child

T A B L E 17.1 Hash Keys of Models in Figure 17.1 in a Sample 4-Digit Identifier Space

Hash Key	Directory Path
1211	/computer
0230	/computer/systems
3211	/computer/hardware
2011	/computer/systems/network
1000	/computer/systems/processor
1013	/computer/systems/network/architecture
0012	/computer/systems/network/protocol
2111	Protocol
0211	TCP
1201	IP
2003	Cluster
0012	Grid
0032	P2P

directory information, allowing the directory to be extended dynamically while browsing. An overlay node also stores keywords that are hashed to it and links the keywords with related ontology domains. Figure 17.2 shows how the directory model above is stored into an example Pastry network.

Since nodes might fail and network connections might break, the ontology model stored on its corresponding overlay nodes are replicated on its neighbors in the Pastry identifier space. This can be done by setting the replica factor f. Whenever a node receives a directory storing request, it will not only store the directory locally but also store it to its f immediate leaf nodes. If any node fails or its connection breaks, its leaf neighbors will detect it by using the keep-alive messages.

17.3.3 Ontology Directory Lookup and VO Register

We provide three kinds of lookup interfaces for users: exact lookups, browser-based lookups, and keyword-based lookups. A node can use these three interfaces to locate VOs they are interested in and join these VOs.

17.3.3.1 Exact Lookups. This is the simplest form of a lookup. This type of query contains the complete directory path of the interest domain, for example, *"/computer/system/network/architecture"*. This complete directory path is hashed to a key and then a corresponding lookup of the hashed key on the Pastry overlay is executed.

17.3.3.2 Browser-Based Lookups. In this case, users do not need to remember the directory path to locate the directory domain of interest. Instead, they can navigate from the root of each hierarchy down to the leaves to reach the directory of interest. A user first uses the root ID as the key to locate the node storing the root of the ontology

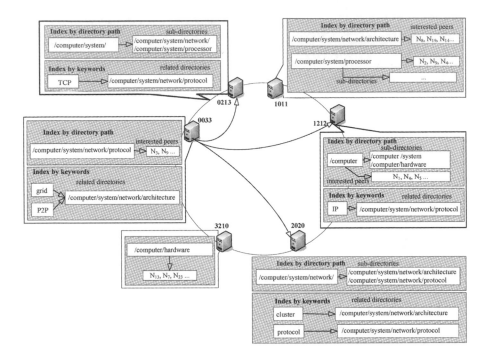

<u>Figure 17.2</u>   Storing the ontology model into a Pastry network of 6 nodes in an example 8-bit identifier space.

model. Since a node is storing a directory entry also storing the next level children, users can dynamically expand a directory tree node to browse its child branches. After the user chooses an interested branch, the directory path of that branch is used as a key to lookup the next level directory. In this way, the tree is expanded until users find the desired directory entries. In reality, the root and top-level categories are widely cached in most of the nodes in the network; therefore, they can be quickly located without going through the overlay network.

17.3.3.3 *Keyword-Based Lookups.* Users can also specify one or more key concepts of their local ontology and use the concepts as keys to lookup the corresponding directory in the overlay. Since overlay nodes in charge of the keywords keep links to the corresponding directory entries, a keyword-based lookup can be converted into an exact lookup. When a user provides multiple keywords, each of them may correspond to multiple directories, the intersection (or union) of all directories related to these keywords is returned to the user. Domain ontologies and/or external generic ontologies like WordNet [14] can be used for keyword semantic query expansion or keyword conceptual indexing in order to improve retrieval performance.

17.3.3.4 *VO Register.* Since an overlay node in charge of an ontology directory also keeps a cache storing information about nodes interested in that ontology directory, a querying node can get contacts of others sharing the same interest through this overlay node. The new node can then join the VO by connecting to those contacts. At the same time, if its ontology matches the ontology of the VO, this new node can register with the VO by adding itself to the cache of the directory overlay node; therefore, in the future, others can find it. A node with multiple interests can register with multiple VOs. There are several special cases for a node's registration: (1) If a new registering node cannot get enough contacts from the interested domain (i.e., the VO is very small), it explicitly routes to the upper- and/or lower-level categories to register and get more contacts. (2) If a node cannot find suitable categories satisfying its interest (i.e., it is the first node registering this interest), it will try to add this category by applying from an authoritative organization.

17.3.3.5 Directory Overlay Maintenance.
The directory overlay nodes are also user nodes. We utilize the heterogeneity of grid nodes, and promote those stable and powerful ones to join the directory overlay. Excluding ephemeral nodes from the directory overlay avoids unnecessary maintenance costs. The maintenance of the directory overlay mainly includes adding new directory entries. We assume deleting and updating do not occur frequently. When a new joining node cannot find its category of interest, it may try to apply to create a new category. If the application is approved by the authoritative organizations in the grid, the node will create this category by hashing the directory path to an overlay node and informing the parent node to add this entry. Then it hashes each of its main key concepts in the ontology to the overlay network. A node joins the directory overlay only when three conditions are satisfied. (1) it satisfies the capacity requirements, that is, it is powerful enough; (2) it is stable for a threshold time period; (3) the directory load balancing algorithm requires it to do so [39].

17.4 SEMANTICS-BASED RESOURCE DISCOVERY IN VIRTUAL ORGANIZATIONS

The ontology-based model facilitates nodes in forming virtual organizations (VOs). The next task is to efficiently share and search inside VOs. Searching and sharing within VOs is still challenging, since the heterogeneous, distributed, dynamic, and large-scale properties of the problem still exist. Previously, we proposed an infrastructure named OntoSum [36] for efficiently sharing and discovering resources inside VOs. OntoSum was inspired by a widely held belief of "small-world" pertaining to social networks, in which that any two people in the world are connected via a chain of six acquaintances (*six-degrees of separation*) [15]. Because of the similarity between grid networks and social networks and the fact that human users of grid networks direct grid nodes' links, we believe that grid networks can also utilize this phenomenon to discover resources.

OntoSum organizes nodes to form a small-world topology from a semantic perspective. It makes the system's dynamic topology match the semantic clustering of peers. The distance metric of OntoSum was determined by nodes' semantic similarity. With the semantics-based small-world constructed, a query can be efficiently resolved in the semantic cluster neighborhood through short semantic paths. This would allow queries to quickly propagate among relevant peers as soon as one of them is reached.

17.4.1 Semantic Similarity

There has been extensive research [17, 18] focusing on measuring the semantic similarity between two objects in the field of information retrieval and information integration. However, their methods are extremely comprehensive and computationally intensive. In our work, we propose a simple method to compute the semantic similarity between two peers. In our similarity measurement, we extract each peer's T-Box [19] as its semantic characteristics. The T-Box [19] part of an ontology defines high-level concepts and their relationships like the schema of a database. It is a good abstraction of the ontology's semantics and structure. For each node, we extract the class and property labels from its T-Box ontology, and put them into a set. This set is called this node's Ontology Signature Set (OSS). We can measure the similarity of two ontologies by comparing the elements of their OSSs. OSS is simple and concise, but on the other hand, it is not precise; it ignores the inherent relationships between T-Box concepts and thus damages the semantic meaning of each concept. To improve the precision, we use the lexical database, WordNet [14], to extend the OSS to include words that are semantically related to the concepts from the original set. We lookup each concept in the WordNet lexicon and extend each concept with its synonyms in the synset. In this way, two semantically related ontologies would have common WordNet terms in their extended OSSs. Besides synonyms, WordNet also includes other lexical semantic relations, such as *is-a*, *kind-of*, and *part-of*. Among these relations, *is-a* (represented by hyponym/hypernym in WordNet) is the most important relationship; it explains a concept by a more general concept. Therefore, we also extend OSS concepts with their hypernyms.

After extension, an OSS may get a large number of synonyms for each concept. However, not all of these synonyms should be included in the set, because each concept may have many senses (meanings), and not all of them are related to the ontology context. A problem causing the ambiguity of concepts in OSS is that the extension does not make use of any relations in the ontology. Because the dominant semantic relation in an ontology is the subsumption relation (super-class, the converse of is-a, is-subtype-of, or is-subclass-of), we use the subsumption relation and the sense disambiguation information provided by WordNet to refine OSSs. It is based on a principle that a concept's semantic meaning should be consistent with its super-class's meaning. We use this principle to remove those inconsistent meanings. We create the refined OSS by adding the appropriate sense set of each ontology concept based on the *sub-class/super-class* relationships between the parent concepts and child concepts. For every concept in an ontology, we check each of its senses; if a sense's hypernym has an overlap with this concept's parent's senses, then we add this sense and the overlapped parent's sense to the OSS set. In this way, we can refine the OSS and reduce imprecision. Besides the *is-a* relation, ontologies often include additional types of domain-specific relationships that further refine the semantics they model.

To compare two ontologies, we define an ontology similarity function based on the refined OSS. The definition is based on Tversky's "Ratio Model" [20], which is evaluated by set operations and is in agreement with an information-theoretic definition of similarity [21]. Our similarity function is based on the normalization of Tversky's model to give a numeric measurement of ontology similarity. Assume A and B are two peers, and their extended Ontology Signature Sets are $S(A)$ and $S(B)$, respectively. The semantic similarity between peer A and peer B is defined as:

$$sim(A, B) = \frac{|S(A) \cap S(B)|}{|S(A) \cap S(B)| + \alpha|S(A) - S(B)| + \beta|S(B) - S(A)|}$$

In the above equations, "∩" denotes set intersection, "–" is set difference, while "||" represents set cardinality, and "α" and "β" are parameters that provide for differences in focus on the different components. The similarity sim, between A and B, is defined in terms of the semantic concepts common to OSS of A and B: $S(A) \cap S(B)$, the concepts that are distinctive to A: $S(A)–S(B)$, and the features that are distinctive to B: $S(B) - S(A)$. The parameters α and β are non-negative, determining the relative weights of these two components. Two nodes, node A and node B, are said to be semantically equivalent if their semantic similarity measure, $sim(A,B)$, equals 1 (implying $sim(B,A) = 1$ as well). Node A is said to be semantically related to node B if $sim(A,B)$ exceeds the user-defined similarity threshold $t(0 < t = 1)$. Node A is semantically unrelated to node B if $sim(A,B) < t$.

17.4.2 Illustrative Example

We use an example to further illustrate how to use the refined OSS and similarity function to measure the semantic similarity between two peers. Figure 17.3 shows two partial ontology definitions about automobiles. Detailed ontology definitions are omitted here. Table 17.2 and Table 17.3 list the ontology concepts and their synonyms and hypernyms from all senses extracted from WordNet.

The primitive OSSs of these two ontologies are:

$$SA = \{auto, truck, racer\}$$
$$SB = \{car, racecar, motortruck\}$$

These two sets share no common terms, and literally they are totally different. If the similarity function is applied to these two sets, the result is 0, meaning they are totally unrelated. Table 17.2 and Table 17.3 illustrate how to extend the OSSs with right WordNet senses.

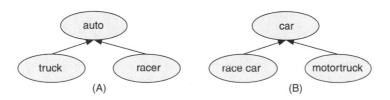

Figure 17.3 Parts of two ontologies.

T A B L E 17.2 WordNet Senses and Hypernyms for Ontology A

Concept	Parent-Concept	WordNet Senses/Synset	Hypernyms of Senses in WordNet	Right Sense?
auto		car, auto, automobile, machine, motorcar	motor vehicle, automotive vehicle	yes
truck	auto	truck, motortruck	motor vehicle, automotive vehicle	yes
		hand truck, truck	handcart, pushcart, cart, go-cart	no
racer	auto	race driver, automobile driver	driver	no
		racer, race car, racing car	car, auto, automobile, machine, motorcar	yes
		racer (an animal that races)	animal, animate being, beast, brute, creature, fauna	no
		racer (slender fast-moving North American snakes)	colubrid snake, colubrid	no

By extending the two primitive OSSs: S_A and S_B, we get the extended OSSs: SA' and SB':

$$S'_A = \{auto, car, automobile, machine, motorcar, truck, motortruck,$$
$$racer, racecar, racingcar\}$$
$$S'_B = \{car, auto, automobile, machine, motorcar, racer, racecar,$$
$$racingcar, truck, motortruck\}$$

T A B L E 17.3 WordNet Senses and Hypernyms for Ontology B

Concept	Parent-Concept	WordNet Senses/Synset	Hypernym of Senses WordNet	Right Sense?
car		auto, automobile, machine, motorcar	motor vehicle, automotive vehicle	yes
		railcar, railway car, railroad car	wheeled vehicle	no
		gondola	compartment	no
		cable car, car	compartment	no
race car	car	racer, race car, racing car	car, auto, automobile, machine, motorcar	yes
motortruck	car	truck, motortruck	motor vehicle, automotive vehicle	yes

Now we can see that these two sets share exactly the same semantic concepts! The similarity function based on the extended OSSs are:

$$sim(A, B) = \frac{|S(A) \cap S(B)|}{|S(A) \cap S(B)| + \alpha|S(A) - S(B)| + \beta|S(B) - S(A)|}$$

$$= \frac{11}{11 + 0\alpha + 0\beta} = 1$$

$$sim(B, A) = \frac{|S(A) \cap S(B)|}{|S(A) \cap S(B)| + \alpha|S(B) - S(A)| + \beta|S(A) - S(B)|}$$

$$= \frac{11}{11 + 0\alpha + 0\beta} = 1$$

This means ontology A and ontology B are semantically equivalent. Note: the equivalent is independent of α and β. With the semantic similarity function defined, we can measure the semantic distance between nodes and reconfigure the network topology accordingly to form semantic small-worlds. The next section gives a brief overview of our semantic small-world topology.

17.4.3 Semantics-Based Topology Adaptation and Search

With the semantic similarity measurement defined, the grid network topology can be constructed based on the semantic similarity. Our previous works have presented strategies of topology adaptation based on semantics [37]. The basic idea is to let each node actively find its semantically related neighbors to connect with. With the semantic small-world topology constructed, resource discovery can be efficiently performed, because queries reflect the querying node's ontology interest, and semantically related nodes are within the neighborhood of the querying node.

17.5 PROTOTYPE IMPLEMENTATION AND EVALUATION

We evaluate the operability of the presented architecture by implementing a prototype system. In this section we discuss the experiences gained and the lessons learned while developing and implementing the prototype, GONID toolkit.

17.5.1 Implementation

The architecture of the GONID toolkit is divided into three layers, namely the communication layer, the semantic layer, and the GUI layer, as shown in Figure 17.4. The communication layer is dedicated to managing the underlying P2P overlay communication, specifically, the directory overlay and the VO overlays. The directory overlay and the VO overlay are implemented in the same P2P network. The semantic layer manages local ontology knowledge. Its functions include knowledge storing, reasoning, mapping, querying, and indexing. The third layer of the system provides a user-friendly graphic interface, through which users can browse the existing ontology directories in the network, join interested VOs, create and edit ontology metadata, map ontologies, and issue

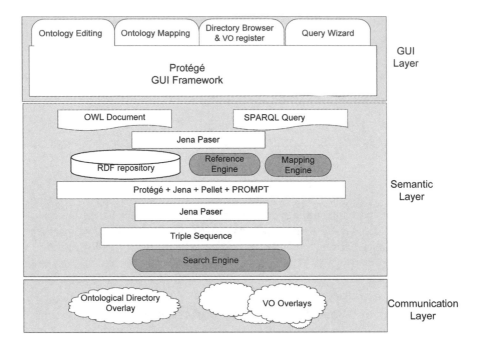

Figure 17.4   Architecture of the GONID toolkit.

complex queries. The implementation of the semantic layer and the GUI layer is built on top of Protégé [85] a free, open source ontology editor and knowledge-base framework. Protégé is written in Java and provides a plug-and-play environment that makes it a flexible base for rapid prototyping and application development. We implement our functionalities as Protégé plug-ins and all components of the system are integrated in the Protégé framework.

The system's graphical user interface builds on top of the available plug-ins of the Protégé user interface and provides additional graphical components for managing the distributed resource metadata. The GONID toolkit extends Protégé by adding two plug-in tabs: (1) the *ontology directory browser and VO register tab* and (2) the *VO ontological query tab*. Figure 17.5 shows a screenshot of the current state of the *directory browser and VO register* plugin. The main functionality of the ontology browser is to let the user browse the existing ontology hierarchy graphically. There are three panels from left to the right in the tab: the domain ontology browsing panel, class browsing panel, and node browsing panel. In the domain ontology browsing panel, when a user selects a domain/category, subdomains within the selected domain are listed in an alphabetical order. The class browser shows all the classes and class hierarchies defined in a particular ontology domain. When clicking a class, its detailed definition is listed in a pop-up window. Corresponding to each class, the node browser lists nodes using that class. A user can choose one or more categories and join their corresponding virtual organizations. The *query tab* shown in Figure 17.6 provides a query interface to support sharing and

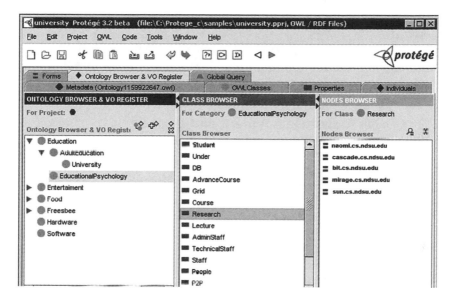

Figure 17.5 A screenshot of the directory browser and VO register tab.

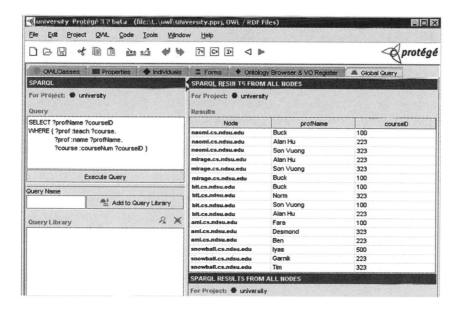

Figure 17.6 A screenshot of the query tab.

discovering knowledge in VOs. In the query panel on the left, users can enter queries in the SPARQL syntax. After a user presses the *Execute Query* button, the query results will be shown on the right panel. Double-clicking on a result entry will navigate to the particular individual in the *Individuals* tab. A more user-friendly query interface (e.g., a query wizard) is part of our ongoing work.

17.5.2 GONID Toolkit Deployment and Evaluation

We installed the GONID Toolkit software on six WinXP computers and six Linux SUSE computers. Each physical node runs three copies of the software and simulates three virtual nodes, therefore, we have in total 36 nodes in the system.

We create an experimental scenario to show that GONID does improve the performance of searching. We use two Information Retrieval (IR) standards: *precision* and *recall* as the performance metrics. *Precision* is defined in Equation 17.1. It measures the purity of the search results, or how well a search avoids returning results that are not relevant. The "document" in the IR definition represents a resource in our experiment. *Recall* refers to completeness of retrieval of relevant items, as defined in Equation 17.2.

$$precision = \frac{|relevantDocuments \cap retrievedDocuments|}{|retrievedDocuments|} \qquad (17.1)$$

$$recall = \frac{|relevantDocuments \cap retrievedDocuments|}{|relevantDocuments|} \qquad (17.2)$$

Our experiments try to justify two hypotheses: (1) grouping semantically related nodes into VOs and using domain ontologies helps to eliminate the semantic ambiguity, thus improving the search precision; (2) mappings between parties with different ontologies and reasoning help to extend a concept's semantic meaning, thus improving the search recall.

To make the experiment easy to control, we simplify the ontology data: we use a small-sized vocabulary set to generate the ontology data. We fix the mapping relation to the *equivalentClass* relation and ignore all other mapping relations. Specifically, the data is generated as follows:

- We generate a dictionary D containing N words. It provides all the vocabulary for the system's ontologies.
- In dictionary D, we create a set of semantically equivalent categories, C. In each category, we have c keywords which are assumed to represent the same semantic meaning, that is, any two keywords refer to the same meaning. In addition, we randomly pick s words, representing polysemy or homonymy (words with multiple meanings); if these words appear in different VOs, they represent different meanings.
- We created $V(V = 3)$ VOs. Each VO has $O(O = 10)$ ontologies, and each ontology includes k $(k=5)$ classes. The ontologies are created with the following process:

TABLE 17.4 Performance Comparison of GONID Search and Exact-Match Search

	Exact-Match	GONID ($m = 1$)	GONID ($m = 2$)	GONID ($m = 3$)
Precision	57%	100%	100%	100%
Recall	33%	64%	89%	100%

```
for class number  i=1 to k
    for ontology num  j=1 to O
        ontology  onto_j set its class  class_i as a keyword
            randomly picked from a category  Ci
    end for
end for
```

This procedure creates O semantically related ontologies that can be mapped mutually, because each class in an ontology can find mappings from other ontologies. In addition, each class has i $(i=6)$ instances.

- Each node joins to *1-3* VOs and keeps one ontology for each VO; it also maintains $m(1 \leq m \leq 3)$ mapping neighbors, that is, neighbors that map corresponding equivalent classes. The equivalent mapping is published so that the query engine can use the mapping to reformulate the query.

The following simple query form has been used in our experiment:

```
SELECT ?x
WHERE ?x rdfs:type ClassX;
```

We compare the GONID ontology-based search with semantics-free exact-match-based search. For the exact-match-based search, a query only matches a keyword without caring about the keyword's specific meaning in a VO and the mappings between nodes. For GONID searching, we vary the number of mapping neighbors (m) a node maintains from 1 to 3. For all the results returned, we compute the *precision* and *recall*. The results are shown in Table 17.4.

As shown in Table 17.4, GONID dramatically outperforms exact-match in both precision and recall. Because GONID search is executed in semantic VOs, it eliminates the semantic ambiguity problem such as polysemy and homonymy. Therefore, all the results returned by GONID search are relevant and the precision is 100%. When the number of mappings increases, the recall also increases, as most of the relevant relations can be identified. In fact, when each node maintains about three mapping neighbors, GONID search achieves a 100% recall rate. The result shows that the proposed GONID strategy is effective in improving the quality of search.

17.5.3 Evaluation Based on Simulation

Because of the limited experimental environment: with only 12 physical nodes in a LAN, we leave the scalability evaluation to simulations. The performance is measured using

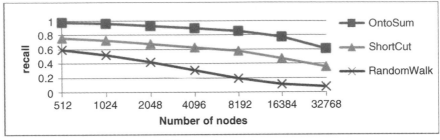

(a) Static environment

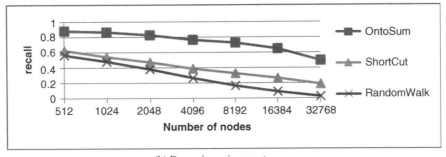

(b) Dynamic environment

Figure 17.7   Recall rate vs. network size.

the metric of recall rate, which is defined as the number of results returned divided by the number of results actually available in the network. For comparison, we also implement the learning-based ShortCut algorithm and random-walk based Gnutella algorithm. For the ShortCut approach, we collect query results after sufficient learning has been done. To simulate dynamic factors, in each time slice every node has a 5% probability to issue a query, and a 2% probability to leave the system. The probability of new nodes with new resources joining the system is the same as the probability of a node leaving. First, we vary the number of nodes from 2^9 to 2^{15} to test the scalability of the routing scheme.

The results are listed in Figure 17.7. As expected, our OntoSum searching scheme performs well as measured by recall rate in both static and dynamic networks. OntoSum's small-world topology effectively reduces the search space, and its ontology summary guides the query in the right direction. Therefore, OntoSum can locate results faster and more accurately. Besides all these reasons, another factor contributing OntoSum's overall better recall rate is that OntoSum is able to locate semantically related results that cannot be located by the ShortCut and random-walk. Because of the semantic heterogeneity of our experimental setup, relevant resources may be represented with different ontologies. OntoSum may use its ontology signature set to find semantically related nodes and use the mapping defined to translate the query. Therefore, it can locate most of the relevant results. However, for ShortCut and random-walk, they have no way to find semantically related resources. Therefore, they can only locate resources represented in the same ontology as the ontology of the querying node.

17.6 CONCLUSION

This chapter focuses on resource discovery in a global-scale grid environment. We have demonstrated that it is possible to meet both the scalability and searchability challenges faced by the resource discovery problem in this target environment. Towards this end, we have designed, implemented, and evaluated distributed discovery systems that are fully decentralized, scalable to the number of users and resources involved, adaptive to heterogeneous resource representations, and capable of handling complex queries.

Important problems in large-scale resource discovery remain to be solved. We identify several limitations of our work and research directions for future work. Some research directions are a natural continuation of this chapter; others are more general problems in resource discovery.

Our search system focuses on relatively static resource information; however, sometimes we need to consider very dynamic information. For example, in computational grids, a scheduler may need to find available computational resources with both relatively static requirements, such as system architecture, OS version, and access policy, and more dynamic requirements, such as instantaneous load and predictions of future availability.

In OntoSum, finding semantically related neighbors is accomplished according to their semantic similarity, which is defined by comparing the extended Ontology Signature Set. This simple similarity can be improved by considering other factors such as nodes' ontological structure, definitions of concepts, and instances of classes.

In our current system, query results are returned to requesters without using any ranking mechanisms. There are many techniques for ranking entities on the web, for example, PageRank 32] and HITS [33], on XML documents [34], and on the Semantic Web [35]. However, these techniques cannot be used directly to rank our search results because of the different problem nature. We plan to investigate the result-ranking problem, so that query results can be ordered based on relevance and importance for users. The ranking problem involves a rich blend of semantic and information-theoretic techniques. The ordering of the results should be able to vary according to user need.

REFERENCES

[1] H. Casanova, "Distributed Computing Research Issues in Grid," Computing, typescript, Univ. of California, San Diego, 2002.

[2] Globus Toolkit, http://www.globus.org/toolkit/.

[3] M. Cai, M. Frank, J. Chen, and P. Szekely, "MAAN: A multi-attribute addressable network for grid information services." The 4th International Workshop on Grid Computing, 2003.

[4] A. Iamnitchi and I. Foster, "On fully decentralized resource discovery in grid environments," in *Proceeding of the 2nd IEEE/ACM International Workshop on Grid Computing 2001*, Denver, 2001.

[5] S. Fitzgerald, I. Foster, C. Kesselman, G. von Laszewski, W. Smith, and S. Tuecke. "A directory service for configuring high-performance distributed computations." In *Proceedings*

of the 6th IEEE Symp. on High-Performance Distributed Computing, pages 365–375. IEEE Computer Society, 1997.

[6] W. Smith and D. Gunter. "Simple LDAP schemas for grid monitoring." Global Grid Forum, GWD-Perf-13-1, June 2001.

[7] I. Foster, C. Kesselman, J.M. Nick, and S. Tuecke. "The physiology of the grid. An open grid services architecture for distributed systems integration." Technical report, *Open Grid Service Infrastructure WG*, Global Grid Forum, June 2002.

[8] R. Raman, M. Livny, and M. Solomon, "Matchmaking: Distributed resource management for high throughput computing." In *Proceeding of IEEE Intel. Symp. On High Performance Distributed Computing*, Chicago, USA, 1998.

[9] S.J. Chapin, D. Katramatos, J. Karpovich, and A. Grimshaw. "The Legion resource management system." In *Proceedings of the 5th Workshop on Job Scheduling Strategies for Parallel Processing*, San Juan, Puerto Rico, 1999.

[10] G. Aloisio, M. Cafaro, S. Fiore, M. Mirto, and S. Vadacca. "GRelC data gather service: A step towards P2P production grids," In *Proceedings of 22nd ACM Symposium on Applied Computing*, 2009.

[11] DMOZ Open Directory Project, http://www.dmoz.org/

[12] DHT, http://en.wikipedia.org/wiki/Distributed_hash_table

[13] A. Rowstron and P. Druschel. "Pastry: Scalable, distributed object location and routing for large-scale peer-to-peer systems," In *Proceedings of the IFIP/ACM International Conference on Distributed Systems Platforms*, Middleware, 2001.

[14] G.A. Miller, R. Beckwith, C. Fellbaum, D. Gross, and K.J. Miller. "Introduction to WordNet: An on-line lexical database." *International Journal of Lexicography*, 3(4):235–312, 1993.

[15] A.L. Barabási, *Linked: How Everything Is Connected to Everything Else and What It Means for Business, Science, and Everyday Life*. New York, Plume, 2003.

[16] J. Kleinberg, "Navigation in a small world," *Nature*, No. 406, p. 845, 2000.

[17] M.A. Rodriguez and M. J. Egenhofer, "Determining semantic similarity among entity classes from different ontologies," *IEEE Transactions on Knowledge and Data Engineering*, Vol. 15, No. 2, March/April, 2003.

[18] J. Lee, M. Kim, and Y. Lee, "Information retrieval based on conceptual distance in IS-A hierarchies," *J. Documentation*, Vol. 49, pp. 188–207, 1993.

[19] OWL Web Ontology Language Overview. W3C Recommendation 10 February 2004, http://www.w3.org/TR/owl-features/

[20] A. Tversky. "Features of similarity." *Psychological Review*, 84(4):327–352, 1977.

[21] D. Lin. "An information-theoretic definition of similarity." In *Proceeding of the 15th International Conf. on Machine Learning*, pages 296–304. San Francisco, CA, 1998.

[22] B. Bloom. "Space/time tradeoffs in hash coding with allowable errors." *Communications of the ACM*, 13(7):422–426, July 1970.

[23] X. Tempich, S. Staab, and A. Wranik, "REMINDIN: Semantic query routing in peer-to-peer networks based on social metaphors," in *Proceedings of the International World Wide Web Conference (WWW)*, New York, USA, 2004.

[24] Gnutella website, http://gnutella.wego.com/

[25] K. Sripanidkulchai, B. Maggs, and H. Zhang. "Efficient content location using interest-based locality in peer-to-peer systems," in *Proceedings of the INFOCOM'03*, 2003.

[26] S. Castano, A. Ferrara, S. Montanelli, and D. Zucchelli. "Helios: A general framework for ontology-based knowledge sharing and evolution in P2P systems." In *Proceedings of IEEE DEXA WEBS 2003 Workshop*, Prague, Czech Republic, September 2003.

[27] A. Castano, S. Ferrara, S. Montanelli, E. Pagani, and G. Rossi, "Ontology addressable contents in P2P networks," in *Proceedings of the WWW'03 Workshop on Semantics in Peer-to-Peer and Grid Computing*, 2003.

[28] D. Watts and S. Strogatz. "Collective dynamics of 'small-world' networks." *Nature*, 1998.

[29] A. Iamnitchi, M. Ripeanu, and I. Foster. "Small-world filesharing communities." In *Proceedings of the Infocom*, Hong Kong, China, 2004.

[30] X. Tempich, S. Staab, and A. Wranik, "REMINDIN: Semantic query routing in peer-to-peer networks based on social metaphors," in *Proceedings of the International World Wide Web Conference (WWW)*, New York, USA, 2004.

[31] D. Stutzbach and R. Rejaie. "Understanding churn in peer-to-peer networks." In *Proceeding of the Internet Measurement Conference (IMC)*, Oct. 2006.

[32] S. Brin and L. Page, "The anatomy of a large-scale hypertextual Web search engine." In *Proceeding of WWW1998*, pages 107-117. Brisbane, Australia, 1998.

[33] J. Kleinberg, "Athorative sources in a hyperlinked environment." *J. ACM*, 48:604–632, 1999.

[34] V. Hristidis, Y. Papakonstantinou, and A. Balmin, "Keyword proximity search on XML graphs." In *Proceedings of the IEEE ICDE*, 2003.

[35] A. Sheth, B. Aleman-Meza, I.B. Arpinar, C. Halaschek, C. Ramakrishnan, C. Bertram, Y. Warke, D. Avant, F.S. Arpinar, K. Anyanwu, and K. Kochut, "Semantic association identification and knowledge discovery for national security applications." *Journal of Database Management*, 16(1), pp. 33–53, Jan-Mar 2005.

[36] J. Li, "Grid resource discovery based on semantically linked virtual organizations," *Journal of Future Generation Computer Systems*, Vol. 26, No. 3, 2010.

[37] J. Li and S. Vuong, "SOON: A scalable self-organized overlay network for distributed information retrieval," in *Proceedings of the 19th IFIP/IEEE International Workshop on Distributed Systems: Operations and Management Managing Large Scale Service Deployment (DSOM 2008)*, Samos Island, Greece, September 2008.

[38] J. Li and S. Vuong, "An ontological framework for large-scale grid resource discovery," in *Proceedings of the IEEE Symposium on Computers and Communications (ISCC'07)*, Aveiro, Portugal, July, 2007.

[39] J. Li, "Ontological directory and directory load-balancing for large scale grids," *International Journal of Applied Research on Information Technology and Computing*, Vol. 1, No. 1, January-April 2010.

18

GAME-BASED MODELS OF GRID USER'S DECISIONS IN SECURITY-AWARE SCHEDULING

Joanna Kolodziej, Samee U. Khan, Lizhe Wang, and Dan Chen

CONTENTS

Large Scale Network-Centric Distributed Systems, First Edition. Edited by Hamid Sarbazi-Azad and Albert Y. Zomaya.
© 2014 John Wiley & Sons, Inc. Published 2014 by John Wiley & Sons, Inc.

18.1 INTRODUCTION

The concept of the modern grid environment has grown far beyond the original Foster's grid idea of simple extension of conventional power networks. Today's grids are not just restricted to the physical infrastructure managed and utilized by the highly distributed users. Future generation grid environments are composed of various services and physical clusters in order to proceed the large amounts of data and information in an intelligent way. The management techniques in such systems should be able to group, predict, and classify different sets of rules, configuration directives, and environmental conditions. This management model must effectively deal with uncertainties in system information that may be incomplete, imprecise, or fragmentary.

The key scheduling objectives in today's computational grids, such as the maximization of the resource utilization and profits of the resource owners [9], may conflict with the users' requirements on security awareness in scheduling and system reliability at different levels of the grid global architecture [6]. Various system infections and external attacks may lead to unpredictable failures of the machines during the task executions. On the other hand, grid end users may define their own individual preferences and security conditions for protection and personalization of their data and applications processed by the system. An effective grid scheduler must be security-driven and resilient in response to all scheduling and risky conditions. It means that, to achieve the successful tasks executions according the specified users' requirements, the relation between the assurance of secure computing services and the behavior of a resource node must be defined and analyzed [3]. The scheduler must be able to analyze and realize the users' decisions.

In many decision-making problems, most of the information is provided by humans, which is inherently non-numeric. Game-theoretical models, besides fuzzy logic methods [14, 26, 27], are the most promising technologies for illustrating and analyzing numerous users' decisions and behavior in highly parametrized heterogeneous environments [13]. In grid scheduling, game theory supports the analysis of the various users' strategies in multi-criteria resource allocation process. All scheduling criteria can be aggregated and defined as cumulative users' cost or pay-off functions. Game-based models combined with the economic theory can capture many realistic scenarios in computational markets, computational auctions, grid, and P2P systems.

This chapter summarizes the recent work of the authors on the game-theoretic models of the grid users behavior in security aware scheduling [5, 15, 17, 19, 20]. The scheduling process may be realized in two alternate scenarios, namely *risky* and *secure* modes. In the former, security conditions are ignored by the users, while in the later, the users allocate their tasks to available machines assuring task security demands. The specification of the security demand can be realized in two different ways: (a) tasks can have security demands on resources to be allocated at and (b) resources can have security demands on tasks to be assigned to them. In this work we focus on the condition (a) of security requirements. The users' cost functions in the game are interpreted as the total costs of the secure execution of their tasks and the costs of the utilization of resources. The cumulative game cost function can be implemented as a two-step hierarchical optimization procedure and can be effectively minimized by conventional global optimization methods, as well as by using the metaheuristics, recommended in large-scale dynamic systems such as grids and clouds.

The effectiveness of the GA-based grid schedulers in solving the security aware games of the grid users is illustrated in the case study provided in Section 18.4. We simulated a simple symmetric game of the end users and minimized their cost functions by using four genetic schedulers working in risky and secure scenarios. All considered instances of grid system and game scenarios have been simulated using the *Sim-G-Batch* grid simulator.

18.2 SECURITY-AWARE SCHEDULING PROBLEMS IN COMPUTATIONAL GRIDS

Today's modern grid environment can be viewed as a complex, highly parametrized distributed computing system that combines the infrastructure of an intelligent computational platform and numerous services for the users and system administrators. Solving the scheduling problems in such an environment can be a big challenge for researchers and engineers, mainly due to the sheer size of the grid and its complex nature. Different types of scheduling problems in grids can be defined with respect to various grid characteristics and the requirements of the system administrators and system end users. All information generated by the numerous system components and received from all system "actors" must be "embedded" into the scheduling mechanism in order to achieve the desired performance of the grid [1, 18, 34].

Four main scheduling attributes are usually set up to specify the particular grid scheduling problem, namely: (a) the environment, (b) grid architecture, (c) task processing policy, and (d) tasks' interrelations. The type of grid environment can be static, where the number of the submitted applications and the available resources remain constant in a considered time interval, or dynamic, where states of the tasks and resources in the system may change over time.

The resource management and scheduling is usually organized in a hierarchical mode that is a compromise among centralized and decentralized scenarios. In a *centralized model* there is a central authority, which has a full knowledge of the system. The primary disadvantages of this model is its limited scalability, lack of fault tolerance, and the difficulty in accommodating multiple local policies imposed by the resource owners. In a *decentralized model*, local schedulers interact with each other to manage the tasks pool. In this model, there is no central authority responsible for resource allocation. In a *hierarchical model*, few central meta-schedulers (or meta-brokers) interact with local job dispatchers in order to define the optimal schedules. The local schedulers have knowledge about resource clusters, but they cannot monitor the whole system. The high-level schedulers can communicate and exchange data and information by using an additional network infrastructure (usually the Internet).

A specification of the tasks' processing policy is important in the identification of the particular scheduling problem. In the instantaneous mode, the tasks are scheduled as soon as they are entered into the system. In batch scheduling, the submitted tasks are grouped into batches and the scheduler assigns each batch to the resources. Additionally, there can be some internal relations among submitted tasks, or each task can be processed independently to another.

18.2.1 Generic Model of Secure Grid Clusters

A general security-aware grid model is based on the conventional hierarchical multilevel grid architecture [22]. However, the role of the particular meta-scheduler is different when security is considered as an additional criterion in the scheduling process. The meta-scheduler must analyze the security requirements for the execution of tasks and requests of the CG users for trustful resources available within the system. The local system brokers analyze "reputation" indexes of the machines received from the resource managers, send their suggestions to the meta-schedulers, and control the resource allocation and communication between CG users and resource owners (or providers).

Figure 18.1 depicts the three-level architecture of a single security-aware grid cluster. The communication (and management) of different clusters can be realized at both meta-scheduler and local secure cluster manager levels.

The trust level and security demand parameters are generated by aggregation of several scheduling and system attributes, as is presented in Fig. 18.2. These attributes can be divided into two major classes: (1) behavioral and security attributes needed for the specification of trust levels of the grid resources, and (2) attributes necessary for specification of the security demand of the grid applications (see also [30]).

Song et al. [29] have developed a fuzzy-logic trust model, where the major behavioral and intrinsic security attributes are represented as single scalar parameters. The task security demand in this model is supplied by the user's applications as request for authentication, data encryption, access control, and so on. The trust level parameters of the resources are aggregated through a two-level hierarchical fuzzy-logic based trust

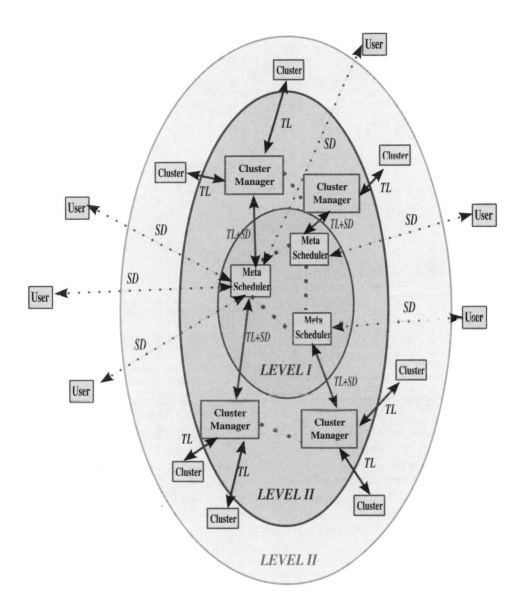

Figure 18.1   Model of a secure grid cluster.

procedure. Song et al. have used their model in online scheduling, however, it can be easily adapted to the other types of grid scheduling problems. In independent batch scheduling, it is used for the specification of new characteristics of tasks and resources in the grid system, namely security demand and trust level vectors. The *security demand vector*, denoted by $SD = [sd_1, \ldots, sd_n]$, where sd_j denotes the security demand parameter of task j. The *trust level vector*, denoted by $TL = [tl_1, \ldots, tl_m]$, is defined as a vector

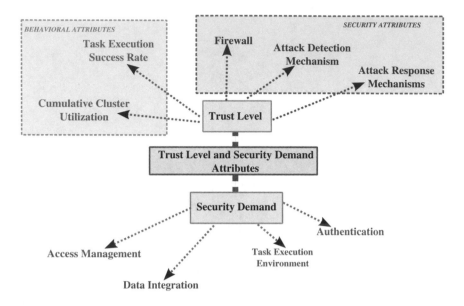

Figure 18.2 Major attributes affecting the trust level and security demand in grid systems.

of trust level parameters tl_i for all resources in the system. The trust level parameters specify how much a grid user can trust the resource manager. The local cluster managers maintain the status of machines in their clusters and monitor the execution of the tasks assigned to those machines. The values of the sd_j and tl_i parameters are real fractions within the range [0,1], with 0 representing the lowest and 1 the highest security requirements for a task execution and the most risky and fully trusted machine, respectively. A task can be successfully completed at a resource when a *security assurance condition* is satisfied. That is to say that $sd_j \leq tl_i$ for a given (j, i) task-machine pair.

The probability of failure of a given machine (i) during the execution of a given task (j) is denoted by $P_f[j][i]$ and can be defined by the negative exponential distribution function in the following way:

$$Pr_f[j][i] = \begin{cases} 0 & , \quad sd_j \leq tl_i \\ 1 - e^{-\alpha(sd_j - tl_i)} & , \quad sd_j > tl_i \end{cases} \tag{18.1}$$

where α is interpreted as a failure coefficient and is a global parameter of the model.

The matrix of failure probabilities calculated for all possible task-machine pairs (j, i) is called as a *Machine Failure Probability* matrix and is denoted by Pr_f.

The process of matching sd_j with tl_i is similar to that of a real-life scenario where users of some portals, such as Yahoo!, are required to specify the security level of the login session.

18.2.2 Security Criterion in Grid Scheduling

Various scheduling problems specified by different combinations of the scheduling attributes can be, in fact, modeled by using one general methodology. To our best knowledge, there is no commonly used notation for the classification of the grid scheduling problems and the conventional scheduling notation of Graham et al. [11] is insufficient for the dynamic scheduling in large–scale distributed environments. In this chapter, we focus on the fundamental type of the scheduling problem in computational grids, namely independent batch scheduling, where it is assumed that tasks are clustered and grouped into batches and there is no inter-relation among them. The trust level and security demand parameters introduced in the previous section are used for the specification of tasks and machines in the system, which can be characterized by the following structures:

(a) **Tasks**:

– *set of tasks' labels* $N = \{1, \ldots, n\}$, (n – number of tasks in the batch)

– *workload vector* $WL = [wl_1, \ldots, wl_n]$, where wl_j – workload parameter of task j expressed in millions of instructions (MI)

– *security demand vector* – $SD = [sd_1, \ldots, sd_n]$

(b) **Machines**:

– *set of machine labels* – $M = \{1, \ldots, m\}$, (m – total number of machines in the batch)

– *computing capacity vector* – $CC = [cc_1, \ldots, cc_m]$, where cc_i – computing capacity parameter of machine i expressed in millions of instructions per second (MIPS)

– *ready times vector* – *ready_times* $= [ready_1, \ldots, ready_m]$, where $ready_i$ is a ready time of machine i, which expresses the time needed for reloading this machine after finishing the last assigned task

– *trust level vector* – $TL = [tl_1, \ldots, tl_m]$

Tasks in this model may be considered as monolithic applications or meta-tasks with no dependencies among the components. The workloads of tasks are usually estimated by using some system prediction methodologies [12], historical data, or users' specification. The term "machine" in this work is related to a single or multiprocessor computing unit or even to a local small-area network.

For each pair (j, i) of task-machine labels, the coordinates of WL and CC vectors can be used for an approximation of the completion time of the task j on machine i. This completion time is denoted by $ETC[j][i]$ and can be calculated in the following way:

$$ETC[j][i] = \frac{wl_j}{cc_i}. \tag{18.2}$$

All $ETC[j][i]$ parameters are defined as the elements of an ETC matrix , $ETC = \left[ETC[j][i] \right]_{n \times m}$ in ETC matrix model [2]. The elements in the rows of the ETC matrix define the estimated completion times of a given task on particular machines, and elements in the column of the matrix are interpreted as approximate times of the completion of particular tasks on a given machine.

The ETC matrix model can be used for the formal implementation of the main scheduling criteria, namely *Makespan* and *Flowtime*. Let us first introduce two representations of the schedules in the system. Let S_∞ denotes the set of all permutations **with repetition** of the length n over the set of machine labels M. An element $Sch(1) \in S_\infty$ is termed a *schedule* and it is encoded by the following vector:

$$Sch(1) = [i_1, \ldots, i_n]^T, \tag{18.3}$$

where $i_j \in M$ denotes the number of the machine on which the task labeled by j is executed.

This encoding method is called *direct representation* of the schedule and can be easily transformed into into *permutation-based representation*, which is defined as a vector $Sch(2)$ of labels of tasks assigned to the machines. For each machine the labels of the tasks assigned to this machine are sorted in ascending order by the completion times of the tasks. Formally, this kind of schedule encoding method can be defined in the following way.

Let us denote by S_2 the set of all permutations **without repetitions** of the length n over the set of task labels N. A permutation $Sch \in S_2$ is called a *permutation-based representation* of a schedule in CG and can be defined by the following vector:

$$Sch(2) = [Sch_1, \ldots, Sch_n]^T, \tag{18.4}$$

where $Sch_i \in N, i = 1, \ldots, n$.

In this representation some additional information about the numbers of tasks assigned to each machine is required. The total total number of tasks assigned to a machine i is denoted by $\widetilde{Sch}_i$ and is interpreted as the i-th coordinate of an assignment vector $\widetilde{Sch(2)} = [\widetilde{Sch}_1, \ldots, \widetilde{Sch}_m]^T$, which defines the loads of grid machines.

The *Makespan* and *Flowtime* are considered in this chapter as the main scheduling criteria and may be expressed in terms of the completion times of the machines by using the ETC matrix model. A *completion time* $C[i]$ of the machine i is defined as the sum of the ready time parameters for this machine and a cumulative execution time of all tasks actually assigned to this machine, that is to say,

$$C[i] = ready_i + \sum_{j \in Task(i)} ETC[j][i], \tag{18.5}$$

where $Task(i)$ is the set of tasks assigned to the machine i.

The C_i parameters are the coordinates of the following completion vector:

$$C = [C[1], \ldots, C[m]]^T \tag{18.6}$$

Vector C is used for calculating the *Makespan* C_{max} in the following way:

$$C_{max} = \max_{i \in M} C[i]. \tag{18.7}$$

In terms of ETC matrix model, a *Flowtime* for a machine i can be calculated as a workflow of the sequence of tasks on a given machine i, that is to say,

$$F[i] = ready_i + \sum_{j \in Sorted[i]} ETC[j][i] \tag{18.8}$$

where $Sorted(i)$ is the set of tasks assigned to the machine i sorted in ascending order by the corresponding ETC values.

The cumulative *Flowtime* in the whole system is defined as the sum of $F[i]$ parameters, that is,

$$F = \sum_{i \in M} F[i] \tag{18.9}$$

In security-aware scheduling, the grid cluster or the grid resource may be not accessible to the global meta-scheduler when being infected with intrusions or by malicious attacks. The scheduler may analyze the machine failure probability matrix Pf_r in order to minimize the failure probabilities for task-machine pairs, or can the scheduler perform an "ordinary" scheduling without any preliminary analysis of the security conditions. The scheduler's strategies give rise to two modes of processing the grid applications, namely *secure* and *risky* modes.

In the secure scenario, all security and resource reliability conditions are verified for all possible task-machine pairs before the scheduling process is initialized. Each meta-scheduler tries to assign the tasks to the machines with possible minimal probabilities of failures of the machines during the executions of these tasks. There is some additional "cost" of the verification of security assurance condition for a given task-machine pair, which can be defined as the product of the probability $Pr_f[j][i]$ and the time $ETC[j][i]$. In this case, the completion time of the machine i is denoted by $C^s[i]$ and can be calculated as follows:

$$C^s[i] = ready_i + \sum_{\{j \in Tasks(i)\}} (1 + Pr_f[j][i])ETC[j][i]) \tag{18.10}$$

where $Tasks(i)$ denotes the set of tasks assigned to the machine i in a given batch.

In this mode the *Makespan* and *Flowtime* can be expressed as follows:

$$C^s_{max} = \max_{i \in M} C^s[i]. \tag{18.11}$$

$$F^s = \sum_{i \in M} F^s[i] \tag{18.12}$$

where

$$F^s[i] = ready_i + \sum_{j \in Sorted[i]} (1 + Pr_f[j][i])ETC[j][i]) \tag{18.13}$$

and $Sorted[i]$ denotes the set tasks assigned to the machine i sorted in ascending order by the corresponding ETC values.

18.2.2.1 Risky Mode. In this scenario, all secure and failing conditions are ignored by the meta-schedulers. The tasks are assigned to the machines based on the analysis of the *ETC* matrix. The estimated completion times of machines are calculated as in Eq. (18.5). If failures of machines are observed, then the unfinished tasks are temporarily moved into the backlog set and then rescheduled in the same way as in the secure mode. The total completion time of machine $i(i \in M)$ in this case can be defined as follows:

$$C^r[i] = C[i] + C^s_{res}[i] \tag{18.14}$$

where $C[i]$ is calculated by using the Eq. (18.5) for tasks primarily assigned to the machine i , and $C^s_{res}[i]$ is the completion time of machine i calculated by using the Eq. (18.10) for rescheduled tasks, that is, the tasks reassigned to the machine i from the other resources.

The formulas for *Makespan* and *Flowtime* in this mode are defined in the following way:

$$C^r_{max} = \max_{i \in M} C^r[i]. \tag{18.15}$$

$$F^r = \sum_{i \in M} F^r[i] \tag{18.16}$$

where

$$F^r[i] = ready_i + \sum_{j \in Sorted[i]} ETC[j][i] + \sum_{j \in Sorted_{res}[i]} (1 + Pr_f[j][i])ETC[j][i]) \tag{18.17}$$

and $Sorted_{res}[i]$ denotes the set of *rescheduled* tasks assigned to the machine i sorted in ascending order by the corresponding *ETC* values.

18.2.3 Requirements of Grid End Users for Scheduling

The complexity of the scheduling scenarios and the roles of the system administrators, service providers, and grid power users strongly depend on the end users' Quality of Service (QoS) requirements and specific scheduling and task execution criteria, such as requirements for specifying their tasks as monolithic, atomic applications, or meta-tasks, access to the remote data, or detailed characteristics of the system resources. The users would like to know the "reputation" indexes of the grid clusters. These parameters can be specified by the local cluster managers or resource owners as trust-level parameters (see Sec. 18.2.1). The user may wish to target particular types of resources (e.g., SMP machines), but should not be concerned with the type of resource management on the grid, nor with the resource management systems on individual resources on the grid.

The trust indexes can be used in the specification of *reliability of grid resources*. In some cases, the machines can fail during the task execution or may be unavailable for some users or some types of applications due to restrictions and special access policies defined by the owners. The information about the current state and reliability of grid resources is needed for an effective management of the users' tasks and for the reduction of costs of possible resource failures. In the case of resource failure, the system administrators can activate rescheduling or task migration procedures, and preemption policies. On the other hand, the end users may specify some special requirements on the assignment of their tasks to the most trustful resources, no matter how expensive this assignment is. Based on the values of trust indexes, the users should be able to estimate the security demands for their tasks on the available resources. In today's grid, the users should be able to monitor the current status of their tasks and applications. The secure access to the system information, internal services, and data requires the specification of some standardized authentication and authorization mechanisms. These standardized authentication certificates can be digitally signed by a certificate authority, and kept in a user's repository that is recognized by the resources and resource owners. All such certificates can be automatically created by the user's interface application during the submission of tasks.

Trying to satisfy the QoS requirements of the end users, the grid managers can work in one of the following scenarios:

- *Cooperativeness:* In this case, the system "actors" can form a coalition to plan in advance their actions.
- *Non-cooperativeness:* In this scenario, all system users and managers act independently of one another.
- *Semi-cooperativeness:* In this model, each user can select a partner for cooperation.

The above-mentioned relations can also show us some brief characteristics of the end users behavior and decisions. In most of the scheduling scenarios, it is assumed that the end users submit their tasks independently. However, in some cases the local coalition of the end users can improve the effectiveness of the system, especially in the cases of considering security to be an extra scheduling criterion embedded into the scheduling model. The strategies and decisions of the grid users and managers of all types can be modeled by using game theory.

18.3 GAME MODELS IN SECURITY-AWARE GRID SCHEDULING

Modeling of the autonomous decisions of the grid users and personalization of the users' data and requirements are among the most important issues in today's grid scheduling. This modeling may be difficult due to the different access policies and sometimes conflicting requirements of the end users. Game-based models, which can be additionally supported sometimes by the economic strategies, can capture many realistic scheduling scenarios and allow aggregation of all scheduling criteria into the cumulative users' cost or pay-off functions, which makes such models very useful in the analysis of the various users' strategies in the resource allocation process.

A short description of the relations of grid managers and administrators provided in the previous section may be used also for the characteristics of the games of the grid users of all types, not just the end users. Therefore, we may define three basic types of grid user games, namely *non-cooperative*, *cooperative*, and *semi-cooperative* games [4], in the following way:

- *Non-cooperative game:* In this game, the players take autonomous decisions, independently, one another. In fact, in the realistic grid environments the end users usually are unable to cooperate due to the sheer size of the whole infrastructure and sometimes conflict of their interests. Also, resource owners and providers try to increase their own profits and keep their resources busy for a long time.
- *Cooperative game:* In this scenario, the players can form the coalition and make the collective decisions on the assignments of their tasks. The whole coalition can specify its own strategies. This game model can be very useful for illustrating the negotiations of the meta-schedulers from different clusters and local cluster managers.
- *Semi-cooperative game:* In this case, each user can choose (randomly) another user (player) for cooperation. This game is usually proposed as a multi-round auction to incorporate the task rescheduling in the case of failures of machines.

Each grid user at various system levels can have different privileges and access to the resources. Therefore, the two following scenarios can be additionally considered in each of the above-mentioned games:

- *Symmetric scenario*. In this case, there are no special privileges in the resource usage for the grid users.
- *Asymmetric scenario*. In this case, there is a privileged user (Leader), who can have full access to resources as opposed to the rest of users who can be granted only limited access to resources. The tasks submitted by the Leader are scheduled first.

In the following subsections we provide brief characteristics of the above-mentioned scenarios in the context of both end users' and system managers' games.

18.3.1 Symmetric and Asymmetric Non-cooperative Games of the End Users

One of the main benefits of the game-based scheduling and resource management in CGs is that it enables a scalability and personalization of the decision-making processes of grid end users. Due to the sheer scale of grid systems, the non-cooperative game is a potential model for integrating security and resource reliability requirements in grid scheduling. This section presents two different general scenarios of the non-cooperative grid users' behaviors, namely *symmetric* and *asymmetric* strategic game models.

18.3.1.1 Non-cooperative Symmetric Game.

In the *symmetric* non-cooperative users' game, the users are selfish and do not make any collective decisions. Also, there are no priorities and privileges in their access to the resources. An illustrative example of the symmetric game can be a scheduling scenario in which each player submits an approximately equal amount of tasks. This game can be defined by the following parameters:

$$G_A = (A; \{X_a\}_{a=1,...,A}; \{Q_a\}_{a=1,...,A}), \text{ where:}$$

- A is the number of grid users;
- $\{X_1, \ldots, X_A\}$; are the sets of users' strategies;
- $\{Q_1, \ldots, Q_A\}; Q_a : X_1 \times \ldots \times X_A \to \mathbb{R}; \forall_{a=1,...,A}$ is the set of users' cost functions.

The elements of sets X_a ($a = 1, \ldots, A$) are defined as users' strategy vectors and are denoted by $Pl_1, \ldots, Pl_A$. Function Q_a estimates the cumulative cost of scheduling all tasks submitted by user a. The players try to minimize simultaneously their cost functions Q_a in the game.

An optimal state of the whole game is called **an equilibrium state (point)** and it is represented by the multi-vector $(\widehat{Pl_1}, \ldots, \widehat{Pl_A})$ of the users' strategies, for which the following condition holds:

$$
\begin{aligned}
Q_a\left(\widehat{Pl_1}, \ldots, \widehat{Pl_A}\right) &= \\
= \min_{Pl_a \in X_a} Q_a\left(\widehat{Pl_1}, \ldots, \widehat{Pl_{(a-1)}}, Pl_a, \widehat{Pl_{(a+1)}}, \ldots, \widehat{Pl_A}\right)
\end{aligned}
\tag{18.18}
$$

for all $a = 1, \ldots, A$.

The equilibrium point can be interpreted as a steady state of the strategic game, in which each player holds correct expectations concerning the other players' behavior.[1]

It can be observed from Eq. (18.18) that the problem of generation of the equilibrium points is a multi-objective global optimization task, and the equilibrium states of the game should be Pareto-optimal [25, 31]. Usually, in the complex game scenarios it is very hard to verify this Pareto-optimality. In this chapter, we focus on the non-zero sum games, where the strategies of the players are not opposite, that is, the sum or the values of all players cost functions Q_a is not 0. In such a case, the equilibrium points are the results of minimization of a *multi-cost game function* Q defined as follows.

---

[1]In the case of continuous players' cost functions, the equilibrium state of the game is called the *Nash equilibrium* [7].

Let us denote by $minQ_a, (a = 1, \ldots, A)$ the minimal value of the function Q_a calculated for each user a, that is to say:

$$minQ_a = \min_{Pl_a \in X_a} \{Q_a(Pl_1, \ldots, Pl_A)\}. \qquad (18.19)$$

The results of the global minimization of the following *game multi-cost* function $Q : X_1 \times \cdots \times X_A \to \mathbb{R}$:

$$Q(Pl_1, \ldots, Pl_A) = \sum_{a=1}^{A} \frac{1}{A}(Q_a(Pl_1, \ldots, Pl_A) - minQ_a), \qquad (18.20)$$

is an equilibrium state of a non-cooperative non-zero sum symmetric game of the grid users, which satisfies the condition of Pareto-optimality [25]. It should be noted that the function Q is a special case of the weighed distance L^p metric function with $p = 1$ [32]. The values of all Q_a functions are non-negative, and the weight coordinates are strictly positive, which means that the global solutions of the problem defined in Eq. (18.20) are Pareto-optimal.

18.3.1.2 Asymmetric Scenario—Stackelberg Game. Although the symmetric game is easy to implement, it can be difficult sometimes to realize this scenario in practical applications. Due to the cross-domain access, authorization, and resource management features of the grid system, the grid users have different access policies to the resources and their relations are rather asymmetric with regard to resource usage privileges. Also, the number of particular tasks submitted by the users may be different.

A Stackelberg game is one of the simplest and best-studied models for illustrating the asymmetric scenario of the behavior of non-cooperative grid users. In this game, one user acts as a *Leader*, and the rest of players (users) are the *Followers*.

The Stackelberg games have been well studied in the game theory literature (see, e.g., [4]). Roughgarden [28] used the Stackelberg game model for scheduling in peer-to-peer networks of machines with load-dependent latencies. The total latency of the system has been minimized in that game.

The following examples illustrate some real-life grid scenarios where the Stackelberg game model can be applied (see also [20]):

- One user (Leader) may have the full access to resources, while the other users have only limited access.
- Some tasks can have critical deadlines (especially in online scheduling) and they can be sent by the Leader to schedule them first.
- One user (Leader) can be the owner of a large portion of the tasks in the batch.
- The Leader can have some special requirements on the "reputation" of the available resources. They may wish to schedule their tasks to the most trustful resources (secure machines).
- The high heterogeneity of tasks in grid usually has a great impact on the system performance. Therefore, the Leader could create a small batch of the most

time-consuming tasks as the backlog set of grid applications, in order to "balance" the computational loads of machines during the scheduling.

Formally, the Stackelberg game of the grid users can be defined as two-level procedure as follows [20]:

- **Leader's action I**: The game is initialized by the Leader and the initial strategy is denoted by $\widetilde{Pl}_1 = [\widetilde{j}_1, \ldots, \widetilde{j}_{k_1}]$, where k_1 is the number of tasks submitted by the Leader.
- **Followers' action:** Followers minimize simultaneously their cost functions relative to the Leader's action I:

$$
\begin{cases}
Pl_2^{Fol} = arg \min_{(Pl_2 \in X_2)} \{Q_2(\widetilde{Pl}_1, Pl_2, \ldots, Pl_A)\} \\
\vdots \\
Pl_A^{Fol} = arg \min_{(Pl_A) \in X_A} \{Q_A(\widetilde{Pl}_1, \ldots, Pl_A)\}
\end{cases}
\tag{18.21}
$$

- **Leader's action II**: Leader updates the strategy by minimizing the cost function Q_1 (see also Eq. (18.30)) taking into account the result of Followers' actions. The following vector $Pl^G = \left[Pl^{Lead}, Pl_2^{Fol}, \ldots, Pl_A^{Fol} \right]$, where:

$$
Pl^{Lead} = arg \min_{(Pl_1 \in X_1)} Q_1 \left(Pl_1, Pl_2^{Fol}, \ldots, Pl_A^{Fol} \right)
\tag{18.22}
$$

is a solution of the whole game.

In the above formulas X_1 denotes the set of the Leader's strategies and $Pl^{Fol} = \left[\widetilde{Pl}_1, Pl_2^{Fol}, \ldots, Pl_A^{Fol} \right]$ denotes a *Followers' Vector*, which is interpreted as the result of the Followers' action. It should be noted that the Followers play an "ordinary" non-cooperative symmetric game, but they must know the Leader's action. The game multi-cost function Q in this case can be defined in the following way:

$$
Q_{Stac} = \frac{1}{A} Q_1 + Q_{Fol};
\tag{18.23}
$$

where Q_1 is the Leader's cost function and

$$
Q_{Fol} := \frac{A-1}{A} \sum_{a=2}^{A} Q_a;
\tag{18.24}
$$

is a *Followers' cost function*. An optimal solution of the whole game is called the *Stackelberg Equilibrium*.

Non-cooperative games are commonly used for modeling the end users' relations. However, those games can be also applied for illustrating the realistic relations of the resource owners. Indeed, in many cases the main aim of the machine owners is to achieve the high profits from renting their computational infrastructure and they usually send their offers to the local service and resource providers independently.

18.3.2 Cooperative and Semi-cooperative Game Scenarios

In practical applications, various levels of the cooperativeness of the grid users can be modeled by using the auction mechanism. In auctions there are two main groups of participants: sellers (resource owners) and buyers (grid end-users). Cooperation between users to form a coalition and win the auction is possible, but usually the users behave selfishly. The auction mechanism can be defined in many ways (e.g., English, Dutch, First and Second Price auctions). A task is awarded to the highest bidder, meaning that the user or system manager that is the best fit to execute the task wins. For the work done, each grid user is compensated by side-payments. All differ in terms of whether they are performed as open or closed auctions and the offer price for the highest bidder. The users' strategies in particular auctions are discussed, for example, in [10].

Khan et al. [16] observed that, in the case of conventional resource providing in the grid systems and data centers, the auction mechanism is effective in the case of semi-cooperation or cooperation of the grid users. Especially in the case of immediate rejection of tasks, the semi-cooperative p-round sealed-bid auction incorporates task reallocation. The user who is unable to execute the task, at random, chooses another user and passes the unexecutable task to it. If the newly chosen user can execute the task, then the reallocating procedure finishes, otherwise, another user is selected at random. This process is repeated $p - 1$ times, where p is the number of the users.

Another proposal of Khan is the cooperative scenario [15], where all users collectively negotiate and deliberate to come up with a task allocation that is beneficial to the system as a whole. In such a scenario, some individual users may not be content with the decision of the coalition, but the resulting allocation is efficient in the sense that it aims to reduce the *Makespan* and *Energy* consumed by the system, and provides a load-balanced task allocation.

Both semi-cooperative and cooperative scenarios presented by Khan et al. [16] may be adapted to modeling the behavior of meta-schedulers and local job dispatchers in hierarchical grid model presented in Fig. 18.1. In this model, the end users can specify their requirements and the task and resource managers are responsible for seeking and selecting the best offer for their "clients" according to the security scheduling criteria.

18.3.3 Online Scheduling Games

The idea of the simple auction models used in batch scheduling has been extended by Kwok et al. [21] to online scheduling. It is model resource management and global scheduling policies are specified at the intra- and inter-site levels in the three-level hierarchical grid structure. In the intra-site bidding, each machine owner in the site, who acts selfishly, declares the "execution capability" of the resource. The local manager monitors these amounts and sends a single value to the global scheduler. In the inter-site bidding, the global scheduler should allocate tasks according to the values sent by the local dispatchers. Formally, the users' decisions can be planned and executed at three different levels and therefore three different game theoretic task allocation and execution problems:

- *Intra-Site Task Execution Strategies:* This problem concerns the strategies of the participating computers inside a local grid cluster (site). Specifically, although the various computers "participate" in making up of the grid cluster, the owner of each individual machine acts selfish in that they only want to execute tasks from local users but do not want to contribute to the execution of remote jobs.

- *Intra-Site Bidding:* This problem concerns the determination of the advertised "execution capabilities" for tasks submitted to one global meta-scheduler. The meta-scheduler needs to know all the sites' execution capabilities. The local job dispatcher can then "moderate" all declarations about the trust levels and computational capacities of the machines and send the offers to the global scheduler. For example, if the local job dispatcher is aggressive in task execution, it could use the "minimization" approach, taking the minimum value of the declarations from all the machine owners. The best strategies for the resource owners can be selected using the auction theory.

- *Inter-Site Bidding:* Similar to the intra-site situation, at the inter-site level, the various local job dispatchers also need to formulate game theoretic strategies for computing the single representative value of the job execution time to be sent to the global scheduler.

Song et al. [29, 30] showed that different combinations of the above games result in different grid management structures. For a semi-selfish grid, the intra-site games are non-cooperative while the inter-site game is cooperative. This model fits most of today's grid and cloud environments, because these infrastructures are usually initialized and built after some cooperative negotiations at the organization level. The results presented in [30] are extended by Wu et al. [33]. The authors consider the heterogeneity of a fault-tolerance mechanism in security-assured grid job scheduling and define four types of GA-based online schedulers for the simulation of fault-tolerance mechanisms.

18.4 CASE STUDY: APPROXIMATING THE EQUILIBRIUM STATES OF THE END USERS' SYMMETRIC GAME USING THE GENETIC METAHEURISTICS

The problem of solving the finite strategic game remains challenging, especially in real-life approaches. The values of the game cost functions Q defined in Eqs. (18.20) and (18.23) can be computed if the cost functions of all players have been first minimized. Therefore, the problem of the minimization of Q function can be defined as a two-level hierarchical global optimization procedure that requires some simple and fast optimization methodologies implemented at each level.

In this section, we provide as a simple case study a simulation of a symmetric non-cooperative game of the grid end users. The cumulative time of the execution of tasks submitted to the system, the cost of the utilization of the resources, and the cost of the verification of security condition (or the failures of the machines during the task executions) are interpreted as a cumulative cost of playing the game and are specified for each user as its game cost function. The Q function has been minimized by using four types of genetic-based, risk-resilient metaheuristics.

18.4.1 Specification of the Game

18.4.1.1 Characteristics of Game Players and Decision Variables. We assume that the general scenario of the game is identical to that defined in Section 18.3.1.1, and A denotes the number of grid users (players). The total number of tasks $n \in N$ in a given batch can be expressed as the sum of tasks submitted by all users, that is,

$$n = \sum_{a=1}^{A} k_a, \tag{18.25}$$

where k_a is the number of tasks of the user $a = 1, \ldots, A$.

Each user a controls their strategic variables. These variables are expressed by the labels of the tasks submitted by a given user and defined as the following *user's strategy vector*:

$$Pl_a = \left[j_{(\widehat{k_{(a-1)}}+1)}, \ldots, j_{(\widehat{k_{(a-1)}}+k_a)} \right], \tag{18.26}$$

where $\widehat{k_{(a-1)}} = k_1 + \ldots + k_{(a-1)}$.

The schedules can be then expressed by the following vectors of the users' parameters:

$$Sch(1) = \left[i_1^1, \ldots, i_{k_1}^1, \ldots, i_{(\widehat{k_{(a-1)}}+1)}^a, \ldots, i_{(\widehat{k_{(a-1)}}+k_a)}^a, \ldots \ldots i_{k_A}^A \right], \tag{18.27}$$

in the direct representation, and

$$Sch(2) = [Pl_1, \ldots, Pl_A], \tag{18.28}$$

in permutation-based representation (see Section 18.2.2).

18.4.1.2 Solving the Grid Users' Game. The general idea of the optimization of the game cost function Q presented in Fig. 18.3. The optimization procedure is composed of two cooperating modules: the **Global Module**, where the values of the function Q are calculated and optimized, and the **Players' Module**, where the users' cost functions Q_a are optimized.

The communication procedure between *Global* and *Players' Modules* can be defined as follows: Let us denote by $Sch^{(0)}$ permutation-based representation of an initial schedule generated in the Global Module, that is, $Sch^{(0)} = [Pl_1^{(0)}, \ldots, Pl_{Play}^{(0)}]$, where $Pl_a^{(0)}$ is the initial strategy vector of the user a (see Eq. (18.26)). Vector $Sch^{(0)}$ is replicated and its copies are sent to the *Players' Module*, one copy per user. Then, each user

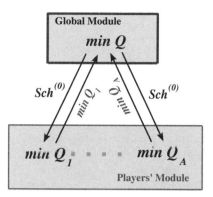

Figure 18.3 Hierarchical procedure of solving non-cooperative symmetric game of grid users.

independently optimizes their game cost function[2] by changing the allocations of just his own tasks. As the result of this minimization, the optimal values of the Q_a cost functions are calculated:

$$
\begin{cases}
min\, Q_a{}^{(0)} = \min_{(Pl_1 \in X_1)} Q_1 \left(Pl_1, Pl_2^{(0)}, \ldots, Pl_A^{(0)} \right) \\
\;\;\vdots \\
min\, Q_A{}^{(0)} = \min_{(Pl_A \subset X_A)} Q_A \left(Pl_1^{(0)}, \ldots, Pl_{A-1}^{(0)}, Pl_A \right)
\end{cases}
\tag{18.29}
$$

These values are sent back to the **Global Module**, where the objective function for the whole game Q is calculated for the schedule $Sch^{(0)}$. A similar procedure can be defined for the direct representation of the schedules.

18.4.1.3 Game Cost Functions. The cost functions Q_a $(a = 1, \ldots, A)$ calculated for all users must, beyond the conventional scheduling criteria such as *Makespan*, *Flowtime*, and the resource utilization [9], express the estimated costs of the verification of the security conditions and possible machine failures. The users have to "pay" an additional "fee" for the secure allocation of their tasks in the machines. Therefore, functions $Q_a, a \in \{1, \ldots, A\}$ can be defined as weighed or simply the direct sum of the following three components:

$$
Q_a = Q_a^{(ex)} + Q_a^{(util)} + Q_a^{(sec)},
\tag{18.30}
$$

---

[2]Note that the users' costs optimization in the **Players' Module** can be implemented as a parallel multi-threaded procedure, which can speed up the whole process.

where:

- $Q_a^{(ex)}$ indicates the user's task execution cost,
- $Q_a^{(util)}$ denotes the resource utilization cost, and
- $Q_a^{(sec)}$ is the cost of security-assured allocation of the user tasks.

Similarly as for conventional scheduling objectives in independent batch scheduling, the ETC matrix model is useful for the specification of all cost functions of the grid users.

18.4.1.4 Task Execution Cost. The cumulative cost of execution of the tasks submitted by particular users can be calculated as an average completion time of their tasks. In terms of the completion times of machines (see Eq. (18.5)) the task execution cost $Q_a^{(ex)}$ for user a can be defined as follows:

$$Q_a^{(ex)} = \frac{\sum_{j=k_{a-1}+1}^{k_a} C[j][i]}{C_m \cdot k_a}, \tag{18.31}$$

where $C[j][i]$ denotes the completion time of a task j on machine i and and it is calculated in the following way:

$$C[j][i] = ETC[j][i] + ready[i], \tag{18.32}$$

and C_m is the maximal completion time of all tasks submitted by the user a.

18.4.1.5 Resource Utilization Cost. The grid user's utility function is usually defined as a cost of buying free CPU cycles [9]. In this work, the utilization cost paid by the user a is calculated as amount of average idle time of machines on which their tasks are executed. This amount depends (is proportional) of the total time spent for execution of their tasks on those machines. This cost depends on the completion times of the user's tasks. The utility function $Q_a^{(util)}$ is defined as follows:

$$Q_a^{(util)} = \sum_{i \in machines(a)} \left(1 - \frac{C_{(a)}[i]}{C_{max}}\right) \cdot Iddle\_Factor[i], \tag{18.33}$$

where $machines(a)$ denotes the set of machines to which all tasks of the user a are assigned and C_{max} refers to the *Makespan*. The completion time of a given machine $i \in machines(a)$, denoted by $C_{(a)}[i]$, is calculated in the following way:

$$C_{(a)}[i] = ready[i] + \sum_{\substack{j \in N: \\ Sch_j(1)=i}} ETC[j][i] \tag{18.34}$$

where $Sch_j(1)$ is the value of j-th coordinate in a given schedule vector $Sch(1)$—or $Sch(2)$—both implementations of the schedules may be used in Eq. (18.34).

The following expression:

$$\left(1 - \frac{C_{(a)}[i]}{C_{max}}\right) \cdot Idle\_Factor[i], \tag{18.35}$$

in Eq. (18.33) is interpreted as an idle time of machine i calculated for a given user a. This is just a "portion" of the total idle time of machine i, and it is proportional to the time of execution of all tasks of the user a assigned to this machine. This proportion is specified by the coefficient $Idle\_Factor[i]$ in the following way:

$$Idle\_Factor[i] = \frac{\sum_{j \in Tasks_{(a)}[i]} ETC[j][i]}{C_{(a)}[i]} \tag{18.36}$$

where $Tasks_{(a)}[i]$ is the set of the tasks of the user a assigned to the machine i.

18.4.1.6 Security-Assurance Cost.
The security-assurance cost of scheduling the tasks of the user a, denoted by $Q_a^{(sec)}$ in Eq. (18.30), depends on the scheduling scenario (risky or secure) and the result of the verification of security condition by the local cluster manager.

In the **Risky mode** the "security" components of the functions Q_a are in fact not calculated, that is, $Q_a^{(sec)} = 0, \forall a = 1, \ldots, A$. However, some machines may fail during task execution and the rescheduling procedure of those tasks must be activated. Therefore, the security cost in this case is calculated as follows:

$$Q_l^{(sec)}[ris] = \sum_{j \in Res(a)} \frac{P_f[j][i] \cdot ETC[j][i]}{(ETC)_{m(a)} \cdot \sharp(Res(a))}, \tag{18.37}$$

where $Res(a)$ is the set of the tasks of the user a that must be rescheduled, and $(ETC)_{m(a)}$ is the (expected) maximal computation time of the tasks of the user a in a considered schedule, that is,

$$(ETC)_{m(a)} = \max_{\substack{j \in Task(a) \\ i \in machines(a)}} ETC[j][i]. \tag{18.38}$$

In **Secure mode**, the users must pay the cost of the verification of the security condition for their tasks. The cost of possible failures of machines during the tasks executions are calculated as the products of the failure probabilities and the expected times of computation of the tasks on the inaccessible machines. The secure cost function $Q_a^{(sec)}$ in this case is defined as follows:

$$Q_a^{(sec)}[secure] = \sum_{j=k_{a-1}+1}^{k_a} \frac{P_f[j][i] \cdot ETC[j][i]}{(ETC)_{m(a)} \cdot k_a}. \tag{18.39}$$

T A B L E 18.1   Hybrid Meta-Heuristics for Risky and Secure-Assured Scheduling

Meta-heuristic	Global Module	Players' Module
RGA-GA	RGA	PGA
RGA-PMCT	RGA	PMCT
SGA-GA	SGA	PGA
SGA-PMCT	SGA	PMCT

18.4.2   Genetic-Based Resolution Methods for Game Models

Due to multiple constraints and different preferences of the grid users, genetic-based heuristic approaches seem to be the best candidate methodologies for solving the users' games. However, different from the classical genetic-based schedulers (see [8]), in this case the main framework of the scheduler must be extended by the hybridization of genetic algorithm (GA) working in the **Global Module** with some other heuristic method implemented in the **Players' Module** (see Fig. 18.3).

Four hybrid GA-based schedulers have been defined for solving the symmetric grid users' games (see also [20]). The combinations of the heuristic components of these hybrids are presented in Table 18.1.

The GA-based meta-heuristics may work as global and local optimizers in the **Global** and **Players' Modules**. Similarly to the methodologies presented in [20], each hybrid algorithm is defined as a combination of two methods, namely *Risky Genetic Algorithm (RGA)* and *Secure Genetic Algorithm (SGA)*, in the **Global Module**; and two local level optimizers, namely *Player's Genetic Algorithm (PGA)* and *Player's Minimum Completion Time (PMCT)*, in the **Players' Module**. The performance of the **Players' Module** can be improved by receiving from the **Global Module** and updating just the changes in machine completion times for each player. Therefore, the general procedure of **Players'** algorithm may be defined as it is demonstrated in Fig. 18.4.

18.4.2.1   Schedulers Implemented in Global Module.   The template of the main GA-based engine implemented in **Global Module** is presented in Fig. 18.5.

The main difference between *RGA* and *SGA* algorithms is the method of the evaluation of the population by using the users' cost functions Q_a, which is different in the **Risky** (RGA) and **Secure** (SGA) scheduling scenarios.

1: Send the ready_times vectors to the individual players;
2: Individual players compute the $minQ_a$ values;
3: Receive the $minQ_a$ values from the individual players;
4: Send the $minQ_a$ values to Global Module;

Figure 18.4   The optimization procedure in **Player's Module**.

1: Generate the initial population P^0 of size μ;
2: Send the ready times vectors of the machines corresponding to the individuals
   of the population P^0 to the Player's Module;
3: Receive the $minQ_a$ values from the Player's Module;
4: Evaluate P^0;
5: while not termination-condition do
6:     Select the parental pool T^t of size λ; $T^t := Select(P^t)$;
7:     Perform crossover procedure on pars of individuals in T^t with probability pc; $P^t_c := Cross(T^t)$;
8:     Perform mutation procedure on individuals in P^t_c with probability pm; $P^t_m := Mutate(P^t_c)$;
9:     Send the ready times vectors of the machines corresponding to the individuals
       of the population P^t_m to the Player's Module;
10:    Receive the values $minQ_a$ from the Players' Module;
11:    Evaluate P^t_m;
12:    Create a new population P^{t+1} of size μ from individuals in P^t and/or P^t_m;
13:    $t := t+1$;
14: end while
15: return Best found individual as solution;

Figure 18.5 Genetic algorithm template.

18.4.2.2 Local Schedulers in Players' Module.
Schedulers implemented in the **Players' Module** should be simple and fast in the optimization of the players' cost functions. In fact, each of these functions depends only on the decision variables of the user for whom the function was defined. For the purpose of the simple case study presented in this chapter, we have implemented two heuristic grid schedulers, namely *Player's Genetic Algorithm (PGA)* and *Player's Minimum Completion Time (PMCT)*.

The *Player's Genetic Algorithm* is a simple extension of the classical GA-based scheduler defined in Fig. 18.5, applied independently for each user a with the cost function Q_a as the fitness measure. The genetic operations are executed on subschedules of the length k_u labeled just by the tasks submitted by user a. *PMCT* algorithm is a modification of *Minimum Completion Time (MCT)* method. In this method, a task is assigned to the machine yielding the earliest (shortest) completion time. The process is repeated until all tasks are scheduled. The template of the main mechanism of *PMCT* procedure is defined in Fig. 18.6.

1: Receive the population of schedules and ready_times of the machines from the Global Module;
2: for all Schedule in the population do
3:     Calculate the completion times of the machines in a given schedule;
4:     for all Individual user a do
5:         for all User's Task do
6:             Find the machine that gives minimum completion time;
7:             Assign task to its best machine;
8:             Update the machine completion time;
9:         end for
10:        Calculate the $minQ_a$ value for a given schedule;
11:    end for
12:    Send the $minQ_a$ values to the Global Module;
13: end for

Figure 18.6 PMCT algorithm template.

18.4.3 Empirical Setup

Four hybrid meta-heuristics defined in Table 18.1 have been integrated with the *Sim-G-Batch* simulator in order to reflect the various grid scenarios. The *Sim-G-Batch* simulator is an event-based grid tool that allows an easy adaptation to all dynamical changes of the systems and tasks states and characteristics. The main concept of the security-aware version of *Sim-G-Batch* simulator is presented in Fig. 18.7.

The *Sim-G-Batch* simulator generates an instance of the scheduling problem by using the following input data:

- Workload vector of tasks
- Computing capacity vector of machines
- Vector of prior loads of machines
- *ETC* matrix of estimated execution times of tasks on machines
- Trust level and security demand vectors for machines and tasks in a given batch

The capacity of the resources and the workload of tasks are randomly generated by using the Gaussian distribution [23]. It is also assumed that all tasks submitted to the system must be scheduled and all machines in the system can be used.

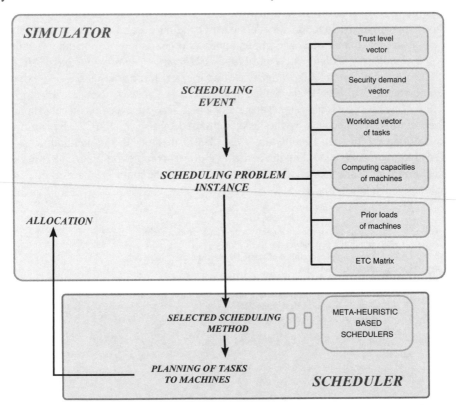

Figure 18.7 General flowchart of the secure *Sim-G-Batch* simulator linked to scheduling.

T A B L E 18.2 Values of Key Parameters of the Grid Simulator in Static and Dynamic Cases

	Small	Medium	Large	Very Large
		Static Case		
No. of machines	32	64	128	256
Resource cap.				
(in MHz CPU)		$N(5000,875)$		
Total no. of tasks	512	1024	2048	4096
Workload of tasks		$N(250000000, 43750000)$		
Security demands sd$_j$		$U[0.6; 0.9]$		
Trust levels tl$_i$		$U[0.3; 1]$		
Failure coefficient α		3		
		Dynamic Case		
Init. no. of machines	32	64	128	256
Max no. of machines	37	70	135	264
Min no. of machines	27	58	121	248
Resource cap.				
(in MHz CPU)		$N(5000, 875)$		
Add machine	$N(625000,$ $93750)$	$N(562500, 84375)$	$N(500000, 75000)$	$N(437500,$ $65625)$
Delete machine		$N(625000, 93750)$		
Max no. of tasks	512	1024	2048	4096
Init. no. of tasks	384	768	1536	3072
Workload		$N(250000000, 43750000)$		
Security demands sd$_j$		$U[0.6; 0.9]$		
Trust levels tl$_i$		$U[0.3; 1]$		
Failure coefficient α		3		

The structure of the *Sim-G-Batch* application is based on the two-module *HyperSim-G* simulator architecture [36], and it is composed of *Simulator* and *Scheduler* modules. The instance of the scheduling problems generated by the *Simulator* are passed on to the *Scheduler*, where the scheduling method selected and activated. The *Scheduler* generates the optimal schedules according to the specified scheduling criteria and sends the schedules back to the *Simulator*. The *Simulator* makes the allocation of the grid resources and reschedules any tasks assigned to machines that are unavailable in the system.

Table 18.2 presents the key input parameters of the simulator in static and dynamic cases in four considered grid size scenarios, namely *Small, Medium, Large*, and *Very Large* in static and dynamic modes.[3] Most of those parameters (excluding the numbers of tasks and machines) were tuned in empirical analysis presented in [21, 29, 30] and some recent publications of the authors of this chapter on security-aware grid scheduling supported by the game-theoretical models [5, 19, 20].

There are 16 players in the game. The parameters of all genetic schedulers working in **Global** and **Players'** Modules are defined in Table 18.3.

---

[3]The notation $N(a, b)$ and $E(c, d)$ is used for Gaussian and exponential probability distributions.

T A B L E 18.3   GA Settings in the **Global** and **Players' Modules** for Large Static and Dynamic Benchmarks

Parameter	Global Module		Players' Module
number of executed genetic epochs	$(5 * (n))$		$(\lceil 0.5 * (n) \rceil)$
population size (*pop_size*)	60	20	
intermediate pop.	48		14
selection method	LinearRanking		
crossover method	Cycle (CX)		
cross probab.	0.8	0.8	
mutation method	Rebalancing		
mutation probab.	0.2		
initialization	LJFR-SJFR + Random		
max_time_to_spend	500 secs (*static*)/800 secs (*dynamic*)		

The combination of the genetic operators presented in Table 18.3 has been specified based on the empirical tuning process provided in [18, 19]. In *LJFR-SJFR + Random* initialization method by two individuals are selected randomly. These two individuals are generated using the *Longest Job to Fastest Resource - Shortest Job to Fastest Resource (LJFR-SJFR)* heuristic [35], where initially the number of m tasks with the highest workload are assigned to the available m machines sorted in ascending order by the computing capacity criterion. Then, the remaining unassigned tasks are allocated to the fastest available machines. In the *Linear Ranking* method, a selection probability for each individual in a population is proportional to the rank of the individual. The rank of the worst individual is defined as zero, while the best rank is defined as $pop\_size - 1$, where pop_size is the size of the population. In *Cycle Crossover (CX)* [24], first, a cycle of alleles is identified. The crossover operator leaves the cycles unchanged, while the remaining segments in the parental strings are exchanged. In the *Rebalancing* mutation method, first, the most overloaded machine is selected. Two tasks, j and $\hat{j}$, are identified in the following way: j is assigned to another machine i', $\hat{j}$ is assigned to i and $ETC[j][i'] \leq ETC[\hat{j}][i]$. Then the assignments are interchanged for tasks j and $\hat{j}$.

18.4.3.1   *Performance Measures.*   The performances of all schedulers in empirical analysis were evaluated under the following three metrics:

- *Makespan* – the dominant scheduling criterion
- *Flowtime* – the second (in the hierarchy) scheduling criterion
- *FailureRate Fail$_r$* parameter, defined as follows:

$$Fail_r = \frac{n_{failed}}{n} \cdot 100\%, \qquad (18.40)$$

where n_{failed} is the number of unfinished tasks that must be rescheduled.

T A B L E 18.4 Average Values of Failure Rate, $Fail_r$, Parameter for four Genetic Schedulers [$\pm s.d.$], ($s.d.$ = standard deviation)

Strategy	Small	Medium	Large	Very Large
		Static Instances		
RGA-GA	4.278%	4.766%	6.976%	7.522%
	[± 0.99]	[± 1.80]	[± 1.34]	[± 1.89]
RGA-PMCT	3.993%	4.089%	**6.436%**	7.336%
	[± 1.04]	[± 1.98]	**[± 1.35]**	[± 2.23]
SGA-GA	3.877%	4.356%	6.543%	8.015%
	[± 0.98]	[± 1.26]	[± 1.89]	[± 1.53]
SGA-PMCT	**3.738%**	**4.005%**	6.456%	**6.832%**
	[± 0.92]	**[± 1.05]**	[± 1.35]	**[± 1.56]**
		Dynamic Instances		
RGA-GA	5.904%	8.469%	8.546%	9.546%
	[± 1.24]	[± 1.56]	[± 1.42]	[± 1.67]
RGA-PMCT	4.880%	6.097%	7.456%	**7.126%**
	[± 0.98]	[± 1.62]	[± 1.32]	**[± 2.11]**
SGA-GA	4.423%	5.533%	6.944%	7.354%
	[± 0.73]	[± 0.69]	[± 0.98]	[± 1.44]
SGA-PMCT	**3.875%**	**4.542%**	**5.953%**	7.211%
	[± 0.88]	**[± 1.03]**	**[± 1.21]**	[± 1.95]

Both *Makespan* and *Flowtime* measures are expressed in arbitrary time units specified for the scheduling.

18.4.4 Results

Each experiment was repeated 30 times under the same configuration of parameters and operators.

The histograms of the average values of *Makespan* and *Flowtime* achieved by four hybrid meta-heuristics designed for solving the users game are presented in Fig. 18.8 and Fig. 18.9.

Table 18.4 presents the comparison of the average values of failure rate, $Fail_r$, parameter for all considered meta-heuristics

The best results for *Makespan* and *Flowtime* in all considered grid scenarios were achieved by *SGA-GA* scheduler. Especially in a static "Small" grid, this method is effective in *Makespan* reduction. The differences in the *Flowtime* results achieved by all hybrid meta-heuristics are not so significant, while in the case of *Makespan* both *SGA* hybrids significantly outperform **risky** hybrids in all grid scenarios. The lowest failure rates were observed for another hybrid of *SGA*, with the *PMCT* algorithm in the **Players' Module**. This method achieved the best results in all but two instances.

(a)

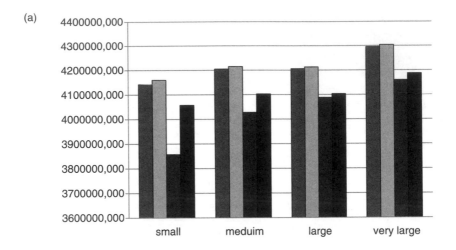

(b)

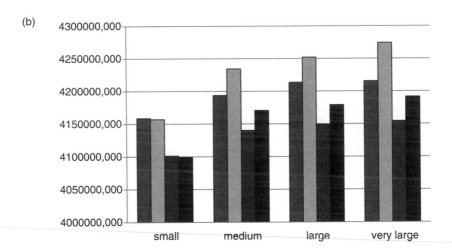

Figure 18.8 Empirical average *Makespan* results for non-cooperative symmetric game: (a) in static case, (b) in dynamic case.

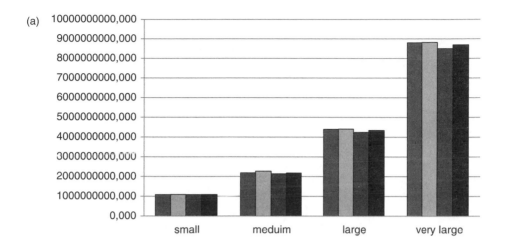

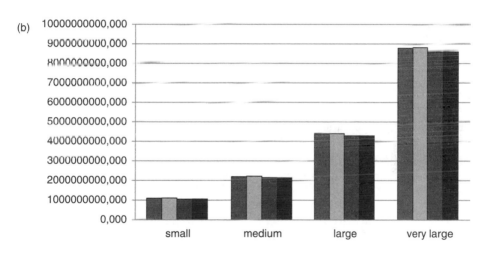

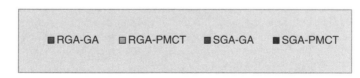

Figure 18.9 Empirical average *Flowtime* results for non-cooperative symmetric game: (a) in static case, (b) in dynamic case.

The results of these simple experiments lead to the following conclusion: *although the security requirements would imply some additional cost to the users of the grid system, it is worth assuming this cost in order to allocate tasks to trustful resources.*

18.5 CONCLUSION

This chapter illustrated various security-aware scheduling scenarios in today's grid systems, where the autonomous decisions and individual strategies of the users have a great impact on the optimization of the cumulative costs of scheduling their tasks. Game-theoretic models have been characterized as the effective methodologies for supporting the grid users' decisions in the large-scale dynamic grid environment. The users' behavior can be effectively translated into the computational model linked to the grid scheduling.

The procedures of simulation and solving even very simple users' games may be very complex, mainly due to the high system dynamics and large amount of strategic parameters that must be specified. However, our simple empirical case study showed the high efficiency of heuristic-based resolution methods for the considered game-based models, especially in the case of additional security costs paid by the users. We believe that for a variety of the real-life game scenarios, the game-based model concepts can be also successfully implemented in cloud environments, where secure scheduling and information management remain as open and challenging research problems.

REFERENCES

[1] A. Abraham, R. Buyya, and B. Nath. "Nature's heuristics for scheduling jobs on computational grids." In *Proc. of the 8th IEEE International Conference on Advanced Computing and Communications, India*, pp. 45–52, 2000.

[2] S. Ali, H.J. Siegel, M. Maheswaran, S. Ali, and D. Hensgen. "Task execution time modeling for heterogeneous computing systems." In *Proc. of the Workshop on Heterogeneous Computing*, pp. 185–199, 2000.

[3] F. Azzedin and M. Maheswaran. "Integrating trust into grid resource management systems." In *Proc. Int. Conf. Parallel Processing*, 2002.

[4] T. Baçsar and G.J. Olsder. *Dynamic Non-cooperative Game Theory*. Academic Press, London, 2nd edition, 1995.

[5] M. Bogdański, J. Kołodziej, and F. Xhafa. "Supporting the security awareness of ga-based grid schedulers by artificial neural networks." In *Proc. of International Conference on Complex, Intelligent, and Software Intensive Systems (CISIS 2011), Seoul, 30.06-2.07.2011*, pp. 277–284. IEEE Soc. Press, Los Alamitos.

[6] E. Cody, R. Sharman, R. H. Rao, and S. Upadhyaya. "Security in grid computing: A review and synthesis." *Decision Support Systems*, Vol. 44:749–764, 2008.

[7] L.E. Edlefsen and C.B. Millham. "On a formulation of discrete n-person non-cooperative games." *Metrika*, Vol. 18, No 1:31–34, 1972.

[8] Y. Gao, H. Rong, and J.Z. Huang. "Adaptive grid job scheduling with genetic algorithms." *Future Generation Computer Systems*, Vol. 21, No. 1:151–161, 2005.

[9] S.K. Garg, R. Buyya, and H.J. Segel. "Scheduling parallel aplications on utility grids: Time and cost trade-off management." In *Proc. 32nd Australasian Computer Science Conference (ACSC) 2009)*, Wellington, & NZ, 2009.

[10] P. Ghosh, N. Roy, K. Basu, and S.K. Das. A game theory based pricing strategy for job allocation in mobile grids. In *Proc. of the 18th IEEE International Parallel and Distributed Processing Symposium (IPDPS 04)*, Santa Fe, New Mexico, 2004.

[11] R.L. Graham, E.L. Lawler, J.K. Lenstra, and A.H.G. Rinnooy Kan. "Optimization and approximation in deterministic sequencing and scheduling: a survey." *Annals of Discrete Mathematics*, Vol. 5:287–326, 1979.

[12] S. Hotovy. "Workload evolution on the cornell theory center IBM SP2." In *Proc. of the Workshop on Job Scheduling Strategies for Parallel, IPPS'96*, pp. 27–40, 1996.

[13] M. Humphrey and M.R. Thompson. "Security implications of typical grid computing usage scenarios." In *Proc. of the Conf. on High Performance Distributed Computing*, 2001.

[14] J. Kacprzyk. *Multistage Decision Making under Fuzziness*. Verlag TUV, Rheinland, Cologne, 1983.

[15] S. U. Khan and I. Ahmad. "A cooperative game theoretical technique for joint optimization of energy consumption and response time in computational grids." *IEEE Tran.on Parallel and Distributed Systems*, Vol. 20, No. 3:346–360, 2009.

[16] S.U. Khan and I. Ahmad. "Non-cooperative, semi-cooperative, and cooperative games-based grid resource allocation." In *Proceedings of International Parallel and Distributed Proceedings Symposium (IPDPS 2006)*, pp. 101–104, 2006.

[17] J. Kołodziej and F. Xhafa. "A game-theoretic and hybrid genetic meta heuristic model for security-assured scheduling of independent jobs in computational grids." In *Proc. of CISIS 2010, Cracow, 15-18.02.2010, in L. Barolli, F. Xhafa and S. Venticinque eds.*, pp. 93–100, 2010.

[18] J. Kołodziej and F. Xhafa. "Enhancing the genetic-based scheduling in computational grids by a structured hierarchical population." *Future Generation Computer Systems*, 27:1035–1046, 2011.

[19] J. Kołodziej and F. Xhafa. "Meeting security and user behaviour requirements in grid scheduling." *Simulation Modelling Practice and Theory*, Vol. 19, No. 1:213–226, 2011.

[20] J. Kołodziej and F. Xhafa. "Modern approaches to modelling user requirements on resource and task allocation in hierarchical computational grids." *Int. J. on Appled Mathematics and Computer Science*, Vol. 21, No. 2:243–257, 2011.

[21] Y.-K. Kwok, K. Hwang, and S. Song. "Selfish grids: Game-theoretic modeling and nas/psa benchmark evaluation." *IEEE Tran. on Parallel and Distributing Systems*, Vol. 18, No. 5: 1–16, 2007.

[22] G. Laccetti and G. Schmidb. "A framework model for grid security." *Future Generation Computer Systems*, Vol. 23 (2007):702–713, 2007.

[23] P.S. Mann. *Introductory Statistics, 7th ed.* John Wiley & Sons, 2010.

[24] I. Olivier, D. Smith, and J. Holland. "A study of permutation crossover operators on the travelling salesman problem." In *Proc. of the ICGA 1987, Cambridge, MA*, pp. 224–230, 1987.

[25] N.G. Pavlidis, K.E. Parsopoulos, and M.N. Vrahatis. "Computing nash equilibria through computational intelligence methods." *Journal of Computational and Applied Mathematics*, Vol. 175:113–136, 2005.

[26] A. Pedrycz. "Finite cut-based approximation of fuzzy sets and its evolutionary optimization." *Fuzzy Sets and Systems*, Vol. 160, No. 24, 2009.

[27] W. Pedrycz. "Statistically grounded logic operators in fuzzy sets." *European Journal of Operational Research*, Vol. 193, No. 2:520–529, 2009.

[28] T. Roughgarden. "Stackelberg scheduling strategies." *SIAM Journal on Computing*, Vol. 33, No. 2:332–350, 2004.

[29] S. Song, K. Hwang, and Y.K. Kwok. "Trusted grid computing with security binding and trust integration." *J. of Grid Computing*, Vol. 3, No. 1-2:53–73, 2005.

[30] S. Song, K. Hwang, and Y.K. Kwok. "Risk-resilient heuristics and genetic algorithms for security-assured grid job scheduling." *IEEE Tran. on Computers*, Vol. 55, No. 6:703–719, 2006.

[31] P.D. Straffin. *Game Theory and Strategy*. Mathematical Association of America Textbooks, 1996.

[32] E-G. Talbi. *Metaheuristics: From Design to Implementation*. John Wiley & Sons, 2009.

[33] C.-C. Wu and R.-Y. Sun. "An integrated security-aware job scheduling strategy for large-scale computational grids." *Future Generation Computer Systems*, Vol. 26 (2010):198–206, 2010.

[34] F. Xhafa and A. Abraham. "Computational models and heuristic methods for grid scheduling problems." *Future Generation Computer Systems*, Vol. 26 (2010):608–621, 2010.

[35] F. Xhafa, J. Carretero, and A. Abraham. "Genetic algorithm based schedulers for grid computing systems." *Int. J. of Innovative Computing, Information and Control*, Vol. 3, No. 5:1053–1071, 2007.

[36] F. Xhafa, J. Carretero, L. Barolli, and A. Durresi. "Requirements for an event-based simulation package for grid systems." *Journal of Interconnection Networks*, Vol. 8, No. 2:163–178, 2007.

19

ADDRESSING OPEN ISSUES ON PERFORMANCE EVALUATION IN CLOUD COMPUTING

Beniamino Di Martino, Massimo Ficco, Massimiliano Rak, and Salvatore Venticinque

CONTENTS

Large Scale Network-Centric Distributed Systems, First Edition. Edited by Hamid Sarbazi-Azad and Albert Y. Zomaya.
© 2014 John Wiley & Sons, Inc. Published 2014 by John Wiley & Sons, Inc.

19.1 INTRODUCTION

Cloud computing is an emerging paradigm that allows customers to easily obtain services according to a pay-per-use business model. The current Cloud providers include Quality of Service (QoS) guarantees in their Service Level Agreement (SLA) proposals [1]. In general, they offer guarantees in terms of service availability and performance during a time period of months or a year. The provisioning contracts regulate the cost that customers have to pay for provided services and resources. Cloud service provider must pay a penalty if the customer's requirements are not satisfied. For example, the Cloud provider is liable to pay a penalty for service requests that are rejected due to unavailability of resources, or if the average service response time exceeds a fixed threshold. In order to support this model, the Cloud infrastructure must continually adapt to changing customer demands and operation conditions. For example, to prevent service availability violations additional standby resources may be required to handle a given number of failures, whereas to prevent performance violations it may be necessary to scale up or move a virtual machine (VM) to another physical machine if the current machine is overloaded. Therefore, this on-demand characteristic is one aspect that complicates QoS provisioning and SLA management in the Cloud computing paradigm.

A side effect of such a model is that customers need to clearly evaluate the performance of their Cloud service to assess whether they are paying the right price for the resources actually used. Such an evaluation can only be based on well-designed benchmarks. A benchmark is a program that generates a well-known workload on the system under test and enables an expert to measure a set of predefined performance indexes. In general, benchmarking activities perform static performance index evaluations that fit the flexibility and dynamicity of the Cloud paradigm.

Monitoring performance and availability of services is mandatory because of charge-back, control, and provisioning. In the Cloud context, the monitoring of service levels becomes critical because of the conflicts of interest that might occur between provider and customer in case of an outage. Because the Cloud is conceived of as a market utility, it is necessary grant that vendor and consumer meet the conditions of the achieved agreement, which can have financial or legal consequences. One issue is what to monitor. This depends on the terms of services included in the SLA, but customers may also be interested in a number of metrics that depend on the kind of application they will run in the Cloud, such as throughput, reliability, load balancing, and elasticity. Another problem to be addressed is how and by whom monitoring should be performed. Monitoring and tools are available for real and virtualized resources, but different scenarios have to be considered. In a private Cloud, everything is available to users; whereas in a public

Cloud, customers can only access to their virtual resources and the provider manages the hardware and hypervisor.

Finally, cyber attacks that aim to exhaust target resources have special effects on service performance in Cloud, due to the pay-per-use business model. The Cloud management system must implement specific countermeasures to avoid paying credits in case of accidental or deliberate intrusion that causes violations of QoS guarantees negotiated with the customers.

In this chapter, the roles of benchmarking and monitoring of service performance in Cloud computing as well as the effects of cyber attack on Cloud service provisioning are discussed. Moreover, a survey on the proposed solutions and technologies to face such issues is presented.

19.2 BENCHMARKING APPROACHES

To date, few solutions effectively exist that confront the problem of benchmarking in the Cloud environment, even though many different approaches exist in different contexts. This section describes benchmark results and products from different points of view and offers a brief critical analysis of proposed solutions, outlining the open research problems.

19.2.1 HPC-Like Benchmarking

High Performance Computing (HPC) has always adopted benchmarks to compare different systems and help developers evaluate and compare different solutions. As a consequence, many stable suites exist, such as NAS Parallel Benchmarks (NPB), Parkbench, SkaMPI, and LinPack. Such benchmarks were adopted in HPC systems to compare HPC systems, like the one in the Top500 list, and to have a summary idea of the power of an elaboration system.

Although big Cloud providers only recently started to offer HPC-oriented services (like the Amazon HPC service), HPC users were interested in the Cloud paradigm from its inception (as shown by the large number of discussions comparing GRID and Cloud). To understand the applicability of Cloud resources to HPC problems, the approach followed was simply to apply typical HPC benchmarks to Cloud-based resources. The most relevant work is the one proposed by Walker et al. [28], which outlined the real performances of Cloud-based clusters; the results are now outdated, but the approach is interesting. Ostermann et al. [29] proposed systematic benchmarking of clusters of virtual machines, obtained from IaaS Cloud providers, and offered some interesting considerations about perceived performance. The primary and well-known limit of such analysis is, what is the real goal of these benchmarks? All the presented works, while offer interesting approaches for obtaining a complete analysis of a cluster systems, lack in real reusable results. They simply point out that clusters of virtual machines connected through a high-latency network have performance that is noncomparable with an HPC system (mainly due to the presence of high-speed, low-latency networks).

19.2.2 Benchmark Standards

In business environments, benchmarks are usually defined through common standards, developed by independent consortiums, which can be used as a clear reference to compare different solutions. No standard currently exists for Cloud benchmarking. In this section, we focus on two of the most important benchmark consortiums that are addressing Cloud-related benchmarking problems: SPEC [4] and TPC [3].

- *SPEC* is the best known and probably most accepted consortium dedicated to development of benchmarks. In March 2011, a subcommittee dedicated to the Cloud was formed that is working on Cloud-related benchmarking problems. No results are yet available. The only applicable standards that can be considered of interest for Cloud-oriented contexts are SPECvirt and SPA SOA. Such benchmarks aim to evaluate the performance of virtualization and service-oriented layers, which are among the enabling technologies of the Cloud. The SPECweb benchmark focuses on Web servers and application servers and is of great interest.

- An alternative to SPEC are the solutions proposed by *TPC-Benchmark*, a nonprofit corporation founded to define transaction processing and database benchmarks and disseminate objective data to the industry. In the context of the Cloud, which was developed to offer transactional services, TPC-Benchmarks are of interest. TPC-Benchmarks can be considered an application-level benchmark in the Cloud environment, used to evaluate the effective performances offered by standard transactional software on the top of IaaS-delivered machines.

19.2.3 Cloud-Oriented Benchmarks

Recently, new benchmarking approaches have been developed that aim to propose benchmarks oriented to the Cloud's dynamic features. Such proposals are based on the idea of building up frameworks, which helps Cloud users to define custom benchmarks that compare, in a clear and transparent way, different providers. Few Cloud-specific proposals exist in the literature: Cloudstone [8], CloudCmp [5, 7], and mOSAIC Benchmarking Framework [8]. These are academic projects that aim to offer flexible frameworks, able to build up custom workloads to be run in the Cloud environment.

- *Cloudstone* is an academic open source project from the University of California, Berkeley. It provides a framework for testing realistic performance. The project has not yet published comparative results across Clouds, but provides users with the framework that allows them to do so. The reference application is a social Web 2.0-style application. The Cloudstone stack can be divided into three subcategories: web application, database, and load generator. When running benchmarks, the load generator generates load against the Web application, which in turn makes use of the database. The application used in Cloudstone is Olio, an open source social-events application with both PHP and Ruby implementations. Nginx and HAProxy are used to load balance between the many Rails servers.

- *CloudCmp* is a framework to compare different Cloud computing providers. It was developed by researchers from Duke University and Microsoft Research. The declared objective of the Cloud CMP project is to enable "comparison shopping" across Cloud providers, both IaaS and PaaS, and to do so for a number of application use cases and workloads. To that end, the project combines straight performance benchmarks with cost-performance analysis. The project has already measured computational, storage, Intra-cloud, and WAN performance for three Cloud providers (two IaaS and one PaaS) and intends to expand. CloudCmp is organized in a two-step methodology: at the first level, it uses standard tools to benchmark the services offered by different Cloud providers, including computation, storage, and network services; at the second level, it uses the benchmarking results to estimate the performance and costs of an application, if it is deployed on a particular Cloud provider.

- *mOSAIC Benchmark Framework* is designed in the context of the mOSAIC project and proposes a new way to develop Cloud-oriented applications. A mOSAIC application is a component-based distributed application that can be developed independently of the Cloud providers. It can be tested locally and then deployed "on the Cloud." The mOSAIC Benchmarking framework aims to offer a set of open-source mOSAIC components that can be used to build custom benchmarks at many different levels (Cloud resources, Cloud components, Cloud applications). The benchmark can be, in this way, built together with the Cloud applications, offering to the developer a simple way to compare different providers before deploying the applications.

19.2.4 Benchmark as a Service Approach

Adoption of benchmarks, as described above, is useful in making comparisons of the offerings from different Cloud providers, mainly at the IaaS level. The main drawback of the benchmarks is that they are not well suited to dealing with the elasticity of Cloud offerings. Benchmarks offer a static evaluation of a delivered system, as it is; they have difficulty providing a clear evaluation of systems that dynamically change and whose performance highly varies over time. As a consequence, an *as a service* approach can be applied to the benchmarking methodology.

Cloud-oriented benchmarking frameworks, like the ones presented above, can be considered the development environment to be used as a basis for building such services by using solutions like *CloudHarmony* and *CloudSleuth* [6]. CloudHarmony is probably the most interesting offering of this kind. It offers a large collection of benchmarks that are continuously applied on remote resources. Users are able to build their own custom set of benchmarks and related reports, which are generated on the basis of continuously applied benchmarks on the target resources. The solution is interesting and looks similar to the ones adopted for monitoring. While CloudHarmony is a benchmark collector, which just reproduces standard benchmark, an alternative approach is proposed by CloudSleuth, which builds a Cloud application benchmark, which generates a fairly standard workload on target services in order to perform comparisons.

19.2.5 Considerations

The presented solutions clearly state the main problem of benchmarking in a Cloud environment: How does one represent with a single (or few) indexes the dynamicity of a Cloud environment? How useful is it to perform few static measurements?

At present, the main direction in performance evaluation of the Cloud is oriented to monitoring resource offerings. Benchmarking solutions, like the ones proposed commercially by CloudHarmony or CloudSleuth, try to adapt benchmarking solutions to typical monitoring approaches. Moreover, it is currently impossible to identify a single workload representing the use of the huge variety of Cloud services offered. The direction adopted is to reuse benchmarks targeted for specific services and to deliver them in a more flexible way, as proposed in Kossomann et al. [9], which used TPC-W to evaluate the Cloud services delivered. It should be noted that benchmark results are not reliable in a Cloud environment when the same request of resource may result in resources offering completely different behaviors, as shown in [10]. This means that benchmarking should be applied on the single specific resource, more than on generic resources offered by a given Cloud provider. This approach has a high impact on the costs: Is it acceptable to pay for a resource usage that is only targeted to execute a benchmark? Benchmarking is hardly needed when choosing a Cloud provider for the first time, when no historical data are available. In such a case, before choosing a provider, the only way is to build a test that is well targeted for the final user needs.

A summary benchmark, modeled as an off-line measurement of Cloud services, should be more flexible than the benchmark commonly adopted in other environments. Adoption of single performance indexes is no longer acceptable and workload definition should be customized by the benchmark user. Different users have different needs from a benchmark, and a clear statement of benchmark goals should be made for different class of users.

19.3 MONITORING IN CLOUD COMPUTING

To support and perform monitoring in Cloud computing, several issues must be addressed: What should be monitored to verify that the vendor and consumer meet the conditions of the agreement? How and by whom should monitoring be performed?

19.3.1 What Should Be Monitored

All Cloud services must be metered and monitored for cost control, chargeback and provisioning [11]. On the provider side, monitoring is necessary for effective utilization of computing resources, to check service levels that have been agreed to with the customer, and to lead negotiation strategies, such as overbooking, to maximize total income. Here, monitoring addresses both hardware resources and virtual ones. Consumers should monitor their resources to check that service levels are continuously respected and to detect underutilization or overloading conditions of their resources so that they can renegotiate the agreement if necessary.

Monitoring is required at each Cloud level: infrastructure, platform, and application.

T A B L E 19.1   Monitored Parameters and Performance Indexes at the IaaS Level

IaaS Service	Monitored Parameters and Performance Indexes	Example
Compute	Cumulative availability (connectivity uptime)	99.5%, 99%
	Role instance uptime	99.9%, 99%
	Outage length	Monthly time
	Server reboot time	< 15 minutes
Network	Availability	100%
	Packet loss	0.1% per month
	Latency within the Cloud network or within the same VLAN	< 1 ms
	Mean jitter, maximum jitter	0.5 ms within any 15-minute period
	Bandwidth	Mb/s, Gb/s
Storage	IOPS	Number of input/output per second
	Latency with the internal compute resource	< 1 ms
	Bandwidth with the internal compute resource	Gbs
	Processing time (does not include transferring)	Time to copy a blob < 60s Time to process data < 2s (x amount of MB to be processed) List tables returns or continues within 10 s
	Maximum restore time	Number of minutes
	Uptime	If < 99.9% refund 10% credits If <99% refund 25% credits

19.3.1.1 Infrastructure as a Service (IaaS).

IaaS delivers a computing hardware infrastructure over the Internet and is able to split, assign, and dynamically resize these resources to build custom infrastructures, as demanded by customers. Cloud IaaS SLAs are similar to SLAs for network services, hosting, and data center outsourcing. The main issues with IaaS concern the mapping of high-level application requirements on monitored parameters that measure low-level service levels. For IaaS, there are many standardization efforts, including the Open Cloud Computing Interface[1] (OCCI), the Service-Oriented Cloud-Computing Infrastructure[2] (SOCCI) by The Open Group, and the ISO Study Group on Cloud Computing (SGCC). Moreover, there is de facto industry alignment on IaaS service-level objectives, warranties, guarantees, and performance metrics. Compute, network, and storage are the main abstractions of services at this level.

Table 19.1 shows the main parameters that can be monitored. For example, the monitored parameters for compute are *cumulative availability*, *outage length*, and

[1] Open Cloud Computing Interface, available at: http://www.occi.org.

[2] Service-Oriented Cloud-Computing Infrastructure, available at: http://www.opengroup.org/projects/soa-soi/.

server reboot time, which are used to check the service-level objectives. Usually, there are no service levels for compute performance; customers are simply guaranteed to have the compute for which they paid, with technical enforcement at the hypervisor level. However, performance information at hypervisor level is always available to vendors and sometimes to customers. As providers usually offer a network SLA, monitoring information regarding the Cloud provider's data center connectivity to the Internet is provided. This information can also be monitored and provided for internal networks between devices within the provider's data center, and if the provider has multiple data centers, among those data centers. Values of key performance indicators are usually related to geographical locations. For storage, monitoring covers availability and performance, however, sometimes a storage performance profile will actually be an internal network profile, covering latency between compute and storage. Finally, security is currently not offered as a service level. In general, it is granted by the availability of protection mechanisms, which are accessible only to providers for administration purposes. However, as will be described in Section 10.3.2, several research works have proposed new solutions.

19.3.1.2   *Platform as a Service (PaaS).* PaaS offers an additional abstraction level: rather than supplying a virtualized hardware infrastructure, a software platform is provided, where consumer services can be run. Sizing of the hardware resources demanded by the execution of consumer services is made by the PaaS provider in a manner transparent to the consumer. PaaS providers offer a wide array of services that cover the development, deployment, and execution of applications. Application stacks, like Ruby on Rails, Java, and LAMP, are examples of PaaS services. The advantage of PaaS is that the developer can leverage a fully functional development and/or production environment. Additional examples of PaaS services include load balancing, domain name services, access control, content delivery networks, databases, and communication mechanisms like queues.

Examples of parameters to be monitored for PaaS are shown in Table 19.2. Unfortunately, at this level performance indexes, which are not necessary to check service levels, are not available. On the other hand, customers of PaaS Clouds are developers who can instrument their own codes to get custom measures of application performance.

19.3.1.3   *Service as a Service (SaaS).* SaaS groups together Cloud systems in order to deliver a complete aggregated service. These services are software products that typically appeal to a wide variety of users. Examples of SaaS services include a webmail client, a document editor, a personal organizer, and an e-book reader. Resources at this level are complete applications. Here, there is not the problem of mapping low-level monitoring information to the application level. The objective of monitoring is to understand how the application works.

Relevant parameters include monthly cumulative application downtime, maximum error response to a valid query during two or more consecutive time-defined intervals, error rates of content delivery, and average download time less than a specified value. However, it is difficult to provide here a comprehensive and representative list of performance parameters. Table 19.3 provides a list of desired performance parameters for SaaS, and one for an example of a file server.

T A B L E 19.2 Monitored Parameters and Performance Indexes at the PaaS Level

PaaS Service	Monitored Parameters	Example
SQL Database	Connection time	< 30s
	Number of read/write/query failures after connection	N.A.
Load Balancing	Latency from VIP to server	< 05 ms
	Throughout (Mb/s or reference transaction per second)	500 Mb/s, 5000 transactions per second
	Concurrent transactions	10.000
CDN (Content Delivery Network)	Number of transactions without error	50 KB-1 M HTTP sample objects are performed in a month by a commercial test application of a third party
Access Control	Cumulative service downtime	Sum of intervals during which the all customer's attempts to establish a connection to Access Control Service fail

I A B L E 19.3 Example of Monitored Parameters and Performance Indexes at the SaaS Level

SAAS Service	Service Objective	Example
General	Service availability	< 0.01% per month
	Response time	Seconds
	Service outage resolution time, failover window for disaster recovery	The time necessary to recover the service after an outage, or after the outage of all the data center.
	RFO	Reason for outage
	Customer service response time, customer service availability	Time needed for reacting to a request by customer service and time of the day, days of week during which the service is available.
	Reclaiming customer data	Possibility to get back the data after the end of the agreement, and eventual support for migration.
	Maintenance notification, proactive service outage notification	Time within which an outage (minutes), or scheduled or special maintenance are notified.
File Server	Connection uptime	99.9%
	Server error	Server error after two or more consecutive 90-s intervals
	Average download time	Fails to download a reference 1-byte document 0.3 sec.

19.3.2 How to Monitor

Monitoring performance and quality indexes in a distribute infrastructure presents important challenges. As resource usage and service workload can change frequently, a continuous and updated answer must be provided to the customer by efficiently monitoring the environment (e.g., a change in the answer must be detected as soon as possible while minimizing the communication cost). Furthermore, the Cloud elasticity allows for the possibility to change dynamically over time the system configuration, and so the distributed monitoring must adapt itself quickly to the new requirements. Infrastructure-level resource monitoring [13] aims to measure and report system parameters related to real or virtual infrastructure services offered to the customer (e.g., CPU, RAM, and data storage parameters). Of course, the support of different performance measurements depends on the actual Cloud provider that is being monitored and on the monitoring technology it is using. Many available tools need to run on the physical machine and use facilities of the hypervisor. In a private Cloud, they can be used for management purpose, but in a public Cloud, they are controlled by the Cloud vendor. They could be used to monitor the usage of resources by applications, but customers cannot trust the providers for checking the respect to the agreed SLA.

With regard to trust, another approach to getting monitoring information in a distributed system uses third-party technologies or services. If the vendor and the customer trust a third-party technology, the IaaS provider can make available an appliance to be installed on the Virtual Machine, whose monitoring information is available both to the customer and to the provider. Of course, its overhead should be minimized in order to not affect the performance of the computing service. Content delivery by RackSpace is an example of a service at PaaS that uses a third-party measuring service to monitor its own service levels. At the application level, the nature of the monitored parameters, and the way their values should be retrieved, depend on the actual software being monitored and not on the Cloud infrastructure it is running on.

Regardless of the level of parameters being monitored, a general monitoring infrastructure is required to collect and process the information provided by the monitored components. Such an infrastructure is provided by the Lattice framework [14] (also utilized in the RESERVOIR project [15]), which has a minimal run-time footprint and is not intrusive, so as not to adversely affect the performance of the system itself or any running applications. The framework defines a system of data sources, data consumers, and control strategies that influence the collection of monitoring data. The monitoring data can be transported over IP multicast solutions, Event Service Bus, or a publish/subscribe mechanism. This is a flexible framework that is tailored towards distributed applications but not Cloud applications.

The open Grid Forum has proposed the Open Cloud Computing Interface (OCCI [16]) as a standard for the Cloud infrastructures level. In particular, an extension of OCCI to support mechanisms for monitoring and SLA agreement negotiation is described in [17]. In [18], the authors claim that an approach based on software agents is a natural way to tackle the monitoring tasks in the aforementioned distributed environments. Agents move and distribute themselves to perform their monitoring tasks leads. In [19], an optimal control of mobile monitoring agents in artificial-immune-system-based

(AIS-based) monitoring networks has been studied. The generation of mobile monitoring agents is optimized to minimize the response time for the mobile monitoring agents to diagnose structural damage in a subnetwork and maximize the average affinity of monitoring agents' receptors to the damaged sensor data.

Many research activities focus on mapping of low-level to high-level parameters [20], but these are still open issues. The more effective solution is to develop custom components and instrumented applications to collect information at different levels.

19.3.2.1 Supporting Tools.
Cloud monitoring means collection and analysis of performance information of virtual resources. Cloud providers can obtain performance information using tools that access hypervisor mechanisms to monitor the execution of virtual machines. A subset of information is sometimes provided to the customers by monitoring services. Furthermore, monitoring of hardware resources is necessary for balancing the workload of Cloud services and to plan their negotiation and booking. As an example, a reason for performance degradation of a virtual machine could be found by detecting lack of space on a physical drive.

In a public Cloud, customers use monitoring information to check the workload of their resources and the compliance of service levels with terms of services in the signed agreements. This can be done either by using monitoring services provided by the Cloud provider, when they are available, or by their own tools installed in the Cloud and outside. The second choice is necessary if customers do not wish to trust the provider twice for the same service. In a private Cloud, customers can access both hardware and virtual resources but have the burden of managing both of them.

Traditional monitoring technologies for single machines or Clusters are restricted to locality and homogeneity of monitored objects and, therefore, cannot be applied in the Cloud in an appropriate manner [21]. There are currently many tools that provide Cloud monitoring facilities, like Cloudkick, Nimsoft Monitor, Monitis, Opnet, and RevealCloud.[3] All of them are proprietary solutions and do not aim to define a standard for monitoring interoperability. Some technologies for monitoring network and host, like s-flow, have been extended to support the transport of monitoring information of virtualized resources. For example, Host-sflow exports physical and virtual server performance metrics using the sFlow protocol. Ganglia and other collectors of performance measures are already compliant with its specification. Some of the better-advertised Cloud-monitoring solutions include the Nimsoft Monitor [22], Monitis [23], and the Tap in Cloud Management Service [24].

For PaaS monitoring, there are two different solutions for monitoring support. In the first case, an API needs to be provided that allow users either to develop an ad hoc monitoring service inside their own application, or to bind applications to monitoring services from a third party. In this case, as an example, CloudBees [25] uses a set of shared services that the externally facing services depend on. For example, an application might use the CloudBees MySQL database service and a Partner Service like New

---

[3]Respectively available at: http://cloudkick.com, http://www.nimsoft.com/the-nimsoft- cloud-monitor, http://portal.monitis.com,http://www.opnet.com, http://www.copperegg.com/product/cloud-monitoring/.

Relic monitoring.[4] In the second case, the PaaS provider provides information about memory, bandwidth, and I/O utilization of deployed applications. An example of this is Jelastic.[5]

VMware vFabric Hyperic [13] specializes in web-application monitoring. It is capable of monitoring applications that utilize any supported web technologies. A more general approach is to utilize the JMX Java framework [27], which is employed by most Java application containers and is capable of providing information on the status of the application running in the container. However, it requires that the application is written in Java and publishes information through the JMX subsystem.

19.4 ATTACK COUNTERMEASURES IN CLOUD COMPUTING

Several works in the literature present models and mechanisms for monitoring and assuring service performance and availability guarantees in the Cloud computing context [27–29]. Cloud applications, due to their openness to the Internet, are prone to cyber attacks, such as Denial of Service (DoS) and distributed DoS (DDoS), which aim at reducing the service's availability and performance by exhausting the resources of the service's host system (including memory, processing resources, and network bandwidth). Such attacks have special effects in Cloud due to the pay-per-use business model described above, that is, the attacks have direct effects on the application costs and not only on the performance perceived by users. Specifically, ensuring the determined performance levels is not easy in the Cloud. Additional resources should be either already acquired to support peak loads or acquired dynamically on demand. Such resources are not free, however, and a cyber attack could make it economically prohibitive. Such a scenario can be called *"economic denial of sustainability."* The inability of the Cloud service infrastructure to diagnose the causes of service performance degradation (i.e., whether it is due to an attack or overloading), can be considered a security vulnerability, which can be exploited by attackers in order to exhaust all the Cloud resources allocated to satisfy the negotiated QoS. It is clear that the SLA availability and performance parameters alone are not enough to ensure the satisfactory of service delivery. Several works explore SLAs for security and analyze security metrics in new paradigms like Cloud computing [30–34]. Incorporating security parameters in the resource requests can improve the QoS of the service being delivered [35]. These requests have profound implications, however, for the security solution (in terms of intrusion detection and diagnosis) to be implemented and delivered to protect the provided Cloud services.

Although several distributed Intrusion Detection System (IDS) solutions has been proposed to deal with security aspects in large-scale networks, their utilization in Cloud computing remains a challenging task. The security of applications and services provided in Cloud against cyber attacks is hard to achieve due to the complexity and heterogeneity

---

[4]Relic monitoring, available at: http://newrelic.com/.

[5]Jelastic, available at: http://jelastic.com.

of such systems. Moreover, the presence of different kinds of users leads to different security requirements. For example, an important issue for Cloud users is the lack of full
control over the used infrastructure. They need to know whether the service performance degradation is due to attacks against their application and whether the acquired
resources and services have been compromised to penetrate other hosts. Each user can
require different types of information, sensors, configurations, and thresholds to monitor
their virtualized components. Therefore, Cloud providers must contemplate the possibility that end users can fully control the resources. But Cloud providers also want to detect
attacks on both the virtualized components and the underlying infrastructure. These attacks can be performed by an external attacker or by a malicious user or a virtualized
component that may have been compromised (i.e., they need to know whether their infrastructure is being used by attackers to penetrate other victims). The techniques adopted
as countermeasures to typical resource exhaustion cyber attacks can be categorized as
either "reactive" or "proactive" [36].

Reactive techniques detect attacks on the target system by using knowledge- or
anomaly-based methods, which analyze some system behaviors (such as network traffic,
resources consumption, and application requests). If an attack is identified, specific countermeasures are triggered, which can be based on several methods, including filtering,
source traceback, and reconfiguration.

- *Filtering methods*: These consist of filtering all the requests identified as malicious. This approach can be performed either by a router enabled to accumulate
  sufficient knowledge to distinguish between legitimate and illegitimate addresses,
  or by a proxy server and software sensors enabled to distinguish between legitimate and illegitimate service requests. In general, filtering techniques suffer from
  some problems: (1) The mechanisms used to react must process a large number
  of flows simultaneously; in a Cloud context, this involves a large additional cost
  in terms of resources needed to carry out the countermeasure. (2) The accuracy
  of the performed countermeasure is linked to the ability to distinguish between
  legitimate and illegitimate traffic; however, the characteristics of heterogeneity,
  dynamism, and adaptability of a Cloud paradigm (in terms of users, provided services, and involved resources) make it difficult to identify known behaviors (e.g.,
  known attack patterns or statistical anomalies) that can be used to filter malicious
  traffic. (3) The use of routers, proxies, and sensors requires either the control and
  knowledge of the system infrastructure, or the possibility to deploy in the Cloud
  infrastructure a specific software component, which, as previously described, is
  not always permitted to Cloud users.
- *Source traceback methods:* These include request-based marking, link testing,
  and verifying logging [37]. They are implemented by two procedures. The first
  generates traceback information, marking the request either by using routers in
  the network or IP control information, such as link-testing messages and verifiable
  logging messages. The second procedure is performed by the victims that use this
  information to trace the attack back to the actual source. However, such techniques
  have some problems: (1) Adopted mechanisms suffer a long delay to react and

block the attack, which could not be tolerated by many customers' business-critical services offered through the Cloud; moreover, they involve large resource consumption in terms of control message processing, storage, and communication. (2) They do not address the distributed attacks, like DDoS, which are one of the more common attacks in Cloud. (3) The source of the attack could be not a real attacker but a host or a virtual component of the Cloud that has been compromised (a zombie machine) and cannot simply be blocked or disconnected by the network because it is used by the customer.

- *Reconfiguration* can be both reactive and proactive. During an intrusion, reconfiguration mechanisms dynamically adapt and reconfigure the system so that the service can be uninterrupted and can maintain performance requirements. In the Cloud paradigm, a wide variety of reconfiguration strategies can be employed given the simplicity with which the virtual components can be moved and reconfigured. A major challenge in designing the reconfiguration mechanism is to protect the Cloud systems from being (mis)used by the attacker, therefore, it is important that this process not be predictable, thus making the system less vulnerable to attacks on its reconfiguration mechanisms. An attacker could exploit this vulnerability in order to trigger a streak of reconfigurations that can involve a significant performance penalty. Moreover, such mechanisms must be resilient to oscillations due to transient effects (*e.g.*, overloaded due to workload peaks), which are very common in a system as complex as the Cloud and may lead to unnecessary reconfigurations, thereby driving the system to an inconsistent state.

Proactive Techniques do not require detection mechanisms. They prevent systems from cyber attacks either by considering rate control techniques or by using an interface layer between client and virtual components that provides the services.

- *Rate control methods*: Because in many cases, it is difficult to distinguish between resource exhaustion attacks and insufficient service performance, rate control mechanisms identify the processing cost for different types of service requests and limit the flow rates such that the target does not go into an overload situation. Different rate limiting policies can be applied to different classes of service based on the resources they consume. However, the main problem with this approach is that its effectiveness is reduced when either the number of attacks is large or the types of requests are different, which are typical situations in the Cloud, where the more common attack is the DDoS, and a multitude of heterogeneous services can be deployed.

- *Indirection methods*: These provide the virtual components (that offer services) the capability to hide their location and operations. Therefore, indirection prevents cyber attacks, which exploit knowledge of the victim's characteristics. There are a wide variety of solutions based on indirection, but they have a common goal: protection by separating clients and servers with an additional layer. Because the indirection is hidden outside of the black box system, clients see only what looks like a COTS server. Indirection mechanisms can be categorized as two main types:

the first interposes additional components between the client and the server, for example, proxies, wrappers, and sandboxes. The second one uses virtualizations and configuration approaches. For example, the VM can be organized as an overlay network, which is used to mediate all communications among virtual components. The overlay network is the only public interface for accessing the provided services, and the host system cannot be directly attacked. However, indirection adds additional overhead, thus increasing latency and costs [38].

In summary, each cyber attack countermeasure has its strengths and weaknesses. Therefore, a solution can be combining the strengths of all solutions and letting them compensate each other's weaknesses. In the literature, several research works propose solutions based on the techniques described above [39–43]. They face security problems involved with the usage of public and private Cloud infrastructures. In the following, some countermeasures proposed in the literature are described.

Cheng et al. [44] present a distributed IDS architecture for the Cloud. They propose separating the IDS for each user from the actual component being monitored. In particular, each virtual component should be secured by a separated IDS sensor, which is responsible for one virtual machine. The intrusion detection message exchange format (IDMEF) standard has been used for communication between different IDS sensors. The Cloud user is responsible for configuring and managing the IDS running on its virtual machine. Additionally, to correlate and analyze alerts generated on multiple distributed sensors deployed in the Cloud, a central management unit is provided. It can also be used by a user to configure the IDSs. The Cloud provider is responsible for enabling different IDS (e.g., network-based and host-based IDS for the infrastructure and platform layers, as well as network-based IDS for the application layer), and provide the possibility to connect them to a virtual component. Moreover, it can recognize attacks on the virtual components of their users by using the IDS management system as well as detect large-scale attacks on several users by correlating the incoming alerts.

A similar solution has been proposed by Chi-Chun et al. [45]. In order to protect the Cloud environment from DoS or DDoS attacks, they propose a federation defense approach, in which IDSs are deployed in each Cloud computing region. IDSs cooperate with each other by exchanging alerts, and implement a judgment criterion to evaluate the trustworthiness of these alerts. As Figure 19.1 shows, the IDS architecture is composed of several modules, which perform the following activities: intrusion detection, alert clustering. threshold computation and comparison, intrusion response and blocking, and cooperative operations. A cooperative agent is used to exchange alert messages from other IDSs. A majority vote method is used to judge the trustworthiness of an alert.

Park et al. [46] propose a multi-level IDS and log management method based on consumer behavior for applying IDS effectively to a Cloud computing system. The multi-level IDS applies differentiated levels of security strength to uses according to the degree of their trustworthiness. On the basis of risk level policies, risk points are assigned to users in proportion to risk of anomaly behaviors. Users are judged by their previous

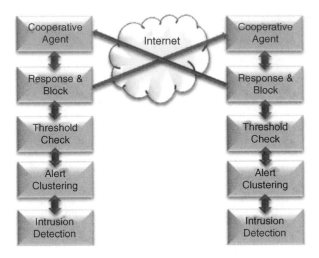

Figure 19.1 The cooperative IDSs system architecture.

personal usage history and assigned virtual components with the security level derived by the judgment. The virtual component assigned to a user may change according to the anomaly behavior level of the user, and migration can occur. Moreover, IDS sensors to be installed on the assigned user guest OS image are chosen on the basis of the security level corresponding to the user's anomaly level.

Ficco et al. [47] propose IaaS services enriched with ad hoc solutions for protecting the delivered resources against a set of security attacks. The goal is to enable the customer to negotiate with the provider the level of security offered, so that the service acquired (e.g., a Web server) will be protected against a given set of attacks. The customer pays for the additional security service, but he/she is guaranteed that the services is able to tolerate a specific set of DoSs attacks (i.e., it continues to work even under attack), and the additional load generated is not charged. The proposed architecture is composed of two subsystems with distinct properties (Fig. 19.2). The first subsystem is *Application System VM*, which hosts the application to protect, whereas the second subsystem, named *ITmOS*, is the VM that hosts the guest OS image to which are

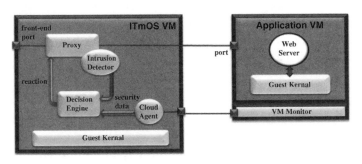

Figure 19.2 ITmOS node architecture.

added intrusion-tolerant mechanisms. The two subsystems are connected through a secure channel isolated from other connections. The interaction of the application with
the outside world is done only through the network, using a *Proxy* hosted on the IT-
mOS VM. A *VM Monitor* monitors the application system VM. It is used to collect
information on consumption of system resources (including CPU, memory, disk). An
Intrusion Detector module collects data from the Proxy and alerts the *Decision Engine*
component when an anomalous behavior is observed. The Decision Engine is a centralized engine that receives and correlates security data. It determines whether the monitored
data are malicious behaviors, and what the effects are on the monitored subsystem. It is responsible for identifying the best action to take in order to mitigate the attack effects on the
target application. In particular, it analyzes the received data and performs the reactions
by the Proxy in response to the attacks, filtering messages to the guest system as needed.

A different implementation of the previous solution is proposed by Rak et al. [48].
It is an open-source framework and platform to develop Cloud applications, called
mOSAIC. Using the programming model offered by mOSAIC, it is possible to add
intrusion tolerance features in a mOSAIC application in a transparent way with respect
to the final user. A mOSAIC application is composed of a set of distributed components,
which cooperate through messages exchanged on message queue Cloud resources. An
example of a solution implemented by the mOSAIC framework is presented in Fig. 19.3.

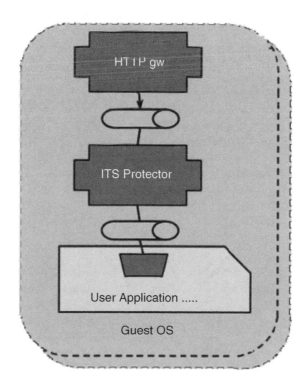

Figure 19.3   mOSAIC node architecture.

It consists of a HTTPgw component that accepts HTTP requests from the Internet and forwards them on internal queues. An ITSprotector component is interposed between the HTTPgw and the application components. This additional component acts as a filter, cutting away attack messages on the basis of specific roles, which are defined according to the type of attack that must be tolerated.

19.5 CONCLUSION

In the Cloud paradigm, resources are dynamically acquired and charged on the basis of a pay-per-use model. The Cloud management system must automatically scale and allocate new resources to match the SLAs. Such activities require a mapping between low-level resource information and high-level SLA parameters as well as mechanisms to adapt the resources on the fly to avoid a SLA violation. This becomes even more effective, but very complex, in a scenario of dynamic provisioning, where the monitoring and evaluation of service performance plays an important role, allowing the possibility to always maintain the best resource allocation that satisfies the application requirements. Evaluation and monitoring of provided services allows for an accurate assessment of system performance, workload distribution, overloads, bottleneck, underused resources, and malicious resource exhaustion, which have special effects in the Cloud because of the pay-per-use business model. This chapter has outlined the additional problems that such issues raise in the Cloud and presented an overview of current solutions and future technologies proposed to face them.

REFERENCES

[1] C.B. Westphall and F.R. Lamin. "SLA perspective in security management for cloud computing." In *Proc. of the Int. Conf. on Networking and Services (ICNS)*, 2010. pp. 212–217.

[2] D.A. Menasce. "Performance and availability of Internet data centers." In *IEEE Internet Computing*, Vol. 8, No. 2, Jun. 2004. pp. 94–96.

[3] TCP - Transaction Processing Performance Council, Available at http://www.tpc.org/default.asp (accessed Apr. 2012).

[4] SPEC - Standard Performance Evaluation Corporation, Available at http://www.spec.org/ (accessed Apr. 2012).

[5] A. Li, X. Yang, S. Kandula, and M. Zhang. "CloudCmp: Comparing public cloud providers." In *Proc. of the Int. Conf. on Internet Measurement Conference*, Nov 2010.

[6] Cloudsleuth - Cloud Performance Analyzer, Available at https://cloudsleuth.net/ (accessed Apr. 2012).

[7] A.A. Li, X. Yang, S. Kandula, and M. Zhang. "CloudCmp: Shopping for a cloud made easy." In *Proc. of the 2nd USENIX Workshop on Hot Topics in Cloud Computing (HotCloud)*, June 2010.

[8] W. Sobel, S. Subramanyam, A. Sucharitakul, J. Nguyen, H. Wong, A. Klepchukov, S. Patil, A. Fox, and D. Patterson. "Cloudstone: Multi-platform, multi-language benchmark and measurement tools for Web 2.0." In *Proc. of 1st Workshop on Cloud Computing*, 2008.

[9] Massimiliano Rak et al., "*D1.6, mOSAIC Tests and Benchamrks*", mOSAIC Public Deliverable, Available at http://www.mosaic-cloud.eu.

[10] J. Dejun, G. Pierre, and C.-H. Chi. "Resource provisioning of web applications in heterogeneous clouds." In *Proc. of the 2nd USENIX Conference on Web Application Development*, 2011.

[11] E. Sciore. "SimpleDB: a simple java-based multiuser syst for teaching database internals." In *Proc. of the 38th SIGCSE Technical Symposium on Computer Science Education*, 2007.

[12] M. Ahronovitz et al. "Cloud Computing Use Cases, A White Paper Produced by the Cloud Computing Use Case Discussion Group, Available at http://opencloudmanitesto.org/Cloud_Computing_Use_Cases_Whitepaper-4_0.pdf (accessed July 2010).

[13] S. Clayman, A. Galis, C. Chapman, and G. Toffetti. *Monitoring Service Clouds in the Future Internet*. IOS Press Books Online, 2010. pp. 115–126.

[14] Lattice Framework. Available at http://clayfour.ee.ucl.ac.k/lattice/.

[15] M. Lindner, F. Marquez, C. Chapman, S. Clayman, D. Henriksson, and E. Elmroth. "The cloud supply chain: A framework for information, monitoring, accounting and billing." In *Proc. of the 2nd Int. ICST Conference on Cloud Computing (CloudComp'10)*. Springer Verlag, 2010.

[16] T. Metsch, A. Edmonds, et al. "Open cloud computing interface core and models." Standards Track, no. GFD-R in *The Open Grid Forum Document Series, Open Cloud Computing Interface (OCCI) Working Group*, 2011.

[17] T. Metsch, V. Bayon, A. Edmonds, and A. Papaspyrou. *SLA Agreement, Negotiation, Execution and Monitoring Using OCCI*.

[18] S. Ilarri, E. Mena, and A. Illarramendi. "Using cooperative mobile agents to monitor distributed and dynamic environments." *Information Sciences*, Vol. 178, No. 9, May 2008. pp. 2105–2127.

[19] W. Liu and B. Chen. "Optimal control of mobile monitoring agents in immune-inspired wireless monitoring networks." *Network Computing Application*, Vol. 34, No. 6, Nov. 2011. pp. 1818–1826.

[20] V. Emeakaroha et al. "Low level metrics to high level SLAs - LoM2HiS framework: Bridging the gap between monitored metrics and SLA parameters." In *Cloud Environments, Information Systems Journal*, Vol. 2, 2010, IEEE. pp. 48–54.

[21] Monitis. 2011. Available at http://portal.monitis.com/.

[22] Nimsoft monitor. 2011. Available at http://www.nimsoft.com/solutions/nimsoft-monitor.

[23] Tap in Cloud Management Service. 2011. Available at: http://www.tapinsystems.com/cloud-services/tap-in-cloud-management-service-overview/.

[24] CloudBees Inc., CloudBees AnyCloud:Business Value, Architecture and Technology, CloudBees White Paper. Available at: http://www.cloudbees.com.

[25] Vmware vfabric hyperic. 2011. Available at http://www.vmware.com/products/vfabric-hyperic/.

[26] Jmx, Java management framework. 2011. Available at http://www.oracle.com/technetwork/java/javase/tech/javamanagement-140525.html.

[27] D. Kossmann, T. Kraska, and S. Loesing. "An evaluation of alternative architectures for transaction processing in the cloud." In *Proc. of the Int. Conf. on Management of Data*. 2010.

[28] V. C. Emeakaroha, M. Maurer, S. Dustdar, S. Acs, A. Kertesz, and G. Kecskemeti. "LAYSI: A layered approach for SLA-violation propagation in self-manageble cloud infrastructures."

In *Proc. of the IEEE 34th Conf. on Computer Software and Applications*, Nov. 2010. pp. 365–370.

[29] E. Walker, "Benchmarking Amazon EC2." In *ph;LOGIN*, Oct. 2008. pp. 18–23.

[30] S. Ostermann, A. Iosup, N. Yigitbasi, R. Prodan, T. Fahringer, and D. Epema. An Early Performance Analysis of Cloud Computing Services for Scientific Computing. TU Delft/PDS Technical Report PDS-2008-12, Dec 2008.

[31] P.R. Barbosa, R.R. Righi, and D.L. Kreutz. "Defining metrics to Sec-SLA agreements in conformance to international security standards." In *23rd Latin American Informatics Conference*, 2007. pp. 36–47.

[32] R.R. Righi, D.L. Kreutz, and C.B. Westphall. "Sec-Mon: An architecture for monitoring and controlling security service level agreements." In *Proc. of the 9th Workshop on Managing and Operating Networks and Services*. pp. 73–84.

[33] R.R. Henning. "Security service level agreements: quantifiable security for the enterprise." In *Proc. of the 9th ACM Workshop on New Security Paradigms*, 2000. pp. 54–60.

[34] C. Irvine and T. Levin. "Quality of security service." In *Proc. of the 9th ACM Workshop on New Security Paradigms*, 2000. pp. 91–99.

[35] R.R. Righi, F.R. Pelissari, and C.B. Westphall. "Sec-SLA: Specification and validation of metrics to security service level agreements." In *Proc. of the Workshop on Computer System Security*, 2004, pp. 199–210.

[36] GoGrid: Scalable Load-Balanced Windows and LinuxCloud-Server Hosting. 2011. Available at http://www.gogrid.com.

[37] H. Beitollahi and G. Deconinck. "An overlay protection layer against denial-of-service attack." In *Proc. of Int. Symp. on Parallel and Distributed Processing*, Apr. 2008. pp 1–8.

[38] S. Savage, D. Wetherall, A. karlin, and T. Anderson. "Network support for IP traceback." In *ACM/IEEE Transactions on Networking*, Vol. 9, No. 3, June 2001. pp. 226–237.

[39] A. Stavrou. "Websos: An overlay-based system for protecting web servers from denial of service attacks." *Computer and Telecommunications Networking*, Vol. 48, No. 5, Aug. 2005. pp 781–807.

[40] S. Ramgovind, M. Eloff, and E. Smith. "The management of security in cloud computing." In *Proc. of the Int. Conf. on Information Security for South Africa*, 2010.

[41] K. Schulter. "Intrusion detection for grid and cloud computing." *IEEE IT Professional Journal*, July 2010.

[42] R. Bhadauria, R. Chaki, N. Chaki, and S. Sanyal. A Survey on Security Issues in Cloud Computing, Available at http://arxiv.org/abs/1109.5388 (accessed Sept. 2011).

[43] R. Zhang, W. Xie, W. Qian, and A. Zhou. "Security and privacy in cloud computing: A survey." In *Proc. of the 6th Int. Conf. on Semantics Knowledge and Grid*, Nov. 2010. pp. 105–112.

[44] I. Gul and M. Hussain. "Distributed cloud intrusion detection model." *Int. Journal of Advanced Science and Technology*, Vol. 34, 2011. pp. 71–82.

[45] F. Cheng and C. Meinel. "Intrusion detection in the cloud." In *Proc. of the IEEE Int. Conf. on Dependable, Autonomic and Secure Computing*, Dec. 2009. pp. 729–734.

[46] C.-C. Lo, C.-C. Huang, and Joy Ku. "A cooperative intrusion detection system framework for cloud computing networks." In *Proc. of the 39th Int. Conf. on Parallel Processing*, Sept. 2010. IEEE CS Press, pp. 280–284.

[47] M.-W. Park and J.-H. Eom. "Multi-level intrusion detection system and log management in cloud computing." In *Proc. of the 13th Int. Conf. on Advanced Communication Technology.* Feb. 2011. IEEE CS Press, pp. 552–555.

[48] M. Ficco and M. Rak. "Intrusion tolerance as a Service: A SLA-based solution." In *Proc. of the 2nd Int. Conf. on Cloud Computing and Services Science*, Apr. 2012. IEEE CS Press.

[49] M. Ficco and M. Rak. "Intrusion tolerance in cloud applications: The mOSAIC approach." In *Proc. of the 6th Int. Conf. on Complex, Intelligent, and Software Intensive Systems*, 2012.

20

BROKER-MEDIATED CLOUD-AGGREGATION MECHANISM USING MARKOVIAN QUEUES FOR SCHEDULING BAG-OF-TASKS (BOT) APPLICATIONS

Ganesh Neelakanta Iyer and Bharadwaj Veeravalli

CONTENTS

Large Scale Network-Centric Distributed Systems, First Edition. Edited by Hamid Sarbazi-Azad and Albert Y. Zomaya.
© 2014 John Wiley & Sons, Inc. Published 2014 by John Wiley & Sons, Inc.

20.1 INTRODUCTION

Many data-intensive applications from several fields, including data mining [1] and computational biology [2], have been modeled as Bag-of-Tasks (BoT) applications. BoT applications are parallel applications whose tasks are independent of each other [3, 4]. In other words, a BoT application is an application that executes in terms of tasks [5]. Examples include simulation of a large number of independent trials or events and processing of independent media frames and matching of DNA to independent known sequences [6]. A task may consists of some instructions or data of arbitrary size and complexity. In a BoT application, the tasks do not communicate with each other during execution. Based on the results obtained from the execution of some of the tasks, other tasks may be canceled or modified. Hence, Cloud computing is an attractive platform for running such BoT applications due to its inherent characteristics such as elasticity, utility computing model, and scalability.

These applications can be executed in parallel on multiple providers to meet some objectives such as task-deadline and/or budget requirements. Further, these applications often need high-end compute resources wherein the resource requirements vary over time based on the number of tasks present or the amount of data to be processed. The Cloud computing paradigm [7, 8] offers users the ability to elastically change their resource requirements and use a variety of resources with varying characteristics based on user requirements. With a plethora of Cloud Service Providers (CSPs) offering various kinds of services [9], it can be difficult for a new user to choose an appropriate CSP or a set of CSPs for doing a particular job.

The concept of using a Broker to connect CSPs and users was first introduced in [10]. According to [11], there are three categories of opportunities for Cloud Brokers. The first is *Cloud Service Intermediation*, wherein the Broker can build services on top of the services offered by the CSPs, such as additional security or management capabilities. The second is *Aggregation*, in which the Broker deploys customer services over multiple CSPs. Finally, *Cloud Service Arbitrage* is where the Broker supplies flexibile and opportunistic choices for users and fosters competition between Clouds. We consider the second category in our model. In other words, the Cloud Broker creates a layer of abstraction between the users and the CSPs with which multiple Clouds can be managed. Based on a survey by [12], most Cloud customers indicated that a Broker plays a critical role in their business decisions.

In this chapter, we introduce a Broker-mediated Cloud Aggregation mechanism for BoT applications wherein users can submit their applications along with the task execution requirements to the Broker and the Broker distributes the tasks to various CSPs based on these requirements. We consider various task parameters, such as task execution time and budget constraints, in order to derive an optimal task scheduling pattern for distributing tasks to CSPs.

This chapter is organized as follows: Section 20.2 briefly describes the relevant literature on Cloud brokering mechanisms, models for deploying tasks on multiple Clouds, and our contributions. In Section 20.3, the problem setting and notations are explained. The proposed Cloud aggregation mechanism is detailed in Section 20.4, wherein we describe the markovian queue-based optimization problem and derive optimal load fractions for task distribution in order to minimize task execution time. Later, we also describe a heuristic algorithm to take into account the user's budget constraints. In Section 20.5, we describe the performance evaluation and explain the results. Some important points about the proposed model are described in Section 20.6. Finally Section 20.7 concludes the chapter and provides some future insights.

20.2 LITERATURE REVIEW AND CONTRIBUTIONS

20.2.1 Literature Review

At the time of writing this chapter, the research on Broker-mediated strategies for connecting multiple CSPs and users is still in its infancy. In [13] and [14], the authors describe a static and dynamic Cloud brokering mechanism for placing virtual machines over multiple CSPs. They consider a 0-1 integer programming formulation for the total infrastructure capacity and the total price and map it to a general assignment problem that is shown to be NP-hard. They evaluate the feasibility of the proposed approach by deploying and benchmarking some sample service configurations.

In [15], the authors propose a Cloud-bank agency, which provides analysis and guidance about the price to users in the system. A pricing model based on historical usage of the resources has also been proposed. In [16], the authors propose a resource and revenue sharing mechanism with coalition formation among the CSPs. They formulate a coalitional-game and the solutions are also described.

In [17], the authors propose a software architecture model based on binary integer programming for hybrid Cloud scheduling. In case of a hybrid Cloud, there are cases wherein the problem solve time exceeded even 5 days without getting an optimal solution. In [18] and [19], the authors propose a model for Cloud-aggregation by a Broker. They describe this as one of the many ways customers can make use of their OPTIMIS toolkit, but they do not give any details of the Cloud-aggregation mechanism.

In [20], the authors propose an approach to model, deploy, and configure complex applications across multiple Clouds. Their approach is based on open Cloud standards such as Open Virtualization Format (OVF) [21] and Open Cloud Computing Interface (OCCI) [22], but it does not consider any user parameters such as cost and task execution time. In [23], the authors propose a service broker architecture for Cloud computing and ad hoc networks. This architecture is sufficiently flexible in handling various requirements of the providers. But they neither describe a mathematical model nor perform any performance evaluation of the proposed architecture.

In [24], the authors propose a layered model for Cloud federation where negotiation is constrained to well-defined sets of parameters. They also give a motivational scenario to illustrate their ideas. In [25], a Cross-Cloud federation architecture is presented to connect different CSPs in order to achieve economies of scale and enlargement of their capabilities. The model proposes a complex three-phase model: discovery (looking for other Clouds), match-making (selecting the Clouds that match their requirements), and authentication (establishing a trust contest with selected Clouds). But the model does not specify any analytical performance evaluation or real implementation.

20.2.2 Contributions and Scope of This Chapter

Our contributions in this chapter are multifold. We propose a Broker-mediated Cloud-aggregation mechanism that connects various CSPs and users through a Broker. Users can submit their BoT application requirements, such as number of tasks, to the Broker. The Broker in turn derives the optimal task distribution pattern that distributes the tasks into multiple CSPs such that overall application execution time is minimized. We model the CSPs as independent M/M/1 queues, formulate an optimization problem to minimize the task execution time, and derive optimal solutions. We use integer approximation techniques to approximate the task distribution values to obtain suboptimal results. Then we adopt a strategy to determine the cases wherein some of the CSPs having lower resource capabilities are eliminated, keeping the overall task execution time to a minimum.

We further propose a heuristic algorithm to consider user's budget requirements in addition to the task execution time in order to calculate the task distribution. We also evaluate the performance of our schemes through rigorous simulation studies. We describe the applicability of our model for executing large-scale divisible load applications and show that our scheme is flexible in handling varying user requirements, such as security, trust, and reputation of CSPs. We evaluate the performance of our schemes in terms of task execution time, task distribution, and total user expenditure for varying budget requirements. Our schemes can take into account users' restrictions on using the Cloud in terms of governing laws and jurisdiction. Further, our schemes can handle various Cloud characteristics such as auto-elasticity, massive scalability, multiple services offered by the CSPs, and consumption-based billing.

We restrict the scope of this work to formulating the optimization problem and deriving an optimal task allocation pattern for Cloud-aggregation considering various parameters such as task execution time and budget requirements. It is beyond the scope of this work to do an experimental realization.

20.3 PROBLEM SETTING AND NOTATIONS

Our model consists of N users $\{C_1, C_2, .., C_N\}$ and M Cloud Service Providers (CSPs) $\{P_1, P_2, .., P_M\}$ that are connected together through a Broker. Each CSP P_j has an arrival rate λ_j and a service rate μ_j (main notations are listed in Table 20.1). A Broker accepts the application requirements from the users such as number of tasks in the application, deadline, and budget constraints and then makes a task schedule based on

T A B L E 20.1 Table of Major Notations

Symbol	Meaning
M	Total number of CSPs in the system
X	Total number of tasks submitted by the user
B	Budget specified by the user
μ_0	Rate of dispatcher
p_j	Fraction of job sent to CSP j
λ_j	Arrival rate of tasks in CSP j
μ_j	Service Rate of CSP j
N_j	Number of tasks in CSP j
t_j	Average time a task spent in CSP j
T_j	Total amount of time spent by all tasks that are assigned to CSP j
D_j	Unit cost per resource per time unit
D_{tot}	Total expenditure for the execution of one BoT application

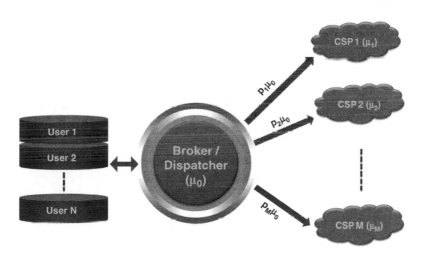

Figure 20.1   Proposed architecture for the Broker-mediated Cloud-aggregation mechanism.

all these constraints. Without any loss of generality, we assume that all CSPs will be able to service any incoming job request and that CSPs have different service rates and price offers for their resources. Later, we show that, if CSPs offer multiple services, our schemes can handle them seamlessly. Architecture of the proposed Cloud-Aggregation mechanism is shown in Fig. 20.1.

20.4 PROPOSED CLOUD AGGREGATION MECHANISM

In this section, we describe the proposed Cloud-Aggregation mechanism in detail. At any point of time, a user C_i can submit a BoT application request having X tasks to the Broker. The Broker maintains information pertaining to the CSPs such as the price offers and service rates. Using this information, the Broker makes a task schedule and distributes the tasks to various CSPs based on this schedule. We first derive optimal values for the task distribution in order to minimize the overall application completion time and then describe heuristics that consider both time and budget constraints.

20.4.1 Task Distribution to Minimize the Application Completion Time

Now, we derive optimal fraction of tasks to be sent out to various CSPs in order to minimize the time spent by various tasks of a BoT application in the system. If p_j is the fraction of job to be send to CSP j, then $\lambda_j = p_j \mu_0$. Further, if N_j is the number of tasks in CSP j, then,

$$N_j = p_j X \tag{20.1}$$

Further, considering each queue as an independent M/M/1 queue, it follows [26] that

$$t_j = \frac{1}{\mu_j - p_j \mu_0} \tag{20.2}$$

Further, we can calculate total time all N_j tasks spent in the system as

$$T_j = N_j t_j \tag{20.3}$$

So we formulate the optimization problem as follows:
    minimize

$$\sum_{j=1}^{M} N_j T_j \tag{20.4}$$

that is, minimize

$$\sum_{j=1}^{M} \frac{p_j X}{\mu_j - p_j \mu_0} \tag{20.5}$$

subject to

$$\sum_{j=1}^{M} p_j = 1 \tag{20.6}$$

$$p_j \geq 0 \forall j = 1, 2, \ldots, M \tag{20.7}$$

Temporarily relaxing the constraint (20.7) and applying the Lagrange multiplier K for the optimization problem, the augmented cost function could be written as

$$L = \sum_{j=1}^{M} \frac{p_j X}{\mu_j - p_j \mu_0} - K \left(\sum_{j=1}^{M} p_j - 1 \right) \tag{20.8}$$

Now, taking the partial derivative of L with respect to each p_j and setting the derivative to zero, we can obtain

$$\frac{\partial L}{\partial p_i} = 0 \Rightarrow K = \frac{X \mu_j}{(\mu_j - p_j \mu_0)^2} \tag{20.9}$$

Further simplifying, we obtain,

$$p_j = \frac{\mu_j}{\mu_0} - \frac{1}{\mu_0} \sqrt{\frac{X \mu_j}{K}} \tag{20.10}$$

Since $\sum p_j = 1$, it follows that

$$\sum \left(\frac{\mu_j}{\mu_0} - \frac{1}{\mu_0} \sqrt{\frac{X \mu_j}{K}} \right) = 1 \tag{20.11}$$

and we obtain the value of K as

$$K = \frac{X \left(\sum \sqrt{\mu_j} \right)^2}{\left(\sum \mu_j - \mu_0 \right)^2} \tag{20.12}$$

Substituting the value of K from Equation (20.12) in Equation (20.10), we obtain a closed form solution for the individual load fractions p_j for each CSP P_j as

$$p_j = \frac{\mu_j}{\mu_0} - \frac{\sqrt{\mu_j} \left(\sum \mu_j - \mu_0 \right)}{\mu_0 \sum \sqrt{\mu_j}} \tag{20.13}$$

Thus, we can calculate the number of tasks to be sent out to each CSP N_j using Equation (20.1).

We illustrate this through an example. Assume $X = 500$, $M = 5$, and $\mu_0 = 70$, then various values obtained based on our results are summarized in Table 20.2. We can observe that the constraints are specified by Equations (20.6) and (20.7). Further, values of p_j's are in proportion to the service rates of various CSPs.

20.4.1.1 Integer Approximation Techniques.
Note that the values of N_j obtained need not be integer quantities. In reality, the assigned load fraction will be in terms of integer quantums. Thus, without loss of generality, we can assume that the minimum possible granularity for any N_j that can be assigned to a CSP as 1. In our context, there should be at least 1 task for a processor. We use the integer approximation technique to ensure that each processor gets an integer load quantum. The pseudo-code for the integer approximation algorithm proposed in [27], which runs in $O(M)$, is

T A B L E 20.2 Example Illustrating the Mathematical Model

CSP (j)	Service rate (μ_j)	Job Fraction (p_j)	No. of Tasks (N_j)	Unit Cost (D_j)	Total Task Execution Time (T_j)	Total Cost ($N_j D_i$)
1	75	0.21	107	0.5	1.79	53.50
2	65	0.13	66	0.4	1.17	26.40
3	77	0.23	116	0.7	1.91	81.20
4	70	0.17	86	0.6	1.49	51.60
5	79	0.25	125	0.5	2.03	62.50
Total task execution time ($max(T_j)$) and total expenditure ($\sum N_j D_i$)					2.03	275.20

summarized in Table 20.3 for the sake of continuity. In this algorithm, $No\_Of\_Jobs[1, m]$ contains values of N_j obtained by Equation (20.1) and $Approx\_Jobs[1, m]$ contains values of N_j after the integer approximation has been performed. This algorithm makes sure that the fraction of the load assigned to each processor is an integer quantity.

20.4.1.2 Eliminating CSPs with Lower Resource Capabilities.
Note that when we derived the optimal values for p_j's, we relaxed the constraint specified by (20.7). This means that values of all p_j's need not be always greater than zero. For example, consider the above example with $\mu_2 = 35$ instead of 65. Then the values of p_j's obtained are summarized in Table 20.4. From Table 20.4, we can see that for a CSP that offers low service rate, the value of p_j becomes negative. In such cases, we propose avoiding such slow CSPs and recalculating the values of p_j. Avoiding CSP 2 in the above example, we obtain various values, as given in Table 20.5. In this case, we obtain the values such that $\sum_{j=1}^{M} p_j = 1$ and that $p_j \geq 0 \forall j = 1, 2, \ldots, M$. We can also observe that, as the number of CSPs processing the tasks decreases, the total task execution time increases.

T A B L E 20.3 Pseudo-code for Integer-Approximation Algorithm [27]

```
1) Initialize the matrix Approx_Jobs[1, m] = 0
2) Approx_Jobs[1] = ceil(No_Of_Jobs[1])
3) sum = Approx_Jobs[1] − No_Of_Jobs[1]
4) for i = 2 to m
5)    Approx_Jobs[i] = ceil(No_Of_Jobs[i])
6)    if (sum + ceil(Approx_Jobs[i] − No_Of_Jobs[i]) < 1 )
7)       Approx_Jobs[i] =ceil(No_Of_Jobs[i])
8)    else
9)       Approx_Jobs[i] =floor(No_Of_Jobs[i])
10)   end
11)   sum+ = Approx_Jobs[i] − No_Of_Jobs[i]
12) end
```

T A B L E 20.4 Example Illustrating Drop-out Condition

CSP (j)	Service Rate (μ_j)	Job Fraction (p_j)
1	75	0.26
2	35	−0.05
3	77	0.28
4	70	0.22
5	79	0.30

T A B L E 20.5 Example Drop-out Condition: Avoiding Slow CSPs

CSP (j)	Service Rate (μ_j)	Job Fraction (p_j)	No. of Tasks (N_j)	Unit Cost (D_j)	Total Task Execution Time (T_j)	Total Cost ($N_j D_i$)
1	75	0.25	124	0.5	2.15	62.00
2	35	0	0	0.4	0	0
3	77	0.27	133	0.7	2.27	93.10
4	70	0.20	102	0.6	1.83	61.20
5	79	0.28	142	0.5	2.39	71.00
Total task execution time ($max(T_j)$) and total expenditure ($\sum N_j D_i$)					2.03	287.30

20.4.2 Task Distribution Based on Budget Requirements

We now describe a simple but effective heuristic to find a task distribution that can handle the user's budget requirements in addition to the application execution time. When the optimal allocation obtained in Section 20.4.1 exceeds the user budget, we opt out the CSP that has the highest cost per resource and recalculate the optimal allocation for the minimization problem described in Section 20.4.1. We repeat this process until the total expenditure is less than or equal to the budget requirements specified by the user. The pseudo-code for this algorithm is summarized in Table 20.6.

T A B L E 20.6 Pseudo-code for Heuristic Algorithm for Task Distribution Based on Budget Requirements

1) Input user budget B
2) Calculate N_j's based on the derivations in Section 20.4.1
3) Calculate total expenditure D_{tot}
4) WHILE $D_{tot} > B$ THEN
5)   Eliminate the CSP which correspond to $max(D_j)$
6)   Calculate all N_j's excluding this CSP
7)   Apply integer approximations to N_j
8)   Recalculate total expenditure D_{tot}
9) END
10) Output the task distribution obtained at present

T A B L E 20.7 Recomputed Optimal Values Without P_3 in Example 1

CSP (j)	Service Rate (μ_j)	Job Fraction (p_j)	No. of Tasks (N_j)	Unit Cost (D_j)	Total Task Execution Time (T_j)	Total Cost ($N_j D_i$)
1	75	0.27	137	0.5	2.45	68.50
2	65	0.19	93	0.4	1.79	37.20
3	77	0	0	0.7	0	0
4	70	0.23	115	0.6	2.13	69.00
5	79	0.31	155	0.5	2.71	77.50
Total task execution time ($max(T_j)$) and total expenditure ($\sum N_j D_i$)					2.71	252.20

T A B L E 20.8 Recomputed Optimal Values Without P_3 and P_4 in Example 1

CSP (j)	Service Rate (μ_j)	Job Fraction (p_j)	No. of Tasks (N_j)	Unit Cost (D_j)	Total Task Execution Time (T_j)	Total Cost ($N_j D_i$)
1	75	0.35	176	0.5	3.49	88.00
2	65	0.26	129	0.4	2.76	51.60
3	77	0	0	0.7	0	0
4	70	0	0	0.6	0	0
5	79	0.39	195	0.5	3.77	97.50
Total task execution time ($max(T_j)$) and total expenditure ($\sum N_j D_i$)					3.77	237.10

For example, consider the example problem described in Table 20.2. The total cost for that allocation is 275.20. Now, suppose the user budget requirements specify that the total expenditure shall not exceed 240.00. So we avoid CSP P_3, which has the highest unit price per resource (0.7), and recalculate the optimal allocation. We obtain the values as shown in Table 20.7.

However, the total expenditure obtained based on this distribution (252.20) does not satisfy the budget requirements (240.00). So we avoid one more CSP (P_4), which has the next highest unit price per resource (0.6), and recalculate the optimal allocation. We obtain the values as shown in Table 20.8.

Note that the total expenditure now satisfies the budget requirements and hence the algorithm stops here. Further, it is evident from these tables that, as we reduce the number of CSPs required for the task distribution, the total application execution time increases.

20.5 PERFORMANCE EVALUATION AND DISCUSSIONS

In this section, we perform rigorous simulation experiments to evaluate the performance of the proposed scheme. We conduct experiments to evaluate the task execution time, total

TABLE 20.9 Major Simulation Parameters

Parameter	Value	Parameter	Value
M	10	X	1000
B	[450,600]	μ_0	100
μ_1	61	D_1	0.5
μ_2	67	D_2	0.4
μ_3	77	D_3	0.7
μ_4	60	D_4	0.6
μ_5	79	D_5	0.5
μ_6	54	D_6	0.75
μ_7	74	D_7	0.55
μ_8	58	D_8	0.6
μ_9	72	D_9	0.65
μ_{10}	64	D_{10}	0.7

expenditure, and the task distribution pattern for large-scale Broker-mediated multiple Cloud environments. The simulation parameters are summarized in Table 20.9.

20.5.1 Analysis of Task Execution Time vs. Budget Requirements

We analyze the task execution time for various user budget requirements, and the results are plotted in Figure 20.2. We can observe that, when no budget requirements are specified, all 10 CSPs are used and the total task execution time is 2.79 units. As the user imposes higher budget restrictions, the total task execution time increases. This

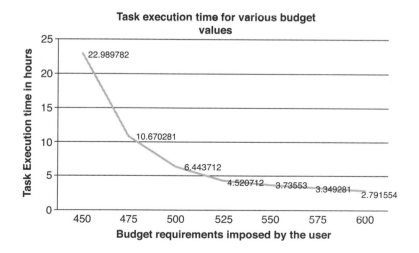

Figure 20.2 Task execution time.

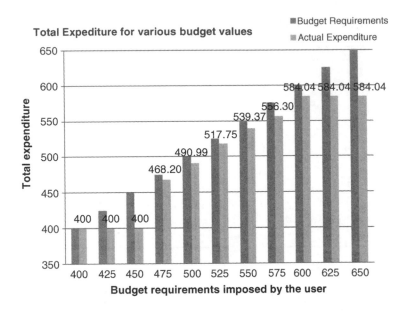

Figure 20.3 Expenditure.

is because, when higher budget restrictions are imposed, tasks are distributed to fewer CSPs and hence it takes more time to complete the same tasks.

20.5.2 Analysis of the Total User Expenditure vs. Budget Requirements

We now compare the total user expenditure for various budget requirements imposed by the user. The results are plotted in Figure 20.3. It can be observed that, in all cases, the expenditure is lower than the user budget requirements. We can also observe that a minimum cost is involved when all the tasks are submitted to only one CSP that offers the lowest price for the resource, and the maximum expenditure can be determined based on the task distribution derived from our optimization problem.

20.5.3 Analysis of Task Distribution Based on Budget Requirements

In this section, we analyze the distribution of tasks to different CSPs based on various user budget requirements and results are plotted in Figure 20.4. In figure, for example, *CSP1(0.5,61)* means that *CSP*1 has a price offer 0.5 and a service rate 61. From Figure 20.4, we can understand that, when a user is flexible with his/her budget, tasks are distributed evenly among the CSPs available for the task execution. But as the user imposes more budget restrictions, the tasks are distributed among fewer CSPs and hence more resources are used from these CSPs to complete the same number of tasks.

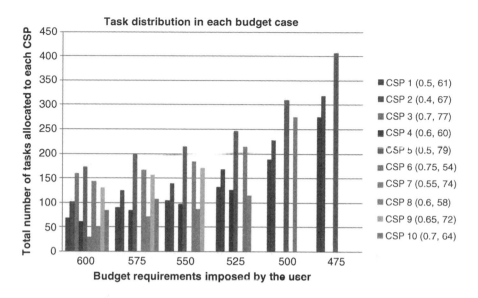

Figure 20.4 Task distribution.

20.6 DISCUSSIONS

20.6.1 Applicability of Our Model to Divisible Load Applications

We can observe that large-scale, data-intensive divisible load applications[1] such as image processing [28, 29] and biological computing [30, 31] applications can also use our model for execution to satisfy various constraints such as budget constraints and application execution time. In the case of divisible load applications, we calculate the optimal amount of data to be distributed to each CSP instead of determining the number of tasks to be distributed. Once the optimal amount of data to be transferred is calculated, the data can be distributed among multiple CSPs and then the application can be executed in parallel among those CSPs.

20.6.2 Flexibility in Considering More User Requirements

In addition to application execution time and budget constraints, users have many other considerations, such as security, trust, and reputation of the CSP [32]. The Broker in our model can seamlessly integrate these features by maintaining databases pertaining to these features of CSPs. For example, whenever a user deploys its tasks to few CSPs, it can submit feedback about those CSPs to the Broker and Broker can maintain these information. Later, when a user submits a new application request, it can also specify some requirements in terms of the desired security level and/or trust level. The Broker

---

[1]Divisible load scheduling theory is referred to as Divisible Load Theory (DLT) in the literature.

can consider a subset of all the CSPs satisfying these criteria to derive the optimal task distribution.

Further, CSPs offer different types of services. We can broadly classify them into three [7] types: Software as a Service (SaaS), Platform as a Service (PaaS), and Infrastructure as a Service (IaaS). For example, Amazon Web Services [33] has three kinds of IaaS offerings: Amazon Elastic Compute Cloud (EC2), SimpleDB, and Amazon simple Storage Service (S3). Similarly, Google has both SaaS (Google Apps) [34] and PaaS (Google App Engine) [35] offerings, and Microsoft Cloud has both SaaS (Microsoft Office 365) and PaaS (Microsoft Windows Azure Platform) [36]. We can observe that, in our model, a user can specify the type of service it wants and a Broker can apply the optimization problem for all CSPs that can offer that service. In a similar manner, our scheme can take into account issues such as governing laws and regulations [37] that may restrict the customer's data and/or code to be deployed within a particular region of the globe for example.

20.6.3 Consideration of Cloud Characteristics

Cloud computing is characterized by various factors such as auto-elasticity, massive scalability, and consumption-based billing. Cloud environments have abundant computational resources, and resources are assigned as and when demand exists, which is referred to as *auto-elasticity*. When BoT applications are executed, based on the results obtained from the execution of some of the tasks, other tasks may be canceled or modified. We can observe that, if customer demand changes (i.e., some of the tasks in the BoT applications are dropped after the execution started or some new tasks are added to the application), a Broker can recalculate the optimal task scheduling pattern and allocate more resources or free some of the resources based on the demand. Further, users have to pay only for the amount of resources they have used for a period of time. Hence, our schemes can effectively handle the Cloud characteristics.

20.7 CONCLUSION

In this chapter, we proposed a mechanism that connects various CSPs and users through a Broker, which deploys user applications to multiple CSPs. Users can submit their BoT application requirements, such as number of tasks, to the Broker. The Broker, in turn, derives the optimal task distribution pattern that distributes the tasks to multiple CSPs such that overall application execution time is minimized. We modeled the CSPs as independent M/M/1 queues, formulated an optimization problem to minimize the task execution time, and derived optimal solutions for task distribution. We used integer approximation techniques to approximate the task distribution values in order to obtain suboptimal results. Then we adopted a strategy to determine the cases wherein some of the CSPs having lower resource capabilities are eliminated, keeping the overall task execution time to be minimum.

We further proposed a heuristic algorithm that considers not only the task execution time, but also the user's budget requirements in order to derive the task distribution.

We described the applicability of our model for executing large-scale divisible load applications that are propounded in the literature and showed that our scheme is flexible in handling varying user requirements such as security, trust, and reputation of CSPs, as well as user's restriction on using Cloud in terms of governing laws and jurisdictions. We evaluated the performance of our schemes in terms of task execution time, task distribution, and total user expenditure for varying budget requirements. We also described that user applications can make use of various Cloud properties such as auto-elasticity and consumption-based billing in order to maximize the benefits of using Cloud environments. Similarly, our Broker-mediated model can handle situations in which CSPs offer multiple services such as compute, storage, and data services seamlessly.

To this end, we designed and analyzed a task distribution strategy for deploying tasks in BoT applications and validated our findings via rigorous simulation experiments. We used Markovian queueing models to model the CSPs in all our simulations. As an immediate extension to this work, one can attempt to consider CSPs adopting dynamic pricing strategies based on market price for attracting more customers. It would also be interesting to incorporate Cloud-Service Intermediation features at the Broker to build new services on top of the services offered by the CSPs.

REFERENCES

[1] F.A.B. da Silva, S. Carvalho, and E.R. Hruschka, "A scheduling algorithm for running bag-of-tasks data mining applications on the grid," *Euro-Par 2004 Parallel Processing, Lecture Notes in Computer Science*, 2004, Vol. 3149/2004, 254–262.

[2] E.N. Cáceres, H. Mongelli, L. Loureiro, C. Nishibe, and S.W. Song, (2010), "Performance results of running parallel applications on the InteGrade. *Concurrency and Computation: Practice and Experience*, 22: 375–393.

[3] W. Cirne, F. Brasileiro, J. Sauve, N. Andrade, D. Paranhos, E. Santos-Neto, and R. Medeiros, "Grid computing for bag of tasks applications," *Proceedings of the 3rd IFIP Conference on E-Commerce, E-Business and E-Government*, September 2003.

[4] F.A.B. da Silva and H. Senger. "Improving scalability of bag-of-tasks applications running on master-slave platforms." *Journal of Parallel Computing* 35, 2 (Feb. 2009), 57–71.

[5] B.D. Steinmacher-Burow. "Dividing the application definition from the execution." *Computing in Science and Eng.* 2, 3 (May 2000), 78–83.

[6] D. Bozdag, C.C. Barbacioru, and U. Catalyurek, "Parallel short sequence mapping for high throughput genome sequencing," *Parallel & Distributed Processing, 2009. IPDPS 2009. IEEE International Symposium on*, May 23–29, 2009, Vol., No., pp. 1–10.

[7] K. Hwang, G.C. Fox, and J.J. Dongarra, *Distributed and Cloud Computing from Parallel Processing to the Internet of Things*, Morgan Kaufmann Publishers, Elsevier Inc. 2012

[8] S. Srinivasan and V. Getov, "Navigating the cloud computing landscape technologies, services, and adopters," *Computer*, March 2011, Vol. 44, No. 3, pp. 22–23.

[9] B.P. Rimal and E.C. Lumb I, "A taxonomy and survey of cloud computing systems," *INC, IMS and IDC, 2009. NCM '09. Fifth International Joint Conference on*, Aug. 25–27 2009, pp. 44–51.

[10] R. Buyya, C.S. Yeo, S. Venugopal, J. Broberg, and I. Brandic. "Cloud computing and emerg-ing IT platforms: Vision, hype, and reality for delivering computing as the 5th Utility," *Future Generation Computer Systems*, Vol. 25, No. 6, June 2009, pp 599–616, Elsevier Science, Am-sterdam, The Netherlands.

[11] D.C. Plummer and L.F. Kenney, Three Types of Cloud Brokerages Will Enhance Cloud Services, white paper, Gartner Inc., 2009.

[12] B.J. Lheureux and D.C. Plummer, Cloud Services Brokerage Proliferates, white paper, Gart-ner Inc., December 2011.

[13] J. Tordsson, R.S. Montero, R. Moreno-Vozmediano, and I.M. Llorente. "Cloud brokering mechanisms for optimized placement of virtual machines across multiple providers." *Future Generation Computer Systems 28*, 2 (February 2012), 358–367.

[14] W. Li, J. Tordsson, and E. Elmroth, "Modeling for dynamic cloud scheduling via migration of virtual machines," *Cloud Computing Technology and Science (CloudCom), 2011 IEEE Third International Conference on*, Nov. 29, 2011-Dec. 1, 2011, pp. 163–171.

[15] H. Li, J. Liu, and G. Tang, "A pricing algorithm for cloud computing resources." In *Proceed-ings of the 2011 International Conference on Network Computing and Information Security - Vol. 01 (NCIS '11)*, IEEE Computer Society, Washington, DC, pp. 69–73.

[16] D. Niyato, Z. Kun, and A. V. Vasilakos, "Resource and revenue sharing with coalition for-mation of cloud providers: Game theoretic approach," in *Proceedings of IEEE International Symposium on Cluster Computing and the Grid (CCGrid)*, Newport Beach, CA, USA, May 23–26, 2011.

[17] R. Van den Bossche, K. Vanmechelen, and J. Broeckhove, "Cost-optimal scheduling in hybrid IaaS clouds for deadline constrained workloads," *Cloud Computing (CLOUD), 2010 IEEE 3rd International Conference on*, July 5–10, 2010, pp. 228–235.

[18] A.J. Ferrer, F. Hernández, J. Tordsson, E. Elmroth, A. Ali-Eldin, C. Zsigri, R. Sirvent, J. Guitart, R.M. Badia, K. Djemame, W. Ziegler, T. Dimitrakos, S.K. Nair, G. Kousiouris, K. Konstanteli, T. Varvarigou, B. Hudzia, A. Kipp, S. Wesner, M. Corrales, N. Forgó, T. Sharif, and C. Sheridan, "OPTIMIS: A holistic approach to cloud service provisioning." Future Generation Computer Systems, Vol. 28, No. 1, pp. 66–77, 2012.

[19] S.K Nair, S. Porwal, T. Dimitrakos, A.J Ferrer, J. Tordsson, T. Sharif, C. Sheridan, M. Rajarajan and A.U. Khan, "Towards secure cloud bursting, brokerage and aggrega-tion," *Web Services (ECOWS), 2010 IEEE 8th European Conference on*, Dec. 1–3, 2010, pp. 189–196.

[20] A. Sampaio and N. Mendonça, "Uni4Cloud: An approach based on open standards for de-ployment and management of multi-cloud applications," *Proceedings of the 2nd Interna-tional Workshop on Software Engineering for Cloud Computing (SECLOUD '11)*, ACM, USA, 2011, pp. 15–21.

[21] Open Virtualization Format (OVF). Available at: http://www.dmtf.org/standards/ovf.

[22] Open Cloud Computing Interface (OCCI). Available at: http://occi-wg.org/.

[23] K.E. Cheng, Y.M. Gottlieb, G.M. Levin, and F.J. Lin, "Service brokering and mediation: enabling next generation market and customer driven service delivery," *Proceedings of the 10th International Symposium on Autonomous Decentralized Systems (ISADS '11)*, IEEE Computer Society, USA, 2011, pp. 525–530.

[24] D. Villegas, N. Bobroff, I. Rodero, J. Delgado, Y. Liu, A. Devarakonda, L. Fong, S.M. Sadjadi, and M. Parashar, "Cloud federation in a layered service model," *Journal of Computer and System Sciences*, January 5, 2012.

[25] A. Celesti, F. Tusa, M. Villari, and A. Puliafito, "How to enhance cloud architectures to enable cross-federation," *Proceedings of the 3rd International Conference on Cloud Computing (CLOUD '10)*, IEEE Computer Society, Washington, DC, USA, 2010.

[26] D. Bertsekas and R. Gallager, *Data Networks*, Prentice-Hall, Inc., 1992.

[27] V. Bharadwaj and N. Vishwanadham, "Suboptimal solutions using integer approximation techniques for scheduling divisible loads on distributed bus network," *IEEE Transactions on System, Man and Cybernatics—Part A: Systems And Humans*, Vol. 30, No. 6, November 2000.

[28] D. Altilar and Y. Paker, "An optimal scheduling algorithm for parallel video processing," *in IEEE International Conference on Multimedia Computing and Systems*, IEEE Computer Society, Silver Spring, MD, USA, 1998.

[29] G.N. Iyer, B. Veeravalli, and S.G. Krishnamoorthy, "On handling large-scale polynomial multiplications in compute cloud environments using divisible load paradigm," *IEEE Transactions on Aerospace and Electronic Systems*, Vol. 48, No. 1, Jan. 2012, pp. 820–831.

[30] J. Yongchang, D.C. Marinescu, W. Zhang, X. Zhang, X. Yan, and T.S. Baker, "A model-based parallel origin and orientation refinement algorithm for cryoTEM and its application to the study of virus structures," *Journal of Structural Biology*, Vol. 154, No. 1, 2006, pp. 1–19.

[31] A. Legrand, A. Su, and F. Vivien, "Minimizing the stretch when scheduling flows of biological requests," Research Report RR2005, Ecole Normale Superieure de Lyon, 2005, 48 pp.

[32] S. Pearson and A. Benameur, "Privacy, Security and Trust Issues Arising from Cloud Computing," *Proceedings of the 2nd International Conference on Cloud Computing*, 2010, pp. 693–702.

[33] J. Murty, *Programming Amazon Web Services: S3, EC2, SQS, FPS, and Simple DB*, O'Reilly Media, March 2008, 602 pp.

[34] M. Morel, M. Alves, and P. Cadet, *Google Apps: Mastering Integration and Customization*, Packt Publishing, Sept. 2011, 268 pp.

[35] C. Severance, *Using Google App Engine: Building Web Applications*, O'Reilly Media, May 2009, 272 pp.

[36] T. Rizzo, M. van Otegem, Z. Tejada, R. bin Rais, D. Bishop, G. Durzi, and D. Mann, *Programming Microsoft's Clouds: Azure and Office 365*, John Wiley & Sons, 2012, 528 pp.

[37] M.D. Parrilli, "Legal issues in grid and cloud computing," in *Grid and Cloud Computing*, Springer, Berlin, 2010, pp. 97–118.

21

ON THE DESIGN OF A BUDGET-CONSCIOUS ADAPTIVE SCHEDULER FOR HANDLING LARGE-SCALE MANY-TASK WORKFLOW APPLICATIONS IN CLOUDS

Bharadwaj Veeravalli, Lingfang Zeng, and Xiaorong Li

CONTENTS

Large Scale Network-Centric Distributed Systems, First Edition. Edited by Hamid Sarbazi-Azad and Albert Y. Zomaya.
© 2014 John Wiley & Sons, Inc. Published 2014 by John Wiley & Sons, Inc.

21.1 INTRODUCTION

Clouds have emerged as a new service provisioning model and are capable of supporting diverse services (servers, storage, network, and applications) over a global network. For Cloud computing–based services, users consume the services when they need to and pay only for what they use. With an economic incentive, Cloud computing encourages individuals and organizations to remotely access resources offered by Cloud Service Providers (CSPs). Therefore, it facilitates individuals and organizations in developing their own core activities without maintaining and developing fundamental infrastructure. Cloud infrastructure enables users to consume services transparently over a secured, shared, scalable, sustainable, and standard worldwide network environment. In addition to this flexibility, Cloud infrastructure services create the illusion of unlimited resources for users to access [1]. CSPs allow users to either allocate one machine for many hours or many machines for one hour, while the costs remain the same. So research organizations or companies with large batch-oriented tasks can get results as quickly as their programs can scale. Without paying a premium for large scale, this elasticity of resources is unprecedented in the history of Information Technology [2].

The various commercial offerings differ not only in pricing but also in the types of machines that can be allocated. For example, for Amazon's EC2, the choice is between "Small," "Large," "Extra Large," "High CPU (Medium)," and "High CPU (Large)" instance types [3]. The efficient use of these payment-services is a crucial issue, because different types of machines may have different rent (pricing). Moreover, different services, belonging to different CSPs, may have different policies for pricing. Users would like to pay a price that is commensurate with the budget they can have. However, currently, the problem of allocating the right number of machines, of the right type, for the right time frame, strongly depends on the application program, and is left to the user to solve.

Given this motivation, we focus on developing an efficient many-task workflow (MTW) scheduling algorithm based on user's time and budget constraints. In general, processing time and economic cost are two typical constraints for MTW execution on Cloud services. In this chapter, we present a budget-conscious adaptive scheduler, which minimizes MTW execution time within a certain budget. The proposed MTW scheduling approach can be used by both end users and CSPs. End users can use the approach to orchestrate Cloud services, whereas CSPs can outsource computing resources to meet customers' service-level requirements.

The remainder of the chapter is organized as follows. We introduce the problem overview and related work in Section 21.2. In Section 21.3, the system model and schedule problem definition are provided. In Section 21.4 we present the proposed scheduling algorithm. In Section 21.5 we conduct performance evaluation approaches and present experimental details and results. In Section 21.6, we conclude the chapter with directions for further work.

21.2 RELATED WORK AND MOTIVATION

As MTW applications are the most typical application model in scientific and engineering fields, much work has been conducted on these (e.g., [4–10], and [11–13] specifically on Cloud environments). However, most efforts in task scheduling have focused on two issues: the minimization of application completion time (makespan/schedule length) and time complexity. It is only recently that much attention has been paid to economic cost in scheduling, particularly for Grids [14, 15].

MTWs can be modeled as Directed Acyclic Graphs (DAGs) [16–20], in which each node represents an executable task and each directed edge represents a precedence constraint between two tasks (data or control dependence). Edges are annotated with a value, which indicates the amount of data that need to be communicated from a parent node to a child node. Given the amount of execution time to run a task on each available machines and the communication time for data transfer from node to node, most traditional studies aim to assign tasks onto machines so as to meet the precedence constraints and minimize the overall schedule length. The existing approaches can address only certain variants of the multi-criteria workflow scheduling problem, usually considering up to two contradicting criteria ([21] and [10], for example) being scheduled in some specific Grid environments. Zhu et al. [22] showed that multi-criteria scheduling on the Grid is a complex problem for which multiple variants can be distinguished based on different possible aspects. So, it is not feasible in general to develop a single scheduling approach that works efficiently for all classes of the problem.

Clouds are emerging as a promising solution for computation and resource demanding applications. MTW has the skew of the distribution [23], and Clouds' distinctive elasticity feature suits MTW to attain efficient use of the computational resources. Users would like to pay a price that is commensurate to the budget they have. So, the commercialization of the Cloud requires policies that can take into account user requirements and budget considerations, in particular. Most existing work is based on a "best effort, free access" model or some specific Grid environments, such as dynamic cost models and market equilibrium. There has been little work examining issues related to budget constraints in a Cloud context.

Sakellariou et al. [24] developed scheduling approaches, LOSS and GAIN, to adjust a schedule that is generated by a time-optimized heuristic and a cost-optimized heuristic to meet users' budget constraints, respectively. However, both LOSS and GAIN should be supported by other scheduling algorithms. References [14] and [25] focus on using genetic algorithms to solve the scheduling problems to meet the budget and deadline constraints. In contrast, we propose bi-criteria heuristic algorithms to schedule MTW within the budget constraints. BaTS [13], a budget and time-constrained scheduler, can schedule large bags of *independent* tasks onto multiple Clouds. A mixture of robustness optimization, satisfying makespan, and price constraints is presented in [26]; it assumes a fixed onetime cost per machine type. Recently, Hybrid Cloud Optimized Cost (HCOC) [27] discussed workflow execution in a Cloud context. HCOC reduces monetary cost while achieving the established desired execution time by deciding which resources should be leased from the public Cloud or which resources should be used in the private Cloud. Byun et al. [28] provided PBTS (Partitioned Balanced Time Scheduling), which estimates the minimum number of computing hosts required to execute a workflow within a user-specified finish time. However, the computing hosts are used as the same monetary cost per time unit. As such, fine-grained management for elastic Cloud resources is not practical yet.

In general, the primary performance goal of supercomputers or Grids has focused on reducing the execution time of applications while increasing the throughput. This performance goal has been mostly achieved by the development of scale out or scale up cluster or multicluster systems. However, this free access model does not considered pricing. Clouds have progressed towards a service-oriented paradigm that enables a new way of service provisioning based on a "pay-as-you-go" model. With the development of Clouds, in the future, more and more large-scale MTWs may be suited for execution on Clouds due to its "scale-*" requirement (scale up—high-performance node, scale out—more nodes for task parallelism, and scale down—short-term usage node of tasks should be released). For example, in the context of scheduling, the long tail of task durations occurs in real-world MTW applications [23], and requires "scale-" to improve system utilization and shorten the time to solution.

In this chapter, we address the problem of scheduling MTW applications in a Cloud and present a budget-conscious scheduling algorithm, referred to as *ScaleStar* (or Scale-*). The ScaleStar algorithm assigns the selected task to the VM with a higher *comparative advantage* (CA), a novel objective function, which effectively balances the execution time and monetary cost. In addition, an adjustment policy (referred to as *DeSlack*) is proposed to eliminate part of idle times without adversely affecting the overall makespan and the total monetary cost.

21.3 SYSTEM MODEL AND PROBLEM SETTING

In this section, we first describe a system model in a Cloud scheduling environment and then illustrate the scheduling problem followed by an example of MTW scheduling. Major notations used in this chapter are summarized in Table 21.1.

21.3.1 System Model

We assume a system model that consists of physical clusters with a fixed number of interconnected servers in a datacenter. Each physical server can be mounted with multiple *virtual machines* (VMs). The communication overhead between two tasks scheduled on the same VM is taken as zero. Without any loss of generality, we denote $\mathbb{V}=v_1,v_2,\ldots,v_V$, where V is the number of VMs, a set of computational VMs participating in a Cloud.

TABLE 21.1 Major Notations Used in this Chapter

Symbol	Definition
$\mathbb{N}$	A set of tasks
$\mathbb{E}$	A set of edges
$\mathbb{V}$	A set of VMs
$\mathbb{P}$	A set of prices (per hour to execute tasks on a VM)
n_i	The i-th task
v_i	The i-th VM
p_i	The price per hour to execute a task on a VM v_i
N	The number of tasks in an MTW
$e_{i,j}$	Inter-task communication between task n_i and task n_j
ω_i	A weight, the execution time of a task n_i
$\epsilon_{i,j}$	The amount of data to be transmitted from VM v_i to VM v_j
$count(n_i)$	The number of required VMs of a P-task
n_{entry}	A task with no predecessors is called an *entry task*
n_{exit}	An exit task
$est(n_i, v_j)$	Earliest start time of task n_i on a VM v_j
$eft(n_i, v_j)$	Earliest finish time of task n_i on a VM v_j
$pred(n_i)$	The set of immediate predecessor tasks of a task n_i
$avail(k)$	The time that VM v_k completed the execution of a task
$Cost_l$	The computation monetary cost of the task n_i on a VM v_j
$Cost_{comp}$	The total computation monetary cost of an MTW
$T_{makespan}$	The total execution time of an MTW
B	The value of budget

We assume that an MTW application is composed of a number of tasks. Our scheme is to schedule a large number of such MTW tasks onto a given Cloud platform. Without loss of generality, an MTW application can be represented by a DAG $\mathbb{G} = (\mathbb{N}, \mathbb{E})$, where $\mathbb{N}$ is a set of tasks (the terms *task* and *node* have been used interchangeably in the chapter), and $\mathbb{E}$ is a set of edges. The edges usually represent precedence constraints: each edge $e_{i,j} = (n_i, n_j) \in \mathbb{E}$ represents a precedence constraint that indicates that task n_i should complete its execution before task n_j starts. $e_{i,j}$ also represents inter-task communication, which is the amount of data (in bytes) that task n_i must send to task n_j in order for task n_j to start its execution. We call n_j the successor of n_i and n_i as the predecessor of n_j. Note that, in addition to data communication itself, overhead may be involved for data redistribution, for example, when task n_i is executed on a different number of VMs. However, when two tasks are assigned to different VMs, a communication cost is required. We ignore the communication cost when tasks are assigned to the same VM. A task n_i has a weight ω_i ($1 \le i \le N$, N is the number of tasks in an MTW), corresponding to the execution time of task n_i on a baseline VM platform, and an edge $e_{i,j}$ ($1 \le i, j \le N$) has a weight $\epsilon_{i,j}$, which corresponds to the amount of data to be transmitted from VM v_i to VM v_j.

If a task n_i simultaneously occupies throughout its execution, for example, a parallel processing task such as an MPI-task requires a fixed number of fully connected computing

CPUs at the same time (as shown in Fig. 21.2(e), task *Adcirc11* requires 256 CPUs), the required VMs are viewed as a special "virtual machine" with an equal price for all required VMs of the task. In this chapter, we term a parallel processing task as a *P-task*. We use $count(n_i)$ to compute the fixed number of required VMs of a *P-task*. For instance, $count(Adcirc11)=256$ represents task *Adcirc11* needs 256 CPUs. For the ease of developing the algorithm and to avoid any confusion in mathematical expression representations, the above 256 CPUs can look like a single VM.

We assume that $\mathbb{G}$ has a single entry task and a single exit task. A task with no predecessors is called an *entry task*, n_{entry}, whereas an exit task, n_{exit}, is one that does not have any successors. If there is more than one exit (entry) task, they are connected to a zero-cost pseudo exit (entry) task with zero-cost edge, which does not affect the schedule. A task is called a *ready task* if all of its predecessors have been completed. The longest path of a task graph $\mathbb{G}$ is the critical path (CP). The overall execution time of $\mathbb{G}$, or *makespan*, is defined as the time between the beginning of $\mathbb{G}$'s entry task and the completion of $\mathbb{G}$'s exit task.

Our monetary cost model assumes that all VM reservation cycles, expressed in hours, are identical for all VMs. Each VM, however, has its own monetary cost per hour, expressed in dollars. Note that these VMs constitute the Cloud, which can be a heterogeneous environment. The target Cloud systems used in this chapter consists of a set $\mathbb{V}$ of V heterogeneous VMs. Each VM $v_i \in \mathbb{V}$ has different VM rents with different configurations; in other words, VM can be chosen according to a user's budget. Then, for each VM $v_i \in \mathbb{V}$, a set $\mathbb{P}$ of p_i the price per hour to execute a task on a VM v_i.

Under these assumptions we formulate the following problem: Given the above application and computation cost model, how can an MTW application be scheduled on a collection of VMs such that it meets a user-given budget while maximizing the performance (minimizing makespan of the execution)?

As defined above, as N is the number of tasks in an MTW, it takes $w_{i,j}$ time units to execute a task n_i on the VM v_j with price p_j. Therefore, the computation monetary cost of a task n_i on a VM v_j can be calculated as:

$$Cost_i = cost(n_i, v_j) = w_{i,j} \cdot p_j \tag{21.1}$$

where p_j is the monetary cost per hour to execute a task n_i on a VM v_j, $w_{i,j}$ is the execution time of a task n_i on the VM v_j.

The total computation monetary cost of an MTW $Cost_{comp}$ can be calculated as:

$$Cost_{comp} = \sum_{j=1}^{V} \left(\left(\sum_{i=1}^{N} w_{i,j} \right) \cdot p_j \right) \tag{21.2}$$

where $w_{i,j}$ is the execution time of a task n_i on the VM v_j (if the task n_i is assigned on the VM v_j with price p_j, $w_{i,j} = \omega_i$; else, $w_{i,j} = 0$) and V is the number of VMs.

In practice, if a VM is not released to CSPs, the user will still be charged even if the VM is idle. Thus, Eq. (21.2) can be redefined as follows:

$$Cost_{comp} = \sum_{k=1}^{V}((eft_{n_j,v_k} - est_{n_i,v_k}) \cdot p_k) \qquad (21.3)$$

where eft_{n_j,v_k} is the earliest finish time of the last task n_j in the kth VM with price p_k, est_{n_i,v_k} is the earliest start time of the first task n_i in the kth VM, and V is the number of VMs.

The total execution time of the MTW, $T_{makespan}$, can be calculated as:

$$T_{makespan} = max\{eft(n_{exit})\} \qquad (21.4)$$

where, eft is defined in Eq. (21.8).

When an MTW is submitted to a Cloud, the scheduler allocates tasks one by one to a VM. Our goal is to model Cloud services considering monetary cost and performance constraints.

$$minimize(T_{makespan}), subject\ to,$$
$$Cost_{comp} + Cost_{tran} + Cost_{stor} + Cost_{spinup} \leq B \qquad (21.5)$$

where B is the user-given constraints on monetary cost, $Cost_{tran}$ denotes the monetary cost of transferring input or output data, $Cost_{stor}$ denotes the monetary cost of permanent storage for input or output data, and $Cost_{spinup}$ represents the monetary cost of system initialization. Although $Cost_{tran}$, $Cost_{stor}$, and $Cost_{spinup}$ are important in user's economic constraints, they are not directly related to MTW scheduling. Hence, we focus on $Cost_{comp}$ in this chapter.

In addition, most commercial CSPs have a minimum billable cost unit. The dimensions of the cost terms in Eq. (21.2) are different from the ones used in resource allocation. For example, the typical unit of computation time is expressed in seconds while that of a *charge time unit* is an hour. As such, the actual monetary cost is calculated by dividing the total cost by the charge unit, and then multiplying the unit cost: For Eq. (21.2), let $\sum_{i=1}^{N} w_{i,j}$ be 30000 and the unit of $w_{i,j}$ be a second. If the CSP charges $p_j = 0.4\$/hour$ for one-hour usage of a VM v_j, the actual monetary cost is $\lceil 30000/3600 \rceil \times 0.4$ dollars.

21.3.2 Many-Task Workflow Scheduling Problem

Given a DAG $\mathbb{G}$ and a Cloud system $\mathbb{C}$, the problem addressed is to find a feasible schedule, defined as a mapping from $\mathbb{G}$ onto $\mathbb{C}$: scheduling of a set of interdependent tasks onto a set of heterogeneous VMs dispersed across multiple data centers in a Cloud. A simple task graph is shown in Fig. 21.1.

Usually, *b-level* and *t-level* attributes are used for assigning priority [29]. The *t-level* of a task n_i is the length of a longest path (there can be more than one longest path) from an *entry* task to n_i (excluding n_i). The *b-level* of a task n_i is the length of a longest path from n_i to an *exit* task. The *b-level* and *t-level* parameters are very important for assigning priority to tasks. For example, if we want to schedule tasks in CP first, tasks

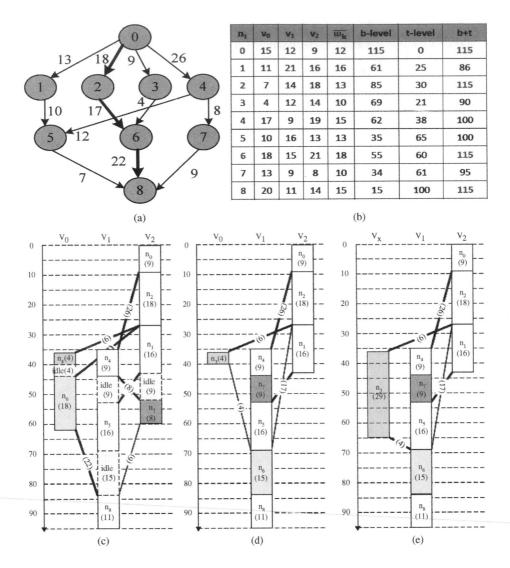

n_i	v_0	v_1	v_2	$\overline{w_k}$	b-level	t-level	b+t
0	15	12	9	12	115	0	115
1	11	21	16	16	61	25	86
2	7	14	18	13	85	30	115
3	4	12	14	10	69	21	90
4	17	9	19	15	62	38	100
5	10	16	13	13	35	65	100
6	18	15	21	18	55	60	115
7	13	9	8	10	34	61	95
8	20	11	14	15	15	100	115

(a)   (b)

Figure 21.1   An example of scheduling in a DAG (assume the monetary cost per time unit of v_0, v_1, v_2, and v_x is 0.1, 0.5, 1, and 0.01 respectively): (a) A simple DAG representing precedence-constrained MTW; (b) Execution time of nodes on three different VMs, average execution time, b-level, t-level, and b-level+t-level of nodes; (c) HEFT algorithm ($T_{makespan}$=95, Cost=92.6 (including idle times), Cost=71.2 (excluding idle times)); (d) Budget-conscious algorithm ($T_{makespan}$=95, Cost=73.4 (including idle times), Cost=73.4 (excluding idle times)); (e) Budget-conscious algorithm ($T_{makespan}$=95, Cost=73.04 (including idle times), Cost=73.04 (excluding idle times)).

can be scheduled in a descending order of *b-level*. If we want to schedule tasks in a topological order, tasks can be scheduled in an ascending order of *t-level*. Consider the DAG shown in Fig. 21.1(a). In this DAG there exists only one CP which comprises tasks n_0, n_2, n_6, and n_8 (the edges in the CP are shown with thick arrows). The values of *b-level*, *t-level*, and *b-level+t-level* are shown in Fig. 21.1(b).

We assume that the target Cloud environment consists of a set $\mathbb{V}$ of V heterogeneous VMs connected in a fully connected topology in which all inter-VM communications are assumed to perform without contention. In our model, it is also assumed that computation can be overlapped with communication. Additionally, task executions of a given MTW are assumed to be nonpreemptive. Before scheduling, the tasks are labeled with the average execution times:

$$\overline{\omega_k} = \frac{\sum_{j=1}^{V} w_{k,j}}{V} \tag{21.6}$$

The earliest start time $est(n_i, v_k)$ and earliest finish time $eft(n_i, v_k)$ of a task n_i on a VM v_k are defined as:

$$est(n_i, v_k) = \begin{cases} 0 & \text{if } n_i = n_{entry}, \\ \max\{avail(k), (\max_{n_x \in pred(n_i)} (eft(n_x, v_m) + \epsilon_{i,j} \cdot \lambda_{v_m,v_k}))\} \\ & \text{otherwise}, \end{cases} \tag{21.7}$$

$$eft(n_i, v_k) = est(n_i, v_k) + \omega_{i,k} \tag{21.8}$$

where v_k is the VM scheduled to task n_i, v_m is the VM scheduled to task n_x, $pred(n_i)$ is the set of immediate predecessor tasks of task n_i, $avail(k)$ is the earliest time at which VM v_k is ready for task execution, and λ_{v_m,v_k} is the inverse of the bandwidth of the link between VM v_m and VM v_k. If n_x is the last assigned task on VM v_k, then $avail(k)$ is the time that VM v_k completed the execution of the task n_x and it is ready to execute another task when we have a non-insertion-based scheduling policy. The inner *max* block in the *est* equation returns the *ready time*, that is, the time when all data needed by n_i has arrived at VM v_k.

The makespan ($T_{makespan}$) is obtained after the scheduling of N tasks in a task graph $\mathbb{G}$ is completed. Since the two objectives (minimization of makespan and monetary cost) in our scheduling model conflict with each other, scheduling decisions should be made accounting for the impact of each of those objectives on the quality of schedule.

Traditional studies from the literature aim to assign tasks onto machines in such a way that the overall schedule length is minimized and precedence constraints are met. For an example of a DAG, the makspan produced using a well-known heuristic HEFT [16], is shown in Fig. 21.1(c). For the example from Figure 21.1(c), we note that there are two lines, bold and fine. The bold line signifies the fact that the earliest start time of a task cannot be scheduled in advance if there is a bold line from an other task. The fine line signifies the fact that a task can be scheduled ahead of the current time provided it satisfies the time constraint on the line and also if there is not any bold line from an other task. In additional, the pricing model of CSPs has an effect on calculating the monetary cost of MTW execution. In Fig. 21.1(c), CSPs charge 92.6 by leasing time (including idle times), but charge only 71.2 by usage time(excluding idle times). If a user is charged by the leasing time, the scheduling algorithm should try to eliminate the idle time or the user should release the machine(s) to CSPs provided the installing machine time is far less than the idle time.

The slack [30] of each task indicates the maximal value that can be added to the execution time of this task without affecting the overall makespan of the schedule. If CSPs charge fees even when a VM is idle, it might be efficient to eliminate idle times without affecting the schedule's makespan. In Fig. 21.1(c), the slack of node 8 is 0, and the slack of node 6 is also 0 (computed as the slack of node 8 plus the spare time between 6 and 8, which is 0). Node 4 has a spare time of 4 with node 6 and a spare time of 44 with node 8 (its two immediate successors in the DAG and the VM where it is executing). Since the slack of both nodes 6 and 8 is 0, the slack of node 4 is 4, which is the maximal time that the finish time of node 4 can be delayed without affecting the schedule's makespan. In Fig. 21.1(d), compared with Fig. 21.1(c), we note that node 6 is reassigned from VM v_0 to VM v_1, the overall makespan remains unaltered while the monetary cost gets reduced. Similarly in Fig. 21.1(e), the makespan remains unaltered but the monetary cost is reduced further. In this case, the node 3 is assigned to the VM v_x, which has a cheaper monetary cost per time unit than VM v_0.

21.4 PROPOSED SCHEDULING ALGORITHM

In this section, we propose both static and dynamic strategies for MTW scheduling. We first present a static method, referred to as static ScaleStar, wherein the tasks are scheduled using their given execution times. This would be an initial solution to the problem, assuming there are no runtime changes for every task scheduled. However, in real-life situations, the execution times may vary during runtime. Hence, each scheduled (but not executed) task might need to be rescheduled according to the runtime resource performance. This is referred to as a dynamic case. For those dynamic scenarios, we then propose a dynamic strategy that adapts to the dynamic demands of the tasks.

21.4.1 Static ScaleStar

As discussed in the previous section, the total computation cost of running an MTW $Cost_{comp}$ can be calculated either by Eq. (21.2) or Eq. (21.3). Eq. (21.2) considers a pricing model in which users pay only for running tasks on VMs. Eq. (21.3) considers a pricing model in which idle times of VMs will be charged unless users release those resources.

It may be noted that it has been a challenging task to schedule MTWs in a distributed system and adding budget constraints makes the problem even more complex. The quality of MTW schedules in Clouds should be measured explicitly by considering both makespan and monetary cost. In order to achieve a time-cost optimization, we introduce a novel objective function, referred to as *Comparative Advantage* (CA), which is incorporated into ScaleStar to deal with such a trade-off. We now describe the computations involved in determining the scheduling solution by calculating the value of CA.

Static ScaleStar algorithm is composed of three phases. In the first phase, an initial schedule S is generated with a $CA1$ value to measure the quality of an MTW schedule in term of monetary cost and task execution time. In the second phase, it adjusts the schedule S according to $CA2$: if the total cost is larger than the budget, we reassign a task to a VM with the smallest non-zero value $CA2$; if the total cost is less than or equal to the budget, we reassign a task to a VM with the largest non-zero value $CA2$. In the third phase, we use the *DeSlack* policy (to be described later in Section 21.4.1.3) to partially eliminate the idle times in the nodes.

21.4.1.1 Initial Assignment Phase.

In the initial assignment phase, we calculate CA1, the comparative advantage of assigning a task n_i to a VM v_j against assigning a task n_i to a "best" available VM v'. For a given task n_i, the value of $CA1(n_i, v_j, v')$ is defined as

$$CA1(n_i, v_j, v') = \frac{cost(n_i,v')-cost(n_i,v_j)}{cost(n_i,v_j)} + \frac{eft(n_i,v')-eft(n_i,v_j)}{eft(n_i,v_j)-est(n_i,v_j)} \qquad (21.9)$$

where $cost(n_i, v_j)$ and $cost(n_i, v')$, calculated using Eq. (21.1), are the respective monetary cost of assigning n_i to v_j and monetary cost of assigning n_i to v'. Similarly, $eft(n_i, v_j)$, $eft(n_i, v')$, $est(n_i, v_j)$, and $est(n_i, v')$ denote the earliest finish/start time of assigning n_i to v_j and that of assigning n_i to v', respectively. The value of $CA1$ is positive for a valid scheduling. For a given task, the "best" available VM will be updated after each comparison of VM v_j and v'. The best assignment is selected when the maximum $CA1$ value is obtained (Steps 3–6 in Table 21.2).

21.4.1.2 Task Reassignment Phase.

In Phase 2, the task reassignment phase, we calculate the comparative advantage ($CA2$). Let $makespan_{new}$ be the makespan to execute task n_i on the new assigned VM v_j and $makespan_{old}$ be the makespan to execute task n_i on the VM assigned by previous schedule S. Also, let the cost associated with $makespan_{new}$ be denoted as $cost_{new}$, and let the cost associated with $makespan_{old}$ be denoted as $cost_{old}$, respectively, which are calculated by Eq. (21.3). Then, CA2 is derived by the following equation:

$$CA2(n_i, v_j) = \frac{makespan_{new} - makespan_{old}}{cost_{old} - cost_{new}} \qquad (21.10)$$

By Eq. (21.10), we calculate CA2 for all possible assignments by assigning n_i to all available VMs v_j. We tabulate all the CA2 values. If $cost_{old}$ is less than or equal to $cost_{new}$ the value of $CA2$ is considered zero. If $makespan_{new}$ is greater than $makespan_{old}$, we assign a $CA2$ value of zero. We compare the total cost with the budget and reassign tasks to VMs. The algorithm keeps trying reassignment by considering the smallest or biggest values of the $CA2$ for all tasks and VMs (Steps 18–22 in Table 21.2).

21.4.1.3 DeSlack Policy.

The idea of *DeSlack* (Step 24 in Table 21.2) is to adjust the start time of each task in the schedule S so as to eliminate idle times (shown as "idle"

T A B L E 21.2 Algorithm: **Static ScaleStar**

Input: A DAG $\mathbb{G} = (\mathbb{N}, \mathbb{E})$ with task execution time and communication.
A set $\mathbb{V}$ of V VMs with cost of executing tasks and available Budget B.
Output: A DAG schedule S of $\mathbb{G}$ onto $\mathbb{V}$.
01. Compute *b-level* of $\forall n_i \in \mathbb{N}$, sort $\mathbb{N}$ in decreasing order by *b-level* value;
02. Build an array $A[N][V]$;
03. **for** $\forall n_i \in \mathbb{N}$ and $\forall v_j \in \mathbb{V}$ **do** {
04.   Compute $CA1(n_i, v_j, v')$ and $CA1(n_i, v', v_j)$ value with v' use Eq.(21.9);
05.   **if** $CA1(n_i, v_j, v') > CA1(n_i, v', v_j)$
06.   Replace v' with v_j, assign n_i on v'; }
07. Compute $makespan_{old}$ and $cost_{old}$ according to S;
08. **for** $\forall n_i \in \mathbb{N}$ and $\forall v_j \in \mathbb{V}$ **do** {
09.   **if** task n_i is assigned to VM v_j
10. $A[i][j]=0$;
11.   **else** {
12.   Compute $makespan_{new}$ assume n_i is assigned to VM v_j;
13.   Compute $cost_{new}$ assume n_i is assigned to VM v_j;
14. $A[i][j]=CA2(i,j)$; }}
15. Assign all the non-zero values of A to a set $\mathbb{A}$;
16. Sort A in increasing order by $CA2$ value;
17. $cost$ = the current total execution monetary cost;
18. **while** ($\mathbb{A}$ is not empty) **do** {
19.   **if** ($cost > B$), get the first element value $A[i][j]$ (and remove it) from $\mathbb{A}$;
20.   **if** ($cost \leq B$), get the last element value $A[i][j]$ (and remove it) from $\mathbb{A}$;
21.   Reassign task i to VM j and calculate new monetary cost of schedule S;
22.   **if** ($cost > B$), invalidate previous reassignment for task i to VM j; }
23. **if** ($cost > B$), use cheapest assignment for S;
24. Call *DeSlack* policy;
25. Return S;

---

in Fig. 21.1) as much as possible to further reduce the cost. The input of this policy is a schedule S. The DeSlack policy (Table 21.3) maintains a schedule S and keeps track of the tasks that have been assigned to a VM. It recalculates the cost by adjusting the start/finishing time of each task so as to eliminate the idle times on a VM. In Table 21.3, est_n and est_{idl} are the earliest start time of task (n) and idle times (idl), respectively. ω_j is the execution time of task (n) on the new selected VM v_j. Note that task (n) and idle times (idl) are in the same VM v_j, and Step (4) in Table 21.3 calculates the total monetary cost using Eq. (21.3).

21.4.2 Dynamic Adaptive Strategy

We propose a dynamic strategy of MTW scheduling as shown in Table 21.4. Firstly, static ScaleStar generates a static solution as an initial schedule. Then, the algorithm obtains the set $\mathbb{N}_{CP}$, which comprises the set of nodes in the critical path (CP). Note that these nodes ($\in \mathbb{N}_{CP}$) have the same biggest value of (*b-level* + *t-level*), for example a critical path formed by a set of nodes $\{n_0, n_2, n_6, n_8\}$ as shown in Fig. 21.1(b).

TABLE 21.3 **DeSlack** Policy

1. Except the entry task and the exit task, compute eft and est
for each task and each "idle" according to the schedule S;
2. Except the entry task and the exit task, find the first tasks or the last
tasks, form a $Candidate_{task}$ set, and sort $Candidate_{task}$ in
decreasing order by the length of execution time ($eft_{task} - est_{task}$);
3. Selected all "idle" and form a $Candidate_{idle}$ set, and sort $Candidate_{idle}$
in increasing order by the length of idle times ($eft_{idle} - est_{idle}$);
4. Compute the total monetary cost, $cost_{old}$;
5. while ($Candidate_{task}$ is not empty) **do** {
    $n \leftarrow$ first task (node) in $Candidate_{task}$;
    while ($Candidate_{idle}$ is not empty) **do** {
        $idl \leftarrow$ first "idle" in $Candidate_{idle}$;
        Compute the total monetary cost, $cost_{new}$, assume
        task n is assigned to a same VM (for a idle idl);
        if ($est_n \geq est_{idl}$, $\omega_{idl} \geq \omega_n$, $\omega_{idl} - \omega_n$
        is the minimum value, and $cost_{new} \leq cost_{old}$) {
            Task n is allocated to the VM where the
            idle idl is, go to **(1)**; }
        Eliminate the idle idl from the $Candidate_{idle}$; }
    Remove task n from the $Candidate_{task}$; }

To adapt to the dynamic scenarios, the algorithm first selects a part of the DAG to execute. Each time, it sets a variable EFT according to the earliest finish time (eft) of a node in the critical path n_j ($\in N_{CP}$), and all the taks whose earliest finish time are no more than EFT are dispatched according to the initial schedule S. As the tasks are being executed,

TABLE 21.4 Algorithm: **Dynamic Adaptive ScaleStar**

Input: A DAG $\mathbb{G} = (\mathbb{N}, \mathbb{E})$ with task execution time and communication.
A set $\mathbb{V}$ of V VMs with cost of executing tasks and available Budget B.
Output: All the tasks are finished.
01. Schedule DAG $\mathbb{G}$ using *static ScaleStar* algorithm and get
    a DAG schedule S;
02. Compute *b-level*, *t-level*, and *b-level* + *t-level* of $\forall n_i \in \mathbb{N}$;
03. Get the set $\mathbb{N}_{CP}$ of nodes in the critical path;
04. while $\exists n_i \in \mathbb{N} \mid n_i$ is not dispatched **do** {
05.   Get the node n_j ($\in \mathbb{N}_{CP}$) with the biggest *b-level*;
06. $EFT = eft_j$;
07.   Dispatch all $n_i \in \mathbb{N}$ such that $eft_i \leq EFT$ according to S;
08.   Remove all dispatched tasks from $\mathbb{N}$;
09.   Remove task n_j from $\mathbb{N}_{CP}$;
10.   If n_j begins to execute and any n_i's $eft_i + \omega_j + threshold > EFT$ {
11.   Update the set $\mathbb{V}$ of V VMs and available Budget B;
12.   Reschedule not started tasks ($\in \mathbb{N}$) with *static ScaleStar*
         algorithm and get a new DAG schedule S;
13. } }

the scheduler compares the real execution time with the estimated one in the original schedule. If the performance loss is higher than a *threshold* (e.g., 10%), it reschedules the remaining tasks using *static ScaleStar* algorithm and generates a new schedule S. At the same time, the information of VM performance and remaining budget is updated according to the measured performance. The process ends when all the tasks are executed.

21.5   PERFORMANCE EVALUATION AND RESULTS

In this section, we evaluate the performance of our algorithms and discuss how efficiently they can adapt to a Cloud system dynamically.

21.5.1   Evaluation Methodology

We built a simulation environment for a Cloud system and conducted rigorous tests for extensive performance analysis. The heterogeneous processors are connected via a fully connected network with transmission rates 1Gbits/sec. Parallel application graphs are based on both real-world MTW applications and randomly generated DAGs by varying parameters such as communication to computation ratios (CCR) and parallelism factor α (see subsection 21.5.3). The performance metrics include *makespan* (in Eq. (21.4)), *budget spend ratio* (in Eq. (21.12)), and *average normalized difference* (in Eq. (21.13)). The qualitative analysis allows us to have a better understanding of the performance and gives suggestive solutions for MTW scheduling.

To study the performance under budget constraints, we define OC as a total optimum monetary cost (OC) and set the value of budget B to vary by different times of OC. The value of OC can be calculated as

$$OC = \sum_{i=1}^{N}(et_{n_i} \cdot count(n_i) \cdot p_h) \qquad (21.11)$$

where et_{n_i} is the execution time of a task n_i; (generally, the execution of a task consists of three phases: downloading of input data from the storage system, running the task, and transferring output data to the storage system); $count(n_i)$ is the number of required types of physical host h for task n_i (e.g., *P-task*); and p_h is the monetary cost per hour of host h. The value OC serves as a lower bound of total monetary cost. We compare the performance of our proposed algorithms with LOSS3 [24] and HEFT [16] and show the importance of an algorithm being aware of the elasticity of the Cloud.

Besides *makespan*, we also evaluate the performance of other two important metrics: BSR and AND.

Budget Spend Ratio (BSR): For a given task graph, we examine the efficiency of a schedule based on the ratio of makespan and monetary cost of the tasks along the critical path (CP) without considering communication costs:

$$BSR = \frac{Cost_{comp}}{\sum_{n_i \in \mathbb{N}_{CP}} min_{v_j \in \mathbb{V}}\{w_{i,j} \cdot p_j\}} \qquad (21.12)$$

where $Cost_{comp}$ is calculated by Eq. (21.3), $\mathbb{N}_{\mathbb{CP}}$ is a set of critical path tasks of $\mathbb{G}$, $\mathbb{V}$ is the set of VMs, and task n_i with execution time $w_{i,j}$ is assigned to VM v_j with price p_j.

Average Normalized Difference (AND) [24] is another performance metric that uses HEFT [16], a well-known workflow scheduling algorithm, as a performance baseline for performance evaluation:

$$AND_x = \frac{1}{R_x} \sum_{i=1}^{R_x} \left(\frac{M_x^i - M_{cheapest}^i}{M_{base}^i - M_{cheapest}^i} \right) \tag{?1.13}$$

where $M_{cheapest}$ is the makespan of the cheapest assignment, M_x is the makespan returned by a target algorithm, M_{base} is the shortest makespan by HEFT [16], and i denotes the i-th run. We use the average value of multiple runs, R_x, to eliminate the randomness of running a heuristic algorithm.

21.5.2 Real-World MTW Applications

For real-world MTW applications, we select six DAGs, namely, Gene2Life [6], LIGO [32], SIPHT [33], Motif [34], NCFS [35], and PSMerge [36]. The structure of each MTW with the computation time and input/output data size of each task summarized in Fig. 21.2.

Gene2Life workflow [6] takes an input DNA sequence to discover genes that match the sequence. This workflow has two parallel sequences to determine the number of identified sequences that satisfy the selection criteria. The outputs of *blast* trigger the launch of *clustalw* for a global alignment analysis. These outputs are then passed through parsimony programs *dnapars* and *protpars* [6]. In the last step of the workflow, *drawgram* generates plots to visualize the results.

LIGO Inspiral Analysis Workflow [32] is used by the Laser Interferometer Gravitational Wave Observatory to detect gravitational waves in the universe. The detected events are divided into smaller blocks for analysis.

SIPHT [33] automates the search for SRNA encoding-genes for all bacterial replicons in the National Center for Biotechnology Information database. It is composed of a variety of ordered individual programs.

Motif workflow [34] is a computationally intensive application that consists of various stages. The first stage of the workflow assembles input data and does preprocessing. This preprocessing stage spawns a set of parallel tasks that operate on subsets of the data. In the second stage, *InterProScan* processes each subset of data. The executions of InterProScan can be handled by Taverna and scripts. Finally, the results from the parallel tasks are merged and then fed into a multi-processor application.

NCFS workflow[35] is developed to accurately simulate storm surges in the coastal areas of North Carolina. It is a four-model system that consists of Hurricane Boundary Layer (HBL) model for winds, Wave Watch III and SWAN for ocean and near-shore wind waves, and *Adcirc* for storm surge. The models require good coverage of the parameter space describing tropical storm characteristics in a given region for accurate flood plain mapping and analysis. Computational and storage requirements for these workflows are

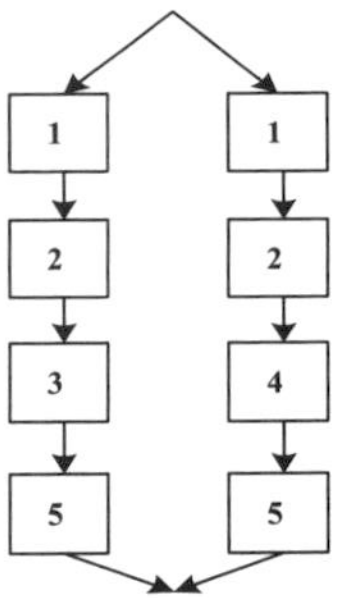

(a) Gene2Life

ID	Task	CT(s)	Input	Output
1	blast	180	0.1MB	1MB
2	clus talw	300	0.1MB	0.1MB
3	dnapars	30	4KB	4KB
4	proipars	30	4KB	4KB
5	drawgram	30	4KB	35KB

(b) LIGO

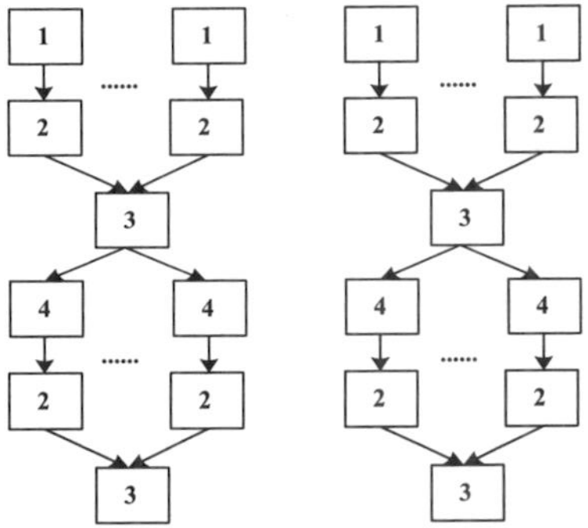

ID	Task	CT(s)	Input	Output
1	TmpltBank (34)	19	70MB	1MB
2	Inspiral (76)	460	75MB	300KB
3	Thinca (14)	6	16MB	30KB
4	TrigBank (42)	6	14KB	10KB

(c) SIPHT

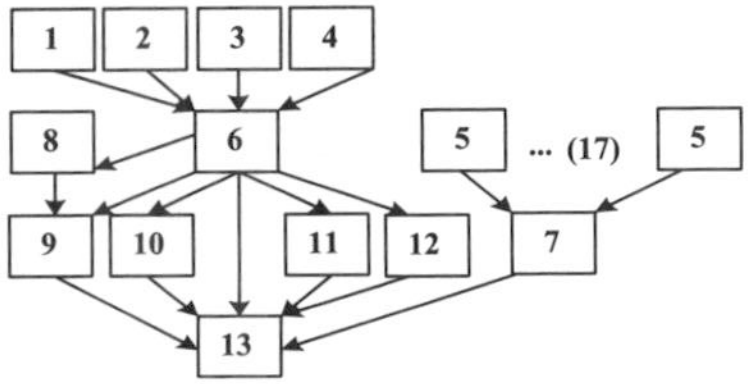

ID	Task	CT(s)	Input	Output
1	Transterm	33	4.65MB	435KB
2	Findterm	975	5MB	46MB
3	RNAMotif	44	5KB	1MB
4	Blast	3331	270MB	5MB
5	Patser (17)	2	4.3MB	10KB
6	SRNA	307	23MB	5MB
7	Patser conate	1	120KB	120KB
8	FFN parse	25	5MB	0.83MB
9	Blast synteny	33	4MB	1.35MB
10	Blast candidate	62	2MB	12KB
11	Blast QRNA	13445	259MB	5MB
12	Blast paralogues	5	1MB	1.24MB
13	SRNA annotate	24	4MB	1.1MB

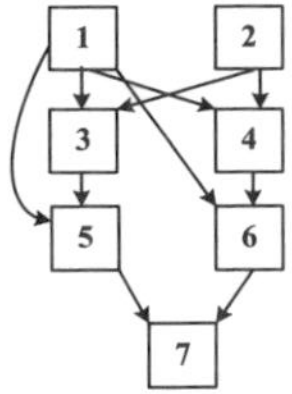

ID	Task	CT(hr)	Input	Output
1	Adcirc	11(256CPUs)	534MB	215277MB
2	Wave Watch III	1(256CPUs)	810MB	27660MB
3	SWAN Outer South	8(10CPUs)	24293MB	14MB
4	SWAN Outer North	130(8CPUs)	24327MB	16338MB
5	SWAN Inner South	3(192CPUs)	215575MB	4.4GB
6	SWAN Inner North	4(160CPUs)	6383.42MB	3.8GB
7	Adcirc	.5(256CPUs)	8.734GB	6510MB

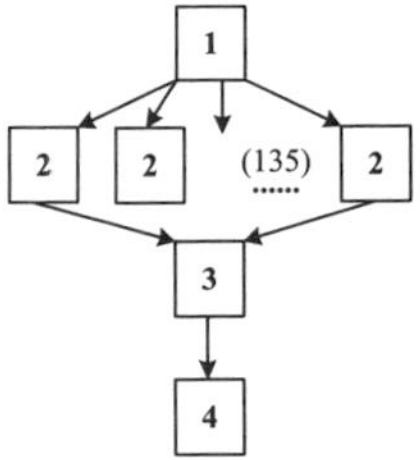

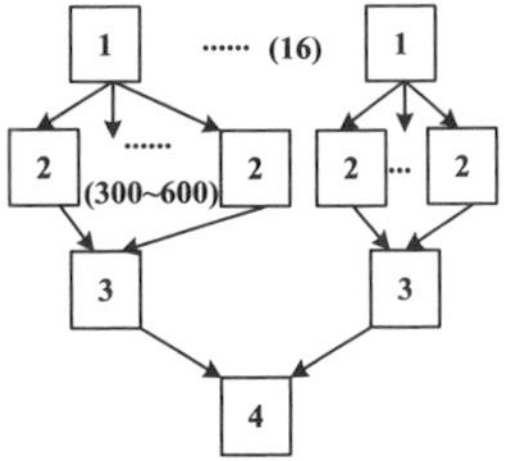

ID	Task	CT(s)	Input	Output
1	Pre Interproscan	30	13MB	10KB
2	Interproscan	5400	100KBS	00KB
3	Post Interproscan	60	67.5MB	599MB
	Motif	3600(256CPUs)	71MB	1432MB

ID	Task	CT	Input	Output
1	ColdDB&LoadDB	5mins	100MB	100MB
2	Merge DB	3hrs	2TB+100MB	~2TB
3	Validate Merge	1min	~2TB	~2.03TB
4	Update Production DB	1hr	~2.03TB	N/A

Figure 21.2 Workflow structures of six MTW applications with the information on computation time (CT) and input/output data size of each task [31] and [6].

fairly large. Hence, it requires careful resource planning. An instance of this workflow is expected to run for over a day.

PSMerge workflow [36] is a data-intensive application. It partitions the data into a substantial number of subsets. Hence, its workflow contains multiple tasks with a high degree of parallelism.

Note that the computation time and the data size of tasks in Fig. 21.2 are representative. We can reconfigure them according to the problem size while the workflow structure remains the same. Further information on these MTWs is available in [31] and [6].

21.5.3 Synthetic MTWs

Since the six MTW applications discussed in the previous subsection cannot cover the characteristics of all MTW applications, we also consider complex MTWs of various structures. We use the procedure described in [37] to generate multiple random MTWs. The set of parameters to define an MTW includes the number of tasks N, the number of edges, the range of computing/execution time, the range of VM requirements for a P task, and the percentage of P-task. The execution time and VM requirement of each task are randomly generated with a uniform distribution over the range. The parameters of ranges are selected to cover as many cases as possible.

Besides the above parameters, the *parallelism factor*, α, and *communication to computation ratios* (CCRs) are used to generate DAGs with different characteristics [16]. The value of α reflects the degree of parallelism of a randomly generated DAG. It defines the depth (by a uniform distribution with a mean value of $\lfloor \frac{\sqrt{N}}{\alpha} \rfloor$) and the height of a DAG (by a uniform distribution with a mean value of $\lfloor \alpha \times \sqrt{N} \rfloor$). A low α value leads to a DAG with a low degree of parallelism [38].

The *communication to computation rato* (CCR) [16] is defined as the ratio of average communication cost to the average computation cost of a DAG. A low CCR value means the workflow is computation intensive rather than communication intensive. In this study, the weight of task is generated randomly with a uniform distribution within the range of [0.1, 1.9]. We study the performance of different scheduling algorithms with respect to those workflows of low communication (CCR=0.1), medium communication (CCR=1.0), and high communication (CCR=2.0). Every set of the above parameters is used to generate several random graphs in order to avoid scattering effects. Each datum presented is the average of the results obtained from 100 randomly generated MTWs with 30000 tasks.

21.5.4 Static Strategy Evaluation

The performance comparison of different algorithms is shown in Fig. 21.3, Fig. 21.4, and Fig. 21.5, which evaluate the performance based on real-world MTW applications and randomly generated MTWs according to various CCR, α, percentage of *P-task*, and budget constraints.

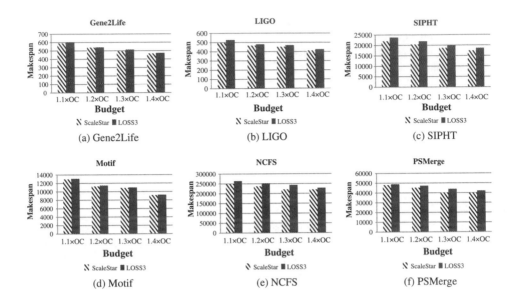

Figure 21.3 Comparison of the makespan of ScaleStar and LOSS3 for Figure 21.2.

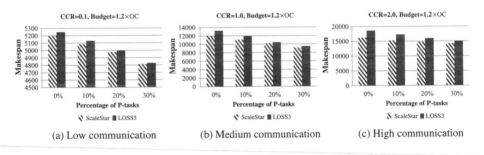

Figure 21.4 Comparison of the makespan of ScaleStar and LOSS3 for synthetic workflows.
(a) CCR=0.1; (b) CCR=1.0; (c) CCR=2.0.

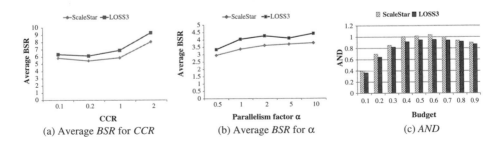

Figure 21.5 ScaleStar vs. LOSS3.

We compare static ScaleStar with LOSS3 for the six types of MTWs and calculate the makespan under different budget constraints. As shown in Fig. 21.3, the results indicate that ScaleStar outperforms LOSS3 with less makespan in most cases. The makespans can be reduced further as the increase of the budget constraints, especially for NCFS and PSMerge workflows. ScaleStar is able to achieve less makespan than LOSS3 for SIPHT because it removes most idle times by adopting *DeSlack* policy. Similarly, ScaleStar is better than LOSS3 for LIGO, whose degree of parallelism can vary widely. ScaleStar is comparable to or slightly better than LOSS3 for Gene2Life and Motif, as both assign the tasks to VMs with similar performance.

Figure 21.4 shows the average makespan of 100 synthetic workflows with different percentages of P-task. The results show that ScaleStar can achieve up to 14.3% performance improvement, and it is consistently better than LOSS3 for MTWs with low, medium, or high communication to computation ratios (CCRs). Moreover, under the same CCR value, ScaleStar is better than LOSS3, especially when the percentage of P-task is small. This result is consistent with those for the six real-world MTW applications.

In Fig. 21.5(a), we note that the monetary cost of the schedules generated by static ScaleStar is comparable with that by LOSS3 when MTWs are less computation intensive (CCR=0.1). The ScaleStar outperforms LOSS3 by a lot, especially when CCR increases, as ScaleStar is better in dealing with the communication-intensive MTWs. Figure 21.5(b) compares the BSR of ScaleStar and LOSS3 with respect to parallelism factor α. We observe that there are steady improvements of the performance by ScaleStar as the parallelism factor α increases. It shows that ScaleStar is good in scheduling highly parallelized applications. In Fig. 21.5(c), the performance of ScaleStar and LOSS3 are compared in terms of AND based on the schedule generated by HEFT. We considered nine possible budgets in [0.1, 0.9]. The value AND reflects the performance gain of a schedule against HEFT in term of makespan. Under a certain budget constraint, ScaleStar can reduce the makespan further to achieve a bigger value of AND than LOSS3. The above experiments indicate that the algorithm proposed in this chapter is able to find affordable assignments with short makespan. The ScaleStar approach applies *CA* to an assignment. Moreover, in the ScaleStar approach, the *DeSlack* policy is used to partly eliminate the idle times to reduce the monetary cost. However, in cases where the available budget is close to the cheapest budget, both ScaleStar and LOSS3 give worse makespan than that close to the money cost for the schedule generated by HEFT. This observation can contribute to the optimization in the performance of the ScaleStar algorithm.

21.5.5 Dynamic Strategy Evaluation

In the previous section, static ScaleStar is able to obtain a good performance of MTW scheduling. However, it is conducted in a static environment where there is no variation of the resource availability and information of communication time and execution time of tasks are always accurate. In a real cloud environment, the actual execution time can fluctuate at runtime. As a result, the makespan of a workflow may vary and the resources can be wasted in case of overprovisioning. In this section, we attempt to study the performance of ScaleStar under dynamic conditions. We assume that the actual execution

TABLE 21.5 The Relative Makespan of Static to Dynamic ScaleStar While the Budget is $1.2 \times OC$ ($Makespan_{static}/Makespan_{dynamic}$)

Workflows	$\mu = 1.2, \sigma = 0.2$	$\mu = 0.8, \sigma = 0.2$
Gene2Life	1.084	1.272
LIGO	1.097	1.315
SIPHT	1.018	1.131
Motif	1.009	1.124
NCFS	1.036	1.179
PSMerge	1.003	1.118

time of a task may not be the same as the estimated one. It follows a normal distribution where the estimated execution times can be shorter or longer than the actual task execution times. We conduct a series of tests and evaluate the performance of dynamic and static ScaleStar. We use a relative makespan, the ratio of makespan generated by static ScaleStar to that by dynamic ScaleStar, to study the performance improvement by the dynamic strategy. Table 21.5 summarizes the results for several MTW applications shown in Fig. 21.2.

In the first scenario, we assume that the average of actual execution times of tasks is longer than the estimated one. The second column in Table 21.5 shows the relative makespan of the static to the dynamic strategy with a mean of μ=1.2 and a standard deviation of σ=0.2. The mean of μ=1.2 means that the average value of actual execution time is 1.2 times greater than the estimated ones. The results show that dynamic strategy has little improvement over static strategy even with the runtime information. This is because it is difficult handle the cases that the actual execution time of tasks on the CP is longer than the estimated one.

In the second scenario, we assume that the average of actual execution times of tasks is shorter than the estimated one. In the third column in Table 21.5, the mean value μ=0.8 means that the average of actual execution times is 0.8 times the estimated ones. With the runtime information, the dynamic ScaleStar algorithm is able further shorten the makespan than can the static method. This scenario represents the cases that the performance of allocated resources is faster than the users' estimation. As shown in the third column in Table 21.5, dynamic strategy successfully reduces the makespan and achieves 27.2% and 31.5% improvement for Gene2Life and LIGO, respectively, compared with the static strategy. So, given the worst case execution time, the dynamic characteristic of ScaleStar allows users to add features to improve the makespan, whereas it is not easy with static strategy. So, we can apply ScaleStar more conservatively with longer execution time of tasks.

21.6 CONCLUSION

In this chapter, we addressed an important issue of scheduling large-scale MTWs on Clouds. We present budget-conscious scheduling algorithms that schedule MTWs with the consideration of the budget constraints. They allow the resources to scale up or down to maximize the performance in terms of time and cost. Static ScaleStar allocates the tasks to those VMs with higher comparative advantage (CA) and eliminates the idle times as much as possible so as to minimize the makespan as well as the monetary cost within a certain budget constraint. Dynamic ScaleStar is more flexible, to adapt to the dynamic situations where the actual execution time of tasks may be different from the estimated ones. Extensive comparative studies have been conducted to compare the performance of MTW scheduling algorithms for various real-world MTWs and synthetic MTWs of randomly generated DAGs. Results show that our proposed methods are efficient to handle various types of MTWs with considerable improvement in terms of both makespan and monetary costs.

While we addressed issues and presented strategies related to MTW handling, what needs to be done in the immediate future is to address the problem collectively with fault-tolerance and security aspects. This is especially crucial when one considers MTW applications that demand services that are remotely available and also when service disruption happens. This study is currently underway.

REFERENCES

[1] J. Kupferman, J. Silverman, P. Jara, and J. Browne. (2009) Scaling into the cloud. [Online]. Available: http://cs.ucsb.edu/jkupferman/docs/ScalingIntoTheClouds.pdf.

[2] M. Armbrust, A. Fox, R. Griffith, A. D. Joseph, R. Katz, A. Konwinski, G. Lee, D. Patterson, A. Rabkin, I. Stoica, and M. Zaharia, "A view of cloud computing," *Communications of the ACM*, Vol. 53, No. 4, pp. 50–58, April 2010.

[3] Amazon.com. (2010) Amazon elastic compute cloud. [Online]. Available: http://aws.amazon.com/ec2/.

[4] N. Doulamis, A. Doulamis, A. Litke, A. Panagakis, T. Varvarigou, and E. Varvarigos, "Adjusted fair scheduling and non-linear workload prediction for qos guarantees in grid computing," *Computer Communications*, Vol. 30, pp. 499–515, 2007.

[5] A. Mandal, K. Kennedy, C. Koelbel, G. Marin, J. Mellor-Crummey, B. Liu, and L. Johnsson, "Scheduling strategies for mapping application workflows onto the grid," in *Proc. 14th IEEE Int. Symp. High Performance Distributed Computing (HPDC)*, 2005, pp. 125–134.

[6] L. Ramakrishnan and B. Plale, "A multi-dimensional classification model for workflow characteristics," in *Workflow Approaches to New Data-centric Science, with ACM SIGMOD*, 2010, pp. 1–12.

[7] H. Zhao and R. Sakellariou, "Scheduling multiple DAGs onto heterogeneous systems," in *Proc. 20th International Parallel and Distributed Processing Symposium (IPDPS)*, 2006.

[8] Z. Yu and W. Shi, "An adaptive rescheduling strategy for grid workflow applications," in *Proc. of the IEEE International Parallel and Distributed Processing Symposium (IPDPS)*, 2007, pp. 1–8.

[9] S.X. Sun, Q. Zeng, and H. Wang, "Process-mining-based workflow model fragmentation for distributed execution," *IEEE Transactions on Systems, Man and Cybernetics, Part A: Systems and Humans*, Vol. 41, No. 2, pp. 294–310, 2011.

[10] R. Prodan and M. Wieczorek, "Bi-criteria scheduling of scientific grid workflows," *IEEE Transactions on Automation Science and Engineering*, Vol. 7, No. 2, pp. 364–376, 2010.

[11] A. Quiroz, H. Kim, M. Parashar, N. Gnanasambandam, and N. Sharma, "Towards autonomic workload provisioning for enterprise grids and clouds," in *Proc. 10th IEEE/ACM Int Grid Computing Conf*, 2009, pp. 50–57.

[12] G. Juve, E. Deelman, K. Vahi, G. Mehta, B. Berriman, B. P. Berman, and P. Maechling, "Scientific workflow applications on amazon EC2," in *Proc. 5th IEEE International Conference on E-Science Workshops*, 2009, pp. 59–66.

[13] A. Oprescu and T. Kielmann, "Bag-of-tasks scheduling under budget constraints," in *Proc. IEEE Second Int Cloud Computing Technology and Science Conf*, 2010, pp. 351–359.

[14] G. Gharooni-fard, F. Moein-darbari, H. Deldari, and A. Morvaridi, "Scheduling of scientific workflows using a chaos-genetic algorithm," *International Conference on Computational Science (ICCS)*, Vol. 1, No. 1, pp. 1445–1454, May 2010.

[15] P. Sugavanam, H.J. Siegel, A.A. Maciejewski, J. Zhang, M. Shestak, M. Raskey, A. Pippin, R. Pichel, M. Oltikar, A. Mehta, P. Lee, Y. Krishnamurthy, A. Horiuchi, K. Guru, M.Aydin, M. Al-Otaibi, and S. Ali, "Robust processor allocation for independent tasks when dollar cost for processors is a constraint," in *Proc. IEEE Int. Cluster Computing*, 2005, pp. 1–10.

[16] H. Topcuoglu, S. Hariri, and M.-Y. Wu, "Performance-effective and low complexity task scheduling for heterogeneous computing," *IEEE Transactions on Parallel and Distributed Systems*, Vol. 13, No. 3, pp. 260–274, 2002.

[17] J. Ding, Y. Wang, J. Le, and Y. Jin, "Dynamic scheduling for workflow applications over virtualized optical networks," in *IEEE Conference on Computer Communications Workshops*, 2011, pp. 127–132.

[18] P.-F. Dutot, T. N'Takpe, F. Suter, and H. Casanova, "Scheduling parallel task graphs on (almost) homogeneous multicluster platforms," *IEEE Transactions on Parallel and Distributed Systems*, Vol. 20, No. 7, pp. 940–952, 2009.

[19] S.C. Kim, S. Lee, and J. Hahm, "Push-pull: Deterministic search-based DAG scheduling for heterogeneous cluster systems," *IEEE Transactions on Parallel and Distributed Systems*, Vol. 18, No. 11, pp. 1489–1502, 2007.

[20] Y.C. Lee and A.Y. Zomaya, "On effective slack reclamation in task scheduling for energy reduction," *Journal of Information Processing Systems*, Vol. 5, No. 4, pp. 175–186, 2009.

[21] Y.C. Lee, R. Subrata, and A.Y. Zomaya, "On the performance of a dual-objective optimization model for workflow applications on grid platforms," *IEEE Transactions on Parallel and Distributed Systems*, Vol. 20, No. 9, pp. 1273–1284, 2009.

[22] Q. Zhu and G. Agrawal, "A resource allocation approach for supporting time-critical applications in grid environments," in *Proc. IEEE Int. Symp. Parallel & Distributed Processing*, 2009, pp. 1–12.

[23] T.G. Armstrong, Z. Zhang, D.S. Katz, M. Wilde, and I.T. Foster, "Scheduling many-task workloads on supercomputers: Dealing with trailing tasks," in *Proc. IEEE Workshop Many-Task Computing Grids and Supercomputers*, 2010, pp. 1–10.

[24] R. Sakellariou, H. Zhao, E. Tsiakkouri, and M.D. Dikaiakos, "Scheduling workflows with budget constraints," in *Integrated Research in Grid Computing*, ser. CoreGrid, S. Gorlatch and M. Danelutto, Eds. Pisa, Italy: Springer-Verlag, Nov. 2007.

[25] J. Yu and R. Buyya, "A budget constrained scheduling of workflow applications on utility grids using genetic algorithms," in *Proc. Workshop Workflows in Support of Large-Scale Science*, 2006, pp. 1–10.

[26] P. Sugavanam, H. J. Siegel, A.A. Maciejewski, M. Oltikar, A.M. Mehta, R. Pichel, A. Horiuchi, V. Shestak, M. Al-Otaibi, Y.G. Krishnamurthy, S.A. Ali, J. Zhang, M. Aydin, K.G. P. Lee, M. Raskey, and A.J. Pippin, "Robust static allocation of resources for independent tasks under makespan and dollar cost constraints," *Journal of Parallel and Distributed Computing*, Vol. 67(4), pp. 400–416, 2007.

[27] L.F. Bittencourt and E.R.M. Madeira, "HCOC: A cost optimization algorithm for workflow scheduling in hybrid clouds," *Journal of Internet Services and Applications*, Vol. 2, No. 3, pp. 207–227, 2011.

[28] E.-K. Byuna, Y.-S. Keeb, J. S. Kimc, and S. Maeng, "Cost optimized provisioning of elastic resources for application workflows," *Future Generation Computer Systems*, Vol. 27, No. 8, pp. 1011–1026, Oct. 2011.

[29] Y. kwong Kwok and I. Ahmad, "Static scheduling algorithms for allocating directed task graphs to multiprocessors," *ACM Computing Surveys*, Vol. 31, No. 4, pp. 406–471, 1999.

[30] R. Sakellariou and H. Zhao, "A low-cost rescheduling policy for efficient mapping of workflows on grid systems," *Journal of Scientific Programming*, Vol. 12, No. 4, pp. 253–262, 2004.

[31] S. Bharathi, A. Chervenak, E. Deelman, G. Mehta, M. Su, and K. Vahi, "Characterization of scientific workflows," in *Proc. of the 3rd Workshop on Workflows in Support of Large-Scale Science*, 2008.

[32] D. Brown, A.D. P. Brady, J. Cao, B. Johnson, and J. McNabb, "A case study on the use of workflow technologies for scientific analysis: gravitational wave data analysis." In *Workflows for e-Science*, Springer, 2006.

[33] J. Livny, H. Teonadi, M. Livny, and M. Waldor, "High-throughput, kingdom-wide prediction and annotation of bacterial non-coding rnas," *PLoS ONE*, Vol. 3, No. 9, 2008.

[34] J.L. Tilson, G. Rendon, M.-F. Ger, and E. Jakobsson, "Motifnetwork: A grid-enabled workflow for high-throughput domain analysis of biological sequences: Implications for annotation and study of phylogeny, protein interactions, and intraspecies variation," in *Proc. 7th IEEE Int. Conf. Bioinformatics and Bioengineering BIBE 2007*, 2007, pp. 620–627.

[35] B. Blanton, H. Lander, R. Luettich, M. Reed, K. Gamiel, and K. Galluppi, "Computational aspects of storm surge simulation," in *Ocean Sciences Meeting*, 2008.

[36] V. Lynch, J. Cobb, E. Farhi, S. Miller, and M. Taylor, "Virtual experiments on the neutron science teragrid gateway," in *TeraGrid*, 2008.

[37] X. Tang, K. Li, Z. Zeng, and B. Veeravalli, "A novel security-driven scheduling algorithm for precedence constrained tasks in heterogeneous distributed systems," *IEEE Transactions on Computers*, Vol. 60, No. 7, pp. 1017–1029, July 2011.

[38] M.I. Daoud and N. Kharma, "A high performance algorithm for static task scheduling in heterogeneous distributed computing systems," *Journal of Parallel and Distributed Computing*, Vol. 68 (4), pp. 399–409, 2008.

22

VIRTUALIZED ENVIRONMENT ISSUES IN THE CONTEXT OF A SCIENTIFIC PRIVATE CLOUD

Bruno Schulze, Henrique de Medeiros Klôh,
Matheus Bousquet Bandini, Antonio Roberto Mury,
Daniel Massami Muniz Yokoyama, Victor Dias de Oliveira,
Fábio André Machado Porto, and
Giacomo Victor McEvoy Valenzano

CONTENTS

Large Scale Network-Centric Distributed Systems, First Edition. Edited by Hamid Sarbazi-Azad and Albert Y. Zomaya.
© 2014 John Wiley & Sons, Inc. Published 2014 by John Wiley & Sons, Inc.

22.1 INTRODUCTION

Science and technology are becoming increasingly dependent on resources with high computing power and storage capacity. The growing development of research activities in various areas of science and industry are generating even larger and more complex data sets, making the use of high-performance computing essential to data analysis, storage, and the quick and efficient sharing of these data and results.

Cloud computing has emerged as a tool to provide access to resources meeting these demands. However, to accomplish this goal, there are still several difficulties related to information security, availability, and performance.

In this study, we focus on aspects related to performance in private Clouds, in support to scientific applications, verifying the influence of the hypervisor used, its relationship with the type of application being executed, and the overall architecture of the environment. Several works have been identified concerning the performance analysis, with the focus only on the performance of the virtual environment, not addressing the aspects concerning the operating system, the processor architecture, and their impact on performance.

In this chapter, we also present an approach differing from the others in the literature, using the virtualization advancements developed so far, the knowledge obtained by tests results to verify the use of hybrid virtual environments, that is, composed of two types of hypervisors/VMM, to support scientific applications. These hybrid models are created based on characteristics of the running applications, combining the use of different types of hypervisors, at the same time, using the best features of each one, to improve the execution performance. In our study, to facilitate the understanding, we call both the hypervisor and the VMM as "hypervisors." Also, we do not cite their brand since we are not concerned with a benchmark evaluation between them, but rather are interested in showing how the use of different hypervisors may impact the performance of the virtual environment and consequently its use in Clouds in support to scientific applications.

The study and the evaluation of the use of these hybrid models and their analysis were motivated by a real demand, to provide access to a Cloud Appliance with a graphical interface (GUI) for distributed image-processing applications. The basic idea is to offer users remote access to virtualized platforms dedicated to their needs and hosted in a Cloud environment.

22.2 RELATED WORKS

Clouds emerge as an alternative environment to support scientific computing by enabling the supply of massive, on-demand computer power just-in-time. The classical HPC model is only possible through the acquisition and immobilization of dedicated resources that eventually do not meet the specific needs of all their users. The Cloud model proposes an utility-based usage with a dynamic provisioning infrastructure (computing resources, storage and applications) to the users, being able to assist them in many ways, varying from the consolidation of the resources and the optimization of their use, to the dynamic escalation of these resources meeting their on-demand needs [1].

According to their intrinsic characteristics, clouds may change the use pattern of HPC environments. The search for high-performance environments is likely to coexist with increasingly on demand and cost-effective scientific-oriented environments, more adaptable to the needs and skills of users and more compatible with applications, albeit with loss of performance due to virtualization overheads and contention [2].

There are several related works regarding the potential use of Clouds as HPC environments, as for instance the NASA Nebula project [3], where resources are being used, for data processing, in scientific research related to ecological and economic fields, as well as in climate disaster prevention and assistance.

The Magellan Project points to the usage of Clouds in HPC, since, among its proposals, it intends to assess whether or not specific science disciplines or algorithms are well-suited to cloud computing environments. Concerning this type of use and evaluation, researchers from the Argonne Leadership Computing Facility at Argonne National Laboratory (ANL) and National Energy Research Scientific Computing Center at Lawrence Berkeley National Laboratory (NERSC) present a report pointing out that Clouds present advantages such as the capacity to allow access to additional resources, the ability to control these resources, and the sharing of these environments with other users. These are not all present in a classical HPC environment. The study results also indicate that some applications are better suited than others if considering their usage in a Cloud environment [4].

Concerning the loss of performance caused by the hypervisor, [5] shows the performance benchmark analysis between three types of hypervisors, assessing their usability in HPC environments. Analyzing their results, they notice that their hypervisor caused a loss of approximately 33% in peak performance if compared to native bare-metal. They also highlighted a high variance degree present in one of them, which may impact the performance metrics for HPC considered applications and cause errors and delays. In their analysis, they show that one of the hypervisors presents the best performance result (for Linpack and fast Fourier transform benchmarks), while another one has the best results for bandwidth and latency tests (for PingPong benchmark).

The above analysis is supported by the extensive work in [6], that performed a deeper analysis with results pointing to the diverse demands of Cloud environments facing scientific and commercial applications. Using Clouds to support HPC demands a review of the metrics used to evaluate the performance of the environments. The existing contention problems affect the overall performance, particularly communication. The results of a series of tests indicates other aspects, in addition to communication, such as: the variability of the environment, the cores' context exchange, the type of processor architecture, the virtual machine type and particularly the type of application being executed. A similar conclusion about the influence of communication, contention and type of application is observed in [7], [8], and [9]. In [10], there is a detailed analysis of the performance loss resulting from the contention effects in a virtualized environment and of the influence of the message type traffic.

From the point of view of HPC environments, the influence of the system architecture and resource contention is well presented in the work in [11], which analyzes the data obtained for two years and lists the following factors as variability causes: symmetric multiprocessing (SMP) resource contention, communication among and within the nodes, kernel process scheduling, cross-application contention, and system activities. These factors become critical if there are multiple virtual machines, and consequently many "HPC environments," which end up competing for the same resources.

The research presented so far shows the need for a deeper analysis of the effects of the hypervisor being used, its relation to the application being executed in the virtual environment, and the overall contention effects. This work presents references regarding the load of the virtual environment and its ability to pin threads to the cores, also the influence of the variability of the environment in the stability and reliability of the results. They all pose questions about the influence of the management capability of the hypervisor, its relationship to the host system, its ability to manage this relation, and how the application characteristics may contribute to the performance results.

The work in [12] presents a study of the influence of the hypervisor in a real-time operating system running in a virtual environment. It presents how the setting up of the Linux kernel may reduce the losses caused by the hypervisor and its management capability. Another aspect they addressed is the relationship among the application, the hypervisor and the host's hardware characteristics. In addition to Skinner and Krammer's work, there is the analysis of the effects of multi-core architectures. The work in [13], states the effects of data temporal locality and spatial locality and the performance degradation according to the stride size used in the read and write memory operations.

Zhuravlev et al. [14] also addressed the effects of multi-core architectures and how operating systems (OS) may interfere in the performance. They highlight how the execution time variability influences the OS scheduler trying to balance the executing threads among the cores, mostly when the cores are on the same chip, and point out cache contention and thread migration across cores. Along with cache contention, they list memory controller contention, memory bus contention, and prefetching contention as causes of performance degradation. They also present how the degree of these contentions varies from benchmark to benchmark.

The work Diamond et al. [15] adds three other elements at the architectural level influencing performance regarding multi-core processors: shared cache capacity, shared off-chip bandwidth, and DRAM page conflicts stating the nondeterministic interaction among the cores on a chip or nodes.

The related works cited above are some of the research done on performance, virtualization effects, and multi-core architecture, thus highlighting some aspects of using Clouds in support of HPC:

1. Clouds may meet an increase in demand of environments compatible with the users' skills and applications.

2. Clouds may provide resources on demand with cost-effectiveness, albeit with a loss of performance.
3. The fact that there are applications that are better suited for Cloud environments.
4. The fact that the variability in the environmental contention impacts significantly the results.
5. The relationship among the type of hypervisor, the application, the hardware architecture, and the obtained performance.

Based on the knowledge above and the experiments presented in the next section, we show how the impact of the hypervisor may be either positive or negative, depending on the type of environment architecture and application. For comparison, different types of hypervisors were used, with different approaches to dealing with the real resources (preemption policy, processing capacity, bandwidth capacity, and I/O management). The test results suggest that a hybrid virtual environment, with various types of hypervisors at the same time, chosen according to their characteristics, host architecture, and application type, may achieve a better performance and less variability in comparison to a single type.

22.3 METHODOLOGY

Three different experiments with different sets of tests are carried out to assess the influence of the hypervisor type and the application type running in the environment. We create and compare the results of a hybrid virtual environment and how this approach may contribute to reduce the performance loss. The last experiment evaluates the performance of a database application.

22.3.1 Experiments and Objectives

The tests and analysis are focused at the application level. The first experiment, the most common one, uses two types of benchmarks to evaluate processing and communication capabilities. The second experiment uses a hybrid environment approach based on a cluster composed of a hypervisor type for the head node and another type for the working nodes. Both experiments use a graphical application to explore the influence of graphical access on the performance and to verify how the hypervisor deals with this type of overhead. The third experiment evaluates the use of virtual environments supporting database applications by testing the transaction processing and the communication capability.

22.3.2 Experimental Infrastructure

The first experiment uses five servers, each one with two quad core Xeon 5520 (2.26GHz) with hyper-threading (HT) technology and virtualization instructions, 12 GB of DDR3 RAM (1333), and Gigabit Ethernet connection. The second uses five servers, each one with two six core Xeon 5650 (2.67GHz) with hyper-threading (HT) technology and virtualization instructions, 24 GB of DDR3 RAM (1333), and Gigabit Ethernet connection. The used benchmark packages for these two experiments are:

1. The ParPac benchmark tool, evaluating the processing capability of both the virtualized and the real environments. The ParPac Application Benchmark is a lattice Boltzmann code, simulating the dynamics of a fluid streaming through a porous structure. It calculates the structure's permeability and returns the performance calculation in Gflops. The package provides automatic domain decomposition, load balancing and optimization of the communication among the nodes [16].
2. The B_eff benchmark [17] measures the accumulated bandwidth of the communication network for a parallel and/or distributed computing systems. Several message sizes, communication patterns, and methods are used. The algorithm uses an average to take into account short and long messages being transferred with different bandwidth values in real applications.

The third experiment uses four servers, each one with two quad core Xeon 5520 (2.26GHz) with hyper-threading capability and virtualization instructions, 12 GB of DDR3 RAM (1333), and Gigabit Ethernet.

This experiment uses two different database benchmark packages:

1. One package is the Pg-Bench benchmark, which is an implementation based on the TPC-B benchmark. The TPC-B benchmark is a database benchmark approved by the Transaction Processing Performance Council (TPC) [18]. The Pg-Bench allows database stress tests, measuring the system transaction capability (transactions per second). The tests use Pg-bench tools [19], to simplify the benchmark execution. Uses a script that executes a number of tests defined by the user, collecting the results and calculating the average number of transactions per second.
2. The Blender and DrQueue applications. The Blender is an integrated application that allows the creation of 2D and 3D contents, providing modeling, texturing, lighting, animation, and video post-processing [20]. DrQueue is an open source distributed render farm manager and is used to distribute the jobs among the nodes [21].
3. The second database benchmark package is the DBT-5 (DataBase Test 5), which is an open-source implementation of the TPC-E benchmark. The DBT-5 is an online transaction processing system (OLTP), executing multiple transaction types, with a balanced mixture of disk input/output and processor usage [22].
4. The last database test simulates an exclusively virtualized data access environment analyzing the behavior of a database server against the gradual increase in the number of connected clients, checking the need to expand the infrastructure by adding more virtual servers as soon as the performance degrades. This experiment is not intended to assess and compare the performance of a virtual database server with native bare-metal, but rather to set a baseline for the number of clients

that the server is able to attend, identifying the optimal situation to expand or to contract the virtual infrastructure.

22.4 EXPERIMENTS

The first experiment uses two hypervisor types chosen for their same virtualization technology (full virtualization), open source, already incorporated "libvirt" libraries, and the possibility of installation and usage without modification of the host OS kernel. All hypervisors and applications are installed as-is, without any special settings to improve performance. We generate 30 samples for each test and evaluate based on the average, considering the 95% confidence interval.

22.4.1 Experiment 1: Influence of the Hypervisors on Performance

This experiment addresses the influence of the chosen hypervisor and access type by comparing the application performance in each one with native bare-metal. In this experiment it is possible to detail the loss caused by the access type to the virtual environment: by SSH (Secure Shell), for both types of hypervisor used, by Remote Desktop Protocol (RDP), for just one type; or by VNC (Virtual Network Computing), for the other one. The goal is to determine the effect on performance, caused by these type of accesses on the virtual environment. The protocol used in each experiment is the native protocol supported by the hypervisor used.

The virtual environments are all created with the same settings. Each one has 8 cores and 10 GB of memory, since one hypervisor type does not allow allocation of all the available real memory, in order to reserve some memory to the host OS. Despite this limitation in memory allocation, the tests conducted with ParPac do not influence the final results. Figure 22.1 presents the average values in Gflops for each test.

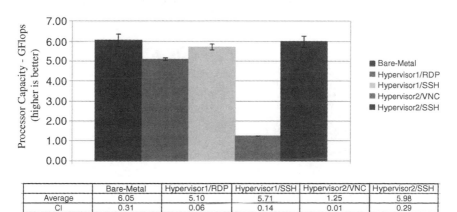

	Bare-Metal	Hypervisor1/RDP	Hypervisor1/SSH	Hypervisor2/VNC	Hypervisor2/SSH
Average	6.05	5.10	5.71	1.25	5.98
CI	0.31	0.06	0.14	0.01	0.29

Figure 22.1 Native bare-metal–virtual environments comparison: SSH–GUI access (higher is better).

The results indicate that both hypervisors, with SSH access, are very similar in terms of performance to native bare-metal. The Hypervisor1 presents a loss of 5.6% and the Hypervisor2 presents a loss of 1.2%. For the Hypervisor2, considering the confidence interval, the loss is statistically null. However, for the Hypervisor2 accessing its virtual environment through a GUI, the performance loss is 79%, while for Hypervisor1 is 15%.

Results in Figure 22.1 indicate that the most appropriate connection via graphical interface (GUI) is for Hypervisor1, with a loss up to 15%. Without such a demand, the use of Hypervisor2 is the more appropriate, with practically no loss. The loss recorded for Hypervisor1 and Hypervisor2, concerning SSH access, is due to their management capabilities and the hosting OS (I/O management and mapping between virtual and real memory).

With a GUI for Hypervisor2, there is a loss due to the VNC protocol that depends on the pixel format and the synchronization between client and server. When using VNC access, there is a race condition between the VNC protocol and the ParPac messages caused by a loss of synchronization due to an intensive message exchange in the environment. As a result, the performance of the Hypervisor2 is reduced 4.8 times, in comparison to its performance with SSH.

Although the use of a GUI is not obligatory in HPC environments, the test intends to evaluate the hybrid hypervisor architecture in another ongoing project [23]. In this context, we need to allow GUI access to virtual appliances running simulations.

To determine the effects of the concurrent usage, we compare the tests of two instances of the ParPac benchmark running concurrently in native bare-metal, with two instances running separately, each one in a virtual environment in the same native bare-metal at the same time. The virtual environments are created using both hypervisors connected via SSH.

Figure 22.2 presents the results (AVERAGE in Gflops and CI the confidence interval) for the concurrent executions of the ParPac benchmark. Hypervisor2 presents better results than those for native bare-metal (11.3% better) and 23.2% better than for Hypervisor1. Hypervisor1 presents a loss in performance of 10%, in comparison to native

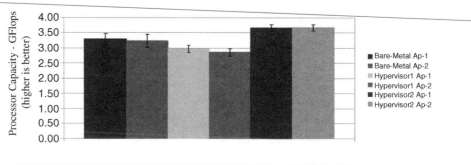

	Bare-Metal Ap-1	Bare-Metal Ap-2	Hypervisor1 Ap-1	Hypervisor1 Ap-2	Hypervisor2 Ap-1	Hypervisor2 Ap-2
Average	3.29	3.23	2.97	2.86	3.66	3.67
CI	0.18	0.21	0.12	0.12	0.11	0.10

Figure 22.2 Concurrency effect on native bare-metal and virtual environment (higher is better).

bare-metal. This may be explained by maintaining the process/virtualized environment on the same core, reducing the loss caused by the preemption of the processes, the context changes between cores, and the associated memory reading/writing [24]. In this case, Hypervisor1 is not able to manage the concurrency and presents an increased loss: 13% in the worst case and 8% in the best case.

These results for Hypervisor2 confirm the advantages that may be achieved in using virtualization, that is, the encapsulation of the task in a virtual environment, reducing concurrency, and preemption effects. These experiments show that Hypervisor2 presents better performance results when accessing a virtual environment via SSH (processing only). But when there is the need of a GUI access, the loss becomes significant for Hypervisor2, and Hypervisor1 shows better performance.

22.4.2 Experiment 2: Hybrid Virtualized Environment Evaluation

Based on the results of the work listed in Section 22.2 and the results for Experiment 1, we create a virtual environment for this experiment using two different hypervisors at the same time. This is to verify the performance of the hybrid approach. Blender and DrQueue perform the same type of tests for Experiment 1 (processing and communication intensive) with an application using a GUI and a distributed processing environment.

Figure 22.3 presents an example of the hybrid model architecture, consisting of a virtual cluster, with the master node based on a Hypervisor1 virtual environment and the working nodes based on Hypervisor2 virtual environments.

This second experiment addresses the performance of the hybrid cluster (using two different types of hypervisors) in comparison to the virtual clusters that use only one type of hypervisor. It intends to verify the influence of the hypervisor characteristics regarding the type of application running on the virtual environment.

The master node is created with 16 cores and 16 GB of memory. It is not possible to create a virtual machine with all memory offered by native bare-metal due to the restriction already mentioned before. The limitation of eight cores in the working nodes is due to the Blender demand of 1.5GB of memory for each rendering. This test uses a "Diskless VM," which is a type of virtual environment without any real disk space, and created during the execution, using only the host memory and processor power.

In this experiment, each sample processes 160 frames, each frame uses an average of 1.4 GB of memory per process, and the processing load at each core reaches 100%.

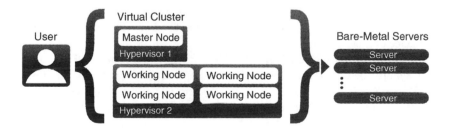

Figure 22.3 Hybrid model architecture.

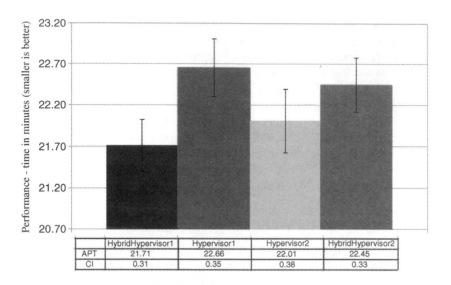

	HybridHypervisor1	Hypervisor1	Hypervisor2	HybridHypervisor2
APT	21.71	22.66	22.01	22.45
CI	0.31	0.35	0.38	0.33

Figure 22.4 Virtual environments performance comparison (smaller is better).

The results in Figure 22.4 indicate the average processing time (APT) for each sample and the corresponding confidence interval (CI).

Four virtualized cluster environments are created: the HybridHypervisor1 model with the master node based on Hypervisor1 type and the working nodes based on Hypervisor2 type: the Hypervisor1 model with all cluster nodes based on Hypervisor1 type; the Hypervisor2 model with all cluster nodes based on Hypervisor2 type; and a Hybrid-Hypervisor2 model with the master node based on Hypervisor2 type and the working nodes based on Hypervisor1 type.

The HybridHypervisor1 model achieves an average performance slightly better than the other ones, 4% better if compared to Hypervisor1, 1% better if compared to Hypervisor2, and 3% if compared to Hybrid Hypervisor2 model, but if considering the confidence interval it only outperforms Hypervisor1 model.

However, if considering 30 samples and measuring the difference in a time basis, the second best processing model (Hypervisor2) spends 9 minutes more in processing time, which is almost half of the time of one sample of the HybridHypervisor1. This result confirms the need for a more detailed knowledge of the characteristics of the application and the hypervisor used to virtualize the environment and how this may contribute to the performance of an application execution.

Despite the performance advantage being not so significant, the HybridHypervisor1 model proves to be much more stable. The number of frames with failures for the HybridHypervisor1 model is 67% less than for the Hypervisor2 model. These failure rates may be attributed to the communication management capability handled by the master node, as presented in Experiment 1.

For a better understanding of why the values for the HybridHypervisor1 model and the Hypervisor2 model are quite close, it is necessary to understand the test and its

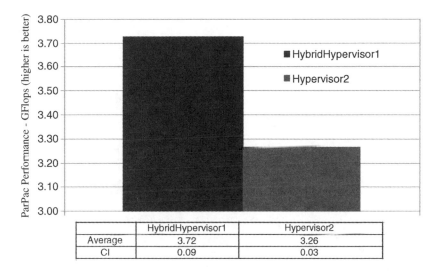

	HybridHypervisor1	Hypervisor2
Average	3.72	3.26
CI	0.09	0.03

Figure 22.5 ParPac Benchmark Hybrid–Hypervisor2-Hybrid model (higher is better).

meaning. In Experiment 2 above, Blender is used to render the frames in the nodes and DrQueue is responsible for managing and scheduling the tasks between them. In this configuration, the master node is responsible for managing the task without a large load and to provide GUI access. All the processing is done with Blender in the working nodes. In this case, with the load in the master node not so high, the influence of the VNC access is not so significant.

Analyzing the communication process between Blender and DrQueue, it is necessary to state that Blender does not participate in the communication process, being only responsible for processing the frames. The entire communication process is managed by DrQueue in the master node. These results indicate that the best option may be an architecture having Hypervisor1 responsible for all communication and control, and Hypervisor2 for the working nodes.

Figure 22.5 presents the comparison between the HybridHypervisor1 and Hypervisor2 model using the ParPac Benchmark. In this case, the processing load of the master node is much higher than in the previous experiment, and thus the influence of the VNC access is much more noticeable. The Hypervisor2 performance loss, in this case, increases to 12% when compared to the Hybrid model. The difference in a time basis with 30 samples has 53.25 minutes less processing time for the HybridHypervisor1 model than for the Hypervisor2 model.

Another important aspect observed during the tests is the performance variability observed in each environment. Occurrence of flaws is possible during the frame rendering. DrQueue registers these failures and the nodes where the failure occurred, in order to resubmit the frame. Reviewing the record of a failure and comparing this record with the values of the variance in each environment, it is possible to observe a direct relationship between them. Figure 22.6 presents the normalized values of fault, variance, and performance. We observe that the greater the number of failures recorded, the greater

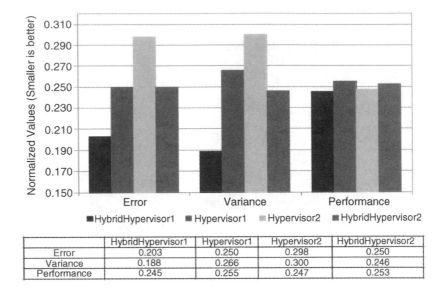

	HybridHypervisor1	Hypervisor1	Hypervisor2	HybridHypervisor2
Error	0.203	0.250	0.298	0.250
Variance	0.188	0.266	0.300	0.246
Performance	0.245	0.255	0.247	0.253

Figure 22.6   Error, variability, and performance comparison (smaller is better).

the variance of the environment (the Pearson product-moment correlation coefficient is 0.86). Thus, the variance value in this case reflects the stability and the quality of the environment in dealing with the problem.

The Hybrid environment presents the best quality result, since it has the lowest variance value. In Figure 22.6, regarding performance, there is no relation between the overall performance value and the variance. We believe this is due to the type of application being executed and the reprocessing error capabilities in each environment and despite the Hypervisor2 model having the greatest amount of error and variance, this is offset by its performance.

For the tests with ParPac, all nodes are subject to a processing load with a communication rate much more intensive than for the tests with Blender/DrQueue. The size of the message block is also different: for ParPac, high rates and short blocks; for Blender/DrQueue, low rates and longer blocks. This type of influence is also noticed and detailed in [10]. The clusters used to run the tests are the same ones used in the previous experiment.

For the B_eff benchmark, the results indicate one of the great restrictions about using Clouds—the bandwidth capacity. In this case, the real environment is 2.2 times the capacity of the best virtualized environment (Fig. 22.7). Evaluating only the virtualized environment, both of the hybrid architectures have less transfer rate capacity than the ones using a single hypervisor (between 5% and 27% less). The reason for these results is the communication bottleneck in the hypervisor and the different capacity in receiving and treating different message sizes.

The cluster with the Hypervisor2 as master node (HybridHypervisor2) is the best among the hybrids, because the working nodes composed by Hypervisor1 offsets the

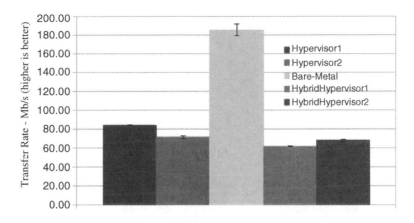

Figure 22.7   B_eff benchmark–Transfer rate–Mb/s (higher is better).

limitation of the master node, treating more efficiently the different message sizes. Although the hybrid cluster has nodes with Hypervisor1, the Hypervisor2 cluster is better, even with the communication bottleneck. This is because of the master node and the working nodes has the same virtual environment and in this case, compatible message protocol.

22.4.3 Experiment 3: Virtualized Database

This experiment presents the influence of the hypervisor in a database application running in a virtual environment. Two database benchmark packages are used, Pg-Bench and DBT-5.

The Pg-Bench benchmark is characterized by the execution of a sequence of SQL commands, (five times the following commands: SELECT, INSERT, and UPDATE, per transaction) by the repeated execution of this sequence, stressing the transaction capacity of the database. After each sequence, it calculates the average rate of transactions per second) [19].

The above sequence of commands is made in four different scales (1,10,100,1000), where the scale 1 corresponds to 100,000 tuples of the tables, and for each scale there is the simulation of concurrent access of 1, 2, 4, 8, 16, and 32 users.

The architecture of native bare-metal used in these tests allowed using hyper-threading technology (HT). To verify the effects of HT in the virtual environments, tests are conducted enabling (disabling) HT in native bare-metal and changing the number of cores in the virtual resources accordingly. Concerning the created virtual environments, there is one with 8 cores, corresponding to the actual number of cores of the bare metal server, and another with 16 cores, corresponding to the total real and virtual cores created with the use of HT.

This experiment tests another type of virtualization approach (BareVZ), characterized by the nonexistence of a hypervisor, where the virtualization is achieved by the creation of isolated containers, each one corresponding to a virtual environment, running over native bare-metal.

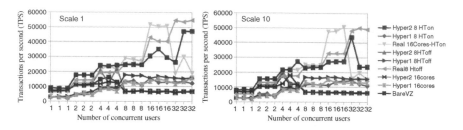

Figure 22.8   Scales 1 and 10 transactions per second evaluation.

Figure 22.8 shows the results of scales 1 and 10, and Fig. 22.9 the results of scales 100 and 1000. An initial analysis of the graphics indicate that scales 1, 10, and 100 have two regions that stand out against the others: the region related to 4 concurrent users and the region of 16 and 32 concurrent users.

The scale 1000 corresponds to the saturation region of native bare-metal and virtual environments, being possible to notice that the BareVZ has the best performance between the virtualized environment. Ranging from 15% better performance for 1 user, to approximately equal for 4 concurrent users, up to a performance loss of 20% for 32 concurrent users if compared to native bare-metal with HT disabled. If compared to native bare-metal with HT enabled, BareVZ presents a gain ranging from 53% for one user, to practically equal for 16 concurrent users, until a loss of performance of 7% for 32 concurrent users. Hypervisor2 has the best performance between the hypervisors, ranging from a 14% (average) better performance for one user to practically equal (5% in the best case) for two concurrent users and to a loss of performance of 25% for 32 concurrent users, if compared to native bare-metal with HT enabled.

It is important to note that the transactions per second (TPS) for this scale is much lower if compared to the other scales. In this scale, the maximum rate achieves 400 TPS, unlike the other scales that reach 55,000 TPS. The better performance observed in this case results from the processing capacity and not from the I /O capacity.

Regarding the other scales (1, 10, 100), by analyzing the region with four concurrent users (Fig. 22.10 indicates a sample in Scale 10), this region presents a very interesting information related to the virtual environments processing management by the hosting OS. Although Hypervisor2 presents a better performance than the Hypervisor1 (34%),

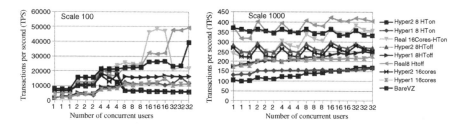

Figure 22.9   Scales 100 and 1000 transactions per second (TPS) evaluation.

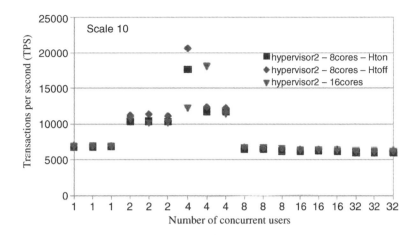

<u>Figure 22.10</u>   Scale 10 sample—Variability with four concurrent users.

its variability is much larger (with an average deviation of 3000 TPS compared to a 450 TPS average deviation for Hypervisor1). To understand the reason for this variability, it is necessary to know that Hypervisor1 pins its processes to a particular core as default configuration and runs its process with the same privileges of the OS process. Hypervisor2, as a default configuration, does not pin its process and they execute as a normal user process by the hosting OS. So during the process execution these differences explain this variability when associated with the number of cores in each processor (4), the allocation of the process and preemption rules used by the hosting OS.

The region encompassing 16 to 32 users also presents important results. These results are noteworthy, although not linked to the effects of virtualization, object of this work. Analyzing the results of native bare-metal in this region, it indicates the effect of enabling (disabling) of HT. For the specific case of these tests, with 16 concurrent users for native bare-metal, with HT disabled, results in 36% less performance if compared to native bare-metal with HT enabled. With 32 users this situation is reversed, and native bare-metal performance with HT disabled is about three times better than native bare-metal performance with HT enabled. The reason for this change in the results is due to:

- For 32 concurrent users, since the number of process with HT enabled is twice the number of real cores, it results in two "stress" processes per core competing with each other, causing a significant loss in performance, as indicated in Fig. 22.9.
- For 16 concurrent users, since this is a stress test, HT enabled contributes positively to the management of the processes. Since the number of concurrent stress processes (users) is equal to the number of real cores, the hosting OS may schedule each process to a real core, avoiding the problem of contention.

Figure 22.11 presents the same effect reported before, but within a virtualized environment. The virtual machine runs with 8 cores in native bare-metal and with HT disabled resulting in a better performance than the same virtual machine running in

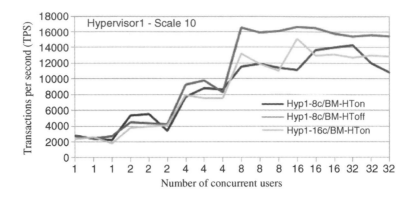

Figure 22.11   Hypervisor 1—Scale 10 sample: Hyper-threading use comparison.

native bare-metal with HT enabled, and still better when running with 16 cores. The reason is the concurrency between the process at the same core, since the hosting OS is unaware of the real and the virtual cores. When the competition between the processes is not significant, the losses suffered by the virtual environment is around 11%, and as soon as the competition between the processes arises, the maximum loss reaches 75% for scale 100.

In the DBT-5 tests (Fig. 22.12), one can see that all three virtual environments have almost the same response, ranging the performance loss from 72% (1, 2, and 4 concurrent users), to 90% for 8 users and to 68% for 16 users. For 64 users, native bare-metal and virtual environments begin to saturate, and, in this case, the virtual environment has a slight improvement ranging from 10% (Hypervisor2) to 20% BareVZ. For 128 users, all the environments saturate, and although the results for Hypervisor1 is better than for native bare-metal, it only completes half of the tests. After 20 tests, the virtual environments are unavailable, due to a damage in the file system.

The last experiment simulates an exclusively virtualized data access environment analyzing the behavior of a database server against a gradual increase of the number

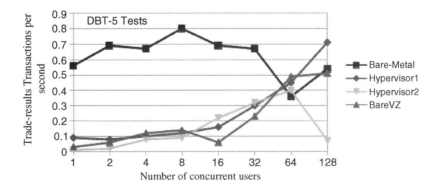

Figure 22.12   Trade-results transactions in DBT-5 tests.

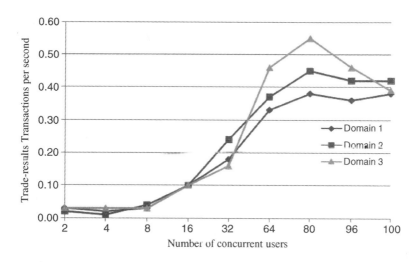

Figure 22.13   Trade-results transactions domain tests.

of connected clients. A metric for this experiment is the number of TPS to analyze the behavior of a virtual database server under stress. The server receiving requests from three different domains, simulated by DBT-5 hosted in three different virtual machines with the same hypervisor. The number of clients varying from 2, 4, 8, 16, 32, 64, 80, 96, and 100 for each of the three domains.

For these experiments, some configuration parameters were identified, allowing the maximization of the database server usage. A PostgreSQL parameter needs to be modified to allow it to receive up to 400 simultaneous connections, supporting up to 300 for the three domains (100 each). Moreover, it is necessary to increase the OS kernel shared memory, by changing the maximum size of a shared memory segment (SHMMAX) and the maximum page allocation for shared memory (SHMALL).

In Fig. 22.13, considering the results related to TPS, the system presents a scalable behavior between 48 clients (16 per domain) and 240 clients (80 per domain), representing the best usage rate of the database server. Above 240 clients, the server tends to limit the performance gain in accordance to the consumption of database server resources.

Also noteworthy is that, from experiments involving 64 simultaneous connections per domain, the use of memory swap by the DBMS results in order to meet the demand. For this reason, in this test set, it is possible to conclude that the maximized usage of a database server in an exclusively virtualized environment occurs when it attends between 192 and 240 simultaneous connections, depending on the system available memory and swap.

22.4.4   Result Analysis

In Experiment 1, Hypervisor2 has a better performance than Hypervisor1 and, depending on the application, even better than native bare-metal environment. This is because the Hypervisor2 is able to encapsulate the virtual environment, making the application less subject to the variability of the external environment. However, in this study case, the Hypervisor2 does not have a good performance when GUI access to the virtual environment is required. In Experiment 1, when this type of connection is implemented, the performance is drastically reduced.

Experiment 2 shows how the relation between the type of hypervisor and the type of application may cause a significant difference in performance. It also shows how the knowledge of their characteristics and the use of the correct configuration (Hypervisor plus application type) can improve the performance. Specifically in this work, the results also indicate that the use of a hybrid virtualized environment may be a solution, since the best features of each type of Hypervisor may be used, according to the application.

Regarding the communication tests, the difference among the hypervisors communication buffer plays the major role in the performance results. Results indicate the constraints of the virtualized environments demanding further development. Results also indicate that the hybrid model suffers more, because the influence of the different capacities in dealing with the message sizes and rates, resulting in a loss in performance.

For the case of the Database Experiment, the use of virtualization, however, should be done carefully, aiming to minimize the performance problems that may occur due to the hypervisor. For relational database servers, the I/O operations in the executed transactions should be considered. Moreover, one should consider how the hypervisors and the OS manage the concurrent requests in the virtualized database server.

Considering the database systems' performance evaluation, some issues, such as the chosen database management system (DBMS) and the hardware architecture, may impact directly on the system's performance. These characteristics, however, may be controlled by the system's administrator, as they may be changed taking the necessary precautions, thus reducing their criticality for the system. The factor outside control that affects the performance of database systems is the number of clients that simultaneously access a database server. The system's inability to behave in a scalable way may compromise its integrity, impacting its performance, or causing services to be unavailable.

By analyzing this information, it is possible to measure whether a virtual database server is able to comply with quality criteria, as well as to define if and when a new virtual server is needed, in order to avoid resource idleness. It mainly allows one to conclude whether it is relevant to use virtualized resources to provide a database server infrastructure aiming to enable load balance and to reduce costs. For this purpose, the possibility arises of using virtual resources, within the paradigm of cloud computing, as a strategy to make it possible to efficiently manage computing resources. This can be achieved throughout the activation or deactivation of virtual database servers, according to the number of requests, allowing one to reduce the acquisition costs and to maximize the usage of physical servers.

22.5 CONCLUSION

The work being done regarding the creation, deployment, and management of virtualized environments and the questions raised about the real benefits that it may represent to the research being done and for scientific applications provided the motivation for this study.

The Magellan Report answers some questions about how to improve the performance of virtual environments, to the benefit of the scientific community, while also posing new ones. To better address these questions, it is necessary to extend the understanding of, but not limited to, the processor architecture, the hypervisor, and the application types.

The understanding of the processor architecture, mostly the multi-core processors, memory layers/contention, and how the scheduling OS process works gives us the basis to better understand the hypervisors and how they interact with the processes/applications running within the virtual environment.

Some limitations of this work are the few types of applications tested thus far, but these preliminary results indicate that the performance of the virtual environment may be improved by use of a pool of hypervisors, with those that best fit the applications to be executed. The main purpose of this chapter is to highlight the relation between the hypervisors and the application types being executed, indicating that a hybrid model that combines more than one hypervisor, in some cases, may improve the performance results and the stability of the environment, using the best characteristics of each hypervisor.

We believe that this knowledge contributes to the understanding of how to better use Clouds as a HPC environment supporting scientific applications and the decisions that should be taken into account before porting these applications to this environment:

1. Which should be the processor architecture to be used in the hosting environment?
2. Which should be the workload of these environments and which preemptive policies should be used?
3. Which type of application may be hosted, whether processor intensive, communication intensive, database application, and others?
4. Which should be the variability of the environment?

From the analysis of the results, regarding the use of Clouds as a HPC environment to support scientific applications, we point out the following:

1. Further studies are needed to determine the classes of applications that should be ported to the Clouds, contributing to the optimization of the usage of the resources and for better performance.
2. Clouds represent a great opportunity to make widespread the use of distributed applications, whether for research, teaching, testing, or development.
3. The relation between the characteristics of the application and the characteristics of the type of the hypervisor should be considered in the development of Clouds schedulers.
4. Further analysis about the influence of the processor architecture and the use of virtualized GPU architectures is needed.

We conclude that Clouds represent a useful addition of resources, supplying the increasing demand of computational power to solve scientific application problems. Some issues that remain, however, concern the virtual environments themselves, the computer architecture to be used in native bare-metal servers, and the communication management capability. Many advances are being observed right now, concerning these issues, but even with these advances, we consider that the evaluation and knowledge of the variability of the Cloud environment, and choosing the best hypervisor/computer architecture fitting the application needs, is essential before porting scientific applications to a Cloud environment.

22.6 GLOSSARY

APT (Average Processing Time)—Statistical measure of the arithmetic mean of the data set time values, spent to execute one sample or one round of the experiment.

CI (Confidence Interval)—The interval in which a measure of a sample may be contained into a given probability.

DBMS (Database Management System)

HPC (High-Performance Computing)—Use of massive computational power for developing and running parallel processing algorithms.

HT (Hyper-threading)—Intel's proprietary technology created to improve the parallelization. It consists of duplicating certain sections of the real processor, creating two virtual processors for each real one, allowing the OS sharing the workload between them.

Hypervisor—Same as VMM, it is one of hardware virtualization types, consisting of a software layer between the hardware and operating system of the virtual machine or virtual environment, responsible for compatibility and management of host's real resources by the virtual environments.

Native Bare-Metal—Real server used to running application without any virtualization layer.

OS (Operating System(s))

RDP (Remote Desktop Protocol)—Microsoft proprietary protocol, developed to give access to another computer trough a Graphical User Interface.

RTOS (Real Time Operating System)—A computer operating system designed and configured to respond to a input within a specific time limit.

SMP (Symmetric Multiprocessing)—Computer architecture that provides multiple computer processor units and shared memory, controlled by a single OS instance, able to processes a single application simultaneously.

SQL (Structured Query Language)—Is a relational database programing language.

TPS (Transactions per Second)

VMM (Virtual Machine Management)—Same as Hypervisor, it is one of hardware virtualization types consisting of a software layer between the hardware and operating system of the virtual machine or virtual environment, responsible for compatibility and management of host's real resources by the virtual environments.

VNC (Virtual Network Computing)—A Olivetti Research Laboratory protocol developed to give access to another computer through a Graphical Interface. Currently an open source GNU General Public License.

ACKNOWLEDGMENTS

This work has been supported by the Brazilian Ministry of Science and Technology and Innovation (MCTI) and the National Council for Technological and Scientific Development (CNPq - PCI/LNCC) and Research Foundation of the State of Rio de Janeiro (Faperj - E-26/112.221/2008).

REFERENCES

[1] C. Vecchiola, S. Pandey, and R. Buyya (2009). "High-performance cloud computing: A view of scientific applications." *2009 10th International Symposium on Pervasive Systems Algorithms and Networks*, p. 13.

[2] C.A. Lee (2010). "A perspective on scientific cloud computing." In *Proceedings of the 19th ACM International Symposium on High Performance Distributed Computing, HPDC '10*, pp. 451–459, New York, ACM.

[3] NASA (2011). Nasa nebula cloud. http://nebula.nasa.gov/about/,

[4] DoF (2011). U.S. Department of Energy - The Magellan Report on cloud computing for science. http://magellan.alcf.anl.gov/.

[5] A.J. Younge, R. Henschel, J.T. Brown, G. von Laszewski, J. Qiu, and G.C. Fox (2011). "Analysis of virtualization technologies for high performance computing environments." In *Proc. of the 4th Intl. Conf. on Cloud Computing (Cloud 2011)*, Washington, DC. IEEE.

[6] P. Bientinesi, R. Iakymchuk, and J. Napper, (2010). *HPC on Competitive Cloud Resources.* Springer US.

[7] K.R. Jackson (2010). "Performance of hpc applications on the Amazon web services cloud." *The 2nd Intl. Conference on Cloud Computing 2010 - Cloudcom2010.*

[8] Q. He, S. Zhou, B. Kobler, D. Duffy, and T. McGlynn (2010). "Case study for running HPC applications in public clouds." In *Proceedings of the 19th ACM International Symposium on High Performance Distributed Computing, HPDC '10*, pp. 395–401, New York, ACM.

[9] Y. El-Khamra, H. Kim, S. Jha, and M. Parashar (2010). "Exploring the performance fluctuations of hpc workloads on clouds." *Analysis*, pp. 383–387.

[10] J. Ekanayake and G. Fox (2009). "High performance parallel computing with clouds and cloud technologies." *Cloud Computing and Software Services Theory and Techniques*, (Vm):20–38.

[11] D. Skinner and W. Kramer (2005). "Understanding the causes of performance variability in hpc workloads." In *Workload Characterization Symposium, 2005. Proceedings of the IEEE International*, pp. 137–149.

[12] J. Zhang, K. Chen, B. Zuo, R. Ma, Y. Dong, and H. Guan (2010). "Performance analysis towards a kvm-based embedded real-time virtualization architecture." In *Computer Sciences and Convergence Information Technology (ICCIT)*, 2010 5th Intl. Conf. on, pp. 421–426.

[13] T.A. Simon and J.W. McGalliard (2009). "Observation and analysis of the multicore performance impact on scientific applications." *Concurrency and Computation: Practice and Experience*, 21(17):2213–2231.

[14] S. Zhuravlev, S. Blagodurov, and A. Fedorova (2010). "Addressing shared resource contention in multicore processors via scheduling." In *ASPLOS*, pp. 129–142.

[15] J.R. Diamond, M. Burtscher, J.D. McCalpin, B.-D. Kim, S.W. Keckler, and J.C. Browne (2011). "Evaluation and optimization of multicore performance bottlenecks in supercomputing applications." In *ISPASS*, pages 32–43.

[16] ParPac (2011). Integrated performance analysis of computer systems. http://www.ipacs-benchmark.org.

[17] Beff (2011). Effective bandwidth benchmark. http://www.ipacs-benchmark.org.

[18] TCPBenchmark (2012). Transaction processing performance council. http://www.tpc.org/.

[19] PostgreSQL (2012). Postgresql benchmark. http://www.postgresql.org/docs/devel/static/pgbench.html.

[20] BlenderFoundation (2011). Blender. http://www.blender.org.

[21] DrQueue (2011). http://www.drqueue.org. DrQueue distributed render manager services.

[22] R.O. Nascimento and P.R.M. Maciel (2010). "Dbt-5: An open-source tpc-e implementation for global performance measurement of computer systems." *Computing and Informatics*, 29(5):719–740.

[23] J.F. Fernandes, B. Schulze, and A.R. Mury (2011). "Neblina—espacos virtuais de trabalho para uso em aplicacoes cientificas." In *Simposio Brasileiro de Redes de Computadores - SBRC 2011 - Salao de Ferramentas*.

[24] J.R. Shameen Akhter (2006). *Multi-core Programming: Increasing Performance Through Software Multi-threading*. Intel Press, US.

Part 5

OTHER TOPICS RELATED TO NETWORK-CENTRIC COMPUTING AND ITS APPLICATIONS

23

IN-ADVANCE BANDWIDTH SCHEDULING IN e-SCIENCE NETWORKS

Yan Li, Eunsung Jung, Sanjay Ranka,
Nageswara S. Rao, and Sartaj Sahni

CONTENTS

Large Scale Network-Centric Distributed Systems, First Edition. Edited by Hamid Sarbazi-Azad and
Albert Y. Zomaya.
© 2014 John Wiley & Sons, Inc. Published 2014 by John Wiley & Sons, Inc.

23.1 INTRODUCTION

Many large-scale scientific and commercial applications produce large amounts of data, of the order of terabytes to petabytes, which must be transferred across wide-area networks. For example, for an e-Science application, data sets produced on a supercomputer in Los Angeles may need to be streamed to a remote storage center in Houston for analysis. The results are then sent to Atlanta and visualized there to guide the next round of experiments. When data providers and consumers are geographically distributed, dedicated connections are needed to effectively support a variety of remote tasks [2]. More specifically, dedicated bandwidth channels are critical in these tasks to offer (i) large capacity for massive data transfer operations, and (ii) dynamically stable bandwidth for monitoring and steering operations. It is important that these channels be available when the data is or will be ready to be transferred. Thus, the ability to reserve such dedicated bandwidth connections either on-demand or in-advance is critical to both classes of operations.

To provide dedicated network connection service between sites, the manager of the high-speed network that connects these sites must address the following issues:

1. Resource monitoring and management. To provide a resource reservation service on a network, it is fundamental to acknowledge the status of available resources and reserve them for a certain period of time.

2. Dynamic and scalable resource model. As the link capacity of a network is shared by different requests at any given time, a dynamic resource model that represents the changing status of the network's available resources is needed.

3. Efficient scheduling algorithms for various reservation requests. Based on the above resource model, algorithms are needed to find paths that fulfill users' requests. User requests generally specify source and destination nodes as well as bandwidth and duration. When the job start time is the primary concern, the bandwidth scheduler needs to find the earliest start time for which a feasible network path is available. When the job requires a large amount of bandwidth, multi-path scheduling is needed to fulfill the resource requirement. When the required path is not available due to link outage, an alterative path needs to be computed and allocated.

The importance of dedicated connection capabilities has been recognized, and several network research projects are currently underway to develop resource scheduling capabilities. These include User Controlled Light Paths (UCLP) [6], UltraScience Net (USN) [7], Circuit-switched High-speed End-to-End Transport ArcHitecture (CHEE-TAH) [8], Enlightened [31], Dynamic Resource Allocation via GMPLS Optical Networks (DRAGON) [9], Japanese Gigabit Network II [5], Bandwidth on Demand (BoD) on Geant2 network [10], On-demand Secure Circuits and Advance Reservation System (OSCARS) [11] of ESnet, Hybrid Optical and Packet Infrastructure (HOPI) [3], Bandwidth Brokers [12], and others. In addition, production networks at the national and international scale with such capabilities are being deployed by Internet2 and LHCNet [13]. Such deployments are expected to increase and proliferate into both shared and private network infrastructures across the globe in the coming years.

Bandwidth reservation systems operate in one of two modes:

1. In **on-demand** scheduling, bandwidth is reserved for a time period that begins at the current time.

2. In **in-advance** scheduling, bandwidth is reserved for a time period that begins at some future time.

In reality, on-demand scheduling is a special case of in-advance scheduling; the future time for each scheduling request is separated from the time at which the request is made by a time interval of zero. Hence, in this chapter, we explicitly consider only the in-advance scheduling mode. Our development is naturally adapted to the on-demand mode.

Much of the research on bandwidth scheduling has focused on reserving a single path for a specified bandwidth request. For on-demand scheduling, this is typically supported by Multiple Protocol Label Switching (MPLS) [14, 15] at layer 3 and by Generalized MPLS (GMPLS) [16] at layers 1 and 2. Algorithms for on-demand scheduling are described in [17–20], and implemented by CHEETAH, DRAGON, HOPI, UCLP, and JGN. GeantII, OSCARS, USN, and Enlighten support in-advance scheduling and algorithms for in-advance scheduling are described in [2, 7, 21–24, 39–41], for example.

On the other hand, it is well known that using multiple paths can utilize the available network resources more effectively [1]. The multi-path reservation problem is formulated in [1] as a network flow problem with the objective of minimizing link congestion. Algorithms for delay-constrained file transfer using multiple paths are proposed in [25]. Multi-path file transfer with both link utilization constraints and path length constraints is considered in [26]. A maximum concurrent flow formulation is used in [27] to solve the large file transfer problem with fixed start and end times. Its objective is to maximize network throughput. Reference [27] also develops linear programming models to maximize network throughput and proposes two heuristics for multi-path routing. The first heuristic, k-Shortest Paths (KSP), uses the k-shortest paths algorithm of [28] to compute k not necessarily disjoint paths from the source to the destination. The scheduling of the file transfer is restricted to these k paths. The second heuristic, k-Disjoint Paths (KDP), computes k disjoint paths from source to destination by eliminating the links contained in previously computed paths before computing the next path; each path computation generates the shortest path in the remaining network.

Our network model is described in Section 23.2. In Section 23.3, a set of in-advance scheduling problems are defined and corresponding algorithms are proposed and evaluated. In Section 23.4, a multiple path scheduling problem *Earliest Finish Time File Transfer Problem* (EFTFTP) is proposed and solved by both optimal solutions and heuristics.

23.2 TEMPORAL NETWORK MODEL

We assume that the network is represented as a graph $G = (V, E)$. Each node of this graph represents a device such as a switch for layers 1-2 and a router for layer 3; and each edge represents a link such as SONET or Ethernet. When developing an in-advance reservation system one must decide on a representation of time. The options are to either consider time as divided into equal size slots as is done in [21, 22, 30, 36, 37] or to consider time as being continuous as in [2, 7, 23, 24, 38].

23.2.1 Slotted Time

Explicit in the slotted model of [21, 22] is the use of an array to store link status for each time slot. So, for example, we may use a two-dimensional array b such that $b[l, t]$ gives the bandwidth available on link l in slot t. The use of this model of time has several merits and demerits. The merits include its simplicity and the fact that the status of a link l in any slot t may be determined in $O(1)$ time. Some of the demerits are:

1. We need to decide the granularity of a time slot. Does a slot represent a minute, an hour, a day, or a week of time? The granularity of a time slot determines the number of time slots we need to provision for in our array b. So, if the advance scheduler permits reservations to be made up to a year in advance of the job completion time, the number of time slots (i.e., size of the second dimension of our array), b, will need to be 52 in case a time slot represents a week and 525,600 in case a time slot is 1 minute (we assume a 365-day year). Assuming that it takes 4 bytes to store the available bandwidth of a link and a network with 1000 links, the memory required for the link status array b is 208,000 bytes when we

employ a 1-week granularity and is about 2GB for a 1-minute granularity. On the other hand, the potential to waste a lot of resources is high when we use a 1-week granularity. This is because the scheduler can allocate only an integral number of slots to a reservation request. So, if a task needs a fractional number of slots, the scheduler must round to the nearest integer. A request for (say) 1.1 slots results in the allocation of 2 slots. With a 1-week granularity, a 1-minute task, which ties up a source-destination path for 1-week results in a 0.01% utilization!

2. The run-time of reservation algorithms is often a function of T, the total number of slots, or τ, the duration of a reservation request or both. So, for example, it takes $O(\tau)$ time to determine whether link l has bandwidth b available in each of slots $t, \dots, t + \tau - 1$. This determination is to be made to verify that link l is available for a bandwidth b reservation of duration τ beginning at slot t. To find the first slot during which link l has a bandwidth of at least b available takes $O(T)$ time.

3. The exact time of day/week/year represented by slot t cannot be fixed. In other words the slot $b[l, t]$ cannot be associated with (say) week t of a year when using a slot granularity of 1 week. This is because the reservation system needs to operate essentially forever using the same array. As time advances from 1 week to the next we need to drop the slot that represented the elapsed week and add a slot to represent the week that is now a year away. To do this efficiently, we must use the slots associated with each link in a circular manner as is done in the circular array-representation of a queue [29].

23.2.2 Continuous Time

In the continuous time model adopted by [2, 7, 23, 24, 38], the status of each link l is maintained using a time-bandwidth list (TB list) $TB[l]$ that is comprised of tuples of the form (t_i, b_i), where t_i is a time and b_i is a bandwidth. The tuples on a TB list are in increasing order of t_i. If (t_i, b_i) is a tuple of $TB[l]$ (other than the last one), then the bandwidth available on link l from t_i to t_{i+1} is b_i. When (t_i, b_i) is the last tuple, a bandwidth of b is available from t_i to ∞. Consider the link shown in Figure 23.1. The graph is a pictorial

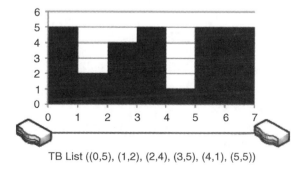

TB List ((0,5), (1,2), (2,4), (3,5), (4,1), (5,5))

Figure 23.1   Time-bandwidth list.

representation of the bandwidth available on this link as a function of time. So, for example, a bandwidth of 5 is available from time 0 to time 1 and the available bandwidth from 2 to 3 is 4. The corresponding TB list is $[(0, 5), (1, 2), (2, 4), (3, 5), (4, 1), (5, 5)]$.

We note that TB lists may be used in the slotted model of time as well with t_i representing a slot rather than a time. In this case, $TB[4] = [(2, 10), (9, 5), (20, 50)]$ would mean that link 4 has an available bandwidth of 10 in slots 2 through 8, a bandwidth of 5 in slots 9 through 19, and a bandwidth of 50 in slots 20 and beyond; the link is not available in slot 1.

Each TB list may be represented as an array linear list using dynamic array resizing as described in [29] or as a linked list.

The demerits of the continuous time model include its relative complexity (linear lists are somewhat more difficult to handle than arrays) and the complexity of determining the status of a link at any given time. The latter can be done in $O(\log I |TB[l]|)$ time using a binary search in case of an array linear list and in $O(|TB[l]|)$ time in case of a linked TB list. Some of the merits of this time model are:

1. There is no need to pick a time granularity or to place a bound on the length of the *book ahead* period (i.e., we don't need to limit ourselves to reservations that complete within a year (say)).
2. The memory required to represent a link state (i.e., the TB list) is a function of the time variation in link bandwidth availability rather than the scheduling horizon T. So, for example, a link with bandwidth capacity 100 and no reservations is represented by the TB list $[(0, 100)]$ irrespective of how far ahead one can schedule. On the other hand, if the available bandwidth changes at times 0, 10, and 40, the TB list will have 3 tuples. We note that the time variation in link bandwidth is loosely related to the number of tasks scheduled on that link.
3. The run-time of reservation algorithms is not a function of the scheduling horizon. Instead, it is a function of the size of the TB lists, which, in turn, depends on the number of tasks that have been scheduled.

Because of the correspondence between a slot and time, we often use the two terms interchangeably.

23.3 SINGLE-PATH SCHEDULING

23.3.1 Problem Definitions

The following problems are of interest in the context of in-advance scheduling.

1. **Fixed Slot:** Reserve a path with bandwidth b from the source s to the destination d from time t_{start} to time t_{end}.
2. **Maximum Bandwidth in Slot:** Find the largest bandwidth b such that there is a bandwidth b path from the source s to the destination d from time t_{start} to time t_{end}. Reserve such a path.

3. **Maximum Duration:** Find the maximum duration τ such that there is a band-width b path from the source s to the destination d from time t_{start} to time $t_{start} + \tau$. Reserve such a path.

4. **First Slot:** Find the least t for which there is a path with bandwidth b from the source s to the destination d from time t to time $t + \tau$, where τ is the duration for which the path is desired. Reserve such a path.

5. **All Slots:** Find all ranges r such that for every $t \in r$, there is a bandwidth b path from the source s to the destination d from time t to time $t + \tau$. Reserve such a path for a user selected t in one of the found ranges.

6. **All Pairs All Slots:** For every source-destination pair (s, d), find all ranges r such that for every $t \in r$, there is a bandwidth b path from s to d from time t to time $t + \tau$.

The fixed-slot problem is referred to as the connection feasibility problem in [22]. The soonest completion problem formulated in [22] is referred to as the *first available transmission period* in [21]; both are identical to the first-slot problem stated above.

In addition to the path problems defined above, an in-advance reservation system may implement aggregate path reservation algorithms in which the available bandwidth on the reserved path may change during the course of the reservation interval. The integral of the available bandwidth over the reservation interval is to meet a prespecified requirement. Aggregate data reservation algorithms are useful in data transfer applications where we are not concerned with transferring data at a uniform rate but just with completing the transfer by (say) a given deadline. Reference [22] shows that the aggregate path reservation problem is NP-hard.

23.3.2 Path Computation Algorithms

We describe only the algorithms needed to compute the paths for the various problems described in Section 23.3.1. The actual scheduling or reservation of the found path requires us to update the TB lists or the b-array entries for the links on the path as well as to signal the routers on the path at the reserved time. The former is a relatively straightforward process and the latter requires the use of specific signaling protocols .

23.3.2.1 Fixed Slot. Of the problems listed in Section 23.3.1, the fixed-slot problem is the most studied. The algorithms that have been proposed are described below.

1. **Feasible Path (FP):** A link of the network is *feasible* for fixed-slot scheduling iff the available bandwidth on the link at all times in the interval $[t_{start}, t_{end}]$ is $\geq b$. Let p be a path from the source s to the destination d. p is a *feasible* path iff it is comprised only of feasible links. In FP scheduling, a feasible path is reserved. Such a path may be found by performing a search (depth- or breadth-first, for example [29]) on the subgraph of G, called the *feasible subgraph*, obtained from G by eliminating all links that are not feasible. FP scheduling is done in [22].

2. **Minimum Hop Feasible Path (MHFP):** The number of links on a path is its hop count. In MHFP scheduling, a minimum-hop feasible path is reserved. Such a path may be found by performing a breadth-first search on the feasible subgraph of G. Notice that FP scheduling is the same as MHFP scheduling when the search method used by FP scheduling is breadth first. MHFP scheduling is used in USN and the path computation algorithm is formally stated in [24].

3. **Widest/Shortest Feasible Path (WSFP):** This is an adaptation of the widest-shortest method proposed in [17] for on-demand scheduling. Let p be a feasible path. Let $b_{min} \geq b$ be the minimum bandwidth available on any link of p at any instant in the scheduling interval $[t_{start}, t_{end}]$. In WSFP scheduling, we use the minimum-hop feasible path that has the maximum b_{min} value. Ties are broken arbitrarily. Notice that WSFP scheduling is MHFP scheduling with a specified tie breaker. WSFP scheduling is suggested in [21]. A WSFP may be found by running a modified Bellman-Ford algorithm on the feasible subgraph of G [17]; the weight of a link is the minimum bandwidth available on that link during the interval $[t_{start}, t_{end}]$ or by running a modified version of Dijkstra's shortest path algorithm on this feasible subgraph [19]. In the latter case, when selecting the next shortest path, priority is given to next-path candidates with least hop count and ties are broken by using the b_{min} value of the path.

4. **Shortest/Widest Feasible Path (SWFP):** This is a variant of WSFP scheduling that was first proposed for on-demand scheduling [20]. We select a feasible path that has maximum b_{min} value. Ties are broken by favoring paths with smaller hop counts. An SWFP path may be found [19] by first running Dijkstra's shortest path algorithm modified to find a path with maximum b_{min} and then doing a breadth-first search to find a minimum-hop path with this maximum b_{min} value; the breadth-first search ignores links that violate this b_{min} requirement.

5. **Shortest Distance Feasible Path Algorithms (SDFP):** These algorithms find a shortest path (the length of a path being the sum of the weights of the links on that path) in the feasible subgraph of G. An SDFP path may be found using Dijkstra's shortest path algorithm.

   SDFP algorithms differ in their selection of a cost metric for feasible links. SDFP-min (minimum SDFP) is an extension of the shortest distance path algorithm for on-demand scheduling [18] to the case of in-advance scheduling. The weight of a feasible link is the reciprocal of the minimum bandwidth available on that link during the scheduling interval $[t_{start}, t_{end}]$.

   In SDFP-avg (average SDFP), the weight of a feasible link is the reciprocal of the average (rather than the minimum) bandwidth available on that link during the period $[t_{start}, t_{end}]$.

6. **Dynamic Alternative Feasible Path (DAFP):** Again, this is an adaptation of the dynamic alternative path algorithm originally proposed for on-demand scheduling [19]. Let h be the number of hops in the MHFP. In DAFP, we use a widest feasible path (i.e., one with maximum b_{min} value) that has no more than $h + 1$ hops. Such a path may be found [19] by restricting the Bellman-Ford algorithm proposed for WSFP to use no path with more than $h + 1$ hops. We note that

while DAFP guarantees to find a feasible path whenever such a path exists, the dynamic alternative path algorithm of [19] provides no such guarantee.

7. **OSPF-Like Algorithms:** These are shortest path algorithms that work on G or some subgraph of G other than the feasible subgraph. They differ in how the link weights are defined and/or in how the subgraph is defined. Since these algorithms do not work on the feasible subgraph of G, they may generate an infeasible path and so fail to schedule a request in some cases where one of the aforementioned feasible path algorithms succeed. The shortest path may be found using Dijkstra's algorithm.

In most implementations of the OSPF algorithm, the weight of a link is defined to be the reciprocal of its bandwidth capacity. Note that this bandwidth is not the link's available bandwidth at any given time but the link's nominal unloaded bandwidth. So, the weight of a 10 Gb link is 1/10 regardless of the already scheduled load on that link. The OSPF path is the shortest path in the graph G using these link weights. In case the OSPF path is not feasible for fixed-slot scheduling, the reservation request is denied.

In the version of OSPF-TE implemented in OSCARS [11], you remove from the network graph G those links that do not have an available bandwidth that is at least b at the time the scheduling request is processed (not at time t_{start}); link weights are as for OSPF. The shortest path in this reduced graph is found and an attempt is made to schedule the reservation request on this path. As with OSPF, the OSPF-TE path may not be feasible. Note that even though the OSPF-TE path has enough bandwidth at the time the path is computed, it may not have sufficient bandwidth during the reservation period $[t_{start}, t_{end}]$. The feasibility of the OSPF-TE path is verified, in OSCARS, by using a database of previously made reservations. In case the OSPF-TE path is infeasible, the scheduling request is denied.

8. **k Dynamic Paths (kDP):** These algorithms are an extension of OSPF-like algorithms. Recognizing that an OSPF-like algorithm may fail to find a feasible path in a network that has a feasible path, kDP algorithms generate additional paths with the hope that one of the additional paths will be feasible. An OSPF-like algorithm generates a shortest path and succeeds when this shortest path is feasible and fails otherwise. In a kDP algorithm, when the generated path is infeasible, we reduce the current graph by removing from it links on the generated infeasible path whose available bandwidth during the reservation interval $[t_{start}, t_{end}]$ is less than b. We then find the shortest s to d path in this reduced graph. This path computation and graph reduction process is repeated at most k times. The process terminates when the first feasible path is found or when k infeasible paths have been generated.

kDP-OSPF and kDP-OSPF-TE are natural extensions of OSPF and OSPF-TE. kDP-LOAD is an adaptation of the algorithms used in [30] for in-advance scheduling of optical networks. In kDP-LOAD, each link is assigned a weight equal to the total load already scheduled on that link. More precisely, a link's weight is the aggregate allocated bandwidth on the link beginning at the current

```
MaxBandwidth(s,d,prev)
{
```
$bw[i] = b[s][i], 1 \leq i \leq n.$
$prev[i] = s, 1 \leq i \leq n.$
$prev[s] = 0.$
Initialize L to be a list with all vertices other than s.
for $(i = 1, i < n - 1, i + +)$
{

Delete a vertex w from L with maximum bw.
if $(w == d)$ return.
for (each u adjacent from w)
    if $(bw[u] < \min\{bw[w], b[w][u]\})$
    {

$bw[u] = \min\{bw[w], b[w][u]\}.$
$prev[u] = w.$
    }

}
}

Figure 23.2 Modified Dijkstra's algorithm.

time and going up to the latest scheduled time. Some other adaptations are kDPA-min in which the link weight is the reciprocal of the minimum bandwidth available in the interval $[t_{start}, t_{end}]$ (as in SDFP-min) and kDP-avg in which the link weight is the reciprocal of the average bandwidth available in this interval (as in SDFP-avg).

9. **k Static Paths (kSP):** In this algorithm, we have up to k precomputed paths between every pair of source-destination vertices. To schedule a path between s and d, we examine, in some order, the up to k precomputed paths for the pair (s, t) and select the first that is feasible for the interval $[t_{start}, t_{end}]$. If none is feasible, the scheduling request is denied.

23.3.2.2 *Maximum Bandwidth in a Slot.*
This computation is achieved by modifying Dijkstra's shortest path algorithm [29] as shown in Figure 23.2. Here, $b[u][v]$ is the minimum bandwidth available on the edge (u, v) during the specified interval/slot and $bw[u]$ is the maximum bandwidth along paths from the source s to vertex u under the constraint that these paths go through only those vertices to which a maximum bandwidth path has been found already. The complexity of the algorithm is $O(n^2)$ for a general n vertex graph. However, practical network graphs have $O(n)$ edges and the complexity becomes $O(n \log n)$ when a max heap (for example) is used to maintain the bw values.

23.3.2.3 *Maximum Duration.*
As noted in [22], the maximum duration problem is very similar to the widest path problem, which in turn is identical to the maximum bandwidth problem. The weight of a link is set to the maximum duration, beginning at t_{start} for which the link has a bandwidth of b or more available. The widest s to d path in this weighted graph is the maximum duration path. The path is found using a modified Dijkstra's algorithm as for the maximum bandwidth in slot problem.

23.3.2.4 First Slot. Three different algorithms have been proposed for the first slot problem [22, 24, 30].

1. **Slotted Sliding Window (SSW):** The sliding window first algorithm proposed in [30] for optical networks is a variation of the soonest completion algorithm proposed in [22]. Both these algorithms try the slots t_{start}, $t_{start} + 1, \ldots$, in this order, to find the least t for which the graph G has a feasible path (i.e., an s to d path with bandwidth b for the duration from t to $t + \tau$). The existence of a feasible path for any t may be done using a fixed-slot algorithm such as FP that guarantees to find a feasible path whenever such a path exists or by using a kDP (as in the case of [30]) or kSP algorithm that does not provide such a guarantee.

2. **List Sliding Window (LSW):** This is similar to SSW except that it was developed for the continuous time model in which there is no concept of discrete time intervals (i.e., slots). For each link in the network, we define a start-time list, ST, that is comprised of pairs of the form (a, b) with the property that for every $t \in [a, b]$, the link has bandwidth b available from t to $t + \tau$. Let $a_1 < a_2 < \cdots < a_q$ be the distinct a values in the union of the ST lists of all links. It is easy to see that the earliest time t for which the network has a path from s to d with bandwidth b from time t to time $t + \tau$ is one of the a_is. The LSW algorithm of [24] examines the a_is in the order $a_1, a_2, \ldots$ stopping at the first a_i for which a feasible path is found. The search for a feasible path is done using a breadth-first search as is done by the MHFP algorithm. Some optimization is possible since the breadth first search for a_i follows that for $a_{i-1} < a_i$. Since the breadth-first search must scan the ST list of each link that is traversed during the search, this scan may begin where the most recent scan of this list (from the breadth-first search for an earlier a_i) left off rather than from the front of the ST list.

   Although LSW was developed for the continuous time model, it may be used also in the slotted time model regardless of whether TB lists or an array is used to represent link status.

3. **Extended Bellman Ford (EBF):** This algorithm for first slot was proposed in [24]. First, we extend the notion of an ST list for a link to that for a path in the natural way. Next, define $st(k, u)$ to be the union of the ST lists for all paths from vertex s to vertex u that have at most k edges on them. Clearly, $st(0, u) = \emptyset$ for $u \neq s$ and $st(0, s) = [0, \infty]$. Also, $st(1, u) = ST(s, u)$ for $u \neq s$ and $st(1, s) = st(0, s)$. For $k > 1$ (actually also for $k = 1$), we obtain the following recurrence

$$st(k, u) = st(k - 1, u) \cup \{\cup_v \text{ such that } (v,u) \text{ is an edge}\{st(k - 1, v) \cap ST(v, u)\}\}$$
$$(23.1)$$

where $\cup$ and $\cap$ are list union and intersection operations. For an n-vertex graph, $st(n - 1, d)$ gives the start times of all paths from s to d that have bandwidth b available for a duration τ. The a value of the first (a, b) pair in $st(n - 1, d)$ gives the desired first slot.

The Bellman-Ford algorithm [29] may be extended to compute $st(n - 1, d)$. The extension merely works with st lists rather than with scalars and is described in [24].

23.3.2.5 All Slots. There appears to be just one algorithm that has been proposed for the all slots problem. This is the extended Bellman-Ford algorithm [24] to compute $st(n - 1, d)$ (see preceding discussion of first slot algorithms). As noted above, $st(n - 1, d)$ gives the start times of all paths from s to d that have bandwidth b available for a duration τ.

23.3.2.6 All Pairs, All Slots. The extended Bellman-Ford (*EBF*) algorithm of Section 23.3.2.4 computes $st(u) = st(n - 1, u)$ for a given source vertex s and all u in $O(nel)$ time. $st(u)$ gives the start time of all available slots of duration d and bandwidth b. So, in $O(nel)$, using *EBF*, we are able to determine all available slots from s to every other vertex u (including vertex d). Furthermore, to determine all available slots between all pairs of vertices, we may run the *EBF* algorithm for n times, once with each vertex as the source vertex s. So, the time needed to determine all slots between all pairs of vertices is $O(n^2 el)$. An alternative strategy to determine all available slots between all pairs of vertices is to extend Floyd's all-pairs shortest path algorithm [29] as is done in [7]. Figure 23.3 gives the resulting extension. Here, $st(u, v)$ is the *ST* list for paths from u to v. Initially, $st(u, v) = ST(u, v)$. On termination, $st(u, v)$ gives all possible start times for paths from u to v.

23.3.3 Performance Metrics

In addition to the traditional metrics of space and time complexity, the effectiveness of an in-advance scheduling algorithm in accommodating reservation requests is critical. The space complexity needs to be "reasonable." That is, the space requirement should not exceed the available memory on the computer on which the bandwidth management system is to run. The time complexity is important as this influences the response time of the bandwidth management system and, in turn, determines how many reservation requests this system can process per unit time. Scheduling effectiveness is, of course, critical as revenue is generated only from tasks that are actually scheduled.

Although many of the proposed algorithms may be run in distributed mode (for example, those based on breadth-first search and Bellman-Ford), current implementa-

```
algorithm ExtendedFloyd()
{
    for (int k = 1; k < n; k++)
        for (int i = 1; i < n; k++)
            for (int j = 1; j < n; k++)
                st(i, j) = st(i, j) ∪ {st(i, k) ∩ st(k, j)};
}
```

Figure 23.3 Pseudocode for extended Floyd algorithm.

tions of these algorithms in in-advance reservation systems such as GeantII, OSCARS, USN, and Enlighten are centralized. Therefore, we limit our discussion of the complexity metric to centralized implementations of the proposed algorithms.

23.3.3.1 Space Complexity.

When using the slotted-array model, the status of link l is stored in array position $b[l][i]$, $1 \le i \le T$, where T is the number of slots in the scheduling horizon.[1] The memory required for link status information is, therefore, $\Theta(eT)$, where e is the number of links in the network. In the continuous time model, where TB lists are used to store link status, we need $O(\sum_i |TB[i]|)$, where $|TB[i]|$ is the size of the TB list for link i. As noted in Chapter 2, the slotted model is a special case of the continuous model and TB lists may also be used for this latter model. When this is done, the size of each TB list is bounded by T and the TB list representation takes $O(eT)$ memory. For a lightly loaded system in which the size of TB list is much less than its maximum possible size of T, the TB-list scheme uses much less memory than is used by the slotted-array representation. In fact, when no tasks are scheduled, the TB-list representation uses $\Theta(e)$ memory vs. $\Theta(T)$ memory for the slotted-array representation. At the other extreme where each TB list has T pairs, the TB-list representation takes about twice the memory taken by the array representation (note that each entry on a TB list is a pair while each array entry is a singleton).

In addition to the memory required to store network status, memory is needed to run the path computation algorithms. Algorithms employing a graph search strategy such as breadth-first search need $O(n)$ space to keep track of which vertices have or have not been visited so far. Note that we may determine whether or not a link is feasible while the breadth-first search algorithm is running and so no additional space is needed to maintain the feasible subgraph of G. Those that use some version of Dijkstra's shortest path algorithm, need $O(n)$ space for a priority queue and $O(e)$ space for the link weights that are in use.

For Bellman-Ford extensions, we need space for the link ST lists and the path st lists. The number of link ST lists is e. Although there are $O(n^2)$ path st lists, the computation of $st(k, *)$ can be done in-place (i.e., using the same space as used by $st(k-1, *)$ [24]). So, space for $O(n)$ st lists is needed. For the slotted model, T is an upper bound on the size of an ST/st list. So, Bellman-Ford extensions require an additional $O((n+e)T)$ memory to run. In lightly loaded systems, the size of an st list is much less than T and correspondingly less memory is needed. For the continuous model, the size of an ST/st list could be as large as the number of tasks scheduled so far. However, in realistic applications, we expect the size to be considerably less than the T value for a corresponding slotted system.

The Floyd extension used in the all-pairs all-slots problem requires an $n \times n$ array of st lists. The memory for this array corresponds to that for $O(n^2)$ st lists. Bounds on the size of an st list were discussed in the previous paragraph.

23.3.3.2 Time Complexity.

Figure 23.4 summarizes the time complexity of each of the algorithms described in Section 23.3.2. We assume also that the number of

---

[1] This representation is an extension of the packed adjacency list representation of a graph described in [29]. The extension requires us to keep an array $b[l][*]$ of slots with each link l rather than a scalar weight.

Problem	Algorithm	SlottedArray	Continuous	
Fixed Slot	FP	$O(e\tau)$	$O(e + L)$	
	MHFP	$O(e\tau)$	$O(e + L)$	
	WSFP	$O(e\tau + n\log n)$	$O(e + L + n\log n)$	
	SWFP	$O(e\tau + n\log n)$	$O(e + L + n\log n)$	
	SDFP	$O(e\tau + n\log n)$	$O(e + L + n\log n)$	
	DAFP	$O(e\tau + n\log n)$	$O(e + L + n\log n)$	
	OSPF	$O(e + n(\tau + \log n))$	$O(e + L + n\log n)$	
	kDP	$O(ke + \min\{kn, e\}\tau + kn\log n))$	$O(ke + L + kn\log n)$	l = size of longest st list
	kSP	$O(\min\{kn, e\}\tau + kn)$	$O(L + kn)$	
Max Bandwidth	Dijkstra	$O(e\tau + n\log n)$	$O(e + L + n\log n)$	
Max Duration	Dijkstra	$O(eT + n\log n)$	$O(e + L + n\log n)$	
First Slot	SSW-MHFP	$O(eT)$	—	
	LSW	$O((q + T)e)$	$O(qe + L)$	
	EBF	$O(nel + eT)$	$O(nel + L)$	
All Slots	EBF	$O(nel + eT)$	$O(nel + L)$	
All Pairs All Slots	Floyd	$O(n^3 l + eT)$	$O(n^3 l + L)$	

q = number of different a_is in the ST lists
L = sum of lengths of TB lists

Figure 23.4 Algorithm time complexities.

links e is at least equal to the number of nodes n. The algorithms of Section 23.3.2 that work on the feasible subgraph of G may be implemented to either begin by identifying the feasible links of G or may check each link for feasibility when the link is first examined. In either case, $O(e\tau)$ time is spent on link feasibility checks when the slotted-array model is used. In the continuous model, feasibility checks take $O(L)$ time, where L is the sum of the lengths of the TB lists. In either case, the remainder of the algorithm takes $O(e)$ time.

When the number of previously scheduled jobs is small, the TB lists also are small in size. However, in the worst case, the size of a TB list may be T. So, for lightly loaded systems, we expect the continuous version of an algorithm to outperform (in terms of run time and memory) the corresponding slotted-array version. This is the typical trade-off between sparse and dense data-structure representations. Additionally, the slotted-array versions for the fixed slot and max bandwidth problems are expected to outperform the corresponding continuous versions when the requested reservation duration τ is small.

23.3.3.3 Effectiveness.
There are two aspects to effectiveness–guarantees and utilization. Guarantees has to do with whether or not the scheduling algorithm provides any guarantee on its result. For example, does a fixed-slot algorithm guarantee to find a feasible whenever such a path exits? Does a first-slot algorithm actually find the earliest feasible path? For the fixed-slot problem, all algorithms other than the OSPF-like, k dynamic paths, and k static paths algorithms provide a guarantee. For the remaining in-advance scheduling problems, all algorithms described in Section 23.3.2, other than the first-slot algorithm of [30], provide a guarantee. Figure 23.5 gives a possible hierarchical classification of the fixed-slot algorithms of Section 23.3.2.1.

Since the scheduling algorithms work in an online mode (i.e., scheduling requests are processed in the order they arrive at the bandwidth management system and a decision on whether or not to make the requested reservation made on the basis of link states at the time the reservation request is processed without regard to future requests), the link

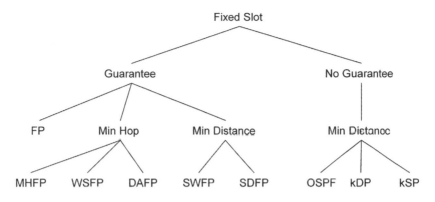

Figure 23.5 Classification of fixed-slot algorithms.

status at the time a decision is made on the current request being processed depends on decisions made in the past. These past decisions are a function of the path computation algorithm(s) in use. Suppose that fixed-slot reservation requests A, B, and C arrive at the bandwidth management system in this order. Request A may be denied by OSPF-TE (as OSPF-TE provides no guarantee) and accepted by FP. As a result, the network state following the processing of request A is different when the bandwidth management system uses OSPF-TE for fixed-slot reservation than when it uses FP. Consequently, it is entirely possible that OSPF-TE then accepts B and C while FP rejects both B and C. Hence, network utilization as measured by the number of accepted requests or total network bandwidth that has been scheduled may be more using OSPF-TE that provides no guarantee than when using FP that provides a guarantee!

Burchard [21] considers two utilization metrics–request blocking ratio (RBR) and bandwidth blocking ratio (BBR), which, for any measurement interval, are defined as:

$$RBR = \frac{\text{number of rejected requests}}{\text{total number of requests}}$$

$$BBR = \frac{\text{sum of bandwidth-duration products of rejected requests}}{\text{sum of bandwidth-duration products of all requests}}$$

Equivalently, we may use request acceptance (RAR) and bandwidth acceptance (BAR) ratios, which are defined as:

$$RAR = 1 - RBR$$
$$BAR = 1 - BBR$$

We note that BBR also has been used in the context of on-demand scheduling (see [19], for example).

23.3.4 Experiments

For each of the max bandwidth, max duration, all slots, and all pairs all slots problems, only one algorithm has been proposed and so no relative effectiveness comparison is possible. For the first slot problem, there are three algorithms–SSW-MHFP, LSW, and EBF. All three guarantee to find the first slot correctly. Hence, barring differences resulting from their possible implementation using different tie breakers, each is just as effective. Of course, there will be some difference in the computer-time taken to execute each algorithm (as indicated in Section 23.3.3.2). Therefore an experimental evaluation of effectiveness is needed only for the various algorithms proposed for the fixed slot problem.

We programmed the various fixed slot algorithms in C++ and measured the effectiveness of each using the RAR and BAR metrics. Although we experimented with both variants (SDFP-min and SDFP-avg) of SDFP, we report only the results for SDFP-min as there the results for both variants are comparable. For OSPF, we programmed the OSPF-TE variant that is used in OSCARS [11]. The kDP variant tested by us is kDP-LOAD with $k = 4$. We used this variant as it is the variant used in Enlightened [31]. Finally, for kSP, we set k to 4 and used 4 shortest paths.

For test networks, we used the the Abilene network [32], 19-node MCI network and the 16-node cluster network of [19], the 11-node network of [21], and several randomly generated topologies. The backbone of the Abilene network used by us has 11 nodes as shown in Figure 23.6(a) and each backbone node has a 5-node stub network attached to

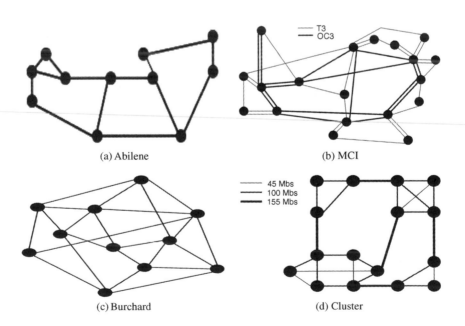

(a) Abilene   (b) MCI

(c) Burchard   (d) Cluster

Figure 23.6 Topologies of Abilene network, MCI network, Burchard's network, and Cluster networks.

it. The bandwidth of each link is 155 Mbps. The bandwidth of each link in the network of [21] (Figure 23.6(c)) is 100 Mbps. Figures 23.6(b) and 23.6(d) give the MCI and cluster topologies together with the link bandwidths. The random networks we tried had 200, 400, or 800 nodes and the out-degree of each node was randomly selected to be between 3 and 7. To ensure network connectivity, the random network has bidirectional links between nodes i and $i + 1$ for every $1 \leq i < n$, where n is the number of nodes. The bandwidth of each link in a randomly generated network was randomly selected from the set 50 Mbps (OC1), 155 Mbps (OC3), 620 Mbps (OC12), 1000 Mbps (1 G Ethernet), 1245 Mbps (OC24), 2490 Mbps (OC48), 4975 Mbps (OC96), 9950 Mbps (OC192), and 10000 Mbps (10 G Ethernet).

We generated a synthetic set of reservation requests. Each request is described by the 6-tuple (source node, destination node, time at which the request is made, requested start time, duration, bandwidth). The source and destination nodes for each request were randomly selected using a uniform random number generator. The time at which the request is made followed a Poisson distribution. The requested start time was set to be the time at which the request is made plus a randomly generated lag. Since the results are relatively insensitive to the lag time, we arbitrarily set the mean lag time to be 100 units.

For our experiments, we had three control parameters—number of requests in the study interval, mean duration of a scheduling request, and mean bandwidth of a request. The study interval was arbitrarily set to 2000 time units; the number of requests in the study interval was set to one of the values 200, 400, 600, 800, and 1000 for the random networks and to one of 100, 200, 300, 400, and 500 for the remaining networks; the allowable mean request durations were 200, 400, 600, 800, and 1000 time units; and the allowable mean request bandwidths were 500, 1000, 1500, 2000, and 2500 Mbps for the random networks and 10, 30, 50, 70 and 90 Mbps for the remaining networks. For each setting of the three control parameters, we ran 10 trials. In the case of random networks, the network topology was randomly regenerated for each of the 10 trials. For each trial, we measured the request acceptance and bandwidth acceptance ratios (RAR and BAR). In reporting our results, we computed the average RAR for all conducted experiments with a given network and fixed value for one of the three control parameters. So, for example, we computed the average RAR for the 250 (5 request durations * 5 request bandwidths * 10 trials) experiments done on the MCI network with the number of requests in the study interval being 100.

Since the relative performance of the fixed-slot algorithms is rather insensitive to whether we use the RAR or BAR metric, we report only on the RAR results. Figure 23.7 and Figure 23.8 give the average acceptance ratios for the fixed-slot algorithms of Section 23.3.2.1 as a function of the number of requests in the study interval. On networks such as the MCI, Cluster, and Burchard networks, that have a relatively small number nodes, the dynamic alternative feasible path algorithm (DAFP) gives best performance consistently across the range of number of requests tested by us. The minimum hop feasible path algorithm (MHFP) is consistently second best. However, on larger networks such as the Abilene network, which has 66 nodes, and the random networks that have 200+ nodes, MHFP is consistently superior to DAFP. For the tested larger networks, MHFP is best and DAFP is second best. Generally, the fixed-slot algorithms OSPF, kDP, and kSP

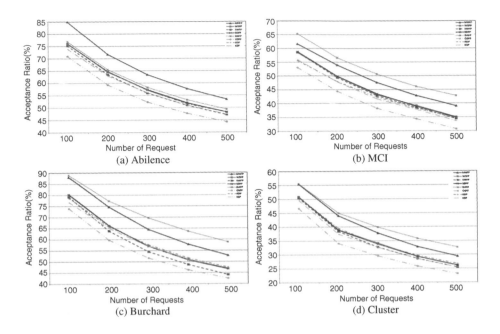

Figure 23.7 Acceptance ratio vs requests number in Abilene, MCI, Burchard, and Cluster networks.

that do not guarantee to make a reservation when such a reservation is possible fared worse than the algorithms that provide such a guarantee. However, at times, the performance of the best "no guarantee algorithm" was quite close to or slightly better than that of the worst "guarantee algorithm." On our non-random networks, OSPF consistently had the worst performance. However, on our random networks, kDP was consistently worst and, often, by quite a margin. As expected, as the network gets saturated (i.e., the number of requests in the study interval increases), the RAR for all algorithms declines and the rate of decline is about the same for all algorithms.

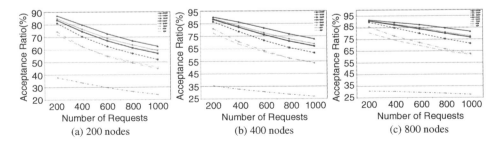

Figure 23.8 Acceptance ratio vs requests number in various random topologies.

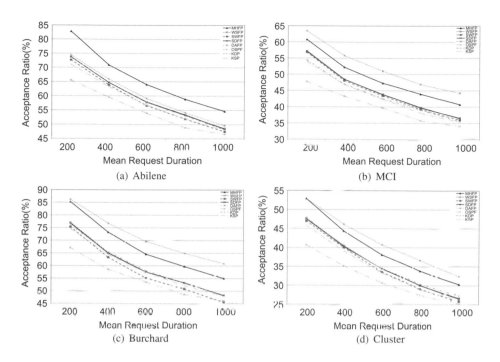

Figure 23.9 Acceptance ratio vs mean requests duration in Abilene, MCI, Burchard, and Cluster networks.

Figures 23.9–23.10 give the average acceptance ratios for the fixed-slot algorithms of Section 23.3.2.1 as a function of the mean request duration. The relative performance of the algorithms is the same as for the case when we fixed the number of requests rather than the mean request duration.

Figures 23.11–23.12 give the average acceptance ratios as a function of the mean request bandwidth. The relative performance of the algorithms is the same as for the case when we fixed either the number of requests or the mean request duration.

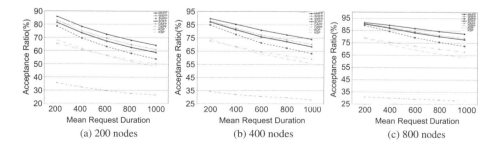

Figure 23.10 Acceptance ratio vs mean requests duration in various random topologies.

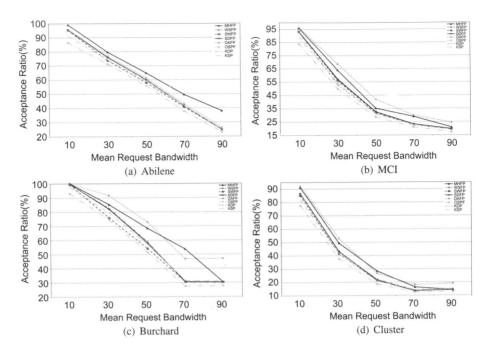

Figure 23.11 Acceptance ratio vs mean requests bandwidth in Abilene, MCI, Burchard, and Cluster networks.

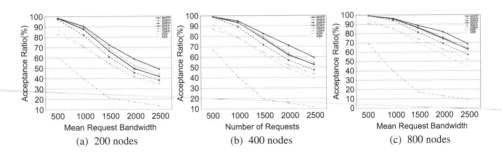

Figure 23.12 Acceptance ratio vs mean requests bandwidth in various random topologies.

23.4 MULTIPLE-PATH SCHEDULING

23.4.1 Problem Definition

Consider the Fusion experiments [34], which are done collaboratively by researchers in different European countries. After each round of experiments, the simulation data are generated in different sites and processed by supercomputers across the continent. Moreover, the data transfer and processing time is limited since the next round of experiments will be guided by the results from the previous ones. Thus, the file transfer time may become a major bottleneck to improve the experiment's efficiency. The delay of any file transfer in the batch will delay the whole project. In this section, we model this problem as the *Batched-File Path Scheduling Problem (BFPSP)*, where the goal is to minimize the overall transfer time of multiple one-to-one file transfers. Without losing generality, we assume that all the file transfer requests are pre-specified before scheduling starts. Clearly, such an algorithm can also be used by batching the newly arrived requests at appropriate intervals. In *in-advanced scheduling* [22], each file transfer may have a different start time. Their earliest start time can be defined by the use in their requests. But actual start time is decided by the scheduling algorithms at runtime. In this section, we provide both optimal and approximate solutions for this problem.

All scheduling approaches can be considered as an variation of **Batch Scheduling**. We assume that all requests are collected as a batch in the scheduler; the requests in a batch are scheduled as a group with certain periodicity. Obviously, if all file transfer requests are batched as one group, the solution is optimal, which is denoted as *All-Batch*. *All-Batch* is very time consuming for large batch sizes. Also, it is not realistic as the arrival time of the requests may not be the same. We present a number of heuristics that have much lower time complexity than using *All-Batch*, but have similar performance and the added benefit that the requests need not be known beforehand. The proposed approach, *N-Batch*, groups requests into batches of constant size N and schedules each batch separately. For the special case of batch size equal to 1, the scheduling is equivalent to **Online Scheduling**. For this case, we develop two sets of heuristics: *GOS* and *k Path*.

We have compared all these algorithms for a variety of scenarios and performance metrics. Our simulations show that both *N-Batch* and *GOS* provides schedules that are comparable in quality to using *All-Batch*, but require significantly less scheduling time than using *All-Batch*. *GOS* is comparable to *N-Batch* but requires significantly less computation time. We also investigate *GOS-E* algorithms that minimize path switching overhead, which is a variant of *GOS*. *GOS-E* is known to have good performance when path switching overhead cannot be ignored.

23.4.1.1 *Data Structures.*

We use the Time-Bandwidth List (TB List) data structure introduced earlier in this chapter. Let $T = [T_0, T_1, \cdots]$, $T_0 < T_1 < \cdots$, be the union of time component of the (t_i, b_i) tuples in the TB lists of all links in the network. We refer to T as the *global time list*. It is easy to see that the available bandwidth on each link of the network is unchanged in the interval $[T_i, T_{i+1})$. Figure 23.13 shows the TB lists for 2 links. For this simple example, assume these are the only two links in the network. The TB list for the first link is $[(0, 5), (1, 2), (2, 5)]$ and that for the second link is $[(0, 5), (1.5, 3), (2, 5)]$. The global time list for our example is $[0, 1, 1.5, 2]$. In the interval $[0,1)$, the available bandwidth on the two links is 5 whereas in the interval $[1,1.5)$, the first link has an available bandwidth of 2 while the second link's available bandwidth is 5, and neither of links' bandwidth changes within this basic interval.

The intervals $[T_0, T_1)$, $[T_1, T_2)$, $\cdots$ in the global time list are referred as *basic intervals*. At any time within a certain basic interval, each edge has a constant amount of available bandwidth. Basic intervals obtained from the global time list can be ordered

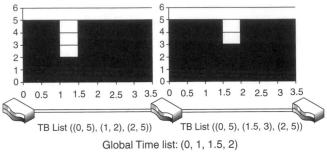

TB List ((0, 5), (1, 2), (2, 5))   TB List ((0, 5), (1.5, 3), (2, 5))

Global Time list: (0, 1, 1.5, 2)

Basic intervals: (0, 1), (1, 1.5), (1.5, 2) and (2, Inf)

Figure 23.13 Basic intervals.

using the relationship $[a, b) < [c, d)$ iff $b \leq c$ (note that the basic intervals of a global time list are disjoint and that $a < b$ for each basic interval $[a, b)$).

File transfer requests are characterized by a 4-tuple (s_i, d_i, f_i, S_i) where s_i is the source location of the file that is to be transferred; d_i is the destination to which the file is to be sent; f_i is the size of the file; and S_i, which is the time at which the file becomes available for transfer, specifies the earliest time at which the file transfer may begin.

23.4.2 Optimal Solution and *N-Batch* Heuristics

In periodic batch scheduling, requests are collected/batched in a centralized scheduler; the collected/batched requests are scheduled as a group. To find out the earliest finish time of a batch of files, We develop a two-step algorithm to optimally (i.e., minimize the maximum finish time) schedule a set of file transfer requests. The two steps are:

Step 1: Determine the minimum finish time, *min Finish Time*.

Step 2: Determine a file transfer schedule that achieves this minimum finish time.

To find out the minimum finish time, we construct a global time list from the TB lists of all links as before and then construct the basic intervals from this global time list. The basic interval $[T_i, T_{i+1})$ is referred to simply as basic interval i. To determine the minimum finish time, we use a linear programming (LP) model to determine, for a specified basic interval i, the minimum time within this basic interval by which it is possible to complete all file transfers in the given request set F. This LP model will have no feasible solution for basic intervals i if it isn't possible to complete the file transfer by time T_{i+1}. In this case, *min Finish Time* must lie in a basic interval $q > i$. Suppose the value of LP's objective function ft is a valid time within the basic interval i. Then all the jobs in the batch F can be finished by ft. Now, $T_i \leq ft \leq T_{i+1}$. If $ft > T_i$, *min Finish Time* $= ft$. However, when $ft = T_i$, it is possible to complete the file transfers in an interval $q < i$. So, using the LP model, we can conduct a binary search over the basic intervals to determine the value of *min Finish Time*.

Equations 23.2 through 23.8 give our LP model to find $minFinishTime$ within $[T_i, T_{i+1})$.

$$\min \quad ft \tag{23.2}$$

$$\text{subject to} \quad \sum_{k:(l,k)\in E} f_{lk}^j(q) - \sum_{k:(k,l)\in E} f_{kl}^j(q) = 0$$

$$\forall j \in F, \forall l \in V, l \neq s_j, l \neq d_j, 0 \leq q \leq i \tag{23.3}$$

$$\sum_{q=0}^{i} \left(\sum_{k:(l,k)\in E} f_{lk}^j(q) - \sum_{k:(k,l)\in E} f_{kl}^j(q) \right) =$$

$$\begin{cases} f_j & \text{if } l = s_j \\ -f_j & \text{if } l = d_j \end{cases} \forall j \in F \tag{23.4}$$

$$\sum_{j\in F} f_{lk}^j(q) \leq b_{lk}(T_q) * (T_{q+1} - T_q), \forall (l,k) \in E, q < i \tag{23.5}$$

$$\sum_{j\in F} f_{lk}^j(i) \leq b_{lk}(T_i) * (ft - T_i), \forall (l,k) \in E \tag{23.6}$$

$$f_{lk}^j(q) \geq 0, [T_q, T_{q+1}] \subseteq [S_j, T_{q+1}], \forall (l,k) \in E, \forall j \in F \tag{23.7}$$

$$f_{lk}^j(q) = 0, [T_q, T_{q+1}] \not\subseteq [S_j, T_{q+1}], \forall (l,k) \in E, \forall j \in F \tag{23.8}$$

In this formulation, $ft \subset [T_i, T_{i+1})$ denotes the time by which all file transfers complete. $f_{lk}^j(q)$ is the amount of file transferred for request $j \in F$ on link $(l,k) \in E$ in the basic interval q. $b_{lk}(q)$ is the bandwidth available on link (l,k) in the basic interval q. Equation 23.3 ensures that for each transfer request $j \in F$, for each node l that is neither the source nor the destination node, and for each basic interval q, $0 \leq q \leq i$, the amount of file j that leaves node l equals the amount that enters this node; i.e., nodes other than the source or destination may not create or store data and data cannot be buffered at these nodes for transfer in later basic intervals. Equation 23.4 requires the source node of request j to send a net f_j units of file j out over all permissible basic intervals and requires the destination node to receive a net f_i units. Equations 23.5 and 23.6 ensure that the amount of traffic on each link in each basic interval does not exceed the available capacity of any link in any basic interval. Equation 23.7 ensures that file transfer amounts are non-negative in permissible basic intervals and Equation 23.8 ensures that the file transfer amounts are 0 in non-permissible basic intervals.

One can verify that each solution to Equation 23.3 through 23.8 defines a valid file transfer schedule for all requests in F and that the finish time of this schedule is at most ft. Further, the inclusion of Equation 23.2 determines the minimum finish time under the constraint that no file transfer may take place in intervals $q > i$. Also, Equations 23.3 through 23.8 have no feasible solution iff the file transfers cannot be scheduled so as to complete by time T_{i+1}.

As noted above, since fractional flow is allowed, $minFinishTime$ is polynomially solvable [33]. A binary search over the basic intervals is needed to determine the interval where $min\,Finish\,Time$ is located and also exact value of $min\,Finish\,Time$. This requires us to solve $O(\log B)$ LPs, where B is the number of basic intervals.

Although the $f_{lk}^{j}(q)$s that determine $min\,Finish\,Time$ define a file transfer schedule that achieves this finish time, these $f_{lk}^{j}(q)$s may define a transfer schedule that includes cycles. That is, we have portions of a file being moved from node a to node b and back to node a, for example, in the same basic interval. While these cyclic flows do not negatively impact the overall finish time, they affect available bandwidth capacity and so negatively impact our ability to schedule file transfers in future periods.

In Step 2, we overcome the deficiencies of the file transfer schedule obtained from Step 1 by using a slightly different LP formulation that is given by Equations 23.9 through 23.14. In this formulation, we minimizes the sum of the $f_{lk}^{j}(q)$ values across all basic intervals. The value $U = min\,Finish\,Time$ computed in Step 1 is used to limit the file transfers' start and end times. We also use i to denote the basic interval for which $T_i \leq min\,Finish\,Time \leq T_{i+1}$. It is obvious that the solution to Equations 23.10 through 23.14 may contain no cycle, or it can not be optimal, since we can always remove cycles and produce a better solution.

$$\min \quad \sum_{j \in J} \sum_{(l,k) \in E} \sum_{q=0}^{i} f_{lk}^{j}(q) \qquad (23.9)$$

$$\text{subject to} \quad \sum_{k:(l,k) \in E} f_{lk}^{j}(q) - \sum_{k:(k,l) \in E} f_{kl}^{j}(q) = 0$$

$$\forall j \in F, \forall l \in V, l \neq s_j, l \neq d_j, 0 \leq q \leq i \qquad (23.10)$$

$$\sum_{q=0}^{i} \left(\sum_{k:(l,k) \in E} f_{lk}^{j}(q) - \sum_{k:(k,l) \in E} f_{kl}^{j}(q) \right) =$$

$$\begin{cases} f_j & \text{if } l = s_j \\ -f_j & \text{if } l = d_j \end{cases} \forall j \in F \qquad (23.11)$$

$$\sum_{j \in F} f_{lk}^{j}(q) \leq b_{lk}(T_q) * (T_{q+1} - T_q), \forall (l,k) \in E, q \leq i \qquad (23.12)$$

$$f_{lk}^{j}(q) \geq 0, [T_q, T_{q+1}] \subseteq [S_j, U], \forall (l,k) \in E, \forall j \in F \qquad (23.13)$$

$$f_{lk}^{j}(q) = 0, [T_q, T_{q+1}] \nsubseteq [S_j, U], \forall (l,k) \in E, \forall j \in F \qquad (23.14)$$

We note that while the LP of Equations 23.2 through 23.8 is solved $O(\log B)$ (B is the number of basic intervals) times, the LP of Equations 23.9 through 23.14 is solved only once as a minimum-cost flow problem. Using the Successive Shortest Path algorithm[33], this flow problem can be solved with $O(E * log(U))$, where E is number of links in the network while U is the largest amount of flow. The just described two-step batch scheduling algorithm is referred to as algorithm *All-Batch*.

23.4.2.1 N-Batch *Heuristics.* As we will see in Section 23.4.4, the computing time required to compute the optimal schedule using algorithm *All-Batch* is very high.

One way to decrease the computation time is to divide the set of file transfers into smaller batches of size N and process them one by one. When $N > 1$, the corresponding heuristic is called *N-Batch*. The solution for *N-Batch* is as follows. The batches are processed one at a time sequentially in an increasing order of the batch's collecting times. When computing the optimal schedule for a given batch, the start time for that batch is given by the end time (the time of the last scheduled job) of the previous batch. The overall finish time is the finish time of the last batch scheduled.

As we use the greedy approach to process all the requests, one of the key issues is to decide the greedy selection criterion. [35] suggested that Largest File First (LFF) is a reasonable and quite effective heuristic to select the request(s) greedily. This approach is based on the intuition that the larger files will take more time to transfer. When scheduling the largest N files first, the larger files are given more priority in the the resource contention, which results in a potentially earlier finish time for the large file transfers. Since these long transfers actually determine the overall finish time often, this heuristic is expected to improve the overall finish time. This expectation is borne out in our experimentaal evaluation and the observed finish times are close to those of the optimal solutions generated by *All-Batch*.

23.4.3 Online Scheduling Algorithms

When the batch size equals 1, the *BFPSP* turns into an instance of Online Scheduling, where all file transfers are scheduled one by one without using any knowledge of the transfers scheduled later in the sequence.

We describe six online file transfer scheduling algorithms. In Sections 23.4.3.1 and 23.4.3.2 , we describe the *GOS* and *GOS-E* algorithms. The remaining four algorithms are variations of the *k-Path* heuristics and are described in Section 23.4.3.3. The greedy algorithm, *GOS*, employs network flows to minimize the finish time of each single file transfer being scheduled. *GOS-E* considers the path switching overhead. The four *k-Path* heuristics use the the *k*-shortest paths or *k*-disjoint paths to compute the schedule on a smaller network than the original one. These adaptations reduce the complexity of the scheduling algorithm, but yield little in maximum finish time.

23.4.3.1 Greedy Algorithm. The greedy online algorithm, *GOS*, schedules a file transfer (s_i, d_i, f_i, S_i) by examining the basic intervals in the network's current global time list in increasing order. The examination begins with the basic interval that includes the time S_i. In each examined interval, we transfer as much of the file as is possible. This maximum amount can be determined using a max-flow algorithm (see [33], for example). The examination of basic intervals stops when all f_i bytes of the file have been scheduled. Figure 23.14 gives the procedure of our greedy online algorithm, *GOS*, to schedule the ith request. In the specification of this algorithm, we construct a reduced graph N from G with only the links have some available bandwidth in current basic interval. we use the term *max flow links* to denote those edges of N that have a non-zero flow in the max flow solution for N. Also, note that *maxFlow* may be zero in some basic intervals and care needs to be taken when programming algorithm *GOS* to avoid a divide by zero error when computing $rfs/maxFlow$.

```
GOS (i, G)
{
        Construct the current global time list T from the
            TB lists;
        Delete from T all T_i ≤ S_i;
        Insert S_i and ∞ into T and relabel the members of T in
            ascending order beginning with the label T_0;
        rfs = f_i;        //remaining file size
        j = 0;        //basic interval index;
        while (rfs > 0)
        {
                Let N be the network derived from G by assigning
                    to each link a capacity equals to its available
                    bandwidth in the basic interval [T_j, T_{j+1}),
                Remove the links with 0 capacity from N;
                maxFlow = Max flow from s_i to d_i in N;
                maxTime = min{T_j + rfs/maxFlow, T_{j+1}};
                size = (maxTime − T_j) * maxFlow;
                Schedule the transfer of size bytes from T_j to
                    maxTime using the max flow links;
                Update the TB lists of the max flow links;
                rfs − = size;
                j + +;
        }
}
```

Figure 23.14   Greedy online scheduling algorithm *GOS*.

The complexity of algorithm *GOS* is determined by the complexity of the max flow algorithm that is used as well as by the number of basic intervals in the global time list. The complexity of the push-relabel max flow algorithm described in [33] is $O(n^3)$, where n is the number of vertices in the network flow graph. For networks with few edges, the sparse graph network flow algorithm of Sleator and Tarjan (see [33], for example) may be used. The complexity of this algorithm is $O(nm \log n)$, where m is the number of links in the network. When scheduling the ith file transfer, the size of the global time list is at most $2i$, since each previously scheduled request will increase the size of global time list by at most 2: job's start and end time. So, the complexity of *GOS* is $O(n^3 i)$ when the push-relabel max flow algorithm is used and $O(nmi \log n)$ when the sparse graph max flow algorithm is used. Since typical computer networks are generally sparse and have only $O(n)$ links, using the sparse graph max flow algorithm results in a complexity of $O(n^2 i \log n)$ for *GOS*.

23.4.3.2 *Greedy Scheduling with Finish Time Extension* (GOS-E). In the *GOS* algorithm, the network flow is computed for each basic interval. This implies that, for a file transfer that lasts n consecutive basic intervals, up to n establishing and tearing down operations on flow path would take place in the network. Moreover, given the fact that multi-paths are required for each flow, the path switching overhead would significantly affect the *GOS*'s performance in practice.

Theorem 23.1

If G has a path from s_i to d_i, then Algorithm GOS schedules the ith file transfer request (s_i, d_i, f_i, S_i) so as to complete at the earliest possible time.

Proof. From the following facts (a) G has a path from s_i to d_i, (b) the rated capacity of each link of G is more than 0, (c) the last basic interval of the global time list always extends to ∞, and (d) the available bandwidth of each link is its rated capacity during this last basic interval, it follows that the max flow from s_i to d_i in the last basic interval is non-zero and so the remaining file size rfs can always be scheduled for transfer in this last basic interval. Hence, GOS is able to schedule every file transfer request.

Let the finish time of a file transfer schedule constructed by GOS be ft. Note that ft is the value of *maxTime* when GOS terminates. We show, by contradiction, that ft is the earliest possible time at which this file transfer can complete. Suppose there is another transfer schedule, S, for the same request that completes the transfer by time $ft' < ft$. Let q be such that $T_q \leq ft < T_{q+1}$ (all global time references in this proof are to times as relabeled by GOS) and let q' be such that $T_{q'} \leq ft' < T_{q'+1}$. Note that $q' \leq q$. If $q' < q$, then there is a basic interval $u < q$ such that the amount of f_i scheduled for transfer in interval u by schedule S is more than that scheduled for transfer in u by the GOS schedule. This isn't possible since the GOS schedule transfers the maximum possible amount in each basic interval prior to q. If $q' = q$, then since $ft' < ft$, the amount scheduled for transfer by S from T_q to ft' is less than that scheduled for transfer by the GOS schedule from T_q to ft, or the flow used by GOS schedule after T_q could not be the maximum flow. Hence, there must be a basic interval $u < q = q'$ in which more of f_i is scheduled for transfer by S than by the GOS schedule. As noted earlier, this isn't possible. Hence, there is no transfer schedule S with $ft' < ft$. $\square$

To decrease the switching overhead, *GOS-E* is proposed to reduce the number of path switchings by reducing the total number of basic intervals in the network. In *GOS-E*, we tried to extend the current job's finish time to the the end of nearest later basic interval t_i, if t_i is not too far away from ft, which is the earliest finish time computed from *GOS*. The extension can be done by either directly over-reserving the bandwidth in the last basic interval involved in the file transfer according to the original reservation plan from *GOS*, or reduce the amount of required bandwidth in the last interval to cope with the longer transfer time, which will not waste bandwidth. As bandwidth resources are limited in our scenario, we take the second approach. The extension scope should be limited to a certain range so that the performance on a single file transfer is not greatly affected.

With *GOS-E*, we are able to eliminate the small basic intervals by merging them into the previous large intervals by reducing its link bandwidth. As small intervals generally perform smaller amount of file transfers than large intervals, this merging process actually costs little additional network throughput but provides the potential to reduce the overall path switching overhead. In the evaluation section, we will test this heuristic and compare with the original *GOS* algorithm, Also, the relationship between the extension scope and algorithm performance is discussed.

23.4.3.3 K-Path Algorithms. Another approach to accelerate the algorithm is to reduce the problem size. We incorporate the idea behind *KSP* [28] and *KDP* [27] scheduling into algorithm *GOS* so as to compute the max-flow in a reduced network. In the *KSP* and *KDP* adaptations, when scheduling the request (s_i, d_i, f_i, S_i), we limit our resource allocations to a subgraph defined by the k paths from s_i to d_i. In the case of the *KDP* adaptation, since the k paths are disjoint, the max flow from s_i to d_i in any basic interval is easily seen to be the sum of the minimum available capacity of a link on each of the k paths. So, we avoid running a complex network flow algorithm to determine the max flow. In the case of the *KSP* adaptation, since the paths are not disjoint, we still need to run the *GOS* algorithm on the network formed by these k paths. However, since the size of the network being considered is smaller, run time is reduced.

For both the *KSP* and *KDP* adaptations, we define a static and a dynamic variant. In the *static variant* the cost of a link is defined to be its rated capacity (alternatively, some other non-changing cost may be assigned) and the k paths between every pair of nodes, whether disjoint or not, are computed once at the first time a request arrives for this pair of nodes and use directly for the scheduling request between the same source/destination pair afterward. In the *dynamic variant*, links are assigned a cost each time a scheduling request arrives and the k shortest paths to use are computed using these newly assigned link costs. The cost assigned to a link in the dynamic variant is proportional to the fraction of its rated capacity that has been committed from the current time to the finish time of the last finishing file transfer so far scheduled in the network. In both static and dynamic variants, the length of a path is the sum of the link costs. The static and dynamic variants of the *KSP* and *KDP* adaptations of *GOS* are referred to as *KSP-S, KSP-D, KDP-S,* and *KDP-D*, respectively.

23.4.4 Experimental Evaluation

23.4.4.1 Experimental Framework. In this section, we measure the performance of the batch scheduling algorithm described in Section 23.4.2 and online scheduling algorithms described in Section 23.4.3. For our experiments, we used the MCI network and random topologies that generated at run time.

File transfer requests were synthetically generated. Each request is described by the 4-tuple (source node, destination node, file size, request start time). The source and destination nodes for each request were selected using a uniform random number generator. The file size is also uniformly distributed between 10 GB and 100 GB. The earliest time at which a file transfer can start followed a Poisson distribution and the request arrival rate (request density) varied from 0.05 requests/time unit to 10 requests/time unit. Our experiments started with a clean network (i.e., no existing scheduled transfers) and simulated the job arrival process for 100 time units. So, for example, with a request density of 5 requests/time unit, one run of our experiment would process approximately 500 requests.

We used the max finish time (MFT), that is, the time when all file transfers in the sequence finish as the performance metric. The execution time of an algorithm is measured in seconds. For *GOS-E*, the extension scope is set to be either 2%, 5%, or

10% of the current file transfer's duration. Suppose that the file transfer J_i, with start and end time S_i and E_i, respectively, is being scheduled. Suppose that E_i's nearest future basic interval ends at T. Then, the extension of E_i to T is performed when $(T - E_i) \leq (E_i - S_i) * Extension\,Scope$.

For the *KSP* and *KDP* variants of *GOS*, we set k, the number of paths, to 16. This setting is consistent with the results of [27], which show that not much improvement can be obtained from using a higher k, and is also consistent with our own experiments on scheduling file transfers that indicate 16 to be a good choice for k.

23.4.4.2 *Single Start Time Scheduling (SSTS).*
A special case of *BFPSP* has all files ready for transfer at the same time, which means all requests in the batch have the same S_i. This special case arises, for example, when all file tranfer requests originate from a single group of users. For this experiment, we set $S_i = 0$ for all transfer requests. The number of files to be scheduled varies from 200 to 1000. The size of the random network varies from 100 nodes to 500 nodes.

Figures 23.15 and 23.16 show the maximum finish time of the schedules for various number of files on the MCI network and a 100-node random network, respectively. All the algorithms proposed in Sections 23.4.2 and 23.4.3 are compared except for *GOS E*. The main objective of *GOS E* is to reduce the path switching overhead. This is not addressed by the other algorithms. Figure 23.17 shows how the scheduling results change as network size increases and the number of requests is fixed at 400. We make the following observations.

1. Batch scheduling performs better than online scheduling in all cases. The larger the batch size, the better the relative performance of batch scheduling. In large networks like random-100, larger batch size has significantly larger improvements on the overall performance; however, in small networks like MCI, the impact of batch size is relatively small.

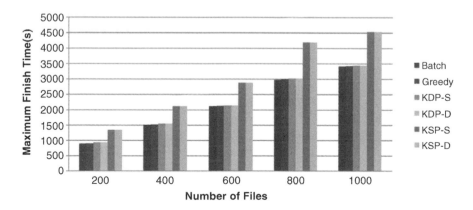

Figure 23.15 Comparison of different algorithms' MFT for different number of files in MCI using *SSTS*.

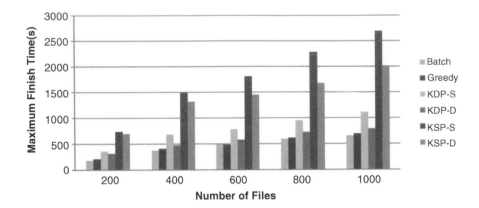

Figure 23.16 Comparison of different algorithms' MFT for different number of files in 100 nodes random topology using *SSTS*.

2. When batch size is 50, *N-Batch* performs as well as the optimal batch schedule in most cases. *GOS* has the best performance among online scheduling algorithms in all cases. In small networks, *GOS* performs almost as well as the optimal solution. In large networks, the improvement acheived by using *All-Batch* is usually no more than 5% over *GOS*.

3. Among the 4 *k-Path* heuristics, two *KDP* heuristics perform better than the *KSP* heuristics and dynamic link cost can improve the performance. This can be partly attributed to the congestion avoidance mechanism that dynamic link cost provided. Without doubt, *KDP-D* provides the best performance among the 4 *k-Path* heuristics. Although not comparable to *GOS* algorithm for large networks, their performance gap is small enough to be acceptable for small topologies.

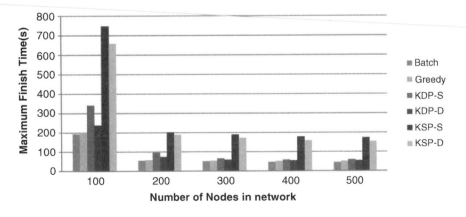

Figure 23.17 Comparison of different algorithms' MFT random topologies of different size using *SSTS*.

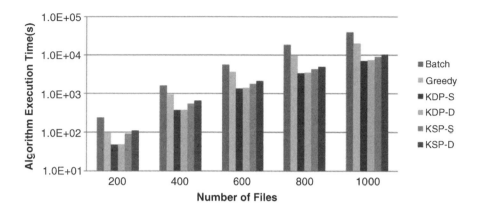

Figure 23.18 Comparison of different algorithms' execution time on different numbers of files on MCI network using *SSTS*.

4. The MFT increases as the number of files increases. The amount of this increase is faster in small networks than in large ones, as small networks are become congested and fully loaded sooner. On the other hand, MFT decreases as the network size increase, as the network provides more bandwidth resources in a global view.

In summary, the *All-Batch*'s advantage over *N-Batch* and *GOS* is not obvious, especially in small networks. When the batch size *N* reaches 50, the performance gap is relatively small and can be ignored in many practical scenarios.

The heuristics described in this section solve an easier max-flow problem than the complex and time-consuming LP formulation solved by *All-Batch*. Figures 23.18 and 23.19 show the execution time for the MCI network and for a random network with

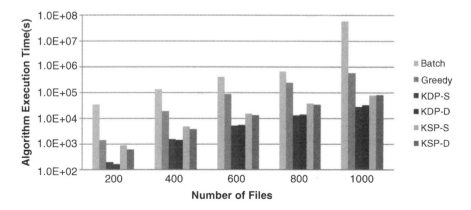

Figure 23.19 Comparison of different algorithms' execution time on different numbers of files on 100 nodes random topology using *SSTS*.

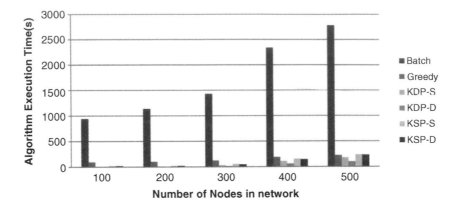

Figure 23.20 Comparison of different algorithms' MFT execution time on random topologies with different size using *SSTS*.

100 nodes, respectively. The horizontal axis is the number of files to be scheduled. The execution time is measured in seconds.

In all cases, the execution time of the online algorithms is much less than that of the batch algorithm. In small networks, the scheduling time is acceptable for all algorithms. Less than 2 minutes are taken to obtain the optimal schedule in MCI for 1000 file requests; the online algorithms take several seconds. In large networks, our online heuristics are dramatically faster than the bacth scheduling algorithm.

Figure 23.20 shows the algorithms' execution time for various network sizes. During the test, we scheduled 400 jobs using *SSTS*. We observed that, although every algorithms' execution time increases with network size, the time required by *All-Batch* and *N-Batch* actually increase much faster than that required by the online algorithms. This is due to the lower complexity of the online algorithms. In the 500 node topology, *GOS* only takes several minutes, but *All-Batch* takes about 2 hours to compute the optimal schedule, which exceeds the actual file transfer time in our experiments.

23.4.4.3 Multiple Start Time Scheduling (MSTS). *BFPSP* actually does not require all the file transfers to start at the same time. When jobs start at various times, the total traffic load is expected to be less intensive than the *SSTS* case, since the file transfers are less overlapped due to the difference in their start time.

Figures 23.21 to 23.26 give the experimental results using *MSTS*. Figures 23.21, 23.22 and 23.23 show how the maximum finish time changes with number of requests and network size. Figures 23.24, 23.25 and 23.26 show the algorithms scalability with increasing number of requests or network size. The observations from *MSTS* are similar to those for *SSTS*. The batch algorithms outperform online ones in terms of MFT value, but require significantly longer computation time. The batch algorithms also show worse scalability with both network size and number of requests. *GOS* performs better than all other online heuristics and provides very good schedules with very small execution time.

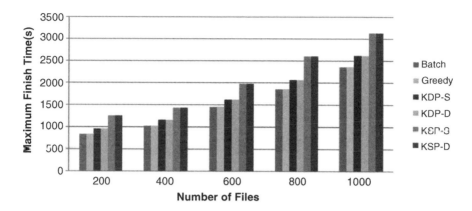

Figure 23.21 Comparison of different algorithms' MFT for different number of files in MCI using *MSTS*.

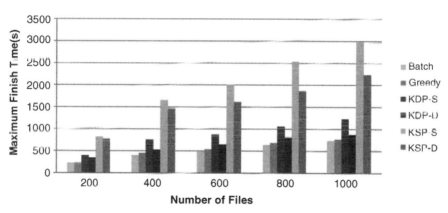

Figure 23.22 Comparison of different algorithms' MFT for different number of files in 100 nodes random topology using *MSTS*.

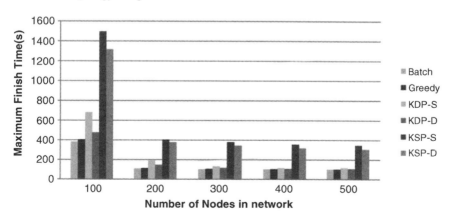

Figure 23.23 Comparison of different algorithms' MFT in random topologies of different size using *MSTS*.

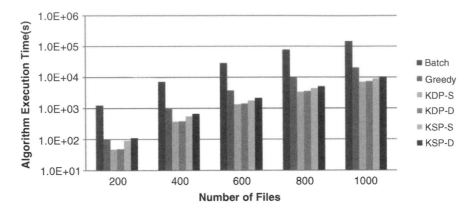

Figure 23.24 Comparison of different algorithms' execution time in MCI network using *MSTS*.

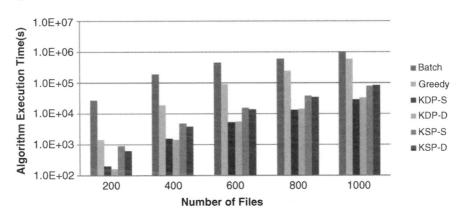

Figure 23.25 Comparison of different algorithms' execution time in 100 nodes random topology using *MSTS*.

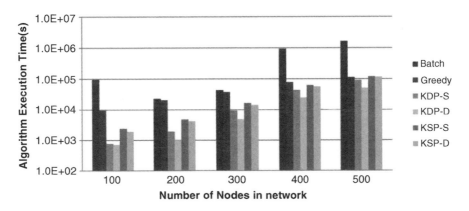

Figure 23.26 Comparison of different algorithms' execution time on random topologies with different size using *MSTS*.

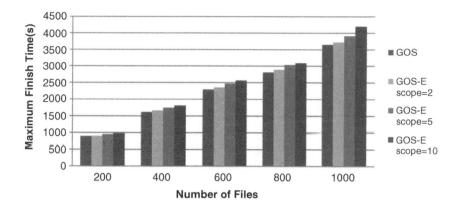

Figure 23.27 Comparison on number of Max-Flows is computed by *GOS-E* and *GOS* in 100 node random network.

23.4.4.4 GOS vs. GOS-E. When path switching overhead is considered, the *GOS*'s potential to switch path for every basic interval can possibly become its major drawback. This problem is more severe when the file is transferred using multiple paths. In this section, *GOS-E* is evaluated and compared with the original *GOS* algorithm.

When performing the test, one of the important issues is to simulate the path switching overhead. From the previous section, we know that path switching happens only between two adjacent basic intervals. So we add a lag of t_l in our simulation between each basic interval to represent the delay due to path switching. In our experiments, we set the delay to be 1 second for establishing and tearing down an optical path. That is, if the schedule for a certain file transfer changes its routes m times during the transfer, a delay of $2 * m$ seconds will be added to its finish time.

The test is performed on *GOS* and three *GOS-E* variants with different extension scopes: 2%, 5%, and 10%, which means *GOS-E* can search for the next existing basic interval and extend the current schedule in the range of 2%, 5%, and 10%, respectively. Figures 23.27 and 23.28 show the MFT performance for all four algorithms, with and

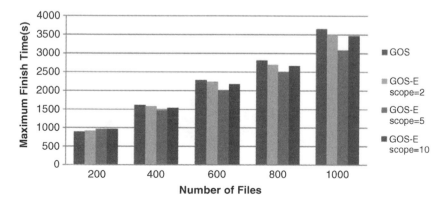

Figure 23.28 Comparison on execution time used by *GOS-E* and *GOS* in 100-node random network.

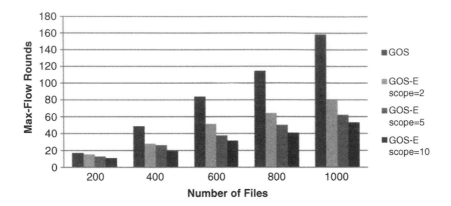

Figure 23.29 Comparison on number of Max-Flows is computed by *GOS-E* and *GOS* in 100 node random network.

without path switching delay counted. We can see that when the path switching delay is not accounted for, the schedules generated by *GOS-E* take more time to complete the file transfers, but when the path switching delay is accounted for, *GOS-E* actually outperforms *GOS*. We also notice that a larger extension scope does not imply better MFT, as *GOS-E* with 5% extension scope generates better schedules than with an extension scope of 10%. Although the switching overhead can be reduced using a larger extension scope, the actual file transfer time increases, which compromises the benefit of fewer path switchings.

Figure 23.29 compares the average rounds of max-flow computation for each request in *GOS-E* with *GOS*, while Figure 23.30 compares their execution times. These results show that bacause of the reduction in the number of max-flow computation rounds, the execution time for *GOS-E* is lower as compared to the *GOS* algorithm. Also, the execution time is further reduced with larger extension scopes albeit at a price of longer

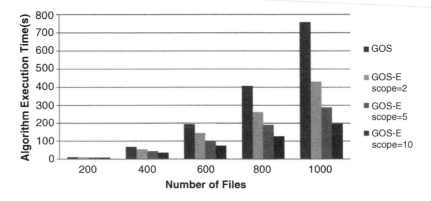

Figure 23.30 Comparison on execution time used by *GOS-E* and *GOS* in 100-node random network.

MFT. However, in large networks, this degradation is considerably small. This makes *GOS-E* more attractive for large networks.

23.5 CONCLUSION

We have categorized the different bandwidth algorithms that have been proposed for in-advance scheduling by both the problem being addressed (fixed slot, maximum bandwidth in slot, maximum duration, first slot, all slots, all-pairs all-slots). In addition, we have proposed several new algorithms (SWFP, SDFP, DAFP, kDP, and kSP) for the fixed-slot problem that are adaptations of algorithms proposed earlier for on-demand scheduling. Although the DAFP algorithm proposed by us is an adaptation of the dynamic adaptive path algorithm proposed for on-demand scheduling in [19], DAFP guarantees to find a feasible path whenever such a path exists, whereas the dynamic adaptive path algorithm of [19] does not provide such a guarantee.

We have conducted extensive experiments with the various fixed-slot algorithms for in-advance scheduling. Our experiments indicate that the minimum-hop feasible path algorithm proposed by us in [24] is the best (in the sense of maximizing network utilization) of these on large networks. For networks with a small number of nodes (say 20 or less), the DAFP algorithm proposed in this chapter is best. From the standpoint of algorithmic complexity, MHFP is considerably faster than DAFP. We have developed several multi-path reservation algorithms for in-advance scheduling of single and multiple file transfers in connection-oriented optical networks. A novel two-step solution, *All-Batch*, has been developed to compute schedules with minimum finish time (i.e., optimal schedules). An *N-Batch* heuristic was developed to enable batch scheduling in more realistic scenarios. We also proposed a new max-flow based greedy algorithm (*GOS*) and four variants of *k-path* algorithms to reduce computation time. These heuristics schedule an individual file transfer to complete at the earliest possible time.

Extensive simulations using both real-world networks and random topologies show that *GOS* presents a good balance among maximum finish time, mean finish time, and computation time. Further reduction in computation time by sacrificing maximum finish time may be obtained using our *k-Path* variants. Of these, *KDP-D* works best. When path switching overhead is considered, *GOS-E* provides good performance.

ACKNOWLEDGMENT

This work was supported, in part, by the National Science Foundation under grants NETS 0963812, NETS 1115184, High-Performance Networking Program, Office of Science of U.S. Department of Energy, and a GRO award from Samsung.

REFERENCES

[1] R. Banner and A. Orda, "Multipath routing algorithms for congestion minimization." *IEEE/ACM Trans. Network* 15 (2007): 413–424.

[2] N.S. Rao, S.M. Carter, Q. Wu, W.R. Wing, M. Zhu, A. Mezzacappa, M. Veeraraghavan, and J.M. Blondin, "Networking for large-scale science: Infrastructure, provisioning, transport and application mapping." *Proceedings of SciDAC Meeting.* 2005.

[3] hopi. Hybrid Optical and Packet Infrastructure, http://networks.internet2.edu/hopi.

[4] internet2. "Internet2." http://www.internet2.edu.

[5] jgn2. JGN II: Advanced Network Testbed for Research and Development, http://www.jgn. nict.go.jp.

[6] UCLP. User Controlled Light Path Provisioning, http://phi.badlab.crc.ca/uclp.

[7] N.S.V. Rao, W.R. Wing, S.M. Carter, and Q. Wu, "UltraScience net: Network testbed for large-scale science applications." *IEEE Communications Magazine* (2005).

[8] X. Zheng, M. Veeraraghavan, N.S.V. Rao, Q. Wu, and M. Zhu, "CHEETAH: Circuit-switched high-speed end-to-end transport architecture testbed." *IEEE Communications Magazine* (2005).

[9] "Dynamic resource allocation via GMPLS optical networks." http://dragon.maxgigapop.net.

[10] geant. Geant2, http://www.geant2.net.

[11] "On-demand Secure Circuits and Advance Reservation System." http://www.es.net/oscars.

[12] Z.L. Zhang, Z. Duan, and Y.T. Hou, "Decoupling QoS control from core routers: A novel bandwidth broker architecture for scalable support of guaranteed services." *Proc. ACM SIG-COMM.* 2000.

[13] lhcnet. LHCNet: Transatlantic Networking for the LHC and the U.S. HEP Community, http://lhcnet.caltech.edu/.

[14] U. Black, *MPLS and Label Switching Networks.* Prentice-Hall, 2002.

[15] P. Aukia, M. Kodialam, P.V.N. Koppol, T.V. Lakshman, H. Sarin, and B. Suter, "RATES: A server for MPLS traffic engineering." *IEEE Network* (March/April 2000): 34–41.

[16] N. Yamanaka, K. Shiomoto, and E. Oki, *GMPLS Technologies.* CRC Taylor Francis, 2006.

[17] R. Guerin, A. Orda, and D. Williams, "QoS routing mechanisms and OSPF extensions." *IETF Internet Draft.* 1996.

[18] Q. Ma, P. Steenkiste, and H. Zhang, "Routing high-bandwidth traffic in max-min fair share networks." *ACM SIGCOMM.* 1996. 115–126.

[19] Q. Ma and P. Steenkiste, "On path selection for traffic with bandwidth guarantees." *5th Intl. Conf. on Network Protocols (ICNP).* 1997. 191–204.

[20] Z. Wang and J. Crowcroft, "Quality-of-service routing for supporting multimedia applications." *IEEE JSAC.* 1996. 1228–1234.

[21] L.O. Burchard, "On the performance of networks with advance reservations: Applications, architecture, and performance." *Journal of Network and Systems Management.* 2005.

[22] R. Guerin and A. Orda, "Networks with advance reservations: The routing perspective." *Proceedings of the 19th Annual Joint Conference of the IEEE Computer and Communications Societies INFOCOM.* 2000. 118–127.

[23] N.S.V. Rao, Q. Wu, S.M. Carter, W.R. Wing, A. Banerjee, D. Ghosal, and B. Mukherjee, "Control plane for advance bandwidth scheduling in ultra high-speed networks." *INFOCOM 2006 Workshop on Terabits Networks.* 2006.

[24] S. Sahni, N. Rao, S. Ranka, Y. Li, E.-S. Jung, and N. Kamath. "Bandwidth scheduling and path computation algorithms for connection-oriented networks." *Sixth International Conference on Networking (ICN'07).* 2007. 47.

[25] N.S.V. Rao and S. G. Batsell, "QoS routing via multiple paths using bandwidth reservation." *INFOCOM*. 1998, 11–18.

[26] Y. Lee, Y. Seok, Y. Choi, and C. Kim, "A constrained multipath traffic engineering scheme for MPLS networks." *Communications, 2002. ICC 2002. IEEE International Conference on*. Vol. 4. 2002, 2431–2436.

[27] K. Rajah, S. Ranka, and Y. Xia, "Scheduling bulk file transfers with start and end times." *6th IEEE International Symposium on Network Computing and Applications*. 2007, 295–298.

[28] J.Y. Yen, "Finding the k shortest loopless paths in a network." *Management Science*. 1971.

[29] S. Sahni, *Data Structures, Algorithms, and Applications in C++ 2nd Ed.* Silicon Press, 2005.

[30] S. Tanwir, L. Battestilli, H. Perros, and G. Karmous-Edwards, "Dynamic scheduling of network resources with advance reservation in optical grids." *International Journal of Network Management*. vol. 18. 2008. 79–105.

[31] enlightened. Enlightened Computing, http://www.enlightenedcomputing.org/.

[32] Abilene. "Abilene." http://abilene.internet2.edu.

[33] R. Ahuja, T. Magnanti, and J. Orin, *Network Flows: Theory, Algorithms, and Applications*. Prentice Hall, 1993.

[34] Fusion. "International Thermonuclear Experimental Reactor." http://www.iter.org.

[35] A. Banerjee, W. Chun Feng, D, Ghosal, and B. Mukherjee, "Algorithms for Integrated routing and scheduling for aggregating data from distributed resources on a lambda grid." *IEEE Trans. Parallel Distrib. Syst. 19*. 2008. 24–34.

[36] I. Foster, C. Kesselman, C. Lee, R. Lindell, K. Nahrstedt, and A. Roy, "A distributed resource management architecture that supports advance reservations and co-allocation." *7th Intl. Workshop on Quality of Service (IWQoS)* (1999): 27–36.

[37] G. Schelen and S. Pink, "An agent-based architecture for advance reservations." *22nd Annual Conference on Computer Networks*. 1997.

[38] J. Zheng, B. Zhang, and H.T. Mouftah, "Toward automated provisioning of advance reservation service in next-generation optical internet." *IEEE Communications Magazine* 44 (2006). 12: 68–74.

[39] B.H. Ramaprasad, A. Soman, and V.M. Vokkarane, "Dynamic non-continuous single slot advance reservation over wavelength routed networks," *International Conference on Computing, Networking and Communications*, 2012.

[40] M. Balman, E. Chaniotakis, A. Shoshani, A. Sim, "A flexible reservation algorithm for advance network provisioning," *Supercomputing Conference*, 2010.

[41] S. Sharma, D. Katramatos, and D. Yu, "End-to-end network QoS via scheduling of flexible resource reservation requests," *Supercomputing Conference*, 2012.

24

ROUTING AND WAVELENGTH ASSIGNMENT IN OPTICAL NETWORKS

Yan Li, Sanjay Ranka, and Sartaj Sahni

CONTENTS

Large Scale Network-Centric Distributed Systems, First Edition. Edited by Hamid Sarbazi-Azad and Albert Y. Zomaya.
© 2014 John Wiley & Sons, Inc. Published 2014 by John Wiley & Sons, Inc.

24.1 INTRODUCTION

Dedicated connections are needed to effectively support a variety of geographically distributed application tasks. Many high-speed networks that provide dedicated connections are based on optical interconnects and optical switches. For these networks, the bandwidth along a given link can be decomposed into multiple wavelengths. The bandwidth scheduling and path computation problem in the context of optical networks is usually called RWA (Routing and Wavelength Assignment) [1]. Algorithms for RWA may have to adhere to one or more of the following constraints:

1. Wavelength continuity constraint: This constraint forces a single lightpath to occupy the same wavelength throughout all the links that it spans. This constraint is not required when an optical network is equipped with wavelength converters. When such converters are present, the network is called *wavelength convertible* network. The algorithms presented in this chapter assume that either wavelength conversion is available at all switches or not available at any switch.

2. Wavelength sharing constraint: For many deployments, it is most effective to consider the bandwidth on a link as consisting of integer multiples of wavelength and a single wavelength as a unit for assignment, that is, one wavelength is occupied by only one reservation at a certain point of time. The algorithms in this chapter assume that this constraint needs to be satisfied. It is worth noting that techniques based on Time Division Multiplexing (TDM)/Wavelength Division Multiplexing (WDM) [7] allow for decomposing the bandwidth on a wavelength.

The Enlightened project [2] has developed several routing algorithms for optical networks assuming wavelength convertibility and no wavelength sharing constraints.

They are developed using the Flexible Advance Reservation Model (FARM) [5] that tries to reduce the blocking probability of requests by assigning a scheduling window for each request [3]. The algorithms developed in the Enlightened project can be termed as k Dynamic Paths (kDP) algorithms according to the classification of [8]. These algorithms do not guaranteed to find a feasible path whenever such a path is present.

The wavelength assignment problem is a relatively orthogonal problem from the routing problem and many heuristics have been developed for its solution [1]. For our experimental comparisons, we use the wavelength assignment policy as proposed for that given routing algorithm.

In Section 24.2, we extended the Extended Bellman-Ford (EBF) algorithm to incorporate the wavelength sharing and wavelength continuity constraints. We also propose modified versions of the algorithms in the Enlightened system for continuous time model. These algorithms are called Modified Switch Path First (MSPF) and Modified Switch Window First (MSWF). MSPF tries to find the earliest path within the scheduling window, while MSWF tries to find the shortest path within the scheduling window. Moreover, a deferred wavelength assignment strategy is presented. This strategy only counts the number of wavelengths that are used on a link. The actual assignment of the wavelength is done when the request is actually fulfilled.

Although the design and implementation of a full-conversion scheduler is relatively straightforward, the high cost and the added latency introduced by wavelength converters make sparse-conversion more attractive in practice. Existing research on *On-Demand* scheduling has shown that wavelength converters have the potential to improve blocking performance significantly and that it is necessary only for a relatively small fraction of the nodes to have a wavelength converter to achieve blocking performance comparable to that of full wavelength conversion [9–11]. Since on-demand scheduling reserves a path for a fixed time slot, this result applies directly to the Fixed-Slot scenario.

In Section 24.3, we present a new network model that that can emulate the existing full-conversion algorithms when only a subset of nodes have a wavelength converter. We demonstrate the utility of this approach using the *Extended Bellman-Ford (EBF)* and *k-Alternative Path (k-Path)* algorithms. We evaluate the algorithms on three performances metrics: blocking probability, average start time and scheduling overhead. Blocking probability, which measures the ratio of blocked requests to the number of scheduled requests, is the primary metric used to evaluate a scheduling algorithm. Average start time, which presents how early the requested lightpath is available, is of special importance in the First-Slot scenario. Scheduling overhead, which compares algorithms according to their computation costs, is an important metric for the algorithms practicality.

24.2 SCHEDULING IN FULL-WAVELENGTH CONVERSION NETWORK

24.2.1 Problem Definition

An optical network topology is represented as a graph $G = (V, E, W)$ where V is the set of nodes, E is the set of links and W is the set of wavelengths supported by each link. An in-advance reservation request for a lightpath can be made between any two nodes on G. Algorithms for RWA may have to adhere to the wavelength continuity and wavelength sharing constraints as described in the introduction. We use the Flexible Advance Reservation Model (FARM). This model tries to reduce the blocking probability of requests by assigning a scheduling window for each request [3].

In this section, we address the following queries:

1. Find the least time t within the scheduling window for which there is a path with an available wavelength from the source s to the destination d from time t to time $t + dur$ and reserve such a path. This is a variation of the First-Slot Problem in [6].

2. Find the shortest path with an available bandwidth from a source s to a destination d within the scheduling window and reserve such a path.

Each request R for a single lightpath is defined as follows: $R = [s, d, dur, start, end]$, where s is the source node of the lightpath, d is the destination node of the lightpath, dur is the reservation duration, and $start$ and end are the start time and end time of the scheduling window, respectively. The scheduling window must be larger than the reservation duration d. The scheduler must check if a path is available during any possible interval in the scheduling window. In slotted time model, the intervals will be $[start + t, start + t + dur]$ where $t = 0, 1, 2, \ldots, end - start - dur$. In the continuous time model, a discrete sliding approach may miss intermediate start times.

The algorithms presented in [5] do not guarantee finding a feasible solution even if a solution is present. The algorithms developed in this section provide such guarantees. We compare the time requirements and the effectiveness of these algorithms in the following sections. The routing and the wavelength assignment portions of these algorithms are presented in separate subsections.

24.2.2 Routing Algorithms

The goal of the first query is to find the path with the least start time during a scheduling window, while the goal of the second query is to find the path with shortest distance/hop during a scheduling window. We develop two algorithms—Modified Switch Path First (MSPF) and List Sliding Window (LSW)—for answering the first query. We also develop two algorithms—Modified Slide Window First Algorithm (MSWF) and Extended Bellman-Ford Algorithm (EBF)—for answering the second query. These are described in detail in the rest of this section.

The algorithms developed in [5] can be termed as k Dynamic Paths (kDP) algorithm according to the classification of [8]. These algorithms check k dynamic paths based on the current network status and test them for their feasibility. If more than one path is found to be feasible, ties are broken appropriately. These algorithms do not guarantee to find a feasible solution even if a solution is present. Experimental results [5] showed that when the link costs are dynamically updated to incorporate current allocation and provide Load Balancing (LB), the blocking rate is significantly reduced. The Load Balancing (LB) scheme [5] assigns the cost of a link with no reservation to be equal to 1. This cost is incremented as additional reservations are assigned to the link. The two versions based on load balancing using the different approaches to choose between multiple paths are called Switch Path First (LB-SPF) and Switch Window First (LB-SWF) algorithm. LB-SPF tries to find the path starting earliest within the scheduling window, while LB-SWF tries to find the shortest path within the scheduling window. We have extended these algorithms for the continuous time model to provide comparisons with our algorithms and are called MSPF and MSWF respectively.

24.2.2.1 Modified Switch Path First Algorithm (MSPF).
For the slotted time model, this algorithm starts at the beginning of the scheduling window. It computes the shortest path using Dijkstra's algorithm. If this path is feasible, it assigns an available wavelength along the path; else, it deletes the busy links on the path and recomputes the shortest path. For a given fixed reservation interval $[t_{start}, t_{start} + duration]$, this shortest path computation has to be repeated at most k times. If no feasible path is found, the reservation interval is incremented by one slot until the interval's end time equals the scheduling window's end time. To adapt this approach to the continuous time model, we advance to the next start time in the *ST* list instead of sliding the reservation interval by one time slot. The modified algorithm is as follows:

Step 1: Sort all a values in the *ST* list of each link in the network. For each a_i in the sorted list, repeat Steps 2 and 3 at most k times.

Step 2: Compute the shortest path based on current link costs. Verify feasibility for reservation interval starting at time a_i.

Step 3: If the path is feasible, stop the algorithm and return this path; else delete all the busy links on the path.

24.2.2.2 Modified Switch Window First Algorithm (MSWF).
The original SWF algorithm is similar to SPF except that it slides the reservation interval before switching the path. This requires a check on all the possible reservation intervals within the scheduling window for one path before checking the next path. For the continuous time model, modified algorithms can be implemented in several ways. One possible variation is as follows.

The intersection of all the *ST* lists on a path can be used to derive the feasibility of a given path. If the path is feasible, an earliest start time can be easily derived by using the smallest number in the intersected list. The algorithm attempts at most k different paths and check all the possible start time for each path as follows:

Step 1: Compute the shortest path and it associated ST lists. Verify the path by intersecting all these ST lists.

Step 2: If intersected ST list is not empty, return this path with first possible start time, else remove the busiest link during the window.

Step 3: Repeat steps 1 and 2 for k times. If none of the path is feasible, reject the request.

If the network is equipped with wavelength converters, one single ST list can be managed per one link. For networks with no wavelength converters, a single path has to be treated as multiple sub-paths corresponding to each wavelength and repeat the process over all sub-paths.

The MSPF and MSWF algorithms are not guaranteed to find a solution even if one exists. They only try k dynamic paths, where k is arbitrarily specified in advance. In the following, we describe two algorithms, List Sliding Window (LSW) and Extended Bellman Ford (EBF), that are guaranteed to find a feasible path if one exists.

We also modify two algorithms from previous chapter to provide a guarantee on finding a feasible path if one exists:

1. **List Sliding Window (LSW)** The LSW algorithm [8] finds the path with the least start time. This algorithm sorts all the a values in ST lists of each link in the network. It determines the smallest a_i for which a feasible path is available by scanning this list sequentially. The search for a feasible path uses a breadth-first search [8]. The execution time can be improved by saving and utilizing the breadth-first search computations from the prior start times. For example, the breadth-first search for a_i can use the search computations required for the breadth first search of a_{i-1} utilizing the following observation: The breadth-first search must scan the ST list of each wavelength on each link that is traversed during the search, this scan may begin where the most recent scan of this list (from the breadth-first search for an earlier a_i) was completed.

2. **Extended Bellman-Ford (EBF)** This algorithm finds the minimum hop path within a scheduling window. It was originally proposed for the First Slot and All-Available Slots problems in [6]. We develop a modified version of the original EBF algorithm so that it can stop as soon as the ST list at the destination node is not empty. It also extends the notion of an ST list for a link to incorporate lightpaths. The resulting start time corresponds to the solution with minimum hop path.

24.2.3 Wavelength Assignment Algorithms

Once a path is found, the wavelength assignment algorithm is applied. This algorithm is relatively orthogonal to the routing algorithm, although it shares with it the current reservation information. When no wavelength conversion is allowed, we extended each algorithm by applying the routine to each wavelength sequentially, that is, a First-Fit wavelength assignment scheme is used.

When wavelength conversion is allowed, flexible heuristics can be designed since we can choose any available wavelength in a link. Several metrics such as min-leading or min-trailing gap [5] can be used in addition to path-wide metrics. To pick up the most appropriate wavelength among possible wavelengths, the Min-Leading-Gap strategy bases its decision on the leading gap between the new and previous reservations. We use the Min-Leading-Gap strategy [5] for the MSPF and MSWF algorithm; we always choose the one that produces the minimum leading gap with the assignment of the current task. This strategy was shown to have the best performance in [5] for link utilization and acceptance ratio.

For LSW and EBF algorithms, we propose a new mechanism called *deferred wavelength assignment*. This mechanism defers assigning a specific wavelength at reservation time. A deferred strategy only counts the number of wavelengths that are used on a link. The actual assignment of the wavelength is done at the time of the request is actually fulfilled. A deferred wavelength strategy can be shown to always guarantee a feasible solution as long as the total amount of reserved bandwidth does not exceed the total capacity of bandwidth of a link at a specific point of time. This alleviates the need to keep track of bandwidth allocation status of each wavelength. Only, a count needs to be maintained for each link.

An algorithm based on the left-edge algorithm for channel assignment in the VLSI routing context [12] can be used for this purpose. Although, this algorithm was for batch assignment, it may be adapted to our context as below:

1. Assign jobs so long as no link has more than k jobs assigned at any time, where k is the number of wavelengths.
2. At current time t, assign each job that begins at time t to any one of the available wavelength on the path reserved for this job; the wavelength is the same for each link on the reserved path. Consider any link e. If the link has q jobs scheduled to start at t, it can have at most $k - q$ jobs continuing from before t. Hence there are at least q wavelengths available on e from t to ∞.

Thus, it can be shown that if the reserved number of wavelengths does not exceed the maximum number of wavelengths of a link, all requests can be accommodated with deferred wavelength assignment.

Figure 24.1 shows an example of arriving requests; the network has only two nodes n_0 and n_1 that are connected to each other by a link with 3 wavelengths (λ_1, λ_2 and λ_3). The requests are sorted in ascending order of arrival time, that is, R_1 arrived before R_2. A pictorial comparison between min-leading gap and deferred wavelength assignment is shown in Figure 24.2. The min-leading gap wavelength assignment scheme schedules requests in a first-come-first-serve fashion, i.e., $R_1 \rightarrow R_2 \rightarrow R_3 \rightarrow R_4 \rightarrow R_5$. This results in a situation that R_2 is scheduled on λ_1, R_3 on λ_2, R_4 on λ_3 and finally R_5 fails to be scheduled. Using a deferred wavelength assignment, all requests are accepted since the link is computed to be available for the period $[t_2, t_5]$. During this period the number of allocated wavelengths is less than or equal to 2. The deferred wavelength assignment

Req ID	Source	Destination	Start Time	End Time
R_1	n_0	n_1	t_0	t_2
R_2	n_0	n_1	t_4	t_6
R_3	n_0	n_1	t_0	t_3
R_4	n_0	n_1	t_2	t_5
R_5	n_0	n_1	t_2	t_5

Figure 24.1   A request table with five requests.

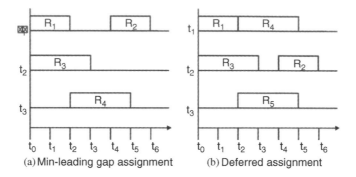

(a) Min-leading gap assignment   (b) Deferred assignment

Figure 24.2 Comparison of wavelength assignment using different schemes for request table of Figure 24.1.

scheme (Figure 24.2(b)) schedules requests according to start times of accepted requests. At t_0, R_1 and R_3 are activated, and scheduled on λ_1 and λ_2, respectively. R_4 and R_5 are scheduled on λ_1 and λ_3 at t_2. Finally at t_4, there is still room at λ_2 for R_2 and R_2 is scheduled.

24.2.4 Performance Evaluation

In addition to the traditional metrics of space and time complexity, the effectiveness of an in-advance scheduling algorithm in accommodating reservation requests is critical. The space complexity needs to be "reasonable." That is, the space requirement should not exceed the available memory on the computer on which the bandwidth management system is to run. The time complexity is important as this influences the response time of the bandwidth management system and, in turn, determines how many reservation requests this system can process per unit time. Scheduling effectiveness is, of course, critical as revenue is generated only from tasks that are actually scheduled.

Figure 24.3 summarizes the time complexity of each of the algorithms. If *deferred wavelength assignment* is used for a wavelength assignment algorithm combined with a certain routing algorithm on a *wavelength convertible network*, all above mentioned complexities will be smaller by the factor of W since it only counts the number of wavelengths that are used on a link.

Problem	Algorithm	Slotted Array	Continuous
First Slot	SPF	$O(\tau k(n \log n + W dn))$	$O(qk(n \log n + L))$
	LSW	$O(\tau ed)$	$O(q(e + L)))$
Any Slot	SWF	$O(\tau k(n \log n + W dn))$	$O(qk(n \log n + L))$
	EBF	$O(nel + ew)$	$O(nel + L)$

d = duration of a request, k = number of paths to try, l = size of longest st list within a scheduling window, q = number of different a_is in the ST lists within a period, L = sum of lengths of TB lists, τ = end of scheduling window - d, w = size of scheduling window.

Figure 24.3 Time complexity of different algorithms.

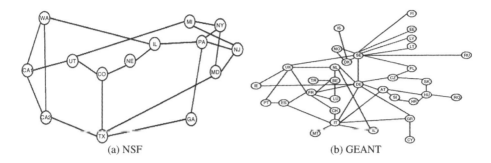

(a) NSF   (b) GEANT

Figure 24.4   NSF and GEANT network.

24.2.5 Experiments

In this section, we first briefly present our simulation environment including the network topologies used and the request generation process. We then present the key variations that were implemented and compared. This is followed by our experimental results and observations.

24.2.5.1 Simulation Environment. For test networks, we used the 24-node NSF network (Figure 24.4(a)) and 33-node GEANT network (Figure 24.4(b)) of [5], the 19-node MCI network and the 16 node cluster network of [13], the 11-node network of [4], the Abilene network [14], and several randomly generated topologies. Although many of these networks (except NSF and GEANT) do not use optical interconnects, we converted these networks into optical networks by setting the number of wavelengths based on the original bandwidth of links. For example, the MCI network that has bandwidths ranging from 45Mbps to 310Mbps was converted to a corresponding optical network by dividing the bandwidth of each link by 5.

The random networks we used for our simulations had 200, 400, or 800 nodes. The out-degree of each node was randomly selected to be between 3 and 5. To ensure network connectivity, the random network had bidirectional links between nodes i and $i + 1$ for every $1 \leq i < n$, where n is the number of nodes. The number of wavelengths for each link was randomly selected between 5 and 10.

We generated a synthetic set of reservation requests in the same way as in previous chapters. For each trial, we measured the request acceptance and bandwidth acceptance ratios for 10 times and presents the average value of the results.

24.2.5.2 Evaluated Algorithms. There are several variants for each basic algorithm that is described in the previous section based on the properties of network (converters or lack of converters) and whether or not a deferred strategy was used for wavelength assignment. For example, the three variant of Modified Switch Path First (MSPF) are as follows:

1. MSPF w/ converter and w/ wavelength assignment

2. MSPF w/ converter and deferred wavelength assignment
3. MSPF w/o converter

Similar variations can also be derived for Modified Switch Window First (MSWF) algorithms.

List Sliding Window (LSW) and Extended Bellman-Ford (EBF) algorithms have two variants depending on the presence or absence of wavelength converters in the optical network. For these algorithms, deferred wavelength assignment is assumed for the networks without converters. For example, the variations for LSW are labeled as LSW w/Conv and LSW w/oConv, respectively. We programmed all the reasonable variants for each basic algorithms in C++ and measured their effectiveness. We also studied the impact of using converters on the effectiveness.

24.2.5.3 Results and Observations. Figures 24.5 and 24.6 provide the average acceptance ratios for the algorithms as a function of the number of requests in

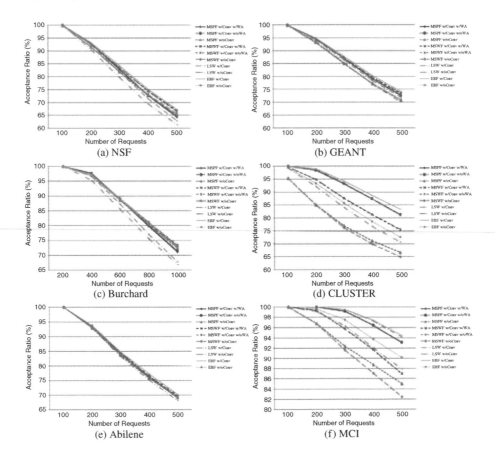

Figure 24.5 Network acceptance ratio vs number of requests.

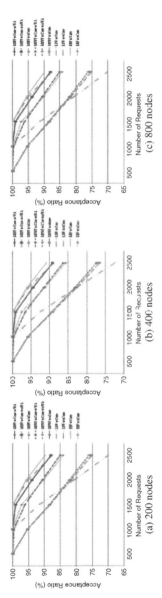

Figure 24.6 Acceptance ratio vs requests number in various random topologies.

the study interval for two network topologies. The average acceptance ratios for these algorithms as a function of the mean request duration for the various network topologies were similar.

Our experimental results show the following:

1. EBF consistently outperformed all other algorithms. For the remaining algorithms, the relative performance varies based on network properties. For homogeneous network topologies (NSF, GEANT, Burchard, and Abilene) (results not presented due to space limitations) that have same number of wavelengths on all the links, MSWF performs better than MSPF and LSW. However, for non-homogeneous network topologies (MCI, cluster, and random networks), LSW has better performance than MSWF and MSPF.

2. For non-homogeneous topologies, the algorithms that do not guarantee to find feasible reservations (MSPF and MSWF) fared worse than the algorithms that provide such a guarantee. However, at times, the performance of the best "no guarantee algorithm" was quite close to or slightly better than that of the worst "guarantee algorithm." As the network got saturated (i.e., the number of requests in the study interval increases), the RAR for all algorithms declined and the rate of decline for the "no guarantee algorithm" was found to be higher than "guarantee algorithm" algorithms.

3. The relative performance of the algorithms does not change significantly with mean request duration. However, the performance gap grows larger as the mean request duration decreases. The performance difference using deferred wavelength assignment method or not using it was not significant.

4. The use of wavelength converters generally led to better performance. Thus, the additional flexibility that wavelength converters provide in a network is worthwhile.

24.2.6 Conclusions

In this chapter, we conducted extensive simulations to evaluate the performance of algorithms for a variety of request patterns and network topologies. Our results show that Extended Bellman Ford (EBF) algorithm has consistently better performance than other algorithms. For non-homogonous networks, LSW also provided comparable solutions; while for homogeneous networks MSPF and MSWF provide comparable solutions.

Our simulations were performed for presence or absence of converters that can be used to convert from a given wavelength to another wavelength. Our experimental results showed that the use of wavelength converters generally led to better performance. Thus, the additional flexibility that wavelength converters provide in a network is worthwhile.

We also showed that a deferred wavelength assignment strategy can be effectively used in conjunction with the routing algorithms. A deferred strategy only counts the number of wavelengths that are used on a link. Since the actual assignment of the wavelength is done at the time of the request fulfillment, this alleviates the need of keeping track of bandwidth allocation status of each wavelength. A deferred wavelength strategy always guarantees to find a feasible solution as long as the total amount of reserved bandwidth does not exceed the total capacity of bandwidth of a link at a specific point of time.

24.3 SCHEDULING IN SPARSE WAVELENGTH CONVERSION NETWORK

24.3.1 Problem Description

In optical network scheduling, the primary concern is routing and wavelength assignment (RWA). Wavelength division multiplexing (WDM) allows multiple lightpaths from different users to share one optical fiber simultaneously. Normally, a feasible lighpath in the optical network has to fulfill the *wavelength continuity constraint*, which forces a single lightpath to occupy the same wavelength throughout all the links that it spans. However, this constraint is relaxed in an optical network that is equipped with wavelength converters. The signals received by a wavelength converter may be transmitted on a different wavelength in the next hop. When every node in the network is equipped with a wavelength converter, the network supports *full wavelength conversion*. When only some of the network nodes have a wavelength converter, the network supports *sparse wavelength conversion*.

The impact of wavelength converters in all-optical routing has be widely studied. Reference [9] showed that for certain topologies and fixed-path routing, sparse wavelength conversion is almost as effective as full wavelength conversion. References [10, 15] have investigated the performance of the *k-Alternative Paths* algorithms in the presence of wavelength converters. Their focus is the blocking probability of sparse wavelength conversion for on on-demand scheduling. Reference [16] considers in-advance scheduling using a continuous time model and evaluates the various algorithms' blocking performance for full wavelength conversion and low workload.

In this section, our primary goal is to study the impact of wavelength converters on First-Slot scheduling and to analyze the temporal behavior of typical RWA algorithms in the context of sparse wavelength conversion. Extensive experimental results are presented in this chapter. According to our test results, increasing the fraction of nodes with wavelength converters is of greater value for blocking performance in relatively low traffic cases than in the high workload cases. However, the average start times are almost unaffected by wavelength converters ratio except for the marginally improvement in small topologies.

Another key consideration here is to explore the advantages and disadvantages of the two scheduling strategies represented by *EBF* and *k-Path*, respectively. Intuitively, always accepting a request whenever there is a feasible lightpath in the network, which is done by *EBF*, should provide better performance than limiting the search for a feasible path to a small set of candidate paths as is done in *k-Path*. However, our results show that this statement is only true when the overall workload is small compared to network capacity. *EBF* often schedules a request on a longer path than used by the *k-Path*. So, when the workload is high, the additional resources utilized by *EBF* to accept a request negatively impacts the acceptance of future requests. Our results clearly demonstrate these tradeoffs: *EBF* performs better when network capacity is ample for the requested workload, but *k-Path* outperforms when the traffics congest the network. This observation leads us to propose a hybrid approach that automatically switches between the two algorithms based on current network traffic.

We also study different tie-breaking approaches when multiple paths are feasible and the impact of different tie-breaking schemes on overall performance in the presence of sparse wavelength conversion. A *slack* tie-breaking scheme is proposed and its performance relative to other widely used strategies is analyzed.

24.3.2 Extended Network Model

The topology of a optical network with sparse conversion is represented as a graph $G = (V, E, W)$, where V is the set of optical switches or routers, E is the set of optical links, and W is the number of wavelengths supported by each link. Each node n in V is associated with a boolean function $F(n)$, which is true if and only if the node is equipped with wavelength converter. To emulate the full-conversion algorithms, we first convert the above graph into a new graph $G' = (V', E')$. To map node set G to G', for a node $n \in V$, if n equips a wavelength converter (i.e., F(n) is true), a corresponding node n' will be inserted into V'. If F(n) is false, W pseudo-nodes $(n'_1, n'_2, \ldots, n'_w)$ will be inserted. W is the number of wavelengths defined in G. For a link $l \in E$, if e connects two nodes with converters, it will be mapped to a link l' in E'; else, l will be mapped into W pseudo-links $(l'_1, l'_2, \ldots, l'_w)$ and each pseudo-link stands for a specific wavelength that carried in l. In the extended model, l'_i is incident to n'_i iff l is incident to n in the original graph and l'_i and n'_i is their i_{th} pseudo copy, respectively.

Figure 24.7 shows a example of a 4-node ring topology. The network contains two wavelength converters, nodes A and B. Each link carries two wavelengths. Its extended presentation, shown on the right side, contains six nodes and seven links. Each non-converter nodes are split into two pseudo-nodes(nodes {C1, C2} for node C and {D1, D2} for node D). Each optical link that is incident to a non-converter node is split into two pseudo-links and each pseudo-link stands for one individual wavelength (link(B, C1) and (B, C2) for link (B, C), for example). Two pseudo-nodes that are adjacent in the

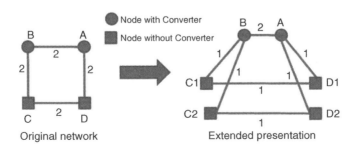

Figure 24.7   Extended network model.

extended model must fulfill two conditions: (1) their corresponding nodes are adjacent in the original graph, and (2) they are either converter nodes or their wavelength index matches.

The extended graph G' is equivalent to the original graph G. Every feasible lightpath in G has a corresponding path in G' and vice versa. The wavelength continuity constraint is also preserved in the extended model. If node n has no wavelength converter in G, every corresponding pseudo-node n'_i in G' is incident by and only by the pseudo-links of wavelength index i. Hence, we can directly apply the RWA algorithms that originally designed for full-conversion/no-conversion networks to the sparse conversion scenario with little adaptation.

When scheduling a request, if the source or destination nodes are extended to multiple pseudo-nodes, the RWA algorithm needs to check every corresponding pseudo-source-destination pairs. So at most W^2 rounds of the original algorithm are needed in the extended model, where W is the maximum number of wavelength carried by a link in the network. Also, during the model extension, the graph size can increase by at most W times for its link and node number. Therefore, an algorithm's computation time on the extended model G' is bounded by a constant ratio (a polynomial of W) of the computation time for that algorithm in full-conversion scenarios, which runs on the original network G. So, the adapted algorithm has the same asymptotic complexity as its original version.

In this chapter, we employ *Extended Bellman-Ford* algorithm and *k-Alternative path* algorithm as our RWA algorithms. The detail of the algorithms will be presented in Section 24.3.3.

24.3.3 Routing and Wavelength Assignment Algorithms

The RWA algorithm for First-Slot problem usually contains three steps:

1. Identify the earliest start time.
2. Find the shortest path that provides such start time.
3. Assign the wavelength.

As the wavelength assignment are independent from the first two steps, most RWA algorithms handle this step separately. In our chapter, *EBF* and *k-path* algorithm proceed the first two steps. A wavelength assignment strategy called *Least Conversion Assignment* is explained in Section 24.3.3.4.

24.3.3.1 Extended Bellman-Ford Algorithm for Sparse Wavelength Conversion. The *extended Bellman-Ford* algorithm [6] applies the Bellman-Ford shortest path algorithm [17] to the ST lists on links that may connect source and destination. The key steps of the algorithm are as follows:

1. Let st(k, u) represent the union of the ST lists for all lightpaths from vertex s to vertex u that have at most k edges. Clearly, $st(0, u) = \emptyset$ for $u \neq s$ and

$st(0, s) = [0, \infty]$. Also, $st(1, u) = ST(s, u)$ for $u \neq s$ and $st(1, s) = st(0, s)$. For $k >= 1$, the following recurrence can be derived:

$$st(k, u) = st(k - 1, u) \cup$$
$$\{\cup_{v,(v,u) \in E} \{st(k - 1, v) \cap ST(v, u)\}\}$$

2. Construct the list $st(n - 1, d)$, which gives the start times of all paths from s to d that have bandwidth BW available for a duration Dur. If $st(n - 1, d)$ is not empty, a in its first (a, b) pair is the earliest start time for this current source/destination pair, denoted as est_i.

3. For all possible source/destination pairs, find the minimum est_i as the earliest start time for the request and the corresponding source/destination pair (s_i, d_i) are recorded.

4. Remove the links that can not provide the requested bandwidth at the earliest finish time.

5. Run Breath-First Search [17] on the extended model and find a shortest route from the s_i to d_i, map the route back to the original graph.

The complexity of intersection and union operation is linear to the length of the current ST List. For each iteration of constructing $st(k, d)$ for $st(k - 1, d)$, we need to compute the ST List for each link and each computation takes $O(L)$ time, where L is the length of the longest st list. Since the construction iterates at most $N - 1$ times, the complexity of the extended Bellman-Ford algorithm is $O(N * E * L)$, where N and E are the number of nodes and links in the graph.

24.3.3.2 k-Alternative Path Algorithm.

The *k-Alternative path* algorithm is extended from the shortest path algorithms routing used by $OSPF$ in Internet routing. Recognizing that an OSPF-like algorithm may fail to find a feasible path in a network that has a feasible path, k-Path algorithm generates additional disjoint paths with the hope that one of the additional paths will be feasible. By constructing ST List on each path, it is easy to decide which path provides earliest start time. If the all generated path is infeasible, the request is rejected.

The k paths can be either fixed or dynamically generated. k-Fixed paths are computed for each node pair before the first scheduling begins according to some given link costs. The k-dynamic paths are computed for every request according to current network status. Usually, the most congested link will have the largest cost so as to avoid the path computation. Reference [18] showed the k-Dynamic paths can provide a much larger network throughput than k-Fixed paths, especially when the traffic load is relatively large for the network's capacity. So, in this chapter, we adopt the this k-Dynamic paths algorithm and call it *KDP*.

24.3.3.3 Breaking the Ties in Path Selection.

When multiple paths can satisfy a user's request, a tie-breaking scheme is needed to select one of them as the actual scheduled path. The most straightforward scheme breaks ties based on *first-fit (FF)* strategy or *Shortest Path (SP)* strategy. *First-fit* strategy terminates the path selection once a

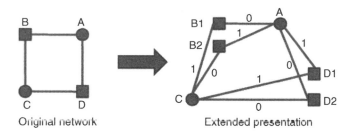

Figure 24.8 Extended network model.

successful path is found. The *shortest-path* strategy choses the path with minimum hop number. Both strategies are widely used in nonconversion and full-conversion scenarios, but using them directly in Sparse wavelength conversion needs careful consideration as these paths are computed on extended models.

In the extended model, the shortest path does not necessarily corresponds to the shortest path in the original graph for same source/destination pairs. Figure 24.8 gives an example of a 4-node ring with only two converters, nodes A and C. Each link consists two wavelengths. At some conjuncture, the available wavelengths are shown in extended graph on the right side. For a request of one wavelength of capacity from node B to A. Two candidate paths are available: $B_1 \rightarrow C \rightarrow D_1 \rightarrow A$ and $B_2 \rightarrow A$. Assume that both path provides the same start time, The *First-Fit* tie-breaking scheme will choose the pair (B_1, A) as source and destination when the node pairs are checked in lexical order and the *Shortest Path* tie breaking scheme will choose the 3-hop path as it is the one available B_1 to A.

A tie-breaking scheme that chooses the shortest path by examining all source-destination pairs, rather than the first successful pair, would solve the problem. However, considering only the path length would not be enough in the context of sparse conversion. In networks without wavelength conversion, a shorter path is more likely have common wavelengths, and therefore is less likely to block the requests. However, the presence of wavelength converters reduces the correlation between path length and path capacities due to the elimination of the wavelength continuity constraint. Hence, in terms of load balancing, choosing a longer-path with higher capacity may also reduce the potential congestion by alleviating the traffic in the short paths. In this chapter, instead of using *First-Fit* strategy in original *EBF* and *KDP* algorithm, we employ a *slack* tie-breaking scheme that selects the path that is most h hops longer than the shortest path but has the most free wavelengths among all the paths that have fewer or equal hop counts. We call these variants *EBF-S* and *KDP-S*.

Intuitively, h should not be too large or the benefit of load balancing would be canceled by the waste of link capacities on longer paths. In Section 24.3.4, we will compare the *First-Fit* scheme with *Slack* scheme and perform a numeric analysis on the choice of h in different scenarios.

24.3.3.4 Wavelength Assignment. With the presence of wavelength converters, wavelength assignment becomes less important in optical routing. However, as wavelength conversion contributes a considerable delay in the optical transmission [15], a proper wavelength assignment would potentially reduce such overheads.

For those links that connect to a non-converter nodes, the wavelength assignment is quite straightforward, as the specific wavelength has been already identified with the lightpath during the path selection process. However, for those links connecting two wavelength converters, we apply the *least conversion assignment* rather than the *first-fit* algorithm used in most RWA algorithms. In *least conversion assignment*, the link that connects two converters will use the same wavelength either as its previous hop or as it next hop unless neither wavelength is available. For instance, let $l \in E$ connect two wavelength converters, w_i be the wavelength assigned for the previous link on the path, and $\{w_n\}$ be the set of common wavelength of both l and l's next link. If w_i is available on l, we assign this w_i to the lightpath, else we assign any wavelength in $\{w_n\}$ if $\{w_n\} \neq \emptyset$. If neither is available, a random available wavelength in assigned. This strategy can always guarantee a feasible solution while avoiding the unnecessary conversions.

24.3.4 Experimental Evaluation

24.3.4.1 Experimental Framework. In this section, we measure the performance of the scheduling algorithms described in Section 24.3.3 and analyze how wavelength converters affects the algorithms' performance in various scenarios. We compare the tie-breaking schemes in Section 24.3.3.3 to show the effectiveness of our *slack* strategy; We analyze the performance of RWA algorithms for three metrics: blocking probability, average start time, and execution time. In our experiments, blocking probability is measured by ratio of rejected requests comparing to the total submitted request. Average start time is measured by the average delay between the reservation window's start time for a job and its actual start time. Execution time measures the convergence speed of each algorithm and how it varies with network size and workloads. We also proposed a self-adaptive algorithm switching strategy that dynamically chooses the suitable algorithm according to the current workload. The performance of this switch strategy is tested in various scenarios.

To simulate an e-Science backbone, we use a 10-node ring topology, a 25-node mesh-torus topology, a real work 11-node Abilene network (Figure 24.9), and several

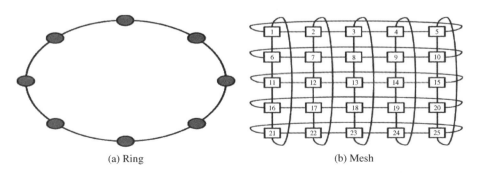

(a) Ring   (b) Mesh

Figure 24.9 Network topologies.

randomly generated topologies. Each link is assumed to carry 10 wavelengths. For randomly generated topologies, we set the out-degree of each node to be random integers between 3 and 7. To ensure network connectivity, the random network has bidirectional links between nodes i and $i + 1$ for every $1 \leq i < n$, where n is the number of nodes. During the results analysis, we found that the test data from Ring and Abilene topology are very similar to each other, while Mesh-Torus and random topology also results in almost the same observations. Thus, in this chapter, we only present the results from Ring and Random topology to avoid redundant diagrams. The full analysis on data from all four topologies can be found in our technical report [19].

Besides the ratio of nodes that have converters, their placement in the network is also an important consideration and extensive studies have been performed [20–23]. Here, we do not employ any specific wavelength converter placement policies for following reasons: (1) most converter placement strategies are closely related to traffic distribution in the network, but the traffics pattern are not precisely known at the network design time; and (2) we assume that topology and converter placement are predefined. The scheduler cannot make changes. Instead, a simple placement strategy is used in our evaluation. A node is capable of wavelength conversion with probability of q independent of the other nodes. The number of wavelength converters in a network of N nodes is binomially distributed with an expectation of Nq. In our simulation, we use *WLC Ratio* to indicate the percentage of nodes that are equipped with wavelength converters. We will compare the algorithms performance under different *WLC Ratio* to plot the impact of wavelength converters. Although a simple strategy is applied here, our expectation is that a performance comparison between different approaches should be applicable even when a more sophisticated placement is used.

File transfer requests are synthetically generated. Each request is described by the 6-tuple $(s_i, d_i, BW_i, Dur_i, ST_i, ET_i)$. The source and destination nodes for each request were selected using a uniform random number generator so that the workload is distributed uniformly among different node pairs. Without loss of generality, we assume each request asks for a capacity of only 1 wavelength. The duration is uniformly distributed within a range of 100 to 500 time units. The arrival of the request follows a Poisson distribution with rate α. The reservation window starts at some time after the requests' arrival. As the results are relatively insensitive for this lag, we arbitrarily chose it as 100 time units. The length of the window is randomly select from 2 to 4 times of the request duration.

We assume that the requests arrive in a Poisson process for each source/destination pair with an arrival rate α. Following the experimental setting in [9], α is picked in the range from 0.01 requests/time unit to 0.1 requests/time unit for each node pair. So, for example, with a arrival rate of 0.05 requests/time unit, one run of our experiment on a 100 node random topology would process approximately $5 * 10^5$ requests during the tests which lasts 1000 time units. All our experiment assume that we start with no load, that is, no existing scheduled transfers.

24.3.4.2 Slack *Tie-Breaking Scheme.* Recall that in Section 24.3.3.3, to select the best candidate path, we consider all the paths that are at most h hops longer than the shortest path. Hence, to evaluate the performance of these heuristics, we must first

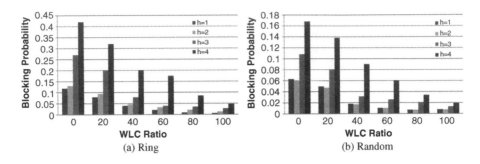

Figure 24.10   Different *h* values for different topologies. Network Traffic Load: $\alpha = 0.05$.

decide the value of the *h*. Figure 24.10 explores how *h*'s value influence the blocking performance of $EBF - S$ in various topologies. In the small topology like an 8-node ring, $h = 1$ provides the best performance, while in the 100-node random network, the $h = 2$ case is marginally better than $h = 1$. Also, large *h* values like 3 or 4 actually deteriorate the performance as the link capacity is wasted by choosing long paths. In our test, $h = 1$ is also the best choice for Mesh-Torus and Abilene. Similar results (not presented here) were also observed for $KDP - S$. In the following tests, we chose $h = 1$ in for Ring, Abilene, and Mesh-Torus topologies and $h = 2$ for random network.

Figure 24.11 depicts the wavelength converters' impact on blocking performance by varying the wavelength converter ratio for various topologies. *EBF-S* and *KDP-S* use the simple *First-Fit* tie-breaking scheme but *EBF-S* and *KDP-S* employ *slack* scheme. We observe that the algorithms with *slack* scheme work much better than the algorithms using *FF* scheme in all cases. Thus, choosing a longer path in presence of excess capacity benefits the blocking performance for sparse wavelength conversion. Another observation is that when *WLC Ratio* equals 20%, the blocking probability of *First-Fit* algorithms is worse than not having any converters. This phenomenon can be explained as follows: when no wavelength converter is available, many requests are rejected due to lack of continuous wavelength, but the accepted request are more evenly distributed among all wavelengths and long lightpaths are less likely to be established. When a small number

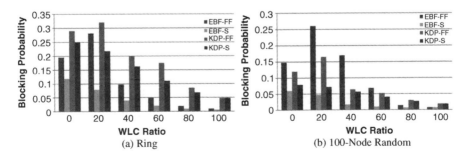

Figure 24.11   Benefit of *slack* tie-breaking scheme in various topologies. Network Traffic Load: $\alpha = 0.05$.

of nodes are equipped with converters, the traffic scheduled by *First-Fit* strategy are more likely to use those long paths between with wavelengths of lower index, as shown in Section 24.3.3.3. The additional benefit from having 20% converters is not enough to cover the degradation due to the wasted capacity of long paths. Although this degradation can be compensated by either inserting more converters, as plotted in Figure 24.11, using the *slack* scheme is obviously more effective and economical. We also notice that the improvement brought by the *slack* scheme in the Ring and Abilene topology is not as much as in the mesh-torus and random topology. This is consistent with the conclusion in [9], which states that wavelength conversion can help more in the topologies with more divergence and connectivity, as more variants in the paths are available.

In the test for both Figure 24.17 and Figure 24.11, the network traffic load is set to a moderate degree: $\alpha = 0.05$. However, similar results are also observed under different workloads.

24.3.4.3 Blocking Probability. In this section, the blocking performance of *EBF-S* and *KDP-S* are evaluated and compared with the *Fixed-Shortest Path* routing algorithm. For *Fixed-Shortest Path* routing, no tie-break is specified as only one path is available. However, as *First-Fit* wavelength assignment is applied, *Fixed-Shortest Path* routing is denoted as *SP-FF* in our diagrams. Figure 24.12 and Figure 24.13 depict the how the blocking probabilities changed with wavelength converter ratio in Ring, Mesh-Torus, Abilene, and Random-100 topology. Figure 24.12 present the results obtained when the network's traffic load is relatively low: $\alpha \in [0.01, 0.05]$, while Figure 24.13 present the result when workload is relatively high: $\alpha \in (0.05, 0.1]$.

From Figure 24.12 and Figure 24.13, we note that Increasing the wavelength converter ratio can decrease the blocking probabilities for all algorithms. However, the improvement is also dependent on the network's traffic load. When network traffic load is relatively low, *EBF* only needs about 40% of wavelength converters to provide a satisfactory blocking performance, but the blocking probabilities of *KDP* and *SP* decreases more gradually with the increase of WLC Ratio. When traffic load is high, increasing the wavelength converters has only marginal improvement on all algorithms. This can be explained as follows. *EBF* explores the network more thoroughly for an available

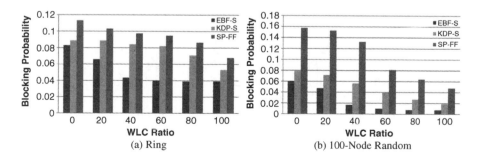

Figure 24.12 Blocking Probability vs. Wavelength Converter Ratio in various topology with low traffic load.

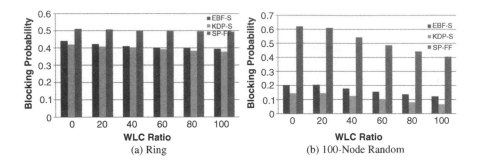

Figure 24.13 Blocking Probability vs. Wavelength Converter Ratio in various topology with high traffic load.

path than *KDP* and *SP*. With a small amount of converters, *EBF* is able to satisfy the traffic demands but *KDP* and *SP* cannot. However, when traffic load is high, the majority of blocking occurs due to lack of link capacities but not the availability of continuous wavelengths. Hence, increasing wavelength converters has little impact in heavy loads.

We also note that in all topologies, *EBF-S* and *KDP-S* algorithms can achieve a much smaller blocking probability compared to *SP-FF* algorithm. In simple topologies like Ring (Figure 24.12(a) and 24.13(a)), *EBF-S* and *KDP-S* leads *SP-FF* for about 2-5% on blocking probability, while in those more complex topologies like random network (Figure 24.12(b) and 24.13(b)), the advantages are doubled. This is consistent with the results in [10], where shortest-path routing is less likely to be improved due to the small number of alternative lightpaths.

Another important observation is that *EBF* outperforms *KDP* in low traffic workloads (Figure 24.12), but *KDP* leads *EBF* in high-traffic workloads (Figure 24.13). This can be explained as follows: *EBF* tries to find any possible path for current request if it exists, but *KDP* only tests no more than *k* paths. When the long-term traffic load is low, the network's capacity is able to accommodate most requests, and the *EBF* that acts greedily would accept more requests than *KDP*. However, when traffic load is high, limiting the routes to only those short paths and rejecting some long paths would definitely benefit the schedule of future requests. In that case, the more conservative *KDP* would provide a better performance in the long run.

This observation can also be supported by the fact that *EBF* actually consumes network bandwidth faster than *KDP* does. Figure 24.14 depicts the total amounts of link capacities that *EBF* and *KDP* consume under different workloads. The total resource amounts are defined as $\sum_{p \in RLP}(Dur(p) \cdot length(p))$, where RLP is the set of all established lightpaths, $Dur(p)$ is lightpath *p*'s duration and $length(p)$ is *p*'s hop count. We see that, for the same request set, *EBF* consumes more link capacities than *KDP* in low-workload cases, as *KDP* rejects those long-path requests while *EBF* accepts them. When the workload is high, *KDP*, which rejects some early long-path requests, substantially accepts more requests in the long run. Therefore, the total amounts of link capacities both algorithms consumes are almost equal in high workload.

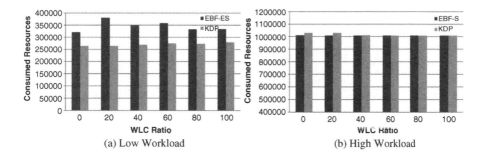

Figure 24.14 Total resource consumption in a 100-node random network under different workload.

24.3.4.4 Requests' Average Start Time.
In the all-optical routing area, blocking probability is always the primary concern, but for this special case of First-Slot scheduling, the availability of earlier start time may also be an important metric to evaluate a scheduler's performance. Figure 24.15 and Figure 24.16 present the influence of wavelength converter ratio on the requests' average start time. Similar with the previous section, Figure 24.15 shows the start time performance in the low traffic case and Figure 24.16 shows the test result in high workload cases.

To exclude the impact of blocked requests on the average request start time, we set the reservation window for each request to a large enough time interval such that every request will be accepted at some time within the window. From the above figures, we can observe that increasing wavelength converters has positive impacts on the requests' start time, but the improvements are not as obvious as the impact on blocking performance, especially for *EBF-S* and *KDP-S*. In Ring topology, the improvement from 0% WLC ratio to 100% WLC ratio is only about 5% in low traffic load case, and 15% in high traffic load cases. In random topology, the improvements are almost negligible.

We also note that *EBF-S* and *KDP-S* lead the average start time over *SP-FF* in all cases. The advantages are larger in random topology than in Ring topology and they increase as the workload increases. This shows that *EBF-S* and *KDP-S* have the ability to

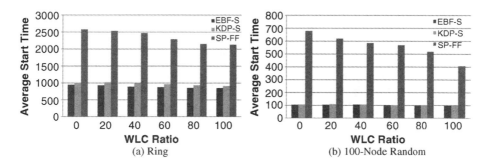

Figure 24.15 Average request start time vs. wavelength converter ratio in various topology with low-traffic load.

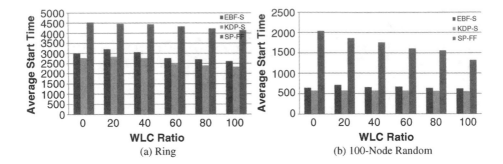

Figure 24.16 Average request start time vs. wavelength converter ratio in various topology with high-traffic load.

schedule the requests in a more parallel way than *SP-FF*. When the network capacities are ample for the requests, *EBF-S* and *KDP-S* provide much faster schedules. When the traffic congests the network, those forthcoming requests have to wait for previous requests to finish due to lack of network capacity, which reduces *EBF-S* and *KDP-S*'s advantages.

Similar to the results in previous sections, *EBF-S* again outperformed *KDP-S* in low workload cases on average start time, and *KDP-S* gains better performance for a conservative reservation strategy in the heavy workload. When the networks' capacity is relatively ample compared to the requested workload, *EBF-S* has the ability to start the job earlier than *KDP-S*, but their performances are very close in large topologies. When the work network is under congestion by high request rates, *KDP-S* leads the average start time in all topologies and its advantage are more observable in large networks.

24.3.4.5 Scheduling Overhead. In this section, we discuss the scheduling overhead of our RWA algorithms. Figure 24.17 presents comparisons on the scheduling overhead of *EBF-S* and *KDP-S* with various WLC ratios and network sizes. These results show that *EBF-S* is about 2–5 times slower than *KDP-S* and its computation time grows faster than *KDP-S* with the increase of network size. The execution time decreases with

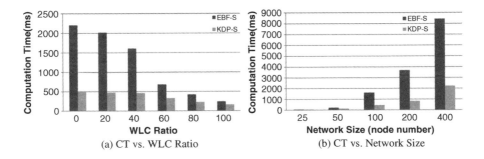

Figure 24.17 Average computation time of *EBF-S* and *KDP-S*.

the increase in WLC ratio, as the size of the extended network is smaller. However, even for a 400-node topology, *EBF-S* can on average schedule a request within several seconds. This should be acceptable in most scenarios.

In summary, equipping the network with some wavelength converters does improve the blocking performance, but adding more converters after a certain threshold does not bring more benefits. Meanwhile, the traffic load and network topology also cast great influence on the blocking probability. For the average start time, we found that the effect of wavelength converter ratio is minor for both *EBF-S* and *KDP-S*, but the traffic load and network topology have more evident influences on this metric. Comparing two algorithms, *EBF-S* generally performs better in the low traffic cases, but *KDP-S* is a better choice when the traffic load is heavy. *KDP-S* is faster than *EBF-S* in all cases, but in even in the worst case, *EBF-S* can still schedule the requests at an acceptable speed.

24.3.4.6 Algorithm Switching Strategy. We found out in Section 24.3.4.3 and Section 24.3.4.5 that the greedy approach *EBF-S* has better performance when the traffic load is comparably light, while the conservative approach *KDP-S* works more effectively in the high workload case. In this section, we propose a self-adaptive algorithm switching strategy that automatically chooses *EBF-S* or *KDP-S* according to current traffic load in the network.

The main idea of the switch strategy is as follows. The time domain is divided into equal-length time slots. The scheduler runs both algorithms simultaneously on each request, and the choice of whose result to apply in current time slot is made at the beginning of this slot, assuming current traffic has the similar pattern as in last slot. The performances of the candidate algorithms can be evaluated by either their blocking performance, the average start time of the requests scheduled in the last slot, or a combination of the two. Comparing the statistical performance of both algorithms in the last slot, the algorithm that performed better in the last slot takes effect in the current slot. If it does not perform as well as the other one in the current slot, the schedule will switch to its alternative at the beginning of the next slot.

To evaluate the performance of our algorithm switch strategy, we designed two scenarios: slow traffic pattern switching (*STPS*) and fast traffic pattern switching (*FTPS*). In our test, we assume the request arrival rate α is randomly selected from the range $[0.01, 0.1]$ and the length of each time slot is 10 time units. In the *STPS* scenario, the arrival rate α changes its value with 50% probability every 100 time unites. In the *FTPS* scenario, the arrival rate changes its range with 50% probability every 10 time units.

Figure 24.18 and Figure 24.19 depict the blocking and start time performance of our switch strategy in both scenarios in a 100-node random topology. *DS-SS* algorithm stands for the switch strategy worked in the *STPS* scenario, while *DS-FS* algorithm stands for the switch strategy worked in the *FTPS* scenario. The results show that the hybrid algorithm worked in the *STPS* scenario, *DS-SS*, has the best performance on both metrics, as the history information from last slot predicted the current traffic pattern quite accurately. On the other hand, the performance of *DS-FS* algorithm that worked in *FTPS* scenario degraded dramatically due to the increasing probability of inaccurate predictions in *FTPS* scenario. In some cases, *DS-FS* even provides the worst performance. So, when the traffic pattern remains static or changes infrequently, our algorithm switch strategy can provide

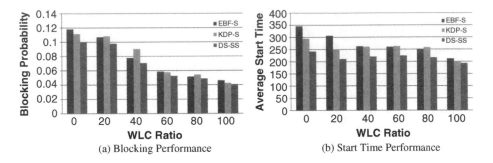

(a) Blocking Performance   (b) Start Time Performance

Figure 24.18   Performance of algorithm switching strategy in slow traffic pattern switching.

fairly good performance by synthesizing the merits of both algorithms. However, when the traffic pattern is changing frequently, the switch strategy does not guarantee any improvement compared to either *EBF-S* or *KDP-S*.

24.3.5 Conclusions

In this section, we examined the impact of sparse wavelength conversion on First-Slot scheduling. We proposed a new network model to emulate the full-conversion algorithms in sparse conversion networks. Using this model, we conducted extensive experiments to assess the impact of wavelength converters on First-Slot RWA algorithms' performance. This assessment used three metrics: blocking probability, average start time, and scheduling overhead. Our experiments have indicated that increasing wavelength converters has a positive impact on blocking performance, but very little impact on the availability of earlier start times. Meanwhile, as most improvements are achieved by having no more than 60% nodes with converters, deploying too many wavelength converters may not be worth the additional cost. We also proposed a *Slack* tie-breaking scheme when multiple feasible paths are available. This tie-breaking scheme is shown to have much better performance than the traditional *First-Fit* or *Shortest-Path* tie-breaking schemes. The comparisons between *EBF* and *KDP* also lead to the conclusion that accepting requests

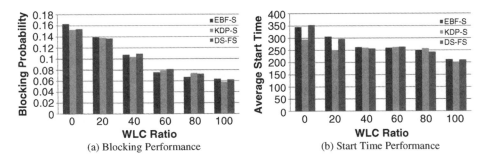

(a) Blocking Performance   (b) Start Time Performance

Figure 24.19   Performance algorithm switching strategy in fast traffic pattern switching.

greedily would provide better performance in a low traffic load case, but rejecting some requests with a long path can be a superior strategy when workload is high. An algorithm switching strategy that adapts the scheduling algorithm as the current workload changes is proposed. When the network traffic pattern changes slowly, this strategy has considerable advantages over static algorithms. Overall, our results show that adding a small number of wavelength converters may have a limited positive impact on First-Slot scheduling. However, this impact should be carefully weighed against the additional costs.

ACKNOWLEDGMENT

This work was supported, in part, by the National Science Foundation under grants NETS 0963812 and NETS 1115184, and by a GRO award from Samsung.

REFERENCES

[1] H. Zang, J.P. Jue, and B. Mukherjee, "A review of routing and wavelength assignment approaches for wavelength-routed optical WDM networks." *Optical Networks Magazine.* 2000.

[2] enlightencd. Enlightened Computing, http://www.enlightenedcomputing.org/.

[3] E. He, X. Wang, and J. Leigh, "A flexible advance reservation model for multi-domain wdm optical networks." *IEEE GRIDNETS 2006.* 2006.

[4] L.O. Burchard, "On the performance of networks with advance reservations: Applications, architecture, and performance." *Journal of Network and Systems Management.* 2005.

[5] S. Tanwir, L. Battestilli, H. Perros, and G. Karmous-Edwards, "Dynamic scheduling of network resources with advance reservation in optical grids." *International Journal of Network Management.* Vol. 18. 2008. 79–105.

[6] S. Sahni, N. Rao, S. Ranka, Y. Li, E.-S. Jung, and N. Kamath, "Bandwidth scheduling and path computation algorithms for connection-oriented networks." *Sixth International Conference on Networking (ICN'07).* 2007. 47.

[7] J. Zheng, B. Zhang, and H.T. Mouftah, "Toward automated provisioning of advance reservation service in next-generation optical internet." *IEEE Communications Magazine* 44 (2006). 12: 68–74.

[8] E. Jung, Y. Li, S. Ranka, and S. Sahni, "An evaluation of in-advance bandwidth scheduling algorithms for connection-oriented networks." *Proceedings of International Symposium on Parallel Architectures, Algorithms, and Networks.* 2008.

[9] S. Subramaniam, M. Azizoglu, and A.K. Somani, "All-optical networks with sparse wavelength conversion." *IEEE/ACM Trans. Netw.* 4 (1996).4: 544–557.

[10] X. Chu and B. Li, "A dynamic RWA algorithm in a wavelength-routed all-optical network with wavelength converters." *INFOCOM.* 2003.

[11] M. Kovacevic and A.S. Acampora, "Benefits of wavelength translation in all-optical clear-channel networks." *IEEE Journal on Selected Areas in Communications* 14 (1996). 5: 868–880.

[12] A. Hashimoto and J. Stevens, "Wire routing by optimizing channel assignment within large apertures." *Proc. 8th Deasign Automation Workshop.* 1971. 155–163.

[13] Q. Ma and P. Steenkiste, "On path selection for traffic with bandwidth guarantees." *5th Intl. Conf. on Network Protocols (ICNP).* 1997. 191–204.

[14] Abilene. "Abilene." http://abilene.internet2.edu.

[15] X. Chu, J. Liu, and Z. Zhan, "Analysis of sparse-partial wavelength conversion in wavelength-routed WDM networks." *INFOCOM.* 2004.

[16] E. Jung, Y. Li, S. Ranka, and S. Sahni, "Performance evaluation of routing and wavelength assignment algorithms for optical networks." *13th IEEE Symposium on Computers and Communications.* 2008.

[17] T.H. Cormen, C.E. Leiserson, R.L. Rivest, and C. Stein, *Introduction to Algorithms.* New York: The MIT Press, 2001.

[18] K. Rajah, S. Ranka, and Y. Xia, "Scheduling bulk file transfers with start and end times." *6th IEEE International Symposium on Network Computing and Applications.* 2007, 295–298.

[19] Y. Li, S. Ranka, and S. Sahni, "Tech Report of CISE UF: In-Advanced First-Slot Scheduling with Spare Wavelength Conversion for e-Science Applications." (2009).

[20] X. Chu, B. Li, and I. Chlamtac, "Wavelength converter placement under different RWA algorithms in wavelength-routed all-optical networks." *IEEE Transaction on Communications* 51 (2003).5: 607–617.

[21] S. Subramaniam, M. Azizoglu, and A.K. Somani, "On the optimal placement of wavelength converters in wavelength-routed networks." *INFOCOM.* 1998, 902–909.

[22] J.M. Yates, M.P. Rumsewicz, and J.P.R. Lacey, "Wavelength converters in dynamically-reconfigurable WDM networks." *IEEE Communications Surveys and Tutorials* 2 (1999), 2.

[23] H. Zang, R. Huang, and J. Pan, "Designing a hybrid shared-mesh protected WDM networks with sparse wavelength conversion and regeneration." (2002).

25

COMPUTATIONAL GRAPH ANALYTICS FOR MASSIVE STREAMING DATA*

David Ediger, Jason Riedy, David A. Bader,
and Henning Meyerhenke

CONTENTS

*Parts of this work have been published in a preliminary form in the proceedings of the 2010 Workshop on Multithreaded Architectures and Applications (MTAAP 2010), in conjunction with the 24th IEEE International Parallel & Distributed Processing Symposium [13], and in the proceedings of the 2011 Workshop on Multithreaded Architectures and Applications (MTAAP 2011), in conjunction with the 25th IEEE International Parallel & Distributed Processing Symposium [14].

25.1 INTRODUCTION

The data deluge from a wide range of application domains, from business and finance to computational biology and computer security, requires development of new analysis tools and algorithms to retrieve the information stored within the data. With the Facebook user base containing over 500 million people [17], Twitter boasting more than four billion tweets [32], over 150 million tracked blogs on the Internet [8], and the NYSE processing over four billion traded shares per day [27], massive graph data sets must be analyzed faster than ever before. Studying these massive data sets will lead to insights about community structure and anomaly detection unavailable within smaller samples.

Current large graph analysis tools like Pajek [4] are primarily designed for static graphs. For dynamic inputs these tools assume the properties to change slowly relative to execution time. Data sets from the literature like web crawls of a particular domain [2], email correspondence between colleagues [25], patent and literature citations [21], and biological networks [22] often are static and small relative to the current massive data sources. Many static graph algorithms demonstrated on these smaller data sets are difficult to scale to massive, real-world data and do not use parallel architectures efficiently. Also, existing approaches do not address interesting temporal properties of real-world, dynamic data sets.

Social networks like Facebook and Twitter as well as a variety of other networks observed in nature and human society have the *scale-free* property [26]. A scale-free graph has low diameter, and the number of neighbors to each vertex follows a power law distribution. Many vertices have a small number of neighbors, while a few vertices are connected with a large part of the graph. Scale-free graphs lack small separators and present unique challenges for parallel algorithms. The degree distribution also creates an imbalance in workload when scheduling vertices among processors. Incorporating dynamic information itself poses new challenges to algorithm design and implementation.

We address the challenges posed by massive streaming input of spatio-temporal data represented by scale-free dynamic graphs with new algorithmic approaches and new data structures. Computing incremental updates and tolerating temporary noncoherence opens up parallel algorithmic performance. We use a new data structure for analyzing complex graphs and networks with possibly billions of vertices that accumulates as much of the recent graph data as possible in main memory. Once the reserved memory is full, older or uninteresting edges are aged off and removed. We update analytical kernels after each new edge or block of edges and attempt to detect significant changes in the corresponding metrics. We refer to this new approach as *massive streaming data analytics*.

To accommodate a stream of edge data, we present a new, extensible, and flexible data structure for massive graphs called STINGER (Spatio-Temporal Interaction Networks and Graphs (STING) Extensible Representation) in Section 25.2, where we also outline assumptions and methods for extracting parallelism when dealing with massive streaming graphs. The STINGER data structure provides a compromise between list- and array-based graph representations supporting both efficient updates and efficient analysis.

Two algorithmic case studies demonstrate the effectiveness of the streaming approach to computation and the STINGER dynamic graph representation. Section 25.3 presents the first study, computing a widely used network analysis metric called clustering coefficients. Global and local (per-vertex) clustering coefficients quantify the "small world-ness" of the graph [34]. The metric is derived from counting a graph's triangles. We present an efficient multithreaded algorithm and its implementation to calculate and maintain the clustering coefficients in an undirected, unweighted graph with a stream of input edge insertions and removals.

Section 25.4 presents the second study, our approach for tracking connected components given a stream of edge insertions and removals. We highlight optimizations afforded by the scale-free nature of the graph. Computing the set of connected components is a well-studied graph analytical metric that is representative of both the structure of the graph as well as the connectivity between vertices. As edges are inserted into and removed from the graph, several metrics are of interest: the number of connected components, the mapping between vertices and components, the size distribution of components, and the point in time when components merge or separate. In scale-free networks, we often observe that most vertices lie in a single, large component while a large number of small components consist of very few vertices. As edges are inserted and deleted over time, most changes occur inside of a given component joining low-degree vertices to high-degree vertices.

The multithreaded platforms we use in our tests, both the massively multithreaded Cray XMT as well as the more common platform built on Intel's Nehalem architecture, are described in Section 25.5 together with their idiosyncracies and our implementation. Experimental results on the Cray XMT are presented in Section 25.6, with a comparison to the Intel Nehalem platform for the clustering coefficient problem. Despite the challenges posed by the input data, we show that the scale-free structure of social networks can be exploited to accelerate local and global graph analysis queries in light of a stream of deletions. On a synthetic social network with over 16 million vertices and 135 million edges, we are able to maintain persistent queries about the connected components of the graph with an input rate of 240,000 updates per second, a three-fold increase over previous methods. Regarding clustering coefficients, a similar rate of 200,000 updates per second can be maintained on the Cray XMT. Related work is described in Section 25.7.

Our new framework built on incremental computation rather than recomputation enables scaling to massive data sizes on massively parallel, multithreaded supercomputing architectures. Studying massive dynamic graphs with more complex methods based on our algorithmic kernels will lead to insights about community and anomaly detection unavailable within smaller samples.

25.2 STINGER: A GENERAL-PURPOSE DATA STRUCTURE FOR DYNAMIC GRAPHS

25.2.1 Related Graph Data Structures

Traditional graph data structures choose between efficient traversal or efficient modification. For example, a full-adjacency matrix permits $O(1)$ edge insertion or removal but requires $O(n^2)$ storage and $O(n)$ time to traverse all edges from any vertex, where n is the number of vertices. Adjacency lists or arrays require only $O(n + m)$ storage, where m is the number of edges, and permit $O(d_v)$ traversal of edges out of vertex v, where d_v is the degree of vertex v. Modifying the graph, however, can require $O(n + m)$ time for arrays, whereas lists have the drawback of poor locality in memory. The primary traditional approach for representing dynamic graphs uses a linked list for storing end vertices. Insertion and deletion while supporting concurrent readers is well-understood [33]. However, list traversal is expensive, and many graph analysis kernels spend most of their time traversing the edge lists.

Data structures that focus on graph traversal store edges or destination vertices in a packed array. The most common high-performance structure for static graph analysis borrows from sparse matrices and uses a compressed sparse row format (CSR). In CSR form, each edge's end vertex is stored in a single, packed array within a contiguous section corresponding to the edge's source vertex. Inserting or deleting edges requires changing the end vertex array's length and shifting data throughout that array. This not only requires a large amount of data motion but also complicates concurrent access by readers. For more related work see Section 25.7.2.

25.2.2 The STINGER Data Structure

The STINGER data structure we propose here has been developed to support a wide variety of algorithms and efficient edge insertion and deletion with concurrent readers

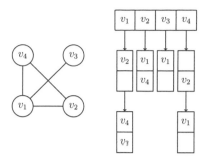

Figure 25.1 An undirected graph and an example representation in STINGER with edge blocks holding two edges. The blanks are holes storing negative numbers rather than end vertex indices. Our tests use a block size of 100 and include additional per-vertex and per-edge data.

in massive graphs with a single in-memory structure. STINGER is a compromise that permits dynamic updates while supporting a wide variety of analytical algorithms on a single copy. It takes the efficient element of CSR, storing end vertices in arrays, and loosens other requirements. STINGER also borrows from the list structure and stores edge end vertices as a list of arrays. Each vertex points to a list of fixed-size end vertex arrays; see Fig. 25.1 for a sketch of how STINGER represents a small graph. This is a common mechanism for representing dynamically sized lists or arrays while supporting rapid traversal.

The arrays are permitted to have holes or blanks represented by storing a negative entry in the end vertex slot. To delete an edge, the end vertex is found and replaced by a negative number. Inserting an edge requires replacing an empty slot or possibly adding a new edge block into the linked list. We assume that a single process manages all graph updates and ensures writing does not suffer from race conditions.

Insertion and deletion can occur concurrently with reader access. By default, low-level consistency is not enforced. In a massive sparse graph, graph updates will very rarely conflict with readers. For our applications, the graph is already assumed to be an approximate model of some real-world phenomenon, and analysis kernels must account for or be resilient to some inconsistencies. The inconsistencies do not corrupt the data structure itself. Examples of tolerated inconsistencies include changing adjacency lists and edge or vertex auxiliary information. A kernel that makes multiple passes over a vertex's neighbors may see different information on each pass. None of the inconsistencies cause infinite loops or other structure access faults.

Other information is associated with each edge: a weight and the most recent time stamp. We do not use this information here and do not discuss the relevant consistency issues. STINGER models multi-graphs, graphs with multiple, distinct edges between the same vertices, by associating a numeric type value with each edge. We do not use these edge types in this chapter; multiple edges are treated as a single connection. Extra information is stored with the per-vertex index, including current in- and out-degrees. The degrees are updated by atomic operations but are not necessarily consistent with respect to the edge list. Analysis kernels must handle extra or missing edges when walking the edge list.

25.2.3 Finding Parallelism in Streams and Analytics

We consider a single, unified input stream of edge insertions and deletions. This provides a synchronization point for analysis but also a bottleneck. For high performance, we need both to expose parallelism within the analytic kernels and to extract some parallelism from the sequential stream for updating the STINGER structure. We make two primary assumptions that help extract parallelism from streaming data: Changes in the stream are scattered widely enough in the massive graph that batches of them are sufficiently independent to expose parallelism. Analysis kernels have small support and small effect, and so a change to the graph only requires access to local portions and affects only a small portion of the output.

To extract parallelism from the stream, we assume the changes are somewhat scattered in the graph. In a low-diameter graph with high-degree vertices, as is the case with many social networks, changes may not be completely independent, but there is potential for updating separate STINGER edge lists simultaneously. Considering the stream as batches of updates loses temporal resolution but exposes more parallelism in data structure and kernel updates. If the graph updates do not interact, then there is little temporal information lost by executing the updates together.

Analytical kernels with small support lend themselves to similar scattering across the graph. For example, per-vertex scores that depend on a fixed radius like Section 25.3's local clustering coefficients naturally parallelize over batches of affected vertices. On graphs with millions or billions of vertices, the number of changes to the vertex scores will be only slightly more than the batch size for a particular set of edge insertions or deletions.

Large-support kernels like k-betweenness centrality [23] pose a more difficult challenge. They depend on paths potentially crossing the entire graph and require large-scale recalculation. A small change may update analysis results across the entire graph. Experience with k-betweenness centrality performance leads us to limit ourselves currently to kernels with small to medium support.

We expect typical massive graph streaming analytics to fit into the following framework:

1. Take a section of the incoming stream as a batch.
2. Split the batch into per-vertex STINGER updates.
3. If necessary, save data (*e.g.*, degrees) to permit incremental computation.
4. Process all the data structure updates.
5. Update analytics on the altered portion of the graph.
6. Transfer changed results to a monitoring process.

Sections 25.5.3 and 25.6.1 investigate steps 2–5 for a simple analytic: local clustering coefficients. In the second case study, see Sections 25.5.4 and 25.6.2, these steps are considered when monitoring a global graph property, the connected components.

Figure 25.2 There are two triplets around v in this unweighted, undirected graph. The triplet (m, v, n) is open, there is no edge $\langle m, n \rangle$. The triplet (i, v, j) is closed.

25.3 ALGORITHM FOR UPDATING CLUSTERING COEFFICIENTS

25.3.1 Generic Algorithm

Clustering coefficients measure the density of closed triangles in a network and are one method for determining if a graph is a small-world graph [34]. We adopt the terminology of [34] and limit our focus to *undirected* and unweighted graphs. A triplet is an ordered set of three vertices, (i, v, j), where v is considered the focal point and there are undirected edges $\langle i, v \rangle$ and $\langle v, j \rangle$. An open triplet is defined as three vertices in which only the required two are connected, for example, the triplet (m, v, n) in Figure 25.2. A closed triplet is defined as three vertices in which there are three edges, or Figure 25.2's triplet (i, v, j). A triangle is made up of three closed triplets, one for each vertex of the triangle.

The global clustering coefficient C is a single number describing the number of closed triplets over the total number of triplets,

$$C = \frac{\text{number of closed triplets}}{\text{number of triplets}} = \frac{3 \times \text{number of triangles}}{\text{number of triplets}}. \quad (25.1)$$

The local clustering coefficient C_v is defined similarly for each vertex v,

$$C_v = \frac{\text{number of closed triplets centered around } v}{\text{number of triplets centered around } v}. \quad (25.2)$$

Let $N(v)$ be the set of neighbors of vertex v, possibly containing a self-loop. Also let $|N(v)|$ be the size of set $N(v)$. The degree of v is denoted by d_v, $d_v = |N(v)|$. Using the triangle count T_v (which counts each triangle exactly twice), the local clustering coefficient C_v can be expressed as

$$C_v = \frac{\sum_{u \in N(v)} |N(u) \cap (N(v) \setminus \{v\})|}{d_v(d_v - 1)} = \frac{T_v}{d_v(d_v - 1)}. \quad (25.3)$$

To update C_v as edges are inserted and deleted, we maintain the values d_v and T_v separately.

For the remainder of this section, we concentrate on the calculation of local clustering coefficients. Computing the global clustering coefficient requires an additional sum reduction over the numerators and denominators.

An inserted edge increments the degree of each adjacent vertex, and a deleted edge decrements the degrees. Updating the triangle count T_v is more complicated. Algorithm 25.1 provides the general framework. Acting on edge $\langle u, v \rangle$ affects the degrees only of u and v but may affect the triangle counts of all neighbors. With atomic increment operations available on most high-performance platforms, loops in Algorithm 25.1 can be parallelized fully.

The search in line 5 can be implemented many different ways. A brute-force method simply iterates over every element in $N(v)$ for each x, explicitly searching for all new closed triplets given a new edge $\langle u, v \rangle$. The running time of the algorithm is $O(d_u d_v)$, which may be problematic when two high-degree vertices are affected.

Algorithm 25.1   An algorithmic framework for updating local clustering coefficients. Loops can use atomic increment and decrement instructions to decouple iterations.

Input: Edge $\langle u, v \rangle$ to be inserted (+) or deleted (−), local clustering coefficient numerators T, and degrees d
Output: Updated local triangle counts T and degrees d

1: $d_u \leftarrow d_u \pm 1$
2: $d_v \leftarrow d_v \pm 1$
3: $count \leftarrow 0$
4: **for all** $x \in N(v)$ **do**
5:   **if** $x \in N(u)$ **then**
6:     $T_x \leftarrow T_x \pm 1$
7:     $count \leftarrow count \pm 1$
8: $T_u \leftarrow T_u \pm count$
9: $T_v \leftarrow T_v \pm count$

If the edge list is kept sorted as in a static computation, the intersection could be computed more efficiently in $O(d_u + d_v)$ time. However, the cost of keeping our dynamic data structure sorted outweighs the update cost. We can, however, accelerate the method to $O((d_u + d_v) \log d_u)$ by sorting the current edge list of d_v and searching for neighbors with bisection. The sorting routine can employ a parallel sort, and iterations of the search loop can be run in parallel given atomic addition / subtraction operations.

25.3.2 Approximating Clustering Coefficients Using a Bloom Filter

We present a novel set intersection approximation algorithm with constant-time search and query properties and an extremely high degree of accuracy. In addition to our dynamic data structure described in Section 25.2, we summarize neighbor lists with Bloom filters [9], a probabilistic data structure that gives false positives (but never false negatives) with some known probability.

Edge arrays could be represented as bit arrays. In one extreme, each neighbor list could be an array using one bit per vertex as well as an edge list. Then $|N(u) \cap N(v)|$ can be computed in $O(min\{d_u, d_v\})$ time by iterating over the shorter edge list and checking the bit array. However, maintaining $O(n)$ storage per source vertex is infeasible for massive graphs. Instead, we approximate an edge list by inserting its vertices into a

Bloom filter. While a Bloom filter is also a bit array, it uses a smaller number of bits. Each edge list $N(v)$ is summarized with a Bloom filter for v. A hash function maps a vertex $w \in N(v)$ to a specific bit in this much smaller array. With fewer bits, there may be hash collisions where multiple vertices are mapped to the same bit. These will result in an overestimate of the number of intersections.

A Bloom filter attempts to reduce the occurrence of collisions by using k independent hash functions for each entry. When an entry is inserted into the filter, the output of the k hash functions determines k bits to be set in the filter. When querying the filter to determine if an edge exists, the same k hash functions are used and each bit place is checked. If any bit is set to 0, the edge cannot exist. If all bits are set to 1, the edge exists with a high probability.

Bloom filters have several parameters useful to fix a given probability of failure. An in-depth description of Bloom filter theory is beyond the scope of this chapter, but a few useful features include the following: Bloom filters never yield false negatives where an edge is ignored, only false positives where a nonexistent edge is counted. The probability of falsely returning membership is approximately $(1 - e^{-kd_u/m})^k$, where m is the length of the filter. This can be optimized by setting k to an integer near $\ln 2 \cdot m/d$ [18], choosing d according to the expected degrees in the graph. Our initial implementation uses two hash functions, $k = 2$, and a 1 MiB filter. The probability of a false-positive will vary depending on the degree of the vertex. In a scale-free graph with an average degree of 30 and a maximum degree of 200,000, the average false-positive rate will be $5 \cdot 10^{-11}$ and the worst-case rate will be $2 \cdot 10^{-3}$.

When intersecting two high-degree vertices, the Bloom filter holds a slight asymptotic edge over sorting one edge list, but a multithreaded implementation benefits from additional parallelism throughout the Bloom filter's operations. Note that entries cannot be deleted from a Bloom filter. A new filter is constructed for each application of Algorithm 25.1, so we never need to delete entries.

Modifications to Algorithm 25.1 for supporting a Bloom filter are straight-forward. After line 3, initialize the Bloom filter using vertices in $N(u)$, the filter's bit array B, and hash functions H_i, $1 \leq i \leq k$:

```
1:  B ← (0, . . . , 0)
2:  for all  y ∈ N(u)  do
3:    for  i = 1 → k  do
4:      B[H_i(y)] ← 1
```

Then implement the search in line 5 as follows:

```
1:  for  i = 1 → k  do
2:    if  B[H_i(x)] = 0  then
3:      Skip to next x
```

Our multithreaded implementation of the complete algorithm for the Cray XMT is described in Section 25.5.3. Before that, we present our second case study, the monitoring of connected components in massive streaming graphs with the scale-free property.

25.4 TRACKING CONNECTED COMPONENTS IN SCALE-FREE GRAPHS

As argued in the introduction, scale-free networks pose particular challenges to parallel analytics software. Despite these challenges, we will show that the scale-free structure of social networks can be exploited to accelerate graph connectivity queries in light of a stream of deletions.

To monitor the connected components of a general graph, insertions must only check the component membership of their endpoints to determine if two components have merged. Deletions are much more difficult to handle as the endpoints do not contain information about the topology of the component or any other paths that may reconnect the two vertices. Enumerating all of the possible edge deletions that would separate components, in light of the constant stream of new edges being inserted in the graph, is infeasible. As a result, breadth-first search is often used to re-establish or rule out connectivity between two vertices after a deletion.

25.4.1 Problem Structure

Given an edge to be inserted into a graph and an existing labeling of the connected components, one can quickly determine if it has joined two components. Given a deletion, however, recomputation (through breadth-first search or st-connectivity) is the only known method with subquadratic space complexity to determine if the deleted edge has cleaved one component into two. If the number of deletions that actually cause structural change is very small compared to the total number of deletions (such as in the case of a scale-free network), our goal will be to quickly rule out those deletions that are "safe" (i.e., do not split a component). The framework we propose for this computation will establish a threshold for the number of deletions we have not ruled out between recomputations.

Our approach for tracking components is motivated by several assumptions about the input data stream. First, a very small subset of the vertices are involved in any series of insertions and deletions. Insertions that alter the number of components will usually join a small component to a large component. Likewise, a deletion that affects the structure of the graph typically cleaves off a relatively small number of vertices. We do not anticipate seeing the big component split into two large components. The small diameter implies that connectivity between two vertices can be established in a small number of hops, but the low diameter and power law distribution in the number of neighbors also implies that a breadth-first search quickly consumes all vertices in the component.

Second, we adopt the *massive streaming data analytics* model [13]. We assume that the incoming data stream of edge insertions and deletions is infinite, with no start or end. We store as much of the recent graph topology as can be held in-memory alongside the data structures for the computation. The graph contains inherent error arising from the noisy data of a social network containing false edges as well as missing edges. As a result, we will allow a small amount of error at times during the computation, so long as we can guarantee correct results at specific points. The interval between these points will depend on the tolerance for error. We process the incoming data stream as batches of edge insertions and deletions, but do not go back and replay the data stream.

25.4.2 The Algorithm in Detail

To motivate our approach, we would like to answer, in a persistent manner, the question "do vertex u and vertex v lie in the same component?", while at the same time supporting the ability to insert and delete edges presented as a batch in parallel. We focus our efforts on scale-free networks like those of social networks and other biological networks and capitalize on their structural properties to motivate our algorithm.

The pseudocode of our algorithm appears in Algorithm 25.2. The algorithm consists of four phases that are executed for each batch of edge insertions and deletions that is received. These phases can be summarized as follows: First, the batch of edges is sorted

---

Algorithm 25.2   A parallel algorithm for tracking connected components.

Input: Batch B of edges $\langle u, v \rangle$ to be inserted and deleted, component membership M, threshold R_{thresh}, number of relevant deletions R, bit array A, component graph C
Output: Updated component membership M'
1: Sort(B)   ▷ Phase 1: Prepare batch
2: **for all** $b \in B$ **in parallel do**
3:   **if** b is deletion **then**
4:     Push(Q_{del}, b)
5:   **else**
6:     Push(Q_{ins}, b)
7: StingerDeleteAndInsertEdges(B)   ▷ Phase 2: Update data structure
8: **for all** $b \in Q_{\text{del}}$ **in parallel do**   ▷ Phase 3: Process deletions
9:   $\langle u, v \rangle \leftarrow b$
10:   $A_u \leftarrow \vec{0}$ ▷ All bits set to zero
11:   **for all** $n \in \text{Neighbors}(u)$ **in parallel do**
12:     Set bit n in A_u to 1
13:   $F \leftarrow 0$
14:   **for all** $n \in \text{Neighbors}(v)$ **in parallel do**
15:     **if** bit n in $A_u = 1$ **then**
16:       $F \leftarrow 1$ ▷ Triangle found
17:   **if** $F = 0$ **then**
18:     **atomic** $R \leftarrow R + 1$ ▷ No triangles found
19: **if** $R > R_{\text{thresh}}$ **then**
20:   $R \leftarrow 0$
21:   $M' \leftarrow \text{ConnectedComponents}(G)$
22: **else**   ▷ Phase 4: Process insertions
23:   $C \leftarrow \emptyset$
24:   **for all** $b \in Q_{\text{ins}}$ **in parallel do**
25:     $\langle u, v \rangle \leftarrow b$
26:     Add $\langle M[u], M[v] \rangle$ to C
27:   $T \leftarrow \text{ConnectedComponents}(C)$
28:   **for all** $v \in V$ **in parallel do**
29:     $M'[v] \leftarrow T[v]$

---

by source and destination vertices. Second, the edges are inserted and/or deleted in the STINGER data structure. Third, edge deletions are evaluated for their effect on connectivity. Finally, insertions are processed and the affected components are merged.

We will consider unweighted, undirected graphs, as social networks generally require links to be mutual. The graph data structure, the batch of incoming edges currently being processed, and the metadata used to answer queries fit completely within main memory. We can make this assumption in light of the fact that current high-end computing platforms, like the Cray XMT, provide shared memories on the order of terabytes. We will now examine, in detail, each phase of the algorithm.

In the sort phase, we are given a batch of edges to be inserted and deleted. In our experiments, the size of this batch may range from 1,000 to 1 million edges. We use a negative vertex ID to indicate a deletion. The batch must first be sorted by source vertex and then by destination vertex. On the Cray XMT, we bucket sort by source using atomic fetch-and-add to determine the size of the buckets. Within each bucket, we can sort by destination vertex using an arbitrary sequential sorting algorithm, processing each bucket in parallel. At the end of the sort phase, each vertex's operations are clustered within the batch into a group of deletions and a group of insertions pertaining to that vertex. At this stage, one could carefully reconcile matching insertions with deletions, which is especially important for multigraphs. For our experiments, we will skip reconciliation, processing each inserted and deleted edge, and allowing only the existence or non-existence of a single edge between each pair of vertices.

In Phase 2, the data structure update phase, the STINGER data structure is given the batch of insertions and deletions to be processed. For each vertex, deletions are handled first, followed by insertions. This ordering creates space in the data structure before insertions are added, minimizing the number of new blocks that must be allocated in the data structure and thereby reducing overhead.

After updating the graph, edge deletions identified earlier are checked in Phase 3 to see if they disrupt connectivity. We create a bit array, in which each bit represents a vertex in the graph, for each unique source vertex in the batch of edge deletions. A bit set to 1 indicates that the vertex represented by that bit is a neighbor. Because of the scale-free nature of the graph, the number of bit arrays required for a batch is much less than the number of vertices. Since vertices can be involved in many edge deletions, the fine-grained synchronization available on the Cray XMT enables parallelism in the creation phase and re-use of the bit arrays in the query phase. We compute the intersection of neighbor sets by querying the neighbors of the sink vertices in the source bit array. Given that a social network is a scale-free graph, the rationale is that this intersection will quickly reveal that most of the edge deletions do not disrupt connectivity. Regarding running time and memory consumption, note that a common case bit array intersection for vertices with small degree can be handled by a quick lookup in the sorted list of neighbors and the bit matrix intrinsics of the Cray XMT.

At this point, we can take the remaining edge deletion candidates and further process them to rule out or verify component structure change, likely using a breadth-first search. Otherwise, we will store the number of relevant deletions R seen thus far. After this number has reached a given threshold R_{thresh} determined by the tolerance for inconsistency before recomputation, we will recompute the static connected components to determine the updated structure of the graph given the deletions that have taken place since the last static recomputation.

If we did not exceed R_{thresh} in the previous phase, the insertions must now be processed in Phase 4. For each edge being inserted, we look up the vertex endpoints in the current component mapping and replace them with the component ID to which they belong. In effect, we have taken the batch of insertions and converted it into a component graph. As this is a scale-free network, many of the insertions will now be self-edges in the component graph. The remaining edges will indicate components that have merged. Although it is unlikely, chains of edges, as well as duplicate edges, may exist in the batch. The order of merges is determined by running a static connected components computation on the new component graph.[1] The result is an updated number of components in the graph and an updated vertex-component mapping.

In both the static connected components case and when finding the connected components of the component graph, we use an algorithm similar to Kahan's algorithm [7]. Its first stage, performed from all vertices in the graph, greedily colors neighboring vertices using integers. The second stage repeatedly absorbs higher labeled colors into lower labeled neighbors. Colors are relabeled downward as another series of parallel breadth-first searches. When collisions between colors are no longer produced, the remaining colors specify the components.

25.4.3 Discussion

Unlike prior approaches, our new framework manufactures large amounts of parallelism by considering the input data stream in batches. All of the edge actions within the batch are processed in parallel. Applying any of the breadth-first search-based algorithms to a batch of deletions would result in thousands of concurrent graph traversals, exhausting the memory and computational resources of the machine. We avoid running any breadth-first search by first constructing bit arrays to represent neighbor lists for vertices affected by a deletion in a batch. We take advantage of the low diameter nature of scale-free networks by intersecting these bit arrays to quickly re-establish connectivity using triangles. Our algorithm uses a breadth-first search of the smaller component graph rather than the vertex graph, and is limited by the size of the batch being processed. The scale-free nature of the input data means that most edges in the batch do not span components, so the number of non-self-edges in the component graph for a given batch is very small.

Our novel methods fully utilize the fine-grained synchronization primitives of the Cray XMT to look for triangles in the edge deletions and quickly rule out most of the deletions as inconsequential without performing a single breadth-first search. All of the neighbor intersections can be computed concurrently providing sufficient parallelism for the architecture. Thus, our proposed approach to tracking connected components minimizes graph traversal and static recomputation.

---

[1]In our implementation we use a compressed sparse row (CSR) representation, rather than creating a new graph data structure, as this only requires a sort of the batch of edges and a prefix sum, both done in parallel.

25.5 IMPLEMENTATION

25.5.1 Multithreaded Platforms

Our implementation is based on multithreaded, shared-memory parallelism. The single code base uses different compiler directives, or pragmas, to expose the threaded parallelism. We use Cray's compiler (version 6.3.1) and its pragmas for the massively multithreaded Cray XMT, and we use OpenMP [28] via the GNU C compiler (version 4.4.1) for a comparison on an Intel Nehalem E5530-based commodity platform.

The Cray XMT is a supercomputing platform designed to accelerate massive graph analysis codes. The architecture tolerates high memory latencies using massive multithreading. There is no cache in the processors; all latency is handled by threading. Each Threadstorm processor within a Cray XMT contains 128 *hardware streams* that maintain a thread context. Context switches between threads occur every cycle, with a new thread selected from the pool of streams ready to execute.

A large, globally shared memory enables the analysis of graphs on the order of one billion vertices using a well-understood programming model. Hashing is used to break up locality and reduce hot-spotting. Synchronization takes place at the level of 64-bit words, and lightweight primitives such as atomic fetch-and-add are provided to the programmer. The cost of synchronization is amortized over the cost of memory access. Combined, these features enable the algorithm designer to implement highly scalable parallel algorithms for analyzing massive graphs.

The Cray XMT used for these experiments is located at Pacific Northwest National Lab and contains 128 Threadstorm processors running at 500 MHz. These 128 processors support over 12,000 hardware thread contexts. The globally addressable shared memory totals 1 TiB.

The Intel Nehalem E5530 is a 2.4GHz quad-core processor with *hyperthreading* [3]. Each physical core holds two thread contexts and switches on memory stalls. The context switches are not as frequent as on the Cray XMT, and only two contexts are available to hide memory latencies. Each core has 256 KiB of level two cache, and each processor module shares 8 MiB of level three cache. The platform tested has two E5530s, a total of eight cores and 16 threads, with 12 GiB of main memory.

The experiments presented in Section 25.4 consist of three cases: the two applications for computing local clustering coefficients and tracking connected components, respectively, and the STINGER data structure implementation. Each takes advantage of the unique features of the Cray XMT in different ways, which we detail in the upcoming sections.

25.5.2 The STINGER Data Structure

Our STINGER data structure must provide the ability to easily and efficiently accept edge insertions and edge deletions from a scale-free graph while also permitting fast querying of neighbor information and other metadata about vertices and edges. The STINGER specification does not specify consistency; the programmer must assume that the graph can change underneath the application. The programmer is provided routines to extract a snapshot of a vertex's neighbor list, alleviating this concern at the expense of an additional buffer in memory.

Our STINGER implementation provides a function that gathers the edge list from the various blocks and returns it to the application in an array. This has the double benefit of isolating the application from changes in the data structure as well as making it easy to convert existing static codes that utilize the popular compressed sparse row format to work with STINGER. In the course of developing the connected components code, we observed that this "copy out" strategy resulted in identical or better performance for static codes using STINGER versus the compressed sparse row representation on the Cray XMT.

The block data format of STINGER enables an additional level of parallelism on the Cray XMT. Blocks can be traversed in parallel while using atomic fetch-and-add instructions to update shared variables.

25.5.3 Multithreaded Implementation of Algorithm 25.1 (Clustering Coefficients)

Our threaded implementation is straightforward. Each undirected edge $\langle u, v \rangle$ is added to or removed from the data structure using two threads, one to work from each end vertex. No explicit locking is involved. The STINGER structure requires only ordered, atomic read/write of 64 bit integers (e.g., end vertices, timestamps) and atomic increment/decrement of counters (e.g., degrees, offsets). Both the Cray intrinsics and the OpenMP pragmas can express the specific operations we need. For brevity, we use the GCC/Intel intrinsic functions similar to the Cray intrinsics.

The algorithm to update the triangle counts T above uses appropriate pragmas to parallelize the outer loops. Inner loops are not parallelized under OpenMP; the target platform has insufficient threading resources to benefit from that level of parallelism. However, the inner loops are parallelized on the XMT by a loop collapse [29]. An atomic increment updates the count of a shared neighbor T_w.

Local clustering coefficients' properties help us batch the input data. Recomputing changed coefficients only at the end of the batch's edge actions frees us to reorder the insertions and deletions. Reordering repeated insertions and removals of the same edge may alter the edge's auxiliary data, however, so we must take some care to resolve those in sequence order. After resolving actions on the same edge, we process all removals before all insertions to open edge slots and delay memory allocation.

The batch algorithm is as follows:

1. Transform undirected edges $\langle i, j \rangle$ into pairs of directed edges $i \rightarrow j$ and $j \rightarrow i$ because STINGER stores directed edges.
2. Group edges within the batch by their source vertex.
3. Resolve operations on the same edge in sequence order.
4. Apply all removals, then all insertions to the STINGER structure.
5. Recompute the triangle counts and record which vertices are affected.
6. Recompute the local clustering coefficients of the affected vertices.

In Step 5, we use slight variations of the previous algorithms. The source vertex's neighboring vertices are gathered only once, and the array is reused across the inner loop. The sorted update and Bloom filter update strategies compute their summary data using the source vertex rather than choosing the larger list.

25.5.4 Multithreaded Implementation of Algorithm 25.2 (Connected Components)

Fine-grained synchronization on the Cray XMT enables the connected components code to fully parallelize all loops. Histograms and shared queues can be built in parallel with atomic fetch-and-add instructions. Bit arrays can be built in parallel for different vertices at the coarse level, and neighbors can be set within the individual bit array in parallel using word-level synchronization.

The bit array is a fast data structure that, with the support of fine-grained synchronization, can be built and queried in parallel. Building a bit array for a graph with 2^{24} vertices will require 2 MiB per array. The scale-free nature of the graph means that it suffices to construct relatively few bit arrays. Although there are 16 million vertices, we pre-allocate only 10,000 bit arrays at a cost of about 20 GiB. If the graph were not scale-free, and if the platform lacked sufficient memory, we would likely not have the space to do this for such a large graph. Since high-degree vertices will likely be touched by each batch, a learning algorithm could be used to identify these vertices, update their bit arrays, and reuse the bit array from batch to batch, amortizing the creation cost. If the graph were less sparse or memory footprint is a concern, a Bloom filter (or another low-cost insert/delete representation) could be used to conserve space while introducing the probability for error. A Bloom filter, however, cannot be reused since it does not support deletions.

Batching of the update stream is required on the Cray XMT to create adequate parallelism for the thousands of user hardware streams. Processing in batches has the additional benefit that it bounds the size of temporary arrays needed for making the calculation. By using these space bounds to preallocate data structures before the computation begins, it is not necessary to allocate memory during processing.

The bucket sort implementation takes advantage of the compiler's ability to automatically identify and parallelize reductions and linear recurrences such as parallel prefix sums. These are used to find the size of the buckets in parallel and then reserve space in the output array.

25.6 EXPERIMENTAL RESULTS

25.6.1 Clustering Coefficient Experiments

Our test data is generated by the R-MAT recursive matrix generator [11] with probabilities $A = 0.55$, $B = 0.1$, $C = 0.1$, and $D = 0.25$. Each generated matrix has a few vertices of high degree and many vertices of low degree. Given the R-MAT scale k, the number of vertices $n = 2^k$, and an edge factor f, we generate $e = f \cdot n$ unique edges for our initial graph. We then select a fraction ρe of those edges and add them to a deletion queue. For these experiments, $\rho = 1/16$.

After generating the initial graph, we generate 1024 *actions* (edge insertions or deletions) for edge-by-edge runs and 1 million actions for batched runs. With probability ρ, a deletion is taken from the deletion queue. Otherwise an insertion is generated with the same R-MAT generator and parameters. The edge to be inserted may already exist in the graph. Inserted edges are appended to the deletion queue with probability ρ. There are no self-loops in our generated edges, but the algorithm implementations do handle self-loop cases by ignoring edges $\langle v, v \rangle$.

The Cray XMT applies to far larger problems than the Intel-based platform. The latter is limited to scale $k = 21$ and edge factor $f = 16$ with our current test harness. On the Cray XMT, our current experiments are 16 times larger, with $k = 24$ and $f = 32$, and are limited more by our testing code's structure than the Cray XMT's architecture.

25.6.1.1 Scalability of the Initial Computation.

We begin by computing the correct clustering coefficients for our initial graph. While not the focus of this chapter, performance on the initial computation shows interesting behavior on the two test platforms.

The initial clustering coefficients algorithm simply counts all triangles. For each edge $\langle u, v \rangle$, we count the size of the intersection $|N(u) \cap N(v)|$. This is a static computation, so we use a packed representation with sorted edge arrays for efficiency. The algorithm as a whole runs in $O(\sum_v d_v^2)$ time, where v ranges across the vertices and the structure is pre-sorted. The multithreaded implementation also is straightforward; we parallelize over the vertices. The $2^{21} \approx 2$ million vertices in the smallest case provide sufficient parallelism for both platforms.

The initial computation has not been seriously tuned for performance on either platform. The algorithm itself is somewhat coarse-grained with sufficiently sized chunks of work to amortize run-time overhead. In Figure 25.3, the Cray XMT's performance improves with increasing processors. Thread creation and management overhead appears responsible for the Intel Nehalem's decreasing performance.

25.6.1.2 Number of Individual Updates per Second.

Unlike calculating the triangle counts T for the entire graph, updating T for an individual edge insertion or deletion exposes a variable amount of fine-grained parallelism. We present results showing how aggregate performance of a *single* edge insertion or deletion stays relatively constant.

Table 25.1 summarizes the sequential complexity of our update algorithms. Figure 25.4 presents boxplots summarizing the updates per second achieved on our test platforms. Figure 25.5 shows local recomputation's speed-up of locally relative to globally recomputing the graph's clustering coefficients. Boxes in Figures 25.4 and 25.5 span the 25%–75% quartiles of the update times. The bar through the box shows the median. The lines stretch to the farthest nonoutlier, those within $1.5\times$ the distance between the median and the closest box side. Points are outliers.

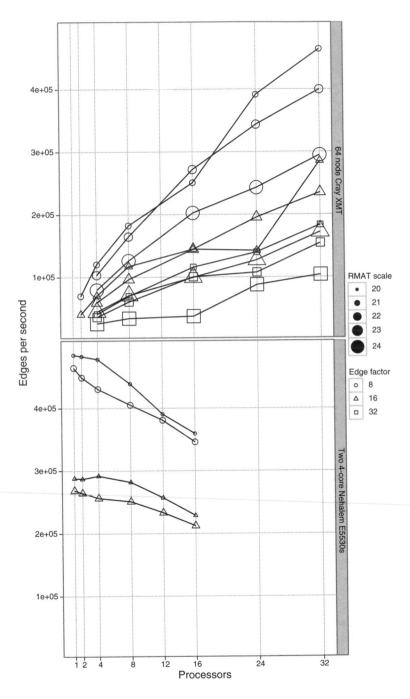

<u>Figure 25.3</u> Performance of the initial clustering coefficient computations, normalized for problem size by presenting the number of edges in the graph divided by the total computation time. The Cray XMT scales well as additional processors are added, while the Nehalem platform's threading overheads decrease performance.

TABLE 25.1 Summary of Update Algorithms

Algorithm	Update Complexity
Brute force	$O(d_u d_v)$
Sorted list	$O((d_u + d_v) \log d_u), d_u < d_v$
Bloom filter	$O(d_u + d_v)$

In Figure 25.4, we see the Cray XMT keeps a steady update rate on this relatively small problem regardless of the number of processors. The outliers with 16 processors are a result of sharing resources with other users. The Bloom filter shows the least variability in performance. Figure 25.5 shows that local recomputation accelerates the update rate typically by a factor of over a thousand.

The Nehalem results degrade with additional threads. The noise at 12 and 16 threads results from overallocation and scheduling from hyperthreading. The Nehalem outperforms the Cray XMT by several orders of magnitude, but can only hold a graph of approximately 8 million vertices and 300 million edges. In comparison, this Cray XMT is capable of holding a graph in memory up to 1 billion vertices and 20 billion edges.

Table 25.2 shows performance obtained from batching operations and extracting parallelism on the Cray XMT. The sorting algorithm was not considered for batching. Notice that increasing the batch size greatly improves performance. For the Bloom filter, this comes at the cost of a proportional increase in memory footprint. A batch size of 4000 required choosing a filter size of 1 MiB to fit within the system's available memory. Even so, we encountered no false positives over 1 million edge actions. Increasing the batch size intuitively improves scalability since data parallelism is increased in the update phase.

25.6.2 Connected Components

The experimental results presented in this section use synthetic R-MAT [11] input graphs derived by sampling from a Kronecker product. We generate two graphs with $2^{20} \approx$ 1 million vertices or $2^{24} \approx$ 16 million vertices, both with an edge factor of 8. Again, we use the R-MAT parameters $a = 0.55$, $b = 0.1$, $c = 0.1$, and $d = 0.25$. For each graph we generate additionally an input stream of edge actions (both insertions and deletions) that, by construction, favors the same vertices as the initial graph. It is this input stream that we will divide into batches. When creating this input stream, we sample from the distribution to create edge insertions. Again, with probability $\rho = 1/16$, we add an edge insertion to a delete queue. We choose an edge from the delete queue to be an edge deletion, rather than choosing a new edge to be inserted, with probability $\rho = 1/16$.

In a real online social network, edge deletions are not independent but are often guided by a kind of pruning based on distance, time, or importance. Since data available to researchers do not include deletions, we resort to artificial networks in order to fully demonstrate our ability to track connected components in a streaming fashion. We are unaware of any other edge stream generators for social networks, which is an area ripe for further study.

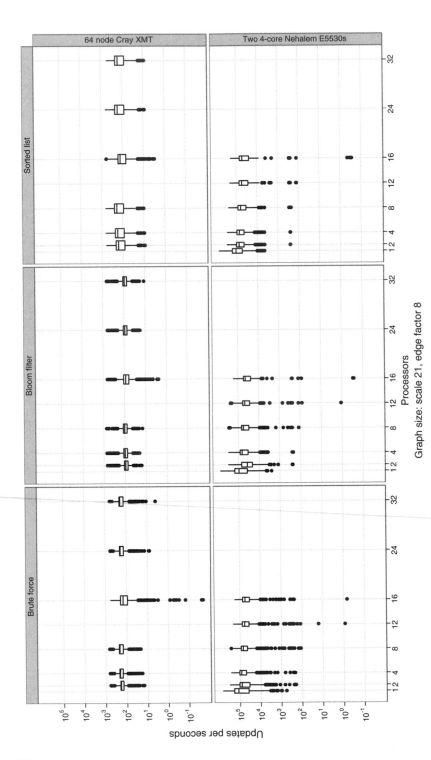

Figure 25.4 Updates per second by algorithm.

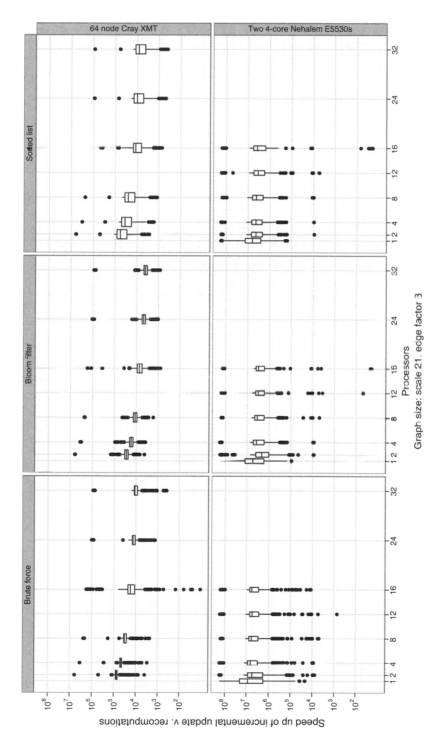

Figure 25.5 Speed-up of incremental, local updates relative to re-computing over the entire graph.

639

T A B L E 25.2 Comparison of Single-Edge Versus Batched Edge Operations on 32 XMT Processors, R-MAT 24 Input, in Updates Per Second

Batch Size	Brute Force	Bloom Filter
Edge by edge	90	60
Batch of 1000	25,100	83,700
Batch of 4000	50,100	193,300

On the Cray XMT, we load the initial graph into memory and create our STINGER data structure. We run a static computation of connected components to establish the initial vertex-component mapping, number of components, and size of components. In effect, we have entered the infinite data stream at some intermediate point to begin tracking connected components. We measure the time it takes for each batch to be processed, the data structure to be updated, and the new component information to be calculated. We report this performance metric in terms of updates per second.

On the 128 processor Cray XMT, we conduct our experiments using 32 processors for two reasons. First, the input graph of 16 million vertices is small relative to the size of the machine. Second, we imagine tracking connected components alongside of other higher-level analysis kernels that subscribe to the results of this computation to aid in their own computation. This frees up resources for other computations to be taking place at the same time. One example is a kernel that samples vertices to create an ongoing approximation of a metric of interest. The kernel may want to ensure that it is sampling vertices from all components or that it samples in proportion to the size of each component. In this way, it is running at the same time as the connected components kernel and receiving the results into its own computation.

Looking closely at the algorithm, one will note that when handling insertions only, the graph data structure does not need to be accessed to update the connected components. We can track the number of components and their sizes using only the vertex-component mapping. The insertions-only algorithm is very fast as the number of "vertices" in the component graph is small compared to the size of the original graph. Additionally, the number of "edges" in the component graph is bounded by the batch size. In Figure 25.6, we observe insertions-only performance of up to 3 million updates per second on a graph with 1 million vertices and nearly 1 million updates per second on the larger graph with 16 million vertices (see Table 25.3 for more data on the larger graph).

STINGER, the data structure, inevitably contributes a small overhead to the processing of updates, but it is scalable with larger batches. The update rate of insertions and the data structure can be viewed as an upper bound on the processing rate once deletions are introduced. One method that has been used for handling temporal updates is to recompute static connected components after each edge or batch of edges. This update rate can be viewed as a lower bound on processing once deletions are introduced. Any method that will decrease the number or frequency of recomputations will increase the rate at which streaming edges can be processed.

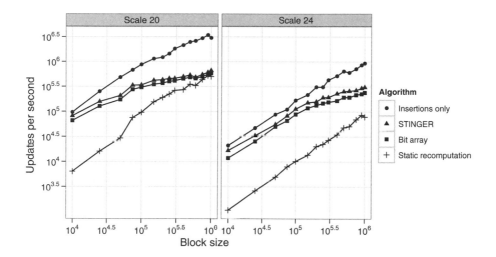

<u>Figure 25.6</u> Update performance for a synthetic, scale-free graph with 1 million vertices (left) and 16 million vertices (right) and edge factor 8 on 32 processors of a 128-processor Cray XMT.

We introduce the bit array intersection method as a means to rule out a large number of deleted edges from the list of deletions that could possibly affect the number of connected components. In the algorithm, we set a threshold R_{thresh} meaning that we will tolerate up to R_{thresh} deletions in which the structure of the graph may have been affected before recomputing static connected components. The performance results for insertions plus STINGER plus the bit array intersection represent the update rate if $R_{\text{thresh}} = \infty$. Choosing R_{thresh} will determine performance between the lower bound and this rate. In practice, reasonable values of R_{thresh} will produce performance closer to the upper rate than the lower bound.

As an example of the effect of the bit array on the number of possibly relevant deletions, our synthetic input graph with 16 million vertices produces approximately 6,000 edge deletions per batch of 100,000 actions. The 12,000 endpoints of these deletions

T A B L E 25.3 Updates Per Second on a Graph Starting with 16M Vertices and Approximately 135M Edges on 32 Processors of a Cray XMT

	Batch Size (Edges)			
	10,000	100,000	250,000	1,000,000
Insertions Only	21,000	168,000	311,000	931,000
Insertions + STINGER	16,700	113,000	191,000	308,000
Insertions + STINGER + Bit Array	11,800	88,300	147,000	240,000
STINGER + Static Connected Components	1,070	10,200	22,400	78,600

contain only about 7,000 unique vertices. Using a bit array to perform an intersection of neighbors, all but approximately 750 of these vertices are ruled out as having no effect on the component structure of the graph. Performing a neighbor of neighbors intersection would likely reduce this number considerably again at the cost of increased complexity. As it is, the synthetic graph used for these experiments has an edge factor of 8, making it extremely sparse and a worst-case scenario for our algorithm. A real-world social network like Facebook would have an edge factor of greater than 100. In a scale-free network, this would reduce the diameter considerably making our bit array intersection more effective. In our graph, less than 1% of deletions cleave off vertices from the big component, while our bit array intersection algorithm rules out almost 90% of deletions at a small cost in performance. Given that we can tolerate R_{thresh} deletions between costly static recomputations, a reduction in the growth rate of R, the number of unsafe deletions, will increase the time between recomputations, increasing throughput accordingly.

The left plot in Figure 25.6 depicts update rates on a synthetic, scale-free graph with approximately 1 million vertices and 8 million edges. Looking at insertions only, or solely component merges without accessing the data structure, peak performance is in excess of 3 million updates per second. The STINGER implementation incurs a small penalty with small batches that does not scale as well as the insertions-only algorithm. The bit array optimization calculation has a very small cost and its performance tracks that of the data structure. Here we see that the static recomputation, when considering very large batches, is almost as fast as the bit array. In this particular test case, we started with 8 million edges, and we process an additional 1 million edge insertions and/or deletions with each batch.

On the right side of Figure 25.6, we consider a similar synthetic, scale-free graph with approximately 16 million vertices and 135 million edges. The insertions-only algorithm outpaces the data structure again, but by a smaller factor with the larger graph. The bit array performance again closely tracks that of the data structure. At this size, we can observe that the static recomputation method is no longer feasible, even for large batches. At this size, there is an order of magnitude difference in performance between the static connected components' re-computation and the insertions-only algorithm.

We observe a decrease in performance in all four experiments as the size of the graph increases from 1 million to 16 million vertices. There are several properties of the graph that change and affect performance. The larger graph has a larger diameter. Longer paths in the graph increase the running time of breadth-first search. As a result, the static connected computations' recomputation time increases. With more vertices to consider, the insertions-only algorithm slows down when merging and relabeling components. The larger graph has a higher maximum degree, so walking the edge list of a vertex in STINGER will require additional time. Likewise, although the average degree remains fixed at 8, there are more vertices with degree larger than 8. Retrieving their neighbor list and performing the neighbor intersection will also see a performance penalty. Given that these steps are $O(n)$ in the worst case and are easily parallelized, we would expect good scalability with increasing graph size. In our experiments, the bit array optimization slowed by a factor of 2 when the graph grew by a factor of 16. The connected components recomputation slowed by a factor of 6 for the same increase in graph size.

25.7 RELATED WORK

25.7.1 Streaming Data

The terms *streaming* [1] and *semi-streaming* [19] in related literature describe an algorithmic model of computation with very restrictive properties on data accesses. In streaming graph algorithms, the graph edges are read one-by-one in an arbitrary, unknown order. Streaming algorithms typically are limited to storing $O(n)$ or $O(n \text{ polylog } n)$ data, where n is the number of vertices, and taking at most $O(\log k)$ many passes over the k-long input edge stream. The metric of interest must be maintained or approximated without access to data other than the edge being observed at any given point in time and the relatively small summary. Streaming models have been applied to the approximation of local clustering coefficients [5, 10]. Current high-performance computer platforms like the Cray XMT and IBM Power 595 support enough main memory to store a significant amount of graph data at once and provide fairly uniform, fast access to that memory. On these platforms, the streaming model's restrictions are overly conservative. Our massive streaming data approach leverages the continued growth in available memory. Also, we assume an effectively infinite input stream and do not take multiple passes over the full input data. The algorithmic streaming model does inspire per-batch approximations.

25.7.2 Graph Data Structures

Alternative graph data structures for dynamic graphs beyond the ones described in Section 25.2.1 include forms of binary trees [24]. Trees pay an extra cost in keeping some order on the edges. On one target platform, the Cray XMT, the maintenance cost is substantial and prohibitive. STINGER's linked array structure permits simple multithreaded traversal and maintenance. Similar work in cache-oblivious algorithms often uses trees where the leaves are ordered arrays with blank entries [6]. The blank entries limit data movement when inserting a new edge into the ordered array. We are investigating whether STINGER can take advantage of a similar technique for accelerating intersections of edge lists. More radical alternatives exist, including representations using sparse certificates specific to different analysis kernels [15]. We consider the multi-use STINGER data structure a better compromise between performance and extensibility to new applications.

25.7.3 Tracking Connected Components

Several algorithms using breadth-first searches have been proposed for tracking connected components in case of deletions. Even and Shiloach [31] spawn two breadth-first searches for each edge deletion. One verifies that the component remains intact while the other determines if the component has been separated. Roditty and Zwick [30] stores the graph as a sequence of graphs that are created with each subsequent insertion. A Union-Find or Least Common Ancestor algorithm establishes connectivity. Henzinger et al. [12] also use a sequence of graphs and a coloring during a connected components computation to determine that a new component has been created after a batch of deletions.

These algorithms do not expose enough parallelism to support the analysis of the massive graphs of interest on massively parallel architectures. A scale-free graph's small diameter implies that a single breadth-first search is an expensive operation that quickly consumes the entire graph. Running one or more traversals for each edge deletion where deletions are unlikely to change the component structure will not support the high data rates of today's input streams.

Another approach partitions the graph to determine components. Henzinger and King [20] create a spectrum of partitions from dense to sparse subgraphs. After a deletion, a search begins within the densest level to re-establish connectivity between the two endpoints. Failure to find a link moves to a sparser level until connectivity is ruled out. Eppstein et al. [16] use partitions according to the average degree and sparsification techniques to maintain a minimum spanning forest of components.

For the social networks of interest, creating a spectrum of subgraphs from dense to sparse is difficult. Facebook, with 500 million vertices and average degree 130, is already very sparse. The Henzinger and King method would create only two levels of subgraphs with the majority of the graph in the first level. Most edge deletions cause what amounts to a static recomputation of connected components. Partitioning according to average degree is difficult because of the power law distribution in the vertex degree.

25.8 CONCLUSION

Our new *massive streaming data analytics* framework for graph analyzes and speeds up two fundamental analysis metrics compared to traditional static recomputation. To store the graph data, we have offered STINGER as a compromise between efficient graph traversal and flexible edge insertions and removals for a wide variety of graph algorithms. We have presented clustering coefficients and connected components as case studies for STINGER and our new analytical framework. Our framework's implementation runs on typical multicore systems like the Intel Nehalem using OpenMP as well as the massively multithreaded Cray XMT and performs well in both environments.

Our algorithms assume that the cost of processing a deletion is high compared to the cost of an insertion. Tolerating a small, *temporary* inconsistency with the static result permits handling deletions lazily and proceeding at insertion speed. When few deletions change the measure of interest, quickly ruling out the inconsequential deletions keeps the temporary inconsistency small and amortizes costly recomputations over many input batches.

Computing clustering coefficients demonstrates our approach's effectiveness. Updating after each edge insertion or deletion duplicates setup time, so the sorted update and Bloom filter algorithms perform relatively poorly. However, the serial stream contains enough parallelism when batched to exploit the Cray XMT's massively multithreaded architecture. We achieve a speed-up of 550× over edge-by-edge updates. The update rates of nearly 200 000 updates per second almost match gigabit Ethernet packet rates.

False positives from Bloom filters may introduce an approximation. A modestly sized filter produces an exact result with no false positives from our sampled scale-free networks. The Bloom filter approach achieved a $4\times$ speed-up over the brute-force method on the Cray XMT for the clustering coefficient case study.

Existing practice shows that the any streaming connected components algorithm should minimize the number of graph traversals necessary to establish or verify connectivity following a deletion. We have contributed a bit array intersection method to reduce drastically the number of deletions that require expensive checks if they cause structural change to the graph. Our experiments on synthetic graphs with millions of vertices and hundreds of millions of edges show that the use of bit array intersection is done at a small cost relative to the cost of static recomputation. The bit array intersection within our connected components algorithm enables graph processing to operate at speeds comparable to those that do not handle deletions at all.

Further work is needed to identify fast data-dependent methods to isolate only those deletions that cause changes in the metric of interest. Regarding connected components, the overwhelming majority of new or deleted edges cause no change in the number or size of connected components for a given batch of insertions and deletions. Additional heuristics could be developed to approximate component size and distribution without requiring expensive graph traversals that are the predominant cost in establishing connectivity after a deletion. Also, more complex algorithmic kernels will yield deeper insights about the structure of streaming networks, for example, for community and anomaly detection.

ACKNOWLEDGMENTS

This work was supported, in part, by the PNNL CASS-MT Center and NSF Grants CNS-0614915 and IIP-0934114. We thank PNNL and Cray for providing access to Cray XMT platforms. We are grateful to Karl Jiang, Kamesh Madduri, Daniel Chavarría, Jonathan Berry, Bruce Hendrickson, John Feo, Jeremy Kepner, and John Gilbert, for discussions on large-scale graph analysis and algorithm design.

REFERENCES

[1] Z. Bar-Yossef, R. Kumar, and D. Sivakumar, "Reductions in streaming algorithms, with an application to counting triangles in graphs," in *Proc. 13th Ann. Symp. Discrete Algorithms (SODA-02)*. San Francisco, CA: Society for Industrial and Applied Mathematics, Jan. 2002, pp. 623–632.

[2] A.-L. Barabási, "Network databases," 2007, http://www.nd.edu/~networks/resources.htm.

[3] K.J. Barker, K. Davis, A. Hoisie, D.J. Kerbyson, M. Lang, S. Pakin, and J.C. Sancho, "A performance evaluation of the Nehalem quad-core processor for scientific computing," *Parallel Processing Letters*, Vol. 18, No. 4, pp. 453–469, 2008.

[4] V. Batagelj and A. Mrvar, "Pajek – program for large network analysis," *Connections*, Vol. 21, No. 2, pp. 47–57, 1998.

[5] L. Becchetti, P. Boldi, C. Castillo, and A. Gionis, "Efficient semi-streaming algorithms for local triangle counting in massive graphs," in *KDD '08: Proceeding of the 14th ACM SIGKDD International Conference on Knowledge Discovery and Data Mining*. New York: ACM, 2008, pp. 16–24.

[6] M.A. Bender, J.T. Fineman, S. Gilbert, and B.C. Kuszmaul, "Concurrent cache-oblivious B-trees," in *SPAA '05: Proceedings of the Seventeenth Annual ACM Symposium on Parallelism in Algorithms and Architectures*. New York: ACM, 2005, pp. 228–237.

[7] J. Berry, B. Hendrickson, S. Kahan, and P. Konecny, "Software and algorithms for graph queries on multithreaded architectures," in *Proc. Workshop on Multithreaded Architectures and Applications (MTAAP)*, Long Beach, CA, March 2007.

[8] Blogpulse, "Blogpulse stats," March 2011, http://www.blogpulse.com/.

[9] B.H. Bloom, "Space/time trade-offs in hash coding with allowable errors," *Commun. ACM*, Vol. 13, No. 7, pp. 422–426, 1970.

[10] L.S. Buriol, G. Frahling, S. Leonardi, A. Marchetti-Spaccamela, and C. Sohler, "Counting triangles in data streams," in *PODS '06: Proceedings of the Twenty-Fifth ACM SIGMOD-SIGACT-SIGART Symposium on Principles of Database Systems*. New York: ACM, 2006, pp. 253–262.

[11] D. Chakrabarti, Y. Zhan, and C. Faloutsos, "R-MAT: A recursive model for graph mining," in *Proc. 4th SIAM Intl. Conf. on Data Mining (SDM)*. Orlando, FL: SIAM, Apr. 2004.

[12] A.T. Computational, M.R. Henzinger, V.K.T, and Y. Warnow, "Constructing a tree from homeomorphic subtrees, with," in *Algorithmica*, 1999, pp. 333–340.

[13] D. Ediger, K. Jiang, J. Riedy, and D.A. Bader, "Massive streaming data analytics: A case study with clustering coefficients," in *Proc. Workshop on Multithreaded Architectures and Applications (MTAAP)*, Atlanta, Georgia, Apr. 2010.

[14] D. Ediger, J. Riedy, D.A. Bader, and H. Meyerhenke, "Tracking structure of streaming social networks," in *Proc. Workshop on Multithreaded Architectures and Applications (MTAAP)*, Anchorage, Alaska, May 2011.

[15] D. Eppstein, Z. Galil, G. Italiano, and A. Nissenzweig, "Sparsification: a technique for speeding up dynamic graph algorithms," *J. ACM*, Vol. 44, No. 5, pp. 669–696, 1997.

[16] D. Eppstein, Z. Galil, G.F. Italiano, and A. Nissenzweig, "Sparsification—a technique for speeding up dynamic graph algorithms," *J. ACM*, Vol. 44, No. 5, pp. 669–696, 1997.

[17] I. Facebook, "User statistics," March 2011, http://www.facebook.com/press/info.php?statistics.

[18] L. Fan, P. Cao, J. Almeida, and A.Z. Broder, "Summary cache: A scalable wide-area web cache sharing protocol," in *IEEE/ACM Transactions on Networking*, 1998, pp. 254–265.

[19] J. Feigenbaum, S. Kannan, A. McGregor, S. Suri, and J. Zhang, "On graph problems in a semi-streaming model," *Theor. Comput. Sci.*, Vol. 348, No. 2, pp. 207–216, 2005.

[20] M.R. Henzinger and V. King, "Randomized fully dynamic graph algorithms with polylogarithmic time per operation," *J. ACM*, Vol. 46, p. 516, 1999.

[21] "Infovis databases," 2005, http://iv.slis.indiana.edu/db/index.html.

[22] H. Jeong, S. Mason, A.-L. Barabási, and Z. Oltvai, "Lethality and centrality in protein networks," *Nature*, Vol. 411, pp. 41–42, 2001.

[23] K. Madduri, D. Ediger, K. Jiang, D. Bader, and D. Chavarría-Miranda, "A faster parallel algorithm and efficient multithreaded implementations for evaluating betweenness centrality

on massive datasets," in *Proc. Workshop on Multithreaded Architectures and Applications (MTAAP)*, Rome, Italy, May 2009.

[24] K. Madduri and D.A. Bader, "Compact graph representations and parallel connectivity algorithms for massive dynamic network analysis," in *23rd IEEE International Parallel and Distributed Processing Symposium (IPDPS)*, Rome, Italy, May 2009.

[25] M. Newman, "Scientific collaboration networks: II. Shortest paths, weighted networks and centrality," *Phys. Rev. E*, Vol. 64, p. 016132, 2001.

[26] M. Newman, "The structure and function of complex networks," *SIAM Review*, Vol. 45, No. 2, pp. 167–256, 2003.

[27] NYSE Euronext, "Consolidated volume in NYSE listed issues, 2010 - current," March 2011, http://www.nyxdata.com/nysedata/asp/factbook/viewer_edition.asp?mode=table&key=3139&category=3.

[28] *OpenMP Application Program Interface; Version 3.0*, OpenMP Architecture Review Board, May 2008.

[29] M. Ringenburg and S.-E. Choi, "Optimizing loop-level parallelism in Cray XMT™ applications," in *Cray User's Group*, May 2009.

[30] L. Roditty and U. Zwick, "A fully dynamic reachability algorithm for directed graphs with an almost linear update time," in *Proc. of ACM Symposium on Theory of Computing*, 2004, pp. 184–191.

[31] Y. Shiloach and S. Even, "An on-line edge-deletion problem," *J. ACM*, Vol. 28, No. 1, pp. 1–4, 1981.

[32] Twitter, Inc., "Happy birthday Twitter!" March 2011, http://blog.twitter.com/2011/03/happy-birthday-twitter.html.

[33] J. Valois, "Lock-free linked lists using compare-and-swap," in *Proc. 14th Ann. ACM Symp. on Principles of Distributed Computing*, Ottowa, Canada, Aug. 1995, pp. 214–222.

[34] D. Watts and S. Strogatz, "Collective dynamics of small world networks," *Nature*, Vol. 393, pp. 440–442, 1998.

26

KNOWLEDGE MANAGEMENT FOR FAULT-TOLERANT WATER DISTRIBUTION

Jing Lin, Ali Hurson, and Sahra Sedigh

CONTENTS

Large Scale Network-Centric Distributed Systems, First Edition. Edited by Hamid Sarbazi-Azad and Albert Y. Zomaya.
© 2014 John Wiley & Sons, Inc. Published 2014 by John Wiley & Sons, Inc.

649

26.1   INTRODUCTION

In environmental management systems, intelligent decision support is utilized in hopes of facilitating more efficacious use of scarce environmental resources, particularly by adapting resource allocation and system operation to user demand, resource availability, and environmental conditions. Intelligent environmental decision support systems (EDSSs), which make use of cyber infrastructure for computing services such as automated reasoning, have been developed to this end. The physical infrastructure that supports environmental management is monitored, controlled, and guided by the cyber infrastructure; creating a *cyber-physical system* (CPS) where embedded computing and communication capabilities are used to streamline and fortify the operation of the physical system [1, 2]. Real-time data collected by sensors from the physical infrastructure and its environment creates situational awareness and enables intelligent decision support and control. As an example, automated reasoning can be used to determine whether a power grid is operating within safety thresholds, and to determine appropriate settings for power electronics devices that control the flow on transmission lines.

Design and development of a reliable, effective, and efficient CPS is contingent upon accurate characterization of the operation of the physical and cyber infrastructures, respectively; as well as the interaction between the two. This is especially critical in the design of EDSSs, where decision support and actuation are needed for allocation of physical resources. Among existing techniques for modeling and representation of complex systems, agent-based modeling holds promise for accurate characterization of the operation of the cyber and physical infrastructures in one integrated model, with high fidelity, and can capture interdependencies among the two infrastructures. This results from the ability of an agent-based model to encapsulate diverse component attributes within a single agent, while accurately capturing the interaction among autonomous, heterogeneous agents that share a common goal achieved in a distributed fashion.

The agent is the key element in our CPS model, in terms of implementing intelligent decision making, which requires autonomous conversion of raw data sensor data to information with the semantics and syntax required by the decision support algorithms. Ontologies can facilitate knowledge extraction by capturing (and presenting) the terminology for and semantic relationships among entities in a given application domain, simplifying the task of an agent responsible for creating useful information from raw data. The semantic relationships that can be captured by an ontology far exceed the "is-a" links typical of taxonomies, whose use is limited to classification of an entity per a predetermined hierarchy.

In this chapter, we propose and validate an EDSS where ontologies are utilized to classify failure events and determine appropriate countermeasures to mitigate their effects. An intelligent water distribution network (WDN) serves as a case study; however, the methodology proposed is applicable to a broad range of environmental management systems.

In a cyber-physical WDN, physical components, for example, valves, pipes, and reservoirs, are coupled with hardware and software that supports intelligent water allocation. Figure 26.1 depicts an example. The primary goal of WDNs is to provide a dependable source of potable water to the public. Information such as demand patterns,

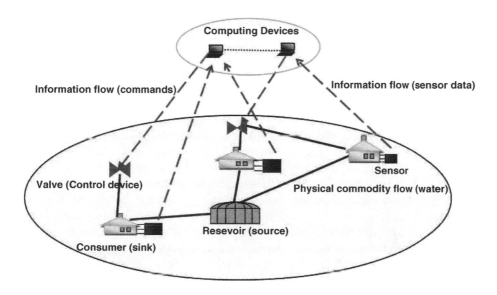

Figure 26.1   An intelligent water distribution network.

water quantity (flow and pressure head), and water quality (contaminants and minerals) is critical in achieving this goal and beneficial in guiding maintenance efforts and identifying vulnerable areas requiring fortification and/or monitoring. Sensors dispersed in the physical infrastructure collect data, which is processed and interpreted by the decision support entities of the cyber infrastructure. Distributed algorithms (e.g., game theory) are used to determine appropriate settings for hardware controllers that are used to manage the allocation (quantity) and chemical composition (quality) of the water. Automated reasoning and computation are implemented through software executing on multiple distributed computing devices. This software is represented by the agents in our model, each of which is capable of perceiving its environment, acting on that perception, and communicating with other agents. Ontologies are presented in this chapter to reflect various aspects of the semantic relationships among components in the intelligent WDN, and their use in automated reasoning is illustrated. The modeling work of ontologies has been submitted in [3].

Our contribution in this chapter includes the presentation of an ontology-based framework to reflect various aspects of the semantic relationships among the components in the intelligent WDN, and illustration of the powerful automatic reasoning capabilities of the ontology. A complete test case scenario is provided to demonstrate the efficacy of the ontology-based service to assist automatic decision-making in cyberinfrastructure when failure occurs in physical infrastructure. By utilizing the ontology to capture the information flow in a complex system, such as CPSs, we can have a more profound and multiperspective understanding of the semantic relationships existing among the interacting components.

To the best of our knowledge, this is the first time that an ontology-based approach has been adopted to assist automatic decision-making based on the raw data collected by sensors in the context of CPSs, particularly in the domain of WDNs. Due to the automated-reasoning capability of ontologies, the ontologies-based framework can be expanded to other CPS domains, such as transportation systems and power grids.

This chapter is structured as follows: Section 26.2 provides an overview of previous related work in environmental decision support systems, agent-based modeling and simulation techniques, knowledge representation capabilities of ontology, and simulation techniques as tools for validation of models for CPSs. Section 26.3 presents the major functional components of a generic CPS, the major components of the derivative WDN, and the agent-based model for WDN operation. Section 26.4 provides a detailed introduction to the class composition of the ontology-based framework and illustrates the automated reasoning based on the defined classes. Section 26.5 presents the object properties for behavior reasoning and the data properties for value reasoning, respectively. Section 26.6 demonstrates the benefits of the ontology-based framework through a test case on an integrated CPS simulator for WDN. Finally, Section 26.7 summarizes the work presented in the chapter and describes future work.

26.2   RELATED WORK

Challenges in the design of EDSSs for management of critical infrastructure have been investigated in several studies; a representative subset is presented in this section. Model formulation of decision support systems for interactive decision making based on environmental data is discussed in [4]. The issue of modeling complex environmental data is discussed in [5]. Strategic decision support for the services industry is described in [6], in which advisors providing a decision support service may use the computerized technique in a competitive environment. Application case studies on utilization of EDSSs include, but are not limited to, contextual role-based access control authorization [7], recognition of driving events [8], and guidance on design of transmission lines [9].

Agent-based modeling and simulation (ABMS) for characterizing systems composed of autonomous, interacting agents is discussed in [10], which points out that ABMS is particularly beneficial to decision-making. The utility of agent-based models for representation of distributed complex systems has been investigated in [11]. The work in [12] adopts a distributed multiagent architecture to analyze observed information in real-time, facilitating adaptation of a multiagent system to the evolution of its environment. A multiagent approach to system assurance is articulated in [13], which demonstrates how to determine the relative importance of any single agent.

Ontologies can be considered a method for modeling and presenting knowledge; they are frequently used to organize and represent knowledge in artificial intelligence. Experts differ on their definitions of "ontology," but every definition encountered by the authors concurs that an ontology is a representation of entities and the relationships among them [14]. A definition given in [15] characterizes an ontology as the specification of conceptualizations that are used to help computers and humans share knowledge. The semantic web and social network research communities have been especially prolific in their use of ontologies [16],[17]. Two well-known examples are FOAF [18] and Flink [19], which have been used to analyze social networks, discover communities of practice [20], and explore "hot" topics [21]. Recent applications of ontologies in automated reasoning include the use of ontologies in improving situational awareness [22].

The simulation methods and techniques to justify the correctness of models for CPSs have been investigated in several studies. Some challenges to the development of a generic framework for the design, modeling, and simulation of CPSs are articulated in [23]. Features described as desirable for such a framework include the integration of existing simulation tools, software reusability, and graphical representation of the modeling and simulation environment. The work presented in [24] meets these criteria. A similar method is proposed in [25], which integrates the ns-2 network simulator with the Modelica framework, a modeling language for large-scale physical systems. The chapter highlights the challenge of two-way synchronization of the simulators. The key difference between [25] and [24] is that a specialized simulator capable of accurately representing the operation of the water infrastructure at high resolution is presented in the latter one.

26.3 AGENT-BASED MODEL FOR WDN OPERATION

The first step in constructing a CPS model is to identify the major functional components of the system. Figure 26.2 depicts the six main functional components of a CPS used for transporting a physical commodity. WDNs, smart grids, and intelligent transportation

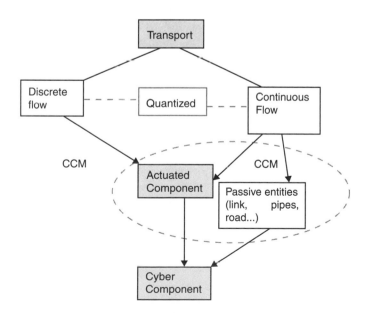

Figure 26.2 Functional model of a transport CPS.

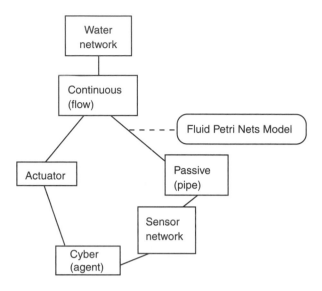

Figure 26.3 Functional model of a WDN.

systems can be abstracted in this fashion, as they transport water, electric power, and vehicles, respectively. In such transport systems, both discrete and continuous flows (the values of which can be quantized) are carried by passive entities and controlled, commanded, and monitored (CCM) by actuated components. The cyber-components (where the agents reside) control both the actuators (directly) and passive entities (indirectly) and provide intelligent decision support for efficient management of the transport system.

Figure 26.3 depicts the instantiation of the functional model of Fig. 26.2 for a WDN.

The functional framework of Fig. 26.3 serves as the basis for qualitative modeling of the WDN, which is carried out with the goal of capturing the interaction between the cyber and physical infrastructures. We use the Uniform Modeling Language (UML) to represent the model, due to the precise semantics offered by this formal specification language. A detailed demonstration of the use of UML for the specification of an agent-based system is presented in [26].

A use case diagram specifies the major functionalities for qualitative system analysis. Each use case captures the interaction of a number of external actors with the system towards the accomplishment of a specific goal. Capturing this functionality facilitates the tracing of information flow through the CPS. Figure 26.4 depicts the actors and use cases involved in a typical WDN. The double circles emphasize the sources of cyber or physical heterogeneity, a significant challenge that has been investigated in [27]. This use case diagram can be readily generalized to other CPSs whose main goal is management of a physical commodity.

The agent is the actor in the use case diagram and is associated with the decision support algorithm. The agent queries the various data sources available to the EDSS (e.g., sensor networks or databases with information on past events). For simplicity, only use

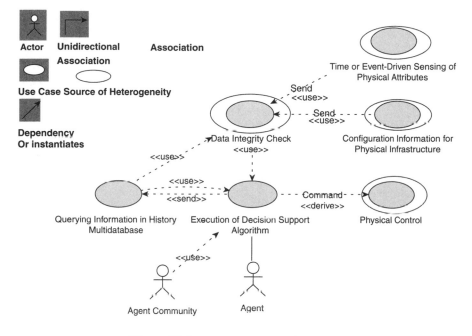

Figure 26.4 Use case diagram for a WDN.

cases associated with one agent are shown in Fig. 26.4; all other agents are associated with similar use cases.

As shown in Fig. 26.4, sensors collect information about the physical operation of the system on a time- or event-triggered basis. As sensors collect data from different areas, the events may occur sporadically, and the data may be represented in different formats. This heterogeneous data is collected by sensors and sent for *Data Integrity Check*, which is a stage of intelligent semantic inference.

The *Data Integrity Check* use case utilizes three main data streams to identify corrupt or invalid sensor data, specifically, (i) real-time data from nearby sensors for the same or related physical attributes, (ii) information about the physical infrastructure, and (iii) data from a (multi)database that maintains historical sensor data. The second and third data streams mentioned are used for corroboration of the first data stream, by checking for discrepancies in the values, whether in variation or in conformance to physical (hydraulic) laws that govern the operation of the physical infrastructure of the WDN. If no data is available from nearby sensors, as would be the case if all nearby sensors are in sleep mode, the history database will serve as the only source of data for corroboration.

The semantic interpretation service is incorporated in the *Data Integrity Check* use case to organize the information into a meaningful hierarchy. The Summary Schema Model (SSM) is an advanced semantic processing model that supports the semantic service by extracting similar semantics of access terms from the underlying local database and forming a hierarchical structure to reduce redundant information. It can provide the ability to perform imprecise queries on the aforementioned data sources by facilitating the identification of semantically similar/dissimilar data.

In concert, use of the semantic interpretation service and the SSM while checking data integrity provides transparent and uniform access to heterogeneous data sources. The SSM maintains a hierarchical (logical) metadata structure based on access terms imported from various local databases, and can be implemented using existing multidatabase technologies, without requiring update or reconfiguration of the local databases. This feature is critical in WDNs, where modifying legacy databases is often infeasible. In this fashion, local autonomy is preserved, while supporting scalability. This approach is well-suited to large WDNs, which are composed of multiple autonomous districts, each of which can potentially have a different local configuration. Utilization of SSM to reconcile data heterogeneity in WDN decision support has been described in [27].

26.4 CLASSES IN WDN ONTOLOGY FRAMEWORK

On the basis of the functional components of Fig. 26.3 and use case diagram of Fig. 26.4, in this section we present the building blocks of the ontology framework—the classes. We use Protégé 4 [28] as the platform for creation of the WDN ontology.

26.4.1 WDN Ontology Class

The topmost classes of the WDN are shown in Fig. 26.5, according to the functionalities identified in Fig. 26.3 and Fig. 26.4. The class *Thing* is the set containing all the subclasses, under which all other classes are defined.

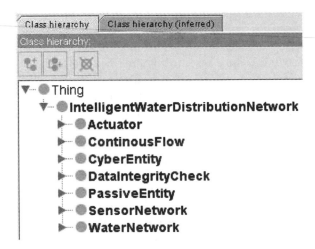

Figure 26.5   Topmost classes of the WDN.

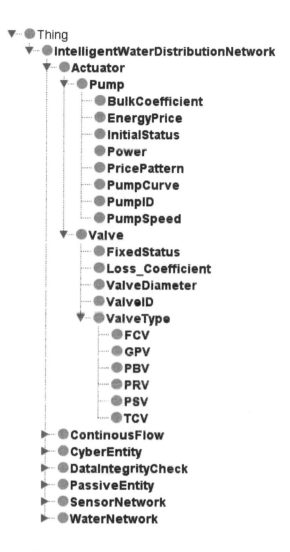

Figure 26.6 Ontologies for actuator class.

Classes can be organized into a superclass-subclass hierarchy, which is quite similar to a taxonomy. We adopt OWL-DL [29] in Protégé to define the superclass-subclass relationships, which can be automatically computed by a reasoner and visualized in diagrams. An automated reasoner can process and parse OWL-DL to understand the relationships among defined classes specifically determining whether a particular class is a subclass of another. The classes we have defined in OWL-DL for the WDN are presented in Fig. 26.6 to Fig. 26.11, where the superclass-subclass relationships are clearly depicted.

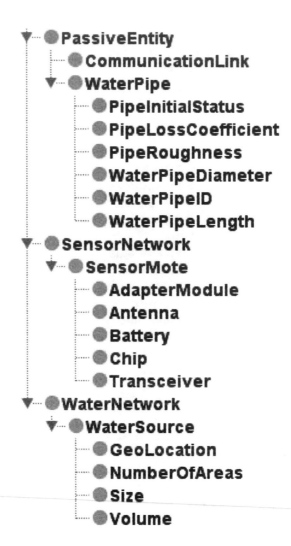

Figure 26.7   Ontologies for passive entity, sensor network and water network classes.

The failure type class is created based on FMEA [30] and fault tree analysis [31]. The *Computer-System-Vulnerability* class is adopted from an existing ontology developed by the Resilience for Survivability group [32]. The mitigation technique database is designed to address a broad range of failure types, and makes reference to [33].

26.4.2   Automatic Reasoning Based on Classes

An automated reasoner can utilize the OWL-DL model to compute the inferred ontology class hierarchy, as depicted in Fig. 26.12. The graph has been gener-ated using OWLViz, a visualization plug-in for Protégé. The rectangle denotes the

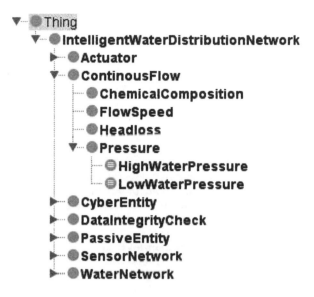

Figure 26.8   Continuous flow class.

selection made when we query the "Decision_MakingFail_Mitigation" class. The hierarchical ontology in OWL-DL facilitates identification of the superclass and subclasses of "Decision_MakingFail_Mitigation". The arcs representing "is-a" relationships have been denoted as such in Fig. 26.12.

As an example, shown in Fig. 26.13, a "PipeOverload" can be automatically identified as a type of failure of the pipe. Once the failure type has been identified, the associated mitigation technique can be determined, and countermeasures can be actuated for the physical components. Identification of the appropriate mitigation technique takes place in a top-down fashion, with higher-level classes being investigated before lower-level classes [34].

26.5   AUTOMATED FAILURE CLASSIFICATION AND MITIGATION

In OWL, properties describe relationships between classes or individuals; instances of the class and the subclass can also be viewed as individuals of the superclass. The two main types of properties in OWL-DL are "object" and "datatype".

26.5.1   Object Properties for Behavior Reasoning

The object properties specify relationships between two classes or individuals. By OWL-DL convention, the properties are prefixed with the word "has" or "is" to clarify the meaning of the property for humans; to take advantage of the "English Prose Tooltip

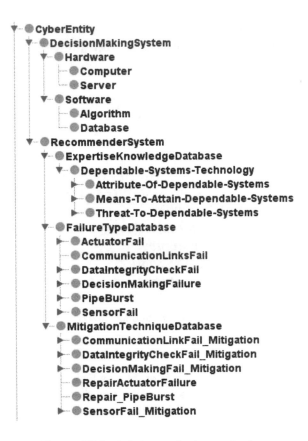

Figure 26.9   Subclasses of cyber entity class.

Generator", which uses this naming convention where possible to generate more human-readable class descriptions [28]; and to facilitate automated reasoning.

The properties we have defined for the WDN ontology are shown in Fig. 26.14.

We can further define characteristics for each object property to enrich its meaning or to constrain its domain or range. More specifically, a property can be characterized as one of the following [28]:

1. *Functional:* A functional property relates a given individual to at most one other individual (e.g., "computer has command over actuator"), and specifies that the computer can send commands to the actuator, as opposed to directly exerting control over the flow transported by the CPS.

2. *Inverse functional:* Properties that measure the inverse properties are functional. For example, if we define an "isCommandedBy" property, then it is the inverse functional property of "actuator is commanded by computer".

3. *Transitive:* If a property relates individual *a* to individual *b*, and also individual *b* to individual *c*, then we can infer that individual *a* is related to individual *c*

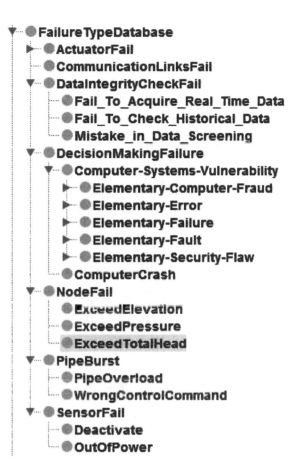

Figure 26.10 Failure type class.

via the same property. For instance, an actuator can be controlled by a computer, and a pipe (passive entity) can in turn be controlled by the actuator; therefore, the "isControlledOf" property can be characterized as transitive.

4. *Symmetric properties:* When individual *a* is related to individual *b* via property *P*, and vice versa, *P* is characterized as symmetric.

5. *Asymmetric properties:* Any property that is not symmetric is characterized as asymmetric. Most of the properties in our WDN ontology are asymmetric.

6. *Reflexive properties:* A property that relates an individual to itself is characterized as reflexive. For instance, in our ontology, the "MitigationTechnique-Database" is reflexively related to "has MitigationIdentification".

7. *Irreflexive properties:* Individuals related by an irreflexive property cannot be the same.

Figure 26.11   Mitigation technique class.

The object properties can be further characterized with a domain and a range, respectively. The object properties link classes (individuals) from the domain to classes (individuals) from the range. In the relationship "computer has command over actuator", the "computer" is the domain and the "actuator" is the range. The domain and the range in OWL-DL are used as "axioms" in reasoning. It is worth noting that an axiom is one of the main components of an ontology; others include concepts, individuals, and relationships, which have been discussed earlier in this chapter. Figure 26.15 shows the characteristics and the description of the domain and range of property "hasCommandOver".

Figure 26.16 depicts an overarching map of the object properties that interconnect various classes and subclasses in the WDN ontology. The map is automatically generated based on the "axioms" used in reasoning. Not all properties have been reflected in this map; it is intended to demonstrate how object properties can be used to infer relationships among different classes. Two types of arcs appear in Fig. 26.16—solid and dashed. A solid arc represents a "superclass-subclass" relationship, such as "software" and "algorithm". A dashed arc represents an object property, for example, if the arrow on the arc between "software" and "continuous flow" is activated, then the object property is highlighted as "Software hasAdvancedComputation of the continuous flow". Similarly, "WaterNetwork" hasFlow of the "ContinuousFlow", "SensorNetwork"

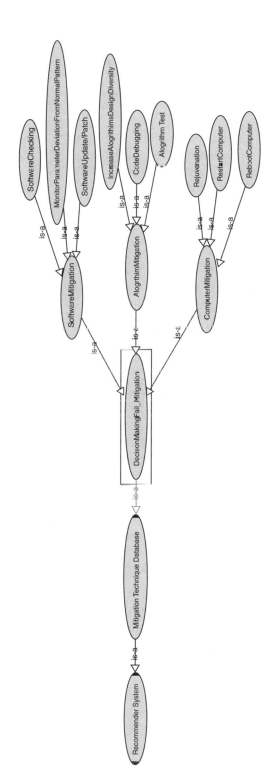

Figure 26.12 Deduced superclass and subclasses of "Decision_MakingFail_Mitigation".

Figure 26.13 Failure type identification based on the reasoning from root class "PipeOverload".

hasMonitorOf the "ContinuousFlow" , "CyberEntity" hasIntegrityDataOf "DataIntegrityCheck", "Computer" hasCommandOver "Acuator", "MitigationTechniqueDatabase" hasSuggestionToComputation for "DecisionMakingSystem", and the "Computer" can send three different types of control command to the valve and the pump (subclasses of the actuator), including "hasIncreaseOriginalValue", "hasDecreaseOriginalValue" and "hasMaintainOriginalValue".

Figure 26.17 depicts the interaction of the major components of the cyber entity class. In this example, once a failure is identified as being of the type "PipeOverload", appropriate countermeasures can be automatically identified and retrieved from the mitigation techniques database. This is reflected by the connection between the "hasMitigationIndentification" property and the failure type database. The mitigation technique database has the reflexive property "hasMitigationIdentification" to facilitate identification of appropriate countermeasures. If a failure is identified as being of type "PipeBurst", the

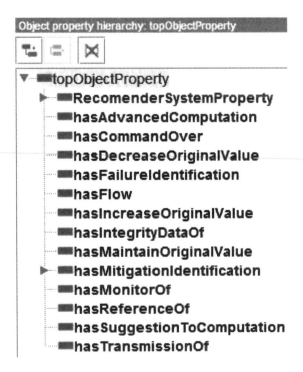

Figure 26.14 Top object properties.

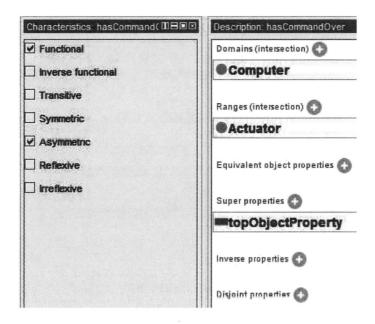

Figure 26.15   Characteristics and description of an object property.

corresponding mitigation technique is determined to be "Repair_PipeBurst". This class will mitigate the pipe burst failure through the object property "hasPipeRepaired". In the meantime, the mitigation technique database will trigger decision support by "hasSuggestionTo Computation", which leads to computation of updated values for the actuator command.

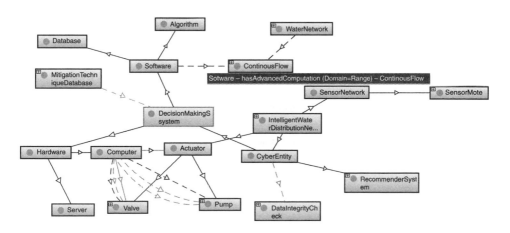

Figure 26.16   Map of object properties in WDN ontology.

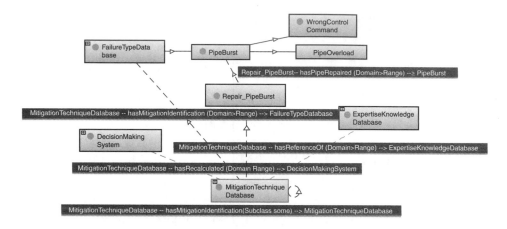

Figure 26.17 Classes and object properties relevant to failure mitigation.

26.5.2 Data Properties for Value Reasoning

Data properties link an individual to an XML schema datatype value, that is, they describe the type of relationship between an individual and data values. For instance, we can use data properties to describe the pressure value of the water flow, specify respective numeric ranges for "high" and "low" flow pressure in a particular water consumption area is high or low, and determine whether the water allocated is sufficient. This judgment capability can be used to improve the dependability of the WDN. For example, we can configure a threshold value for the flow pressure, and once this threshold is exceeded (reflecting potential failure), a mitigation technique can be identified and initiated.

We use "pressure" as an example to demonstrate automated reasoning of values. Initially, we define a data property as "has-flow-pressure-value", shown as Fig. 26.18. We then create four instances within the "Pressure" class and define the properties of each instance.

Figure 26.19 shows the data property definition for "Commercial-Area-Water-Pressure", which is "has-flow-pressure-value 400". This specifies that the average water pressure value in a commercial area is around 400(psi). Similarly, the average pressure values in industrial, residential, and suburban areas are set to 700, 260, and 200, respectively.

We further refine the use of datatypes by adding restrictions on the possible values. We define classes that specify a range of values in which we are interested; for instance, particularly high or low pressure values that may indicate a possible failure. For example, in Fig. 26.20, we specify that when the flow pressure value is greater than 450, then the pressure is identified as a "HighWaterPressure" class. Similarly, the "LowWaterPressure" is specified that "has-flow-pressure-value equal to or lower than 200".

By automatically reasoning based on the data properties defined for each individual and the range specified for each property, the members (instances) of each subclass can be intelligently added. In Fig. 26.21, the individual "industrial-area-water-pressure" (700) is automatically added as a member of "HighWaterPressure" that is more than 450.

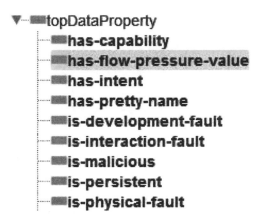

Figure 26.18 Definition of data property.

Figure 26.19 Data property assertion of individual.

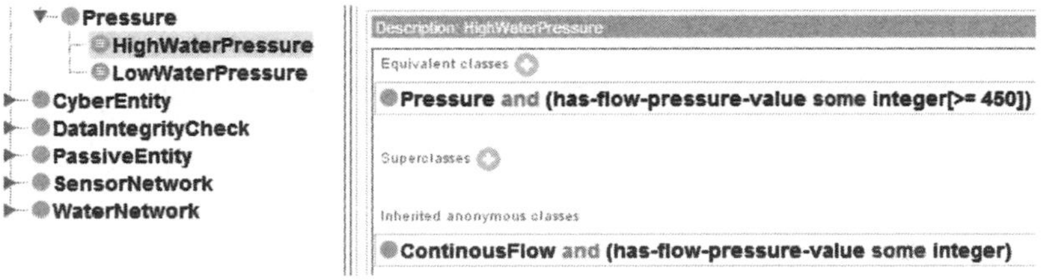

Figure 26.20 Definition of the "HighWaterPressure".

Figure 26.21 Automated classification of an individual.

26.6 VALIDATION OF AUTOMATED FAILURE MITIGATION

The test case scenario can be created on an integrated simulator for the intelligent WDN, which is composed of EPANET and MATLAB, to represent the physical water distribution network and the decision support algorithms, respectively. Communication between the two simulators replicates the interactions between cyber and physical components of WDNs and facilitates the observation of physical manifestations of intelligent control decisions. This communication between the simulators takes place without user intervention, as all information relevant to each simulator has been identified and extracted from the output of the other. Information flows from the physical simulator to the cyber simulator, replicating the operation of sensors in the physical infrastructure. The cyber simulator processes this data, and provides decision support for water allocation, in the form of setting for control elements in the physical infrastructure. This information is provided to the physical simulator, which applies these settings. The details for the design of the simulator and the working flow can be found in [24].

In this section, we present and analyze an empirical test case used to validate the automated failure mitigation technique of Section 26.5. The integrated cyber-physical WDN simulator developed in [24] was utilized. The sensor data was generated by EPANET, which is used to simulate the physical infrastructure. Identification of the failure type is carried out using the ontology model, as is determination of the corresponding failure mitigation technique. The automated reasoning procedure is represented by an OWL-DL script; the reasoned result is converted into a readable .txt format that can be parsed by MATLAB, which simulates the intelligent decision support and determines appropriate settings for physical components. These settings are fed back to EPANET, completing the control cycle. The entire simulation working flow is shown in Fig. 26.22.

26.6.1 Initial Configuration and Normal Operation

The topology assumed in EPANET for the physical infrastructure is shown in Fig. 26.23. The main criteria for creating the topology follow two aspects: the water distribution

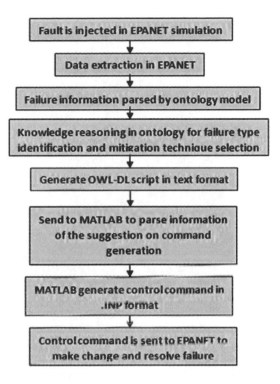

Figure 26.22   Validation flow.

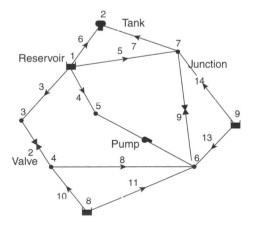

Figure 26.23   Topology assumed for physical infrastructure.

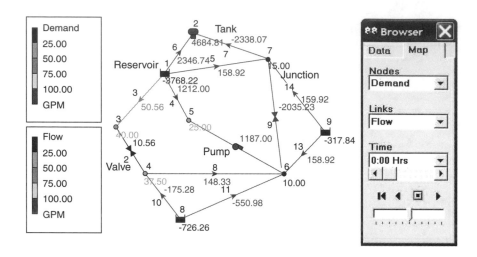

<u>Figure 26.24</u>   Values of demand and flow at time 0.

network should have three actuators, either pump or valve, in charge of different areas; the water distribution network should have three reservoirs, representing that three agents are in charge of providing or retrieving water from their neighbors.

Based on this topology (and the laws of hydraulics), EPANET determined the initial demand (node labels) and flow (link labels) to be as depicted in Fig. 26.24.

The time span and time step of simulation are configured as 24 hours and 1 hour, respectively. Throughout the time span, it is possible to change the settings configured for any component in the physical infrastructure, or for the system as a whole. As an example, it is possible to set the value of "total head", which is the hydraulic head (elevation + pressure head) of water in the reservoir and a required property for simulation. Fluids possess energy and the total energy associated with a fluid per unit weight of the fluid is denoted as the fluid's "head", which is expressed in units of height. On many occasions, energy needs to be added to a hydraulic system to overcome elevation differences, friction losses, and other minor losses. A pump is a device to which mechanical energy is applied and transferred to the water as total head, therefore, it can add more energy to the fluid. From the simulation results, shown in Fig. 26.25, when no error occurs in the simulation, the status of the nodes and links in each time span can be displayed in EPANET. It can be concluded that when the total head is configured as 100 ft, reservoir 8 (node at the bottom of the map) is operating normally at time 0.

The status of an actuator (a pump or valve) in different time slots can also be observed. The pressure values at 0 and 10 hours, respectively, are as shown as node labels in Fig. 26.26 and Fig. 26.27.

26.6.2   Failure Scenario and Automated Mitigation

Fault injection was carried out to validate the automated failure mitigation technique. The specific fault injected was decreasing the total head from 100 to 50 ft, which corresponds

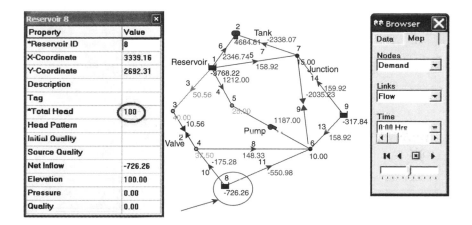

Figure 26.25 Status of reservoir 8 at time 0, when total head = 100 ft.

to a failure at reservoir 8. This is because the total head is an energy parameter associated with elevation. If the elevation of the reservoir cannot sustain the updated total head value, the excessive energy will be distributed to its neighbors. This energy release can lead to excessive flow in neighboring links of the physical infrastructure, including both pipes and pumps. EPANET reflects this failure by displaying a warning message with information about overloaded links, as shown in Fig. 26.28. The complete warning message has been omitted in the interest of brevity.

Detection of this failure by EPANET should trigger automated failure mitigation, using the ontologies of Section 26.4 for identification of the failure type and determination

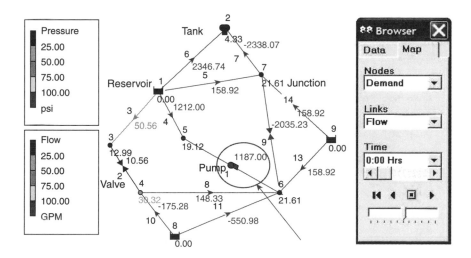

Figure 26.26 Pressure values (node labels) at time 0.

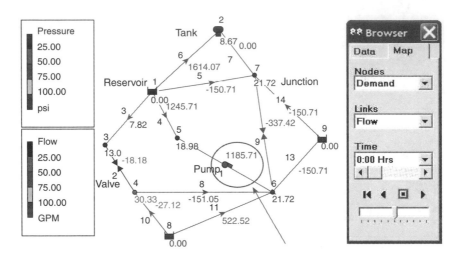

Figure 26.27   Pressure values (node labels) at 10 hours.

of the appropriate countermeasure. As our fault injection was limited to the physical infrastructure, the countermeasures applied are changes in physical device settings. In the overload scenario described above, the cyber infrastructure determines settings for actuators that regulate the water flow.

Identification of the failure type is the first step in failure mitigation, and takes place based on the warning generated by EPANET. The information embedded in the text file shown in Fig. 26.28 is interpreted to denote a failure caused by "exceeds maximum flow", which corresponds to the failure type of "Exceed Total Head", a node failure in the

```
WARNING: Negative pressures at 0:00:00 hrs.
WARNING: Pump 1 open but exceeds maximum flow at 0:00:00 hrs.

WARNING: Negative pressures at 0:05:39 hrs.
WARNING: Pump 1 open but exceeds maximum flow at 0:05:39 hrs.

WARNING: Negative pressures at 0:34:44 hrs.
WARNING: Pump 1 open but exceeds maximum flow at 0:34:44 hrs.

WARNING: Negative pressures at 0:38:38 hrs.
WARNING: Pump 1 open but exceeds maximum flow at 0:38:38 hrs.

WARNING: Negative pressures at 1:00:00 hrs.
WARNING: Pump 1 open but exceeds maximum flow at 1:00:00 hrs.

WARNING: Negative pressures at 1:04:53 hrs.
WARNING: Pump 1 open but exceeds maximum flow at 1:04:53 hrs.
```

Figure 26.28   EPANET warning message.

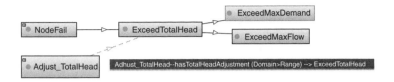

Figure 26.29 Ontology-based reasoning for failure classification.

failure ontology of Fig. 26.10. The reasoning procedure that leads to this determination is shown in Fig. 26.29.

Once the failure type is identified, the associated countermeasure is determined using the mitigation ontology of Fig. 26.11. A snapshot of the resulting mitigation object is shown in Fig. 26.30.

The automated reasoning procedure (an OWL-DL script), from "failure identification" to "mitigation technique identification" is depicted in Fig. 26.31.

In our simulator, the selected countermeasures are recorded in an OWL-DL text file, which can be parsed by MATLAB. For the failure scenario described, the "Adjust_TotalHead" countermeasure leads to configuration of the total head at reservoir 8 to 100 ft—the value under normal operating conditions. This value is calculated by MATLAB and sent to EPANET as the input file shown in Fig. 26.32. The countermeasure does not affect the "Pattern" (an option relevant to time specification), and this value is left blank in the automatically generated file.

Exertion of this countermeasure by EPANET, for a 24-hour simulation with 1-hour time steps (the same parameters as the normal operating case of Fig. 26.24) led to results identical to those depicted in Fig. 26.25, verifying the effectiveness of the countermeasure in restoring normal operation.

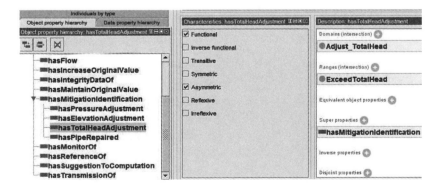

Figure 26.30 Characteristics and description of mitigation technique.

```
<Declaration>
  <Class IRI="#Adjust_TotalHead"/>
</Declaration>
<Declaration>
  <Class IRI="#ExceedTotalHead"/>
</Declaration>
<Declaration>
  <ObjectProperty IRI="#hasTotalHeadAdjustment"/>
</Declaration>
<SubClassOf>
  <Class IRI="#Adjust_TotalHead"/>
  <Class IRI="#NodeFail_Mitigation"/>
</SubClassOf>
<SubClassOf>
  <Class IRI="#ExceedTotalHead"/>
  <Class IRI="#NodeFail"/>
</SubClassOf>
<SubObjectPropertyOf>
  <ObjectProperty IRI="#hasTotalHeadAdjustment"/>
  <ObjectProperty IRI="#hasMitigationIdentification"/>
</SubObjectPropertyOf>
<FunctionalObjectProperty>
  <ObjectProperty IRI="#hasTotalHeadAdjustment"/>
</FunctionalObjectProperty>
<AsymmetricObjectProperty>
  <ObjectProperty IRI="#hasTotalHeadAdjustment"/>
</AsymmetricObjectProperty>
<ObjectPropertyRange>
  <ObjectProperty IRI="#hasTotalHeadAdjustment"/>
  <Class IRI="#ExceedTotalHead"/>
</ObjectPropertyRange>
<ObjectPropertyRange>
  <ObjectProperty IRI="#hasTotalHeadAdjustment"/>
  <Class IRI="#ExceedTotalHead"/>
</ObjectPropertyRange>
```

Figure 26.31   Automated reasoning procedure for failure mitigation.

```
[RESERVOIRS]
;ID                    Head                  Pattern
 1                     100
 8                     100
 9                     100
```

Figure 26.32   Countermeasures provided by MATLAB to EPANET.

26.7 CONCLUSION

The intelligent decision support offered by the cyberinfrastructure is the major motivation of the adoption of CPSs for leveraging environmental management. The utilization of ontology makes further improvement in terms of knowledge engineering on the information flow in the CPSs. An intelligent water distribution network is selected as the case study for the EDSSs in this chapter. On the basis of the agent-based model to identify the major functionalities, the work presented shows the details of the construction of an ontology-based framework, and also shows the benefits of ontology in terms of automatic reasoning, beyond the defined relationship among components. The test case has successfully proved the efficiency and the intelligence that the ontology-based model has to leverage the decision-support in the agents.

Due to the extension and reusability of the ontology, we plan to extend the current framework by continue creating the ontology for other CPS domains, such as power grids and transportation systems. Based on the constructed ontologies, it is anticipated that we can abstract a generic CPS framework that can incorporate all the major CPS domains and facilitate the development of the CPSs, especially in the fields of reliability and security. We also plan to validate the created domain-specific ontologies through an experiment to prove the functional and nonfunctional correctness of the framework.

ACKNOWLEDGMENTS

The authors wish to thank the U.S. National Science Foundation (under Grant No. IIS-0324835) and the Missouri S&T Intelligent Systems Center for support of this work.

REFERENCES

[1] E. Lee, "Cyber physical systems: Design challenges," in *Proceedings of the 11th IEEE International Symposium on Object Oriented Real-Time Distributed Computing (ISORC'08)*, May 2008, pp. 363–369.

[2] J. Sztipanovits, "Composition of cyber-physical systems," in *Proceedings of the 14th Annual IEEE International Conference and Workshops on the Engineering of Computer-Based Systems (ECBS '07)*. Washington, DC: IEEE Computer Society, 2007, pp. 3–6.

[3] J. Lin, S. Sedigh, and A. Hurson, "Ontology-based framework to improve the automatic decision support in intelligent water distribution network," in *Proceedings of the 45th Hawaii International Conference on System Sciences (HICSS-45)*, Grand Wailea, Maui, Hawaii, January 2012.

[4] L. Fang, K.W. Hipel, D. Kilgour, and X. Peng, "A decision support system for interactive decision making—part I: Model formulation," *IEEE Transactions on Systems, Man, and Cybernetics*, Vol. 33, No. 1, Feb 2003.

[5] C.M. Roadknight, G.R. Balls, G. Mills, and D. Palmer-Brown, "Modeling complex environmental data," *IEEE Transactions on Neural Networks*, Vol. 8, No. 4, July 1997.

[6] K.W. Hipel, D.M. Kilgou, L. Fang, and X. Peng, "Strategic decision support for the services industry," *IEEE Transactions on Engineering Management*, Vol. 48, No. 3, Aug 2001.

[7] G.H.M.B. Motta and S.S. Furuie, "A contextual role-based access control authorization model for electronic patient record," *IEEE Transactions on Information Technology in Biomedicine*, Vol. 7, No. 3, Sept 2003.

[8] D. Mitrovic, "A contextual role-based access control authorization model for electronic patient record," *IEEE Transactions on Intelligent Transportation Systems*, Vol. 6, No. 2, June 2005.

[9] G.A. Fenton and N. Sutherland, "Reliability-based transmission line design," *IEEE Transactions on Power Delivery*, Vol. 26, No. 2, April 2011.

[10] C.M. Macal and M.J. North, "Agent-based modeling and simulation," in *Proceedings of the Winter Simulation Conference (WSC' 09)*, Dec 2009, p. 86.

[11] C.M. Macal and M.J. North, "Tutorial on agent-based modeling and simulation Part 2: How to model with agents," in *Proceedings of the 38th Winter Simulation Conference (WSC '06)*, 2006, pp. 73–83.

[12] Z. Guessoum, N. Faci, and J.P. Briot, "Adaptive replication of large-scale multi-agent systems—towards a fault-tolerant multi-agent platform," in *Proceedings of the 4th International Workshop on Software Engineering for Large-Scale Multi-Agent Systems (SELMAS)*. ACM, 2005.

[13] M. de C. Gatti, C. de Lucena, and J. Briot, "On fault tolerance in law-governed multi-agent systems," in *Proceedings of the 5th International Workshop on Software Engineering for Large-Scale Multi-Agent Systems (SELMAS)*. ACM, 2006.

[14] S. Blackburn, *The Oxford Dictionary of Philosophy*. Oxford University Press, 1996.

[15] T.R. Gruber, "Towards principles for the design of ontologies used for knowledge sharing," *International Journal Human-Computer Studies*, Vol. 43, No. 5–6, Nov 1995.

[16] J.J. Jung and J. Euzenat, "Towards semantic social networks," in *Proceedings of the 4th European Semantic Web Conference*, 2007, pp. 267–280.

[17] I. Cantador and P. Castells, "Multilayered semantic social network modeling by ontology-based user profiles clustering: Application to collaborative filtering," in *Proceedings of the 15th International Conference on Managing Knowledge in a World of Networks*. Springer Verlag Lectures Notes in Artificial Intelligence, 2006.

[18] J. Golbeck and M. Rothstein, "Linking social networks on the web with foaf: A semantic web case study," in *Proceedings of the Twenty-Third AAAI Conference on Artificial Intelligence*, July 2008.

[19] P. Mika, "Flink: Semantic web technology for the extraction and analysis of social networks," *Journal of Web Semantics*, Vol. 3, 2005.

[20] H. Alani, S. Dasmahapatra, K. O'Hara, and N. Shadbolt, "Identifying communities of practice through ontology network analysis," *IEEE Intelligent Systems*, Vol. 18, No. 2, 2003.

[21] V. Paola, N. Roberto, and C. Alessandro, "A new content-based model for social network analysis," in *Proceedings of the 2th IEEE International Conference on Semantic Computing*, Aug. 2008.

[22] E. Miguela, P. Patro, K.E. Brown, Y.R. Petillot, and D.M. Lane, "Semantic knowledge-based framework to improve the situation awareness of autonomous underwater vehicles," *IEEE Transactions on Knowledge and Data Engineering*, Vol. 23, No. 5, May 2011.

[23] J.E. Kim and D. Mosse, "Generic framework for design, modeling and simulation of cyber physical systems," *ACM SIGBED Review*, Vol. 5, No. 1, pp. 1–2, Jan. 2008.

[24] J. Lin, S. Sedigh, and A. Miller, "Towards integrated simulation of cyber-physical systems: a case study on intelligent water distribution," in *Proceedings of the 8th IEEE International Conference on Pervasive Intelligence and Computing (PICom '09)*, Chengdu, China, Dec. 2009, pp. 690–695.

[25] A. Al-Hammouri, V. Liberatore, H. Al-Omari, Z. Al-Qudah, M.S. Branicky, and D. Agrawal, "A co-simulation platform for actuator networks," in *Proc. of the 5th Int'l. Conference on Embedded Networked Sensor Systems (SenSys '07)*. New York: ACM, 2007, pp. 383–384.

[26] B. Bauer and J. Odell, "UML 2.0 and agents: How to build agent-based systems with the new UML standard," *Engineering Applications of Artificial Intelligence*, Vol. 18, No. 2, 2005.

[27] J. Lin, S. Sedigh, and A. Hurson, "An agent-based approach to reconciling data heterogeneity in cyber-physical systems," in *20th International Heterogeneity in Computing Workshop in conjunction with 25th IEEE International Parallel and Distributed Processing Symposium*, May 2011.

[28] Standford University, "Protégé," retrieved in March 2012. [Online]. Available: http://protege.stanford.edu/

[29] W3, "OWL Web Ontology Language reference," retrieved in March 2012. [Online]. Available: http://www.w3.org/TR/owl-ref/

[30] FMEA-FMECA.com, "Failure mode and effects analysis," retrieved in March 2012. [Online]. Available: http://www.fmeainfocentre.com/

[31] Isograph, "Fault tree analysis," retrieved in March 2012. [Online]. Available: http://www.faulttree.org/

[32] ReSIST Project, "ReSIST Resilience for Survivability in IST," retrieved in March 2012. [Online]. Available: http://www.rkbexplorer.com/explorer/

[33] K.S. Trivedi, D.S. Kim, A. Roy, and D. Medhi, "Dependability and security models (keynote paper)," in *7th International Workshop on Design of Reliable Communication Networks (DRCN '09)*, Oct. 2009, pp. 11–20.

[34] J. Lin, S. Sedigh, and A. Miller, "Modeling cyber-physical systems with semantic agents," in *Proceedings of the 34th IEEE International Computer Software and Applications Conference (COMPSAC '10)*, 2010.

INDEX

Large Scale Network-Centric Distributed Systems, First Edition. Edited by Hamid Sarbazi-Azad and Albert Y. Zomaya.
© 2014 John Wiley & Sons, Inc. Published 2014 by John Wiley & Sons, Inc.

679

WILEY SERIES ON PARALLEL AND DISTRIBUTED COMPUTING
Series Editor: Albert Y. Zomaya

Parallel and Distributed Simulation Systems / Richard Fujimoto

Mobile Processing in Distributed and Open Environments / Peter Sapaty

Introduction to Parallel Algorithms / C. Xavier and S. S. Iyengar

Solutions to Parallel and Distributed Computing Problems: Lessons from Biological Sciences / Albert Y. Zomaya, Fikret Ercal, and Stephan Olariu (*Editors*)

Parallel and Distributed Computing: A Survey of Models, Paradigms, and Approaches / Claudia Leopold

Fundamentals of Distributed Object Systems: A CORBA Perspective / Zahir Tari and Omran Bukhres

Pipelined Processor Farms: Structured Design for Embedded Parallel Systems / Martin Fleury and Andrew Downton

Handbook of Wireless Networks and Mobile Computing / Ivan Stojmenović (*Editor*)

Internet-Based Workflow Management: Toward a Semantic Web / Dan C. Marinescu

Parallel Computing on Heterogeneous Networks / Alexey L. Lastovetsky

Performance Evaluation and Characteization of Parallel and Distributed Computing Tools / Salim Hariri and Manish Parashar

Distributed Computing: Fundamentals, Simulations and Advanced Topics, *Second Edition* / Hagit Attiya and Jennifer Welch

Smart Environments: Technology, Protocols, and Applications / Diane Cook and Sajal Das

Fundamentals of Computer Organization and Architecture / Mostafa Abd-El-Barr and Hesham El-Rewini

Advanced Computer Architecture and Parallel Processing / Hesham El-Rewini and Mostafa Abd-El-Barr

UPC: Distributed Shared Memory Programming / Tarek El-Ghazawi, William Carlson, Thomas Sterling, and Katherine Yelick

Handbook of Sensor Networks: Algorithms and Architectures / Ivan Stojmenović (*Editor*)

Parallel Metaheuristics: A New Class of Algorithms / Enrique Alba (*Editor*)

Design and Analysis of Distributed Algorithms / Nicola Santoro

Task Scheduling for Parallel Systems / Oliver Sinnen

Computing for Numerical Methods Using Visual C++ / Shaharuddin Salleh, Albert Y. Zomaya, and Sakhinah A. Bakar

Architecture-Independent Programming for Wireless Sensor Networks / Amol B. Bakshi and Viktor K. Prasanna

High-Performance Parallel Database Processing and Grid Databases / David Taniar, Clement Leung, Wenny Rahayu, and Sushant Goel

Algorithms and Protocols for Wireless and Mobile Ad Hoc Networks / Azzedine Boukerche (*Editor*)

Algorithms and Protocols for Wireless Sensor Networks / Azzedine Boukerche (*Editor*)

Optimization Techniques for Solving Complex Problems / Enrique Alba, Christian Blum, Pedro Isasi, Coromoto León, and Juan Antonio Gómez (*Editors*)

Emerging Wireless LANs, Wireless PANs, and Wireless MANs: IEEE 802.11, IEEE 802.15, IEEE 802.16 Wireless Standard Family / Yang Xiao and Yi Pan (*Editors*)

High-Performance Heterogeneous Computing / Alexey L. Lastovetsky and Jack Dongarra

Mobile Intelligence / Laurence T. Yang, Augustinus Borgy Waluyo, Jianhua Ma, Ling Tan, and Bala Srinivasan (*Editors*)

Advanced Computational Infrastructures for Parallel and Distributed Adaptive Applicatons / Manish Parashar and Xiaolin Li (*Editors*)

Market-Oriented Grid and Utility Computing / Rajkumar Buyya and Kris Bubendorfer (*Editors*)

Cloud Computing Principles and Paradigms / Rajkumar Buyya, James Broberg, and Andrzej Goscinski

Energy-Efficient Distributed Computing Systems / Albert Y. Zomaya and Young Choon Lee (*Editors*)

Scalable Computing and Communications: Theory and Practice / Samee U. Khan, Lizhe Wang, and Albert Y. Zomaya

The DATA Bonanza: Improving Knowledge Discovery in Science, Engineering, and Business / Malcolm Atkinson, Rob Baxter, Michelle Galea, Mark Parsons, Peter Brezany, Oscar Corcho, Jano van Hemert, and David Snelling (*Editors*)

Large Scale Network-Centric Distributed Systems / Hamid Sarbazi-Azad and Albert Y. Zomaya (*Editors*)

Verification of Communication Protocols in Web Services: Model-Checking Service Compositions / Zahir Tari, Peter Bertok, and Anshuman Mukherjee